AF809899

Markers of Psychosocial Maturation

Mufid James Hannush

Markers of Psychosocial Maturation

A Dialectically-Informed Approach

palgrave
macmillan

Mufid James Hannush
Psychology
Rosemont College
Rosemont, PA, USA

ISBN 978-3-030-74314-7 ISBN 978-3-030-74315-4 (eBook)
https://doi.org/10.1007/978-3-030-74315-4

© The Editor(s) (if applicable) and The Author(s), under exclusive licence to Springer Nature Switzerland AG 2021, corrected publication 2021
This work is subject to copyright. All rights are solely and exclusively licensed by the Publisher, whether the whole or part of the material is concerned, specifically the rights of translation, reprinting, reuse of illustrations, recitation, broadcasting, reproduction on microfilms or in any other physical way, and transmission or information storage and retrieval, electronic adaptation, computer software, or by similar or dissimilar methodology now known or hereafter developed.
The use of general descriptive names, registered names, trademarks, service marks, etc. in this publication does not imply, even in the absence of a specific statement, that such names are exempt from the relevant protective laws and regulations and therefore free for general use.
The publisher, the authors and the editors are safe to assume that the advice and information in this book are believed to be true and accurate at the date of publication. Neither the publisher nor the authors or the editors give a warranty, expressed or implied, with respect to the material contained herein or for any errors or omissions that may have been made. The publisher remains neutral with regard to jurisdictional claims in published maps and institutional affiliations.

Cover illustration: Patrick Kunkel

This Palgrave Macmillan imprint is published by the registered company Springer Nature Switzerland AG.
The registered company address is: Gewerbestrasse 11, 6330 Cham, Switzerland

Preface

This project began with a basic existential question: *what does it mean to be or become a psychosocially mature person*? In my deep desire to answer this question, I immersed myself in maturation-relevant scholarly sources, primarily derived from psychoanalytic *and* humanistic-existential-phenomenological psychologies and philosophies. Brief biographies, autobiographies, and fictional references were also utilized. I emerged from my re-search, utilizing a dialectically informed hermeneutic approach, with *thirty markers or meanings of maturity*. These constituents or manifestations of maturity were then subsumed under *ten thematic clusters.*

The other side of the basic existential question posed above is *what kind of person do I desire to be*? This question is also an existential inquiry into one's calling. Psychosocial growth is a complex developmental life task. It involves progressions and regressions, setbacks, and slippages. Although it is never fully completed, we are born with the organismic desire to heed the call of maturation, made possible by maturational conditions facilitative of psychosocial growth. Responding resolutely to the call of maturation, however, requires living a life of rigorous self-understanding, self-regulation, and self-cultivation, always in a supportive relational context. Individual maturation and communal maturation are correlative phenomena. In a relatively mature communal context, members help each other become their truer selves, thus becoming more mature. Still, becoming mature requires an ever-renewed and renewable passionate decision on the part of each person to respond to the call of maturation responsibly.

This book reflects my passion, as a psychologist, educator, and who I am as a person, to understand the meanings of psychosocial maturation and to share this provisional learning with others, as I learn about my own maturational journey. It is my hope that the reader will find it a rewarding journey too.

Rosemont, PA, USA Mufid James Hannush

Contents

1

Introduction

The Work's Aim

The aim of this work is to com-prehend (grasp together) the constituents of the phenomenon of psychosocial maturation. It is to provide a portrait of the relatively mature person, for maturation comes in degrees and is never complete. The process is dynamic, experiential, and open-ended. More specifically, the goal is to gain insight into the *markers* or *meanings of psychosocial maturation.* These *markers* or *meanings* are interdependent. They are *co-meanings.* These *co-meanings* of maturity are in dialogue with one another. As Merleau-Ponty (1962) puts it, there is always a "communion … a coition, so to speak, of our body [bodily self] with things [meanings]" (p. 320). Meanings of maturity, therefore, intersect, overlap, interact with, and are transformed into one another to form the whole experience of relative maturity. They are indispensable ingredients of an integrated experience of relative wholeness. This relative integration is itself an essential expression of our level of maturation. I say "relative" because this sense of integrated wholeness, which is the lived experience of maturity, is always in a tension-tinged dialogue with not only our own immaturity, but also the immaturity of others and the unpredictable contingencies of our everyday life. Yet, there is a significant difference between how this tension is endured by the mostly mature person in contradistinction to how it is poorly endured by the mostly immature person. When our maturity outweighs our immaturity, the dark, daunting, and difficult vicissitudes of life are better endured.

This text aims at advancing an integrative approach to understanding the complex phenomenon of psychosocial maturity. It proposes to do this via the

© The Author(s), under exclusive license to Springer Nature Switzerland AG 2021
M. J. Hannush, *Markers of Psychosocial Maturation*,
https://doi.org/10.1007/978-3-030-74315-4_1

introduction of *markers* or *meanings* of psychosocial maturity. The primary mechanism utilized in the application of this approach is *dialectical hermeneutics*. It is a way of interpreting texts that views psychosocial maturation as a dialectical movement between meaning-polarities of existence – such as the need for connectedness *and* separation or the need for dependence *and* independence, toward relative balance or integration (see Hannush, 2007, for the application of this dialectical approach to understanding cultural value-polarities – such as over*valuing* independence and under*valuing* dependence or vice versa, and its implications for multicultural therapeutic practice).

Lived meanings can be viewed as ways of being-in-the-world-with-oneself-and-with-others. "What does it mean for me to be close to and separate from essential others?" "What does it mean for me to be dependent on and independent from essential others?" "How do I embody and enact these meanings?" "How do I integrate or find a balance between these lived, polar meanings?" Relatively mature persons actualize themselves in all these universal (existential) dimensions of life (existence) while adapting them to their own individual, familial, and sociocultural contexts. For we are all like all others, like some others, and like no other even when it comes to the actualization of our own meanings of maturity. It is the unique and dynamic confluence of these lived meanings that constitutes the essential structure of maturity. Again, these lived meanings are interdependent, overlapping, and polymorphous. Maturation as a *whole* syndrome manifests itself in these *partial* ways of being mature, which, together, make up mature Being as a whole. Yet, maturity as a kaleidoscopic whole, while manifesting itself in an oscillating variety of different ways of being-in-the-world-with-others, remains essentially finite, limited, and incomplete.

The Work's Dialectical Approach

The "only way to arrive at a well-founded understanding of the criteria of maturity," believes Boelen (1978), "is in a living dialogue between philosophical and psychological ways of thinking and researching" (p. 192). In this text I take a fresh look at data from various psychoanalytic *and* humanistic-existential-phenomenological sources that are both qualitatively and experientially oriented and will focus on lived meanings of maturity in order to derive a conceptual, theoretical model of psychosocial maturity. The psychoanalytic sources, though diverse, can be subsumed under attachment theory, object relations theory, intersubjective-relational theory, and self-psychology. I will be selectively attuned to psychoanalytic readings that are, at least in part, implicitly existential, humanistic, or phenomenological. The case of Erik Erikson serves as an example.

I believe that Erikson's psychodynamic model of human development is incipiently dialectical, existential, and phenomenological – an experience-near description and depiction of human development. Jerome Bruner describes Erikson's approach as "'literary-phenomenological'" and Erikson as a "'self-styled phenomenologist,' the artist with an eye to life at the borderlines" (quoted in Wallulis, 1990, p. 6). Robert Coles contends that Erikson's "'method' could be called contrapuntal – or in a way, Hegelian, in as much as it displays a certain dialectic, a certain progressive momentum" (quoted in Wallulis, 1990, p. 73). Knowles (1986) provides a creative interpretation of Erikson's psychosocial theory of development from a Heideggerian perspective. Wallulis (1990) describes Erikson's work as a "hermeneutics of life history" whereby the central organizing aim of psychosocial development (maturation) involves seeking and finding a "balance" between "personal [identity] achievement" and "historical belonging." Hoare (2002) is of the conviction that Erikson's writings are not only philosophically dialectical, but also progressively existential in orientation, with their allusions to "existential paradoxes" and "existential conflict[s]" (pp. 102–103). For Erikson, a maturational movement is set in motion "when the adult is most open to the untapped opposite" (p. 103). Here is Hoare describing the affinity between Erikson's "philosophical" orientation and that of Hegel, Heidegger, and Husserl:

> To the extent that Erikson wrote philosophically one finds Blake and Hegel in his work. The dialectics of thesis and antithesis, of conflicting polarities in the self-same stage of development, and life as a series of tensions and contradictions are systematic Hegelian notions. All three of these thinkers – Blake, Hegel, and Erikson – held that life is an evolution of oppositional contraries. As to claims that Erikson was a phenomenologist, if by such a label is meant that he observed and described attributes without bothering to explain them, the criticism is unfounded. His thought does resemble that of the German phenomenologists Heidegger and Husserl … Yet his closeness to them, just as of his similarity to Goethe and Hegel, is due more to a spiritual brotherhood of thought and style than to content. (pp. 216–217)

Our own dialectical model differs from that of Erikson's in three respects. First, Erikson's theory adopts a primarily *stage approach* to understanding human development. Even though the attainment of *basic trust* is a pivotal maturational step in the earliest stage of life, the theme of *trust* and the accompanying *hope* are paramount throughout life. The later Erikson begins to see the significance of the triad of trust-hope-faith in the last stage of life, the stage of integrality.

Second, according to our dialectical model, the interactive tension is not between absolute opposites that are antithetical to each other but are rather *seemingly* oppositional and ultimately *complementary.* For Erikson, trust, for instance, is the syntonic (harmonious) element and mistrust is the dystonic (disruptive) element in the interaction of opposites, even though Erikson acknowledges that *mistrust,* as a relational tendency or orientation, is important for adaptation. From the perspective of the dialectical model presented here, both (optimal) *trust* and (optimal) *caution* are syntonic (harmonious) and complementary. *Trust,* as a relational orientation, can go awry and become excessive, naïve trust that inevitably results in relational betrayals, difficulties, and disappointments. Analogously, *caution,* as a relational orientation, may go awry and become excessive, suspicious caution that inevitably results in relational difficulties or even paranoia.

Third, *trust,* and its accompanying *hope,* is part of an inborn *trusting (hopeful) openness,* a wholehearted directedness (*intentionality*) toward lifeworld's possibilities. I call this primary predisposition of openness toward lifeworld's possibilities *existential trust.* Correlatively, the totality of the lifeworld – *all that is,* manifests itself as trustworthy. Our capacity for *identificatory resonance,* which in turn makes our abilities to mentalize, sympathize, and empathize with others possible, is a manifestation of our original or primordial trusting openness to the lifeworld of which we are a part. In its ecstatic modality, this openness is characterized by a sense of awe and wonderment. Think concretely of an infant's awe-and-wonder-filled gaze at the mesmerizingly beautiful face of his mother. Complementarily, think of the awe-and-wonder-filled loving gaze of the mother as she enthrallingly looks at her beautiful child. They are both passionate participants in the synchronized dance of mutual openness toward each other, a dance of aesthetic reciprocity.

Marcus (2010, 2013) creatively fuses insights from psychoanalysis and the hermeneutic phenomenology of Emanuel Levinas and Gabriel Marcel. Orange (2011) offers a *hermeneutics for everyday clinical practice* integrating insights from psychoanalysis and the writings of, among others, Hans-Georg Gadamer and Emanuel Levinas. Here is what Orange says about D. W. Winnicott, whose work is made use of in this text: his trust-based spontaneous therapeutic interventions "bring out important emotional truth from dialogic engagement [which] provides the best … example possible of Gadamerian hermeneutics" (p. 138) or of "a hermeneutics of development" (p. 145). Moreover, she refers to Heinz Kohut's self-psychology, which we also utilize in our work, as a "phenomenologically informed psychology of the self" (p. 176). As his work develops, Kohut, Orange tells us, relies less and less on interpretation (explanation) and more and more on empathic understanding and on the guiding sense that understanding is developmental. Kahn (1997) sees a significant convergence between the humanistic psychotherapy of Carl Rogers and the self-psychology of Heinz Kohut, particularly in their emphasis on empathic understanding. Thompson (1994) describes a convergence between Sigmund Freud and Martin Heidegger's conceptions of truth and untruth. Leffert (2017) draws on phenomenology – including explications of "the phenomenology of meaning," "the phenomenological self," "the phenomenology of aesthetics," and "the phenomenology of desire" to carve out an understanding of the meaning of "subjective well-being," with intermittent slippages into dualistic and reductionistic explanations derived from neuroscience.

The dialectical approach is present in the psychoanalytic writings of Ogden (1986), Johnson (1994), and, extensively utilized by, Carveth (2018). Ogden (1986) has this to say about the dialectical process as a movement toward integration:

> A dialectic is a process in which each of two opposing concepts creates, informs, preserves, and negates the other, each standing in a dynamic (ever-changing) relationship with the other … The dialectical process moves toward integration, but integration is never complete. Each integration creates a new dialectical opposition and a new dynamic tension. (p. 208)

Ogden goes on to describe how the "dialectical process is centrally involved in the creation of subjectivity" (p. 208), which involves not only the capacity for self-awareness but also one's sense of "I-ness" "the quality [of experience] that one is thinking one's thoughts and feeling one's feelings as opposed to living in a state of reflexive reactivity" (p. 209). The dialectical process is additionally involved in the capacity for wishing (desiring) and meaning making. Paradoxically, the sense of "I-ness" is itself created in the context of an interpersonal dialectic where "I-ness" (of the infant) is made possible in dialogue with the "otherness" of the mother.

Although Johnson (1994) does not even mention the term "dialectic," his approach to understanding "character styles" is incipiently, though not rigorously or systematically, dialectical and "existential" (a term he does use).

In the development of our character style, says Johnson (1994), we all have to face and come to terms with existential life issues expressed in such polarities as "presence-absence," "seeking dependency gratification-providing dependency gratification," "autonomy-enmeshment," "worthlessness-grandiosity," "controlled-controlling," and "sexual-asexual" (Table 1, pp. 12–13). It is in the chapter on the narcissistic character, however, that Johnson focuses on two interrelated "basic human polarities" which the developing person must gradually integrate:

> These polarities are (1) unity-individuation and (2) grandiosity-vulnerability. Even under the best of circumstances this integration is not simple. Significant human psychopathology arises out of those familial situations in which any part of either polarity cannot be freely experienced and then integrated. (p. 158)

The enmeshment-seeking symbiotic character comes about as a consequence of blocking the integration of the unity-individuation polarity. The grandiosity-seeking ("grandiosity" here is used in its unnatural, unhealthy, compensatory sense in contradistinction to the child's original natural and healthy grandiosity) narcissistic character emerges out of blocking the integration of the grandiosity-vulnerability polarity. The healthy character arises from a good-enough relational context that allows the developing person to integrate both polarities. Maturely loving parents accept, prize, and unconditionally regard their loveable child for "all its magnificence and vulnerability" (p. 160). Good-enough parents allow themselves to be "used" by their individuating and separating child while the child remains securely attached to them. They extend empathic "understanding, respect, mirroring, echoing, and love," toward their child while at the same time setting proper limits (p. 159). Simply stated, maturely loving parents are able to attach to their child as a real, separate person. They appreciate their child's magnificence (or what I would prefer to call "wondrousness") while remaining empathically attuned to his or her accepted vulnerabilities. This kind of "love, respect, echoing, and mirroring" is "required for him to discover, accept, develop, and love his true self" (p. 161).

Carveth (2018) describes himself as an existentialist and a Freudian-Kleinian psychoanalyst. He applies a Hegelian dialectical approach to re-visioning Melanie Klein's developmental-therapeutic theory. Conflict, though not exclusively, is of the essence of our psychic and relational lives. In every human conflict there is a thesis and an antithesis that beckon compromise or resolution through a third higher-order, elevating synthesis. In almost every either/or conflictual situation there exists the possibility of a higher-order both/and creative compromise or integrative resolution. Almost every human conflict can be subjected to a "dialectical deconstruction" (p. 67). Carveth (2018) elaborates:

> In dialectical thinking … conflict is recognized as a necessary but intermediate stage in a three-step developmental process in which an initial monism gives way to a dualistic clash of opposites, which is then transcended, however momentarily, in a higher synthesis of some type. … the figure three [the third stands for synthesis] is fundamental in dialectical thought …
>
> In dialectical thinking, development through differentiation and integration is also a reality; [a progressive] evolution [toward an ultimately incompletely knowable whole] is real.
>
> The dialectician's favored image of living systems is the spiral, which in health ascends, but in illness yields to fixation, stasis or premature decline.
>
> … a defining feature of regressive [non-dialectical] mental functioning is the privileging of one or the other pole of … binary oppositions, affirming thesis over antithesis or vice versa.
>
> … the psychoanalytic method may be conceptualized as, in part, a process of dialectical deconstruction … in which the repressed complementarity and mutual dependence of the opposing terms is exposed.
>
> … the mark of mature mental functioning is the capacity to achieve and hold the synthesis in which neither pole is concretized or absolutized. (pp. 104–107)

Carveth (2018) then applies his dialectical thinking to re-visioning Klein's well-known developmental "positions." "Dialectical thinking," Carveth informs us, "is essentially allied to Klein's … depressive position in which the either/or thinking (splitting) characterizing the paranoid-schizoid position is transcended" (p. 105). Carveth, however, does not stop at the point of demarcating the paranoid-schizoid (P-S) position as developmentally deficient (bad) and the depressive (or what Carveth labels as "reparative") position as developmentally mature (good), as mainstream Kleinian psychoanalysts have done.

Developmentally, the paranoid-schizoid position is our first natural or normal position in Kleinian developmental theory. It describes our early infantile state of mind. Because of its utter vulnerability, dependency, and helplessness in infancy and due to being born with a primitive and fragile sense of self (ego), the infant is easily threatened by destructive drives from within or threatening forces from without experienced in consequence of the absence of immediate ministration to its basic needs. The infant is left with no recourse but to make use of primitive defenses such as projection, introjection, and, above all, splitting. This results in an experience of a split in the intentional world structure of the developing child. In an organismic effort to keep itself, more or less, protected, safe, and secure, the infant splits her or his world into a good self-world and a bad self-world. In Kleinian language, the infant experiences the "object" (breast or, later, mother) as either good (loved) or bad (hated). Correlative feelings are experienced in reference to the emerging sense of self. The good-and-loved object must not be contaminated by feelings of hate for the bad object. This alleviates, to some degree, the child's feelings of persecutory anxiety. It precipitates for the child an ordered and less vertiginously chaotic world.

The depressive-reparative (D-R) position is not only a developmental stage that follows the paranoid-schizoid position, but also, similar to the paranoid-schizoid position, a state of mind, a way of organizing experience, a positioning of oneself toward one's intrapersonal and interpersonal world. It is a more mature position because, to a considerable degree, it resolves the either/or splitting stance of the paranoid-schizoid child. It more or less *integrates* the bipolar or split love-and-hate feelings toward the same essential other who is now perceived as a whole and separate person. Loving and hateful feelings are brought into a relationship with one another. The depressive-reparative child is now capable of contemplating her or his ambivalence toward the same important other. She or he realizes that one can have ambivalent feelings not only toward others but also toward the self. Additionally, the depressive-reparative child begins to experience the damage that she or he can perpetrate or has inflicted upon the loved other through her or his own destructive actions that can result in real loss. As a consequence, the now *concerned* child is motivated to undo the damage through acts of creative reparation or "atonement," as Hans Loewald (1988) prefers to call it, which in itself is a creative act of "sublimation."

Placing oneself in a position of being persecuted by part-objects who are perceived one-dimensionally and handled defensively highlights the Paranoid-Schizoid's (P-S) central mode of functioning in the world. Placing oneself in a position of being sensitively attuned to the impact of one's behavior on whole and separate objects who are perceived multidimensionally and handled with care, concern, and with a spirit of confidence in one's preparedness for efficacious reparation highlights the Depressive-Reparative's (D-R) central mode of functioning in the world. Whereas the P-S person has a strong tendency to splitting others or oneself into opposites – for example, people or the self are either all good (caring) or all bad (selfish) – the D-R person is able to manage the tensions involved in bringing opposites together – for example, people or self and can be both good (caring) *and* bad (selfish). The D-R person is able to acknowledge that she or he can both love and hate oneself or the other person. The D-R person is able to manage the dialectical tensions involved in bringing seemingly polar experiences (meanings) together. *These are the signs of psychological maturity.* Achieving and maintaining the D-R position is the mature way of being-in-the-world-with-self-and-others.

Mainstream Kleinians have viewed the movement between the P-S position and the D-R position as being *linear*, with allowances made for temporary regressive oscillations. In applying his dialectical thinking to Klein's theory of development, Carveth (2018) re-visions the movement between P-S and D-R as being circular rather than linear. More importantly, in line with our own dialectical approach, Carveth posits good-and-bad aspects to both the P-S and D-R positions.

The P-S person, Carveth (2018) informs us, is in a position whereby she or he can use the defense mechanism of splitting as an adaptive necessity to defend herself or himself against the imminent transgressions of predators. We can only defend ourselves against a genocidal Hitler by adopting the P-S position. We fall madly in love only when we are captivated by the overpowering passion of the P-S position. All this is an illustration of the positive aspect of the P-S position. "This is where excitement, intensity, passion, falling in love and resolute commitment in a struggle are to be found" (p. 196).

The D-R person, Carveth (2018) continues, is simply too rational and too empathic to the point of rendering her or him in a frozen position, a position of inaction. If I begin thinking of how Hitler was violently traumatized by his father's harsh discipline as a child and of how he loved dogs, then I will end up either appeasing Hitler or being killed as a consequence of his genocidal orders. And if I begin to rationally contemplate the merits and demerits of my fiancée, I will end up unable to resolutely commit myself to marrying her.

Carveth (2018) concludes in stating that out of the conflict between the P-S and D-R positions a creative synthesis of these two polar stances elevates one to a higher level of integration:

> instead of valuing one and devaluing the other, both the merits and demerits of both positions are recognized and a creative synthesis that unites what is valuable and life-enhancing in each is worked out. Here, for example, we might find the passion and intensity of Ps creatively combined with the care and responsibility of D (a synthesis symbolized here as PsD). (p. 201)

We need to "find a way to love, hate, cherish and use more or less simultaneously … this is what appears … to be necessary to be both responsible [in the "I-Thou" mode of relating to others] and exciting [in the "I-it" mode of relating to others]" (p. 203).

Something needs to be said about the concept of *ambivalence* in general and the *capacity for ambivalence* as a maturational achievement that is central to the D-R position in particular. For the early Freud, Carveth tells us, ambivalence meant diffusion or splitting, as in splitting the life-affirming drive

(Eros) from the death or destructive drive (Thanatos). For the later Freud, as well as for Klein, ambivalence came to mean fusion or the overcoming of splitting. Merleau-Ponty (1964), however, re-visions the views of Melanie Klein, a re-vision with which we concur. Whereas for Klein the capacity for ambivalence is a maturational achievement, Merleau-Ponty links ambivalence to psychological rigidity while connecting psychological maturity to the *capacity for ambiguity.*

> As opposed to ambivalence, ambiguity is an adult phenomenon, a phenomenon of maturity, which has nothing pathological about it. It consists in admitting that the same being who is good and generous can also be annoying and imperfect. ... ambiguity is ambivalence that one dares to look at face to face. What is missing in rigid subjects is the capacity to confront squarely the contradictions that exist in their attitudes toward others. (p. 103)

Moreover, for Merleau-Ponty, "emotional ambivalence is what demands the denial of intellectual ambiguity. In subjects whose intellectual ambiguity is strong, it often happens that the emotional foundation is much more subtle than in other subjects" (p. 105). Lastly, Merleau-Ponty brings to our awareness – and this is my own extrapolation – the fact that the *degree* of ambivalence in early childhood and the *extent* of openness to future tolerance of ambiguity are highly context sensitive. In an "authoritarian atmosphere," which is highly conducive to the acquisition of *psychological rigidity*, Merleau-Ponty points out, the child is *sensitized* to "having two alternative images of the same object, the same person, without making any effort to connect them or to notice that in reality they relate to the same object and the same person" (p. 103). In a more benign and authoritative atmosphere, which is highly conducive to the progressive acquisition of *psychological fluidity* or *flexibility*, the degree of ambivalence is attenuated and the movement toward the tolerance of *ambiguity* is enhanced. By viewing ambivalence on a continuum from high-to-low in degree of intensity that is contingent upon the relational context in which it develops, the contradiction in the views of the early and later Freud is eliminated. As simplistically dualistic feelings of ambivalence become attenuated and modulated, they become absorbed, elevated, and integrated into a more complexly mature tolerance of ambiguity – *the capacity for ambiguity.*

Although somewhat differently utilized than our model, Deurzen-Smith (1997) is an existential psychotherapist who has incorporated "dialogue as dialectics" into her therapeutic approach. "The art of dialectics," says Deurzen-Smith, "requires the therapist to be very steady and sure-footed, able to consider the opposite view of whatever the client asserts, and to systematically look for the missing and shadow side of an issue – the things that are not being said and the things that need considering still" (pp. 229–230). Existential therapy, explicates Deurzen-Smith, aims at helping clients "tackle" both sides of an issue – their "original position" and the opposite, shadowy position. Clients need to learn to "include" both positions in order to achieve "the positive outcome of existential psychotherapy" (p. 230). "The objective," she continues, "is never simply to reach some sort of middle-way compromise, or dilute the tension implied in living [in paradox], but rather to maximize one's ability to stand them, and allow them to span one's life from one end of the range to the other" (p. 230). Deurzen-Smith describes her dialectical "map of the world" this way:

> The four dimensions of our existence [bodily, social, personal, and ideological] are each spanned and dominated by polar oppositions. Life can be defined as the activity of movement between these opposites. People find themselves moved and motivated by the forces created in the tension between these extremes ... Existence [for instance,] is the tension between life and death and the lay of forces in-between. (p. 99)

We all typically try to stay near the polar side that offers us a sense of comfort, familiarity, and security. I can, for example, become preoccupied with the hassles and minutiae of everyday life that I become forgetful of my mortality.

> There are, however, also balancing mechanisms built in to life tending to redress the equilibrium and exposing one to the previously neglected side of existence. When the body has engaged in a lot of strenuous effort, it tires and aims for rest. When we have been intensely involved with other people for a significant period of time, we seek peace and quiet. When we have been resolute and self-assertive for long enough, we crave a phase of letting our guard down. When we have been consistently virtuous and good, we are ripe for self-indulgence. (p. 99)

We tend to live on the assumption that our way of living is right (positive), only to find out that it has a negative side. Analogously, we discover that what we thought of as wrong (negative) turns out to have a positive element in it. Deurzen-Smith concludes her chapter on *dialectics* by providing examples of polarities in the different domains of existence (*existential dimensions*) by subsuming them under a **Positive pole** and a **Negative pole**: life (+) versus death (-), representing the **physical dimension**; belonging (+) versus isolation (-), and love (+) versus hate (-), representing the **social dimension**; integrity (+) versus disintegration (-) and confidence (+) versus doubt (-), representing the **personal dimension**; and good (+) versus evil or destructiveness (-), representing the **ideological/spiritual dimension**. In our dialectical model, each pole can be positively (+) *and* negatively (-) valenced.

There is a double sense in which *dialectics* is used in our work: (1) it is used as an integrative and interpretive tool for uncovering the essential markers, meanings, or constituents of psychosocial maturation gleaned from both psychodynamic *and* existential-humanistic-phenomenological sources; and (2) it is described as an essential feature of self-world experience, whereby the self is viewed as being directed to tension-producing polar meanings in its lifeworld and is thus motivated to seek balance in its effort to find better (articulated and individuated) meanings that, under relatively optimal conditions, serve the ultimate purpose of increased psychosocial maturation. Ironically and paradoxically, this dual use, which is akin to the demarcation between *dialectical thinking* (reflecting, interpreting, insight-seeking) and *dialectical living* (acting, doing), is a spurious distinction. With psychosocial maturation, the distinction dissolves regarding concernful involvements that matter. Our concernful way of being-in-the-world-with-others manifests itself in the way we *think-about-and-do-things*. Living authentically involves a dialectical interplay between *reflection* and *action*. Existential-dialectical-dialogical thinking is the kind of thinking that illuminates and keeps lighted before us, especially during dark times, what is most important in life. "Authentic thinking," states Boelen (1978), "is the creative process of man's articulated or dialectical self-disclosure as Being-in-the-world … Thinking cannot be defined in opposition to being. It is essentially an integral constituent of our being-in-the-world" (pp. 45–46). Just as we have to pass through maturational levels to achieve authenticity, so too our thinking has to undergo the same levels of maturational development. Different ways of thinking parallel different ways of being-in-the-world-with-others. They correspond to different *intentionalities*. And "intentionality," May (1969) reminds us, is "the structure by which experience becomes meaningful" (p. 299). "With maturity," adds Deurzen-Smith (1997), "comes the ability to transpose one form of [meaningful] experience to another" (p. 220). Achieving a higher level of thinking entails the emergence of a new way of being-in-the-world, a new way of meaning making, where meanings are not only thought-meanings and emotion-meanings, but also action-meanings. Lest we forget the relational context in which meaning making occurs, Holmes (2010) brings to the fore of our attention that "it is the *mutuality* of meaning-*making* that matters" (p. 53).

The Work's Implications

Positive psychology, though seemingly inspired by humanistic psychology, has moved the research into "character strengths and virtues" back to the forefront of mainstream psychology (see Bolt & Dunn, 2016). However, what qualifies it to belong to mainstream psychology and distances it from humanistic psychology is its adoption of a *quantitative*, natural scientific methodological approach to studying "character strengths and virtues" such as commitment, empathy, friendship, flourishing, happiness, hope, humility, love, meaning, self-control, self-respect, and wisdom (Bolt & Dunn, 2016). Let us see how the character or "human strength" of *meaning making* is handled from a quantitative, natural scientific perspective. Readers, like random subjects have done before them, are invited by Bolt and Dunn (2016) to complete the "Meaning in Life Questionnaire (MLQ)." "*The MLQ*," we are told, "*has two subscales, the Presence [of Meaning] subscale and the Search [for Meaning] subscale*" (p. 224). *Presence of Meaning* is weighted, on a seven-point scale, through the way respondents answer questions, such as "My life has or does not have a clear sense of purpose." *Search for Meanings* is weighted, on a seven-point scale, through the way respondents answer questions, such as "I am searching for meaning in my life." We are then instructed to calculate our *Presence of Meaning* and *Search for Meaning* scores.

> *The Presence of Meaning subscale measures how full respondents feel their lives are of meaning. The Search for Meaning subscale measures how engaged and motivated respondents are in efforts to find meaning or deepen their understanding of meaning in their lives. Presence is positively related to well-being, intrinsic religiosity, extroversion and agreeableness, and negatively related to anxiety and depression. Search is positively related to religious quest, rumination, past-negative and present-fatalistic time perspectives, negative affect, depression, and neuroticism, and negatively related to future time perspective, close[d]-mindedness (i.e., dogmatism), and well-being. Presence is also related to personal growth self-appraisals, and altruistic and spiritual behavior.* (Bolt & Dunn, 2016, pp. 224–225)

Something deeply valuable about having and pursuing a *meaning in life* is lost from the above quantitative and confusingly disjointed approach to understanding such a critical "character strength" as *Meaning in Life*. For one thing, it escapes the constructors of the MLQ that meaning can be discovered not only through a sense of purpose but also, at a minimum, though a sense of efficacy, through appreciation of beauty, through loving relations, and through knowing that one is a good person. Moreover, forcing the answerer to quantify her or his response to the meaning-tapping questioning does not allow the subject to describe what the question means to her or him in light of the answer (marked number). Let us contrast this quantitative approach with a descriptive, qualitative, and phenomenological approach to understanding the phenomenon of *lifeworld meaning.*

"Phenomenological psychology," states Fuller (1990), "begins with the premise that *lifeworld meaning*, which conventional [mainstream] psychology is simply unable to calculate, comes into its *truth*, with an integrity of its own, in existential [lived, not objective] space" (p. 79). "Phenomenological psychology," he continues, "is a [human] science that is dedicated to *understanding* behavior in its total everyday [meaningful] context rather than *explaining* in terms of objective conditions; precisely therein lies its hermeneutic character" (p. 33). It is lived meanings that co-organize our experience. We commune and engage in dialogue with these emotion-and-value-laden and action-packed meanings. Our bodily selves are always already directed to lifeworld meanings – the things and people we deal with in our everyday lives. Others, as variations on ourselves, are also meanings for us – as loveable or despicable, for instance. In a sense, *we are our lifeworld meanings*. We make meanings and meanings make us. Psychosocial maturation on the bodily self side is mirrored in maturation on the meanings side. Meanings grow (differentiate and individuate) as we grow as human *beings*.

Positive psychology is oblivious to this rich phenomenological *understanding* of lifeworld meaning. It only provides us with a simplistic and superficial *explanation* of the meaning of *Meaning of Life*. "*Positive psychology*," state Bolt and Dunn (2016), lifting the definition from the "Positive Psychology Center," "*is the [natural] scientific study of the strengths that enable individuals and communities to lead meaningful and fulfilling lives, to cultivate what is best within themselves, and to enhance their experiences of love, work, and play*" (p. 3). Something is sacrificed in what is learned about "human strengths" when approached from a calculative or quantitative point of view, let alone applying such learning to helping individuals and communities live meaningful lives whereby their capacities for **love**, **work**, and **play** are enhanced – three capacities that emerge as part of thirty essential meanings of psychosocial maturation in our present project.

Contemporary psychoanalysis tends to have one foot grounded in a descriptive approach and another foot grounded in natural scientific approach to understanding important human phenomena. "The cutting edge of contemporary psychoanalytic therapy," holds Holmes (2010), "rests in the combination of accurate phenomenological accounts of what happens in the consulting room with emerging findings from neuroimaging, genetics and child development" (pp. 177–178). "Together," he surmises, "these offer the possibility of psychoanalytic therapy as a [natural] science of intimate relations" (p. 178). Yet, the same Holmes holds that "meaning-making is intrinsic to all therapy," that such meaning-oriented framework brings "order to the intrinsically inchoate experience of [mental] illness," and that "meaning," which can be developmental, relational, and unconscious (implicit), "transcends mere cognition and ultimately derives from bodily experience" (p. 43). Meaning can become our "secure base" (p. 45). Although he does not explicitly make mention of it, Holmes is here saying that some value-and-feeling-laden meanings we hold allow us to belong to the lifeworld, whereby bodily self and lifeworld meanings are bound together as one. Moreover, shared meanings or mutual meaning making can be a source of soothing and comfort, joy and exuberance, consensual validation of social reality, and an impetus to exploring and acquiring knowledge about self-and-other and co-constructing a coherent life narrative. Our bodies, says Holmes, let us know if we are "finding the right meaning" (p. 50). To find the right meaning, I need to (1) be attuned to my own "affective and corporeal sensory-affective world"; (2) describe such sensation in words, thus transforming my "'preconceptions' into conceptions'"; and (3) give full expression to what I mean by taking into account my own affective reactions, my knowledge of my essential other's internal world. Ultimately, "it is the *mutuality* of meaning-making that matters" (p. 53). The "*capacity to find/make shared meanings*" is a hallmark of mental health. This I believe is a rich phenomenological description of the process of mutual meaning making.

If contemporary psychoanalysis is to be a *human science*, then it has to consistently refrain from succumbing to dualistic and reductionistic thinking. Instead, it needs to make consistent use of hermeneutic and dialectical thinking. It needs to utilize rigorous descriptive methods that aim at capturing the *essential meanings* of human phenomena, such as love and loss, without slipping into dualism or reductionism. It needs to adopt more rigorous "phenomenological psychological methods" of investigation (see the pioneering work of phenomenological psychologist Amedeo Giorgi, 2018). Psychoanalysis and phenomenology can both be enriched through a cross-fertilizing dialogue. Similarly, a "communion" between psychoanalysis, in its various forms, and existential-humanistic-phenomenological psychologies can result in the enhancement of our human understanding. This present project is one such endeavor that aims at understanding the phenomenon of psychosocial maturation. In this *qualitative* re-search project I have immersed myself into the maturation-relevant literature of existential-phenomenological psychology and philosophy *and* the psychoanalytic or psychodynamic literature that is incipiently dialectical-dialogical or existential-phenomenological and emerged with thirty *essential meanings or markers of psychosocial maturity*.

Why re-search the phenomenon of psychosocial maturation? What does it *mean* to be an emotionally, psychologically, or psychosocially mature human being? What are the *core characteristics* of the psychosocially mature person? What are the *meanings* or *markers* of psychosocial maturity? How can we describe the process of *becoming* a mature individual? The provisional answer to this question, which is the goal of our project, is important because the impulse that beckons us toward development, growth, and maturation is an existential given. In line with humanistic and existential psychologists, such as Viktor Frankl, Erich Fromm, Abraham Maslow, Rollo May, and Carl Rogers, I hold to the principle that we humans have the potential within us to better ourselves and become more than we are. Moreover, society is made up of individuals who in turn make it up. The more mature we become as individuals the more mature our society becomes. Following the example of Habermas (1971), who maintains that we humans have a fundamental interest in communicating, being understood, and gaining knowledge about ourselves and others, I hold to the assumption that we humans have a fundamental interest in psychosocial maturation. Should the reader concur with this assumption, she or he will hopefully find experiential validation and resonance in her or his own personal quest for psychosocial maturation as she or he journeys with me in my search for the essential structure of psychosocial maturation.

Additionally, all psychotherapeutic approaches aim at contributing to the psychosocial maturation of clients or patients. Implicitly or explicitly, "psychotherapy provides an image of the well-functioning, well-adjusted, healthy, happy person and a method designed to help one to approximate the ideal" (Deurzen-Smith, 1997, p. 124). Psychotherapists themselves need to have acquired a significant level of psychosocial maturation before they embark on assisting clients or patients, even if obliquely, in their personal journey toward emotional, psychological, and relational maturity. A therapeutically helping relationship, says Rogers (1989), is one "in which at least one of the parties has the intent of promoting the growth, development, maturity, improved functioning, improved coping with life of the other" (p. 108). The "optimal helping relationship," continues Rogers, "is the kind of relationship created by a person who is psychologically mature. Or to put it in another way, the degree to which I can create relationships which facilitate the growth of others as separate persons is a measure of the growth I have achieved in myself" (pp. 124–125).

"A mature practitioner," states Jacobs (2010) in his text on psychodynamic psychotherapy, will show, selectively:

> – a mature sense of judgment ...
> – the ability to think ... while containing anxious situations ...
> – the ability to learn from errors and mistakes through non-defensive reflection ...
> – ongoing openness to learning ...
> – ease with not knowing ... together with the confidence in one's competence ...
> – a genuine sense of humility ...
> – self-acceptance ..., consistent commitment ...
> – ongoing personal development and self-knowledge from a variety of experiences. (pp. 72–73)

What are the indicators of more mature development in the patient? Here are, according to Jacobs (1998), some of these indicators of psychosocial maturation:

> – Basic sense of trust and faith in others, the environment and the self; basic sense of the 'world' as good.
> – Healthy mistrust ...
> – ... recognition of ambivalence ['without the negative destroying the positive'], and concern [and care] for others ... receiving care from others ...
> – Containing and working through bad experiences and feelings without being overwhelmed by them in the long run.
> – Healthy self-respect and self-regard, while still able to accept one's shortcomings, own mortality, and weaknesses.
> – A separate identity: able to own thoughts and feelings ...
> – Identifying through empathy and concern for and with others.
> – ... depending appropriately upon others.
> – Capacity to be alone – inner harmony and self-esteem.
> – Putting experiences in perspective, retaining a sense of hope even in adversity.
> – Expressing appropriate anger or assertiveness when frustrated or disconcerted without (fear of) being destructive.
> The internalization of the positive features of others, in the course of relating to them, particularly as part of the grief process after loss or bereavement. (pp. 213–214)

The point to be made here is that psychotherapists need to not only serve as *models of maturity* but also have a *map of maturity* in their efforts to be instrumental in helping others in their maturational journey. Among other goals, this book will aim to provide such as a provisional guiding *map of maturity*. In addition, it not only will hopefully contribute to furthering our understanding of the *meaning of maturity*, but will serve as a guiding light to the existential project of *becoming more mature* that beckons every one of us. If psychotherapy is to provide an "image" of the psychosocially mature person and a "method" for approximating this "ideal," then this present project attempts to make this implicit "image," explicit, while inviting future researchers, doing "qualitative" research, to refine this provisional picture.

The Work's Organization

Guided by my prior research and writings utilizing the dialectical approach, I immersed myself in psychodynamic *and* existential-humanistic-phenomenological literature of relevance to the phenomenon of psychosocial maturation. I took a fresh look at these qualitatively and experientially oriented sources, focusing on lived meanings of maturation. I searched for markers, meanings, principles, themes, essences, and examples of psychosocial maturation. Utilizing a hermeneutic-dialectical process, I aimed at discovering, synthesizing, and portraying the essential constituents of psychosocial maturation. From this qualitative analysis emerged thirty markers, meanings, or constituents of psychosocial maturity. Thereafter, I distilled these thirty "markers" into *ten thematic clusters*.

The reader will discover, as I have, that the thirty core characteristics are constituent parts of the whole phenomenon of psychosocial maturation. Just as the parts are manifestations of the whole, the whole will be manifested in each part. Described differently, these core characteristics of psychosocial maturation partake of one another. They overlap and are not isolated from one another. There is a dynamic interaction and interdependence between them.

The Special Case of Love as a Superordinate Integrative Marker of Maturity

Ultimately, emotional or psychological maturity can be fostered only in a *loving* relational context that is characterized by "*co-wonder*" (a concept that I owe to Boelen, 1978, p. 103) – a shared co-presence to the awe-inspiring miracle that is Life itself. Of all the overlapping markers of maturity, I single out the capacity for love as a superordinate integrative marker of maturity. That is why inordinate space is allotted to love as an essential constituent of maturity. Cultivating the capacity to love maturely or wisely is one of life's ultimate achievements. Maroda (2010) describes the capacity to love as "'the final competence' … one is competent only to the extent and to the degree that one can love" (p. 234). The inability to love maturely is one of life's ultimate failures. Quoting Freud, Carveth (2018) echoes that "in the last resort we must begin to love in order not to fall ill, and we are bound to fall ill if … we are unable to love" (p. 10).

Love is the source of true *integrality* (with its double ethical and integrative connotations), stability, solidity-producing solidarity, harmony, happiness, fulfillment, creativity, and self-and-relational actualization. Love is the most fundamental integrating force in human existence. Still, Boelen (1978), thinking dialectically, reminds us that:

> mature love cannot be achieved without the pain of its primal conflict with indifference, hatred, alienation, egoism, fixation, prejudice, etc. A mature person can have integrity even though he stumbles. Mature … love can only be attained at the cost of a lifetime of self-discipline, constant struggle, arduous effort, and even occasional failure. (p. 168)

Mature love enables us to maintain a life-affirming stance in spite of the ugliness, destructiveness, and deception in human existence.

In a chapter on psychoanalyst "Harold Searles' 'Oedipal Love in the Countertransference' and 'Unconscious Identification,'" Ogden (2012) has this to say:

> Though Searles does not discuss the theoretical underpinnings of his findings, it seems that the therapeutic effect of the expression of the therapist's love for the patient is the meeting of a developmental need for recognition of who the patient is (as opposed to the satisfying of an erotic desire). The latter would lead to increased sexual excitement; the former fosters psychological maturation, including the consolidation of a self that is experienced as both loved and loving. Searles is implicitly, and only implicitly, positing a human developmental need to love and be loved and to be recognized as a separate person whose love is valued. (p. 162)

What both Searles and Ogden are saying here about love in therapy applies to love outside therapeutic settings – what I call *natural therapeutic environments*, such as parent-child relationships, relations between partners or friends, and so on. We all have a universal (existential) need to love and be loved as separate individuals. The capacity to love maturely results in the fostering of "psychological maturation," which includes the "consolidation [or integration] of a self that is experienced as both loved and loving."

The capacity to love, viewed developmentally, can serve as a superordinate integrator. When as children we are properly or maturely (non-possessively or non-narcissistically) loved, we are granted the creative space to separate, individuate, and differentiate, while maintaining our close ties to our essential others. In other words, relatively speaking, we are enabled to transcend the tension-producing dichotomy of subject versus object or the "I" versus the "we." We are able to achieve relative balance between our emerging sense of *agency* and our felt *communion* with our significant others. At the same time, we are also able to achieve a relative balance between relating to the Other as a co-subject and relating to the Other as a use object, with the former outweighing the latter in the resulting optimal ratio. To use Buberian language – after existential philosopher Martin Buber (1970), the "I-Thou" (subject-to-subject) relationship outweighs the "I-It" (subject-to-object) relationship – a relationship that is based on use and not encounter. In fact, in a mature loving relationship, be it between loving partners, parent and child, or friends, the participants allow themselves to be used, a benign allowance lovingly accepted while having its boundaries and limits.

References

Boelen, B. J. (1978). *Personal maturity: The existential dimension*. The Seabury Press.

Bolt, M., & Dunn, D. S. (2016). *Pursuing human strengths: A positive psychology guide* (2nd ed.). Worth Publishers.

Buber, M. (1970). *I and thou*. Charles Scribner's Sons.

Carveth, D. L. (2018). *Psychoanalytic thinking: A dialectical critique of contemporary theory and practice*. Routledge.

Deurzen-Smith, E. V. (1997). *Everyday mysteries: Existential dimensions of psychotherapy*. Routledge.

Fuller, A. R. (1990). *Insight into value: An exploration of the premises of a phenomenological psychology*. State University of New York Press.

Giorgi, A. (2018). *Reflections on certain qualitative and phenomenological psychological methods*. University Professors Press.

Habermas, J. (1971). *Knowledge and human interests*. (J. J. Shapiro, Trans.). Beacon Press.

Hannush, M. J. (2007). An existential-dialectical-phenomenological approach to understanding *cultural tilts*: Implications for multicultural research and practice. *Journal of Phenomenological Psychology, 38*, 7–23.

Hoare, C. H. (2002). *Erikson on development and adulthood: New insights from the unpublished papers*. Oxford University Press.

Holmes, J. (2010). *Exploring in security: Towards an attachment-informed psychoanalytic psychotherapy*. Routledge.

Jacobs, M. (1998). *The presenting past: The core of psychodynamic counselling and therapy* (2nd ed.). Open University Press.

Jacobs, M. (2010). *Psychodynamic counselling in action* (4th ed.). Sage.

Johnson, S. M. (1994). *Character styles*. W. W. Norton.

Kahn, M. (1997). *Between therapist and client: The new relationship* (Rev. ed.). W. H. Freeman.

Knowles, R. T. (1986). *Human development and human possibility: Erikson in the light of Heidegger*. University Press of America.

Leffert, M. (2017). *Positive psychoanalysis: Meaning, aesthetics and subjective well-being*. Routledge.

Loewald, H. W. (1988). *Sublimation: Inquiries into theoretical psychoanalysis*. Yale University Press.

Marcus, P. (2010). *In search of the good life: Emanuel Levinas, psychoanalysis, and the art of living*. Karnac.

Marcus, P. (2013). *In search of the spiritual: Gabriel Marcel, psychoanalysis, and the sacred*. Karnac.

Maroda, K. J. (2010). *Psychodynamic techniques: Working with emotion in the therapeutic relationship*. The Guilford Press.

May, R. (1969). *Love and will*. Dell.

Merleau-Ponty, M. (1962). *Phenomenology of perception* (C. Smith, Trans.). Routledge.

Merleau-Ponty, M. (1964). *The primacy of perception*. Northwestern University Press.

Ogden, T. H. (1986). *The matrix of the mind: Object relations and the psychoanalytic dialogue*. Jason Aronson.

Ogden, T. H. (2012). *Creative readings: Essays on seminal analytic works*. Routledge.

Orange, D. M. (2011). *The suffering stranger: Hermeneutics for everyday clinical practice*. Routledge.

Rogers, C. R. (1989). *The Carl Rogers reader*. Houghton Mifflin.

Thompson, M. G. (1994). *The truth about Freud's technique: The encounter with the real*. New York University Press.

Wallulis, J. (1990). *The hermeneutics of life history: Personal achievement and history in Gadamer, Habermas, and Erikson*. Northwestern University Press.

Part I

The Capacities for Self-Analysis, Self-Understanding, and Self-Transcendence

2

Self-Analysis: The Capacity for *Self-Analysis* Through Self-Reflection

The ability to connect or link lies at the heart of the capacity for self-analysis. To link, state Cabaniss and her colleagues (2013), is to connect patterns of feeling, thinking, and behaving to our developmental history. In their view, "psychodynamic formulation" involves (1) *describing* present patterns, (2) *reviewing* developmental history, and (3) *linking* patterns to history. The focus of their text is on helping clinicians learn to formulate psychodynamically in an effort to understand and treat patients in clinical settings. In this chapter, we will transpose their psychodynamic formulation for the purpose of self-analysis – to understand ourselves and thus to gain self-knowledge.

We are naturally curious about our own developmental history. Some of us, ironically due to the vagaries of our own early life experiences, are more curious than others. Self-analysis involves formulating hypotheses about how our developmental history contributes to making us who we are today. From a dialectical viewpoint, we humans are constructed to raise-questions-and-seek-answers. Like a pendulum, we are forever rhythmically caught between questioning and searching for answers. Sometimes answers are not forthcoming. At other times, we glimpse partial answers. Frequently, answers, always tentatively held, beget more questions. We will set aside the scientific kind of questions, the answers to which humans have made exponential strides, which have yielded countless technological dividends. The pace of progress in finding answers to existentially and psychodynamically relevant questions has been much slower. Here are some examples of such questions, some of which are general, while others are more specific:

© The Author(s), under exclusive license to Springer Nature Switzerland AG 2021

M. J. Hannush, *Markers of Psychosocial Maturation*,
https://doi.org/10.1007/978-3-030-74315-4_2

- *Why is it that my life, at times, seems full of contradictory and seemingly oppositional meanings?*
- *Why is it that I have a rough time balancing my needs for connectedness and intimacy with my needs for separateness and solitude?*
- *Why is it so arduous for me to find a balance between competing-and-cooperating with others?*
- *Why is it so difficult for me to find a balance between being healthily dependent on others and being healthily independent from others?*
- *Why is it that I hold on to people and things and to feelings and thoughts, when it would be beneficial to my mental health to let go or the other way around?*
- *Why am I either overly trusting or overly cautious in my relationships with (essential) others?*

Here are further questions raised by Cabaniss and her colleagues (2013):

- *How might early trauma lead to problems with affect regulation?*
- *How might depression in childhood lead to problems with self-esteem management?*
- *How might an absent mother lead to interpersonal problems in adulthood?*
- *How might having an attuned mother help someone to grapple with a breakup in college?*
- *How might an overly close relationship with a parent lead to sexual inhibitions?* (p. 138)

A self-analysis that will lead to liberating self-knowledge involves the cultivation of the capacity to engage in a never-ending cycle of questioning-and-answering. It requires us to acquire and refine our ability to think dialectically, developmentally, and psychodynamically. We form hypotheses about how our own history might have led to the development of our unique-and-not-so-unique healthy and unhealthy or problematic patterns of feeling, thinking, and behaving. Our healthy patterns include how the cultivation of our capacities and talents comes about. We can identify with our affective, cognitive, and action patterns. We can have relatively coherent and complementary patterns. We also can have contradictory patterns, such as repetitive intense feelings of love-and-hate toward an essential-or-not-so-essential other. In light of this dialectical questioning-and-answering, we become aware of the contradictory and clashing elements in our view of ourselves and/or others. It is important to note that from a dialectical perspective, there are good and bad questions and good and bad answers. Bad questions beget bad (rationalizing and fixed) answers. Good questions beget good (*truthful* and, though painful, liberating) answers.

What makes the acquisition of such *truthful* self-knowledge so difficult is that many of our patterns are unconscious. Still, the line of demarcation between consciousness and unconsciousness is continuous. In other words, we can have vague notions and glimpses about that of which we are not explicitly aware. We may have a vague awareness that our sense of self seems to lack constancy and consistency or that our sense of self-esteem fluctuates dramatically upon not receiving the recognition we desire. We register that our capacity to pause before we respond seems to be frequently elusive. Our bodies try to tell us something. We fail to listen. Our insomnia attempts to reach us, but we are beyond hearing.

To think dialectically and psychodynamically, we need to take notice of our vague notions and glimpses of our seemingly unconscious, automatic, and habitual affective, cognitive, and behavioral patterns. We need to be vigilantly attuned to their "felt meanings." We can be immensely helped in the recognition of the meaning of our unconscious patterns by an essential other. To some degree, our unconscious is in the consciousness of the Other. In other words, especially those who know us well can, at times, "see" our unconscious patterns more clearly than we do. Suppose, for example, we display the habitual relational pattern of always trying to please others. We embody this relational way of being with others sometimes with and at other times without a dim, but fleeting awareness. Others, including our therapists, however, see it clearly. They may, in a safe and secure context, gently bring this to our attention without making us defensive. Or, being dimly aware of this relational tendency, we can make it the focus of our attention. We begin to unravel its "felt meaning" and trace its developmental origin. We can commence to ascertain the difference between proper and improper pleasing and between proper and improper displeasing. Lastly, we begin to translate this *insight into meaning* into action. This is what it means to *think-and-live dialectically and psychodynamically.*

We are *persons* who have *problems*. But we are more and other than our problems. Yet, we, as persons, also identify with our problems. We are our problems. This is our contradictory nature. We say, "I am depressed." The "I" is identifying with the "depression." More foundationally, the "I" identifies with lifelong problematic patterns across domains of functioning, making them seem intransigent. These lifelong patterns, such as the previously mentioned relational pattern of "pleasing others," have become part of who we are. Our path toward emancipation involves dis-identifying from our faulty relational patterns – the characteristic maladaptive ways of feeling, thinking, and behaving. Not only does the "I" identify with our maladaptive relational patterns but also it identifies with our self-enhancing, actual, and potential strengths. Thus we need to strengthen our identification with our already existing strengths, cultivate new strengths with which to identify, and use them to help us counter our unhealthy identification with our limiting problematic patterns.

Self-analysis is made possible by the human capacity for *reflexivity*. In fact, Mann (1994) offers *A Simple Theory of the Self* in which *reflexivity is viewed as the essence of selfhood*: The "self is 'the individual as the object of his own reflective consciousness.' The self is its own observer, simultaneously I and Me, subject and object, to *itself* as well as to others" (pp. 30–31). Our self-awareness is almost always shadowing our waking consciousness. Our mindfully embodied propensity for "self-reflection … is inherent and necessary to our nature" (p. 32). For Mann, then, *reflexivity* and *self-reflection* are interchangeable.

"Reflexivity," Mann (1994) reiterates, "is the engine of consciousness. We are aware that we are aware" (p. 60). "Identity," he emphasizes yet again, "is the product of reflexivity" (p. 60). It is through reflexivity that we can maintain a sense of sameness and continuity that are essential elements in the persistence and integration of our identity. *Identity*, *selfhood*, and *personality* are used interchangeably. Reflexivity spans the domains of consciousness and unconsciousness that extend along a continuum. The "fundamental features of the self," elaborates Mann, are "reflexivity, bodiness, and time" (p. 61). The body-in-time serves as the locus of our capacity for reflexivity. When our capacity for reflexivity becomes skewed, the effect will be noticeable in how we live in body, time, and place. Even "emotion" is viewed as an "amalgam of bodiness and time" (p. 61). Our feeling life "*fuses bodily experience, time, and reflexivity into an irreducible kernel of psychic reality.* Feeling emanates from the center of being, the meeting point of the axes of the self" (p. 63).

Most symptomatic feelings, thoughts, and behaviors, asserts Mann (1994), "reduce ultimately to variations in the reflexive propensity of the self" (p. 61). Psychological symptoms tend to emerge when "the self-reflexive process," elaborates Mann, "becomes restricted or even fixed to certain regions of its range" (p. 76). But what makes reflexivity rigid? Mann's answer is that the self-reflexive process becomes restricted or fixed when the developing person is unable to attain a *balance* between *freedom* and *compliance*. His description is dialectical in nature:

> Psychological health rests on the balance between freedom and compliance. … The healthy self moves freely among possible states, yet belongs to the world and knows itself well enough to return home when need be. Freedom to move, compliance to be moved. Freedom is a privilege of [individual] ownership; compliance, a duty of [social] belonging. (pp. 76–77)

This description flies in the face of the popularity of the mindfulness movement that is in vogue today. One cannot reflexively *will* mindfulness and then expect to reap its long-term ripening fruits of such a mindful daily existence. Our capacity for mindful self-observation and self-analysis is made possible by our own self-reflexive process. Reflexivity, in turn, is contingent upon our ability to attain a delicate dialectical balance between the meaning-laden polarities of freedom ("ownership" or responsible owning) and compliance ("duty of belonging") and, I would add, many other polar meanings of existence that are elucidated throughout this text.

The meaning of freedom, for Mann (1994), manifests itself concretely in "*the principle of ownership*" (p. 109). To be free *is* "to own one's fate" (p. 109). "Owning and disowning describe experiences associated with sorting out what is and is not part of the self" (p. 108). How we own our fate will be mirrored in how we relate to others in our interpersonal world. The way we disown our fate is also a mirror of our embodied way of relating to others. When we disown certain regions of the self, we are simultaneously eclipsing diverse regions of meaning in our lifeworld. A distortion befalls the intentional arc between the subject-and-the-object. *Meanings* become *rigidified and skewed.* Mann's insights are here translated into phenomenological terms. Mann is providing us with a creative fusion of psychoanalysis and a dialectically informed existential-phenomenology.

Our lived freedom (ownership), illuminates Mann (1994), reveals itself in our sense of *agency* or choice-making capacity. "Choice," says Mann, is "the degree of subjective causation of one's own experience. … it signifies … the measure to which the self experiences agency" (p. 80). Those who struggle in assuming ownership cannot tell the difference between an internal locus of control (choice) and an external locus of control (fate). Those who are able to assume ownership *transform* their fate into destiny through the mediation of their sense of agency, while not denying the contingencies of fate.

Our psychological health or psychic maturation is dependent on cultivating the courage to be both compliant and free. As was quoted earlier, "compliance" is "a duty of belonging" (Mann, 1994, p. 77). Although he does not directly state it, Mann is implicitly making a distinction between genuine and false "belonging" (compliance). He uses the Piagetian concepts of *assimilation* and *accommodation* to illustrate the point. As a defense, while growing up, we may *over-assimilate* (excessively comply) in order to adapt and survive – in order to receive the semblance of belonging. Such "defense compromises reflexivity" (p. 92). "By contrast, [creative] accommodation tends to bring subjectivity into line with the object world, thus to heighten reflexivity and to serve the aims of self-ownership" (p. 92). In a good enough environment, "the task of human adaptation involves the struggle for self-possession amid the rigors of belonging to the world. This struggle organizes our experience" (p. 92). Just as there is bad assimilation, there is also bad accommodation. "Accommodation to misinformation about ourselves does not improve self-reflexivity, but potentially erodes it" (p. 93).

In the absence of the attainment of a precarious balance between freedom (ownership, agency) and compliance (belonging), our capacity for reflexivity is compromised. Just as there can be a skewing on the compliance side of the continuum, there can also be a distorted tilting on the freedom side – freedom gone awry. Some of my "struggling" college students who are academically at risk, for example, assert vehemently that they can be *anything* they want (choose) to be even in domains in which they have no proven aptitude, skill, or talent! Without relatively intact reflexivity we cannot *realistically* seek and acquire self-knowledge or knowledge about others – the *truth* about ourselves and about others. Mann calls the opposite of reflexivity *dysreflexia*. Of course, there are degrees of states of dysreflexia.

"When it [reflexivity] falters," says Mann (1994), "identity [and lifeworld, I would add] alters" (p. 60). Dysreflexia fails to maintain a self-world that "conforms well with what our hypothetical neutral observer would see" (p. 60). "Complete dysreflexia defines psychosis" (p. 61). A relatively intact reflexive self remains open to life's *possibilities*. In a dysreflexive mode of being, life possibilities shrink and close. In most psychopathologies, such as addictions and eating disorders, there is a loss of reflexivity. These are bodily selves in whom the accuracy and stability in reflexivity is lacking or wildly fluctuating. In their assessment of threat, for instance, there is a mismatch between their subjective sense and the objective situation.

In the presence of dysreflexia in intimate relationships, stuckness is likely to be experienced as fated. "The less conscious the [relational] pattern," explains Mann (1994), "the more fateful it feels" (p. 74). Compliance, as it appears, for example, in the form of a lifelong pattern of pleasing others, can go awry. "Ownership," on the other side of the continuum, "can go awry in other ways, as well." 'It' can feel like a part of me yet out of my control as in obsessions, compulsions, conversions, addictions, and certain delusions" (p. 91). All our "*defense*," or defensiveness, "*is secured through the sacrifice of reflexivity*. … Each psychological mechanism of defense can be seen as a loss of self through a compromise of reflexivity" (p. 91).

Reflexivity includes the capacity for *meta-meaning* making – making meanings about meanings. A loss in reflexivity involves stiffening in our ability for generative meaning making; it is a loss in perceiving meaning possibilities. Things could mean otherwise. Constriction in meaning possibilities entails a narrowing of our action potential and action range.

From a phenomenological perspective, elucidate Deurzen and Kenward (2005), a distinction is to be made between reflexive and *pre-reflexive consciousness* – "the simple awareness of objects [people and things] … it is what we are aware of before we are aware of ourselves, before we are conscious of the self" (p. 160). *Reflexive consciousness* refers to "consciousness of consciousness" or awareness of awareness (p. 160). The self, here, is present to awareness. But "there is a great range of consciousness" (p. 160). Linking awareness or consciousness to *meaning*, we may or may not be aware of the meanings we intend (are directed to); meanings are lived pre-reflexively or contemplated and then enacted reflexively. *Reflexivity* is a deepened form of self-reflection.

For Habermas (1971), psychoanalysis is "the only tangible example of a science incorporating methodical self-reflection" (p. 214), the aim of which is to overcome distorted communication and fixed ways of living. "Self-reflection," however, "is not a solitary movement; it is tied to the intersubjectivity of linguistic communication with an Other. In the end self-consciousness is constituted only on the basis of mutual recognition" (pp. 344–345). In amending "linguistic" communication by adding "pre-linguistic" communication, Habermas is in synchrony with the insights of Maurice Merleau-Ponty (1962) and Erik Erikson (1963).

Through a deepened, affective self-reflection, situated in mutual social interaction, mutual rational communication, and mutual recognition, I can correct my faulty social self-formation. I can dis-identify from my early maladaptive identifications. I can learn to correct my distorted way of communicating. I can appropriate new and healthy identifications. Through self-reflection, holds Habermas (1971), "the self makes itself transparent to itself as action that returns into itself" (p. 207). In becoming transparent to myself – in learning the emotional-and-relational truth about myself, I emancipate myself. I achieve self-emancipation through deep and feeling-laden self-reflection and self-understanding. Habermas sees this process of renewal of self-formation in psychoanalysis. I believe that Habermas would concur that this kind of self-renewal can occur in social contexts other than psychotherapy. Human beings, holds Habermas, have a *fundamental interest* in acquiring self-and-relational *knowledge* through *understanding-and-being understood.* Moreover, as Rogers (1951) would wholeheartedly affirm, the experience of *being understood* is crucial for our development, growth, and psychosocial maturation.

References

Cabaniss, D. L., Cherry, S., Douglas, C. J., Graver, R. L., & Schwartz, A. R. (2013). *Psychodynamic formulation*. Wiley.

Deurzen, E. V., & Kenward, R. (2005). *Dictionary of existential psychotherapy and counselling*. Sage.

Erikson, E. H. (1963). *Childhood and society* (2nd ed.). W. W. Norton.
Habermas, J. (1971). *Knowledge and human interests.* (J. J. Shapiro, Trans.). Beacon Press.
Mann, D. W. (1994). *A simple theory of the self.* W. W. Norton.
Merleau-Ponty, M. (1962). *Phenomenology of perception* (C. Smith, Trans.). Routledge.
Rogers, C. R. (1951). *Client-centered therapy: Its current practice, implications, and theory.* Houghton Mifflin.

3

Self-Understanding: The Capacity for *Self-Understanding* and Insight into the Self

Why do we think, feel, and behave the way we do? Are we interested in answering questions about the way we think, feel, and behave? Are we even dimly aware of possible answers that seem to hover on the borderline of our consciousness or in the mirroring consciousness of others, especially those close to us? Why do we experience unwelcome repetitive feelings and thoughts? Why do we habitually behave in maladaptive ways thinking that this time the outcome will be different? Why do we deal with anxiety or stress the way we do? Why do we have repetitive difficulties in our work and in our love life? Why can't we enjoy ourselves, have fun, be playful, and take life less seriously? Why do we engage in regressive or self-destructive acts? Why do we hurt the ones we most love? Why is it that sometimes we behave as if earlier conditions from our past are still persistently present? Seeking answers to such questions rigorously can contribute to our continuing maturation and growth.

Our "problems," say Cabaniss and her colleagues (2013), "are often caused by thoughts and feelings that are out of awareness – that is, that are **unconscious**" (p. 4). Becoming aware of our unconscious thoughts and feelings and understanding how they developed are good for our maturation and growth. They are good for our well-being and mental health.

What we need for our continued maturation and growth, says Ogden (2012), is cultivating "the art of looking deeply *into* seemingly ordinary conscious experience" (p. 173). But for Ogden, as it is for phenomenological psychologists, "there is only one consciousness … the unconscious aspect of consciousness is *in* the conscious aspect, not under it or behind it … conscious and unconscious experience are qualities of a unitary consciousness … we gain access to the unconscious dimension of experience by looking *into*

© The Author(s), under exclusive license to Springer Nature Switzerland AG 2021

M. J. Hannush, *Markers of Psychosocial Maturation*,
https://doi.org/10.1007/978-3-030-74315-4_3

conscious experience, not by looking 'behind' it or 'beneath' it" (pp. 173–174). "In other words," continues Ogden, "consciousness and unconsciousness are aspects of a single entity viewed from different vertices… The unconscious is always a dimension of consciousness whether or not it is easily perceptible, just as the stars are always in the sky whether or not they are obscured by the glare of the sun" (p. 177). Our developmental task is to cultivate "a form of consciousness characterized by a seamless continuity of conscious and unconscious experience" (pp. 176–177).

For many, many years I have enjoyed washing my face upon awakening in the morning. Not infrequently, I have had the feeling that it is a sensuous, vitalizing, and hope-laden experience. In difficult, tiring, and trying times, I have found myself washing my face more than once during the day. I have always tacitly known that in my face washing I was identifying with my mother. As an adult, I recollect an image of my young mother – who later died prematurely in a car accident, in my mind's eye, washing her face and being taken by the way she did it. The ritual struck me as not simply serving the pragmatic purpose of cleansing and awakening. I sensed in the ritual of splashing water on the face while bent on the sink the joy of having her face touched by water, the source of life. Like her, I derive from such a simple ritual of face washing a sense of rejuvenation and renewal, however fleeting it may be. For me, there is a touch of beauty, goodness, and truth in repeatedly retrieving this image of my mother and identifying with it. Yet, my way of washing my face every morning and each day is not "identical" to the way my mother gently splashed water on her beautiful face. My "identification" is a creative fusion of her way and my own special way, given that, though similar, we are both unique, and not identical beings. Additionally, the face washing ritual that we share maintains the deep affinity and affection I have always felt for my mother. That is what this morning ritual *means* to me. It is not an "abstract" meaning. It is a lived, existential meaning. As the excavation of my experience of the meaning of face washing delineates – brings to the surface what was at one time mostly "unconscious" – it is a meaning that is inevitably connected to other meanings. But the meaningfulness of the ritual goes beyond the uncovering of related meanings because of the way its meaning *energizes* and *rejuvenates* me. It is a spatiotemporal embodied experience that says "Yes" to life. It says it in renewing and revitalizing action and not just in repeatedly evaporating words.

In order to understand our primary relational patterns and those of others, we need to understand our (and their) developmental histories – how and why we all developed the way we did. We have to observe, listen, inquire, and reflect on what we say and do to ourselves, what others say and do to us, what we say and do to others, and what others say and do to themselves.

One enlightened way of approaching our unconscious is oblique. Here is an incisive description of this indirect approach given by Fiumara (2013):

> As is known, we can only apprehend our unconscious and its conflicts by means of inferences. There is no direct route. There is nothing we can learn by just fighting with our unconscious conflicts; and thus the creative, maturational approach to the unconscious is through acceptance, acknowledgement, consent – paradoxically a surrender to our conflictive vicissitudes … With the acknowledgment and acceptance of our [unconscious] psychic currents also comes a measure of freedom from them. (p. 32)

We need to learn, says Fiumara, to approach our unconscious psychic currents with acceptance, acknowledgment, consent, forgiveness (without a forgiving *agent*, for it is not a form of *willful* forgiveness), and surrender. We need to create a symbolic domain or milieu to give creative expression to our instinctual vicissitudes (learn to sublimate). We have to cultivate an attitude of neutrality as we face our psychic currents. We need to look at our painful conflicts or crises for they conceal within them opportunities for transformational experiences. When we can acceptingly and freely talk to ourselves and/or our therapeutic others, we are making it possible for a still space to surround our unconscious conflicts. Curative talk or healing discourse will begin to replace our combative (self-) talk or discourse. Our thick and conflictive tangles will be transmuted in this transformative space. When our hot buttons are triggered in relational contexts, we can "gladly" accept them to allow another, "ulterior" kind of thinking-feeling-acting to replace the old way of knowing-emoting-and-doing. These "ulterior" ways of knowing-emoting-and-doing "may function like a psychic embrace" (p. 33). We are then welcomingly invited to this transformative space.

Our "unconsciousness is attained [fashioned]," asserts Fiumara (2013), "in order not to know the self-damaging evil [destructiveness] that we do" (p. 68). In order not to know, we fashion "inner disconnections" that "ultimately amounts to damaging one's own self" (p. 68). A "shift" occurs "from integration to fragmentation" (p. 68). "And so vanity [false pride] necessarily leads to projective, splitting policies [strategies]" (p. 68). But "our talent for healing is to invent linking strategies" instead of "falling" for our alluring, yet "damaging projective inclinations – because of course we can only project what we have previously split [or disowned]" (p. 69).

Fiumara's (2013) insight into the fashioning of the unconscious requires a commentary.

1. We need to be reminded that our unconscious is a vital and vitalizing part of our consciousness and that there are degrees of being unconscious. We may have vague stirrings of its presence in the manner of our being-and-doing, to which we conveniently pay no heed. It is therefore more useful to speak of degrees of conscious and unconscious ways of being-in-the-world-with-self-and-others. Stated differently, the bodily self's conscious and unconscious attunement to lifeworld meanings come in degrees.
2. Even seemingly enlightened psychoanalysts fall for reductive mentalism or psychologism, thus emphasizing the inner over the outer. Of course, there are psychologists who fall for reductive environmentalism, thus stressing the outer over the inner. From existential-phenomenology we learn that self-and-world are inseparable. Consequently, if there is a split within, there is invariably a split without. There is no need to make use of "projection" to connect the inner with the outer. "Inner disconnections" have their correlates in our "fragmented/disjointed world." Disconnections-within and disconnections-without go hand-in-hand. Thus, when we do damage (destruction) to ourselves, we invariably do damage (destruction) to our relational world. Anyway, (a) we, relatively unconsciously, do to ourselves what was done unto us; (b) we, relatively unconsciously, do to others what was done unto us; (c) we, relatively unconsciously, invite others to do unto us what was done unto us, and (d) we, relatively unconsciously, provoke others to do unto themselves what was done unto us.
3. Fiumara speaks only of our acknowledged or unacknowledged "shadowy" unconscious. But, as Bollas (2011) repeatedly reminds us, our dark unconscious carries within it the phosphorous light that is the source of our animating (playful) creativity and life-affirming vitality.

Insight into the self, or self-understanding, contends Rogers (1989), is necessary for movement toward integration and full functioning. Rogers describes a client in therapy who comes to the realization ("insight and self-understanding come bubbling to the surface") that he has "no need to be defensive about his negative feelings" (p. 73). "It is this acceptance of both the mature and immature impulses … which gives the individual an opportunity for the first time in his life to understand himself as he is" (p. 72). Rogers reflects: "This insight, this understanding of the self and acceptance of the self … provides the basis on which the individual can go ahead to new levels of integration" (p. 73). Once "emotional understanding" or "insight is achieved," writes Rogers, "the actions that are taken are likely to be admirably suited to the new insight"

(p. 75). Through "more complete and accurate self-understanding," expands Rogers, "the individual gains courage to see more deeply into his own actions" (p. 75). As insight is "increasingly integrated [into] positive action on the part of the client ... [t]here is less fear about making choices, and more confidence in self-directed action" (p. 75). This integrative movement is a response to the call of the "drive to be a better, more mature [person]" (p. 75).

The primary theme of the person-centered approach to therapy, reflects Rogers (1989), is that "the individual has within himself or herself vast resources for self-understanding, for altering his or her self-concept, attitudes, and self-directed behavior" (p. 135). These "resources for self-understanding," Rogers concludes, "can be tapped if only a definable climate of facilitative psychological attitudes can be provided" (p. 135). Three conditions make up this "growth-promoting climate": (1) acceptance, caring, or prizing; (2) congruence, genuineness, or realness; and (3) empathic attunement and understanding.

Hermans and Kempen (1993) provide us with a dialogical-dialectical theory of the self and then offer us a blueprint as to how to gain insight into the dialogical self. The self, they hold, is *reflexive* in that "it can be both subject and object. The self as subject can take itself as object" (p. 102). A subject is not only that which is subjected or "thrown" into unceasing frustration, resistance, and suffering, but also one who, as an embedded and embodied agent, takes initiative and acts upon the world. As the object of its own self-awareness and self-reflection, the subject is capable of gaining insight into the self.

Hermans and Kempen (1993) conceive of the self as "a developing narrative of personal meanings attributed to events considered as relevant to one's individual history" (p. 81). Moreover, "self-narratives imply the interplay of opposite [contrasting, contradictory, colliding] characters [meaning-laden traits]" (p. 163). Here are some descriptive examples of contrasting meanings attributed to characters or traits: "open versus closed, active versus passive, ambitious versus lazy, serious versus playful, masculine versus feminine" (p. 88). The polar meanings of autonomy versus communal connectedness would serve as yet another example. These can be understood as protagonists and antagonists in a dramatic narrative. Every narrative that is infused with polar meanings is lived dialogically – intrapersonally and interpersonally. "Dialogue is at the heart of every thought" (p. 43). Symmetrical dialogues involving harmonious affect-and-value-laden meanings give the self a sense of coherence, continuity, and integrity. Asymmetrical dialogues result in self-experiences that are discontinuous, chaotic, confused, contradictory, and dispersive. The "coherence of the self ... is the result of a dialogical relationship between the individual and other persons. In other words, the self is not a given but an emergent" (p. 44). Psychosocial maturation involves "achieving a more symmetrical or synthesized self" (p. 80). "Self" is understood as "synthesizing *activity*" (p. 92). Asymmetrical and discontinuous experiences, when confronted with openness, can disclose "new fields of meaning" (p. 51). Moreover, "conflict and contradiction," "once faced, may extend the experiential field of the person and contribute to its richness" (p. 59). Egalitarian dialogues are more conducive to the self's synthesizing activity. Dominance-based dialogues are less likely to support the self in its goal of achieving symmetry and synthesis. The "self," then, "is a dialogical phenomenon that works according to the principles of intersubjective exchange and [or] dominance" (p. 98). In an intersubjective exchange, participants in the dialogue are willing to *share their agency*.

The self, expand Hermans and Kempen (1993), can also be conceived as revolving around affectively charged and uniquely appropriated familial and societal value-laden meanings with which the self identifies or dis-identifies:

> The people with whom I positively identify and the ones with whom I disidentify are both part of myself. In their opposition and irreconcilability, they call upon a struggle of the Self. The same view applies to myself as part of society. I may identify with some groups, classes, or categories of people and disidentify with other ones … the developing person finds himself somewhere between splitting and synthesis and, therefore, the struggle of synthesis is always associated with a continuous shifting of the self/non-self boundaries. (p. 120)

For Hermans and Kempen (1993), identifications, along with imitations and internalizations, are forms of (internal) dialogue. We gain insight into the self through either partaking of an inner or, better yet, relational dialogue concerning the developmental history of our meaning making constructions. Have I achieved, relatively speaking, a balanced synthesis between the personalized meanings of self-enhancement, on the one hand, and communal enhancement, on the other? The "Western self is not well equipped to deal with polar opposites" (p. 163). Under relatively optimal dialogical conditions of open exchange, I can become receptive to a new emotional understanding of my previously held either/or meaning attributions and gain a heart-felt insight that now includes new and transforming both/and meaning attributions: that self-enhancement and communal enhancement require and are not antagonistic to each other. "Meaning emerges from dialogical movements" – movements in meaning that occur as a consequence of being a co-participant in an egalitarian dialogue, say, with a significant other. The "*dialogical movement* … transforms meaning into meaning making, or meaning construction"

(p. 167). Gaining insight into the self as a center for meaning synthesis involves the recognition that "*there are always neglected and suppressed meanings*" (p. 168). If one sedimented meaning habit – say, "If I do not *dominate*, I am nothing" – is an intrinsic feature of a dialogical style, then "the prevalence of one meaning implies the necessary neglect or suppression of other ones" (p. 168). Meanings can become neglected for reasons implicated by one's own personal, developmental, familial, and cultural history.

Gaining insight into the *dialogical self* through *monitoring its meaning movements* is an approach that is in synchrony with Fuller's (1990) *phenomenological theory of insight* (pp. 164–170). "Phenomenological psychology," writes Fuller, "finds that ... an activity of insight does indeed make a difference in the meanings we actually grasp; that insight is an invariantly required co-organizer of meaning; that insight [just like meaning] has a standing of its own" (p. 164). "Insight is an immediate awareness of 'the structure of a situation' ... of how one meaning stands with regard to another –or perhaps how a meaning affects the self" (pp. 158–159). "Insight," he continues, "is the openness of [to] events of meaning presencing" as a lifeworld event (p. 165). "The insightful self" releases meaning possibilities in one's existential lifeworld. To "exist," expounds Fuller, "is to be in openness to events of meaning presencing ... [it is to] *let* meanings *be* ... [to] let meanings matter" (p. 166). It is to be open to other meanings. As meanings "grow," so does Dasein (human *being*). There is a *becoming* in the being of Dasein and, correlatively, there is a *becoming* in the *being* of meanings in the lifeworld.

Meanings are affect-and-value-laden events. Experiencing polar meanings, states Fuller (1990), involves being "affected by the tension thus set in motion" (p. 167). It necessitates being caught in "the play of tensions (stretches) between them" (p. 167). "Insight partakes of the original having it out of meaning's phenomenal tensions" (p. 167). The embedded, embodied, insightful self seeks to actualize itself through the "coactualization of meanings in accordance with structural demands of their own" (p. 169). "Insight," which is an interpretive activity, says Fuller, "is responsible answering to meaning, a responding that disposes itself to the structural necessity of meaning events" (p. 196). Responsibility is an attitude of opening oneself to releasing meaning's possibilities. "Insight interpretively releases a meaning's tensions to their everrenewed [sic] pursuit of balanced possibilities" (p. 172). **Positive meanings** are experienced as, or provide us with, a sense of *balance, balanced fulfillment, clarity, equilibrium, equilibrated belonging, calmness, incisiveness, harmony, integrity, peace, purity, regularity, rightness, simplicity, stability, tranquility*, and *symmetry* (pp. 105–131). **Negative meanings** – meanings charged with negative affect and are disvalued – trigger in us opposite experiences.

Negative meanings create restless tension. These meanings are "not at peace" (p. 122). When we are confronted with a bad meaning, we wish it to be otherwise. Negative meanings, however, "may occasion an increase in the richness and complexity of our meanings, for the law of good gestalt, all the while seeking a state of balance, works to integrate new and disturbing elements into existing wholes of meaning" (pp. 168–169).

Positive meanings, Fuller (1990) tells us, are "meanings 'to be reached,' 'to be supported,' 'to be maintained,'" and negative meanings "are meanings 'to be avoided,' to be changed in the positive direction, 'to be eliminated'" (p. 140). Positive meanings are intrinsically connected with "love, beauty, and moral action [goodness]" (p. 156). Human beings are directed toward *feeling-and-value-laden polar meanings.* "As one of our meanings, a fellow human being is [primarily] another 'myself'" (p. 145) and, I would add, secondarily "not-myself." Whether it is things (events, projects, or people) we are caringly involved with, they all carry *meanings* for us. "Meaning," elaborates Fuller, "is something or someone with which Dasein [*human being*] is preoccupied, about which Dasein cares in some way, precisely as something or someone is brought close in its lived dimensionality" (p. 81).

It turns out that *good meanings*, says Fuller (1990), are analogous to *good gestalts* ["Gestalt is meaning" (p. 98)], toward which we are primarily directed. They are meanings that are experienced as, or provide us with, an *ultimate* sense of *beauty, goodness,* and *truth.* "The law of good gestalt [or good meaning]," Fuller says, "could almost as well be called the law of beauty" (p. 150). There are "meanings that are especially pure and excellent. They are meanings that are outstanding in the *beauty of their goodness*" (p. 151). These meanings *feel right* or *true.* There is a "sheer nonpsychological rightness of … [this kind of] original meaning" (p. 151). "All meaning," expands Fuller, "strives for its own perfection as a good gestalt … A gestalt [meaning] is an action (process) in which tensions are at play in the direction of best meaning (outcome) possible" (p. 114). When we face meanings that are not good enough, we, barring a proclivity to distortion and defensiveness, spontaneously attempt to improve the not-quite-good-enough meaning. The tension between good or good enough meanings with bad or not good enough meanings is at the heart of our everyday psychosocial reality.

There are two forces at work in the self's striving toward good meanings in the lifeworld: "the tendency toward … tension reduction [tendency toward the simplest, most regular, and balanced meaning] with [the tendency toward] tension enhancement [articulation of meaning]" (p. 116). Setting aside the developmentally arresting tendency to deny, distort, or defend against seemingly bad (threatening) meanings in an effort to reduce tension (anxiety), our tolerance for anxiety, unfamiliarity, uncertainty, and ambiguous complexity opens us to new, emergent, individuated, and integrative meanings. For instance, suppose that for me, tender-mindedness means weakness, whereas tough-mindedness means power, being-in-control. In a loving relational context, I may feel safe, secure, and relaxed enough to open myself up to experiencing the empowering feeling of mutual tenderness. The meanings of "tenderness" and "empowerment" have shifted. This instance illustrates the growth-enhancing role of impassioned insight into one's own affect-and-value-laden-meanings.

References

Bollas, C. (2011). *The Christopher Bollas reader*. Routledge.

Cabaniss, D. L., Cherry, S., Douglas, C. J., Graver, R. L., & Schwartz, A. R. (2013). *Psychodynamic formulation*. Wiley.

Fiumara, G. C. (2013). *Psychoanalysis and creativity in everyday life: Ordinary genius*. Routledge.

Fuller, A. R. (1990). *Insight into value: An exploration of the premises of a phenomenological psychology*. State University of New York Press.

Hermans, H. J. M., & Kempen, H. J. G. (1993). *The dialogical self: Meaning as movement*. Academic Press.

Ogden, T. H. (2012). *Creative readings: Essays on seminal analytic works*. Routledge.

Rogers, C. R. (1989). *The Carl Rogers reader*. Houghton Mifflin.

4

Self-Transcendence: The Capacity for *Self-Transcendence* Through the Suspension of Belief/Judgment

Though they approach it differently, the phenomenon of *self-transcendence* or simply *transcendence* is a major theme in the work of humanistic, existential, and phenomenological psychologists and philosophers. Tageson (1982) equates self-transcendence with self-reflexivity, which refers to "the capacity of the mind [self] 'to rise above itself and turn back *critically* on what it normally does without examination or question'" (p. 28). It points to the ability to reflexively stand back or aside to engage, with care, in self-observation in order to take stock of one's life. Without the "experience of reflexive self-awareness," Tageson adds, "the experiences of self-determination [or freedom], or the illusion [distorted version] of it, would be simply impossible" (p. 18). Analogously, without the experience of self-transcendence, awareness of limitedness and mortality would not be possible.

For Rogers (1980), self-transcendence refers to the ability to "advance beyond the ordinary level of consciousness" (p. 128). It is an altered state of consciousness whereby one is "in touch with, and grasp[s] the meaning of … [an] evolutionary flow … [a] tending toward a transcending experience of unity" (p. 128). One experiences oneself as "being dissolved in a whole area of higher values, especially beauty, harmony, and love" (p. 128). It involves a mystical "experience of union with the universal" (p. 128). When experienced in a communal context, one experiences one's "transcendental core" reaching out and touching the "transcendental core" of the Other.

One key characteristic of *self-actualizers* (healthy or mature persons), states Maslow (1968), is having the capacity to experience mystical or "peak" experiences. In such "peak" moments, *the self is transcended* and the peak-experiencing person is gripped with feelings of awe, bliss, confidence, decisiveness, ecstasy,

© The Author(s), under exclusive license to Springer Nature Switzerland AG 2021

M. J. Hannush, *Markers of Psychosocial Maturation*,
https://doi.org/10.1007/978-3-030-74315-4_4

empowerment, and potentiation. Still, peak experiences can vary from mild to intense ones. Healthier persons, however, have more intense peak experiences than persons of average mental health. Maslow calls high "peakers" as "*transcenders*."

Peak experiences, then, are moments in which self-transcendence is experienced. Maslow (1968) defines these momentary experiences of self-transcendence as:

> basic cognitive [knowledge-illuminating or truth-revealing] happenings in the B[ing]-love experience, the parental experience, the mystic, oceanic, or nature experience, the aesthetic perception, the creative moment, the therapeutic or intellectual insight, the orgasmic experience, certain forms of athletic fulfillment, etc. These and other moments of highest happiness and fulfillment I shall call peak experiences. (p. 73)

In addition to peak experiencing, responding to the call of ultimate or Being-values (Beauty, Goodness, Justice, Meaningfulness, Order, Perfection, Playfulness, Simplicity, Truth, Unity, Wholeness, and more) is another pathway to self-transcendence.

Frankl (1969) holds that the search for meaning overrides a search for oneself (pp. 50–79). Through seeking and discovering value-laden meanings, such as those tied to beauty, love, and moral action, humans transcend their psychological states. People strive to actualize meaningful, value-laden goals *beyond* themselves. They are always, already directed to things beyond themselves, "a meaning to fulfill or another human being to encounter lovingly" (p. 78). People are happy when they choose meanings worth living for. For Frankl, the will to meaning is a core characteristic of *reflexive consciousness* that renders humans as *self-transcending* organisms. The basic human orientation toward seeking and discovering meaning is a self-transcending life project. The call-to-meaning beckons a responsible answer from all of us.

Bakewell (2010), herself deeply acquainted with existential-phenomenology, writes that French philosopher Michel de Montaigne (1533–1592), having been touched to the core of his being by classical Greek philosopher Pyrrho (360–270 BC) and his later popularizer, Roman philosopher Sextus Empiricus's (160–210 CE) concept of *epoche* – meaning, "I suspend judgment," had it inscribed in a series of medals "together with his own arms and an emblem of weighing scales [signifying balance] so as to keep this goal in the forefront of his mind" (p. 127). Montaigne's own French rendition of the Greek *epoche* is, *je soutiens*, meaning "I hold back." By suspending judgment, one becomes ataraxic (relaxed) and even joyful. One no longer takes oneself or life too seriously. By suspending judgment, one is freed from the need for certainty. One is more attuned to one's own fallibility. It is okay not to know. It is all right not to have a fix on *the* truth. It is better to view everything – most of all oneself, questioningly. It is far better to take oneself lightly. Montaigne wants to "remind himself both to maintain balance, and to weigh things up rather than merely accepting them" at face value (p. 127). That is why, for Montaigne, the scale is another deeply meaningful symbol that he paired with the term *epoche* in the inscribed medals that he carved out for himself as constant reminders of how he wanted to live.

"If the medal was indeed designed to remind him [Montaigne] of his principles [of how to live]," comments Bakewell (2010), "it worked":

> Skepticism guided him at work, in his home life, and in his writing. The *Essays* [Montaigne's classic work] are suffused with it: he filled his pages with words such as 'perhaps,' 'to some extent,' 'I think,' 'It seems to me,' and so on – words which, as Montaigne said himself, 'soften and moderate the rashness of our propositions' [assumptions], and which embody what the critic Hugo Friedrich has called his [Montaigne's] philosophy of 'unassumingness.'
>
> And of all that was mysterious, nothing amazed him more than himself, the most unfathomable phenomenon of all. Countless times, he noticed himself changing an opinion from one extreme to the other, or shifting from emotion to emotion within seconds. (p. 128)

To illustrate, Bakewell quotes Montaigne directly:

> My footing is so unsteady and so insecure. I find it so vacillating and ready to slip, and my sight is so unreliable, that on an empty stomach I feel myself another man than after a meal. If my health smiles upon me, and the brightness of a beautiful day, I am a fine fellow; if I have a corn bothering my toe, I am surly, unpleasant, and unapproachable. (p. 129)

All philosophy and philosophizing or all psychology and psychologizing for that matter, Montaigne would say, is incarnate. Even my simplest perceptions cannot be depended on. When I am ill, my world is experienced differently, compared to when I am healthy and well. "'The [rabid] dog's saliva could make,'" quoting Montaigne, "'all [of Socrates'] philosophy, if it were incarnate [which it is], raving mad'" (p. 129).

"Montaigne's talent," says Bakewell (2010), lies in "being able to slip out from behind his eyes so as to gaze back upon himself with Pyrrohonian suspension of judgment [epoche]" (p. 129). This opens Montaigne to a "new way of living" whereby "the world becomes a multidimensional landscape in which every point of view must be taken into account" (p. 130). This way, once more quoting Montaigne, we "'become wise at our own expense'" (p. 130). This incipiently phenomenological method in living – this living by the "question everything" rule – necessitates constant effort. As Montaigne puts it, "'we must really strain our soul to be aware of our own fallibility'" (p. 130).

Montaigne's skepticism, Bakewell (2010) informs us, predisposes him to "celebrate his imperfection" (p. 147). His skepticism, however, is practiced not as end in itself. After questioning everything, "he deliberately reaffirms everything that is familiar, uncertain, and ordinary – for that is all we have" (p. 147). With rigor, he tries to (cheerfully) accept whatever happens or has happened – including the things he has made happen in his past:

> Montaigne knew that some of the things he had done in the past no longer made sense to him, but he was content to presume that he must have been a different person at the time, and leave it at that. His past selves were as diverse as a group of people at a party. Just as he would not think of passing judgment on a roomful of acquaintances, all of them had their own reasons and points of view to explain what they had done, so he would not think of judging previous versions of Montaigne. 'We are all patchworks,' he wrote, 'and so shapeless and diverse in composition that each bit, each moment, plays its own game.'
>
> No overall point of view existed he could look back and construct the one consistent Montaigne that he would have liked to be … he did not try to airbrush his previous selves out of life. (pp. 286–287)

In Montaigne, I find not only a nascent phenomenologist but also a consummate dialectician. I will soon show how Michel de Montaigne and pioneering phenomenologist Edmund Husserl (1859–1938) converge in their understanding of the *epoche* – the suspension of judgment. To emphasize yet again, after *doubting* everything, "he deliberately reaffirms everything that is familiar, uncertain, and ordinary – for that is all we have" (Bakewell, 2010, p. 147). This simple sentence discloses Montaigne's dialectical approach to living. He lives by the rule of rational (questioning; doubting) faith (re-affirming things as they are; returning back to basic meanings). Montaigne uses doubt only to return to organismic faith – faith in the human organism as it is, as a guide for living. Montaigne, however, has his slippages. In reflecting on his understanding of the "self" – especially himself – he becomes forgetful of his natural, dialectical grounding. He only focuses one-sidedly on the self as "patchwork," "shapeless," and "diverse." But that is only one meaning pole: Montaigne's discontinuous sense of self or, more accurately, selves. He glosses over the other meaning pole – Montaigne's continuous sense of self, which is in dialectical tension with Montaigne's discontinuous sense of multiple selves. Of course, Montaigne would "celebrate" this slippage. One of Montaigne's favorite rhetorical questions is: "What do I know?"

To retrieve the unadulterated meaning of things – the pure phenomena that appear in human experience, thus the name "phenomenology," Husserl, the father of phenomenology, instructs us to suspend all prior knowledge (theories) or preconceived judgments. Husserl calls this suspension "bracketing" or *epoche*, which means to place all our biases, expectations, preconceptions, prejudgments, and prejudices temporarily into a bracket or holding position. The ultimate aim is to *reduce*, never to totally eliminate, our everyday judgmental (natural) attitude toward the things we experience – to the "natural" way we unreflectively attribute meanings to things and people. Husserl labels this as the "phenomenological reduction." As his work unfolds over time, Husserl envisions a series of progressive *reductive* steps the aim of which is to purify the "natural" flow of consciousness, culminating in a purified transcendental ego (I) experiencing things as they are – *purified meanings*, as much as that is humanly possible (although this is my own condensed interpretive version, see the section on "Edmund Husserl" in the *Encyclopedia of Phenomenology*, edited by Embree and his colleagues (1997) for a detailed description of these reductive steps). To use my own simplifying words, as we neutralize the biased, judgmental selves that we are in our everyday life and identify with a more or less neutral observing Self, we begin to experience the *meanings* of things (persons or happenings) of our world more accurately. Though never totally, we are better poised to understand the *basic or essential meanings* of our interpersonal world. Just as there is a shift in our affective-mental stance on the Self-side, there is simultaneously a switch in what we experience on the World-side. This is a wonderful way of describing how we humans co-constitute or co-create our worlds. This is the arc of intentionality in action. But not only is *intentionality* of the essence of consciousness – consciousness or, better, bodily self – always other (meaning)-directed, so too is its *reflexivity* – the ability to reflectively disengage or distance ourselves from our everyday meaning attributions, which makes it possible for us to assume the reductive stance of the *epoche* – the ability to more or less neutrally observe our everyday meaning attributions.

The so-called Husserlian more-or-less-neutral bracketing – a shifting to a neutral gear, so to speak, that defines the "reductive" epoche – is apparently, to my understanding, re-visioned in the later unpublished manuscripts of Husserl (Melle, 2002). Husserl, according to Melle, comes to view it as an "ethical epoche":

> The concern about my life as a whole becomes an ethical concern through an *ethical epoche*, a bracketing of my whole previous life and a universal critique of it oriented toward a radical renewal according to *ethical ideals*. A person can draw together the totality of her previous life and can come to the insight that her first life was neither happy nor good because it was a life of dispersion and drifting or a naïve life guided by unquestioned traditional acceptances. She can then make a solemn decision that encompasses her entire future life from then on … Husserl calls it 'a personal decision of the active heart.' (pp. 243–244)

The ethical ideal toward which the epoche is oriented has to do with being true to oneself. "A person … is who she is most inwardly [truly] by her love and calling" – the calling of "our individual conscience" (p. 244). "I am who I am by loving" (p. 245). The ever renewable "decision of the active heart" to abide by the calling of love and conscience enables us to "overcome blind fate and evil" and inevitable setbacks (p. 247).

"The rule of *epoche*," says Spinelli (1989), "urges us to impose an 'openness' on our immediate experience so that our subsequent interpretation of it may prove to be more adequate" (p. 17).

> For example, imagine that you are about to meet someone for the first time and that you have been told certain things about this person by others so that, even before your meeting, you have built up a number of expectations and reservations about that person. Chances are that your initial experience of that person will have been already 'set' and constrained by these biases. And, as is often the case under these circumstances, your judgments and conclusions about the person may turn out to be both inadequate and imbalanced.
>
> On the other hand, were you to follow the first step of the phenomenological method [the rule of *epoche*], you would attempt to bracket these biases as far as possible for you so that you had more of an open mind about that person and so that your subsequent conclusions would be based more upon your immediate experience of the person rather than upon prior assumptions and expectations. (p. 17)

In order to reduce our tendency toward judgmentalism, asserts Adams (2009), we need to strengthen our observer self: "Really effective, intentional change begins with strengthening your *observer self.* The better you can see what is already there – that's where the observer self comes in – the better you can apply the right skills and strategies to make the changes you want" (p. 32). To emphasize, when we are in the observer mode – when we are using the observer part of ourselves – we are better able to *clearly see what is already there*. Although she does not use the term, Adams is making use of the rule of *epoche*.

To empower our *observer self*, elaborates Adams (2009), we need to cultivate the sub-capacities of calmness, centeredness, equanimity, presence, and stillness. To become an *observer self*, a person needs to learn:

> how to stand outside himself and nonjudgmentally witness his thoughts, feelings, and actions … we all have this observer capacity. It is sometimes experienced as a feeling of watching a movie in which we are one of the actors. …
>
> From the position of observer, we have the ability to simply notice *what is*, somewhat detached from our own thoughts and feelings. We become more able to distinguish between our own sense of what's true and what's actually happening around us. It is a way of being more 'mindful' of the role our own emotions, opinions, or attachments play in how we view the world. (p. 160)

"Is it ever possible," asks Adams, "to become 100 percent objective and open to what's true and real? Probably not," she answers (p. 161). "But," she adroitly adds, "switching into observer mode, to any degree, is an invaluable skill for negotiating change, making decisions, operating effectively under pressure, and relating well to others" (p. 161).

In my opinion, Adams's (2009) method, though in part phenomenological, is heavily anchored in a fusion of cognitive behavior therapy and the choice theory behind reality therapy. It lacks the rigor of the phenomenological method and the balancing and enriching presence of dialectical thinking and psychodynamic insight seeking. Adams calls her method "Question Thinking or QT" (p. 9). "Thinking" is emphasized from the very beginning. "Questioning" is a form of thinking.

> Much of the time we're barely conscious of asking questions, especially the ones we ask ourselves. But they're a part of our thought processes nearly every moment of our lives. Thinking actually occurs as an internal question and answer process. Not only that, we often answer questions by taking some action. (p. 25)

Simply stated, Adams (2009) asserts that by changing the questions we ask of our selves or others, we change our lives – the way we live. Good questions result in wiser choices, focused and effective actions, and positive bodily sensations and emotions.

Whether we are aware of it or not, we are always asking questions. Some questions place us in the path of "learning"; other questions move us automatically and reactively in the direction of judgmentalism. Moreover, we always have a "choice" as to whether we want to be imprisoned by "judger" questions or freed by "learner" questions. Change involves "switching" from "judger" (judgmental) to "learner" (open-minded) questioning. The only barrier to "switching" is our natural human tendency to be judgmental. Being judgmental ultimately implies either an attack on the self or an attack on others. Here are some "judger" questions: "What's wrong with me? How can I prove I'm right? ... Why is that person so stupid and frustrating? How can I be in control?" And here are some "learner" questions: "What do I want? What can I learn? What are the facts? ... What is the other person thinking, feeling, and wanting? What is the big picture? What is possible?" (p. 50).

To repeat, for Adams (2009), thinking unfolds as "an internal question and answer process." It is interesting to note here that although Adams' description of how the human mind thinks is dialectical in nature, she places a one-sided, skewed emphasis on the questioning aspect of the dialectical relationship between questioning and answering. It does not occur to Adams that there are times when the question remains the same, but an alternative, more truthful (realistic or objective) answer is envisioned at a later time. Additionally, there are other times when preliminary answers themselves invite better questions, and so on. Moreover, Adams does not "question" the etiology of our repetitive, unfruitful, and enslaving question-and-answer spirals that can beset us in our adult lives the origin of which lies in our early life experience. This is what I mean when I say Adams's method could have benefited from an infusion of rigorous phenomenology, dialectical reflection, and psychodynamic understanding of the so-called repetition compulsion. Moreover, from a phenomenological point of view, just as thinking can affect our actions and bodily sensations/emotions, so too can our actions influence our thoughts and bodily sensations/emotions. Similarly, our bodily sensations/emotions can have an impact on our actions and thoughts. Better yet, there is not only a circular relationship between these modalities of being-with-ourselves-and-others, but when thinking is in the foreground of our consciousness, our bodily sensations/emotions and our predisposition to action are in the background. When our action is figural, our bodily sensations/emotions and our thoughts are in the background. When our bodily sensations/emotions are figural, our cognitions and action potential form their ground. To conclude our commentary on Adams's method, change does not simply happen by deliberately willing (choosing) to "switch" from "judger" (judgmental) to "learner" (open-minded) questions. It is too facile to suggest "three simple ways to start empowering your observer capacity" (p. 161): Practice 1: when your telephone rings, stay still and do not answer. Instead, carefully observe your reactions, including your bodily sensations, thoughts, and feelings triggered by the ringing of the telephone. Like clouds, imagine them floating across the sky. Practice 2: when you find yourself in a pressure or stressful situation, simply "step into your observer mode" (pp. 161–162). Defer action until you are "mindful of potential outcomes" (p. 162). Practice 3: next time you find yourself hijacked by your judgmental self, take time to be alone. "Simply observe and note" (p. 162). Again, defer action until you become mindful of potential consequences.

Among others things, say Cabaniss and her colleagues (2017), psychoanalysis aims at strengthening patients' "reflective capacity," "the ability to 'step outside' their immediate thoughts [feelings and behaviors] to look at them critically" (p. 22). Phrased more elaborately, it "refers to the ability to examine one's own thoughts and behaviors, to connect different aspects of experience, to recognize patterns, and to reconcile inconsistent attitudes and feelings" (p. 38). Reflective capacity has two other aspects: psychological mindedness and reality testing. Psychological mindedness is "the ability to think about possible unconscious motivations for one's thoughts, feelings, and behaviors" (p. 38). Reality testing refers to "the ability to differentiate reality from fantasy" (p. 38).

Cabaniss and her colleagues (2017) provide us with an enlarged understanding of this reflective capacity when they focus on it as a requisite for being-and-becoming a good enough psychoanalyst. In this context, they say, "**self-reflection**" is "the counterpart of empathic listening" (p. 124). In other words, to listen empathically, one has to be able to engage in self-reflection. I would add that this is ultimately true for not only the psychoanalyst but also, by extension, the patient. Self-reflection, or the capacity for reflection (reflexivity) in general, is at its ripened best when empathy (care and compassion) is its counterpart. I think that Cabaniss and her colleagues would concur that in addition to empathy, acceptance and honesty are also counterparts to self-reflection.

Our egotistical self's natural way of sustaining itself, observes Barratt (2013), is through being *judgmental*. It is a mode of being-in-the-world-with--others that is the opposite of our "readiness for compassionate witnessing" (p. 133). Although Barratt is focused on patient-analyst relations whereby the "compassionate witnessing" of the analyst becomes over time, through identification I presume, the compassionate witnessing of the patient of his own experiences, I will extrapolate by applying his insights to people in general.

We are not simply neutral self-other observers; we are, at least potentially, caring participant-observers or witnesses of our own as well as others' experiences and behaviors. This brings to mind Heidegger's (1962, 1996) description of the care structure of human existence. We are fundamentally constructed to care about our own being and the being of others. Uncaring and carelessness are deformations of this basic existential structure.

"Integrity" or maturity in a person's relationships, says Barratt (2013), means that "the individual is able to both experience love as well as hate in the engagement with the … Other, and to entertain the possibility that every experience may not simply be the way it seems; that is, to love and hate passionately but also to be the compassionate witness to these experiences" (135). This compassionate witnessing stance may be implicit in Adams's observer self, especially when she advises us to "befriend" our "judger" or judgmental self, but this befriending does not seem to be part of the way she portrays the essence or essential meaning of Selfhood in general or the observer self in particular. Still, viewed dialectically, my inclination is to describe the task of the integrative or mature participant-observer self as involving the management of the tension between stepping outside our identifications with our immediate perceptions (meaning attributions) – of our own thoughts, feelings, and behaviors and those of others and viewing them *critically*, on the one hand, and being a *caring compassionate, and empathic witness* to all of these perceptions (meanings), on the other hand. Just as we are forever challenged to balance the tension between the centripetal Observer Self, which strives for union, harmony, and wholeness, *and* the centrifugal observed selves, which at times vie for separation and even domination, we are also called to modulate the task of being suspended between the two meaning poles of critical *and* compassionate observation of self and others. Succeeding, more or less, at this developmental task strengthens our sense of "transcendental I-ness" and, when mutual, our sense of "transcendental we-ness" and thereby our sense of agency and communion, respectively.

The *repetition compulsion* is a major barrier to the achievement of transcendental I-and-we-ness position-takings that make it possible for us to be simultaneously caring-and-critical observers of our selves and others. In other words, we are entrapped by our own fixed, incomplete, and repetitive meaning attributions or intentionalities that constrict our consciousness, freeze our horizons, and limit our possibilities. Although this may self-deceptively buttress our defensively fragile sense of self either by enabling us to avoid intrapersonal or interpersonal pain or by giving us the illusive promise that with the next repetition the outcome will be positively different, it ultimately makes our lives and the interconnected lives of others miserable.

However, as Barratt (2013) repeatedly reminds us, the compulsion to repeat controls the temporal dimension of the human psyche or soul. Perhaps, what Barratt loses sight of here is that, seen from a dialectical perspective, the proclivity toward *repetitiveness* (following the push of habitual meanings) is one meaning pole that beckons balance with its complementary meaning pole – *spontaneity* (being open to the pull of new, emergent meanings). It is only when the tendency toward repetitiveness severs its link to spontaneity that it becomes *compulsive*. Where Barratt (2013) is at his richest is when he describes, in true Heideggerian form, the dialectical tension between *revelation* and *concealment* of "what was and what is to become":

> In short, pasts that anticipate the possibility of a future different from the present animate the experience of the present itself. 'Past-futures' thus impinge upon the presencing of present experience, its structural transformations and its contents; in this respect, we may conclude that present experience both reveals and conceals what was and what is to become. … What we consciously believe we are thinking and feeling, and why we believe we are having such thoughts and feelings, is never 'all that is the case,' for something 'otherwise' is always being revealed and concealed, and this is a "timeless otherwise." … something 'in but not of' the intentions and meanings that consciousness takes itself to have, is both revealed and concealed repeatedly. (p. 50)

Repetitions, elaborates Barratt (2013), coagulate our consciousness and reassure our egotism of the stability and solidity of our fragile and tenuous identity. These "seemingly incessant repetition[s]," he explains, involve "'micro' narratives, within a 'macro' storyline called 'my life'" (p. 41). Our "egotism," he reflects, "consoles itself with stories that abrogate the definitiveness of death" (p. 42). Our egotism tends to conceal, negate, and disown this painful aspect of our experience, among others. But we humans have the capacity for free associative discourse that can tap into our "felt sense" and disclose what is being concealed. "This," however, "is also seriously troubling to our egotism which insists that it really knows 'what's what'" (p. 47).

"A timeless otherwise," says Barratt (2013), "is always being revealed and concealed" in the stream of our consciousness (p. 50). He expands:

> Through the transformations in the stream of consciousness, something 'in but not of' the intentions and meanings that consciousness takes itself to have , is both revealed and concealed repeatedly and this is evidence of what has been called the 'fundamental heterochrony' or "diachronic heterogeneity" of the psyche. This is the essence of the repetition-compulsivity that governs the temporalities of the psyche or human soul. (p. 50)

However, Barratt importantly adds, "the compulsive-repetitiousness of the human psyche is a ceaseless repetition-with-a-difference" (p. 53). In this "difference" lies the *potential* for change. Although Barratt does not make it explicit, a distinction can be made between a "difference" that makes no radical change in our lives and a "difference" that is creatively life-affirming, life-changing, and life-enhancing. There is a kind of lived repetition in the present, though superficially not identical with the past, that reenacts the past. An example of this would be those regressive violent outbursts in the face of frustration in the present that are variations on the temper tantrums of children who throw them when they do not get what they want. An example of creative repetitions can be glimpsed in those identificatory loving behavioral patterns inherited from the past that are infused with our own unique ways of expressing them. Barratt, incidentally, does not believe that change can occur through the modifications of our identifications, a position with which I respectfully disagree. If identifications are the channels through which our identity, at least in an essential part, is established, a premise with which Barratt concurs, then changing our identifications is *a* (one) creative way of changing our sense of who we are. Identifications are not, as Barratt contends, simply a means through which adaptation or adjustment to the status quo is achieved. Through broadening our identifications – by identifying with our fellow suffering humans, for example – we are creatively stretching the boundaries of our interpersonal identities. Additionally, it seems to me, his distinction between *therapy*, under which he subsumes change-through-identification-with-the-psychoanalyst, and *healing* is spurious. Interestingly, for someone who is ever attentive to the etymological origins of words, the word "therapy" is derived from the Greek "therapeia," the meaning of which is "healing." What is critical here is that identificatory healing occurs in a caring relational context. As Barratt beautifully puts it, our psychosocial ailments (adversities and sufferings) are "the bodymind's call for healing" (p. 132). Moreover, our ailments are manifestations of our alienated relationship to our selves and to others.

Regardless, Barratt (2013) concludes with this. Free associative discourse:

> offers a way of healing as an emancipative freeing of ourselves from the grip of repetition-compulsivity that requires acceptance of the inherent "castratedness" and "deathfulness" of our being-in-the-world. Of course, this is a freedom strenuously and even violently resisted by our egotism with its grandiose ambitions of conquest; our egotism cannot tolerate the abyss that lies within every present moment, as it retroactively reverberates and anticipatorily heralds an otherwise dimension of our being-in-the-world that comes to us incessantly as if from 'elsewhere'. (pp. 61–62)

And that is why, psychoanalysis, with its core method of free associative discourse, is an "existential practice" (p. 60). The healing power of this free associative discourse, of course, occurs in a safe and secure relational context which enables the participants to assume the position of a judgment-suspending caringly observing Self loosened from the tight grip of a compulsively repetitive egotistical self who would rather conceal than reveal.

Barratt (2013), once more, makes an artificial distinction between free associative discourse as a medium of healing occurring in the caring context of compassionate witnessing and the alienating use of the method of free association as an egotistical identificatory mechanism taking place in so-called psychoanalytic therapy:

> [Free associative discourse is] the workplay of listening to oneself (that is, to the bodymind as it speaks itself free-associatively). More accurately, this is the workplay of opening, expressing, listening ... opening, expressing, listening ... and so forth [in spite of intermittent resistances]. Some clinicians have referred to this as evidence of the functioning of the 'self-observing ego.' The problem with this conceptualization of such an ego function is that it traps the patient in a perpetual mode of self-alienation, and idealization of this function usually has the result of equating the patient's 'therapeutic progress' with his or her identification with the clinician. ... the notion of 'compassionate witnessing' seems far more helpful... .In [an authentic] psychoanalytic process, the patient has both to allow free-associative expression and to listen to what is expressed with both care and caring. In this sense, to embark on the psychoanalytic journey, the prospective patient has to have a readiness for compassionate witnessing. (p. 133)

Ultimately, Barratt tells us, compassionate witnessing is a form of love. It appears to me, however, that any good enough psychoanalyst will inevitably listen caringly and compassionately, not in a judgmentally alienating (objectifying) way, to the patient's free associative discourse. Being mirrored thusly, the patient *identifies* with the psychoanalyst's "compassionate witnessing." The patient, like the psychoanalyst whom he realistically idealizes as a relatively mature, yet flawed human being, *becomes* a caring participant-observer to himself and by extension to others and life itself. Although Barratt eschews developmental models of maturity, which he labels as being a form of "developmentalism," he does not shy away from answering the question, "What should I become?" (p. 180). He then provides us with the answer: "To love, to work, and to play" (p. 180). "To love," he explains, "implies our human capacity to respond to powers greater than our egoism" (p. 180). "To work," he continues, "might be understood foremost as the process of making oneself through changing one's reality" (p. 180). "To play," he concludes, is "a surrendering to the whimsically poetizing creativity of the human spirit" (p. 280). These he labels as "the triune dimensions of what we may become" (p. 180).

The critical question that remains is this: how are we to describe the individual who is strengthened in her or his capacity for being-and-becoming a "compassionate witness" or a caring participant-observer to oneself, others, and life itself? It is she or he, Barratt (2013) would agree, who is capable, through interrogative discourse and reflection, of discovering the embodied experience of repressed "meanings that are 'in' but not 'of' those that it [s/he] intends" (p. 31). Or, as I would provisionally put it, it is she or he who is able to disengage, distance, or dis-identify with fixed meanings so as to identify with larger or more encompassing meanings. Returning back to Barratt, a compassionate witness or caring participant-observer is someone who does *not* use her or his "egotism" to console "itself with [compulsively repeated] stories that abrogate the definitiveness of death" (p. 42).

The compassionate witness is someone who, through reflexive (aware) free associative discovery – the "ability [of a person] to be open and to listen to his or her own discourse" (Barratt, 2013, p. 154), experiences emancipation "from the grip of repetition-compulsivity that requires acceptance of the inherent 'castratedness' and 'deathfulness' of [one's] … being-in-the-world" (pp. 61–62). The "passage of healing the human psyche," says Barratt, "necessarily involves the kinetic confrontation of self-consciousness with the castratedness and deathfulness of its constitution" (p. 125). Under "castratedness" are subsumed terms such as "deficiency," "inadequacy," "insufficiency," and "helplessness." Because of our constitutional castratedness, we can never be the full authors or meaning-makers of the unfolding narratives of our lives. The human being's "inherent castratedness" refers to "its inability to claim authority and authorship over its own constructed meanings" (p. 178). Under "deathfulness" are subsumed terms and phrases such as "the inherency of loss," "the abyss of human egotism," and "the ultimate emptiness of 'I.'" The human being's "inherent deathfulness," then, refers to "the emptiness of its identitarian assertions, the 'black hole' of egotism" (p. 178).

The caring participant-observer is someone who *can* "tolerate the abyss that lies within every present moment" as one "retroactively reverberates and anticipatorily heralds an otherwise dimension of our being-in-the-world that comes to [one] … incessantly as if from 'elsewhere'" (Barratt, 2013, p. 62). This something otherwise – our repressed meanings, "that present experience both reveals and conceals what was and what is to become" (p. 50). This timeless and repressed otherwise is "something 'in but not of' the intentions and meanings that consciousness takes itself to have, is both revealed and concealed repeatedly" (p. 50). Compassionate witnessing unfreezes lived time through being open in the present – a form of presencing in the here-and-now – and liberates lived space by making "workplay" possible in creative "transitional space."

In short, the compassionate witness or caring participant-observer is able to tolerate the dialectical tension between concealment (deception, denial, dissimulation, or defensiveness) and revelation (the disclosure of affect-laden intrapersonal and interpersonal truths). It is through reflexive free associative awareness that we come to see "the truthfulness of our being-in-the-world" – "that what we are doing [thinking or feeling] belongs elsewhere, that it was indeed optimal but perhaps in a different time and place (the past-futures that we inhabit) … that we come to understand that these thoughts, feelings and actions may not be the only optimal possible option henceforth" (p. 156). "This," Barratt concludes, "is the gift of freedom from repetition-compulsivity that psychoanalysis offers" (p. 156).

Our path to truth and freedom, says Schalow (2001), involves successfully managing the tension-filled interplay between the darkness of *concealing* and the luminosity of *revealing*. As he puts it, "freedom and truth are understood reciprocally; freedom is the entrance into unconcealment, while truth is the letting be of that event" (p. 125). "The experience of truth," he continues, "as the coming into one's own, indeed, of a more primordial homecoming, always includes this polarity of revealing-concealing and can thereby *lead down many ways in order to return to the origin*" (p. 146).

Just as there are good repetitions, such as healthy habits, there are bad or pernicious repetitions, such as bad habits or addictions. In his text on the *phenomenology of addiction*, Schalow (2017) tells us, "human beings are equally capable of concealment and covering up as they are of disclosedness and self-discovery" (p. 35). It is through care, "the ultimate constitution of human existence," that a "'sense of balance' and 'discretion'" is maintained between the tendency toward concealment and the tendency toward disclosedness, openness, or revelation. When these two meaning poles are balanced, our tendency toward constructive concealment manifests itself through our capacity for awe and *wonder* in the face of the mystery of life, and our tendency toward disclosedness manifests itself through the "capability of standing outside and beyond … [ourselves] toward possibilities, of entering into the openness, as it were" (p. 39). It is this capacity to stand outside and beyond ourselves while being open to possibilities that enables us to perform the *epoche* – to suspend our judgment until further notice. To emphasize, our capacity for wonder, as a manifestation of our tendency toward concealment, forming one meaning pole of the dialectic and our capacity for standing "outside and beyond ourselves while being open to possibilities" as a manifestation of our tendency toward disclosedness, openness, or revelation, forming the complementary meaning pole of the dialectic, are delicately and discerningly balanced by our caring orientation to the world.

Paralleling the dual capacities for concealment/covering and disclosedness/self-discovery is the downward momentum toward "falling" and the upward momentum toward "transcending." Our tendency toward "falling" manifests itself through "blindness" and through "concealment, dissimulation, and deception" (p. 39). However, emphasizes Schalow (2017), the self also has the opposing capacity to stand above and beyond itself, assume an open orientation, and direct itself to new possibilities. This capacity to stand outside and beyond our selves is what is meant by *transcendence*. The accumulation of layers of concealment contracts our openness and intensifies our falling. Our self-disclosedness opens up a "play space," a creative space where a *polyvalency of meanings* and significations abound. To some degree, concealing and falling are inevitable in human experience. Again, with constructive concealing comes a positive sense of mystery; with constructive falling comes a sense of humility in the face of finitude. A sense of "balance" is made possible, by "the ultimate constitution of human existence as 'care'" (p. 35). This dialectical interplay between concealment and revelation lived in the moment in play-or-existential-space is at the heart of human experience. Lived creatively, this dialectical interplay opens us up to possibilities under the shelter of the mystery of human existence.

Schalow (2017) provides us with a prototypical example of the fallen individual who has lost the capacity for judgment suspension and reflexive self-observation: the addict. The addict, Schalow tells us, has lost his "capacity for transcendence" – the ability to stand outside and beyond her or himself. Her or his horizons of meanings have become constricted and closed. The addict lacks the realization that any present moment can "offset the fetish-like pull of immediate gratification" (p. ix). She or he is oblivious to the transformative power of the present moment that always contains the possibility of discovering new, alternative meanings in life. She or he is blind to the potential of the present moment for offering herself or himself the opportunity to reexamine his or her priorities in life and for rediscovering an alternative life trajectory. Simply stated, she or he no longer realizes that things could be otherwise.

The addict is embroiled in self-deceptive practices. The hallmark of addiction, Schalow (2017) says, is the individual's embodiment of the "*tendency toward dissimulation, distortion, and (self-) concealment*" (p. 14). Furthermore, the addict has relinquished her or his power to choose, or more primarily, "choosing to choose." She or he experiences the self as being dispersed among the unchosen "facts" of her or his lifeworld. The addict, therefore, no longer owns her or his existence. Not only does the addict not dwell in the present, with its openness to being otherwise, she or he is closed off to the future. Only the habitual past is compulsively repeated in the absence of owning up to the assumption of responsibility for this repetitive-compulsivity. "The hallmark of this complicity," Schalow reflects, "lies in the willingness and propensity to make excuses for the destructive behavior of the addict" (p. 33).

In the absence of caring self-observation, the addict does not realize that the way she or he cares (or cares less or doesn't care) structures the way she or he lives in time, lives in existential space, and lives in her or his body. The diminishment of caring in the addict, elaborates Schalow (2017), goes hand-in-hand with "falling" along with its "concomitant behaviors of lying, deceiving, and excuse making" (p. 40). The more the addict falls, the more her or his identity becomes inauthentically disowned. In falling the self-unity becomes fragmented and loses its cohesiveness. Instead, the addict seeks the pseudo-solidification of her or his dispersed identity through intensifying her or his escape into craved addictions, possibly buttressed by a sense of pseudo-belonging to a group of fellow addicts. When caring is warped, so does one's bodily desiring. It narrows the object of one's concern or desire. It is in this context that the addict becomes "hooked" on the object of her or his desire: addiction. It is in this circumstance that the addict gives in to her or his compulsive tendency to identify with her/his narrow bodily desire. Schalow asserts, in light of a Heideggerian understanding of freedom and responsibility, that freedom lies in the power of uncovering one's own possibilities and one's own capacity for choosing to choose and that one's responsibility originates from the answers one gives to life's ultimate questions of *how to be*-in-this-world-with-others. Instead of choosing the open path of transcendence, the addict blindly chooses the path of fallenness – the narrow path of fixity and compulsivity. The addict becomes blind to the human capacity to stand outside and beyond oneself and, with humility and care, orient oneself to the openness of possibilities and that through this act of transcendence, one can give birth to a new, authentic self, a self that assumes ownership, responsibility, or answerability to who one truly is as a human *being who is always, at least potentially, becoming*. It is in this kind of *existential logic or thinking* where the salvation of the addict lies.

Under relatively optimal contingencies of existence, authentically repetitive acts of self-transcendence will result in the broadening of our identifications and thus in the stretching of the boundaries of our self-identity. This is one way of describing the path toward psychosocial maturation. However, the road toward becoming relatively mature is always strewn with slippages, especially those that involve unbalanced identifications – such as, contradictory identifications, over-identifications, and under-identifications. Ultimately, our reflective or pre-reflective acts of self-transcendence aim at making us better persons. As Paskow (2004) puts it, under optimal conditions, our self-reflections are in the service of our "potentiality to be."

"Existence," holds Heidegger, "means to step beyond, or, better, having stepped beyond" (quoted in Fuller, 1990, p. 55). Being beyond, and thus surpassing, itself, Dasein (human *being*) is directed toward possibility or *meaning possibilities in its lifeworld.* This moving beyond and toward possibilities of meaning needs to be understood against the backdrop of lifeworld resistance erected by our human finitude, limitedness, and transitoriness. Simply stated, human transcendence has its limitations. Here is how Heidegger puts it: "'On the basis of the upswing into possibility, Dasein is, in each case, beyond beings [things] as we say, but it is beyond in such a way that it, first of all, experiences beings in their resistance, against which transcending Dasein is powerless'" (quoted in Fuller, 1990, p. 56). However, as Schalow has alluded to, within our boundaried existence, given that we have already fallen and thrown into a lifeworld of meanings not of our choosing, we still remain competently open to possibilities of meaning in the present against the backdrop of our past and future. True, the meanings in which we find ourselves embedded determine us; yet, we determine meanings in the way we take them up.

Existence and ecstasy, explicate Deurzen and Kenward (2005), are connected. Ecstasy is derived from the "Greek, *ekstasis*, meaning to stand out, and [is] linked etymologically to **existence** … In existential philosophy the term is used in a similar way to **transcendence** … an essential aspect of human **Being**, and a reference to its being beyond the mere physical [objective] facts of its place" (p. 61). Existence, ecstasy, and transcendence are made possible by our existential temporality – the way we live time in existential (lived) space. Here is Heidegger (1996) describing this essential link:

> Temporality is the primordial 'outside of itself' in and for itself. Thus we call the phenomena of future, having-been, and present, the ecstasis of temporality.
>
> …
>
> The existential and temporal condition of the possibility of the world lies in the fact that temporality, as an ecstatical unity, has something like a horizon … The unity of the horizontal schemata of future, having-been, and present is grounded in the ecstatic unity of temporality. (p. 329; p. 365)

What I have gathered from Schalow's (2001) interpretation of Heidegger is that we humans exist in an "ecstatic play-space" that unravels before us in our unfolding life history (p. 151). I would add, and I am certain that Schalow would concur, that, because they are two aspects to our life-horizon, we exist in *ecstatic play-time*. Each present moment contains the ecstatic possibility of transcending habitual, sedimented meanings and venturing into new meanings – better meanings that are beautiful, good, and true or meanings that are more beautiful (less ugly), fairer (less unfair), and truer (less false), meanings that bring us peace, at least for a while. Then tensions-producing meanings beckon us to seek higher-order meanings that, in turn, provide us with temporary tranquility.

References

Adams, M. (2009). *Change your questions, change your life: 10 powerful tools for life and work*. Berrett-Koehler.

Bakewell, S. (2010). *How to live or a life of Montaigne in one question and twenty attempts at an answer*. Other Press.

Barratt, B. B. (2013). *What is psychoanalysis? 100 years after Freud's 'secret committee'*. Routledge.

Cabaniss, D. L., Cherry, S., Douglas, C. J., & Schwartz, A. (2017). *Psychodynamic psychotherapy: A clinical manual* (2nd ed.). John Wiley & Sons.

Deurzen, E. V., & Kenward, R. (2005). *Dictionary of existential psychotherapy and counselling*. Sage.

Embree, L., et al. (Eds.). (1997). *Encyclopedia of phenomenology*. Kluwer.

Frankl, V. E. (1969). *The will to meaning*. World Publishing Company.

Fuller, A. R. (1990). *Insight into value: An exploration of the premises of a phenomenological psychology*. State University of New York Press.

Heidegger, M. (1962). *Being and time* (J. Macquarrie & E. Robinson, Trans.). Harper and Row.

Heidegger, M. (1996). *Being and time* (J. Stambaugh, Trans.). State University of New York Press.

Maslow, A. H. (1968). *Toward a psychology of being* (2nd ed.). D. Van Nostrand.

Melle, U. (2002). Edmund Husserl: From reason to love. In J. J. Drummond & L. Embree (Eds.), *Phenomenological approaches to moral philosophy: A handbook*. Kluwer.

Paskow, A. (2004). *The paradoxes of art: A phenomenological investigation*. Cambridge University Press.

Rogers, C. R. (1980). *A way of being*. Houghton Mifflin.

Schalow, F. (2001). *Heidegger and the quest for the sacred: From thought to the sanctuary of faith*. Kluwer.

Schalow, F. (2017). *Toward a phenomenology of addiction: Embodiment, technology, transcendence*. Springer.

Spinelli, E. (1989). *The interpreted world: An introduction to phenomenological psychology*. Sage.

Tageson, C. W. (1982). *Humanistic psychology: A synthesis*. The Dorsey Press.

Part II

The Capacities for Balance, Feelings, and Creativity

5

Balance: The Capacity to Establish and Maintain a Dialectical *Balance* Between Polar Lifeworld Meanings

"The secret of good living," reflects Deurzen-Smith (1997), "is to dare to venture and have the ability to restore a satisfactory balance, no matter how shaken and de-centred we become" (p. 95). We define this "ability," as the capacity to sustain a relative, precarious balance between seemingly oppositional or contrasting polar meanings of our identity or selfhood as manifested in our affects, attitudes, beliefs, embodied stances, ideologies, identifications, and values. To be relatively balanced is to be relatively integrated. It is to bring the semblance of coherence, harmony, and wholeness to our sense of being and results in our psychic state of well-being.

In this chapter, I will draw on and at the same time go beyond Erikson's stage-based model of human development (see Hannush, 2002, Chapter 1, pp. 13–22), for I find in his developmental description an incipient dialectics. Let me begin with Erikson's definition of identity or selfhood (identity-in-cultural-context), the center and organizing core of his model of human development.

Erikson (1963) defines identity as "the accrued confidence that the inner sameness and continuity prepared in the past are matched by the sameness and continuity of one's meaning for others" (p. 261). Here is Erikson (1980) ruminating on the multiple meanings of identity: "[Identity, at one time] appear[s] to refer to a conscious *sense of individual identity*; at another to an unconscious striving for a *continuity of personal character*; at a third, as a criterion for the silent doings of *ego synthesis*; and finally, as maintenance of *solidarity* with a group's ideals and identity" (p. 109). Identity-making, says Erikson (1968), is "a process 'located' *in the core of the individual* and yet also *in the core of his communal culture*, a process which establishes, in fact, the identity

© The Author(s), under exclusive license to Springer Nature Switzerland AG 2021

M. J. Hannush, *Markers of Psychosocial Maturation*,
https://doi.org/10.1007/978-3-030-74315-4_5

of those two identities" (p. 22). Identity-formation, he continues, is a byproduct of the "interplay between the psychological and the social, the developmental and the historical" (p. 23).

In a footnote, Erikson (1963) adds that although identity is achieved primarily through our identifications with "given social roles" and through "adaptation to the demands of social change," the "healthy and strong individual, however, adapts these roles to the further processes of his ego [identity], thus doing his share in keeping the process [of change] alive" (p. 412). The emergent and evolving identity of the healthy individual is a creative synthesis of identifications with social roles offered by the group to which one belongs and with which one identifies.

The natural human proclivity toward seeking dialectical balance between (1) being-and-becoming the *same* as a representation of the group (the essential Other) and being-and-becoming *different* from the representation of the group (the essential Other) and (2) seeking *sameness/continuity* and *differentness/discontinuity* within or in relationship to oneself (remaining the same person, yet also changing and becoming different) is already implicitly present in Erikson's theoretical framework. However, in my humble opinion, he does not make it explicit and the topic of rigorous and systematic pursuit. For instance, the major mechanism that makes identity-formation possible, Erikson repeatedly emphasizes, is identification. But he does not stress enough its polar twin: dis-identification in the same breath. The existential "I" desires (chooses) to *be*come *both* like the Other *and* unlike the Other. Here lies the creative tension. Healthy identification goes hand-in-hand with healthy dis-identification. Otherwise, we are left with either unhealthy over-identification (excessive and enslaving sameness and continuity) or unhealthy dis-identification (alienating and destructive differentness and discontinuity).

Where there is the "I am," there also is, potentially, the "I am not." Where there is being, there also is the possibility of nonbeing. I am alive while at the same time in touch with my vitality and in tune with the vibrancy of life. My life is in resonance with Life itself. I can be alive, but leading a deadly existence while living. I am alive, but I also know that one day I will not be. I can be either affirming or dreading my mortality, consciously or unconsciously. Where there is a "Yes," there also is the potential "No." There is a healthy and constructive or an unhealthy and destructive way of saying "Yes." There is a healthy and constructive or an unhealthy and destructive way of saying, "No." Viewed from the perspective of our unfolding healthy and unhealthy identifications and dis-identifications, there is an authentic or inauthentic way of becoming-a-self ("selving") and there is an authentic or inauthentic way of "unselving."

"Identity-formation" or "selving," a term I borrow from the poet Gerard Manly Hopkins, is the heartbeat that gives life to Erikson's developmental model. His eight-stage-theory of human development makes up the core of his contribution. Identity, for Erikson, unfolds across a sequence of eight stages, crises, or turning points, always occurring in a dynamic social context: *basic trust* versus *basic mistrust, autonomy* versus *shame and doubt, initiative* versus *guilt, industry* versus *inferiority, identity* versus *role confusion, intimacy* versus *isolation, generativity* versus *stagnation, ego integrity* versus *despair* (Erikson, 1963, p. 273, 1980, p. 178).

The challenge of each stage is to achieve some *balance* between each of its bipolar dimensions. Achieving cumulative *balance* means movement toward psychosocial health and maturation. Balance is equivalent to synthesis or integration. From the perspective of our dialectical model, there is no such thing as absolute balance to be sought. Harmony-producing balance is always in interplay with tension-producing imbalance. De-integration is always the counterpart of integration. "De-integration" is used to counter the negative connotation of "disintegration." Balance or integration is not only relative, but can also be positively valenced (+) or negatively valenced (-). There is good (fluid, flexible) or bad (rigid, inflexible) balance or integration, and there is good imbalance (in the service of higher synthesis or level of integration) and bad (rigid, ossified) imbalance or de-integration. Moreover, there are degrees of balance or integration. In others words, we are very likely to always be partly balanced (integrated) and partly imbalanced (de-integrated). Imperfect and precarious, but significant balance or integration is good enough. Good-enough integrative balance is truer to life.

The theme of dialectical balance or integration is implicitly present under Erikson's concept of *optimal ratio*. In a critical footnote, Erikson (1980) writes:

> One of the chief misuses of the schema [model of human development] presented here is the connotation that the sense of trust (and all the other *positive* senses to be postulated [autonomy, initiative, industry, identity, intimacy, generativity, and integrity]) is an *achievement*, secured once and for all at a given stage. In fact, some writers are so intent on making an *achievement scale* out of these stages that they blithely omit all the *negative* senses (basic mistrust, etc. [shame/doubt, guilt, inferiority, role confusion, isolation, stagnation, and despair]) which are and remain the dynamic counterpart of the positive senses throughout life...
>
> What the child [adolescent or adult] acquires at a given stage is a certain *ratio* between the positive and the negative which, if the balance is toward the positive, will help him to meet later crises with a better chance for unimpaired total

> development. The idea that at any stage a *goodness* is achieved which is impervious to new conflicts within and changes without is a projection on child [adolescent or adult] development of that success ideology which so dangerously pervades our private and public daydreams and can make us inept in the face of a heightened struggle for a meaningful existence in our time. (p. 182)

Ironically, as revealed in Sue Erikson Bloland's (2005) memoir, Erikson did *over-identify* with the "success ideology" that pervaded his private life and contributed to making him somewhat duplicitous – the idealized public persona with which Erikson identifies in contradistinction to the more complex private, "inept" and "insecure" husband and distant and exacting father that his daughter depicts him to be. His daughter, however, also attests to many of his strengths, including his intellectual brilliance and his capacity for expressing his abiding tender lovingness for his wife, Joan, upon whom he is excessively emotionally dependent. His human fallibilities should not diminish or distract from the complexity, richness, innovativeness, and originality of his theory of psychosocial development. But neither should we be blind to its limitations, some of which may have autobiographical underpinnings, which at the same time fuel his creative achievements and strengths. Erikson and other psychologists and psychoanalysts, such as Heinz Kohut (See Strozier's (2001) discussion of "The Autobiography of Mr. Z," a disguise for Kohut himself) and Rollo May (see Hannush, 1999 and 2010, for a discussion of "The Case of Philip," a disguise for Rollo May himself), are able to lift their personal plight into a universal plane by making creative use and expansion of extant stock of psychological knowledge, thus illuminating for us, in their own unique and original ways, our common human struggles.

To stress, for Erikson, "all the positive senses" of trust, autonomy, initiative, industry, identity, intimacy, generativity, and integrity "are and remain the dynamic counterpart" of "all the negative senses" of mistrust, shame/doubt, guilt, inferiority, role confusion, isolation, stagnation, and despair throughout life. In other words, the positive and negative senses are in continuous dialectical tension. The movement toward development, growth, and maturation challenges and requires of us to find an *optimal ratio* or balance between each pair of the positive and negative senses. In each stage of development, under good-enough conditions, the growing child (adolescent or adult) seeks to position himself or herself along this dialectical trajectory in a way that will allow him or her to continue to develop, grow, and mature.

In anticipation of what is about to be re-visioned, let us take the example of trust versus mistrust. For Erikson, successful or unsuccessful experiences with the primary caregiver (mother) give rise to experiences of trust and mistrust. Curiously, say Mitchell and Black (1995), "Erikson's vision skipped over and left underdeveloped ... the relationships between the child and particular caregivers" (p. 147). Still, they continue, for Erikson, "the mother is the representative of and vehicle for a cultural approach to living that organizes and ranks safety and danger, pleasure and restraint, gratification and frustration" (p. 147).

The sense, position, quality, or capacity of trust-in-tension-with-mistrust is the first to unfold as part of an organismic process involving a series of unfolding dialectical tensions that follow and culminate in the ultimate sense, position, quality, or capacity of integrity (integration)-in-tension-with-despair. Although one dialectical tension is in the foreground in any given stage, all tensions are active in the background throughout the cycle of human development. Still, the final aim of development, growth, and maturation is the gradual psychosocial integration of self-identity. As developing individuals, we all have to confront and come to terms with these dialectical tensions. In a good holding (supportive) environment, the capacity for trust is always in creative tension with mistrust, autonomy with shame and doubt, and so on. Under relatively optimal conditions – optimal indulgences and optimal frustrations – the relationship between each pole in a pair of dialectical tension is complementary. Achieving the final integration (integrity) of the eighth stage requires having achieved a more or less successful resolution of the dialectical tensions of the previous seven stages.

Made more explicit from the perspective of our own dialectical model, "trust" and "mistrust" are *both*, potentially, positively and negatively valenced. There is a healthy way to trust or mistrust, and there is an unhealthy way to trust and mistrust. In a good-enough supportive social environment, the child (adolescent or adult) successfully achieves an *optimal ratio* or *relative balance* between trust and mistrust. Being-and-becoming overly trusting makes us naïve and vulnerable. Being-and-becoming overly mistrustful makes us overly suspicious and paranoid. Knowing when to discerningly trust or discerningly mistrust is one of the manifestations of psychosocial maturity.

In our dialectical scheme, therefore, the opposition or tension is not between a *positive sense* and a *negative sense*. Rather, it is a dialectical tension between two potentially positive senses seeking complementary, creative, dynamic, resonant, and interactive balance. In fact, the word "versus," which Erikson uses, does not quite capture this type of dialectical relationship between the potentially complementary senses, for it implies "readiness to do battle with." In our dialectical scheme, the self is viewed, at its core, as a seeker of integrative balance. It is the center of dialectical initiatives, the aim of which is finding relative balance (integration) between the seemingly conflicting existential issues of life, such as the existential life issues (needs) of connectedness *and* separation, control *and* surrender, love *and* hate, magnificence *and* vulnerability, self-affirmation *and* self-neutralization, specialness *and* ordinariness, and unity *and* individuation.

The achievement of dialectical selfhood involves a selving process involving a back-and-forth balance-seeking movement between seemingly polar existential life issues, such as meeting the existential needs of *both* closeness *and* distance, and unity *and* individuation. This characteristic way of being-in-the-world can be viewed as an index of psychosocial maturation and mental health. Phenomenologically, the intentional structure of such a dialectical consciousness can be metaphorically depicted in a Mobius-like strip with arrows pointing in opposite directions. Persons can best be understood in relation to how they integrate these seemingly opposite existential life issues. Such a work of integration does not occur in a vacuum. It occurs in a relational context that either facilitates or hinders the work of balance and integration.

Allow me to return once more to the existential life issue, which is a foundational stage in Erikson's stage model of development, of trusting and mistrusting oneself or others. I can be cognizant that there are merits and demerits in trusting and mistrusting myself. These are complementary and not oppositional modes of being-in-the-world-with-oneself-or-others. It is easy, on the surface, to say that trusting oneself is good, while mistrusting oneself is bad. There are times, however, when mistrusting oneself can be a sign of emotional maturity. Through painful experience I learn that there are dangerous situations in which I cannot trust myself. Learning from such experience can make me humble and can alert me to take precautions to avoid danger. Then again, if I become too mistrustful of myself, I would not be able to function effectively in this world. For another example, let us briefly take Erikson's opposition of autonomy (independence) versus doubt in the second stage of his developmental scheme. I can be simultaneously aware of my independency needs while questioning the efficacy and impossibility of total independence. Such doubtful self-questioning can serve as a conduit for finding balance in meeting *both* my independency *and* dependency needs. In other words, there are times when self-doubt can be a sign of psychological maturity. Then again, if I become riddled with excessive self-doubt, I would not be able to operate efficaciously in this world.

We view these dialectical tensions not as stages, but as states or ways of being-in-the-world-with-self-and-others. We eliminate the state of grand integrity versus despair (Erikson's eighth stage) and subsume it under the superordinate dialectical tension of *identity-integration-in-relation-to-identity-de-integration*

(Erikson's fifth stage), which is the developmental lifework of the dialectical self. *Selving* involves the existential drive to integrate the dialectical tensions of our evolving and unfolding individual and social identity. To stress again, unlike what we find in Erikson's model, the potentially creative tension is not between a positive meaning pole (e.g., trust) and a negative meaning pole (e.g., mistrust), but rather between one meaning pole that can potentially be positive or negative (e.g., mature, differentiating trust or immature, undifferentiating trust) and another meaning pole that can also potentially be positive or negative (e.g., mature, differentiating mistrust or immature, undifferentiating mistrust). Attaining relative balance or integration between a complementary pair of positive meanings (e.g., mature, differentiating trust *and* mature, differentiating mistrust) entails movement toward psychosocial maturation. A developmental arrest results when movement toward relative balance or integration between positive pairs is not successfully achieved. The consequence is a skewing, twist, or tilt (imbalance) toward one meaning pole of the pair, which simultaneously affects the seemingly opposite meaning pole (e.g., excessive, undifferentiating trust will be reflected in the inability to be discerningly mistrusting). We are ready to re-vision Erikson's stage theory of psychosocial development and modify it to fit our own dialectical scheme.

Trust-in-Dialectical-Relation-to-Caution

Basic trust develops from the early interaction between the emerging self and its primary caregivers. If the primary caregivers are good-enough – attuned, affectionate, available, reliable, and responsive – the infant comes to *expect* or *trust*, on a preverbal, bodily level, to be nourished, nurtured, and that her or his basic needs, though not perfectly, will be taken care of. If the preverbal infant could speak, she would say something like this: "Mom and dad, although you were not perfect, all things considered, you did your best and your best was alright by me. When I was hungry, you fed me. When I was cold, you warmed me up. When I was hot, you cooled me off. When I was in pain, you soothed and comforted me and did your utmost to make the pain go away. When I wanted to play, you played with me. You knew how to alternate, match, or synchronize your responses to mine. But when I became saturated, you sensed and knew when to stop. When I became tired or sleepy and began to fall apart, you held me and eased my transition to rest and sleep. When I smiled, you radiated with smiles. In the gleam of your eyes, I knew in the deepest part of my heart that you loved and valued me and thought I was the most precious child in the world. You 'read' me accurately and responded well to shifts in my mental and physical states, moods, and my changing needs. Also, you were always well attuned to my emerging capacities and competencies, like when I started to say Mama and Dada for the first time or when I started to sit upright and stand or when I began to vocalize and utter my first words. In general, you were there for me when I needed you. I wanted to add one more thing. You taught me that the world was, for the most part, a welcoming place. But you also taught me that there were places in which I had to be vigilant and people around whom I had to be cautious. But, on the whole, I came to expect and trust that life is good and this world is a good place to be in. Mom and Dad, although 'you' had, or better yet, 'we' had our difficult days, you were 'good-enough.' And you know what? I think I will keep your loving goodness inside me for ever!"

Trust is the foundation of close, intimate, or loving relations. In general, it is hoped that two partners in a close relationship trust each other. Although close relationships abound in many domains of life, let us focus on an intimate, heterosexual relationship between two partners. In this imaginary relationship, he trusts her and she trusts him. They both experience times when caution is called for, sometimes warranted, at other times not. Because of their respective temperaments, personalities, and developmental histories, during these times, they display emotion-laden vigilance regarding, say, issues revolving around money (concern about excessive expenditure) or sex (concern about availability or fidelity). But, on the whole, they have been able to establish a precarious balance between mature trust and mature caution between them, punctuated intermittently by slippages into excessive caution or excessive trust. Even their *loving sex* is predicated on a trust-based sense of safety, on what Holmes (2010) calls *hedonic intersubjectivity*, which he defines as "playful, self-affirming, interactive sensuality" (p. 99). Because of their mutual trust-based sense of security, they "make love freely, spontaneously, safely, excitingly, harmoniously, tenderly, and empathically" (pp. 101–102). Their loving sex "combines extreme excitement and absolute relaxation and trust" (p. 102). The "foundations of enjoyable sexuality" or loving sex, "lie in the hedonic intersubjectivity of parent and child in infancy" (p. 107). There is "a mutually pleasurable aspect to the infant-care-giver relationship that I characterize as 'hedonic intersubjectivity'" (p. 115). There is an *aesthetic* dimension to this *hedonic intersubjectivity*, I would add.

"The general state of trust, furthermore," says Erikson (1963), "implies not only one has learned to rely on the sameness and continuity of outer providers, but also that one may trust oneself … and that one is able to consider oneself trustworthy" (p. 248). "Such consistency, continuity, and sameness of experience," he adds, "arouse a feeling of familiarity [with the goodness of outer provision], of having coincided with a feeling of inner goodness" (p. 247). This "inner goodness" co-relates to outer goodness – the consistent tender loving care provided by primary caregivers. "Trust," Erikson asserts, is "born of care" (p. 250). "But," he continues, "even under the most favorable circumstances, this stage [of trust] seems to introduce into psychic life (and become prototypical for) a sense of inner division [comprising of a sense of deprivation and abandonment] and universal nostalgia for paradise forfeited. It is against this powerful combination ... that basic trust must maintain itself throughout life" (p. 250). In other words, even under the most favorable circumstances, the positive quality of trust is never 100 percent pure. It has to deal with the dialectical tension produced by its counterpart, the need for caution, throughout life.

As a correlate to one's trust in the goodness of essential others, Erikson asserts, one comes to trust oneself and one's own inner goodness. However, dialectically speaking, there are times when it is also good to distrust oneself. I do not always find myself trustworthy, especially in trigger situations where I find myself losing my grip on myself and on social reality. Part of the process of psychosocial maturation is learning to "read" and anticipate these trigger situations, which can never be totally evaded, let alone mastered.

The vitalizing "virtue" or "ego strength" that emerges as the outcome of a favorable ratio from the relative resolution of the tension surrounding the primary existential life issue of trust (versus mistrust) is, according to Erikson, "hope." "*Hope*," says Erikson (1964), "*is the enduring belief in the attainability of fervent wishes in spite of the dark urges and rages which mark the beginning of existence.* Hope is the ontogenetic basis of faith, and is nourished by the adult faith which pervades patterns of care" (p. 118). A modulated sense (virtue) of hope, therefore, is one of the basic enlivening qualities of psychological health. Besides "Hope," the other vitalizing virtues are "Will," "Purpose," "Competence," "Fidelity," "Love," "Care," and "Wisdom" (Erikson, 1985, pp. 32–33). Poignantly, Erikson adds, these character strengths "have their counterparts in the spirit of those human institutions which attempt to formalize and to safeguard [the] dealings ... of generations with each other" (Erikson, 1964, p. 155). In other words, there is "a mutual activation and replenishment between the virtues emerging in each individual life cycle and the strengths of human institutions" (p. 155). Erikson concludes by saying that "without the spirit of institutions pervading the patterns of care, love, instruction and training, no virtue could emerge from the sequence of generations" (pp. 155–156).

Trust, faith, hope, and goodness are fragile qualities that need nourishment and sustenance not only at home, but in all larger institutional contexts of which we are a part – our extended network of family and friends; our neighborhood; our educational and religious institutions; our state, local, and national governments; and our world-wide socio-economic and socio-political inter-systems. It is easier to build our virtues when they are in healthy synchronous resonance with virtues that surround us in our ever-widening concentric communal circles. It is much more difficult to refine our emerging character strengths when we are pressured to partake in unhealthy asynchronous dissonance, masquerading as conforming consonance, with the vices found in the cultural air we breathe. It is hard to keep on cultivating our character strengths when we are swimming against the cultural currents of our times. The challenge is to find pockets within the culture of which we are a part that can share with us life-affirming values to live by.

Part of the process of psychosocial maturation involves accepting that our trust, and consequently our hope, is tainted. Trust or hope loses its purity as we become less naïve and more maturely cautious. But Erikson is not the only psychoanalyst to link hope with goodness. "The realm of hope," says Searles (1979), "seems to us a last repository of such innate goodness as human beings possess" (p. 479). "One of the harshest maturational tasks the individual must accomplish to become truly adult," he continues, "is to realize and accept that his hope is 'impure' in two vast ways: first, it is not unitary in nature but multifarious and permeated with ambivalence, with conflict … and second, many of these hopes are devoted not to loving, but rather to destructive ends" (p. 479).

Just as, from the dialectical perspective, a distinction is made between positive (discerning and healthy) trust and negative (excessive and unhealthy) trust, Searles (1979) contrasts constructive to destructive (excessive or misplaced) hope. Any "realistic [mature] hope," says Searles, "as contrasted to unconscious denial-based [immature] hopefulness – must be grounded in the ability to experience loss" (p. 484). "One who has survived the griefs over losses, over disappointments in the past," continues Searles, "has known what it is for hope to triumph over – to survive – despair" (p. 484). "In the same regard," concludes Searles, mature "hope comes into being when one discovers such feelings as disappointments and despair can be shared with a fellow human being – when one discovers, that is, that the sharing of such feelings can foster one's feeling of relatedness with one's fellow human beings" (p. 484).

Growing up in a family that is overly protective, pampering, and idealizing and identifying with the overly optimistic and unrealistic cultural message that one can be anything one wants to be with sheer willpower can lead to what Searles calls "destructive hope." Internalizing a materialistic version of the American Dream can result in an embodied hope that is self-destructive for those who cannot, though they strive mightily to, achieve the so-called Dream. After all, we can ask, "Who's American Dream are we talking about?" The American Dream of the privileged is more realizable than that of the underclass. Additionally, the American Dream of those born with culturally approved bodies equipped with innate gifts and talents is more likely, especially when coupled with available opportunities, privileges, and resources, to actualize their potentials, relatively speaking, and thus their dreams. Of course, a strong drive, high energy, persistence, perseverance, resilience, making optimal use of even limited resources, and even luck are important elements that figure into translating one's realistic hopes into actuality. But the odds are higher for those born into privilege and for those who were properly parented. Ultimately, destructive hope is grounded in the denial or repression of limits. "One is free," says May (1981), "only as one recognizes one's limits" (p. 158).

"Hope," notes Nicholsen (2002), "as an orientation to possibility, is an emotional expression of the ongoing creative process of life. Despair, in contrast, feels like an internal process of destruction, something that attacks the very life in us and propels us toward death rather than toward a future" (p. 183). Nicholsen here is focusing on constructive hope and destructive despair. Dialectically, we can also speak of destructive hope, as Searles does, and potentially constructive despair, the kind of existential dread that can propel us into life-affirming choices and actions. It is like diving deep into the phosphorous dark waters of despair and surfacing into renewed, life-saving air. "Despair," states Nicholsen, "has its hopeful aspects" (p. 184). Despair can counter our blindingly unrealistic hopefulness by positioning us to accept our limitations, dependency, helplessness, and suffering. As Searles (1979) says, hope is "multifarious." Nicholsen (2002) elaborates that hopes can be contradictory, re-vengeful, self-serving and selfish, overly idealistic, and unrealistic. "It is not until hope is tempered with concern and disappointment," adds Nicholsen, "that it becomes … 'mature hope'" (p. 183). Goodness is impossible without mature trust and mature hope. Lest we slip into perfectionistic language, to emphasize, we are not speaking of pure and unalloyed trust, hope, or goodness. The mature or "protean" self, observes Lifton (1993), "even while adrift in its own emotions, can live with partial integration and partial trust in the possibility of constructive [prosocial or good] human action" (p. 100).

The smooth and successful transition from a state of trusting dependency and merging connectedness to a state of gradual, independence-seeking separation is made possible by a relatively solid sense of secure attachment to primary caregivers. In other words, having developed a balanced sense of trust, a trust that is in balance with caution, based on secure attachment with essential others, the path is cleared for the developing child to engage in autonomous strivings in order to separate successfully from his parents and forge, in the spirit of self-determination and in gradual increments, an autonomous (independent) sense of self that is healthily connected.

Independence (Autonomy) in-Dialectical-Relation-to Dependence

Take the seemingly opposite pair: independence (Erikson's "autonomy") versus dependence. As developing human beings we are naturally and always dependent upon others in our efforts not only to survive but also to flourish and thrive in life. In spite of Erikson's effort to understand the positive sense of "autonomy" as a counterpart of the negative senses of "doubt and shame," the relative resolution of the tension between them results in the acquisition of a strong sense of autonomy or independence. In contrast to our dialectical model, Erikson does not dwell on the negative sense of independence and the positive sense of dependence.

To my knowledge, it is Fairbairn (1952) who first offers a theory of psychosocial development that revolves around the theme of *mature dependence*. Here is Fairbairn succinctly describing his dependence-focused developmental theory:

> The outstanding feature of the child's personal relationship to his mother is, however, one of extreme *dependence*; and this dependence is reflected in the psychological process of *primary* [undifferentiated] *identification*, in the light of which separation from his object [mother] becomes the child's greatest source of anxiety... [It] seems most appropriate to describe the first stage as one of Infantile Dependence ...[This] dependence is chiefly manifested in an attitude of oral incorporation [taking in] towards, and an attitude of primary emotional identification with the object [mother]. By contrast, the final stage appears best described as a stage of *Mature Dependence* – 'mature dependence' rather than 'independence' since a capacity for relationships necessarily implies dependence of some sort. What distinguishes mature dependence from infantile dependence is that it is characterized neither by a one-sided attitude of incorporation [taking in] nor by an attitude of primary [undifferentiated] emotional identification. On the contrary, it is characterized by a capacity on the part of a differentiated individual for co-operative relationships with differentiated objects [others]... [It] is a relationship involving evenly matched giving and taking between two differentiated individuals who are mutually dependent, and between whom

> there is no disparity of dependence… At least, this is the ideal picture; but it is, of course, never completely realized in practice, since there is no one whose libidinal development develops without a hitch. The intermediate stage … is *Transitional*; and it appears best so named, since it is a stage of vicissitudes arising out of the difficulties and conflicts of transition. (p. 145)

Human development, for Fairbairn, proceeds from a position of *infantile dependence* on the mother, to a position of *transitional dependence*, and finally to a position of *mature dependence* on others while acknowledging the others' own centers of initiative, separateness, and independence. Psychosocial growth unfolds from an infantile stance of "taking" to a more mature stance of mutual "giving-and-taking" between two differentiated persons. Fairbairn regards the capacities to give-and-take as innate. Personal growth, then, moves from immature to mature dependence. Consequently, even mature (differentiated) individuals will depend on the available responsiveness of essential others throughout life. Successful development or maturation depends on how well the individual negotiates the dialectical tension between being dependent upon and being independent from others.

For Fairbairn, says Seinfeld (1991), "the outcome of development [is viewed] in terms of mature dependence upon a community of relationships in which otherness and separateness are acknowledged while persons share in survival and living tasks" (p. 40). "His views," continues Seinfeld, "do not neglect the importance of individuation but rather emphasize that the individual arrives at independence with a built-in social sense. He explicitly states that in mature dependence an attitude of emotional giving is dominant over the earlier attitude of taking" (pp. 40–41). "Fairbairn felt," conclude Greenberg and Mitchell (1983), "that continued interdependence with others was so central to maturity that he terms psychological health the state of 'mature dependence'" (p. 370).

Just as Fairbairn describes a tension-laden developmental struggle between the push of infantile dependence and the pull of mature dependence, we posit a complementary tension-laden struggle between the push of infantile independence and the pull of mature independence. The optimal outcome for our development and growth involves achieving a relative balance between mature dependence and mature independence. In the absence of the attainment of such a precarious balance, our personality becomes skewed in the direction of either immature dependence or immature independence. Immature independence or pseudo-independence manifests itself, for instance, in acts of blind rebelliousness. Think of the toddler who says "no" indiscriminately simply to assert him-or herself. When this child is not handled delicately and understandingly, then he or she may be on the path toward either immature dependence or immature independence. Imagine the adolescent who tries to prove his or her independence through indulging in acts of risky rebelliousness such as smoking, excessive drinking, reckless driving, and partaking in promiscuous and unsafe sex. Or, yet again, think of the adult who tries to assert his or her autonomy by always being disagreeable, uncooperative, and contentious. Additional manifestations of immature independence may involve the inability to apologize because an apology *means* an assault on one's "autonomy."

Immature dependence, on the other hand, signals a basic lack of differentiation and individuation. It manifests itself in loss of self-other boundaries and lack of assertive decisional autonomy. Like immature independence, it is the outcome of insecure attachment. It is linked to fear of abandonment, rejection, or separation. It is co-related to a fragile sense of self, a low estimation of oneself. It harks back to the longing for embeddedness and enmeshment from which one wishes to drive a sense of belonging and security. It places the self in a highly vulnerable position, which leads to either exploitation due to one-sided excessive neediness or rejection because of the excessive burden that is placed on the shoulders of essential others.

Initiative-Taking (Seeking Adventure Through the Pursuit of New Ways of Being and Doing)-in-Dialectical-Relation-to-Maintenance of Steadiness (Seeking the Steady Safety and Security of Habitual and Routinized Ways of Being and Doing)

"Initiative," says Erikson (1963), "adds to autonomy the quality of undertaking, planning and 'attacking' a task for the sake of being active and on the move … initiative is a necessary part of every act, and man needs a sense of initiative for whatever he learns and does" (p. 255). Children, elaborates Erikson, derive pleasure from "making" and "being on the make." Children (and adults) extract "exuberant enjoyment" from "the goals contemplated and the acts initiated" (p. 255) or from the energetic pursuit of "contemplated initiative" (p. 256). A positive sense of initiative emerges in a supportive context of "mutual regulation" between parent and child. In this context, a child's vibrant sense of initiative is guided by internalized "moral responsibility" and healthy and realistic "work-identification," first with the parent. This "realistic identification [is] based on a spirit of equality experienced in doings things [tasks or projects] together … it also sets the direction toward the possible and tangible which permits the dreams of early childhood to be attached to the goals of an active adult life" (p. 258). Thus, the child absorbs the *economic ethos* of the adult world and the culture at large.

"Patienthood," observes Erikson (1964), "is a condition of inactivation. *Agens* [agency] is the opposite of *patiens* [patiency]" (p. 87). Initiative is a vehicle for "turning passive into active," a phrase Erikson borrows from Sigmund Freud (p. 86). "**Initiative**," note Newman and Newman (2018) in their Eriksonian text, "is an expression of agency – an outgrowth of early experiences of the self as a causal agent" (p. 259). A healthy sense of initiative, they add, goes hand-in-hand with acquired autonomy, creation [creativity], curiosity, desire for discovery, exploration, exuberance, innovation, investigation, playfulness, and self-control. Our "individuality" or "individual position," elaborates Erikson (1964), is "marked by *centrality*, *wholeness*, and *initiative* … these are the attributes of what we call identity" (p. 86). In my re-vision, I would expand on Erikson and say that *trust, autonomy, initiative, industry, intimacy,* and *generativity*, along with other maturational qualities, are all central attributes of our *integrative identity*. Their centrality has to do with their role in making us relatively integrated and whole. *Personal integration* always occurs in the context of and along with *social integration.*

For now, however, we can focus on *initiative* as a central attribute of our developing identity, personality, or selfhood. Coincidentally, like Erikson, Kohut, though viewing the meaning of the concept of the self as ultimately somewhat elusive, similarly assigns centrality to initiative in defining the self. Kohut (1977) refers to the self as "the basis of our sense of being an independent center of initiative and perception" (pp. 176–177). Once again, as with Erikson, initiative is tied to our sense of agency and independence, our need for individuation – our need to carve out an *autonomous identity* while maintaining our *relationship to others*. That is the integrative achievement of a dialectical self. It is a bodily self that is actively oriented, by way of initiative taking, toward attaining balance between seemingly polar lifeworld meanings – such as *trust*-in-relation-to-*caution*, bringing their intrinsic tensions to a most satisfying state of rest. The bodily self is virtually always directed to lifeworld meanings in general and polar lifeworld meanings in particular. The latter always beckon balance. Initiative must be taken to actualize balanced tensions between lifeworld meanings. Our psychosocial maturation lies in the balance. Balance is never achieved once and for all. As meanings of trust-and-caution, dependence-and-independence, initiative-and-steadiness, industriousness-and-leisure, intimacy-and-separation, and other-care-and self-care individuate and grow on the lifeworld side, so do we individuate and grow on the self side.

In complementarity with Erikson's ideas about the self, initiative is grounded in our original vitality and craving for creativity our impulse to create something new. Hence, we can refer to the healthy self as a center of "creative initiative." This creative initiative includes our potential for configuring and re-configuring our lifeworld meanings. Phenomenologically, our bodily self is always reaching out or intending to make meaningful connections out there in our lifeworld. This is always a potentially creative venture. The self therefore can be described as the bodily being that stretches to creatively achieve higher-order meanings that surpass seemingly polar meanings. Our capacities for agency, creativity, and imagination play a pivotal part in our bodily self's orientation to meaning making. We can refine Erikson and Kohut's definitions of the self by viewing the bodily self as a center of an intentional and creative, balance-seeking initiative. "Intentional" here subsumes conscious or unconscious intentions, desires, drives, and motivations. It also refers to the way we reach out, touch, and are touched by lifeworld meanings, including people and things. The attainment of good (balanced) meanings is at the heart of our psychosocial reality. "All in all, the bodily self is a historically situated center of meaning" (Fuller, 1990, pp. 164–165). Thus, defining the self as "a center of meaning," the movement of which is dialectical in nature – an oscillating back-and-forth movement toward relative integrative balance is much more encompassing and inclusive of the definition of the self as simply a "center of initiative."

Regardless, whereas Erikson opposes "initiative" to "guilt," a tension to be reduced or a "crisis" that needs to be resolved during the oedipal stage of development (between the ages of four and five), I contrast "initiative-taking" to "maintenance of steadiness" in our own dialectical model of maturation. I hold that positive initiative requires and is complementary to positive steadiness. Our maturational journey challenges us to find a balance between initiative taking and maintenance of steadiness. It is the balance needed between creativity and repetition. Just as there is a healthy way of taking initiatives, so it is that there is, correlatively, a healthy way of partaking of habitual repetition or repetitive habits. Habits can free us; habits can enslave us. Initiatives gone awry, as when pursued compulsively and manically, wear us out. We need to find that precarious balance between creative initiative and the freeing habits that make up the routines of our everyday life. It is akin to living the cycle of invigorated awakening and restful sleeping. We humans have established many habits and repetitive routines that make our lives efficient, healthy, revitalized, and re-creative, such as working and exercising, followed by the rhythmic return to the safety of our secure home base with its rituals of eating, relaxing, and sleeping. These steadiness-maintaining routines make it possible for us to embark upon our everyday creative initiatives with a sense of adventure and freshness. The development of a sense of adventure-in-balance-with-a-sense-of-steadiness is the achievement of the dialectical self, of living a dialectical (balanced, integrated) life. It is similar to balancing our play-life with our work-life, which we turn to next.

Industriousness (Seeking Investment in Work)-in-Dialectical-Relation-to-Leisure (Seeking Play, Recreation, Relaxation, and Rest)

"With the oncoming of the latency period [the ages between six and eleven or twelve]," says Erikson (1963), the child "learns to win recognition by producing things ... and thus becomes ready to apply himself to given skills and tasks ... He develops a sense of industry" (p. 259). That is, the child, Erikson (1963) elaborates:

> adjusts himself to the inorganic laws of the tool world. He can become an eager and absorbed unit of a productive situation. To bring a productive situation to completion is an aim which gradually supersedes the whims and wishes of play. His ego boundaries include his tools and skills: the work principle ... teaches him the pleasure of work completion by steady attention and persevering diligence ... Thus the *fundamentals of technology* are developed, as the child becomes ready to handle ... the tools [and linguistic and technological artifacts of his culture]. (p. 259)

The latent child, under relatively optimal conditions or encouraging circumstances, being naturally inclined toward industriousness and given his "epigenetic ground plan," cultivates the capacity for industry through "identification" with "tool partners." Tool partners or models can be parents, peers, teachers, mentors, or other figures, fictional or real. "It is at this point that wider society becomes significant in its ways of admitting the child to an understanding of meaningful roles in its technology and economy" (p. 260). Moreover, "industry involves doing things beside and with others, a first sense of division of labor and of differentiated opportunity, that is, a sense of the *technological ethos* of a culture, develops at this time" (p. 260). Erikson here, having already voiced his concern about the danger of under-identification with future work roles, cautions against the danger of over-identification with future work roles:

> But there is another, more fundamental danger, namely man's restriction of himself and constriction of his horizon to include only his work … If he accepts work as his only obligation, and 'what works' as his only criterion of worthwhileness, he may become the conformist and thoughtless slave of his technology and those who are in a position to exploit it. (pp. 260–261)

"Work," says Hoare (2002), "is a gift. It provides access to, contributions in, and inclusion by mainstream society. Work structures time, engaging the mind and psyche, thus work is essential to adult mental health" (p. 129). "The centrality of play in work," continues Hoare, "and of work with playfulness, is Erikson's main theme and requirement" (p. 129).

> To Erikson, each healthy person, at every developmental level, needed engaged work that alone shows one's play. Among children and adults … genuine play renews the psyche; like refreshing sleep, it prepares one to take up new challenges and demands. Among adults, good work provides release from emotional demands; it permits play with content and ideas. (p. 118)

We humans have a basic need to play-and-work. As a consequence, we have a corollary need for a complementary context that makes it possible for us to play-*in*-work, a context that is suitable for our developmental level. For Erikson, "good, free, uninterrupted play was the essence of work, a vital, engaged immersion for all" (Hoare, 2002, p. 118). But of course, inevitably, work also creates constricting demands and requirements. We sense this aspect of work deeply upon retirement from meaningful or purposeful work. The level of our satisfaction relative to work is a byproduct of the ratio of play/enjoyment-to-work restrictions and constrictions.

Play, elaborates Hoare (2002), gives work the "leeway" necessary for being transformed into a creative contribution. Leeway is "the genuine gift of 'free to be, you and me,' a safe harbor for work, imagination, and creativity" (p. 129). We need "the free range of the leeway of play and childlikeness in work" (p. 140). Hoare concludes with an Eriksonian message: "Absence of leeway, in work, in community endeavors, or at home, and limitations in the interplay one is permitted and within which one is considered human – trusted and autonomous – seriously harm the psyche and inhibit functioning" (p. 143).

Instead of opposing play to work, we can speak of "play-work." For instance, like Erikson, I play-in-my-work (present project) ideationally with the polar meanings of our existence; only I, unlike Erikson, co-constitute them, from the very beginning, as potentially complementary and not as oppositional.

Thus, for instance, "industry versus inferiority" becomes industriousness (work)-in-dialectical-relation-to-leisure (play). More than that, I play-in-my-work with other polarities, ones that Erikson did not include in his psychosocial theory of development.

"And yet," points out Browning (1975), "all through Erikson's work is the implication that the creative adult (the generative adult) is precisely the person who can infuse his work with play; he is the person who can stand back from the reality of his work long enough to fantasy a more human way of coping with its confinements, tensions, and dichotomies" (pp. 188–189). We humans are motivated to play with the tension-producing polarities of existence "until they submit to a new synthesis which … enlivens and activates [us]" (p. 189).

> The capacity for meaningful play, which first emerges in late childhood, is never lost for generative [mature] man. In Erikson's thought, play is man's major means of restoration – his preferred therapy. Play is the way the ego [self] repairs itself in the face of the threats and challenges of life which tend to rob the ego of active mastery … For Erikson, there is no great difference between the play of children and the play of adults. Both use play to regain a sense of ego integration, wholeness, and mastery; through play, both the child and the adult attempt to convert the more capricious and obstinate aspects of life into something at least acceptable and manageable if not actively willed. (p. 188)

For Erikson, observes Browning, our capacity for industry (work) builds on and stretches our natural inclination for play. Our capacity for optimal adaptation is "a *synthesis* of play and work" (p. 190). Through this play-work integration, I give expression to my humanity. In integrating work with play, I join together "wisdom as well as pleasure, adaptive strength as well as satisfying expressiveness," and "the instinctive and so-called irrational" with a broadened "concept of rationality" (p. 190).

Work, notes Levine (2010), "is the characteristic activity in which adults have the opportunity to feel alive" (p. 4). And to feel alive is to "experience our unique presence of being" (p. 4). Our self comes alive when we perform meaningful work. Work, he continues, has to do with our sense of agency and efficacy. Thus, "the self 'is the author of the work'" (p. 5). "To combine work and play," continues Levine, "means to escape from servitude [determinism] … To escape from servitude means to 'rove autonomously' [gain limited freedom]" (p. 48).

Identity-Integration-in-Dialectical-Relation-to-Identity-De-integration (Fluidity or Openness to Self-Questioning)

We are born to "selve," to carve out an autonomous and differentiated identity, always in a relational context, to pursue inter-*person*-hood. To "selve" is to interrogatively integrate affect-and-value-laden lifeworld meanings – meanings that we come to embody and enact. Our sense of self is interwoven with our lifeworld meanings. Already existing meanings decide our life; we decide our life's meanings. As Fuller (1990) frames it, "self and meaning circularly determine each other" (p. 198). And again, "the self is relative to the world, determined by it in its impact, and the world is relative to the self, interpretively determined by the self" (p. 196). Therein lies the paradox of our unfolding life narratives. Moreover, *interpreting* is not simply a cognitive act; it is a creative, venturesome, and "imaginative enactment of meaning" (p. 190). "All in all, then," Fuller observes, "people insightfully enact meanings in different ways, in accordance with the varying interpretive competencies they have become in their lifetime" (p. 188).

The "self," states Fuller (1990), can be described "as the openness of [life] events of meaning presencing" (p. 191). More specifically, "the bodily self" is defined as "a historically situated center of meaning" (pp. 164–165). It is always directed to (positive or negative) meanings. "Meaning is something or someone with which Dasein [human *being*] has become preoccupied, about which Dasein cares in some way, precisely as something or someone is brought close in its lived dimensionality" (p. 81). *Meanings matter.* Becoming insightful involves *monitoring the movement of meanings* in our lives.

Insightful selving, Fuller expands, involves "responsible answering to meaning" (p. 196). Responsibility (response-ability) is a disposition of opening oneself to intrinsic emotional-and-valuational meanings. "Responsibility," Fuller elaborates, entails "preparing oneself for their [meanings'] advent, ever-renewed [sic] process of becoming dimensionally responsive" to their actualization (p. 196). We are our meanings; "meaning become us" (p. 174). From our perspective, others *are* what they mean to us. In our own eyes, we *are* what we mean to our selves. The more insightful we become, the more interpretively competent we become in releasing "a meaning's tensions to their ever-renewed [sic] pursuit of a balanced state of fulfillment" (p. 172). The law of good meaning (gestalt) seeks "a state of balance, works to integrate new and disturbing elements [meanings] into existing wholes of meaning" or higher-order meaning (pp. 168–169). Dialectically described, even a seemingly positive meaning can be permeated with negativity or limitation upon deeper examination. Alternately, even a seemingly negative meaning, upon being subjected to open exploration, can be imbued with a positivity or strength, which then can become integrated into a more mature (higher-order) meaning. "If meanings remained neutral or good, if the status quo never manifested its internal and external structural limitations, problems of all sorts could never arise, much less solutions" (p. 169). There would never be a reason for change and growth.

The self then can now be viewed as a center for the co-organization (formation, re-formation, and trans-formation), integration, and co-actualization of meanings. Alternately, it is a center for the de-actualization of outmoded meanings with which we have identified. The self is oriented to seeking good, balanced meanings. "The search for goodness," reflects Fuller (1990), "is a structural invariant of events of meaning presencing" (p. 156). Intrinsically good meanings are "connected with love, beauty, and moral action" (p. 156). "Meanings" are always in "existential motion." Tensions are constitutive of meaning. Moreover, meanings are "always and already in existential space, dynamically stretched to and signifying one another" (p. 152). Good meanings "balance the lifeworld situation out perfectly bringing the tensions intrinsic to its structure to a most satisfying state of rest" (p. 151). Best meanings are "especially pure and excellent. They are meanings that are outstanding *in the beauty of their goodness*" (p. 151). Balance seeking in the movement of meanings can result in either tension reduction or tension enhancement. "A meaning's beauty lies in the excellence with which both tendencies are achieved at once in a meaning" (p. 150). There are times when the balancing of meanings is "nothing short of a moral demand. What is to be achieved is a higher-order meaning" (p. 253). This higher-order meaning is sponsored by a "higher-order insight, higher-order conscience … [which] is a, if not *the* paramount task of our lives" (p. 253). Our integrity, integration, or integrality as persons lies in such *balancing* of a broad and wide range of intrinsic affect-and-value-laden meanings. It lies in the "manner of surpassing to meanings" (p. 254).

"As one of our meanings," explicates Fuller (1990), "a fellow human being is another 'myself.' Other people as such special positively or negatively required meanings are referred to here as *person values*" in contradistinction to *use objects* (p. 145). Then again, person values and use values can become subverted with other people serving as use objects and objects becoming ends in themselves. Other people come to embody affect-and-value-laden meanings for us in a variety of ways:

> as worthy, contemptible, loving, lovable, cheating, friendly, hostile, manipulative, small, aloof, warm, concerned, honest, spiteful, refined, sound, wise, shallow, and so on. Persons as our required others are our friends, our lovers, our enemies, those from whom we have learned something, those who care for us and will hear us out, our parents, our children, those who perform a service for us, those who turn their backs on us. (p. 145)

The ratio of positive to negative meanings that other people embody and enact for us has consequences in that they are either accepted or rejected precisely as selves, as ends in themselves who *are* the totality of meanings we attribute to them. These meaning attributions can change over time. As one psychologist formulates it, upon being asked about what she had learned from being in a very long marriage: "I have had many marriages within this one marriage!" In other words, the meaning of her marriage had evolved over time. We understand others by entering their context of meanings. When we change, our contexts of meanings change.

What we seek in intimate relations are *balanced, harmony-producing, and integrating meaning attributions* that will outweigh *disturbed, disturbing, and de-integrating meaning attributions.* Intrapersonal peace cannot be separated from interpersonal peace. Just as we are condemned to attribute meanings to the comportment of others, so it is that we are forever attributing meanings to our own emotions, thoughts, and behaviors. We long for felt meanings that bring with them a sense of being-at-home-in-our-lifeworld. We seek to embody and enact meanings that will help integrate and harmonize our being-and-becoming, *meanings, small or large, that will bring balance to our lives.*

Let me illustrate. My wife asks me, and sometimes I anticipate the asking, to bring her eyeglasses as she lies down on the sofa, after a hard day's work. I say, "gladly," or "Mr. Gladly at your service." Or, I say, "To Serve with Love," playing on the title of the movie, "To Sir, with Love." This, for me, signifies a small act of love, which is part of the larger meanings of Acts of Love. It is saying "Yes" to love and to life, to a life of living in love, to love of Life. There are times when I say "No" to some requests. I am asserting my autonomy, hopefully discerningly. I am enacting what being autonomous *means* to me. There are times when my "Noes" are not so discerning or are perceived as thoughtless and uncaring. Hopefully, my mature "Yeses" will outweigh my immature "Yeses" and my mature "Noes" will outweigh my immature "Noes." The same applies to my wife's side. Of course, there are times when we agree to disagree and other times when things remain unreconciled and we pray for time to dissipate the aftermath of such unresolvable disagreements. Such is part of the work of *integrating the meanings* of my dependence on and my independence from my wife. We depend on each other in a myriad of ways. We also have our independent existences, our autonomously pursued life preferences and projects. Of course, there are times when I am not there for her when she needs me and the other way around. On average, we are for the most part there for each other. Take for instance our need for touch. We are fortunate that both my wife and I love to touch and be touched. The *co-meanings* of touching-and-being-touched for both of us are in synchrony. I depend on her to give me hugs, expect that my need to be hugged will be for the most part met, and I, in turn, generously give and anticipate her need to be hugged and held. Naturally, our former encounters with meanings of tender touching among loved ones have shaped our alreadiness and preparedness. We both *are* a repertoire of emotional competencies of these specified life-world meanings. Such meanings of touching-and-being-touched, in the way we have uniquely appropriated and enacted them, excite us and have a positive impact on us. One thing I have learned from my psychological knowledge and training is this: when we hold each other well, we are held together well. Embodied solidarity begets psychological solidity.

Let us return to Erikson. The later "existential" Erikson, says Hoare (2002), comes to prefer the use of the term "integrality" over the term "integrity." For Erikson, the term "integrality" connotes both *integrity* and *integration.* "The attainment of integrity" in later adulthood, note Newman and Newman (2018), "is ultimately a result of the balance of all the psychosocial crises that have come earlier [trust versus mistrust, autonomy versus doubt and shame, initiative versus guilt, industry versus inferiority, identity achievement versus identity confusion, intimacy versus isolation, and generativity versus stagnation], accompanied by all the ego strengths [hope, will, purpose, competence, fidelity to others and to values to live by, love, and care] or core pathologies [withdrawal, compulsion, inhibition, inertia, dissociation, repudiation, exclusivity, and rejectivity] that have accumulated along the way" (p. 540). "Integrity," they summarize, "is an ability to integrate one's past history with one's present circumstances and to feel content with the outcome" (p. 540).

Unlike the Eriksonian stage-based model, our dialectical model is cross-sectional. It is more like a revolving wheel where the *explicit* focus is on balancing, for instance, one's need to trust others and one's need to approach others with caution, while other seemingly polar needs are in the background and can become the focus of attention at any time. Erikson himself acknowledges that unresolved polarities of earlier stages can resurface in later stages. What Erikson does not focus upon is the deep connection between the fundamental issues of adolescence and later adulthood. As outlined by Erikson himself, these so-called two stages have significant themes in common. The work of identity integration begun in adolescence never ceases and is a work in progress throughout the lifespan. In our dialectical scheme, selving begins the moment after birth, if not before. Becoming trusting, autonomous, initiating, industrious, intimate, and generative are all parts of a holistic growth movement toward *inter-selving* – becoming differentiated while remaining connected.

Just like the acquisition of integrity in later adulthood, identity achievement in later adolescence, Newman and Newman (2018) inform us, "involves the integration of past, present, and future" (p. 399). Both mature later adolescents and mature later adults reflect upon their past identifications, hold onto the good ones, let go of the bad ones, and add new good ones. All this is done in light of articulating valued life goals and aspirations for the future – for the kind persons they are becoming. In the process they are both forging a balance between their sense of continuity and discontinuity with the past. Erikson tends to weigh too heavily on the side of *continuity* with the past as being central to carving out a solid identity – an identity that is firmly anchored in one's familial-cultural-historical roots. Maturation, however, requires balancing *continuous identifications* with *discontinuous dis-identifications* with the values of the past as one reexamines and revises these identifications in the present and creatively carves out a changing identity into the future.

Both later adolescents and later adults need to find a *balance* between acknowledging and affirming their strengths, while taking into account their limitations in the present. And both need to find a precarious *balance* between their private and public selves, between their authentic (real) and inauthentic (false) selves. This is the work of *integration.* "In the process of achieving personal identity, one must synthesize the private sense of self with the public self derived from the many roles and relationships in which one is embedded" (Newman and Newman, 2018, p. 400).

Both later adolescents and later adults seek to find *equilibrium* between being authentic (being themselves, their genuine, real, and true selves) and being inevitably and inescapably inauthentic. Authenticity and inauthenticity are not all-or-none phenomena. Just as there are degrees of authenticity, there are also degrees of inauthenticity. For Heidegger, as Deurzen and Kenward (2005) explicate it, authenticity means an owned way of existing. "To be authentic," they explain, "requires us to admit to ourselves that our possibilities are our own, and that we therefore have to win [own] our self for ourselves" (p. 11). "Authenticity," however "is only a modification but not a total obliteration of inauthenticity" (p. 11). "For Heidegger," and here they quote Heidegger directly, "'the inauthenticity of Dasein [human *being*] does not signify a 'lesser' being or a 'lower' degree of being. Rather, inauthenticity can determine Da-sein [Being-There] even in its fullest concretion, when it is busy, excited, interested, and capable of pleasure'" (p. 12). Ultimately we become authentic, our true selves, by examining our motivations and intentions, facing our possibilities and limitations, our fragility, fallenness, and finitude, and by listening to the voice of our caring conscience as a guide for living. However, we will always be inauthentically absorbed in the "They-self" – the complying and conforming self. This is what I label as our *compensatory false self*, that is a byproduct of the "conditionality," dutifulness, and self-forgetfulness involved in living and getting along with others. We pay a mental health price for pursuing the Purified-Authentic-Self *and* for pursuing a life swept by the Unreflexive-They-Self.

What Erikson and the Newmans do not emphasize enough is: (1) the im*pulse* toward balance and integration, *integrative balance*, is at the heart of self-formation from the beginning of life; and (2) a skewing of the balance can occur at either end of the polar continuum. What Erikson calls "identity foreclosure" is simply a premature (rigid) integration. Not all integration is good for our maturation or mental health. Similarly, not all de-integration is bad for our maturation and mental health. Some self-questioning, self-doubt, and self-criticalness are good for our continued psychosocial growth. Excessive self-questioning, self-doubt, and self-criticalness are bad for our maturation and mental health.

De-integration or skewing in excess results in fragmentation. The identity center will no longer hold. Compensatory, defensive, or protective, but nevertheless illusory, measures are taken to keep humpty-dumpty together. Such delusionary measures can take the form of what Horney (1970) describes as general pathological ways of being–in-the-world-with-others or maladaptive identifications – such as, inflexibly *moving-toward-others* (always trying to please others), *moving-against-others* (always aggressing against others), and *moving-away-from-others* (always avoiding or withdrawing from others). Or, the one-sided skewer can take refuge in the consumption of specific bad transitory objects such as food, alcohol, tobacco, and drugs. Erikson repeatedly reminds us in his various works that *identity*, at least in crucial part, is made up of *identifications*. Thus, we can surmise that when these *identifications* are faulty, as when we come to *identify* with one inflexible way of being-in-the-world-with-others, there is a *fault* or *fissure* at the center of *identity*.

Intimacy-in-Dialectical-Relation-to-Separation

Erikson (1963) defines intimacy as "the capacity [of the mature individual] to commit himself to concrete affiliations and partnerships and to develop the ethical strength to abide by such commitments, even though they may call for significant sacrifices and compromises" (p. 263). Intimacy, he adds, requires the *fusion* of identities without the fear of loss of one's *separate* identity. The absence of finding balance between "self-abandon" that is a requisite for "the solidarity of close affiliations" (intimacy) *and* the simultaneous maintenance of one's own separate and solid identity will "lead to a deep sense of isolation and consequent self-absorption [or excessive narcissism]" (pp. 263–264).

"The counterpart of intimacy," Erikson (1963) adds, "is distantiation" (p. 264), which he equates one-sidedly with isolation. In our dialectical model, we would make a distinction between, on the one hand, mature (differentiated) intimacy and immature (enmeshed) intimacy and, on the other, mature separation and immature separation. We would subsume Erikson's negative distantiation or isolation, which he defines as "the avoidance of contacts which commit to [mature] intimacy" (p. 266), under immature separation, as in emotional or physical cutoffs. Achieving relative integrative balance involves learning to modulate optimal distancing with optimal closeness.

Resolving the crisis of intimacy versus isolation, Erikson (1963) concludes, results in the acquisition of the core character strength of the capacity to love. "For [John] Bowlby,", observes Holmes (2010), "attachment and love were synonymous" (p. 6). Holmes himself refers to "the attachment/separation dialectic of relationships" (p. 86). His fleeting use of the term *dialectic*, however, lacks the rigor of our own dialectical model. Regardless, if we substitute love or intimacy for attachment, then Holmes is on the right track in describing the dialectical relationship between intimacy (love) and separation. In psychoanalytic attachment theory, the inevitable counterpart of attachment (love or intimacy) is separation. Whereas secure attachment results in mature separation, premature separation is a consequence of insecure attachment.

The needs to *both* attach *and* separate are core, complementary existential issues beckoning balance. Johnson (1994) states that every child is entitled or has the right to have her or his need for attachment (love) optimally indulged and optimally frustrated. Feeling secure in being loved (securely attached), the child is then free to individuate – to achieve a healthy separate autonomous identity. Feeling loved and loveable, she or he experiences being a part of a larger familial whole to which she or he belongs.

Stern (2004) asserts that "belonging versus psychological aloneness" is an essential and universal dimension of our "intersubjective motivational system." Here is Stern in his own words:

> Broadly speaking, the intersubjective motivational system concerns regulating psychological belonging versus psychological aloneness. The poles of this spectrum are, at one end cosmic loneliness, and at the other, mental transparency, fusion, and disappearance of the self. The intersubjective motivational system regulates the zone of intersubjective comfort somewhere between the two poles. The exact point of comfort depends on one's role in the group, whom one is with, and the personal history of the relationship leading up to that moment. The point on the continuum must be negotiated continually with second-to-second fine-tuning. Too much is at stake for it not to be. (p. 100)

Stern goes on to equate belongingness with intimacy, as, when we say to a loved other in a moment of passionate intimacy, "You belong to me." Belonging and intimacy "play a powerful role in group formation and maintenance ... [However,] belonging is different from physical, sexual, attachment, or dependency ties. It is a separate order of relatedness" (p. 100). Viewed in the context of lived experience, it is not always easy to separate the sense of belonging from attachment (love or physical, sexual, nonsexual intimacy) and dependency ties.

Other-Care (Generativity)-in-Dialectical-Relation-to Self-Care

The "term [generativity]," Erikson (1963) informs us, "encompasses the evolutionary development which has made man the teaching and instructing as well as the learning animal" (p. 166). Just as children (the younger generation) depend upon adults, so too adults (the older generation) depend upon children who make up humanity's future. "Mature man," Erikson quickly adds, "needs to be needed" (pp. 266–267). "Generativity then," Erikson expands, "is primarily the concern in establishing and guiding the next generation" (p. 267). "And indeed," Erikson further elaborates, "the concept of generativity is meant to include such more popular synonyms as *productivity* and *creativity*" (p. 267). Cultural, societal, or religious institutions assume the responsibility of creatively codifying "the ethics of generational succession" (p. 267).

Generativity, then, is essentially the *concern* in establishing, guiding, teaching, and instructing the next generation in ways that are creative and productive. Giving birth to and taking good *care* of a child is a generative act that is symbolically imbued with productivity and creativity (pro-creation). It is an act of renewal and re-generation. The "ability to lose oneself in the meeting of bodies and minds," Erikson (1963) waxes poetically, "leads to a gradual expansion of ego [self]-interests and to a libidinal [passionate] investment in that which is being generated" (p. 267). Humans, Erikson reminds us, can be generative and display their *capacity for care-and-concern*, in a myriad of ways other than generating and caring for children. "The mere fact of having children, however, does not 'achieve' generativity" (p. 267). There are multiple ways in which we can creatively and productively *maintain* this precariously precious world of ours. In fact, Erikson reminds us that there are exceptionally generative individuals who renounce their "right to procreate or to produce" by turning to "ultimate concerns" and thus strive "to settle the matter of … their relationship to the Care for the creatures of this world and to the Charity which is felt to transcend it" (pp. 267–268).

Where generativity fails, cautions Erikson (1963), "regression to an obsessive need for pseudo-intimacy takes place with a pervading sense of stagnation and personal impoverishment" (p. 267). Generative failure can be a byproduct of "early childhood impressions; in excessive self-love based on a too strenuously self-made personality; and finally … in the lack of some faith, some 'belief' in the species, which would make a child appear to be a welcome trust of the community" (p. 267). Of course, the family is children's first community. Having been deprived of a welcoming love, children fail to develop a basic belief, faith, or trust in their human community. One possible outcome is that as they develop, they may "begin to indulge themselves as if they were their own – or one another's – one and only child" (p. 267). Being developmentally arrested, they become preoccupied with excessive "self-concern."

Erikson is here juxtaposing generativity (optimal other care-and-concern) with stagnation (excessive self-love and self-concern). Viewing this polar juxtaposition from the perspective of our own dialectical model, we can conclude that it tells only half the story. What Erikson is neglecting is the potentially negative version of Other Care and the potentially positive version of Self-Care.

Other-Care can emerge developmentally as a compensatory defense against conditional love. For instance, an individual may, in a role-reversal, adopt the role of carer of the parent to gain what Erikson describes as "pseudo-intimacy" or pseudo-love, pseudo-empowerment, and pseudo-specialness. Thereafter, she or he over-identifies with this Other-Care role, the enactment of which generalizes to other domains of existence.

Self-concern or Self-Care, when modulated with Other-Care, can be viewed as an index of maturation and mental health. Self-Care involves the capacity to take care of oneself *and* the capacity to seek and allow essential others to take care of oneself. Whereas excessive self-concern is a manifestation of unhealthy narcissism, modulated Self-Care is a necessary complementary condition for modulated Other-Care. Compulsive, compensatory Other-Care is a defensive relational style constructed for the purpose of coping with conditional love. Negotiating an optimal *balance* between Self-Care and Other Care is the mark of the relatively *balanced* or *dialectical self*.

References

Bloland, S. E. (2005). *In the shadow of fame: A memoir by the daughter of Erik H. Erikson*. Viking.

Browning, D. S. (1975). *Generative man: Psychoanalytic perspectives*. A Delta Book/ Dell Publishing.

Deurzen, E. V., & Kenward, R. (2005). *Dictionary of existential psychotherapy and counselling*. Sage.

Deurzen-Smith, E. V. (1997). *Everyday mysteries: Existential dimensions of psychotherapy*. Routledge.

Erikson, E. H. (1963). *Childhood and society* (2nd ed.). W. W. Norton.

Erikson, E. H. (1964). *Insight and responsibility*. W. W. Norton.

Erikson, E. H. (1968). *Identity: Youth and crisis*. W. W. Norton.

Erikson, E. H. (1980). *Identity and the life cycle*. W. W. Norton.

Erikson, E. H. (1985). *The life cycle completed*. W. W. Norton.

Fairbairn, R. W. D. (1952). *Psychoanalytic studies of the personality*. Routledge.

Fuller, A. R. (1990). *Insight into value: An exploration of the premises of a phenomenological psychology*. State University of New York Press.

Greenberg, J. R., & Mitchell, S. A. (1983). *Object relations in psychoanalytic theory*. Harvard University Press.

Hannush, M. J. (1999). An interview with Rollo May. *Review of Existential Psychology and Psychiatry*, Numbers 1, 2, & 3 (pp. 129–141).

Hannush, M. J. (2002). *Becoming good parents: An existential journey*. State University of New York Press.

Hannush, M. J. (2010). Playing with polarities of existence: Toward understanding a pivotal passage in the life and work of Rollo May. In T. F. Cloonan & C. Thiboutot (Eds.), *The redirection of psychology: Essays in honor of Amedeo Giorgi* (pp. 137–162). CIRP.

Hoare, C. H. (2002). *Erikson on development and adulthood: New insights from the unpublished papers*. Oxford University Press.

Holmes, J. (2010). *Exploring in security: Towards an attachment-informed psychoanalytic psychotherapy*. Routledge.

Horney, K. (1970). *Neurosis and human growth: The struggle toward self-realization*. W. W. Norton.

Johnson, S. M. (1994). *Character styles*. W. W. Norton.

Kohut, H. (1977). *The restoration of the self*. International Universities Press.

Levine, D. P. (2010). *Object relations, work, and the self*. Routledge.

Lifton, R. J. (1993). *The protean self: Human resilience in an age of fragmentation*. The University of Chicago Press.

May, R. (1981). *Freedom and destiny*. W. W. Norton.

Mitchell, S. A., & Black, M. J. (1995). *Freud and beyond: A history of modern psychoanalytic thought*. Basic Books.

Newman, B. M., & Newman, P. R. (2018). *Development through life: A psychosocial approach* (13th ed.). Cengage Learning.

Nicholsen, S. W. (2002). *The love of nature and the end of the world: The unspoken dimensions of environmental concern*. The MIT Press.

Searles, H. F. (1979). *Countertransference and related subjects: Selected Papers*. International Universities Press.

Seinfeld, J. (1991). *The empty core: An object relations approach to psychotherapy of the schizoid personality*. Jason Aronson.

Stern, D. N. (2004). *The present moment in psychotherapy and everyday life*. W. W. Norton.

Strozier, C. B. (2001). *Heinz Kohut: The making of a psychoanalyst*. Farrar, Straus and Giroux.

6

Feelings: The Capacity to Balance One's *Feelings* and Come to Terms with the Ambivalences and Ambiguities of Existence

"Ambivalence," states Longhofer (2015), "refers to the coexistence of two opposing feelings, drives, tendencies and impulses, towards the same person, goal or object" (p. 14). Longhofer goes on to make a distinction between "ambivalent instability" (p. 15) and ambivalent stability. *Ambivalent stability* or positive ambivalence is a mental-emotional state that succeeds in integrating and thus tolerating the coexistence of "two opposing feelings, drives, tendencies and impulses." For instance, "the coexistence of love and hate toward the same object [person] can be tolerated" (p. 15). "The critical achievement in the attainment of ambivalence," says Ogden (1986), "is the fact that the person one hates is the *same person* whom one has loved and unconsciously still loves and hopes to openly love again… When one hates, the love that one had felt is still real and is present in the history that one shares with the person hated" (p 89).

To be alive is to be ambivalent about something or someone. However, as we have learned, there is a wide maturational gap between negative, intolerant, or unstable ambivalence and positive, tolerant, or stable ambivalence. Here is an example of *unstable ambivalence*. When I fight with my wife, I am filled with hateful feelings toward her. She becomes my enemy. Winning or losing my argument with her becomes a sum-zero game, a deadly serious duel. I would derive perverse pleasure from eradicating and obliterating her point of view. In the midst of rendering her defenseless, I am totally forgetful of the fact that I also love her. Here is another example of *stable ambivalence*. I am fighting with my wife. But I am not forgetful that she is and will always be my loved life partner. My recollection of my love for her modulates my hateful feelings toward her and allows me to caringly and concernedly "collect"

© The Author(s), under exclusive license to Springer Nature Switzerland AG 2021

M. J. Hannush, *Markers of Psychosocial Maturation*,
https://doi.org/10.1007/978-3-030-74315-4_6

myself. I now remain open to the possibility of understanding her point of view, of entering her context of meaning. I am presently predisposed to quickly repair our momentary relational rupture. It is all right to admit, upon reflection, that I was wrong and apologize; or not to be self-righteous upon realizing that I was right. I am inclined to compromise and conciliate. I am willing to let go and move on without rigidly holding on for too long. I am inclined to see the comical or temporary aspect of our conflictual condition. A tender touch or a knowing smile from her results in a mutual and meltingly tender hug. The capacity to become tolerant of "opposing feelings, drives, tendencies and impulses," in general, and the ability to balance loving and hateful feelings, in particular, are maturational achievements.

Ambivalence is of the essence of our human existence. Consequently, our ambivalence permeates not only our affect-laden relational (relation to self and others) disposition of love versus hate, but also our connectedness (closeness, attachment) versus separateness (distance, detachment), dependence versus independence, self-care versus other-care, initiative (beginning and perseveringly completing projects) versus inertia (relaxing, resting, or doing nothing), and working (seriously contributing) versus playing (having leisurely fun). When these relational dimensions are lived as embodiments of *ambivalent instability*, they become mutually exclusive or either/or polarities. In other words, I am either too closely connected (enmeshed) or separate-and-emotionally distant; I am either excessively dependent or fiercely independent; I am either hyper-initiating projects or I am in a perpetual state of listless inertia; I am either compulsively working hard or perpetually and irresponsibly playing. But when these relational dispositions are lived as embodiments of *ambivalent stability* they become mutually inclusive and complementary or both/and polarities. I am both connected and separate; I am both dependent and independent; I can alternate between states of inertia and initiative in a creative and vitalizing way; I can work-and-play and I can even playfully work.

We need to learn to recognize and tolerate our ambivalence. When we are very young, our ambivalent feelings are experienced in a one-dimensional way. As we mature, we gain greater respect for the power and flux of our feeling-states. Frosh (2011) goes so far as to "suggest that the core of neurosis is the failure to come to terms with one's own feeling states" (p. 21). Our mind, continues Frosh, "strives toward integration" (p. 21). "And the general rule of mental health," he adds, "is directed towards recovering [reintegrating] … split-off emotions" (p. 21). Feeling-states cannot be separated from self-states. Frosh makes reference to a generalized feeling that reflects and reveals our sense of "aliveness" and our "quality of life." When the suffering other communicates to me on a deep level, "Make me feel better," I need to understand this as "an ethical request" (p. 93). This essential other is desperately seeking a *better* quality of life. "Feelings," adds Frosh, "have others at their source (as in sadness due to loss, happiness due to love, fear due to threat)" (p. 9). Feelings are "*social*: they pass between people, infecting each one" (p. 13). Moreover, he elaborates, "the capacity to feel other people's feeling, or at least to understand what they feel, might be central to what makes us human" (p. 9). And although they bring us pain and suffering, this is "what we are for" (p. 9). From the beginning, *feeling felt*, we are enabled to feel for ourselves and for others.

"A successful developmental process," Frosh (2011) tells us, "is marked by the infant moving through a phase of perceiving the world as split between loving and hateful elements ... and then integrating these into a more unified, albeit ambivalent, set of relational states" (p. 17). This maturational process is facilitated by helping the developing child acquire knowledge of her or his feelings and to be able to articulate this knowledge in an atmosphere of safety, security, and trust. The "capacity to experience emotion without hiding from it ... is an important [maturational] marker of ... [personal and relational] integrity" (p. 25). "Having a secure identity," in at least one sense, is equivalent in meaning to "the sense of feeling 'at one' with oneself and with one's community" (p. 32). "So, being at one with oneself would involve being at one with one's surroundings; feeling comfortable in one's identity is a social as well as a personal act" (p. 33). But a feeling "can have the function of throwing one off balance" when the "elements of our lives ... do not quite fit in [cohere]" (p. 34). "Feeling out of sorts could be the beginning of something new" (p. 36). Suddenly losing a loved one, for instance, I am thrown off balance. In the process of mourning my loss, by feeling sad over my loss, I am awakened to the fragility of life. My I-world becomes reconstituted as I begin to discerningly focus on what really matters in light of my loss. Painfully, over time, I regain my sense of stability as I resolve the tension between holding-on-and-letting-go of my lost loved one. I hold on to my deeply felt loving memory of my lost loved one in a usable way that allows me to move forward with my life.

Frosh (2011) differentiates between negative and positive forms of ambivalence or ambivalent feeling-self-states. Splitting in the form of seeing self or others as all bad or all good and experiencing abrupt shifts in between is a negative form of ambivalence. A warm, holding environment in which one feels felt and held allows the developing child and adolescent to face the challenge of change with relative equanimity. In such a "setting in which loss can be recognised but managed allows for the development of feelings of sadness and hope bound up together as a positive form of ambivalence" (p. 81). It permits the developing person "to develop more finely calibrated capacities *for* feeling ('understanding' one's feeling more fully, or showing a deeper capability for feeling anything at all)" (p. 85). This for Frosh is reflective of an *ethical stance* that involves a relational readiness for significant "I-You" encounters not of the instrumental kind – the kind that is not concerned with a particular *use*ful outcome.

A maturing stance, indicates Frosh (2011), "involves coming to terms with ambivalent feelings, and recognizing that the destructive urges we have within ourselves are often directed at the people we love" (p. 4). This mature position "is an active welding [or integrating] together of love and hate, a kind of moral [or ethical] stance in which the damage done is recognized and absorbed and in which the concomitant feelings of sadness is actually a healthy way to do emotional [and relational] work" (pp. 4–5). Feelings of sadness, guilt, or shame can urge us to make reparation for our destructive acts or it may spur us into the pursuit of creative projects. "The capacity to feel," says Frosh, "is a fundamental sign of mental health" and is ultimately "an ethical position" (p. 5). The ability to feel maturely involves making "connections between feeling states (love and hate, for example)" (p. 5). To really live is to feel deeply. "Openness to feeling," however, "clearly means openness to [not only pleasure and joy, but also] hurt [or pain and suffering]; it makes us vulnerable" (p. 5). Maturing means tolerating our vulnerability. From the start of life we are vulnerable because we are utterly dependent on and open to others. "In our dependent state, we learn from early childhood onwards whether others are trustworthy or not; we build conscious and unconscious expectations of how we are going to be treated" (pp. 6–7). By being properly handled, held, and contained, we "gain a sense of ourselves as cared-for and indeed as worthy of care, and others as likely to be supportive and loving" (p. 7). We learn to modulate our excessive infantile feelings. We learn to "tolerate dependency and vulnerability" (p. 7).

We are, however, vulnerable to inevitable feelings of loss even under relatively optimal conditions in which we grow up. Some losses, such as the loss of childhood, are necessary; some are seemingly unnecessary, such as the loss of the permanent presence of a parent due to divorce. Losses may or may not, at least on the surface, be accompanied by gains. As we grow older, we experience "symbolic losses such as the loss of an ideal or of a future possibility; or, of course, loss of love. The lost ideal might even be an idea of oneself" (p. 3). I might feel sad because of my sudden realization of the damage and hurt I have inflicted upon others and thus failed in being the kind of person I might have been. I may feel sad because I have failed in a project in which I have invested myself.

Ambivalence may predate our own birth. Even parents-to-be and parents of newborn infants may experience feelings of ambivalence toward their coming or newly born co-creation. Young toddlers struggle with and can become overwhelmed by powerful ambivalent feelings of love and hate, writes Joyce (2005). In fact, she points out, "*conflict and ambivalence* are the main characteristics of toddler behaviour" (p. 84). On the one hand, the toddler wishes for closeness to his loved-and-loving parents, the attachment figures that constitute the source of her or his safety and security and thus upon whom she or he is totally dependent. On the other hand, the toddler wishes for autonomy, independence, and freedom. For the toddler, this dialectical tension between the need for closeness and dependence and the need for separateness and independence is simply too much to bear.

The toddler is helped to resolve her or his dialectical dilemma (connectedness versus separation; dependence versus independence), explains Joyce (2005), when the parent is tolerant of the young child's "*regressive tendencies* and *autonomous urges*" (p. 84). It is "the mother's love of the toddler and the acceptance of his ambivalence that enable the toddler to develop a sound sense of self-esteem in these circumstances" and to "separate successfully" (p. 84). Through their discerningly loving mediation, which includes age-appropriate limit setting, the parents enable the toddler to transcend her or his confusing helplessness resulting from her or his ambivalence and to integrate her or his passionate feelings of love and hate. It is this capacity for loving understanding through accurate *meaning making* on the part of emotionally available and empathically mirroring parents – what Wilfred Bion calls the capacity for *reverie* and what Neville Symington calls the capacity for *contemplation,* which enables the developing child to modulate her or his overwhelming ambivalent feelings. Through their empathic attunement, mature parents are able to *read the meaning* of their toddler's *dialectical dilemma* accurately. Through their judicious responsiveness, they communicate this accurate meaning making to their loved child. This is what I call *authentic* or *existential communication,* for they are helping their child resolve a universally experienced human conflict that is revisited throughout the life cycle: the deep desire to be securely attached and closely connected versus the equally deep desire to be dignifiedly detached and separately individuated. Similarly, this dialectical dilemma is evident in our need to be *passionate participants* in our lifeworld and our need to be *dispassionate overviewers* of our complex life situations. "These" polar meanings, emphasizes Rayner (2005), when integratively balanced, "are at the heart of mature thoughtfulness and mental integrity" (p. 139).

In an incipiently phenomenological insight, Rose (2005) suggests that "*emotions may be viewed as thoughts that are not yet fully formed*" (p. 190). "An emotion," expands Hart (2009a), "values or devalues 'something' or someone. Emotions … In this sense are founded on … cognition" (p. 207), such as a belief or an expectation. "Anger" for instance, exemplifies Hadreas (2007), "*requires* the belief that an outrage has been experienced. … someone cannot be angry when he thinks himself treated justly" (p. 100). Moreover, an emotion, such as love, adds Hart (2009a), can become a "position-taking" or an ethical "stance": "Love is an emotion that becomes a stance or position-taking but which itself is founded on the position-taking of empathic perception. … Thus the position-taking of empathic perception, i.e., the presencing of the Other as another self-experiencing has the seed of love" (pp. 206–207). Moreover, "empathic perception is always on the verge of a valuation of respect" (p. 207). In loving and being loved our individual essences are revealed. "Love reveals the innermost center of the I of the one loving. In this sense it is a gathering [or integrative] act" (p. 206).

Love becomes an ethical stance. Edmund "Husserl himself," Hart (2009a) hastens to add, "holds a version of this sense of love when he ties it to what he calls the 'one thing necessary' and the absolute Ought which is the single individual's unique calling" (p. 205). In responding resolutely to such a calling of our mature *loving conscience* and in continuously renewing such a resolution we come to *identify* fully with our loving self. My being is overwhelmingly defined by my loving position-taking or stance. I become the agent of the emotional truth of a loving orientation.

What love values (cherishes, delights, and rejoices in), states Hart (2009a), is the beingness, blessedness, ipseity (essential "I-ness"), inherent radiance, or dignity of the Other. But to be empathically loving also requires, paradoxically, an intermittent shifting into a stance or position-taking of what I label as *dignified detachment* or *disengagement* to balance our *passionate attachment* or *engagement*. This is why Hart interprets Husserl as saying that to be empathically present to the Other, I need to assume the double stance of identificatory resonance as well as partaking in the "epoche" – disengaging from "all that can be disengaged or invalidated," such as my own biases and prejudgments (p. 145). Here is Hadreas (2007) delineating the same theme:

> In one remarkable passage Husserl describes the ethical love for others as an analogue of the transcendental reduction [a reduction in our biases and prejudices that transcends our ordinary pre-judgmental self] itself! As the phenomenologist puts objects [taken-for-granted ideas and expectations] 'out of action' in the phenomenological reduction, with ethical love, they analogously suspend

> thematic interests extended to another person. The other person is no longer someone with whom I have an [instrumental] agenda of any sort. This analogue of the *epoche* uncovers persons as occupied in their own strivings. As such, the transcendental connection to the other, as a 'responsive alter Ego' [an Other I] appears. This means that we allow ourselves to accept others in their uniqueness, a transcendental condition for personal love. Finally, uncovered is a permanent, yet worldly, union with the other's individuality. (p. 110)

And here is Melle (2002) writing on a similar theme in his essay, "Edmund Husserl: From Reason to Love":

> The concern about my life as a whole becomes an ethical concern through an ethical epoche, a bracketing of my whole previous life and a universal critique of it oriented toward a radical renewal according to ethical ideals. … The ideal is a life based on a good theoretical, axiological, and practical conscience – a life with no regrets. … [It] is the ideal of a person who would be absolutely true to herself and who would preserve herself in all her acts… A person … is who she is most inwardly by her love and calling. … We have to follow the call of our individual conscience; we have to realize and preserve our true genuine self, to be true to our deeper self, to the absolute ought of our pure love. (pp. 243–344)

This love is no longer *merely* an emotion because for Husserl it involves "personal decision of the active heart" (p. 244). "And since I am who am I [sic] by loving [which is an act of identification], I sacrifice myself in sacrificing this value" (p. 245). Through my choice, which is perpetually reaffirmed, I transform my past fate into my future destiny. My loving, which becomes my life project, is in need of continuous refinement. "In the pursuance of the ethical ideal [of love] we have to cope with regular setbacks" (p. 247). Though my world will be largely infused with the beautiful and the good, I must inevitably struggle with the ugliness and badness that are ever present in myself-and-in-my-lifeworld. Part of my challenging life task is to hold the badness in myself in check and transform whenever humanly possible the ugly into the beautiful, as do artists like Vincent van Gogh and Henri Matisse.

"Human beings," holds Howard (2011), "have a strong tendency to split things into opposites and only see one aspect of a complex situation. In particular, we tend to see others or ourselves as all good or all bad" (p. 17). "It is a sign of psychological maturity," she adds, "when we can manage the tensions involved in bringing opposites together, for example being able to acknowledge that we can *love* and *hate* the same person" (p. 17). Phenomenologically – in adhering unbiasedly, as much as that is humanly possible, to describing lived experience itself, we observe ourselves as having the dual tendency to *simplify* and prematurely *integrate* our world (of people, happenings, and ideas) *meaningfully*. Dichotomizing our world into either/or sub-worlds (what psychoanalysts describe as object-splitting) allows us, in childhood, to adapt to the happenings of our world quickly. But this readiness to dichotomize (rigidly categorize) our lifeworld will soon prevent us, under less than optimal conditions for maturation, from moving beyond our simplistic (either/or) meaning making and advancing toward a more complex (both/and), higher-order meaning making. As we mature, under good enough conditions, we become disposed to stretch and surpass our either/or bipolar meaning making capability. We are now open to integrating feeling-laden meanings such as love *and* hate.

The *simplifying* (dichotomizing, all-or-nothing, either/or) stance reflects a closed, constricting, impulsive, inhibiting, rigidifying way of being-in-the-world-with-self-and-others. The *integrating (both/and) stance* reflects a dignified, flexible, reflective, and thoughtful way of being-in-the-world-with-others. The integrative orientation is a *dignified* position-taking in that it is detached-and-caring at the same time. It is a paradoxical mixture of being close to and being somewhat at a distance from the Self in relation to the Other. More than that, a dignified positioning is, as Hart (2009a, 2009b) describes it, a stance that is respectfully mindful of the presence of the "I-ness" of the Other, the "propertyless myself" in the Other. It is respectful of the center of the Other's "personal I" (*Existenz*). It is an openness to the "Who I am" in the Other as well as oneself. It is affirming the fact that I or the Other is more and other than my or her properties. It is the validation of my or the Other's "unique essence." This dignified stance can be likened to the respectful distance that allows me to hear the voice of my own *existential (caring) conscience*. It can also be likened to Husserl's equation of "ethical love" with the "transcendental reduction" or the "epoche." In others words, as Hadreas (2007) puts it, "ethical love" requires of me to "suspend the thematic [agenda-based] interests … [and respectfully] accept [become attuned to] others in their uniqueness, a transcendental condition for personal love" (p. 110). Only then am I ready for a "union with the other's individuality" (p. 110).

We all fall short of responding *fully* to the call to love ethically summoned by our *caring conscience*. This "holy" calling is our destiny. Falling miserably short is succumbing to our fate – what Heidegger (1962, 1996) calls "thrownness." Thrown into this world, we are buffeted by genetic and environmental forces that suspend us between dialectical tensions that beckon acceptance and resolution – choosing in the face of the unchosen, all in the context of listening, under relatively optimal environmental conditions, to the call of our *caring conscience*. This is how we can, within limits, transform our fate, by way of a responsible owning, into our chosen destiny. Ultimately, we are who we are through our ethical (mature) loving. Still, as Melle (2002) puts it, in "the pursuance of the ethical ideal [of love] we have to cope with regular setbacks" (p. 247). Why? Because this "ideal is an infinite ideal of perfection that we can strive for and work toward and in some sense approximate, but without ever coming closer to its [full] realization" (p. 247). In the face of hate and destruction, we have to maintain our faith-and-belief that our ethical will-to-love counts as an ultimate concern and that the beautiful, good, and true are more primary than the ugly, bad, and false.

What Husserl does not tell us, according to Melle (2002), is how to balance the passion (emotion) of love with the dignified detachment of reason. Incidentally, Husserl's "discourse of [on] love is to be found almost exclusively in [unpublished and untranslated] research manuscripts" (Melle, 2002, p. 247). I would add that, to my knowledge, Husserl does not edify us concretely as to how to balance our love with our hate.

Hate, holds Hart (2009a), is "of necessity ignorant of the Other in herself and knows her only as the postulated source upon which is laminated the vile properties and with which/whom she identifies these properties [attributes, qualities, or traits]" (p. 241). Ironically, the hater presumes to "know" the essence of the hated Other. The hater makes the presumption that the despised properties of the hated Other reveal the essence of who s/he is as a person. But when one loves the essence of who the Other is as a person, the lover "does not permit the Other's negative qualities ever to obliterate the transcendent incomparable splendor of the essential fullness of the ipseity [center of Selfhood; the core Self; essential "I-ness"]. These shortcomings and weaknesses are always balanced by what is regarded as the incommensurate good of the other's ipseity [the essence of who this person is]" (p. 241). In other words, for the relatively mature person, love and hate have *reconcilable meanings*; whereas for the immature individual, love and hate have *irreconcilable meanings*.

"Hatred," notes Gaylin (2003), "is more than emotion. It is also a psychological condition; a disorder of perception; a form of quasi-delusional thinking" (p. 66). As Gaylin describes them, unlike fear, guilt, rage, and shame, love and hate are more than powerful feelings. Unlike feelings, which come and go, love and hate are passions that endure. My sense is that we need to be open to viewing all raw feelings or communicated emotions as having the potential of becoming enduring passions or pervasive affective-and-relational position-takings. Moreover, we need to remain cognizant as to how surface emotions, such as anger or rage, may defensively disguise core affects such as helplessness and shame.

Whereas love individualizes (sees the uniqueness of the Other), says Hadreas (2007), hate generalizes and rigidly categorizes the Other. Whereas personal love conjoins empathies, one after another, hatred, "generalizes and exclusively separates the culpability of the hated person from oneself" and maximizes "the 'us-them' opposition" (p. 99). All types of hatred, he specifies, share two conditions or principles: "First the hater has ill-will for the hated" (p 65). This he labels as the "principle of harm or ill-will." "Second," he continues, "in all types of hatred there is a whole shifting of blame to the hated individual or group" (p. 65). This second condition is labeled as "the principle of blame" or "extra-vituperation." With hatred there is a denial of the Other's individuality. Utilizing key Husserlian concepts, Hadreas traces the developmental origins of love and hatred to our comfort in and attachment to our "home-world" and our discomfort in and detachment from anything resembling an "alien-world." Using my own discourse, we are more at home with that which triggers our identificatory resonance; we are ill-at-ease with that which elicits our dis-identificatory dissonance. The former triggers feelings of likeness-and-liking or even love; the latter elicits feelings of unlikeness-and-dislike or even hate. Hatred is triggered by that which violates that with which we are identificatorily at home. In an effort to make meaning of our feelings of hatred, either we look inside for something lacking within us or, preferably, we look for a cause for blame outside ourselves. The former results in self-hatred; the latter results in hatred of the generalized Other. Hatred of the Other, of course, may be an unconscious compensation for self-hatred. Regardless, hatred of the Other may manifest itself in visceral, non-reflective discrimination, prejudice, and scapegoating.

Hadreas (2007) leaves room for "two relatively benign forms of hatred" (p 94). The first is *civil hatred* and the second is *philosophic misanthropy.* "In *civil hatred*, the targets of hatred are malfeasances clearly harmful to civil society" (p. 94). In *philosophic misanthropy* "the target of hatred is [reprehensible, universal] human behavioral traits in general" (p. 96). "Philosophical misanthropy … targets humanity in general" (p. 97). This distinction between healthy and unhealthy hatred, when paired with our own distinction between healthy (mature) and unhealthy (immature, enmeshed, narcissistic, or possessive) love, matches our dialectical model. Maturity, according to our model, involves finding an integrative balance between healthy love and healthy hate. It necessitates keeping our unhealthy hate in check.

The later Husserl, Hart (2009a) tells us, comes to see that "'love, in the genuine sense, is one of the chief problems of phenomenology'" (p. 204). Both Hart and Hadreas (2007) point to the critical role that *empathy* plays in the Husserlian understanding of personal love. Prior to empathy, however, personal love, Hadreas (2007) elaborates, first requires that the participants to make or be in contact – "establish a consensual openness to affect and be affected by the other person" (p. 13). Second, "personal love" is "based in interactive empathy" (p. 13).

> Departing from ordinary German usage, Husserl coins the term *Nachverstehen* 'understanding one after another', to this purpose. In building *Nachverstehen*, we conjoin empathic understandings. One person's empathy follows upon the empathy of another. This conjoining of empathies transpires 'pre-objectively' [pre-reflectively] even without a conscious judgment of the other person. … the notion of 'person' comes to be constituted through the adjoining of empathies. … personal love establishes the uniqueness of the beloved as a singular subject, with a unique and characteristic physiognomy and style of endeavor. The uniqueness of the beloved arises because the beloved is understood through acts of empathy that, from the beginning, are joined with our own interaction. The singular style of walking, posture or vocal inflection is unique because added on to it is the lover's own empathy. (pp. 13–14)

Husserl goes on to elaborate that lovers are not only conjoined through the medium of cumulative mutual empathy, but "'they bind themselves in a loving partnership' so that '… all the striving of one enters in the striving of the other'" (Hadreas, 2007, p. 16). This appears in a manuscript entitled "Love" that Husserl has written in 1921. Like in "life" itself, "Personal love arises from a bundling together of striving subjects, who take 'security-in-one-another'" (p. 16).

Just as being contactful – being open-endedly receptive to another person – occasions the opportunity to exercise my empathy, so does empathy deepen my open-ended receptivity. Through contact and mutual empathy, I influence ("determine" the other; move the other's "striving or willing") and am influenced by the other. "But 'contact' as an inter-affective venue for communication allows for communication to take place as a reciprocal apprehension of the other's strivings" (Hadreas, 2007, p. 18). Additionally, Hadreas elaborates, mutual contact, empathy, and attunement to the other's strivings results in "a reordering of ourselves and the other person that cannot be foreseen in advance" (p. 19). A "second self grows out of" cumulative empathic interaction (p. 25). I am reminded of Saint Augustine's assertion, "we become what we love." More than that for Husserl, our "'*true value* arises because of what is loved'" (cited in Hadreas, 2007, p. 26). Through my authentic personal love, I discover, with heightened sensitivity, what is truly valuable.

When I understand the uniqueness of the essential other by being open-endedly receptive, empathic, and attuned to her or his strivings, I am at the same time beginning to apprehend this other person's singular "uniqueness as their truth" (p. 29). Such an inter-self state, which is an intensified intersubjective and inter-affective mode of being with the essential other, "establishes joys, 'high' joys" (Hadreas, 2007, p. 31). The "truth" of our character is deepened and widened in each other's eyes.

"But," asks Hadreas (2007), "how can personal love supervene over the griefs, sorrows, not to mention the mottled collection of everyday annoyances and irritations?" (p. 34) Here is his answer: "Regardless of how the loved one occasions pain and sorrow, our personal love concerns the 'truth' of the beloved person that endures in a world that is separate from our ordinary world of … consciousness [or everyday preoccupations and concerns]" (pp. 34–35). What helps me endure the everyday frustrations, irritations, pains, and sorrows is my enduring love of the "truth" of my beloved's essential I-ness or, simply, who s/he is. Even "pain may be 'dominated' by love" (p. 36). When I am in pain I no longer feel isolated which in turn makes the pain more bearable. Again, "personal love, through inter-affective *Nachverstehen* [cumulative, interactive empathic acts of attentiveness, attunement, and care], can establish identities perceived *through* love" (p. 37). Such cumulative, interactive empathy-based personal love allows me to set aside my self-preoccupied and utilitarian "ego" and tolerate and transcend my everyday annoyances, griefs, frustrations, irritations, and sorrows.

By building upon this cumulative inter-empathic relation with an essential other, Hadreas (2007) expounds, we arrive at what Husserl calls "ethical love." "Ethical love is neither instinctual nor natural. It is wholly attentive to the individual and apprehends each individual as unique and exceptional" (p. 106). To exemplify, Hadreas informs us, Husserl uses the "paradigm of motherly love." For the mother, the child has his worth in his individuality. It is a relation between two individualities. All the children are equal in a mother's eyes. They are "equal in that, as their worth is individual, they are beyond comparison" (p. 106). Above and beyond enacting a pattern of contactfulness and empathy over time, ethical love requires "self-forgetfulness." In this self-forgetfulness, "there is full consideration of one's own interests, answered by a choice to act solely on behalf of the friend or beloved" (p. 107). In true personal love there is mutuality. My beloved is for me a "co-subject," a subject "in the field of my ethical solicitude; their true good and bad concerns me and, inversely, mine concerns them, in the measure to which they have understood their significance and form" (p. 109). Additionally, "Husserl postulates a love [an ethical love] that is 'infinite, absolute and universal' ... It is an absolute limit of the possibility of love" (p. 107). Finally, for Husserl, love is grounded not only in our pre-reflective cognitions, such as our complementary beliefs, conations, or "interactive volitions" (wills), but also in our actions, such as our joint "endeavorings," "strivings," and "projects." Shared projects break down "I" versus "You" oppositions.

Goldberg (1999) approaches the themes of love-and-hate from an incipiently dialectical perspective. She describes not only the positive or healthy (cooperative) side of love, but also the negative or unhealthy (uncooperative) side of love. Analogously, she explicates not only the negative or unhealthy (uncooperative) side of hate, but also the positive or healthy (cooperative) side of hate. Cooperative love goes hand-in-hand with cooperative hate. Without cooperative hate there can be no cooperative love.

We have devoted ample space for healthy love and unhealthy hate. We will now focus on unhealthy ("narcissistic" or "destructive") love and healthy hate. "All of our love relationships – family, friends, or lovers," asserts Goldberg (1999), "encompass a potentially destructive side, because within each of us lie the seeds of aggression" (p. 24).

> Although it is true that love can be tender, warm, cozy, nurturing, and supportive, its fulfillment also demands *aggression* – a determined pursuit to *possess* something special, to be near someone, to share interests and lives, to attain security and comfort.
>
> ...
>
> In expecting more from a beloved than he or she is willing or able to give, or thinks of as a part of the 'love contract,' we fall victim to the unrealistic promise of love. When this happens (and it always will), hate emerges out of the darkness, and we find it in its rightful place alongside the positive forces of love. (p. 48)

As a related aside, Ogden (2012) describes "the inevitable destructiveness of love in the sense that love involves a demand on the loved object [person] which may (in fantasy, and at times, in reality) be too much of a strain for the person one loves" (p. 81). We have to come to terms with the depleting, draining, and destructive effects of the essential other's demanding love. It is therefore "necessary," Goldberg (1999) reminds us, "to learn how to love [properly]" in an emotionally balanced fashion (p. 24).

Narcissists, Goldberg (1999) informs us, have never learned to partake in a mutually loving relationship, where both partners participate equally in acts of giving-and-receiving.

> Narcissists can function only in one direction [receiving]. Unlike people who are more emotionally balanced, narcissists cannot both give and receive love. Either they focus solely on their own needs or they focus solely on the other person at the expense of their own needs. Narcissistic people who form relationships based on either of these principles are engaged in what I call *narcissistic love:* a love that never completes its path from pole to pole and thus never matures into a communicative, mutually giving and receiving cooperative love. (pp. 67–68)

The ultimate consequence of narcissistic love, which is a developmental failure, is that the narcissist never acquires *true feelings* for others. Narcissistic lovers never experience the psychosocial movement toward *mature*, productive, responsible, and interdependent relational living. Their immature love is not based on a realistic evaluation of the needs or the emotional or mental states of others. Instead, they are stuck in either a passive-receptive-dependent or an aggressive-intrusive-hyper-or-pseudo-independent relational stance. They feel entitled and therefore experience no gratitude for the care that has been bestowed upon them.

The demanding narcissistic lover, notes Goldberg (1999), expects others to sacrifice on his behalf for he "assumes it is the way of relationships" (p. 102). He feels entitled to the one-sided giving of others. He wants to shape the seemingly loved other into his own likeness. The "loved" other must mirror his expectations, ideas, needs, and sensitivities. The one-sided giving of the self-sacrificing narcissistic lover has its origin in "narcissistic hate that is turned against the self" (p. 102). The self-sacrificing narcissistic lover measures the level of her love-worthiness by the depth of her self-sacrifice and the degree of her self-obliteration. In order to be loved and deemed worthy, she is willing to allow the other to mold her into a shape that mirrors his expectations, ideas, needs, and sensitivities.

Goldberg (1999) equates the term *cooperative* with the word *mature*. Just as there is mature (cooperative) love, so there also is mature (cooperative) hate. As she sees it, there can be no mature (cooperative) love without the attainment of mature (cooperative) hate. The capacity for mature loving and mature hating is to be found in the relatively "integrated personality." "Love and hate cannot be separated, because they are both in us in equal measure" (p. 40). "The ability to recognize hate – to feel it as well as detect it," continues Goldberg, "is an essential ingredient in the building of what I call a strong *psychological immune system*" (p. 40). Hate is a universal human emotion whose denial results in deleterious and dire physical, psychological, and social consequences.

"It was Jesus' insight into the inevitability of this feeling in each of us," comments Goldberg (1999), "that led him to utter these words in Luke 14:26: 'If any man come to me, and hate not his father, and mother, and wife, and children, and brethren, and sisters, yea, and his own life also, he cannot be my disciple'" (p. 46). The suppression of negative feelings, including hate, can result in a host of psychosomatic conditions, such as backaches and headaches. Furthermore, when we hate the hateful feelings within us, we hate an important part of ourselves. "Recognized and used correctly, hate can be healthy" (p. 46). By listening to our own hateful feelings, we gain valuable knowledge "about who we are, the world around us" (p. 46). "Hate," elaborates Goldberg, "is a sign that there is a striving toward individual development. It is a natural byproduct of a healthy process. Hate also sustains us when the pain of loss is too great to tolerate. It intervenes until another [positive] feeling can take its place" (pp. 47–48).

What are we then to do with the feelings of hate that we will inevitably experience in our loving relationships? First, says Goldberg (1999), we have to "accept hate in our relationships" (p. 65). Second, "making hate conscious is the only way to reduce its power over us" (p. 65). There is no such thing as "pure" love. Love "must be tempered with hate to be whole, enduring, and strong" (p. 66). Love must "withstand the wear and tear" of the inevitably accompanying feelings of hate and its masking surrogates, such as disgruntlement and disappointment.

Paradoxically, expounds Goldberg (1999), "hate has the potential to both heal and help, as well as harm or hurt" (p. 63). Conflict (friction) is of the essence of relational life. "All emotional friction (and there is eventually friction in all human interactions) generates aggression and hate" (pp. 63–64). We need to be attuned to "the constructive potential of hate" (p 64). We need to learn to "fuse love and hate" (p. 65). We need to achieve a love that is balanced. I am reminded here of a mini-story from my own life. My wife and I were having dinner at a restaurant with friends – a man and his wife. At one point during our unfolding conversation, the wife spontaneously, but *lovingly* declared, referring to her husband of a decades-long marriage, "There are times when I *hate* him!" I, upon hearing this, said to myself that this expression is a reflection of a true-and-tested love. While acknowledging with passion her occasional deep hateful feelings toward her husband, I glimpsed the gleam of love toward him in her eyes.

The fusion of love and hate is a developmental achievement. Under good-enough conditions, we learn to tolerate our ambivalences toward our essential others. The "capacity of the human mind to tolerate contradictions," comments Goldberg (1999), "paves the way for the fusion of love and hate"

(p. 54). What do love and hate have in common? Here is Goldberg's answer: "We hate when we care and when we want; so, too, when we love. Hate is an active process that implies active involvement; so, too, is love. Hate, like love, stems from an unconscious drive related to self-preservation. Hate, constructively channeled, and love belong together" (p. 56).

As we develop, we need to become exposed to loving parents who reliably demonstrate for us the expression of constructive hate without treating us hatefully. We need to feel and learn to express our hatred without treating others hatefully.

> Mature hate, like mature love, can be a reasonable response based on a realistic appraisal of another person ... Mature cooperative hate, like mature cooperative love, is justified by the other person's own hateful aspects ... Cooperative hate is a realistic response based on a recognition and acceptance of the hateful (or annoying, or infuriating) aspects of the other person. Cooperative hate is, in fact, loving. (Goldberg, 1999, p. 75)

We can learn to respond appropriately to our seemingly destructive hateful feelings. "For most of us," reflects Goldberg (1999), "the hardest part of this process is simply becoming unafraid of constructive hate" (p. 243). This is especially so if we have been conditioned throughout life that hate is bad (evilish). By acknowledging the fact that hate is part of the human condition, we defuse its power over us. We "find that it need not be destructive – that in fact it can be our psychological ally and defender" (p. 243). Its positive aim is to protect and preserve life. It brings us alive. From a phenomenological point of view, the emotion of hate on the "I-side" directs us toward something we disvalue on the "World-side." This connecting of the negative emotions of hate to that which we disvalue in our lifeworld completes the arc of intentionality. Without this connection, we live with an uneasy vague intention that is a source of being ill-at-ease in a confused and confusing or disturbed and disturbing lifeworld in which we are involved. "The more attuned we are to aggression in its various forms, the more adept we become at managing hate and rage constructively. By emptying the caldron of bitterness that boils in our unconscious, we free ourselves to better enjoy the present" (p. 243).

The process of *psychosocial maturation* involves moving from a dichotomizing ambivalence to a positive or benign ambivalence and from thereon to the tolerance of the complex *ambiguity* of lifeworld itself. "Psychoanalysis," says Safran (2012), "tends toward the view that at a fundamental level, human beings are complex creatures whose experience and actions are shaped by multiple and often conflicting conscious and unconscious determinants, as well as by social and cultural forces. Related to this is an emphasis on the importance of tolerance of ambiguity" (p. 50). In other words, life's complexity inevitably brings with it ambiguity, and this triggers our curiosity and challenges us to tolerate the accompanying anxiety as we attempt to achieve partial, but more nuanced understanding of our lives and the lives of others. We will never achieve a totally clear, definitive, unambiguous, and unequivocal understanding of ourselves, let alone of others. However, with curiosity, humility, patience, and determined pursuit of emotional and relational truth, in spite of the pain involved in the process, we can become witness to the unfolding or evolving of our self-and-relational understanding while still remaining tolerant of what will always elude our total grasp – absolute emotional and relational truth.

Holmes (2010) links the capacity for "high level ambiguity" to the imaginative "capacity to evoke multiple meanings" (p. 151). Equipped with "higher level ambiguity," one becomes open to a "wider range of meanings," which in turn makes it possible to "have enhanced options for negotiating the interpersonal jungle of intimate social life" (p. 177). More than that, when this capacity for flexible meaning making and meta-meaning making – reflecting on the meanings of meanings, which is a manifestation of the capacity for "higher level ambiguity" – is shared over time with an essential other, it enhances the level of intimacy. This is why, as indicated before, in contradistinction to the Kleinians, I have a preference for the phrase *higher-level ambiguity* over the phrase *higher-level ambivalence.*

Although we begin to experience feelings when we are infants, say Cabaniss and her colleagues (2013), we "do not know what those feelings are or how to regulate them" (p. 96). They add that it is through our coordinated interactions with our attuned and empathic primary caregivers that we learn to label and modulate our feelings. All this affective attunement and empathic responsiveness initially occurs nonverbally and unconsciously. As infants, our good-enough parents are able to "read" our feeling-states based on our behavior. After reading our affective or mental states accurately, they are able to "perform some coordinated behavior that 'matches' it. For example, if the baby cries, the caregiver might make a gently frowning face. In turn infants must be able to 'read' the caregiver's response as having something to do with their own original feeling experience" (p. 96). "This nonverbal [unconscious and inter-bodily] communication," they continue, "helps children get to know, organize, and regulate their own internal states without being overwhelmed and is essential for the development of anxiety and affect tolerance" (p. 96).

Without *feelings*, conclude Cabaniss and her colleagues (2013), "life would be colorless" (p. 46). Feelings, they add, "help us understand ourselves and others" (p. 46). Feelings, they elaborate, not only vitalize us, but also enable to learn from experience, to have empathy, and to have relationships full of meaning, purpose, and passion. Experiencing, tolerating or managing, and expressing a broad range of feelings are indicators of the degree of our *emotional maturation* and *mental health*.

References

Cabaniss, D. L., Cherry, S., Douglas, C. J., Graver, R. L., & Schwartz, A. R. (2013). *Psychodynamic formulation*. Wiley.
Frosh, S. (2011). *Feelings*. Routledge.
Gaylin, W. (2003). *Hatred: The psychological descent into violence*. Public Affairs Books.
Goldberg, J. G. (1999). *The dark side of love: The positive role of negative feelings*. Transaction.
Hadreas, P. (2007). *A phenomenology of love and hate*. Ashgate.
Hart, J. G. (2009a). *Who one is, Book 1: Meontology of the "I": A transcendental phenomenology*. Springer.
Hart, J. G. (2009b). *Who one is, Book 2: Existenz and transcendental phenomenology*. Springer.
Heidegger, M. (1962). *Being and time* (J. Macquarrie & E. Robinson, Trans.). Harper and Row.
Heidegger, M. (1996). *Being and time* (J. Stambaugh, Trans.). State University of New York Press.
Holmes, J. (2010). *Exploring in security: Towards an attachment-informed psychoanalytic psychotherapy*. Routledge.
Howard, S. (2011). *Psychodynamic counselling in a nutshell* (2nd ed.). Sage.
Joyce, A. (2005). One to two years old: Junior toddlers/Two to three years old: Senior toddlers. In E. Rayner, A. Joyce, J. Rose, M. Twyman, & C. Clulow (Eds.), *Human development: An introduction to the psychodynamics of growth, maturity, and ageing* (4th ed.). Routledge.
Longhofer, J. (2015). *A-Z of psychodynamic practice*. Palgrave Macmillan.
Melle, U. (2002). Edmund Husserl: From reason to love. In J. J. Drummond & L. Embree (Eds.), *Phenomenological approaches to moral philosophy: A handbook*. Kluwer.
Ogden, T. H. (1986). *The matrix of the mind: Object relations and the psychoanalytic dialogue*. Jason Aronson.
Ogden, T. H. (2012). *Creative readings: Essays on seminal analytic works*. Routledge.
Rayner, E. (2005). Three to five years old. In E. Rayner, A. Joyce, J. Rose, M. Twyman, & C. Clulow (Eds.), *Human development: An introduction to the psychodynamics of growth, maturity, and ageing* (4th ed.). Routledge.
Rose, J. (2005). Work, identity, and love. In E. Rayner, A. Joyce, J. Rose, M. Twyman, & C. Clulow (Eds.), *Human development: An introduction to the psychodynamics of growth, maturity, and ageing* (4th ed.). Routledge.
Safran, J. D. (2012). *Psychoanalysis and psychoanalytic therapies*. American Psychological Association.

7

Creativity: The Capacity for *Creativity* and Creative Living

For Freud, sublimation was the basis for creativity and culture. Freud writes:

> Observation of men's daily lives shows us that most people succeed in directing very considerable portions of their sexual instinctual forces to their professional activity. The sexual instinct is particularly well fitted to make contributions of this kind since it is endowed with a capacity for *sublimation*: that is, it has the power to replace its immediate aim by other aims which may be valued more highly and which are not sexual. (quoted in Fiumara, 2013, p. 51)

Creativity, in Freudian terms, is thus defined as "the expression of a sexual impulse in a non-sexual and socially valued way" (Frosh, 1991, p. 79). Creativity, then, is sublimated sexuality. Behind it lies the longing for rest, sleep, and union with mother. "**Sublimation**," more broadly defined, is "a mature defense mechanism in which an unacceptable thought, feeling, or wish is redirected into a constructive, healthy outlet" (Frankland, 2010, p. 179). Freud emphasizes that the capacity for sublimation, and thus for creativity, is available for use for most of us in our everyday lives as we "struggle to make the burden of life more bearable and even desirable" (Fiumara, 2013, p. 51). In short, for Freud, to create is to sublimate.

The original version of this chapter was revised: Reference list was added to the chapter. The erratum to this chapter is available at https://doi.org/10.1007/978-3-030-74315-4_33

© The Author(s), under exclusive license to Springer Nature Switzerland AG 2021, corrected publication 2021

M. J. Hannush, *Markers of Psychosocial Maturation*,
https://doi.org/10.1007/978-3-030-74315-4_7

Reparation, and not Freudian sublimation, is the source of creativity for Klein:

> Reparation is … the basis of the Kleinian theory of creativity, which assumes that the drive to 'make good' that which is experienced as damaged is the source of the artistic impulse and the explanation of the relationship between cultural forms and the psychological processes of the artists who produce them. (Frosh, 2012, p. 148)

The "roots of the creative impulse," says Segal (1979), lies "in the depressive position and the reparative drives associated with it" (p. 138). And again, Segal repeats, "Klein concludes that the anxieties of the depressive position and the reparative urge which they give rise to lie at the root of creativity" (p. 139).

In Klein's theory of human development, the depressive position or orientation to life and living is equated with maturational achievement. Psychosocial or emotional maturation is a byproduct of the acquired *capacity to repair* relational damages incurred by the self and the *capacity to mourn* the depressive (sad) feelings – feelings of *concern*, associated with loss in our developmental trajectory. "The depressive feelings," continues Segal (1979), "are reactivated by every loss, and every step in development implies some loss" (p. 140). The realization of separateness from the breast (mother), weaning, toilet training (which implies giving up the idealized feces), learning how to walk and talk, while developmental gains, imply the loss of symbiotic connectedness to the mother. Struggling for and achieving independence in adolescence and early adulthood signifies loss of dependence. Losing one's youth and losing one's parents are all examples of cumulative and never-ending losses, culminating with the anticipation of the ultimate separation-and-loss, our own death. Between birth and death, one must also deal with symbolic losses, such as the loss of validation, loss of vocation, and loss of major assets. At every step the temptation is to regress, digress, or distract ourselves from coming to terms with anticipated and experienced losses and their accompanying depressive pain. The challenge of maturation lies in "working through of the depressive pain in a way leading to further growth and development" (p. 140).

> In that sense one could say that the depressive position is never entirely worked through: the working through of the depressive position would result in something like the perfectly *mature* individual. But the degree to which the depression has been worked through and internal good objects [internalized representations of our good-enough essential others] securely established within the ego [self] determines the *maturity* and stability of the individual. (p. 140)

An essential part of the maturational process involves working through our inevitable losses and making reparations for the destructive feelings, thoughts, and behaviors we experienced and displayed in protest of what we had to give up and in response to the everyday frustrations we experienced in not always getting what we want or need. It is this working through losses and the acting upon the impulse toward reparation that lie at the root of creativity. In sum, for Klein, to create is to successfully mourn and repair.

Our "creativity," says Winnicott (1971), is universal in that it "belongs to being alive ... to the approach of the individual to ... reality" (p. 68). "It is in playing," he specifies, "that the individual child or adult is able to be creative and to use the *whole personality*, and it is only in being creative that the individual discovers the self" (p. 54). "The creative impulse," Winnicott continues, "is ... something that is present when *anyone* – baby, child, adolescent, adult, old man or woman – looks in a healthy way at anything or does anything deliberately [using his or her sense of agency]" (p. 69). We are our best, joyous, and "true" selves when our creativity is in gear. Our creative impulse is the primal motivator of our spontaneous actions. "The creative impulse," says Winnicott by way of a vivid illustration, "is present in the '*child who is enjoying breathing* as it is in the *inspiration* of an architect who suddenly knows what it is that he wishes to construct'" (p. 69).

According to Winnicott, Frosh (2012) elaborates, "the child's spontaneous desires [and playful actions] ... under the right circumstances [i.e., growing up in an optimally facilitating environment] would flower into a 'true self' capable of creativity and integrity" (p. 111). "Winnicott insists," notes Fiumara (2013), "that there is a creative impulse in each of us, and the exercise of this creativity engenders freedom. Its exercise expands the vistas of the self" (p. 11). Again, for Winnicott (1971), the capacity for creativity is a "universal" human potential. It "is a universal and belongs to being alive" (pp. 67–68). We have two alternative ways of living our lives: we can live creatively or uncreatively. "In a tantalizing way," Winnicott reminds us, "we may have experienced just enough creative living to sadly recognise that for most of the time we have been living uncreatively ... These two alternatives of living creatively or uncreatively can be very sharply contrasted" (p. 65).

Full living involves genuineness, originality, and creativity. For Winnicott, play is at the root of creativity. The impulse to play and be playful is universal. So is the drive to create. According to Winnicott, "*play is in fact neither a matter of inner psychic reality nor a matter of external reality*" (quoted in Tuber, 2008, p. 13). To understand play, phenomenologically – as it is experienced and lived, we need to trace its developmental origin to the play space, or what Winnicott calls "transitional space," of early childhood. This play space emerges from:

> the overlap between the needs of the infant and the devotion of the mother through the mother's provision of an object (such as a soft piece of blanket or stuffed animal) or a bit of behavior (such as a little bedtime tune or ritual). The

> baby, according to Winnicott, is positioned to feel that he or she has *created* the thing provided, and he makes the point of emphasizing that the paradox must not be resolved … From this experiential overlap … develops the whole of cultural experience. (Rodman, 2003, p. 164)

"Play's status as the quintessential embodiment of transitional phenomena in a transitional space," Tuber (2008) tells us, "is what allows creativity, originality, and genuineness to flourish – the three aptitudes that together define for Winnicott the best that life has to offer" (p. 14). The facilitating environment, as originally embodied in the good-enough mother, leads "the child to experience creativity, not just control, as its most important aim" (p. 36). The good-enough mother is a created mother, a mother invented by the developing child. Creativity is a byproduct of this creation. The child's sense of creation has an illusionary aspect, for the child does not realize that his creation is made possible by the mother who generously co-creates the space in which his omnipotent inventiveness freely displays itself. Regardless, the growing child acquires a double (split) consciousness that alternates between grand *omnipotence* and total *dependence*, between *freedom* and *limitation*. Maturation requires a dialectical integrative modulation between these seemingly bipolar meaning-saturated modalities of existence.

Still, in the beginning, the child's creation of the mother "becomes the capacity to invent other actions in other contexts and hence other beings in other contexts" (Tuber, 2008, p. 36). The optimal environment in which this psychosocial evolution and integrative modulation occurs is the lived space of mutual playfulness.

> Playing thereby allows the child to consistently work on the boundary between illusory omnipotence and helplessness and thus has at its essence the quest for mastery over the inner and outer chaotic (that is, not yet understood) aspects of its experience. The fact that the baby has internalized the mother as a precursor to this process means that his play is always simultaneously related in an equally primary vein even while he hones selfhood.
>
> …
>
> Playing is therefore inherently object [other]-related at one and the same time that it allows and ensures privacy; it is the milieu in which baby discovers her True and hence utterly private Self and yet the means by which she engages others and develops rapport. It is the inherent duality of play that it at once creates privacy yet counts on relatedness. (Tuber, 2008, p. 123; p. 122)

The mature mother knows when to fit in in her play with the child and when to introduce her own new ideas for play, while awaiting the welcoming or non-welcoming responsiveness of her child. "'The way is paved,'" Winnicott comments, "'for a playing together in a relationship'" (quoted in Tuber, 2008, p. 122). Ultimately, "this transitional play space is then linked by Winnicott to the formations of culture, religion, art, and so on" (Tuber, 2008, p. 123). Our focus here, however, is on relational creativity. For Winnicott, the capacity for this kind of creativity involves the co-creation of a play space in which two intimate players can be relaxedly and joyously their best (true) selves. In a word, to create is to play and be playful with a playing and playful partner. We need to "remind ourselves of Winnicott's 'gold standard' for [mental] health, the capacity to be creative and authentic" (Tuber, 2008, p. 217).

"The Winnicottian version of object relations," holds Holmes (2010), "views playfulness and creativity as a mark of psychic health" (p. 55). What is not made explicit in Winnicott's link between playfulness, on the one hand, and creativity and authenticity, on the other, is that it is the mutuality of *loving* playfulness between mother-and-child that makes it possible for the developing child to *integrate* her or his seemingly polar needs for sociality (connectedness) *and* privacy (separateness). The achievement of this kind of ongoing integration (dialectical balance) is supremely necessary for becoming a mature, developing person.

For Kohut, it is not simply sublimation, mourning, reparation, or playfulness, but rather the *transformation of narcissism* that is the basis of creativity. Here is Siegel (1996) describing the Kohutian theory of creativity:

> *Creativity*: The creative individual has the child-like capacity to play imaginatively with that individual's surroundings, because such a person tends to be less psychologically separate from the surroundings. The creative work becomes part of the self. Just as a mother idealizes her unborn fetus, so the creative person, in a transformation of narcissism, extends an idealization to his or her work. (p. 62)

In this chapter, the focus is mostly on the kind of creativity that is necessary and indispensable for change, development, growth, or maturation. I will therefore limit my attention to emotional, intrapersonal, and interpersonal or relational creativity. "The creative act," says Symington (2004), is "one whereby I gather all the disparate parts of myself into a new personal synthesis" (p. 176). *The movement toward a new synthesis or integration is itself a form of creativity. Maturational movement is therefore a creative act.* What Symington describes as the gathering of "disparate parts," we would label as the gathering by the bodily self of *disparate lifeworld meanings.*

The Kohutian self-psychological viewpoint posits that our capacity for creativity unfolds naturally when we grow up in a facilitating environment with empathic and need-satisfying essential others. The word "creativity" is related to the word "creation." Creativity involves creating or constructing. It is a fact that we are created through being born and are shaped by the environment in which we are raised. However, it is also true that under relatively good-enough conditions, we are propelled to be become co-creators. At least potentially, we can become active and imaginative participants in constructing our ambitions, goals, and ideals; in our selective use of our skills and talents; and in negotiating the discrepancies between our ambitions *and* talents in a realistic and creative way. In short, given our developing proficiencies and preoccupations, we are *co-creating co-meanings.* Here is Lessem (2005) explicating, in self-psychological terms, the phenomenal experience of *creatively generating new fulfilling meanings*:

> We participate in generating our selfobject experience by scanning the environment to identify potential sources of selfobject sustenance. We then contribute to their shapes and qualities through our own creative emphases and embellishments. We creatively imbue the other with qualities and attributes that assist that person, experience, or [find a] place to meet our self-object needs. (p. 25)

Although the term "selfobject" can be an elusive and slippery concept, just as how Kohut himself views that concept of "self" at times, it still carries a phenomenological richness. Just as self cannot be separated from world – self-in-world, so it is that "object" cannot be separated from "self." Where there is a self, there is an object that is important, in degrees, to the self. The object can be my wife, my daughter, my sister, my friend, and so on – persons that I hold dear to my heart and are an important part of my life. They are "primary" objects for they assume primacy in my life. Moreover, objects can include my writing project, the classical music that I value, the nature (trees, birds, mountains, seas, etc.) with which I commune. These are all enlivening sources of nourishment, and sustenance. With maturity, I imaginatively and creatively broaden and deepen my selfobjects. My self expands as does, simultaneously, my world of "objects." My self-in-world is enriched. Phenomenologically phrased, the bodily self grows as our meanings grow.

Sloppiness, states Stern (2004), is an essential requisite for creativity. "Sloppiness," he expands, "results from the interaction of two minds working in a 'hit-miss-repair-elaborate' fashion to cocreate and share similar worlds" (p. 156). There are, potentially, always elements of spontaneity and unpredictability in any interpersonal interaction. Relational sloppiness carries within it the potential for intrapersonal and interpersonal creativity. Of course, freedom-producing sloppiness is dialectically related to rule-bound orderliness. For example, "fair fighting" is more likely to produce a creative solution to a relational conflict than "unfair fighting." Amidst the sloppiness of "fighting," there are limits to adhere to which aim to preserve the dignity and integrity of the close contestants. Here again is Stern in his own words:

> Progressively they [the interlocutors] cocreated islands of intentional fittedness from the sloppiness. These then coalesced through the same process of utilizing the potential creativity of sloppiness to forge larger spaces of shared implicit knowing. This intersubjective field shifted and new paths opened … It is important to emphasize that sloppiness is potentially creative only when it occurs within a well-established framework. Without that, it is only disorder … [Within a well-established framework] there is a wide degree of freedom for sloppiness to be cocreated. (p. 164)

What Stern labels as "shared implicit knowing," we would describe as *shared lived meanings.* Regardless, sloppiness is the inevitable result of acting upon our longing for "intersubjective contact." Our primordial motive for intersubjective contact is the overarching context that makes co-creativity possible. "The desire for intersubjective contact," continues Stern, "mobilizes the cocreativity of two minds working together at the local level (with short-term and long-term therapeutic [growth-enhancing] goals [implicitly] in mind), to get somewhere" (p. 165).

The ultimate kind of intersubjectivity we desire happens "at the local level" in "moments of meeting." Of course, what happens before between two people prepares the way for these moments of meeting. A moment of meeting, where intersubjective contact is co-created, is characterized by (1) an "intentional fittedness" or a "fittedness of intentions" and (2) a "vitalization of affect" or "affective vitalization" (in the sense of emotional affirmation). At such moments of contact we experience "an affective state of completion" and a "sense of intersubjective sufficiency" or "intersubjective closure." We have moved from sloppiness to creative coherence. A change has occurred. We are not the same. We have imperceptibly moved forward. The quality of our being-and-doing-things-together has been enhanced and enlarged. *New shared meanings have been fulfilled.*

Our "growth," observes Fiumara (2013), "is rooted in creative lived experience" (p. 3). Growth lies primarily in removing "that which separates the person from the creative self he already silently is or could be" (p. 17). Creativity is unveiled in our capacity to see "the extraordinary within the ordinary. It is the inner attitude to do extraordinary – however small – things for oneself and others" (p. 17). "The capacity to secretly dare, or strive, or struggle," she continues, "is in fact the essential feature of the creative potential" (p. 18). In answer to the question "'What is a genius?'" she quotes James Grotstein: "In my eyes a genius is one who sees patterns, structures or gestalten in an incipient or incomplete form … Put another way, a genius is one who sees through the camouflage of images and symbols and is in touch, so to speak, with the 'thing-in-itself'" (p. 3).

Dealing creatively with reality, expounds Fiumara (2013), involves approaches, attitudes, or "efforts to surpass [imitative] compliance and seek ulterior dimensions in common life" (p. 54). She cites Donald W. Winnicott stating, "It is creative appreciation more than anything else that makes the individual feel that life is worth living" (p. 54). *Creative living* involves a deep affirmation of life. Creativity, for Fiumara, is possible in any domain of our existence. Her focus is on our ordinary creativity or our "ordinary genius." Our "ordinary geniuses," she expands, "do often re-create our inter-subjective cosmos; and 'cosmos' means beauty in a way that is essential to the persons involved" (p. 57). In other words, there is *beauty* in the re-creation of our relational field that surpasses our previously repetitive and stagnant interpersonal dynamics. Rayner (1995) reminds us that "*beauty* is experienced whenever deep feelings are truthfully expressed" (p. 16).

Our "ordinary genius," Fiumara (2013) adds, "creates micro-worlds for daily psychic survival" (p. 57). I would add that it not only contributes to our "daily psychic survival," but also to our daily psychosocial flourishing. Even our non-stop internal and external talking, Fiumara says, may serve the "latent function" of our "constant search for both therapy [therapeutic growth] and creativeness" (p. 57). Similarly, following the philosopher Emanuel Kant, our imagination is always a potential source of our creativity and originality, propelling us beyond our compliant and imitative proclivities.

For Fiumara (2013), "creativity enters into virtually every aspect of life. It is not a special 'faculty' but an aspect of our human intelligence in general; it is manifested in everyday abilities… every one of us is creative, to a degree" (p. 10). Even a "turn of phrase" or, I might add, a tilt of head may all of a sudden bring about a shift in how we see ourselves-and-our-lifeworld. These moments of insight may be small or momentous. "And of course," she adds, "renewed outlooks may bring about rapid changes" (p. 2). Even our capacity to appreciate and experiment with sounds and signs are manifestations of our ordinary creativeness. She cites Kant as saying that there are times when we have thought something for ourselves only to discover that we could have learned it from others who preceded us in thinking it out and writing about it. Yet, this should not diminish the excitement surrounding the illumination of the insight for our own lives. We might even feel honored-and-humbled to be in the company of such luminary figures. We do not have to be a poet or a novelist to be an ordinary "master of metaphor" – to be capable of metaphoric creativeness. What is on the line here, states Fiumara, is our "capacity for profound turns of perspective" (p. 6). Our metaphoric approach to reality allows us to "get hold of something fresh" (p. 6). Our kinesthetic, iconic, and linguistic imagination can have "major disruptive effects on previous ways of looking at situations" and thus can "serve to influence a world view" (p. 6). It can give us the impetus to "migrate from one epistemic context to another" (p. 7). "This area of [creative responsiveness] is the space for ordinary inventiveness" (p. 19).

"Creativity," notes Fiumara (2013), "basically refers to what we do at the intentional level" (p. 19). However, she immediately adds a modifier: "The determinist and the intentional attitude are both necessary of course ... The two ... in fact are inseparable in our human species" (p. 19). This is an existential argument for freedom-within-limits. There are three concerns I wish to register here. First, although modified, creativity is still equated with intentionality – in this context meaning "agency" as opposed to "patiency" or passivity. What is lost here is the positive role that "active passivity" can play in creativity and the negative role that hyperactive agency can play in blocking creativity. Second, the overemphasis on the intentional (agentic) attitude as a foundational feature of creativity detracts from the positive role that the unconscious can play in our creative endeavors. To elaborate briefly, "unconscious play work," notes Bollas (2011), "is pivotal for the creative mind" (p. 63). Third, although Fiumara is cognizant of and makes reference to Husserl's theory of intentionality and its intrinsic relevance to creativity, she does not "see" the connection and contradiction to her definition of creativity as a purely "intentional" (agentic) act. She herself describes intentionality – becoming mindful of our habitual orientation to the world, as an "outlook" that allows us to "become free observers of our condition" (p. 77). It is an "inclusive" attitude that permits us to "turn our attention to the way we experience it [our world]" (p. 78). The "creative capacity to include is a foundational feature of intentionality" (p. 78). Bollas, however, reminds us that Freud's inventive and instructive introduction of free associative speaking and listening – listening with an evenly hovering attentiveness, is the means by which we make unconscious intentionality conscious and thus paving the way to therapeutic change and growth. Freud here is ingeniously putting Husserl's phenomenological suspension or neutralization of belief in everyday intentionality into serviceable use. For example, my affect-laden consciousness or, more likely, unconsciousness, is habitually oriented to seeing (interpreting or ascribing meaning to) my enemy in a one-dimensional shadowy light. Bracketing my natural attitude toward my nemesis, I may begin to perceive her or him in a different multidimensional light. Incidentally, as an aside, Freud had attended the lectures given by the charismatic philosopher Franz Brentano, who in turn had exerted a strong influence on the work of Edmund Husserl. Brentano is best known for having introduced the notion of intentionality to contemporary philosophy.

Living in an uncertain world, we, ordinary humans, are humbly challenged to be ever more extraordinarily creative. "There are no forms and institutions," says Fiumara (2013), "that can serve as frames of reference for long-term plans … Such an uncertain world," she continues, "requires us to be flexible and adaptable in our nearly invisible [creative] moves" (p. 31). We need to make honest use of our inferences regarding our unconscious resources. We need to "creatively construct original meanings" (p. 31). Ordinary "creative persons have more efficient [or proficient] capacities for processing [interpreting] toxic elements [*meanings*] into maturational experiences [*integrative higher-order meanings*]" (p. 32). This capacity to beautify the ugly or toxic in our lifeworld is urgently needed. It requires the concomitant capacity to resist the contagion of malignant meanings – toxic others, polluting relations, or pathogenic cultural emissions.

Fiumara (2013) links everyday ordinary creativity to psychological health. She thinks of "psychic health as a sufficiently well connected inner world, and … of 'living creatively' in terms of a capacity to combine, adjoin and integrate personal experiences" (p. 65). Living creatively involves connecting and reconnecting with the conscious and unconscious elements in our "whole personality." It includes linking our "official selves and their 'shadows'" (p. 65). To live creatively, we need to partake of the work of "*bringing them [the elements of personality] together and making something*" (p. 65). It involves connecting parts of the self and making them into a whole. Fiumara fleetingly hints that these elements could be our "identifications." Living creatively, therefore, could be thought of as cultivating the capacity to construct or invent connections between our "dispersed" identifications – *meanings with which we identify*. Focusing on identifications allows us to deemphasize dichotomizing "inner" from outer aspects of living creatively. True to life, identifications are always identifications with someone (or aspects of the Other) or something. Phenomenologically speaking – looking at things from the perspective of lived experience, our identifications are intersubjective and intentional. Fiumara, like most other psychoanalysts, views the work of integration as an "inner project." The work of integration, however, is simultaneously an inner-and-outer project. Inner integration cannot take place in a vacuum. It goes hand-in-hand with social or intersubjective integration or consolidation. The word "con-solidation" is pregnant with multiple meanings, most important of which are inner solidity and interpersonal solidarity.

"Creativeness," for Fiumara (2013), "is the art of increasing connections rather than the sloth to let splitting indefinitely reproduce" (p. 67).

> The labour of the creative act lies in being confronted with these parts [meanings] of ourselves that we tend to disown … [It lies in] the achievement of [ordinary] genius insofar as the end-product is a synthesis of the infantile and adults worlds; of repressed contents and contents that are approved by a demanding self-critical ego; of the rational and the irrational. (p. 67)

Fiumara speaks of "connective creativity." However, not only one connects inner parts into a whole but, at same time, one connects with others to become a part of a whole, a whole of which one is a part. Integrative connectivity requires integrative interconnectedness, healthy interpersonal communion, social integration, or communal solidarity. Fiumara's (2013) model of creativity is compatible with such a balancing extension. Above and beyond being psychoanalytic, it is incipiently dialectical. To be human is to be suspended between polarities of existence (polar meanings) – such as being infantile versus being mature and being rational versus being irrational. Becoming mature entails having to confront and come to terms with these polar meanings of existence again and again. Moreover, we are constructed to co-create new and higher-order meanings. We are born with the potential to live creatively, to find an integrative balance between these lived polar tensions. Maturation or psychosocial growth is itself a co-creative-and-re-creative act. It is giving birth-and-rebirth to the bodily self which is always directed to lifeworld meanings again and again, always in a hopefully supportive social context. "The specificity of our talent for healing," says Fiumara, "is to invent linking strategies" (p. 69). To create, or to live creatively, is to connect-metabolize-and-integrate "parts of the self." "And moreover," she adds, "an essential aspect of being a [whole] person is the creative combination of good and bad components [meanings]; an individual who primarily splits [disconnects from or 'disowns fearsome inner currents' or *disturbing meanings*] and therefore obliterates the 'wickedness' in himself is doomed to be largely a 'non-person'" (p. 69). We connect previously unconnected lifeworld meanings. Fiumara's emphasis tends to be skewed toward the inner and only considers the outer peripherally, although she is not oblivious to it. And, most importantly, not any connection will do. The connection, as Fiumara describes it, needs to be "useful," "fertile," and "life-enhancing." A creative interconnection, I would add, needs to yield *better and more fruitful meanings* to our shared lives.

In the interpersonal domain, for instance, the life-affirming connection needs to be chosen discerningly, always made in light of the disposition of *kindness*. Stated differently, it is the disposition of kindness that makes relational creativity possible. "If we are to discover beauty," in the "I-ness" of the Other, Armstrong (2004) alerts us, "we need to develop a more kindly attitude toward this person" (p. 138). As a consequence, for instance, we become interested in the attractive qualities this other person has. We even begin to notice some pleasing features about that person's posture and other loveable qualities. To summarize succinctly then, for Fiumara, to create is to connect.

Marcus (2013b) defines "emotional creativity" as "the human capacity for using one's emotions, both positive and negative ones, to fashion more aesthetically pleasing, more meaningful, coherent, and inspired contexts [of meaning] for inventive everyday living" (pp. 36–37). I am being emotionally creative, by way of illustration, when I use my imagination to actively transform (sublimate) my anger, grief, or sexual desire into life-affirming, love-laden, and joyful projects, pursuits, and, in my "'for the Other' relationships" (a phrase borrowed from Gabriel Marcel). Echoing Marcel, Marcus reminds us that "a most worthwhile goal for each of us is to be a creator [someone who brings something new, a new meaning into existence], to bear witness to a creation especially through our 'for the Other' relationships" (p. 39). We are called to radiate with creative presence – an imaginative presencing of life-affirming meaning. It is the most worthy contribution we can make to Life. In the ethical or relational sphere, the creative impulse is manifested in acts of admiration, friendship, generosity, hospitality, and love. To be emotionally-and-relationally creative – an affect-laden form of radiant co-presence is to be self-affirming *and* other-regarding at the same time; it is to be giving *and* receiving. Echoing Klein, emotional creativity, Marcus remarks, can be a curative or healing act of reparation or restoration.

Our emotional creativity, maintains Marcus (2013b), "gives us access to the best of what is both 'inside' and 'outside' ourselves, namely, Beauty, Truth, and Goodness" (p. 21). It is creating something "above" or "higher" than ourselves. The "elemental freedom a person has," continues Marcus along Marcelian lines, "is the 'creative power' to decide what kind of person he wants to be":

> Whether to live with reasonable self-control or be a slave to his desires, whether to be receptive, responsive, and responsible to others or inaccessible and self-centric, and whether to live a life mainly devoted to the 'lower' values associated with our over-functionalised, technique-dominated, possession-driven 'mass society', as Marcel called the 'having' mode, or to the 'higher' values of Beauty, Truth, and Goodness, the 'being' mode. 'At bottom, I can validly assert that *I belong to myself* only insofar as I create, as I create myself.' (p. 20)

Following Marcel, Marcus (2013b) connects creativity to our very being – the way we are, and our existence, the way we live. To truly be and to authentically exist is to be creative. Creativity, being, and existence cannot be unlinked. A creative life "is characterized by 'novelty, freshness, revelation [illumination]' … [by] radical perspective-shifting, life-affirming self-transformation, a 'renewal of being' … 'emotional creativity' [is] the psychological bedrock for a 'renewal of being'" (p. 21).

> Simply stated, emotional creativity refers to the capacity for 'novel, effective and authentic' receptiveness, responsiveness, and responsibility, an openness, curiosity, and imagination that leads to a process of 'spiritualization [sublimation] of the passions', to quote Nietzsche again, that is, to 'self-realization and expansion'

> and to increased 'vitality, connectedness and meaningfulness.' In a word, we are talking about self-creation which … always includes an other-directed, other-regarding thrust to it. (p. 21)

Our unconscious, notes Nicholsen (2002), contains a "creative ferment." "Let us call the beyond within," she continues, "our unconscious" (p. 25). She uses the word "wild" to describe the "beyond within" that is our "unconscious." Using phenomenological discourse, creativity happens when the primal bodily self is directed to its natural complement or finds its intentional fulfillment in primal lifeworld meanings out or over there. A sense of delight, exuberance, and joy, fused with a sense of awe, surprise, and wonder, is the natural affective accompaniment of this synchronous mode of being-in-and-encountering the wild world.

Intriguingly, Nicholsen (2002) turns a phosphorous beam of light on the creative use of loss. The mourning process itself can become a channel for creativity. We can make ourselves worthy of the loss of our loved others, not by wallowing in inordinate survival guilt, self-destruction, or self-pity, but by devoting ourselves to "purifying" projects. It is a creative way of affirming life, while at the same time, acknowledging the emotional truth of our own potential for destructiveness. We can all feel and act destructively as well as constructively (creatively). We are being destructive when we satisfy our needs without regard for the rights or welfare of others. We are being destructive when we split our selves or others into being either all good, or all bad, lacking the capacity for integrating our loves and hates. Dialectically, we need to differentiate between benign destructiveness, which is preparatory for constructiveness (creativity), and malignant destructiveness. Analogously, we can become malignantly constructive, when in the realm of relations we well-intendedly impose our so-called altruistic actions upon others who perceive our seemingly constructive (generous) actions as intrusive and unwelcome. Nonetheless, understanding our capacity for being benignly destructive is a requisite for becoming creatively constructive.

Nicholsen (2002) traces the origin of creativity to the early experience of aesthetic reciprocity occurring in the context of a bonding loving relationship that acknowledges difference and separateness between mother-and-child.

> This sense of kinship, of difference-in-unity, is the basis of the baby's capacity for what Winnicott calls creative looking. It is the basis for the baby's confidence in his or her ability to find meaning in the world of seen things – to perceive aesthetically. At first the mother's face is the baby's world. Then the world is extended and it too is a face. … Meaning comes through emotional connection. (p. 98)

The origin of creativity, therefore, lies in the loving and playful interchange between mother-and-child. "Imaginal vision," "aesthetic perception," or creative seeing is "the medium of kinship" (p. 103). I see my beautiful and cherished mother seeing me just as I see her. In this loving kinship, my mother is like me, my kin with whom I identify while retaining my difference and separateness. This allows me to be free to stamp my seeing with my own uniqueness. This is what I understand *creative looking or seeing* to mean. It depicts the essence of the confluence of communion-and-individuation.

"Creativity," observes Nicholsen (2002), is "the process whereby things come into being. … the void is seen as the ground from which beings arise. The notion of emergence from the void provides a way to look at the process of unfolding that is creativity" (p. 105). Creativity, then, involves the meaningful resolution of the dialectical tension between being (such as the presence of an image or word) and nothingness (such as the absence of an image or word). This is why, in part, the very young child delights in the game of peek-a-boo, a game involving the active mastery of the alternating presence and absence of the mother's face. The point to be made, however, is that being at home with silence or void (nothingness) is critical for the origination of the creative response, be it an image, sound, or word. There is something beautiful in companionable and later un-companionable silence that can serve as a gestation period for creative imaging or wording. Silence can also serve as an opportunity for emptying ourselves – a kind of bracketing of the ongoing narrating voice, so that we are open to alternative, images, voices, or perspectives. The "preconceived idea, the idea that is already known, closes up the gap through which newness, the unknown, might emerge" (p. 117). The dialectic here is between the known and the unknown, between the old and the new. We need sources of strength, protection, and patient en*courage*ment early in life in order to become courageous enough to be open to that which is (frighteningly, thrillingly) new and unknown. Similarly, we need to carry with us from childhood the lovingly reassuring felt presence of our parents so that we develop the capacity to be alone (initially in the presence of our parents) and at home with silence which is the seed of potential creativity.

The space between mother-and-child, in kinship, says Nicholsen (2002), is "the locus of creativity" (p. 120). It is the play space that symbolizes the convergence of their union (merger) and separateness. It is a space that is constructed in the context of security and trust. "In this space of play, everything is new and creative to the baby, just as it feels intense and personal" (p. 120). Cultural space, which is experienced later, is viewed as an expansion on this original play space. Quoting Winnicott, "'every detail of the baby's life is an example of creative living'" (p. 120). Just like a good-enough mother, a good-enough culture will offer its members the holding environment needed for the creative pursuit of meaningful projects. Analogously, the provision of reciprocal holding is needed for creative relational living. Reciprocal creative seeing and mutuality in loving intensify our sense of kinship. We need a good communal life in order to flourish creatively. Creative relational living requires of us the capacity for *mentalization* – the ability to be cognizant of our own state of mind while being attuned to the states of minds of others that are seemingly different from ours. This capacity for mentalization, Fonagy (2001) informs us, is made possible by being and becoming securely attached. "Reflective function [mentalization]," he writes, "is closely linked to [secure] attachment" (p. 166). A sense of security or having a secure base, made possible by a developmental history of cumulative loving experiences of being "held" (Winnicott) and "contained" (Bion), is a precondition for the (creative) exploration of the affect-laden mental states of oneself and others. Secure attachment frees our already existing open disposition toward creatively fashioning our emerging lifeworld meanings.

The creative use of our talent, states Nicholsen (2002), requires gratitude, labor, and generosity. Because our talent is a gift, we need to be grateful for it. Because our talent requires effort to cultivate, it is a labor of gratitude. And because it has been received, it needs to be generously given. "A transformational gift ... does its work through the labor of gratitude" (p. 174). This labor of gratitude requires the responsible appropriation, ownership, and fruitful use of the skill or the talent. The creative use of the gift of talent or skill unfolds best in an affirming, supportive, and validating – in short, in a facilitating social environment.

"Life in its creativity," concludes Nicholsen (2002), "unfolds toward what is new and as yet unknown. Hope, as an orientation to possibility, is an emotional expression of the ongoing creative process of life" (p. 183). In a dialectical spirit, guided by the work of Harold Searles, Nicholsen makes an important distinction between *selfish hope* and *mature hope*. *Mature hope* is "tempered with [broadening and deepening] concern and with [edifying] disappointment" (p. 183). Broadened and deepened concern entails the assumption of social responsibility. Edifying disappointment can nudge us to attain *binocular vision* (a term borrowed from Wilfred Bion), which is a form of "creative seeing." "Binocular vision ... requires a safe emotional 'place' in which we can feel supported enough to notice the irrational churning away in ourselves" (p. 196). Through binocular vision "we perceive our connection to the group and at the same time are able to reflect on that connection as separate individuals" (p. 195). By way of binocular vision, we become "aware both of the abyss of infinitude, doubt, uncertainty, and possible disaster *and* of limits and choice, which particularize us into a time that unfolds into the future" (p. 187). In fact, "people's maturity is indicated by the time span they can encompass ... people's time span gets longer as they develop and mature" (p. 187). *Bi-logical thinking* goes hand-in-hand with *binocular vision*. In bi-logical thinking we are attuned to *both* "symmetry (sameness) and asymmetry (difference, which could include similarity)" (p. 188). Whereas asymmetry "localizes and particularizes," symmetry "infinitizes," "assimilates," and "aggregates." "Both symmetry and asymmetry are necessary for [creative] mental life" (p. 188). Being in love is a highly emotional experience that involves the integration of both symmetrical and asymmetrical thinking. It requires binocular vision and bi-logical thinking. When I say to my graduate students in a course entitled Multicultural Counseling, "We are like all others, like some others, and like no other," I am appealing to their bi-logical thinking. When the painter Paul Klee says something like, "One eye sees; the other eye feels," he is making use of the metaphor of binocular vision. Binocular vision and bi-logical thinking generate a mental space for creative thought and a prompting for creative action. "As we become more capable of binocular vision and bi-logic, more capable of tolerating the frightening conjunction of symmetry and asymmetry in our experience, more capable of living in unfolding time, we become the bearers of this continuity [the continuation of creative generativity or generative creativity]" (p. 191). Simply stated, to live life creatively is to perceive and live dialectically.

References

Armstrong, J. (2004). *The secret power of beauty*. Penguin Books.

Bollas, C. (2011). *The Christopher Bollas reader*. Routledge.

Fiumara, G. C. (2013). *Psychoanalysis and creativity in everyday life: Ordinary genius*. Routledge.

Fonagy, P. (2001). *Attachment theory and psychoanalysis*. Other Press.

Frankland, A. G. (2010). *The little psychotherapy book: Object relations in practice*. Oxford University Press.

Frosh, S. (1991). *Identity crisis: Modernity, psychoanalysis, and the self*. Routledge.

Frosh, S. (2012). *A brief introduction to psychoanalytic theory*. Palgrave Macmillan.

Holmes, J. (2010). *Exploring in security: Towards an attachment-informed psychoanalytic psychotherapy*. Routledge.

Lessem, P. A. (2005). *Self psychology: An introduction*. Jason Aronson.

Marcus, P. (2013b). *In search of the spiritual: Gabriel Marcel, psychoanalysis, and the sacred*. Karnac.

Nicholsen, S. W. (2002). *The love of nature and the end of the world: The unspoken dimensions of environmental concern*. The MIT Press.

Rayner, E. (1995). *Unconscious logic: An introduction to Matte Blanco's bi-logic and its uses*. Routledge.

Rodman, F. R. (2003). *Winnicott: Life and work*. Perseus.

Segal, H. (1979). *Melanie Klein*. Penguin Books.

Siegel, A. M. (1996). *Heinz Kohut and the psychology of the self*. Routledge.

Stern, D. N. (2004). *The present moment in psychotherapy and everyday life*. W. W. Norton.

Symington, N. (2004). *The blind man sees: Freud's awakening and other essays*. Karnac.

Tuber, S. (2008). *Attachment, play, and authenticity: A Winnicott primer*. Jason Aronson.

Winnicott, D. W. (1971). *Playing and reality*. Tavistock Publications.

Part III

The Capacities for Aesthetics, Goodness, Kindness, and Truth

8

Aesthetics: The Capacity for Relational *Aesthetics*

Hagman (2010) holds that "aesthetic experience is an aspect of a mature level of self-organization" (p. 13). Leffert (2017) defines aesthetic competence as "the capacity to experience subjectively the good, the true, and the beautiful, an activity which is intimately involved with man's search for meaning … and Subjective Well-Being" (p. 62). There are two aspects of this definition that I wish to modify. The first, I would nullify the hard distinction between the "subjective" and the "intersubjective." There is always an intersubjective element in the seemingly subjective. Second, although I have been movingly inspired by Frankl's (2006) *Man's Search for Meaning* early in my academic career, I have come over time to take issue with his claim that modern human beings are *searching* for meaning in life. I do not believe this position, which Leffert wholeheartedly espouses, is phenomenologically sound.

In the Preface to his *Phenomenology of Perception*, Merleau-Ponty (1962) asserts that we humans are "condemned to meaning." From our developmental beginnings, we are predisposed to perceiving meanings and to meaning making. But just as we make meanings, meanings make us. We are meaning-perceivers and meaning-makers through and through. We will always experience a dialectic between an expectable meaning and an unlimited possibilities of new or emergent meanings. These meanings are originally grounded in our relational, affective, and bodily experiences. Some meanings become more "meaningful" than other meanings. We are capable of making *meta-meanings* – meanings about meanings. Our capacity to generate meanings creatively and flexibility captures a crucial aspect of our psychosocial maturation. From the start of life we are motivated by a fundamental meaning-seeking drive. The more secure we are the better is our capacity for generative meaning making,

© The Author(s), under exclusive license to Springer Nature Switzerland AG 2021

M. J. Hannush, *Markers of Psychosocial Maturation*,
https://doi.org/10.1007/978-3-030-74315-4_8

the more open we are for a wider range of meanings and the closer we are to approximating the fulfillment of affective, developmental, intrapersonal, interpersonal, conscious and not so conscious meanings, meanings that contain emotional and relational *truths*. Succinctly stated, the capacity for *generative meaning and meta-meaning making* or the capacity to *play with meanings* is of the essence of psychosocial maturation.

We may get stuck on narrowly and rigidly constructed meanings that obstruct our movement toward further development and growth. We may hold confused, contradictory, or inconsistent meanings that serve as barriers to our psychosocial maturation. Our negatively valenced meanings of lifeworld events may make us pessimistic and depressed and incline us to see the world darkly. That is altogether a different matter. What we may need for healing is a *different* set of meanings that are wider, more flexible, and less confused, contradictory, or inconsistent. What we may need is a radical transformation in our meaning making capacity; in our whole being-in-the-world-with-others as meaning-makers. Meanings may be a source of human misery. But, beginning in childhood, feeling securely attached (loved), we also experience the exuberance that accompanies the emergence of new meanings, especially *aesthetic meanings*.

Let us return to the varieties of aesthetic experiences themselves. Some of them, says Leffert (2017), "are serious and profoundly moving, while others are lighthearted and playful" (p. 64). Regardless, they are essential to our existence. Our aesthetic experiences can reveal to us insightful emotional and relational truths about the essence of who we are as human beings – about the being of our selfhood. Prior to the Franklian *search for meaning*, however, we are and have been already open and directed to *aesthetic and non-aesthetic meanings* from the very beginning of our lives. This Heideggerian "openness" is essential to the quality of our existence, to what it means to be participants in the lifeworld with others – beginning with our earliest essential m/other.

Leffert (2017) is at his phenomenological best when he traces aesthetic experiencing in our early inter-corporeal existence:

> To the extent that early aesthetic being exists, it must involve the very young child's experience of the mother's body, her appearance, her smell, her skin texture, and the textures and colors of her garments. However aesthetic being begins, it must begin altercentrically, remaining inseparable from the Social. (p. 73)

Leffert (2017), however, cannot maintain the unity of being-aesthetically-oriented-to-the-lifeworld. Why? He repeatedly succumbs to subjectivism by maintaining the dual influence of subject on world and world on subject. "If the aesthetic is best grasped phenomenologically," he states, "it must also be understood as subjective and inextricably engaged with the social" (p. 71). Yet again, "the self and its being are constantly being changed by the world in which it is embedded and are also constantly changing the world" (p. 14). Phenomenologically, self-and-world is a unity that changes simultaneously. Still, Leffert can slip and slide into accurate phenomenological discourse as when he states that "aesthetic familiarity can be soothing, calming, and satisfying as it takes us into a different world" (p. 67).

What escapes Leffert (2017) is that from a phenomenological perspective the *subjective is always already intersubjective.* The loss of aesthetic competence, in response to early trauma, is a developmental failure. This is not merely a consequence of a subjective or intrapsychic aesthetic incompetence. In my view, this results in a constriction or narrowing in the capacity for aesthetic experiencing which simultaneously correlates with a closedness or lack of openness to aesthetic meanings in one's lifeworld. What colors or co-constitutes our closedness or openness to (aesthetic) meanings lies in the style or habitual ways with which we take up the familial, gendered, historical, and socio-political facts of our existence into which we are thrown in the here-and-now. Leffert is phenomenologically on target when he suggests, "aesthetic competence [or the capacity for deep aesthetic experiencing] is one of the endpoints of successful development of [a "Worlding"] Self, maintaining self-regulation and integration, maintaining its thrown being" (p. 72). Experiencing deep aesthetic relational moments are self-regulatory and integrative in nature because these "moments" mean something *beautiful, good, and true* and thus touch us deeply. The now is always potentially creative in that it is pregnant with possibilities of such newly emergent aesthetic meanings.

Yet again, Leffert (2017) slips into *objectivism* when he asserts that "neuroscience has something to offer us" if we are "to develop a deeper understanding of aesthetics" (p. 77). Or, "it is impossible to understand aesthetics without understanding how the brain functions" (p. 77). Based on the research findings available, he concludes that the capacity for aesthetic experiencing "must be mediated by the Mirror Neuron System" (p. 77). Although the Mirror Neuron System may make it possible for us to experience aesthetic sights and sounds, our capacity for aesthetic competence becomes functionally autonomous (becoming more and other than) our Mirror Neuron System.

Under good-enough developmental conditions (of tender loving care), our joyous consciousness becomes naturally attuned to the intensification of aesthetic meanings in our lifeworld. According to Schindler's (2004) interpretive treatise on the work of Hans Urs von Balthasar, when a child is loved properly by his mother, joy comes to constitute the passionate orientation of his consciousness. Correlatively, that which is beautiful, good, and true, as embodied by the Mothering One, becomes the object of the child's joyous consciousness – the epiphanous perception of his lifeworld.

There is a kinship of intentionality or intentional kinship between the so-called subjective (the bodily self side) and the so-called objective (the lifeworld side) in the experience of relational aesthetics. Inspired by Neoplatonistic philosopher Plotinus (204–270 CE), Armstrong (2004) writes:

> To find something beautiful is to register the kinship between the object and the most important part of oneself – one's soul. The beauty of a physical object embodies purity, perfection, harmony and order. And these are, precisely, the qualities that the soul strives to attain in itself. So in the beautiful object we see what should be. But these qualities are more fully realized in beautiful action, in beauty of character or of mind … This thrill, this sense of recognition, is what we call the 'experience of beauty.' (p. 72)

I discover (clearly see) more of myself as I simultaneously deepen my aesthetic experiencing of an "Other" who is a part of my, now, stretched beautiful lifeworld meaning. My beautiful lifeworld meanings expand, as I open my sensuous fleshly presence to that which is movingly beautiful. The "Other" could be an object, event, or person. Plotinus makes a distinction between perceptual (material) and moral beauty – beauty of character or personality. But even physical beauty animatedly points to something beyond itself. The "whole of how we live and who we think we are gets implicated in our apprehension of beauty" (p. 25). Aesthetic selving, moral selving, and maturational selving stand in close proximity to one another. "This is the story of growth. In the encounter with beauty the soul [Self] sees more of itself" (p. 72). In this encounter we experience a resonant synchronicity or a synchronous resonance in meanings, such as balance, harmony, optimal sequencing, order, perfection, proportion, purity, perfection, and serenity. In this encounter we are invited to appropriate, embody, and refine these beautiful qualities of character or personality which are "perhaps, the deepest objects of love" (p. 76).

In the same spirit, Balthasar (1998) intones:

> By developing his soul [self or who one is] according to the images of the objectively beautiful [the beautiful out there in one's interpersonal world], the maturing person gradually learns to acquire the art of discrimination [or discernment], that is, the art of perceiving what is beautiful in itself. In the process of their development, the subjective elements of perception (which, doubtless, include state of mind and fantasy) more and more pass into the service of objective perception. (p. 178)

Beauty, goodness, and truth, explains Schindler (2004), are tension-laden and intrinsically interrelated meanings that are essential to our existence as human beings. Goodness and truth shine through the experience of beauty. "This experience of beauty, then," explicates Schindler, "is clearly the ontological correlate to the interpersonal experience of the mother's smile" (p. 125). The child responds to mother's *loving* smile with his *whole* being. It is a heart-to-heart reciprocal or mutual responsiveness. Tension is at the heart of this mutuality because of the "reciprocal 'needing of each other'" (p. 167). Again, "both reciprocity and tension express the fact of an inward mutual dependence of two things [beings] that cannot be reduced to each other" (p. 391). Even the mother is deeply dependent on the child's recognition in her role as a loving-and-loved mother. Through this mutual recognition mother and child en-joy a union. The smile is not only a "fruit of the union," between mother and child, but also a mirroring of the child's unique belovedness. The loving smile "preserves the unity and difference of the child's personhood or selfhood in relation to that of the mother" (p. 119).

Beauty, goodness, and truth, expounds Schindler (2004), are "modes of encounter" (p. 234). In his encounter with his mother, the child sees, on a pre-reflective level, the embodiment of her beauty, goodness, and truth. If he could speak, when contented and smiling in response to her loving smile, he would say, "Mommy, you are beautiful, good, and true to me." This for the child is an epiphanous aesthetic experience. In this aesthetic encounter there is a natural *movement* on the part of the child toward the mother. This movement of going beyond his nascent bodily self toward the mother is the *ground of intentionality*. The beauty of the mother is an invitation for the child to know (explore) the mother. Relational beauty (aesthetics) is an invitation to relational knowledge (truth). The gradual discovery of relational truth vis-à-vis the mother unveils her goodness. It is easy to conjure an infant mesmerized by the beautiful features of his beloved mother and, before long, reaching out (moving actively toward) to touch the different parts of the alluringly, enthrallingly, and excitingly inviting face of the mother. The child is moving toward what *he is* (in identificatory resonance or union with) and *what he is not* in a double sense: "what he does not yet possess" (p. 398) and what is different and separate from his emerging nascent self.

Something needs to be said about how the mother is herself mesmerized by the beauty of her child. It is therefore an experience of *mutual aesthetic arrest*. Let us take the reciprocal smiling of mother and child as a prototypical example of a primordial encounter between two humans that matter to each other. First, the smiling of the mother cannot be separated from her (unconditional) love for her child. The authenticity (genuineness or truthfulness) and goodness (care and concern for doing what is best for her child's present and future welfare) of the mother shines through the gleam in her loving eyes. Second, just as the child needs the mother – even in the instance of reciprocal smiling, the mother, in turn, *needs to be needed* by her child. Third, both mother and child are enlivened in this loving encounter. Both of their worlds are lit up. Both sets of eyes are gleamed. Fourth, both mother and child are naturally called to move lovingly toward each other. Although unacknowledged, this is the primordial prototype of a *mutually lived intentionality*: the child's bodily self moves joyously and lovingly toward the mother, while the mother, in turn, moves joyously and lovingly toward her child. All other (abstract) instances of intentionality are derivative from this originary mutual movement. The "self comes *to* itself," informs us Schindler (2004), "only by coming *out* of itself or, more concretely, only by *going to another*, indeed by being raised up *by* the other, *to* the other" (p. 112). We are awakened to ourselves by the call of the m/other. The subjectivity of selfhood is made possible, validated, and brought to fruition by the objectivity of the mother's smile. Here is the paradox: I become more of myself through a movement that takes me outside (transcends) my nascent or emerging self. My subjectivity is made possible by a reciprocal intersubjective movement.

"The mother's smile," expands Schindler (2004), "is the outward expression of her *love* for the child and thus her 'self-gift' to the child" (p. 114). The mother "gives her *self*" through her smile. Through her smile, she bestows upon her child her loving and welcoming presence. Her loving and welcoming smile is a "creative call" that allows the child to be and become her or his spontaneous bodily self. The mother's smile, therefore, has *multiple value-laden meanings* for the child. The child apprehends these meanings pre-reflectively through inter-bodily communication and communion. The "child grasps 'that this love,'" which is communicated through the loving smile of the mother, "is the highest good" (p. 115). Here abides a primal relational *truth*: the *beauty* of the mother's loving smile reveals her *goodness*. Just as the smile of the mother awakens the smile of the child, or vice versa, "so does love awaken love" (p. 115). Through the reciprocal loving smile two whole beings are moved or touched at the core of their being. They both are called to "muster all that is best" in each other (p. 117). Through calling and answering, both, mother and child, experience the worthiness of being loved – being worthy of each other's love. Both mother and child experience the "joy of love," an "ek-static being with another" (p. 118). The mood that pervades this mutually felt awareness of beauty is joy. This is why "consciousness *is* essentially joy – *in its very structure* … joy is the first name of consciousness" (p. 127).

The good mother knows when to withdraw her attention, allowing the child time to return to itself. This "preserves the unity and difference of the child's personhood or [emerging] selfhood in relation to that of the mother" (Schindler, 2004, p. 119). The child's consciousness of his sense of "otherness-in-unity" emerges from the mutuality of a discerningly loving communion with the mother. There is a dialectical tension in needing to experience oneness and unity with each other, on the one hand, and in needing to separate, differentiate, and acknowledge the otherness of the other, on the other hand. This is a lifelong delicate balancing act. One can easily slip into a seemingly loving and co-dependent enmeshment or slide into an alienated sense of emotional aloneness and isolation. The mature mother enables such a developmental achievement by being at home with both poles of the meaning continuum. She understands (accurately interprets) the meanings of the child's needs for *connectedness* and *separation* and thus responds responsibly to both needs.

All things unfolding relatively well, there is goodness and truth in the beauty of the loving smile of the mother which is reciprocated by the loving smile of the child. "This experience of beauty, then, is clearly the ontological correlate to the interpersonal experience of the mother's [loving] smile" (Schindler, 2004, p. 125). In the absence of discerning love, there is unfairness, untruth, and ugliness. I say "discerning love," because the fundamental mutuality between mother and child is in the beginning a form of "asymmetrical reciprocity." There is an imbalance in the relative maturity of mother-and-child dyad. Although mother-and-child need and are dependent on each other, the child is much more dependent upon and needful of the mother.

As modes of encounter, being beautiful, being good, and being true (being truthful and truth seeking) go together. This is why Scarry (1999) equates being beautiful (fair) with being just (fair): a single word, "fairness," is used both in referring to loveliness of countenance and to the ethical requirement for "being fair" and "fair distribution" (p. 91). Moreover, Scarry elaborates, "beautiful things" or beautiful people "hold steadily visible the manifest good of equality and balance" (p. 97). Yet again, "equality is the heart of beauty" (p. 98). "Beauty," she expands, "is pacific" (p. 107). It points to the absence of injury and injustice. Moreover, in the presence of beauty, "we undergo a radical decentering" (p. 111). We are no longer the center of our psychosocial universe. We let go of our self-centeredness, egocentrism, and selfishness. It is "an occasion for 'unselfing' and that is what is popularly called beauty" (p. 113). Scarry links *aesthetic fairness* with *ethical fairness*: "It is clear that an *ethical fairness* which requires 'a symmetry of everyone's relation' will be greatly assisted by an *aesthetic fairness* that creates in all participants a state of delight in their own lateralness" (p. 114). In sharing, directly or vicariously, in a symmetrical experience of aesthetic fairness, we derive a sense of delight from this *side-by-side* participation in the contagious spreading of the lived meaning of beauty.

Think of the impact on us of the beautiful character of Atticus Finch from Harper Lee's (1960) *To Kill a Mockingbird* as an exemplar of Scarry's thesis here (see Hannush, 2002). The beauty of Atticus's character is "clearly discernible" in his everyday moral actions. Initially, the beauty of his character causes us to suspend our judgment in awe. Of course, we can make "self-corrections" and "self-adjustments" as we learn more about and digest his character. We continue to scrutinize our judgment of his unfolding character. His beautiful character fills our mind and invites us to search for a larger meaningful life that beckons us beyond ourselves. The "beautiful person," illuminates Scarry (1999), "incites in us the longing for truth" and inspires our willingness "to labor, struggle, wrestle with the world to locate enduring sources of conviction – to locate what is true" (p. 31). Atticus embodies for us beautiful and "enduring sources of conviction." This is why, Scarry asserts, "beauty really is allied with truth" and that beauty "ignites the desire for truth by giving us … the experience of conviction and the experience, as well, of error" (p. 53) – Atticus has his limitations and shortcomings. Yet, his fallibility is extremely minimized in Lee's novel. For instance, upon multiple readings of Lee's novel, I came upon the self-correcting conclusion that Lee had dichotomized or split human nature into the all-good character of Atticus Finch and the all-bad character of Bob Ewell. We are all mixtures of virtues and vices. Our challenge is to maximize the beautiful and the good and minimize (keep in check) the bad and ugly within and between us. With this self-correction in mind, I can still be inspired by and identify with the beauty of Atticus Finch's convictions. Like parents who, upon conceiving a child, wish "the beauty of the beloved, already in the world, to enter the world a second time" (p. 71), we too want to creatively appropriate and pass on Atticus's beautiful, fair, and truthful convictions. The "beauty [of his character]," Scarry would say, "prepares us for justice" (p. 78). Through our exposure to the beauty of his character, we recommit ourselves to a higher standard of care toward all people. As we behold, identify with, and internalize the beauty of Atticus's character, we ourselves become beautiful in the interior-and-exterior of our lives. Even "a sentence of incredible tact delicately spoken," (p. 89) of which there are many in Lee's novel, upon being appropriated, can imbue our character with beauty. Like "a compact, or contract between the beautiful being and the perceiver" (p. 90), "the gift of life" has been conferred upon us.

We can also interpret the beauty of Atticus's character in light of Maslow's (1970) *hierarchy of needs*. From Maslow's (1971) perspective, Atticus would be considered one of those self-actualizing individuals who are said to be "better cognizers and perceivers" of meaning contexts than most (p. 6). He would be more accurate in his perception or interpretation of social reality. He would be someone who lives by *Being-values*, such as *Beauty*, Goodness, Truth, Justice, Completion, Order, Perfection, Playfulness, Simplicity, and Wholeness. What Maslow calls *Being-values* I would describe as *affect-and-value-laden higher-order lived meanings*. As a self-actualizing person he is able to co-organize and co-actualize lifeworld meanings like being kind, fair, and truthful. For Maslow (1968, 1970, 1971), Beauty along with other Being-values are necessities of life. They are the highest requirements for living a life of refined and individuated meanings. Atticus's meta-motivation is "character growth, character expression, *maturation*, and development; in a word self-actualization" (Maslow, 1970, p. 159). Ironically, as a self-actualizing person, Atticus is focused on concerns *outside* himself. In spite of his pain and suffering as a consequence of the resistance he receives in response to his principled living, Atticus, always in a state of being-and-becoming, gives full agonizing and joyous expression to his humanness. Above all, Atticus is responsibly responsive to the call of his vocation and his caring conscience – to uphold the law of justice for everyone. He lives for justice and truth. He devotes his life to the law. Living by Being-values is his "end" goal. Maslow (1971) has found self-actualizing individuals to be:

> working at something which fate has called them to somehow and which they work hard at and which they love, so that the work-joy dichotomy then disappears. One devotes his life to the law, another to justice, another to beauty or truth. All, in one way or another, devote their lives to the search for what I have called the 'being' values. (p. 43)

We, as witnessing readers, are awed and inspired by the beauty of Atticus's character. The experience of such beauty can move readers to change their lives. Many lawyers have attested to having chosen their vocation as a consequence of their identification with the fictional character of Atticus Finch. As readers, having feelingly gained insight into the beauty of Atticus's character, we have responded with admiration and wonder, love, and respect. In response to the beauty of his goodness and truthfulness, our caring conscience has been aroused. We now deeply desire to live by his beautiful *Being-values.*

Something needs to be stated about the dialectical movement, though never fully fulfilled, toward the convergence of beautiful meanings and ugly meanings in our lived lives. In general, being loving is more beautiful than being hateful. Whereas love beautifies us, hate uglifies us. On the whole, telling the truth carries a "beautiful" and "good" meaning for us and not telling the truth carries an "ugly" and "bad" meaning for us. Just as we expect our mother's love, observes Ogden (2012), to remain love, we expect her to be truthful and to embody the truth, a truth "that can be taken utterly for granted" (p. 113). Ogden adds: "There is something about being a mother that doesn't go together with lying. It's not a matter of ethics or sentimentality; it's a feeling that a mother, when she's being a mother, is telling the truth, she *is* the truth" (p. 113). But what Ogden does not make explicit here is that a lie can sometimes be beautiful and in service of the good; love can become possessive and ugly; and hate, as we have seen, can be constructive. Our challenging task in life is to navigate these dialectical tensions between seemingly polar meanings.

Ogden (2012) emphasizes yet again, "being a mother is somehow *to be* what is true" (p. 115). Being a mother is *to be* beautiful and good. Then again, we may be asking too much from our mothers, for being human they are prone to slippages. Like all humans, Ogden asserts, "a slippage [distortion] in meaning … prevents painful recognition of the truth" (p. 136). Ogden adds, "beauty and … horror [ugliness] … constitute human nature" and that our task in life is "to cope with and learn from disturbing [ugly] experience" (p. 132). All of us, including mothers, can transform the ugly slippages in meanings, such as lying, into beautifully restored meanings through acts of reparative "atonement." Quoting Hans Loewald, Ogden observes: "'The self, in its autonomy [and, I would add, in its inter-dependence] is an atonement structure, a structure of reconciliation, and as such a supreme achievement'" (p. 152). The generative act of atonement, which is a beautiful undertaking, counters the ugly slippage in meaning, such as that we "see" in the destructive act of lying. Atonement bridges the gap or tension between connectedness and separateness: "The atonement (at-one-ment) that underlies superego formation involves the metamorphic internalization of an object relationship with the parents as whole and separate objects" (p. 153). Atonement involves a mature form of identificatory resonance that allows for the achievement of a balance between our need for connectedness, oneness, and union, on the one hand, and our need for differentiation, individuation, and separateness, on the other hand. Ultimately, our acts of atonement aim at maintaining and enhancing our love for others. They enable us to continue loving and being loved. The act of atonement maintains a "sense of oneself as a loving and lovable person who recognizes (with a feeling of loss) the constraints [limits] of external [social] reality" (p. 168). There is beauty in that.

Let us now recall, in summary, Schindler's (2004) description of the child's encounter with the mother's loving smile, whereby the child is awakened (becomes open to), on an inter-bodily and pre-reflective level, to four realizations:

> (1) that he is one in love with his mother, even in being other than his mother, therefore all being is one; (2) that love is good, therefore all being is good; (3) that love is true, therefore all being is true; and (4) that love evokes joy, therefore all being is beautiful … the event of reciprocal causality [or mutuality] … lies embedded in each of the transcendentals [Beauty, Goodness, and Truth]. (p. 416)

In life, as we live it, "there is room for 'untruth' and for evil, and the ugliness they imply" (p. 407). However, the negation of ugliness does not override the positivity of beauty, goodness, and truth. "Greater than Angst is joy: and joy is especially tied to beauty, because joy is the ek-stasis and surprise of genuine mutuality. Joy, in other words, is itself another word for reciprocal causality" (p. 407). While beauty "dances" around goodness and truth, love is both the cause and effect of the experience of beauty. All that is painfully harsh, hopeless, humiliating, mediocre, shrill, and vulgar – all that is ugly needs to be humbly "assimilated into a totality which can and must be accepted positively – without artificial sweetening, just as it is" (p. 419). The totality of all that is beautiful, good, and true, unified by, while strengthening, love, needs to be the wider beautiful meaning that assimilates the narrower ugly meanings. This requires of us an ever-renewed commitment to the whole which is beautiful, a beautiful whole that transcends the ugly parts of our daily lives. As the guardians of the whole – of beauty, goodness, and truth – we need to stand for "the meaning of being: its beauty, its goodness – and its truth" (p. 420).

Aesthetic experience, notes Nicholsen (2002), has the potential to unify "our internal and external experience" for it is "the ground of our human life" (p. 2). The aesthetic response, adds Nicholsen, is "a kind of inspiration, a breathing-in of the world, in which we help the individual things [or persons] appear to us in their loveliness by mingling them with our hearts" (p. 40). To be prepared or ready for such "inspiration" requires of us a labor of intimate imagination or imaginative intimacy. Developmentally, it entails growing up in an emotionally sheltering home – a loving home where as children we breathed in the homeworld relaxedly and in*spiringly*. "For we need a [protective] home in order to become a [fluid, yet solid] self" (p. 41) that is capable of a deep aesthetic response to the world. "But intimacy," cautions Nicholsen, "brings with it not only love and loveliness but also hatred and ugliness, pain in many variants" (p. 40). Home can be emotionally and physically harsh, un-sheltering, and ugly. Children may come not to feel at-home in their own so-called home. They may experience a feeling of exile or homelessness in the house in which they grew up. Wounded, they feel marginal. What becomes marginal is diminished, is destroyed, or ends up being destructive. With diminishment, the capacity for an aesthetic response as a unifying force of self-and-its-lifeworld meanings is attenuated. "Reality," as a "process – organization and reorganization, context of meaning succeeding context of meaning" (Fuller, 1990, p. 266), is constricted.

"Aesthetic reciprocity," Nicholsen (2002) informs us, "is the foundation of the baby's development" (p. 63). Nicholsen elaborates:

> The baby's self is formed through passionate interchange with the the mother's body and psyche, based on the baby's perception of the mother as an aesthetic object – but this is possible only if the mother perceives the baby that way as well. Reciprocity … [is] the mutuality of intimate reciprocal relationship. (p. 63)

Reciprocity in this sense, therefore, is akin to a passionately intimate and loving encounter: "The passionate interchange between mother and baby … makes a containing space in which their love making can reverberate and escalate" (p. 64). This form of passionate reciprocity or reciprocal passion is a source of spellbinding *wonder*. "Reciprocity is closer to a love relationship than a commodity of exchange" (p. 65). Reciprocity within the field of interaction has the quality of profound encounter. Within this shared containing field or space, there is room for mutual identificatory resonance and reverberation. Such intimate reciprocity makes us totally *at home* in life and in ourselves. The intimate aesthetic reciprocity between mother-and-child creates a holding space in which "their love making reverberates as each experience is assimilated and leads on to the next in an ongoing process of growth and development" (p. 65). "The ultimate result of this intimate reciprocity," Nicholsen condenses, "is the growth of consciousness" (p. 65).

The experience of beauty is thus grounded in early reciprocal aesthetic perception. "What we perceive as beautiful," Nicholsen (2002) expands, "is experienced as having a face that returns our gaze" (p. 95). That which is beautiful is experienced originally as a felt presence. "In the mutual gaze of mother and baby we see the prototypical instance of aesthetic reciprocity" (p. 95). "Aesthetic experience," therefore, "begins at birth, if not before … [for in] the beginning was the aesthetic object" (pp. 95–96). From the start, the infant experiences his ordinarily devoted mother as physically and mentally beautiful, as an essential other veiled with an aura of mystery. Her beautiful face inspires awe and inspiration – an object that invites amazement, interest, curiosity, wonder, and exploration. "The enigmatic quality of the mother's beauty," however, "gives rise to aesthetic conflict" (p. 96). On the one hand, the infant is passionately attracted to mother's face; on the other hand, he is uneasy in the face of the mysterious unknown that his mother's beauty represents. In her overwhelmingly beautiful presence, he is transfixed or aesthetically arrested. To some degree, he is overwhelmed and cannot bear it. Yet, he also wants to tolerate this aesthetic experience in order to (1) receive the gift of her beauty, (2) know his mother, and (3) respond to the inspirational call of development and growth. How does the developing baby learn to endure his aesthetic conflict? (1) The cumulative experience of aesthetic mutuality itself enables the child to endure the aesthetic conflict. (2) The mother's mental-and-emotional capacity to hold or contain the baby while pondering the meanings of her child's inchoate psychic experiences and communicating her understanding to her child diffuses the aesthetic conflict and makes it less overwhelming.

Just as there is beauty in mature (discerning) love, so there is ugliness in immature (non-discerning) hate. Analogously, and dialectically, there will be moments of ugliness in immature (non-discerning or unwise) love and there may even be beauty in moments of constructive (care-based) hate. Fascinatingly, Nicholsen (2002) enlightens us, whereas mourned losses open us to more clearly see the beauty of our relational world, unmourned losses cloud our vision and sensitize us to see ugliness in our relational world. Similarly, I would conjecture, being forgiving or unforgiving, as modes of being-in-the-world-with-others, have parallel effects. Love, mourning, and forgiveness open us to seeing more *beautiful meanings* in our lifeworld. In our relational encounters, we are either open to higher or lower degrees of reciprocities of beauty or ugliness. Our mental health lies in the balance – the ratio of reciprocities of beauty relative to the reciprocities of ugliness. Just as the good-and-true loving mother has a beautiful face, so does the world. And just as the bad-and-untrue unloving mother has an ugly face, so does the world. The good-enough mother's ugly moments can be easily absorbed into her overall essential beauty – into her infinite emotional meaning as a beautiful face. In a loving environment, where parents participate in a reverberating aesthetic mutuality, there is an abundance of beautiful meanings. An unloving environment, filled with excessive mistrust, shame, and guilt, where parents fail to participate in aesthetic mutuality, will be saturated with *ugly meanings*. Where there is relational failure, there also is reciprocity of ugliness. Where there is deep and joyous relating, there is also aesthetic reciprocity. "Babies see their own aesthetic capacities and their own beauty reflected in their first aesthetic object, the mother's face" (p. 99). "Aesthetic reciprocity takes the form of the field of love between mother and baby" (p. 100). The mother's lovingly smiling face radiates her embodied beneficence in lived, existential space, the space where beautiful meanings commune with one another.

Hagman (2010) holds that aesthetics is "basic to human identity and daily life" (p. 3). He asserts that the capacity for aesthetic experience emerges from the rhythmic interactions between mother-and-child, which include the rhythm of breathing jointly together, the experience of touching and being touched soothingly and excitingly, and the musically vocal communication between them. The synchronous act of lovingly holding and being held is the original medium for aesthetic experience. "The beauty of her child's smile, the shape and color of the child's body, the clothing with which she keeps him or her warm, all are aesthetically based and are chosen out of the mother's engrossment and love" (p. 3). The mother's facial expressions are imbued with beauty. There is an element of aesthetic reciprocity in the mother's rhythmic inter-bodily interactions with her child in ritualistic acts of comfort and play. "The shared love and idealization between mother and baby invests the forms of feeling with beauty and special value. The aesthetic experience of this dyad is intense, exciting, and endlessly variable" (pp. 3–4).

This aesthetics of relatedness that is a source of exuberance and infinite variability and surprise is at the same time a source of soothing calmness, protective security, and predictable familiarity and orderliness. This balanced form of aesthetic relatedness begets *aesthetic meanings* that simultaneously contain and prospectively and adventurously propel us toward the creation of *new aesthetic meanings*. Under less than optimal conditions, we may either get stuck at pseudo-safety producing *rigid meanings* or, at the other end of the dialectical continuum, recklessly seek adventures that falsely promise the yielding of *hyper-euphoric or manic meanings* that obliterate our tortuous sense of selfhood.

Our early experience of holding and being held, Hagman (2010) tells us, provides us with both an "aesthetics of refuge" and "aesthetics of prospect" (p. 124). I call these an "aesthetics of security" and an "aesthetics of adventure." Regardless, here is how Hagman describes the experience of holding and being held:

> The holding of a child by the mother or father in the circle of his or her attention and the firmness of their arms is the developmental source of refuge. A child being held aloft, or swung around the parent like a carousel, or tumbled on the bed is the developmental source of prospect. Both are necessary and both are related. To be held and at the same time allowed to survey the surrounding

> world. To feel the strong grip of the parent as you are held aloft over the beach, suddenly thrilled by the view. These differing but related aesthetic states once again can be characterized as maternal (refuge) and paternal (prospect). (p. 125)

Hagman (2010) agrees with philosopher Theodor Lipps that the concept of empathy can be understood as an aesthetic experience. Thus, Hagman refers to the concept of *aesthetic empathy*. Lipps, in the words of Hagman, characterizes "empathy as the objective enjoyment of self; for him positive empathy (beauty) is where the self is encountered in the object, and negative empathy (ugliness) is where the self is repelled" (p. 115). There is therefore beauty in the emotional union (empathy) between mother and child. This is a "bond of beauty." No wonder then that this "bond of beauty" provides the child with an integrative experience.

The "violation of aesthetic organizations of experience," Hagman (2010) informs us, "is experienced as a sense of ugliness" (p. 6). "In the experience of ugliness," he continues, "the expectation of beauty is radically disrupted. Instead of resonance, there is dissonance. … Harmony and wholeness are replaced by conflict and disintegration" (p. 12). When a child expects love and affection, but instead is shocked to encounter a violation of his or her expectation, she or he then experiences anxiety, revulsion, or, in short, a sense of ugliness. Whereas "aesthetic experience [integrative "bond of beauty"] is an aspect of mature level of self-organization" (p. 13), cumulative unaesthetic (ugly) experiences tip the balance in the direction of immaturity and self-disorganization. "Beauty involves powerful affective and self-states that are of an intensely pleasurable and integrative nature" (p. 117).

There are two concerns I wish to voice regarding Hagman's (2010) conception of aesthetic experience. One has to do with his slippage into idealism: "Beauty," he says, "is about the ideal relationship and the vitality that comes with the experience of a perfect fit, of safety and joy" (p. 137). The relationship does not have to be *ideal*, and the fit does not have to be *perfect* in order to experience a significant *degree* of "vitality," "safety," "joy," and a relative "sense of wholeness and balance that comes with understanding and even love" (p. 137). Beauty comes in degrees, so does ugliness. Beauty can be perceived in *imperfection*. The other concern has to do with the sharp distinction he maintains throughout his text between "maternal aesthetics" and "paternal aesthetics." "The maternal aesthetics," he summarizes, "is what we traditionally think of as beauty. The quality of formal [form-al] balance, pleasing rhythm and harmony … resonates with our unconscious memory (or fantasy) of perfect attunement with mother" (p. 137). "The paternal aesthetics," he condenses:

> reflects dynamic and multiple sets of representations that are organized around the child's experiences of the father. It is what we have come to call the Sublime. The nature of the paternal aesthetics is a quality of formlessness, of vastness, of open space, rather than rounded or enclosed space. It is about movement and power. The paternal aesthetic rather than pleasing and reassuring provokes wonder, awe, even fear.
>
> The Paternal aesthetic found in sublime experience gratifies both the desire and motivation to seek out the new and different and creates the opportunity for us to investigate and discover the world. Our sense of vigor and curiosity intensifies, and the inherent drive to individual [sic, intending "to individuate"] and separate becomes united with the curiosity about the world around us. (p. 137)

This kind of dichotomy reflects a patriarchal division of labor that traditionally and historically relegated women to the *enclosed and disempowering space of home* and freed men to pursue *empowering positions in the open space* of work. Moreover, there are more variations *within* women and men than there are variations *between* women and men regarding the provision of experiences of *parental aesthetics of relatedness*. What is important is that the embodied Other, be it father or mother, stays *for the most part* beautiful and whole despite occasional slippages into ugly modes of being such as empathic failures on the part of parents or enraged attacks upon the parent on the child's part.

References

Armstrong, J. (2004). *The secret power of beauty*. Penguin Books.

Balthasar, H. U. v. (1998). *The glory of the Lord: A theological aesthetics, Volume I: Seeing the form*. Ignatius.

Frankl, V. E. (2006). *Man's search for meaning*. Beacon Press.

Fuller, A. R. (1990). *Insight into value: An exploration of the premises of a phenomenological psychology*. State University of New York Press.

Hagman, G. (2010). *The artist's mind: A psychoanalytic perspective on creativity, modern art and modern artists*. Routledge.

Hannush, M. J. (2002). *Becoming good parents: An existential journey*. State University of New York Press.

Lee, H. (1960). *To kill a mockingbird*. Warner Books.

Leffert, M. (2017). *Positive psychoanalysis: Meaning, aesthetics and subjective well-being*. Routledge.

Maslow, A. H. (1968). *Toward a psychology of being* (2nd ed.). D. Van Nostrand.

Maslow, A. H. (1970). *Motivation and personality* (2nd ed.). Harper and Row.
Maslow, A. H. (1971). *The farther reaches of human nature*. Viking.
Merleau-Ponty, M. (1962). *Phenomenology of perception* (C. Smith, Trans.). Routledge.
Nicholsen, S. W. (2002). *The love of nature and the end of the world: The unspoken dimensions of environmental concern*. The MIT Press.
Ogden, T. H. (2012). *Creative readings: Essays on seminal analytic works*. Routledge.
Scarry, E. (1999). *On beauty and being just*. Princeton University Press.
Schindler, D. C. (2004). *Hans Urs von Balthasar and the dramatic structure of truth: A philosophical interpretation*. Fordham University Press.

9

Goodness: The Capacity for *Goodness*

"Goodness," states Staub (2003), "is the opposite of evil. It refers to actions that bring benefit to individuals or whole groups… goodness can also take the form of persistent engagement in helping people or creating positive social change" (p. 6). Our capacity for goodness, says Staub, "evolves" as we engage in prosocial actions. We are changed by our caring and helpful actions. We "become more caring and helpful" (p. 7). The predisposition toward goodness or caring about and being helpful toward others becomes an integrated part of our selves. "Goodness," stresses Staub, "is likely to be one expression of optimal functioning" (p. 547). The *call of maturation* is at the same time a summons for what Staub calls "inclusive caring," which is a requisite for stretching our capacity for goodness. To "create goodness, extending the boundaries of 'us' is essential" (p. 534).

How can we "generate goodness"? What are the "building blocks of goodness"? In an attempt to answer these critical questions, Staub (2003) provides us with a "basic needs perspective" (p. 531). We "human beings," writes Staub:

> have fundamental, shared needs. These include a need for security, for a positive identity, for a sense of effectiveness, for both positive connection to other people and autonomy, for a comprehension of reality … [and] the need for transcendence … – the need to go beyond one's own material concerns and beyond the self. When these needs are fulfilled, people are well on their way to harmonious, caring relationships with others, as well as continued growth in their lives. (pp. 531–532)

© The Author(s), under exclusive license to Springer Nature Switzerland AG 2021
M. J. Hannush, *Markers of Psychosocial Maturation*,
https://doi.org/10.1007/978-3-030-74315-4_9

Goodness is generated when familial, communal, and social conditions contribute to the fulfillment of our basic human needs. Conditions that frustrate our basic needs, such as abuse, dehumanization, devaluation, disempowerment, discrimination, disrespect, economic impoverishment, harsh treatment, hostility, inequality, inequity, injustice, marginalization, neglect, and rejection (lack of acceptance or recognition), give rise to anger, resentment, and violence. Simply stated, evil is generated through the frustration of our basic, universal needs. For Staub, "evil means human destructiveness" (p. 5). He also equates "evil" with "harmfulness." "On the 'evil' side," Staub elaborates, "individuals and groups harm others in small and big ways" (p. 4).

"Certain practices in families," continues Staub (2003), "are important in fulfilling basic needs. Eating family dinners together and reading to young children can foster connection. However, fostering connection while also allowing and even fostering autonomy [such as allowing developing children for making their own decisions and having time for themselves] is important [especially when they are growing up in an individualistic culture]" (p. 534).

"Inclusive caring" is for Staub (2003) a core manifestation of goodness. He defines it as "the extension of caring to the 'other,' ideally to all human beings" (p. 534). It develops by way of communication through images and words that humanize all of us. We need "the example of models who show caring for people regardless of their group membership, and through one's own experience of connection with varied people" (p. 534). Ultimately we internalize the support of caring others – "like parents who exemplify moral values [and 'moral courage']" (p. 535). "Affirmation when a child or teenager speaks out against cruelty or injustice, or simply expresses beliefs or points of view that are contrary to those of others, can help develop moral courage" (p. 535).

A democratic "society that is just and benevolent," expands Staub (2003), "will reduce violence [destructiveness or evil] and create harmony [or goodness]" (p. 538). Democracy, as we know it today, is rarely, if ever, complete. A capitalistic society that is hyper-individualistic, hyper-competitive, and hyper-materialistic frustrates basic needs. In such a society, even when it claims equal opportunity and equal treatment under the law, many individuals and groups feel that their basic needs and rights are frustrated. They can feel invisible, unheard, unfairly treated, and left at the lower rungs of the ladder of economic success. Not everyone, for instance, can dream the so-called American Dream.

"Difficult conditions of life," states Staub (2003), "can intensify these [basic] needs" (p. 538). "Frustrating needs," for example, results in "problems of identity" (p. 538). Individuals with a negative individual and/or social identity may "seek ways to relinquish a burdensome self" (p. 538).

"Community," and not only family, "is crucial in fulfilling needs for connection and identity" (p. 539). In fact, "nuclear families lack community ... Societies ought to be creative in building communities that help people constructively fulfill basic needs. Institutions of learning and other communities ought to help young people integrate the old and the new ... and constructively participate in social processes" (p. 539).

Aside from "difficult life conditions," even in the course of so-called normal everyday existence, children and adults experience "life injuries." They inevitably, sooner or later, have wounding experiences such as losing friends, being subjected to divorcing parents, and experiencing unmourned losses of loved ones. These experiences can make us mistrusting, vulnerable, and unhappy in life. "Healing from past wounds," says Staub (2003), "diminishes evil and creates goodness" (p. 539). In order to heal we need to work through and come to terms with our painful experiences. We also need to share our pain and suffering with loving-and-loved others who acknowledge our pain and suffering and from whom we receive needed empathy and sympathy. It is this loving connection that contributes to our healing and resilient recovery. "Such corrective experiences can lead to ... 'altruism [and empathy] born of suffering'" (p. 540). Having healed from a specific suffering, I can reach out understandingly to a fellow-sufferer who is now similarly suffering.

When we are focused on our own pain and suffering, we do not pay attention to the pain and suffering of others. But as we heal, and become relatively whole again, we begin to "see the possibilities of human goodness" (Staub, 2003, p. 541). When our own cries are heard, we are then sensitized and are able to respond to the cries of others. Healing enhances our capacity for "empathy, caring, and helping" or, simply, our capacity for goodness.

When the conditions necessary for generating goodness are precariously and confusingly present or glaringly absent, individuals may use destructive means to meet their basic needs for safety and security, loving connection, a sense of efficacy (a feeling of control and a sense of effectiveness), and a positive identity. "Children who are treated by parents or other people with great harshness and who learn to use violence in their defense," elaborates Staub (2003), "may believe that only violence will give them security, a feeling of control, a positive identity" (p. 541). Moreover, they are "unaware of the impact of their [destructive] behavior on others" (p. 545). Becoming aware of the world around us and of our own actions, thoughts, feelings, beliefs, values, and motives, continues Staub, "makes choice and self-control possible" (p. 545). This kind of awareness is snuffed when our basic needs are frustrated and not adequately satisfied.

"Goodness," to repeat Staub's (2003) assertion, "is likely to be one expression of optimal functioning" (p. 547). "By this [optimal functioning] I mean our continued growth as persons, the unfolding and evolution of our positive human and personal potentials. I mean the capacity both to live a full and satisfying interpersonal/emotional life, a fulfilling and constructive [and creative] life" (p. 546). The elements of goodness – caring, helpfulness, reflexive self-awareness, empathy, and respect for other people, are therefore aspects of optimal functioning or, in our terms, *psychosocial maturation*. "Optimal function," in turn, "is an outgrowth of the fulfillment of basic needs" (p. 546).

In his conclusion, Staub (2003) writes: "goodness requires active bystandership by individuals and organizations, communities, and nations" (p. 547). "To be active bystanders requires caring values, a feeling of responsibility, as well as a feeling of efficacy, the belief that one can bring about positive ends. Active bystandership is also facilitated by mutual support, people working together for a shared cause" (p. 547). Although it entails some risk-taking, active bystandership has its own rewards such as "the satisfaction inherent in living up to one's values [and] the gains for one's self, one's children, and grandchildren in living in a more harmonious, caring society and world that one's actions help to create" (p. 548).

Evil (destructiveness), as we have come to see, is the opposite of goodness (constructiveness). Gaining insight into evil illuminates the *meaning* of its opposite, goodness. In his treatise on evil, Kellerman (2014) equates evil (destructive behavior) with symptomatic acting-out behavior. The formulaic explanation for acting-out is deceptively simple. The "pleasure principle of all life," says Kellerman, "contains the '*wish*' for gratification (of all '*wishes*'), along with a potential rage in the thwarting of such gratification of '*wishes*.' Thus, *repressed anger* or rage will, in every case, generate symptoms of acting-out … the psyche's process in the formation of such an acting-out symptom creates the ground out of which evil can take shape" (p. 26). The proclivity toward evil (acting-out) surfaces when the wish for gratification is thwarted and the ensuing rage is repressed. The choice of content for such acting-out is made possible by the social context of such acting-out. In other words, the way we give expression to our predisposition toward evil (acting-out), upon the thwarting of our wishes and the consequent repression of our rage, is facilitated by our social surrounding. Say I am growing up male in an American family. My wish to be loved by my parents is thwarted. I am angered and enraged. I then repress my anger and rage. I am now positioned to act out. I observe that my father in particular and my community and culture in general condone or are tolerant of generalized violence on the part of boys and men, especially toward girls and women. Thus, my family and my culture provide me with a handle on how to indirectly express my repressed rage. I am now ready to act out. Frustrated (unconsciously angered because my wish to be loved is thwarted), I take license from my family and culture to act out (aggress) against vulnerable, visible, and available targets – others in general and girls and women in particular.

As human beings, expands Kellerman (2014), "we are all *wish*-soaked creatures" (p. 4). The pleasure principle translates our aims, ends, goals, or wants into the central concept of *wishes*. The pleasure principle's primary representative is therefore the wish. Freud, Kellerman tells us, came upon the profound and powerful insight that our wishes live on in our own minds (psyches), even when they are thwarted in our everyday life. We, as wishing selves, shall not be denied. Our mind tricks us into allowing our wishes to continue to live on in disguise symbolically as emotional, psychological, or psychosomatic symptoms. This is why "we love our symptoms – even those that are painful – because the symptom represents our *wish* fully gratified, albeit in symbolic form" (p. 4).

"It takes," Kellerman (2014) reflects, "a resilient ego, a warm historical family structure, personal courage, … the presence of sufficient empathy and compassion in the personality … to 'correct' any potential evil choice-making" (p. 6). Similarly, it takes the same set of qualities to resist "mass pressure to conform" or "to support apparent or unmistakable tyranny" (p. 6). Kellerman continues: "in order to make objective choices [and thus avoid 'potential evil choice-making'], one necessarily would need to be sufficiently introspective and ego-strong. It requires strength to face up to one's shortcomings, dissatisfaction, and defeats of life without needing to conceal it all by invoking compensatory fantasies, beliefs, and behaviors" (p. 7).

Such "objectivity" and "strength," required for "good" choice-making, are difficult to come by. Living in a democratic society, we like to believe or, better yet, assume that our choices or decisions are objective and under our conscious control. But our proclivity to unconsciously act-out and make use of truth-distorting defense mechanisms like splitting or self-doubling shows us otherwise. *Acting-out* is "an immature defense mechanism in which intolerable emotions [such as anger, rage, shame, or guilt] are discharged into unhealthy and often impulsive actions" (Frankland, 2010, p. 175). *Splitting* is "an immature defense mechanism that reduces anxiety by keeping notions of good and bad separate in the person's mind" (Frankland, 2010, p. 179). Making use of the immature mechanism of splitting or self-doubling, for example, diminishes or "neutralizes" our capacity for empathy, and thus for "goodness." Making optimal use of *mature* mechanisms such as altruism, humor, sublimation, and suppression (consciously deciding "to temporarily set aside an uncomfortable thought, feeling, or wish") (Frankland, 2010, p. 179) is much more difficult for us humans to achieve, whereas making frequent use of immature mechanisms, such as splitting or projection, comes to us more easily.

Becoming mature is the most difficult overarching developmental task that we humans face. The lure of immaturity looms large in our everyday lives. Like Kellerman (2014) says, it takes resilience, strength, and courage to keep us from acting-out in immature ways. "This sort of courage to face up to things [or to keeping on maturing] is, in the present state of human evolution, seemingly quite underdeveloped, and actually rather thin" (p. 8).

"Acting-out," says Kellerman (2014), "is the attempt to **do** something rather than **know** something … it implicates repression (as well as the vicissitudes of the *wish*)" (p. 17). Whereas for Kellerman it is *acting-out*, for Alford (1997) and Lifton (1993), it is, respectively, *projection* and self-doubling (*splitting*) that is the mechanism of evil (destructiveness). Like acting-out, projection and splitting are immature defense mechanisms. Similar to acting-out, both projection and splitting implicate the mechanism of repression, yet itself another defense mechanism. Having defined acting-out and splitting (or self-doubling), let us add projection and repression to the list of definitions. Projection is "an immature defense mechanism in which an individual attributes unacceptable internal thoughts or feelings to an external source" (Frankland, 2010, p. 178). Repression is "a neurotic [or immature] defense mechanism in which an unacceptable thought, feeling, or wish is kept outside of conscious awareness" (Frankland, 2010, p. 179). In addition to repression, Kellerman (2014) explains, other immature defense mechanisms also make acting-out possible. These are *denial*, *displacement*, *projective identification*, *regression*, *splitting*, and *symbolization*. Through *denial*, "identified as perceptual defense … you see what you want to see and don't see what you don't want to see" (p. 22). *Displacement* permits us "to direct *anger* in a transferential sense to the targeted 'other'" (p. 22). *Projective identification* allows us, in two steps, to see "disavowed qualities of the self [intolerable thoughts or feelings] in the other that are unconsciously repudiated" (p. 22). We do this by applying pressure on the other the aim of which is to induce him or her to take on the intolerable thoughts or feelings. This is the first step in projective identification. "In the second step, the second person thinks, feels, and behaves as if characterized by the projected thought or feeling" (Frankland, 2010, p. 178). *Regression* – reverting "to an earlier developmental functioning in order to avoid discomfort or distress at the current level" (Frankland, 2010, p. 179) – allows us to keep "superego responses in check, thus permitting impulse to be released" (Kellerman, 2014, p. 22). *Splitting* makes it possible for us to divide other people "into good ones and bad ones according to the subject's needs" (Kellerman, 2014, p. 22). *Symbolization* "enables any person (subject) to identify with emblems *who* seem congruent with the subject's needs" (Kellerman, 2014, p. 22). Allow me to quickly differentiate between *unhealthy (immature) identification* and *healthy (mature) identification. Immature identification* refers to "a neurotic defense mechanism in which an individual takes on [unhealthy or immature] qualities of another" (Frankland, 2010, p. 177). In *mature identification*, the individual takes on healthy or mature qualities of another.

Extending upon Kellerman's conceptualization, *symbolization* enables the individual to identify with emblems that are congruent with *either* the false self's needs *or* the true self's needs. Unlike the naturally unfolding needs of the real, true self, *the needs of the false self are compensatory* in nature constructed to complement the *conditional expectations* of essential others. This important distinction eludes Kellerman's concept of symbolic identification or identificatory symbolization.

The way Kellerman (2014) sees it, the immature defense mechanisms of repression (of anger or rage in response to a thwarted wish) *plus* denial, displacement, projective identification, regression, splitting, and symbolization (immature identification) coalesce to make acting-out destructively possible. Although Kellerman recognizes that we humans are "wish-soaked creatures" and that we are naturally drawn to unconscious self-deception in an effort to hold on to our wishes through the use of mechanisms of defense which fuse to incline us to acting-out, he still finds a sliver of hope in the human capacity for "goodness" as a counterweight to our propensity for evil (acting-out destructively). He resonates to Dorothy Martyn's equation of "goodness" with "authentic love" in her *Beyond Deserving*. "Several factors," he tells us, "comprise this sort of love [as summarized from Martyn's text]: (1) Genuine love… (2) 'Participation with'… (3) 'Patience'" (Kellerman, 2014, p. 44). *Authentic love* is the most "genuine" form of love because it is given and is bestowed, even when unearned and *undeserved. Authentic love* "participates" in the distress of the other without taking into account past or future exchange, reciprocity, and equitable fairness. Mercy, in this form of participatory love, triumphs over justice. "The 'withness' [the 'participation' part of *authentic love*] represents the deepest sense of empathetic compassionate sharing" (p. 44). The "patience" part of *authentic love* refers to "the kind of love that knows how to wait, how to accompany and sustain the child [or adult], allowing space and time for the other's own being ['personhood'] to emerge without coercion" (p. 44).

Alford (1997) argues that when we are traumatized into a state of dread, especially early in our lives, we unconsciously project the dread onto others. To use different words, unknowingly, we do unto others what was done unto us. We trigger dread in other people, especially our own loved ones – those who are visible, available, and vulnerable. Evil is the evocation of dread in others. Alford adds that, not only the family but, more critically, our culture ought to contain our daily dread. Art as a cultural artifact, for example, can, creatively, give form to our dread. This "is what the ancient Greeks … did, confronting the sheer terror of existence, their dread, with nothing but beauty, the beauty of their art and the graceful beauty of their lives" (p. 129).

Individually or collectively, constructively or destructively, consciously or, mostly, unconsciously: (1) we do unto ourselves what was done unto us, (2) we do unto others what was done unto us, (3) we invite others to do unto us what was done unto us, and (4) we make others do unto themselves what was done unto us. This is, at least in part, how goodness (constructiveness) and evil (destructiveness) are perpetuated intra-generationally and inter-generationally (within and between generations).

Ricoeur (1995) defines evil as "the incapacity belonging to the capable man, the incapacity that does not abolish capability but presupposes it as the very thing that has ceased to be available to man as we know him historically" (p. 569). "But between this possibility [potential capability] and reality of evil [incapacity]," adds Ricoeur (1986), "there is a gap, a leap in the whole riddle of fault" (p. 142). What Ricoeur is saying here is that we humans are constructed in such a way that there will always be a gap between our capability and incapability and the wider the gap, the more our proclivity for evil, or, in our terms, destructiveness. Our life task, therefore, is to make the disciplined leap across the fault line in order to reduce the gap and thus lead a constructive (good) life. This way we close up to some extent the fissure between our capacity and incapacity and thus relatively, but never fully, resolve the riddle of our existential fault line.

For Ricoeur, then, the gaping fissure between trying to achieve a meaningful *destiny* or a purposeful life through the actualization of our capacities *and* our incapacity to accomplish it is the source of our destructiveness. Goodness or constructiveness results when the gap between our capacity to achieve a meaningful destiny and our incapacity to do so is relatively small. Our sense of self is born out of the tension between our capacities and incapacities. The good self is behind the good acts; the bad (destructive, evil) self is behind the bad acts. "The evil self," says Ricoeur (1966), is "at the root of an evil act" (p. 58). Because the gap between capacity and incapacity will always be there, we are all a fusion of good-and-bad selves. It is just a matter of *ratio* of good-to-bad. However, for Ricoeur, there are two things to keep in mind. One is that the proclivity to goodness is primary. That is our "involuntary" *nature*; that is how we are constructed. The other is that we have some "voluntary" choice-making at our disposal that can be used in the service of keeping our priorities straight while, to a certain degree, freely pursuing our destiny. "Evil," states Ricoeur (1995), "consists in a reversal of priorities, an inversion or subversion on the plane of the maxims of action" (p. 77). These "maxims of action" are "the means by which we hierarchize our preferences" as, for example, when we place "duty above desire, or desire above duty" (p. 77).

Although evil permeates us inside out and outside in, we are still responsible for the choices we make. "Evil," says Ricoeur (1967), "is not symmetrical with the good... However *radical* evil may be, it cannot be as *primordial* as goodness" (p. 156). Evil, then, is to be put in its place, as the polar opposite of superabundant goodness. We need to have *faith* in our primordial capacity for goodness. Faith, for Ricoeur, is what bridges the gap between our capacity for destructiveness and originary capacity for constructiveness. McWilliams (2004) defines faith as "a gut-level confidence in a process, despite inevitable moments of skepticism, confusion, doubt, and even despair" (p. 42). What both Ricoeur and McWilliams are, at least in part, saying or implying is that our movement toward *maturation* and growth is made possible by the faith or confidence essential others have in our capacity for goodness, a faith or confidence that we have internalized as a consequence of a primary process of identificatory resonance. Properly loving or good parents transmit this faith or confidence to and in their children. They in turn identify and resonate with the capacities they themselves awaken in their children (Hannush, 2002).

What I find lacking in Ricoeur, but is present in the writings of Rollo May, is an attunement to the potential destructiveness of good intentions (naïve innocence enacted with seeming good intentions) and the potential constructiveness of the daimonic impulses. Here is Ricoeur (1967) attributing innocence – a perpetuation of a womb-like paradise, to goodness: "Evil is not symmetrical with the good, wickedness is not something that replaces the goodness of a man; it is the staining, the darkening, the disfiguring of an innocence, a light, and a beauty that remain (p. 156). Evil, then, disfigures our "innocence" but does not eradicate it. Although, as far as Ricoeur is concerned, we are all guilty (fallen) for we are born to be destructive (to do evil), our primary innocence cannot be replaced by our secondary, but inevitable guilt-producing destructiveness.

May (1972) is in agreement with Ricoeur that we humans are suspended "in an endless dialectic between good and evil" (p. 202). But he offers a more nuanced view of "goodness" and "evil." Goodness for May is not equated with innocence. "Innocence," he says, "that cannot include the daimonic becomes evil" (p. 50). In May's dialectical model, life is characterized by an ongoing tension between a positive life force (*eros*) and a negative life force (*daimon*). "The daimonic," says May (1969), "is part of eros" (p. 163), but not all eros is daimonic. Daimon is a diabolical force. The term "diabolic," remarks May (1985), "comes from the Greek *dia* plus *ballein* and means to 'tear apart, to confuse, to throw into discord'" (p. 157). The daimonic mode of being "refers to any capacity which has the power to push the individual into disintegrative behavior" (May in Reeves, 1977, p. 305). "The course of human life," for May, "unfolds in a spiraling dialectical movement between integrative and disintegrative powerful passions, partly absorbing and partly being absorbed into each other resulting in different levels of integration and disintegration" (Hannush, 2002, p. 95). We humans have the capacity to *deconstruct old meanings* and *create new meanings*. "Children (and adults) tear existing models apart and put together something new, creative, and original. In this instance, disintegrative power is put (absorbed) in the service of integrative power" (Hannush, 2002, pp. 95–96). "In Charles Dickens's (2001) *Great Expectations*, the character of one of the main protagonists, Estella, is bent and broken, but only to reform into a better shape" (Hannush, 2002, p. 96). May goes so far as to say that "even aggression at times [is] not only unavoidable but healthy in developing love relationships" (May, 1972, p. 118). Sometimes, it is through fair fights (mutually modulated aggressiveness) that we grow and change.

Of course, we humans have the potential to place our daimonic mode of being in the service of becoming destructive, dominant, and exploitative. This type of dominance-seeking aggressiveness or exploitative manipulation develops as a consequence of not having been loved properly in one's early development and having been exposed to faulty models. In that case, "there develops in his [a person's] later aggression a penchant for revenge on the world, a need to destroy the world for others in as much as it was good for him" (May, 1972, p. 159). Such a person may then resort to violence "to prove one's power, to establish the worth of the self" (p. 187). "In his youth, Adolf Hitler is depicted as an aspiring mediocre artist. Regardless of his level of talent, he is struggling to give expression to the creative force within himself. In adulthood, it is abundantly clear that Hitler's creative urge is absorbed into and overtaken by the destructive urge within [the origin of which can be traced to a traumatized childhood, a trauma that is now being inflicted upon the whole of humanity]" (Hannush, 2002, p. 96).

In a previous publication (Hannush, 2002), I devote a chapter to interpreting and revising May's work in an attempt to put forth "an existential theory of parenting" (p. 144). In it, I reflect on the meaning of *psychosocial maturation* in light of May's conception of good and evil:

> Growing up or maturing means becoming sensitive to and accepting of our increased potentiality for both good and evil. It means becoming increasingly aware of our own power. It means owning up to our positive as well as our negative passions. It means forever being vigilant, for our integrity (integration) lies in the delicate balance between our power to be good and our power to be bad. It is out of this (creative) tension between our capacities for good and evil that our individuality or personhood is created. This creation simultaneously mirrors our human universality. Good is that which empowers and affirms the existential worth of the other as well as the self; evil is that which disempowers and denies the existential worth of the other as well as the self... As May sees it, just as humans are mixtures of love and hate, they are simultaneously fusions of good and evil. We are bestowed with the blessings and burdens of the power to pause, to be self-aware, to reflect on ourselves, to be conscientiously self-conscious (and thus called upon to listen to the call of conscience), to make choices and to take actions, and to be responsible for the consequences of our actions. These powers demand from us to muster the courage to confront our destinies and to look into ourselves and become aware of, acknowledge, and own our proclivities toward good as well as evil...
>
> May views human beings as having the power to be both good and evil. They also have the capacity to recognize the good as well as the evil within and outside of themselves. They have the power to pause and choose to cultivate the goodness within [and without]. (pp. 96–97)

Looking back, I now think it is too simplistic to propose that we humans have the *power to pause* (or the *will-to-pause*) and place our weight on the side of constructive goodness, using our daimonic side in the service of constructive goodness, while keeping our disintegrative, disempowering (or pseudo-empowering) daimonic side in check. In spite of his grounding in psychoanalysis and his awareness of the unconscious dimensions of our choices, May, at times, becomes blinded by the fundamental existential error – attributing too much "power" to the will-to-pause and throw one's weight in one decisional direction rather than another. The American poet Robert Frost (1965) concludes his poem, "The Road Not Taken," in which a traveler is faced with a decisional fork in the road and retrospectively looks back upon his decision this way: having once in his travels, long time ago, come upon two divergent paths in a woodland and having *paused* and chosen the one less trodden by previous journeying voyagers, he can now take a deep breath expressing his relief. Why? Because this consequential *pause* in choosing the one rather than the other path *seemingly* resulted in the unfolding of a different life course and a different life narrative.

Many readers and literary critics may easily equate the ending of Frost's poem with May's *will-to-pause*. Frost, however, is simply too sharp and shrewd for this simplistic explanation of life's critical decisions. In reviewing the beginning of the poem carefully, we discover that after carefully weighing both alternate roads, the traveler could have chosen that other path. Why? Because we are told by the poet-narrator that the other path was just as attractive. And even though the chosen path *seemed* somewhat grassier and less worn, the path not chosen is equally good. The choice, in other words, could have been otherwise and just as valid.

There must be more to our *pausing* and *deciding* than meets the initial eye. We like to think that the narrator, with whom we wish to identify, has made the right choice, one that has made all the difference in the unfolding of his life narrative. Thus, we commit what I call the *fundamental existential error*. We like to delude ourselves into thinking, especially those of us living in Western cultures, that we are the sole authors of our developing life story, that we carve out our destiny out of sheer willpower. We tend to underestimate the power of "unconscious" choices. We gloss over, especially when things have unfolded well, co-determining factors in our lives. Looking back, we deceive ourselves into rationalizing our decision in favor of presenting ourselves as heroic journeying selves. We do this by telling ourselves and others that when once faced with two diverging paths, we paused and made the courageous decision in favor of one rather than the other and consequently reaped the beneficial dividends. We attribute too much power to our say in interrupting our unfolding fate. Looking at our lives retrospectively, we convince ourselves that it was our own agency – our decisional acumen, that transformed our given fate into our own created and owned destiny.

Then there are those of us who attribute their fortune or, especially, misfortune to their biologically or environmentally determining fate. More of us are caught up in the dialectical tension between our seemingly fixed fate and our *co-created* destiny. The challenge of *psychosocial maturation* lies in turning our fate into a fairly measured and modulated destiny, while humbly acknowledging our fallibility and limits. That is where Frost's poetic wisdom lies.

Bollas (2011) links evil to "identification with the anti-life" (p. 157). The "evil self" is "identified with the killing of what is good, the destruction of trust, love, and reparation" (p. 160). We can, therefore, infer that goodness goes hand-in-hand with identification with the affirmation of life and that the good self is identified with the generation of what is good, the building of relationships based on trust, love, and reparation. "A person who has a sense of his own evil," says Bollas, "derives it from a [repetitive] pathology which has unconsciously determined him, and from which he develops a logic and turns it into an extreme statement" (p. 155). Bollas attributes the genesis of this unconsciously determined repetitive pathology to early traumatization. Early "loss of love and catastrophic displacement can foster an envious hatred of life, mutating into an identification with anti-life… The prince of darkness [in Milton's *Paradise Lost*] is a traumatized soul who feels condemned to work his trauma upon the human race, trying to bring others to an equivalent fall" (p. 157).

Early traumatization undermines, what Erikson calls, the developing child's "basic trust" in the parents. In agreement with Erikson, Bollas (2011) says that this "basic trust" is "so elemental that it precedes reflective consideration, almost a thoughtless assumption, derived from parental care of a child" (p. 158). But a mature "parental care of a child," adds Bollas, entails withholding "any violent or murderous response" and bearing "the child's greed, omnipotence, empty-headedness, and jealousies" (p. 158). Mature-enough parents survive the child's destructiveness. Abundant love contains and survives the destructiveness of the child. But the child's absolute dependency and therefore vulnerability cannot survive the parent's habitual destructiveness. Parents who survive their children's destructiveness probably had parents who in turn survived their parents' destructiveness. Similarly, parents who are not mature enough to survive their children's destructiveness, in all likelihood, had parents who could not survive the destructiveness of their own children. This attests to a perpetuation of a pattern of generational transmission of destructiveness.

Bollas (2011) traces the birth of the "evil self" (p. 163) to the early loss of parental love – a position of "catastrophic annihilation" in which the child is ruptured "from the folds of nurturance" (p. 157). In the absence of proper love, the child's trustful relation to the providing world is shattered. When proper love is lacking, the child fails to develop "that generative capacity which allows an individual to soothe oneself" (p. 159). The child comes to identify "with the killing of what is good, the destruction of trust" (p. 160). A dark zone is created within the emerging self, "where sudden destructiveness against or from the self arises" (p. 161). From this zone of darkness a vibrant mental and relational life is missing. When in this dark zone, the sense of aliveness, vitality, and love of life is sucked out. When in this hopeless zone, one is caught in "infinite repetitions, but no creative variations… something displaced the true [vital] self and left in its place an irreversible identification with the act committed against the child's self" (p. 161).

Understanding how the "evil self" comes into being sheds light on the birth of the good self. Growing up in a facilitating and properly loving environment, the child comes to identify with what is good, - with trust, love, and reparation. The child is offered life, dependence, and hope based on the somatic belief that his or her most vital needs will be sufficiently satisfied. The child unconsciously identifies with Life – his little life vibrates in relative harmony with Life itself. This is the relational context within which the true self is born from pure potentiality. In such a positively expectable environment, which is good enough, but never perfect, the ratio of emerging true (non-defensive) selfhood to false (defensive) selfhood is heavily in favor of the former. Whereas the true self is the good self, the false self is the bad (potentially evil or destructive) self. True selfhood comes in degrees, so does false selfhood. We all have good and evil selves. Correlatively, goodness comes in degrees; so does badness (evil or destructiveness). It is this ratio that is not sufficiently emphasized, though implied and hinted at, by Bollas and many other psychodynamic theorists. From our own dialectical point of view, goodness can be compromised by what Bollas calls "malignant innocence" and destructiveness can be transformed or sublimated into creative channels and pursuits.

In my reading of Bollas (2011), I sense that he makes a distinction between good identification and bad identification, good (creative) unconscious and bad (repetitive) unconscious, and good (true) self and bad (false) self. Under good- enough, nourishing life circumstances, "the [creative] unconscious … survive[s] one's own [symbolic] death" and consequently one does not have to unwillingly identify "with his own premature [symbolic] mortality" (p. 162). In other words, growing up in a facilitating environment, our emerging true self, which is in touch with our creative unconscious, outlives and outweighs the temptation to identify with a destructive false self that is propelled by an uncreative unconscious. The true self does not have to be projected onto others who become the target of resentment, revenge, and, ultimately, destruction. The true self is in touch with the goodness and the badness within and does not have to act out the partitioned parts of oneself destructively in the theater of life.

To make free use of the language of Bollas (2011), goodness arises from the kind of "generative intercourse" that occurs in facilitating, holding, and supportive environments. It is consonant with identifying with the Life that animates our growing selves. It emerges from the primitive preverbal somatic belief in the goodness of others, from entrusting the good m/other. It arises in light of the child's own *generative* innocence and the parents' tolerance of the child's *malignant* and destructive innocence. Repair in relational ruptures, because of either occasional and inevitable *empathic-and-mentalizing* – becoming aware, imagining, contemplating and reflecting upon, and accurately "reading" the meaning of the mental state of the child – *failures* on the part of the parents or their momentary inability to contain the malignantly innocent badness (narcissistic destructiveness) of the child restores the primacy of goodness. With the end of the age of innocence, the maturing child becomes attuned to his or her own badness and in turn partakes in acts of reparation in an effort to restore his own good image in the eyes of the m/other. Maturing children "bear to own responsibility for their own destructiveness" without having to project their badness onto others (p. 166). For Bollas, however, under relatively good-enough conditions, the original "generative innocence" will not be lost and will serve as source for the regeneration of aliveness and hope in later times of turmoil. Growing up under less than favorable circumstances can result, among other possibilities, in "malignant innocence." Bollas gives the example of "a woman who is battered by her partner," but "continuously return[s] to be victimized yet again" (p. 167). The "malignantly innocent" woman, like an infant or a child, keeps falsely hoping for the miraculously healing, yet fixedly immature, love of her partner.

Levine (2013) describes how the capacity for ethical conduct organizes or structures our inner world. Phenomenologically, I would rephrase this by stating that our capacity for perceiving and enacting *goodness-saturated meanings* organizes *both* our inner and outer world simultaneously. Moreover, Levine elaborates, the realization of an ideal or end in conduct gives the conduct its ethical standing. An ideal (perfected meaning) matters because of what we hope to achieve by attaching ourselves to and identifying with it. In both ethical theory and psychoanalysis we refer to this something to which we hope to attach ourselves the *good* (in psychoanalytic language the *good object*). In existential terms, to be good is to make ourselves worthy of the love that has been bestowed on us. We might, therefore, consider love itself as the ideal of the good, in which case our ideal is ultimately to love and be loved in the most humanly refined way possible. Consequently, it would not be difficult to conclude that the capacity for goodness is grounded in an ethic of love.

Maslow describes goodness as a *being-value* (a *metaneed*) rather than a *deficit value* (a *deficiency need*). Maslow's (1971) list of *metaneeds* or *being-values* include *beauty*, *goodness*, *playfulness*, and *truth*. Hierarchically arranged physiological, safety, belongingness and love, and esteem needs are subsumed under *deficit needs.* We cannot become self-actualizing – making optimal use of our competencies, talents, and potentials, until these lower-level needs have been satisfied to a sufficient degree. "The highest [*being*] motive," Maslow (1970) wrote, "is to be unmotivated and nonstriving" (p. 135). In other words, self-actualizing persons do not strive for the ultimate requiredness of goodness (the highest good) in living. They simply *mature* into it. Goodness for Maslow (1971) refers to characteristics such as benevolence, desirability, honesty, justice, oughtness, rightness, and uprightness.

Being-values, such as beauty, goodness, and truth, Fuller reminds us (1990), are "meanings that are especially pure and excellent" (p. 151). That is why they are the highest in Maslow's hierarchy of needs. These are needs worthy of living by. The *metaneeds* or *metamotives* of beauty, goodness, and truth are essential attributes of existential reality. Fuller deems "Maslow" as being "at one with phenomenology" (p. 155). "All in all," Fuller concludes, "self-actualization consists in an ability possessed by some to coactualize or co-organize certain lifeworld meanings: to discover, cherish, embody, and spread Being values" (p. 155).

References

Alford, C. F. (1997). *What evil means to us*. Cornell University Press.
Bollas, C. (2011). *The Christopher Bollas reader*. Routledge.
Dickens, C. (2001). *Great expectations*. Modern Library.
Frankland, A. G. (2010). *The little psychotherapy book: Object relations in practice*. Oxford University Press.
Frost, R. (1965). *Selected poems of Robert Frost*. Holt, Rinehart and Winston.
Hannush, M. J. (2002). *Becoming good parents: An existential journey*. State University of New York Press.
Kellerman, H. (2014). *Psychoanalysis of evil: Perspectives on destructive behavior*. Springer.
Levine, D. P. (2013). *The capacity for ethical conduct: On psychic existence and the way we relate to others*. Routledge.
Lifton, R. J. (1993). *The protean self: Human resilience in an age of fragmentation*. The University of Chicago Press.
Maslow, A. H. (1970). *Motivation and personality* (2nd ed.). Harper and Row.
Maslow, A. H. (1971). *The farther reaches of human nature*. Viking.
May, R. (1969). *Love and will*. Dell.
May, R. (1972). *Power and innocence*. W. W. Norton.
May, R. (1985). *My quest for beauty*. Saybrook.

McWilliams, N. (2004). *Psychoanalytic psychotherapy: A practitioner's guide*. Guildford.
Reeves, C. (1977). *The psychology of Rollo May*. Jossey-Bass.
Ricoeur, P. (1966). *Freedom and nature: The voluntary and the involuntary*. Northwestern University Press.
Ricoeur, P. (1967). *The symbolism of evil*. Beacon Press.
Ricoeur, P. (1986). *Fallible man*. Fordham University Press.
Ricoeur, P. (1995). *Figuring the sacred*. Fortress.
Staub, E. (2003). *The psychology of good and evil: Why children, adults, and groups help and harm others*. Cambridge University Press.

10

Kindness: The Capacity for *Kindness*

Evolutionary psychology focuses on the biological origin of kindness and traces its roots to within-group survival. Our ancestors who were reciprocally kind to each other were more likely to survive and pass their genes to their progeny than those who shunned such reciprocity. Siassi (2015), reflecting the contemporary intersubjective and object-relations view, traces the origin of kindness to the early mother-infant relationship. Becoming kind results from identifying with and internalizing the good (loving) mother. Having tasted nurturance, the child is naturally inclined to reciprocate nurturance with his mother. A former graduate student of mine once showed me a photograph of herself as a very young child captured in the act of lovingly spoon-feeding her father. The child who is properly cared for, nurtured, and loved by a kindly mother is poised to reciprocate these feelings of care, nurturance, and love. In short, kind parents tend to beget kind children. The child is not only positioned to be kind to her mother/parents but this kindness generalizes naturally toward others. Moreover, the child becomes kind toward herself or himself. Her or his kindness modulates the potential harshness of her or his evolving conscience. Moreover, this kind disposition reduces the need for taking refuge in compensatory defensiveness. Described differently, kindness inclines us to become less defensive or non-defensive in our relational interactions. It makes us aware of our interdependence with others. Using Kleinian language, Siassi concludes by stating that it is the *balance* between the identified with and internalized goodness of the mother *and* the identified with and internalized badness (destructiveness) of the mother – a *balance in favor goodness*, that makes it possible for us to metabolize and tolerate the ambivalence

© The Author(s), under exclusive license to Springer Nature Switzerland AG 2021
M. J. Hannush, *Markers of Psychosocial Maturation*,
https://doi.org/10.1007/978-3-030-74315-4_10

of our loves and hates, to become soft enough to be forgiving and kind enough to be gentle toward ourselves and others.

"Kindness," state Phillips and Taylor (2009), "is the ability to bear the vulnerability of others, and therefore of oneself … Prioritizing the needs of others" is one of its essential elements (p. 8). "Bearing other people's vulnerability," they continue, "means sharing in it imaginatively and practically" (p. 11). The "kind life," they add, "[is] the life lived in instinctive sympathetic identification with the vulnerabilities and attractions of others" (p. 4). Phillips and Taylor equate kindness with "fellow feeling" (p. 48; p. 49), "identification with other people's sufferings and pleasures" (p. 49), "imaginative capacity to identify with other people" (p. 52), "being sympathetic to others" (p. 49; p. 51), "generosity" (p. 50; p. 59), "tenderness" (p. 51), "realistic care and reassurance" (p. 56), "being considerate, thoughtful, [and] sensitive" (p. 70), "regard and consideration" (p. 82), reciprocal empathy between self and others (p. 95), "caring about others" (p. 95), "sympathetic attachments" (p. 95), "sympathy and cooperation" (p. 97), concern for the well-being of others (p. 108), "engaged concern" (p. 109), and healthy reciprocal dependencies between self and others, where autonomy, independence, or self-sufficiency is *balanced with* and is made possible by our need to depend on others.

We have, state Phillips and Taylor (2009), "an innate need for other people as purveyors and objects of kindness" (p. 96). We also have an innate disposition toward aggression and cruelty. Because of our evolutionary heritage, we are wired for both kindness and cruelty. "Kindness comes naturally to us, but so too does cruelty and aggression … Human beings … are ambivalent creatures" (p. 105).

"In one sense," Phillips and Taylor (2009) elaborate, "kindness is always hazardous because it is based on a susceptibility to others, a capacity to identify with their pleasures and sufferings" (p. 5). Though involving a risky exchange, kindness "is fundamental to our sense of well-being" (p. 6). In contemporary culture, however, kindness:

> is incidentally praised while being implicitly discouraged. Kindness … has become a sign of weakness (except of course among saintly people, in whom it is a sign of their exceptionality) … we have become phobic of kindness in our societies, avoiding obvious acts of kindness and producing, as we do with phobias, endless rationalizations to justify our avoidance … [There is a] widespread modern suspicion of kindness: that it is either a higher form of selfishness … or the lowest form of weakness … And what, after all, can kindness help us win, except moral approval; or not even that, in a society where 'respect' for personal status has become a leading value … Most people growing up now, secretly

> believe that kindness is a virtue of losers. But agreeing to talk about winners and losers is part and parcel of phobic avoidance, the contemporary terror of kindness. (pp. 8–9)

Yet, "children begin their lives 'naturally' kind, and ... something happens to this kindness as they grow up in contemporary society" (p. 11). As they grow up, these children, especially male children, learn to equate being kind – being caring, compassionate, and nurturing, with being a loser.

Kindness, which allows us to identify with the joys and sorrows of others and which comes naturally to how mature parents and their children relate to each other, expound Phillips and Taylor (2009), has become a forbidden pleasure. It is becoming more and more difficult to be kind and to practice kindness while living in a hyper-individualistic, hyper-materialistic, and hyper-competitive culture. New-age exhortations for the practice of loving-kindness repeated in well-selling self-help books and weekend retreats sound decontextualized, hollow, sentimental, and wishful despite the best of intentions. The capacity for kindness, a marker of psychosocial maturation, is hard to practice in a culture that is developmentally in its immature adolescent phase – a culture that is unhealthily narcissistic, unrealistically optimistic, and "innocently" blind to its vulnerability to finitude.

We pay so much attention to sentimentalized and idealized versions of love, but not enough to kindness. "Love," say Phillips and Taylor (2009), "never seems to deliver what we want it to do. Love never works as magic, but it can work as kindness" (p. 60). And "only by taking sexuality [love] and aggression [hatred] seriously," continue Phillips and Taylor, can one "begin to take kindness seriously (that is without sentimentalizing it)" (p. 67). "The origins of self-hatred [aggression turned inward]," for example, "are often to be found in failures of kindness" (p. 60).

It helps greatly if we are fortunate enough to carry with us embodied memories of kindness. Because these embodied memories are modes of communication and relatedness – as in a kind gesture – we are then more inclined to engage in general acts of self-kindness and kindness to others. Genuine, as opposed to soppy and wishful, kindness requires not only nurturance, a facilitating environment, but also cultivation in relational contexts. Mature kindness is manifested in the capacity to resist becoming unkind in response to the unkindness of others and to living in a seemingly unkind culture. Neither does one succumb, in a defensive posture, to presenting a false façade of a saccharin kindly self in an effort to ward off repressed and unacceptable feelings of rage-evoking resentment and predispositions toward acts of cruelty and destructiveness.

Intimate partners become forgetful of their love for each other when embroiled in a heated, hatred-triggering conflict. The same loved other becomes re-configured into a hated other. Pushed to one's limits, the eradication of the irreplaceable "I-ness" of one partner would relieve the other partner. It behooves each partner, then, to calmly recollect one's love for the Other in the midst of a heatedly hate-inducing collision. Phillips and Taylor would say that love and hate are simply too close to each other. The inference is that it would be very difficult to summon love in the midst of hate. It would be more prudent and less daunting to summon up kindness.

For Phillips and Taylor (2009), kindness is an essential *integrative* element in all kinds of relations at different levels of intensity. In other words, if I can be kind in diverse relations, then my kindness will be the common denominator that contributes to my intrapersonal and interpersonal integration.

Again, even though kindness is risky because it involves the bearing of the receptive other's as well as our own vulnerability, it is a conduit for our potential transformation, growth, well-being, and happiness – better yet, our relative contentment. "So," comment Phillips and Taylor (2009):

> it is not that real kindness requires people to be selfless, it is rather that real kindness changes people in the doing of it, often in unpredictable ways. Real kindness is an exchange with essentially unpredictable consequences. It is a risk precisely because it mingles our needs and desires with the needs and desires of others, in a way that so-called self-interest never can … Kindness is a way of knowing people beyond our understanding of them … Kindness is potentially far more promiscuous than sexuality. (p. 13)

When I am kind to you, the possibility of a creative exchange between us increases. Whereas self-interest precludes discovery, say Phillips and Taylor (2009), kindness opens us for new discoveries. Among other things, through kindness, we discover the "pleasures" of feeling and acting upon our concern for others. This is why, as parents and as a society, we should never deprive our children from "one of the greatest sources of human happiness" (p. 14). The "child," they point out, "needs the adult and his wider society to help him keep faith with his kindness, that is, to help him discover and enjoy the pleasures of caring for others" (p. 13).

Kindness, observe Phillips and Taylor (2009), "is a developmental achievement. In short, only an adult, who has learned to bear frustration, is capable of putting the needs of someone else before his own" (p. 49). There are degrees in the maturation of our capacity for kindness. Even though kindness comes naturally to mature parents and their children, this kind of kindness has to be cultivated, refined, and ripened. Kindness will not fully ripen until parents and children learn to accept the worst about each other. This is true of all other kinds of relationships. We are kind, continue Phillips and Taylor, because we want or desire to and not because we have to. "Whereas kindness as desire, as something integral to what desiring is, is irresistible. Ordered to be kind, we are likely to be cruel; wanting to be kind, we are likely to discover our generosity" (p. 50). We are likely to experience the pleasure of being kind, for kindness links us to our fellow human beings – our kin. "Fellow feeling joins us to various and diverse other people. Kindness is extravagant" (p. 51).

"Ordinary kindness," elaborate Phillips and Taylor (2009), "is not a manipulative bribe or a magical cure [aimed at rescuing the Other], but rather a simple [intimate] exchange. In a parent-child relationship where no one is looking to the other to rescue him, each can enjoy the other without needing to transform him" (p. 56). The adults are not looking to the child to become the parent and look after their well-being. When this arrangement inevitably fails, they end up feeling needy, vulnerable, frightened, frustrated, disappointed, enraged, and enslaved. In other words, the adult parents are not expecting the child to be committed to "magical kindness – to the avoidance of frustration at all costs – [in this endeavor] parents can only fail" (p. 57). Parents who expect magical kindness from their children are reversing the order of dependencies and thus are "unable to collaborate in the ordinary business of growing up" (p. 56).

We humans, expand Phillips and Taylor (2009), are naturally desiring of kindness. But this desire can go awry. When our needs, including the need to be needed, are not optimally met we construct defenses to protect ourselves, to get crumbs of conditional love, to survive. "What Freud called defenses are the ways we protect ourselves from our desires which are also our relations with others" (p. 57). We can learn as male children, for example, to silence our desire to be kind in order to appropriate a tough persona that is desired by our fathers and our culture. As we grow older we separate tenderness from sexuality and focus on performance and conquest. Our original desire to engage in kindly sensuality becomes usurped. "If kindness … is at the heart of human desiring [then even sex] … becomes one of the more complicated forms of fellow feeling (there is no sex without kindness or its refusal)" (p. 57).

Ironically, comment Phillips and Taylor (2009), the more rare kindness becomes in our culture, the more obsessed we become with parenting. "Talking about child development and about parents may be one of the only ways we have now of talking about fellow feeling [or kindness]" (p. 52). Maturing or "growing up, if anything, is the imaginative elaboration of fellow feeling; the acknowledgment that other people have what we need and their well-being matters to us" (p. 53). Our ultimate failures are "failures of kindness" (p. 60). Conversely, our ultimate successes are successes in kindness – kindly love, kindly care, kindly concern, kindly respect, and so on. We become unkind to ourselves and/or others when we are deprived of the kindly care, concern, and respect of essential others. Our unkindness is a protective, survival-seeking response to the threat or actual loss of kindness. In the process we become alienated, disjointed, isolated, and imprisoned. Kindness or "fellow feeling … [is] what holds people together and what keeps people together" (pp. 66–67). Only by taking love and hate seriously can we begin to take kindness seriously. In other words, mature kindness goes hand-in-hand with the cultivation of the capacity for loving wisely which in turn enables us to contain our proclivities for hostility and harmful hate. "Kindness," reflect Phillips and Taylor (2009), "entails the acknowledgement of hatred. It is kind to see people as they are and not as one would like them to be" (p. 90).

Genuine kindness, emphasize Phillips and Taylor (2009), is a developmental accomplishment. It is to be distinguished from "magical kindness." The latter is evidenced by the "love bribe" that children offer their parents. "The child cares for his parents so that they care for him; his 'kindness' is a magical wishing-away of any anxiety or unhappiness that might interfere with parental solicitude" (p. 109). Genuine kindness emerges from the failure of magical kindness. Authentic or real kindness not only accommodates our conflicts and cruelties but also delivers "the pleasure of mutual enjoyment and exchange" (p. 110). Mature-enough parents help their children make the developmental transition from magical to true or genuine kindness. They do not fear ambivalence. They do not seek to be rescued from it. Rather, they contain it. And just as parents can "prevent this authentic kindness from developing … so, too, can a society that denigrates kindness as weakness, and rewards unkindness" (p. 110). Real kindness does not involve wishing away our aggressive and hateful impulses "in favor of selfless dedication to others" as proselytized by new-age gurus and weekend motivational speakers. "Real kindness 'enlarges' us, and so gratifies our profoundly social natures" (p. 110).

Authentic parental kindness accommodates children's aggressiveness, hatred, and hostility. What makes the relation between children and parents "feel real" is the cultivation of the ability to live through the aroused hatred without damaging their relationship to each other. When children or parents get inevitably frustrated as a consequence of their dealings with each other, they feel hatred toward each other. They both need to survive this fleeting mutual hatred. Good-enough parents do not abandon the frustrated-and-hating child. The parents are able to survive the onslaughts of their hateful child. They are able to move on. The child does not retreat from real engagement and stop making demands. The parents do not turn away from him, withdrawing their love or coercively impose their will upon the will of the child. Good-enough parents, wisely, attempt to coordinate their will with the will of the child. Through this coordination they negotiate their way to a more realistic relationship. "Kindness of this variety," comment Phillips and Taylor (2009), "allow for ambivalence and conflict while false, or magical kindness distorts our perceptions of other people, often by sentimentalizing them, to avoid conflict. Sentimentality is cruelty by other means" (p. 91). "Love," they continue, "freed from hate kills fellow feeling [or kindness]" (p. 92). Authentic kindness absorbs ambivalence. It endures conflict in oneself and others. It takes genuine kindness to care for others as they are.

Although being kind makes us feel good, it also endangers us. It puts us at risk. It makes us vulnerable. "It is kindness," however, "that makes us grow … and growing up is what we want to do" (Phillips & Taylor, 2009, p. 81). Though innate, our predisposition toward kindness needs cultivation in caring contexts. Kindness "easily gets lost in growing up; and this … loss, when it occurs on a wide enough scale, is a cultural disaster" (p. 109). There is a mental, physical, and relational price to be paid for becoming forgetful of our "openheartedness" or, what the philosopher David Hume calls, the movements of our heart. Following the philosopher Jean-Jacques Rousseau, we can say that kindness is a natural extension of our self-love and that through kindness we give expression to our vitality. Through kindness we extend our being, the joy of being alive, to others. There is something deeply gratifying about experiencing the "beneficial difference" that kindness makes in our lives. Kindness makes us more hopeful: "kindness, fundamentally, makes life worth living … [it] demonstrates, in the clearest possible way, that we are vulnerable and dependent animals who have no better resource than each other" (p. 113). We need each other's assurance and reassurance to maintain our "sense of viability."

Acts of kindness, conclude Phillips and Taylor (2009), are not "to be seen as acts of will or effort or moral resolution" (p. 114). Rather, kindness comes from "a revived awareness of something that is already felt and known" (p. 114). It is an extension of our natural inclination "to include ourselves with others," to be "in solidarity" with others.

"The negotiations of reciprocity," states Fiumara (2013), "are often based on our unpretentious capacity to be kind, in the sense that processes of repair can only function in an atmosphere of kindness – indeed an essential catalyst for interpersonal arrangements" (p. 30). Conflicts can spiral out of control with catastrophic consequences in the absence of the "metabolite – kindness."

It is the kindness of others that makes not only our conflicts solvable but also our pains and sorrows bearable.

Genuine (mature) kindness entails accepting of the good-and-bad within ourselves and in others. "It means," continues Fiumara (2013), "embracing the 'saint' and the 'demon' in the other person. But a [mature] 'kindness' that embraces the shadows requires a slow blossoming over years; this is the real measure of our [creative] adventures with one another" (p. 71). Paradoxically, even our capacities for sympathy and empathy can be viewed as predispositions to acts of kindness. Sympathy is a form of "weak kindness" that serves the purpose of engagement in "short" relational moves in which we respond to the similarity between our selves and others. Empathy, in contradistinction to sympathy, serves the purpose of engagement in "extensive" and "creative" relational moves in which we respond to "the difference-bearing features of others" (p. 71).

For Fiumara (2013), kindness and *creativity*, the ability to connect seemingly unconnected domains, go hand-in-hand. The "capacity to link alien domains," she says, "requires an atmosphere of kindness" (p. 74). The common denominator between kindness and creativity is that both are "inclusionary ventures." Kind people are creative because they are inclusive of seemingly foreign elements or dimensions within themselves, and their kindness is inclusive of seemingly different others. They do not restrict their kindness for people who are seemingly similar to them. Fiumara (2013) elaborates:

> But of course kindness makes us seriously vulnerable. Vulnerability is the acceptance of more and more elements to process. If we do not process them we just do not perceive them and exclusion becomes automatic – as if forclusion [sic] were established as a rule … But then, even if the capacity to include may make us vulnerable, perhaps we have more to gain from vulnerability than from exclusionary control. (p. 75)

Even if kindness makes us vulnerable, we need to "take on, to almost welcome, our own turbulence. It is the capacity to be disturbed by our own feelings and to be nourished by the disturbance that [promotes a deeper sanity]" (p. 75). "And thus," she continues, "sanity [or well-being] rests on the patience to connect things and to endure the connection. This is the talent for making patience a creative asset" (p. 76).

We not only can speak in a kindly manner, intones Fiumara (2013), but can also listen in a kindly way, both of which are creative acts. Kindly listening is creative listening in that it is potentially transformative and healing to the recipient who takes in and digests the kindness of the other openheartedly.

This is why, she adds, even traumatized individuals may be enabled to metabolize, or to cycle, their trauma when they are surrounded by the supportive presence and kindly listening of essential others. They are able "to get hold of their shaken personality once again" (p. 92).

"Kindness," expands Fiumara (2013):

> is a form of care that can unfold in the here and now, and that can start at any moment of life; and, of course, we can be kind to others as well as to our own self. Kindness can be an immediate response that sustains any variety of caring ventures and that can instantly function in virtually all interpersonal circumstances; one can be kind in the job of arresting a person, or rude in sexual relations. Kindness is an immediate response; it is to be caring in the here and now … The capacity to kindly bear with the vulnerability of others, and of ourselves [needs to be regarded as a character strength] … To be capable of psychic care in the here and now we must be creative enough to maintain an atmosphere of kindness. … kindness … [is a] pleasure that is fundamental to our sense of well-being. (p. 99)

"Consciousness," concludes Fiumara (2013), "is ultimately the product of kindly creative action" (p. 93). Two points need to be mentioned in response to this concluding statement. First, it is *transformed* or *enlarged* consciousness, and not any consciousness, that is the byproduct of "kindly creative action." Second, there is a circular and not linear relationship between the expansion of consciousness and kindly creative action. Our consciousness is broadened as we habitually engage in kindly creative action and our newly broadened consciousness predisposes us to engage in further kindly creative action. Our habitual acts of kindness are at the same time contributing to the co-creation of a kindly habitat.

Hamrick (2002), using the "phenomenological method," attempts to decipher the "nodal points" that make up the essential meanings of the phenomenon of kindness as it "appears" or experienced (lived) in everyday life. By elucidating the essential meanings of kindness, it is hoped that our lives become not only more "more readable" but also more kindly.

Being a phenomenologist, Hamrick (2002) eschews approaching the phenomenon of kindness in the abstract. Instead he focuses on "the bodied nature of kindness" (p. 16). His aim is to describe "the manifold ways in which kindness appears to us – its unique manner of existing – through bodily actions and omissions to act" (p. 3). He wants to show how our "bodily gestures take on the weight of commitment in kind and unkind relationships with others" (p. xxvi). From the beginning, Hamrick is grounding our kindly and unkindly acts or omissions (inactions) in our bodily and inter-bodily ways of being-in-the-world-with-others – in our gesturing-relational-selves. This is why we are constructed to be exquisitely attuned to the kind or unkind gestures of the Other, beginning with our mother's gesturing face – "the gleam in the mother's eyes." "Kindness," points out Hamrick, "is in the gesture or the speech act just as immediately as is love or joy, with which it often overlaps" (p. 14). Prereflectively and preverbally, our bodies "resonate and respond to the real presence of kindness (and unkindness)" (p. 15). Having gazed into our mother's kind eyes, we are deeply sensitized to detecting the kindness (or unkindness) in the eyes of the Other.

Hamrick (2002) distinguishes between kind acts and "kind omissions to act." There are times when our kindnesses shine through our "omissions to act," which are another type of kindly action. We choose on occasions not to act out of consideration for the welfare of others. But what kind acts of commission and omission have in common is that they must be *intentional* (purposeful), *voluntary*, thus involving our "motivated freedom," and have a *vector quality*: "the actions are done *for* a certain person" (p. 8). An act of kindness, continues Hamrick, "embodies a sensitivity to the need of the other and a resolve to attempt to remedy the need" (p. 8). Being kind means taking interest in and contributing to the other's welfare and "actively seeking the other's … flourishing" (p. 9). I as the recipient of a kindly act realize that my need has registered in the person being kind to me and that s/he is extending assistance to me with care, concern, humility, and gratitude.

To summarize so far, kind acts and omissions are "invested with a motivated freedom, purpose, and sensitivity to my welfare" (p. 21).

In synchrony with a major thesis of our text, like maturity, kindness, for Hamrick (2002), comes in degrees. Correlating kindness to (social) "sensitivity," he states that kind "actions [or omissions] teach us that there are not only corresponding degrees of [social] sensitivity to our welfare but also the resolve to act on those sensitivities" (p. 9). Good Samaritans, for example, can appear to us as "minimally good," "very good," and "splendid." Kindness can manifest itself to us in degrees of considerateness and warm-heartedness. We encounter little or big kindnesses in our daily lives.

To emphasize, kind actions and omissions have our accurate-and-ultimate welfare in mind. This is why, Hamrick (2002) hastens to add, kindness *overlaps* with, but needs to be distinguished from, niceness, courteousness, and gentleness. "Kindness may overlap these qualities, but the connection is always contingent" (p. 22). Parenting provides us with an excellent example. There are times when as a parent I may find myself being not so nice, courteous, or gentle with my child because I am reading her or his needs accurately and I have her or his ultimate welfare in mind. Such instances may sometimes be subsumed under the inflated label of "tough love." Niceness can simply be a manifestation of an internalized cultural script or "can serve as a cover for repressed hostility" (p. 23). Further, "socially constructed niceness … [can be] deeply unkind to both boys and girls, as well as to men and women" (p. 23). I can be gentle, yet indifferent to the pain and suffering of others. An act of kindness can therefore be hurtful to its recipient in an immediate sense, but not harmful in its mediate, long-term consequence for it has the ultimate welfare of the Other in mind.

Above and beyond describing "the phenomenology of kindness" as involving "the habitual performance of kind acts," Hamrick (2002) holds, "there are at least three other qualities that are also essential to being a kind person. These are (1) an active disposition to leading a life of kindness, where possible; (2) a warm generosity; and (3) self-mastery" (p. 33). Let us go over the three characteristics of personal kindness.

1. We do not acquire a disposition toward kindness "through will power, decision making, and conscience alone," says Hamrick (2002); we develop it "through doing kind acts that eventually sediment themselves in this habitual character trait" (p. 75). A kind individual displays a proactive readiness to be of service to others. An existential awareness of our human fragility, vulnerability, and finitude sensitizes us to the suffering of others and consolidates our compassion into kindness. We identify with the plight of our human family. We respond to the call of sympathetic and empathic participation in the lives of others. "This appeal is a calling … for responsibility – answering the call – a disposition to kindness as the capacity for compassion" (p. 36). We commit ourselves responsibly to compassionate action. We open ourselves to the "bond of human solidarity." The "disposition to perform kind acts," continues Hamrick, "originates not in an intellectually constituting consciousness but in an intuitively reasoned feeling that gets expressed in various modes of attunement to the world" (p. 42).
2. Guided by the philosophy of Gabriel Marcel, Hamrick (2002) correlates *warm generosity* to "pure charity." "It is that by which I am 'available' to, 'at the disposal (disponsible) of' the other … [It is being] at the service of the other" (p. 44). Our warm generosity is grounded in our openness to life, in our active receptivity to the Other. It is fueled by the core existential affect of hope. "Hope is … a dynamic, joyful commitment to the other. It creates a concrete relationship with the other that is a 'permeability' in and though which we 'participate' in each other's being" (pp. 44–45). Listening

> can be a way of generous giving. Even smiling can mirror a warm generosity. Ultimately, kindness can be viewed as a life project, a project freely chosen requiring "creative fidelity" and commitment to human solidarity. This kind of kindness can manifest itself not only in "I-Thou" (after Martin Buber) or "I-**You**" (where the "You" is a variation on the "I," another me) encounters, but more commonly in ordinary, functional "I-**y**ou" encounters such as our contacts with "letter carriers, doctors, teachers, store clerks, and the like" (p. 47). Kindness, therefore, can coexist with seemingly objectifying functional roles. Kindness can also coexist with the partial or intermittent objectification and aesthetic appreciation of the body of our intimate partner in sexual encounters. Our kindness can manifest itself in our sexuality.

By "warm," as in "warm generosity," Hamrick (2002) means "genuineness of feeling inscribed in a commitment of service to the other" (p. 50). Warm generosity exudes "a real presence, a strong impression of the persons themselves embodied in the act [of kindness]" (p. 51). The "how" is just as important as the "what" of an act of kindness. "Generosity" is interwoven with attunement to the welfare of the other, benevolence, care, concern, thoughtfulness, love, and magnanimity. "In both look and word, the face of the kind other expresses warm generosity in terms of welcome, peace, and hospitality" (p. 52). The "concern of the kind person" holds Hamrick, is "both to remedy needs and to express a positive desire to enhance the other's flourishing" (p. 53). "In assuming this responsibility, borrowing Marcel's language, I 'participate in the being of the Other … to make the stranger, the widow, the orphan – in brief, the injurable Other – 'at home'" (pp. 53–54). My hospitality toward the Other speaks the voice of my *caring conscience*. "The authentic self is centered on others to whom, and for whom, it finds itself responsible" (p. 54). The Other is experienced by me as reversible. He or she could be me. He or she is equal to me. Responsibility or response-ability "is assigned to me by the other, from the other" (p. 54). "I bear the trace of the other within me (and vice versa) – in my flesh" (p. 55). This *calling for response-ability* is a bodily felt feeling that is inscribed in my flesh – my bodily-being-in-the-world-with-others. It awakens my nascent predisposition of being-for-the-Other. Using the language of Emanuel Levinas, the "animation, the very pneuma of the psyche, alterity in identity, is the identity of a body exposed to the other, becoming 'for the other,' the possibility of giving" (p. 69). The developmental genesis of this can be traced to the inter-bodily mutuality, the nonverbal communication and communion, between mother-and-child. Granted, the balance of reciprocity between the nascent, emerging self of the child and the mother is initially weighted in the direction of the mature mother at this early stage of life. The mother welcomes the solicitations of her child and offers him her solicitude.

It is through this maternal (or simply parental) solicitude that the child's nascent self experiences valuation and worthiness:

> Solicitude is thus internal to self-esteem, because [quoting Paul Ricoeur] it 'unfolds the dialogic dimension of self-esteem … self-esteem and solicitude cannot be experienced or reflected upon without the other' … As a result, there is a dialectic between my own self-esteem and my ability to esteem others, and this creates an equivalence between 'the esteem of the *other as oneself* and the esteem of *oneself as an other*.' (Hamrick, 2002, p. 60)

From the early beginnings of the life cycle, the seeds of child's self-esteem lie in being esteemed by the mother, in the solicitations of the child, and in the welcoming solicitude of the mother, as an essential other. In turn, the primitive loving and solicitous gestures of the child toward the mother affirm the mother's self-esteem. Through solicitude, the mother is attuned to the needs of her child. She is actively seeking the welfare of her child. *Kindness is born of solicitude.*

3. In describing the final essential characteristic of personal kindness, Hamrick (2002) uses "self-mastery," "self-restraint," and "self-withdrawal" interchangeably (pp. 62–63). Acts of kindness or "kind interventions imply some necessary restraint" (p. 63). In order to "take the other's place" or imagine the other's patterns of thoughts and feelings I must undergo a process of "self-transposal." I need to "adopt the whole case" of the other. "In a non-dominating, non-manipulative way, one can slip unobtrusively into the role of facilitating the project of the injured person" (p. 65). Kind people are able and willing "to act for the welfare of the other through imaginative self-transposal" (p. 66). For this to happen, I need to *bracket* my egoistic, impositional self. I need to refrain from coercing the other to talk my talk and walk my walk. I need to avoid imposing my lexicon on him or her. I must not act like "parents who wish to relive their childhoods through their children and hence attempt to understand the latter [their children] in terms of their own criteria and expectations of happiness" (p. 67). I have to divest myself of those parts of my life that are not central to my core selfhood. "This task of 'radical and conscientious abstraction ["bracketing"] from one's own personality' is clearly difficult. It requires a … [process of] coming to detach ourselves from the ways we normally ["naturally"] live" (p. 68). In order to transpose my self I need to experi-

> ence a special kind of *presence-and-absence* at the same time. My improper absence will manifest itself through being uninvolved or coldhearted. My improper presence will reveal itself through being controlling, dominating, imposing, intrusive, and manipulative.

> In contrast, the truly kind person offers us a model of intervening in the lives of others while at the same time refusing to transfer her own mental baggage. Kindness is a way of knowing the other as other, because it requires both closeness and distance, proximity and tactful differentiation, compassionate intervention and appropriate withdrawal. (pp. 68–69)

Using the language of the English novelist George Eliot (1819–1880), kindness is a form of *self-forgetful goodness.* "The appropriate presence and absence of self … [forms] the core of discretion" (p. 69). The "appropriate absence of self in acts of kindness, also implies a positive sense of knowing one's own limitations" (p. 69). Self-restraint or "self-withdrawal also consists of self-imposed limits on the 'occupation' of the other's life" (p. 69). In other words, I need to retract after taking the position or viewpoint of the other. I need to maintain my "own position beyond the other while imaginatively shifting back and forth between us" (p. 70). To be kind is to attach. However, "it is possible to be attached too much and to remain too long" (p. 70). Ties can not only "connect but also violently bind" (p. 70). A *balance* needs to be maintained between the centripetal force of self-directedness (self-contentment, self-gratification, self-enhancement) and the centrifugal force of other-directedness (enhancing the flourishing of the other, meeting the other's true needs, contributing to the other's genuine welfare). When I am centripetally self-absorbed (overly self-involved), I do not see, feel, touch-and-be-touched by the other. When I am centrifugally other-involved (overinvolved), I try to mold the other in my own image. I am inclined to control, colonize (take over), dominate, or totalize (objectify) the other.

"Self-transposal and its necessary complement of self-withdrawal," Hamrick (2002) tells us, "are also crucial in understanding the feeling bonds uniting the kind person with other" (p. 75). Self-withdrawal enhances our fellow-feeling, our "emotional identification" with others. And this in turn, in a circular fashion, motivates us to continue being kind. "Fellow-feeling is not emotional fusion" (p. 76). Becoming hyper-kind will leave us depleted. A *balancing* "rhythmic alternation" between self-and-other directedness is needed here.

> Kindness, like all forms of knowing the other as other, embodies and requires intelligently purposive feelings that conjugate similarity with difference, closeness with distance, proximity with tactful differentiation, unity with diversity, and compassionate intervention with appropriate withdrawal. Both halves of the *dialectic* are inscribed in empathy that, in our chiasmatic relationships with the other, is the crucial epistemological hinge on which kindness turns ... In empathic experience, self-transposal modulates activity and passivity as it moves between one half of the chiasm and the other. (p. 79)

Is it our duty, the reader may ask, to be kind to those with an ugly, unattractive, or unkind character? Hamrick (2002) agrees, "kindness and duty are not necessarily disjuncts" (p. 74). He is also in agreement "that we have a duty to try anyway to perform kind actions toward the unattractive until we determine the effort to be 'fruitless'... The reason is that such acts raise 'the mere beneficent disposition of the will to a higher degree of excellence' and make it more effective" (p. 74).

Kindness can flow from empathy, but *mature empathy* requires good judgment. It involves, notes Hamrick (2002), "*bracketing* one's own frame of reference while opening oneself up to a foreign point of view ... [It requires] assessing the appropriateness of another's joy, sorrow, anger, anxiety, and so on" (p. 80). Kindness makes responsibility possible. Then again, I would add, responsibility makes discerning kindness possible. We "can be both kind and unkind to ourselves" and to others (p. 87). "Kindness is an accomplishment rather than a given, because it requires not only the right sort of disposition but also a factual understanding of the external circumstances that we wish to arrange to our purposes" (p. 88). Simply stated, discerning kindness requires practical wisdom. Such discerning kindness, for instance, "prevents us from being too kind" (p. 88). There are contexts that call forth unreflective acts of kindness based on unreserved availability. There are other (ambiguous) contexts that call upon us to be judicious observers prior to participation in an act of kindness. These uncertain circumstances call on us to be inventive in our charitableness. They may make us meditate "on the relation between happiness and suffering" (p. 91). They may engage us in a reflection on the relation between ethics (of care) and morality (of justice). Or they may make us dwell on the question of how to fail or succeed at *being human*. Lastly, empathic acts of kindness are moored in our "primordial physical and emotional well-being in which is already inscribed the presence of other people" (p. 93). In line with the thought of Maurice Merleau-Ponty (1962), we are all, potentially, reversible and inter-corporeal. Pre-reflectively, I experience the Other as another me and vice versa.

Importantly, Hamrick (2002) makes a distinction between naïve kindness – the kind that can be "corrupted by exploitative power" (p. 237) and "critical kindness" or what I prefer to call *discerning kindness*. The exploitation of kindness, he tells us, can take place on personal, interpersonal, and social levels:

> On an interpersonal plane, my act(s) of kindness to the other(s) can expose me to the risk of being used both directly and indirectly as a mere means to an end … For instance, an act of self-sacrificing kindness might enable that person [an aggressively competitive colleague] to secure advantages over me … On a social plane, there are also various forms of direct and indirect exploitation [by fraudulent or shiftless charities, institutions, or organizations] … [On a personal plane] I must also direct suspicion at myself. For just as I can be an unwitting victim of others, I can unwittingly [or self-deceptively] victimize them both directly and indirectly. Because of self-deception and the rationalizations that stem from them, like … the patriarchal husband, I can also misread myself and the facts … such misreadings stem from not viewing one's own actions from the point of view of the victim … [and/or] because successfully deceived victims do not know that they are victims … As a result, a commitment to avoid victimization entails a willingness to be suspicious of one's own motives even, or especially, if the other party does not. (pp. 238–239)

In the presence of discerning kindness we become realistically hopeful. An outlook of hope, observes Hamrick (2002), "clearly depends on the (re-) establishment of community, for which kindness in a multiplicity of social forms is a necessary condition" (p. xvii). "Contemplating acts of kindness," adds Hamrick, "likewise [as in a work of art] leads us out of our singularity and opens us to what is universally human" (p. 252). Kindness creates communion with our human kin. Witnessing an act of kindness we are moved through imaginative feelings of identification and participation. We are stirred and inspired to turn in the direction of our essential humanness.

Unlike Phillips and Taylor (2009), for whom kindness is amorally instinctive, Hamrick (2002) holds that kindness, like its "allied phenomena of hope, sympathy, and compassion," is a form of moral life that "requires combining the qualities of being a kind person" (p. 240). Conflict is of the essence of moral, let alone all of, life. The discerningly kind person holds together, while tolerating the tension, conflictual, contradictory, and opposing qualities. "Trust must be conjugated with suspicion, openness with closedness, the warmth of generosity with a cautious discipline, the readiness of *disponibilite* [availability] with unreadiness, and activity with passivity … [one possible] result: cautious trust, hesitant openness, a checked readiness, controlled activity" (p. 240). "Both sets of opposites must be kept, [in] tension with each other … This means that either side of a pair of opposites can prevail in a given situation" (p. 241). There are times, then, when I ought to not be kind. For instance, I should not be kind if I sense that my act of kindness will result in direct or indirect coercion or exploitation. I will refrain from being kind if I intuit that my kindness will very likely play into a harm-doer's hands. My availability and readiness to be kind are necessary but not sufficient conditions for *performing* acts of kindness. Similarly, there are times when I ought to refuse the apparently authentic kindness of others, for it too may place me in harm's way even though the intention was initially seemingly good.

It is the task of practical wisdom to mitigate the harm that can possibly be perpetrated upon the doer and/or recipient of the act of kindness. "Practical wisdom," holds Hamrick (2002), "serves as a principle of caution for translating that readiness and its generous warmth into effective ways to help others" (p. 241). The critically (discerningly) kind person, Hamrick tells us, is equipped with practical wisdom. Desiring to be kind may make me enthusiastic and may give me an anticipatory sense of communion with the other, but my practical wisdom offers me the "circumspection, directing control, and effectiveness" needed to discern the real welfare of the person I am attempting to help. My practical wisdom informs me whether the risk I am taking in being kind is reasonable or unreasonable. It reminds me, in general, to give "pride of place" to trust and not to suspicion. Yet, I need to keep both trust and suspicion in tension with each other and, thus, to tolerate the dialectical tension. Placing the weight on trust allows me to retain my care and concern for others and myself.

"The upshot here," Hamrick (2002) notes, "is that kindness is a regulative ideal" (p. 242). I will inevitably experience varying degrees of success in implementing it. Just because I am not always capable of living up to my guiding principle of kindness does not mean that I should cease attempting to bring it about.

There is "a certain type of decision making that is appropriate for this life of critical [discerning] kindness," adds Hamrick (2002, p. 242). It involves "making judgments about how to seek the greatest possible good for the other under the circumstances with the least possible harm" (p. 243). Although this kind of decision-making is guided by guidelines, rules, or "maxims," it has, as in all aesthetic projects, the qualities of integration, inventiveness, and creativity. The decision-making that goes into my acts of kindness helps me integrate my trusting self with my suspicious self. It enables me to transcend my other "polarized interests." It makes it possible for me to bind my wounds and prevents me from becoming alienated. It allows me to embrace other values such as "truth and justice and peace." It provides me with a sense wholeness and personal integrity. It fortifies me against fragmentation into a plethora of functions. It helps me balance "centripetal self-withdrawal by a centrifugal affirmation of myself as a totality of relationships through which I am at the disposal of others" (pp. 243–244).

Discerning kindness, involving good judgment and practical wisdom, clarifies and sharpens my mind. It refines my perception. It enables me to appreciate the good of the Other. It fine-tunes my social sensitivity. The "kind person," posits Hamrick (2002), "lives in the state of feeling attunement to the needs and desires of others" (p. 244). After all, "our flesh is already adapted for relationships" (p. 244). Discerning kindness further fosters our imaginative self and its capacities for empathy, mentalization, perspective taking, and sympathy. It acts as "a preventative for mental problems" (p. 244). Quoting the French phenomenological philosopher Mikel Dufrenne, Hamrick states: "In kindness, as in artistic creation, 'expression is the revelation of the self, simply because it causes us to actually *be* what it expresses'" (p. 245). Through acts of kindness not only is the self altered, but also, correlatively, the world is changed too. A "nimbus of kindness around the kind person … radiates a world of kindness" (p. 246). The world of the discerningly kind person is different from the world of the narcissistically unkind person. Kindness aestheticizes (beautifies) our world. A "life of kindness," holds Hamrick, "is analogous to aesthetic experience" (p. 250). Kindness makes it possible to relate *truth*fully to reality. Kindness moralizes our world. Life is better with kindness. Kindness makes us loving-and-loveable persons who dwell in a loving-and-loveable world. In short, Beauty, Goodness, and Truth are manifestations of kindness and vice versa.

Kindness, says Hamrick (2002), is a life "project of warmly generous service to the other" (p. 248). It is a project worthy of admiration and respect. The depth of our kindness correlates with the depth of our maturity. This depth "opens us up" and "broadens us." Agreeing with the British philosopher David Hume, Hamrick quotes the former stating that there is "'some particle of the dove kneaded into our frame, along with the elements of the wolf and serpent,'" and as a consequence our life project involves the "struggle to re-channel energies into acts of kindness that would have been invested in gaining power over others" (p. 248). This life project challenges us to keep our worst in check while pursuing the "fulfillment of our best possibilities" as human beings. Kindness makes it possible for me to *refine* my humanness. Kindness elevates and ennobles me. It valorizes my everyday actions. It brings *better and more meaning* into my wondrous world. It correlates not only with maturity but also with hope, which is a manifestation of maturity. Kindness as a way of being-in-the-world-with-others brings with it a deep sense of joy in being alive.

Being kind involves making a discerning judgment not only of the Other but also of the Self:

> That is, because acts of kindness honor both agent and recipient, and because kindness is a contingent quality of action for which the agent alone is responsible, kindness also serves as a criterion of self-assessment. But kindness has a wider moral significance, because it can serve as vehicle of self-judgment for those who observe others perform such acts. (Hamrick, 2002, p. 250)

Thus, the ability to be kind becomes a standard of self-evaluation. We are inclined to evaluate the kind other not only as worthy of admiration and respect, but also as a loveable other who is worthy of our love.

Not only is the proclivity toward kindness is prefigured in our bodily existence – in our gestural being, but "the possibility of community is already schematized in our flesh, and the self is solidary, not solitary" (Hamrick, 2002, p. 250). From the beginning our vitalizing bodily self tends toward communion, toward community, toward humanity. From the start, human co-presence is inscribed into our fleshly existence. Quoting the phenomenological sociologist Alfred Schutz, Hamrick notes that, as in the musical experience between listener and performer, there is, in kindness, a "'mutual tuning-in relationship' … by which 'the 'I' and the 'Thou' are experienced by both participants as a 'We' in vivid presence'" (p. 251). We identify with the performer by way of feelings of joyous participation or participatory joy. Contemplating kindness, as in contemplating great music to which we resonate and reverberate, "leads us out of singularity and opens us to what is universally human" (p. 252), as in Beethoven's Ode to Joy. "Here also," continues Hamrick, "we recognize the universally human within us and with and in others … Acts of kindness bring about a [sense] of communion … [and, quoting Marcel,] 'a fundamental existential assurance' that makes hope possible" (p. 252), a condition that allows us to be open to others.

As a discerningly kind person I realistically seek the good of the Other. *To serve with kindness* becomes my motto. I wish to "bring goodness into being" while at the same time remaining "suspicious" (what I call "cautious" in our dialectical model) and attuned to the limits of my situation. Tolerating the tension while doing so is no easy life task. Such a life project is made doubly difficult because, "it is paradoxically and deeply counter-cultural" (Hamrick, 2002, p. 253). Why?

> Our culture continues to stress hardness and toughness, it fosters distrust of anything that looks 'soft,' and mistakenly consigns kindness to that denigrated category. By the same token, it overlooks the real strength required to be kind. In addition, also ingrained in our culture is a radical individualism that … does not logically imply, but is much more congenial to, egoistic indifference [or narcissistic preoccupation, I might add] … The third reason that a life of kindness is counter-cultural is because it has become increasingly difficult to reach the depth of feelings that nourish kindness and that are necessary for an aesthetic humanism. (p. 254)

We live in a hedonistically "juvenile culture" that overvalues youthfulness, that cannot tolerate the tension between young and old (life and death), between memory (past) and anticipation (future). We live in a culture that values "ephemeral success" and not what I call *existential success* (Hannush, 2002) or *maturational success.* We live in a dominant culture that is preoccupied by "frivolous consumption" and typified by "zero-degree thinking," a culture that is "deficient in the capacity for [good or wise] judgment." Such a culture rests "in a large part on narcissistic individualism inscribed in the intertwining cults [worship] of the body and youthful appearance" (Hamrick, 2002, p. 257). This kind of culture is fertile ground for the development of a "self-identity, or individuality, … that … has no depth of character development or other aesthetic depths … Rather this fashionable self … flits from one ephemeral seductive pleasure to another, but this time in an image culture" (pp. 257–258).

Although this type of culture places great obstacles to becoming a kind person, it, ironically, widens "the boundaries of tolerance and autonomy [which] may provide individuals and groups the freedom they need to remain counter-cultural until society changes enough to rediscover the depth of experience beneath the images and ephemeral appearances" (Hamrick, 2002, p. 258). "Concomitantly," Hamrick concludes, "they will come to appreciate the truth of [W. H.] Auden's observation that, 'We must love one another or die' … and that love does not live on appearances alone" (p. 258). Permit me to paraphrase Auden's quotation: "We must be kind to one another or die while living a life of fragmented isolation."

References

Fiumara, G. C. (2013). *Psychoanalysis and creativity in everyday life: Ordinary genius.* Routledge.

Hamrick, W. S. (2002). *Kindness and the good society: Connections of the heart.* State University of New York Press.

Hannush, M. J. (2002). *Becoming good parents: An existential journey*. State University of New York Press.
Merleau-Ponty, M. (1962). *Phenomenology of perception* (C. Smith, Trans.). Routledge.
Phillips, A., & Taylor, B. (2009). *On kindness*. Farrar, Straus and Giroux.
Siassi, S. (2015). Kindness, altruism and forgiveness: Three facets of healthy human relatedness. In S. Akhtar (Ed.), *Human goodness: Origins, manifestations, and clinical implications*. Rowman & Littlefield.

11

Truth: The Capacity to Seek, Find, and Be in the Service of Emotional and Relational *Truth*

Truth, declare Deurzen and Kenward (2005), "is derived from the meaning of the world for the conscious being" (p. 206). "The term *meaning*," says Fuller (1990), "refers … to the things we deal with in daily life. It refers to people, too" (p. 1). As human beings we are always "open to possibilities of meaning" (p. 61). More than that, as Merleau-Ponty (1962) puts it, we are constantly "communing with the meanings themselves" (p. 320). Meanings, Fuller (1990) expands, "reach beyond themselves and commune with one another" (p. 63). Meaning grow into further meanings. In our lived or existential space, we bring some meanings close while keeping some meanings at a distance. "Bringing-close reveals the '*true* world' in all the qualitative richness of its lived dimensionality" (p. 74). We are always either "*truthing*" or retreating from the truth ("*untruthing*") by bringing meanings close or keeping meanings at a distance. When I care about something or someone, I bring it close into my existential space of meaning. This "bringing-close" allows the truth of this something or someone to come into its own. "Phenomenological psychology," states Fuller, "begins with the premise that lifeworld meaning, which conventional psychology is simply unable to calculate, comes into its truth, with an integrity of its own, in existential space" (p. 79).

Truths, which are always perspectival, and thus partial and never absolute, are meanings that are accurate manifestations of psychosocial reality. "Reality," states Fuller (1990), "is process – organization and reorganization, context of meaning, succeeding context of meaning" (p. 266). There is a *becoming* quality to lifeworld meanings. "Reality, with its circular lifeworld signifying, is more like a conversation for existential phenomenology" (p. 102).

© The Author(s), under exclusive license to Springer Nature Switzerland AG 2021

M. J. Hannush, *Markers of Psychosocial Maturation*,
https://doi.org/10.1007/978-3-030-74315-4_11

Meanings are feeling-and-value-laden lifeworld events (including people) that we are directed to and preoccupied with – especially events that we care about and that matter. Positive meanings are valued and thus feelingly approached. Negative meanings are disvalued and thus feelingly avoided or an effort is made to change them in the direction of positive meanings. "*Value is a whole of meaning that is positively or negatively required in its place within a lifeworld context*" (Fuller, 1990, p. 136). A positively value-laden, felt meaning is "something 'to be accepted' – to be loved, welcomed, appreciated, grateful for, respected" and a negatively value-laden, felt meaning is something "to be loathed, pushed away, regretted, looked down upon" (p. 139). Fuller (1990) equates a "good meaning" with a "good gestalt" – a meaning within the broadest lifeworld context. "All in all," elaborates Fuller, "the law of good gestalt [good meaning] presses for truth, the original self-manifestation of things [or people] in accordance with their intrinsic structural law [of requiredness]" (p. 147). "The search for and discovery of moral requiredness in and through the immediate sense we have of ourselves and the structure of our situation is *conscience*" (p. 148). Using my own phrasing, I can only answer the call of a "good or true meaning" by listening to and being guided by my "good conscience." Insight into higher-order meaning is made possible by higher-order conscience. Such "higher-order conscience … is a, if not *the* paramount task of our lives … One's deepest interiority is to be found outside in a certain manner of surpassing to meanings" (pp. 253–254). In step with higher-order meanings, higher-order truths unfold as possibilities. Just as meanings, to use Merleau-Ponty's (1962) words, are in "a communion … a coition, so to speak, of our body [bodily self] with things [meanings]" (p. 320), truths also commune with each other, for "Self-other-things" form a system "as it comes into being" (p. 57).

"The mind," say Symington and Symington (1996), "grows through exposure to truth" (p. 3). Our symptoms, they continue, are covers for and hidden signs of the truth. We are motivated, they add, not primarily by seeking pleasure and avoiding pain, but rather by seeking truth because of our "desire for emotional growth" (pp. 6–7). "Truth is growth-promoting and anti-truth psychically debilitating" (p. 114). Moreover, "[Wilfred] Bion saw thought as in the service of truth where the individual uses it to understand him- or herself" (p. 8). In order to intuit the truth, we need to seek it with "Unprejudiced openness," which is "a very difficult attitude to achieve" (p. 178). We need to cultivate a kind of *binocular vision* "which allows the simultaneous interweaving of unconscious and conscious elements [meanings], giving rise to depth and resonance in thinking and … intuition" (p. 130).

Whereas Bion (1984a) goes on to equate absolute truth with mystical reality, where "ultimate reality [is] represented by terms such as absolute truth, the godhead, the infinite, the thing-in-itself" (p. 26), I will more modestly focus on emotional and relational truths. I will bypass any discussion of "Absolute Truth." Bion (1984b) himself links (intra/interpersonal) truth to affect: "something seems real [or 'true'] only when there are feelings about it" (p. 77). When I reach a point in my emotional understanding whereby I "see" the need to bridge or transcend the divide between a pair of opposites – say, images of my mother and father, where I am able to unite or integrate these two images, where these two maternal and paternal images coalesce harmoniously in my imaginative thinking, then there is something not only intimately emotional, but also *aesthetic* about this moment of appropriation of personal truth.

Good thinking for Bion is akin to good linking, a linking that is *revealing* of emotional and relational truths. From a dialectical point of view, two modifications are offered here to Bion's equation of good thinking to good linking: (1) good thinking involves *both* good linking *and* good de-linking, and (2) *revealing* will always involve an element of *concealing* (mystery).

Truth, states Civitarese (2016), is emotional and therefore corporeal and relational, aesthetic, and, I would add, existential. Truth, he elaborates, can be not only emotional, but also rational (or logical), conscious and unconscious (which is an aspect of our expansive consciousness), creative, and transformational. It "makes no sense," says Civitarese, "to speak of emotions *in isolation from* a relationship and from the meaning it assumes within the relationship" (p. 108). Truth, he continues, can promote "transformations that lead to psychic growth. However, these are not achieved unless they are with emotion" (p. 108). Emotions are the messengers that inform us about the clarity or density of our innermost truths.

Intra-and-interpersonal truths encompass the *accuracy of the meanings* of our perceptions about our selves and others. Some perceptions (meanings attributions) are more accurate and less distortive than others. As human beings motivated to make life more bearable, we have evolved to become masters in deceiving our selves and others. The disciplines of social psychology and psychoanalysis demonstrate again and again how we humans are rationalizing, self-justifying, and delusional (reality-distorting) organisms. We are forever using dishonest and manipulative means to achieve our ends – power, pleasure, and the avoidance of pain.

Existential truths involve the degree to which we *own the meaning attributions* we make about our selves and others – meanings that are central to who we are and who we want to become. They call for higher-order (good) meanings that are in resonance with our higher-order (good) conscience. It is one thing to know or understand something about our selves or others on a cognitive or intellectual level; it is another to *own* it on an emotional level. I may know that we humans are all mortal, but I may live as if I will go on living forever. Of course, there are times, such as when I am in denial, when my awareness of a truth is for the most part cut off even at the cognitive level. On an emotional level, I do not *own* my ephemeral existence – that I will die and that my loved ones will die. I do not *own* my transitoriness. For another example, take our human competence. Many of us have illusions of competence. Many others have illusions of incompetence. The former are unable to own their incompetence. The latter are unable to own their competence. Psychoanalysis has demonstrated again and again our ubiquitous use of distortive, defensive mechanisms and strategies the aim of which is to protect us from pain and to increase our pleasure. Here is a sample of defensive mechanisms presented alphabetically as adapted from Cabaniss and her colleagues (2017, p. 37): acting-out, denial, displacement, emotionality (excessive), dissociation, idealization (unrealistic), devaluation (pathological), externalization, identification (unhealthy), intellectualization, isolation of affect, projection, projective identification, rationalization, reaction formation, regression (unhealthy), repression, sexualization, somatization, splitting, turning against the self, and undoing. Above all, we construct a distorting *false* self in order to *compensate* for the *true* self that has been denied spontaneous expression.

Levine (2013), in synchrony with our version of understanding, focuses on emotional, psychic, or relational truth. He delineates two barriers to truth. The first "obstacle to psychic truth is the need to tell lies, especially lies about the self … [Moreover,] there is an essential link between psychic truth and ethical conduct" (p. 2). In other words, the more we disown psychic truth, the more likely it is for us to engage in ethical misconduct. The second obstacle to psychic truth is the desire to comply with others. Here Levine is guided by D. W. Winnicott's distinction between the "false self" and the "true self." We come to assume a false self through complying with others. My hunch is that both Winnicott and Levine have in mind excessive compliance and not simply any kind of compliance. From our dialectical perspective, we need to make a distinction between healthy compliance and noncompliance and unhealthy compliance and noncompliance. The more we engage in unhealthy or undiscerning compliance or noncompliance, the more likely it is for us to engage in ethical misconduct.

To the question, "What is true about the true self?" Levine (2013), following Winnicott, answers, "the true self is true because in connecting with it we feel that we exist ... in our own right [and that this connection] becomes a secure internal source of [our] being ... a center of initiative" (p. 1). When we have an "emotional connection to what we do and how we relate to others," we are in touch with our vital or emotional center (p. 14). When our true self is in gear, we experience a connection between our inner and outer worlds. We present to others a self that is real, assuring that what is most important about us will be known to them.

Waddell (2002) states that Wilfred Bion

> saw the [essential universal human] conflict as the predicament of having the desire to know and understand the truth about one's own experience on the one hand, and the aversion to that knowing and understanding on the other. The authenticity of the quest for the truth of one's experience is lodged, he maintained, in the capacity actually to have the experience, in the sense of staying with it, of really undergoing and suffering it, rather than seeking to dismiss, or to find some way of bypassing it. (p. 30)

From a Bionian point of view, what enables the developing child to *have* an experience is the kind of reciprocal or mutual interaction between the growing infant and the primary caregiver (mother) that helps the child to move from a nascent dispersed self to a more integrated self. "In this reciprocity of feeling [and pre-thinking] there is a sense both of beauty and of truthfulness" (p. 36). To this reciprocity or mutuality, the mother brings not only her loving and nurturing self, but also her thinking and reflective self. Bion goes so far as to refer to "the thinking breast." It is the bringing of this balanced self to the reciprocal or mutual interaction that *contains* the developing child's chaotic psychic life. Waddell (2002) elaborates:

> In good circumstances, that is if sufficiently held – psychically and emotionally – by a containing presence, the baby slowly derives a sense of having an internal holding capacity of his own, an experience of integration which is a necessary prerequisite to continued development ... [The mother gives] not only loving, nurturing, nourishing qualities to the baby, but also formative mental ones, of the sort that could be drawn on to *make sense* of experience; that could make meaning available and thus could *actively* contribute to the growth of the mind. (pp. 36–37)

Bion, according to Charles (2004), makes an important distinction between:

efforts toward evasion and efforts toward understanding. In his later theorizing, he spoke of a *truth instinct* ... I call it *integrity*. Whatever term we use, we are alluding to an internal reference point that marks these forks in the road we come to, where it is only our essential integrity or instinct for truth that helps to provide markers distinguishing the path of growth from the path of avoidance.

We come to these choice points ... moments when we might choose the more difficult path or avoid it and try to pretend to ourselves that such avoidance is acceptable. Such moments of what [existential philosopher Jean-Paul] Sartre called "bad faith" are palpable. They have their impact ... Part of our job as therapists is to help our patients [or ourselves] to believe that they [or we] might actually take the path of truth without facing imminent annihilation. (p. 29)

As I understand him, Bion sees the development of the self as an expanding search for truth (accurate self-other-meanings) guided by the "truth instinct." The maturing self identifies ever more deeply and widely with the truth. In his very late seventies, Erikson (1981) contemplates the meaning of Jesus's "Existential 'I'" against the backdrop of "the Primal Other" or *primal presence* as a "fundamental counterplayer" (p. 302). This "original interplay of *You* ['the Ultimate Other'] and *I* remains the model for mutual recognition throughout life" (p. 302). Still, "there remains for the *I* a certain existential solitariness" (p. 303). The *way* with which Jesus identifies is the "only one way to see the inner light and that was to love" (p. 301). The inner light of the existential "I" refers to the "luminosity of awareness," an awareness of a "numinous center" (pp. 300–301). The "more aware *I* [is] related to a more universal *We*" (p. 332). Erikson equates "the *I* with an inner eye full of light" (p. 335). Jesus, Erikson concludes, is an exemplar of "the evolution of human *consciousness* and *conscience*" (p. 337). Incremental consciousness of (the) truth(s) goes hand-in-hand with maturing conscience.

The search for truth involves being honest (in "good faith") with oneself and with others. "With increasing cognitive and social maturity," states Nicholas (1994), "one is able to encompass larger social and moral fields, moving from self-centeredness to other-directedness, to institution-dependent, to interdependence" (p. 208). Under relatively optimal, good-enough supportive conditions, Nicholas continues, we cycle "through successive levels of truth in the same way as the child does in the course of his moral development" (p. 208). She adds:

Whether the truth is a feeling, a thought, or a perception; whether it is about oneself or a relationship; whether it is pleasant or painful – facing it opens up more possibilities for genuine affection than could ever exist when there were

> secrets or blocks, not to mention unspoken resentments. Often, the expression of truth brings with it a vulnerability on the part of the discloser, which encourages others [to respond in mutual or reciprocal ways]. (p. 208)

The "expression of truth" not only strengthens my sense of intrapersonal and interpersonal reality, but also brings with it experiences of beauty, goodness, and love (Hannush, 2002):

> Love, reality, and truth go together. In other words, the real and the true are revealed through a proper loving orientation. Refined love unveils that which is real and true and leads to what is good. Goodness shows itself through truthful depiction of reality which is disclosed through love. (p. 38)

> In our sense, that which is beautiful is that which is loved. In the beauty of loving, we, along with our children, learn about ourselves. We discover new dimensions (truths) about ourselves. In the light of a beautiful [loving] interpersonal experience ... [we learn] something deeper and more universal than ourselves. (p. 109)

"Truth," says Nicholas (1994), "tends to join people with one another in positive and loving ways, leading to increased **altruism**, **responsibility**, **egalitarianism**, and **justice** in the relationship" (p. 208). It takes courage to face difficult truths in our everyday lives – "truths ... compel action commensurate with ... insight. Such action ... is usually moral" (p. 209). In part, our search for truth involves analyzing the intent behind our actions so that we can distinguish between our moral and amoral failures. We struggle daily with our failures. We hurt and disappoint others. Others hurt and disappoint us. Did we intend to hurt and disappoint others? Did others intend to hurt and disappoint us? To what degree are we attuned to our unconscious or dimly sensed motivations and choices? Deciphering conscious or unconscious intent goes hand-in-hand with the owning of responsibility (blame) and plays a part in consequent attempts at acceptance, reparation, and forgiveness.

Truth, says Lynch (2004), like love, is worth living by for its own sake. It is an ultimate evaluative standard and constitutive good in itself: "truth is more like love than money. We – at least most of us – care about truth, at least sometimes, for more than instrumental reasons. Truth is deeply normative; it is worth caring about for its own sake" (p. 17). Lynch, however, does not stop here:

> Like many other people, I not only prefer the truth for its own sake, I also don't want to be the sort of person who doesn't – who would prefer the life of illusion. I want to be the sort of person, for example, who has intellectual integrity, who, other things being equal, is willing to pursue what is true even when it is danger-

> ous or inconvenient or expensive to do so. I not only desire the truth, I desire to desire the truth. … desire for the truth … is grounded in what matters to me. I don't just prefer the truth, in other words, I *care* about it. (pp. 18–19)

"To care about the truth," continues Lynch, "entails that one is disposed to act in certain ways" (p. 129).

> [To] the extent that one cares about truth, one manifests particular character traits that are oriented toward the truth. It involves being willing to hear both sides of the story, being open-minded and tolerant of others' opinions, being careful and sensitive to detail, being curious, and paying attention to the evidence. It also involves being willing to question assumptions, giving and asking for reasons, being impartial, and being intellectually courageous. … Like all human characteristics, intellectual virtues are matters of degree. I can be more or less open-minded or curious or careful. I can also manifest some of these virtues to a greater extent than others. (pp. 129–130)

Caring about the truth (e.g., holding true beliefs) is an important part of our happiness. "By happy life, I mean a good or flourishing life, a life lived well" (p. 137). Being "true to life" is a difficult life project. But it is worth embarking upon because it is important to flourishing. Like living a life of loving-and-being loved, living a life of integrity-producing truthfulness is essential for constructing a vital sense of self that is an important part of living a relatively contented and happy life. Having true "self-knowledge is part of happiness. This gives us reason, and an important one, for caring about the truth of some sorts of beliefs for their own sake" (p. 128). Self-knowledge, in turn, requires caringly cultivating a "self-reflective attitudes" that "in turn are elements in the greater good of having a fulfilled and happy life," just as "loving and being loved are parts of a fulfilled and happy life" (p. 128).

What we care about, continues Lynch (2004), constitutes the kind of persons we are. This nexus of our care makes up, in a certain sense, what we call the *self* – "the self that answers questions about who a person is, what that person aims at and cares about" (pp. 145–146). This self is a complexly constructed narrative. We strive to create a comprehensively coherent life narrative. My self-narrative may seem coherent, "but I can be wrong. And if I can make a mistake about who I am, then the truth about who I am is to that degree objective" (p. 146). The truth about who I am, in other words, comes in degrees of truthfulness. We both "create and discover the truth about ourselves" (p. 146). "There are external constraints on the coherency of the narratives we weave about ourselves – our past history, our biology, our cultural circumstances, our emotions, and the views of others, who can point out to us when our sense of self is out of kilter with who we are" (p. 146).

In spite of these constraints, elaborates Lynch (2004), who I am, my sense of self, my unfolding life narrative is a creatively constructed and discovered byproduct of what I am committed to, what I *identify* with. To "live authentically is to identify with one's effective desires" (p. 134). It is to identify with deeply normative and constitutive goods, like love and truth. "But one might stand for what one thinks is right without necessarily identifying with it" (p. 134). Persons are authentic to the extent that they identify with their effective desires or desired goods. Our identities, we learn from Erikson, are made up of our identifications. Our developmental and maturational challenge is to hold on to our healthy identifications, let go of our unhealthy identifications, and appropriate new-and-healthy identifications. Healthy identifications are dynamic, open to refinement, and thus can assume a functional autonomy from their origin – their initial source of appropriation. This process in itself requires truth seeking, truth discovering, truth discerning, and truth appropriating. Maintaining relative constancy in this unfolding life project is no easy task. It is not enough to *think* or *believe* that I am a truthful or a truth-seeking-and-abiding person. I need to go deeper. I need to *identify* with both *meanings of the truth* – truth as affect, truth as knowledge – self-knowledge and other-directed knowledge, and truth as action. At its core, the "I" is identified with being true to oneself-and-others. I *am* truth-fully "*selving*." I am *becoming* my truer inter-self. Becoming mature means refining the accuracy or truthfulness of our (shared) lifeworld *meanings* (or *co-meanings*) – what our selves and others that we care about mean to us. Ultimately, truthful selving, ethical selving, and aesthetic selving unfold together as a unified whole.

Permit me to conclude this chapter by offering a poignant and touching example of how difficult, painful, but at the same time deeply and satisfyingly transforming can the pursuit of truth as a life project be. After decades of undergoing psychotherapy, psychoanalysis, and self-analysis for her lifelong struggle with clinical depression, the essayist and novelist Daphne Merkin (2017) comes upon this dynamically evolving revelation (truth) about her condition – her emotionally impoverished childhood, toward the end of her memoir:

> I was beginning to understand, however tentatively, that my quest for a new and improved childhood was so futile that it was tantamount to a wish to die – to stop the world and get off. The time for absolute caretaking was past, and if I hadn't gotten it [more than] thirty years earlier, I wasn't going to get it now, no matter how implacably I insisted on it. (pp. 294–295)

> There is something I want that I cannot have, a redress that will never come. No one is going to make anything up to me – not now, not then, not ever. This can't be so, but it is so. This simple truth enrages me – I will not make do with such thin gruel! but there is nowhere for my rage to go. If you're a socialized person, you can't go spewing your anger at the nearest available target. You must learn to live with it, sublimate it somehow, or work it out in a counter- productive fashion, by eating or drinking or drugging too much. (p. 280)

Existential truths have to be repeatedly confronted before they sink in and result in concrete consequences, before they contribute to change, growth, and maturation. Merkin needs to face her "simple truth" again and again before she experiences palpable change, not without intermittent regressions:

> I once dreamed of conquering my depression for good, but I have come to understand that it is a chronic condition, as much a part of me as my literary bent. … I have learned the hard way to give it, ephemeral as it may seem, its due. … If I can't quite declare victory over my depression, I am giving it a run for its money, navigating around it, reminding myself that the opposite of depression is not a state of unimaginable happiness but a state of approximate contentment, of relative all-right-ness. (pp. 282–283)

Notice how absorbing and appropriating her "simple truth," bit-by-bit, allows Merkin to "see" her depression differently. The *meaning* she attributes to her depression is stretched and widened. The phantasy-based wish to eradicate her depression one day, once and for all, disappears. The presence and absence of depression are no longer viewed in either/or fashion: I am either depressed or happy. Rather, she is now open to experiencing depression and happiness on a continuum with "approximate contentment" and "relative all-right-ness" in between. Merkin is now able to *play with her pain*. She is able to *play with the meanings* of her depression. Depression's *horizon of meaning* has been creatively and imaginatively broadened. She begins to entertain the *possibility* that life is not only a burden to shoulder, but, as she tells her daughter in the very last chapter of her memoir, "Life is a gift … A great gift… [and, she reflects] … anything else seems ungrateful – even to me" (p. 283). Merkin then ends her autobiography with a scene in which she has invited two friends and her daughter to her rented summer home with a swimming pool, a scene which she "cannot imagine having arranged until recently, one that requires me to take the helm instead of hoping [unrealistically] that someone else will manage things for me" (p. 284). It is worth noting that Merkin is countering the passivity that typifies depression by taking a life-affirming initiative, a purposive and more *meaningful initiative* that is a manifestation of an affirmative stance toward life – a Yes-saying to life, which is the counter of the No-saying to life and a Yes-saying to death, which has plagued her for decades. Merkin cites the following experience:

> I stand up in the pool with the intention of doing few laps when suddenly somewhere in the sky I could swear I feel my [dead] mother's presence, more benign than not. For a moment I feel her loss intensely, and when I'm sure no one is watching I look up and give her a little wave, just in case. (p. 284)

In contradistinction to her previous not-so-benign remembrances of her mother, as the one who "blighted" her life and "destroyed" her, Merkin now experiences her mother "more benign than not." The *meaning* of "mother" is changing. She ends her book with a recollection of a line from a poem by Charles Olson, as she drifts to sleep that night while reflecting on the blessings of the day and the day to come: "'I have had to learn the simplest things / last. Which made for difficulties'" and concludes with a life-affirming exclamation mark that contains part of the title of the book: "Whoever thought I'd be this close to happy" (p. 285)!

References

Bion, W. (1984a). *Attention and interpretation*. Karnac.

Bion, W. (1984b). *Transformations*. Karnac.

Cabaniss, D. L., Cherry, S., Douglas, C. J., & Schwartz, A. (2017). *Psychodynamic psychotherapy: A clinical manual* (2nd ed.). John Wiley & Sons.

Charles, M. (2004). *Learning from experience: A guidebook for clinicians*. The Analytic Press.

Civitarese, G. (2016). *Truth and the unconscious in psychoanalysis*. Routledge.

Deurzen, E. V., & Kenward, R. (2005). *Dictionary of existential psychotherapy and counselling*. Sage.

Erikson, E. H. (1981). The Galilean sayings and the sense of "I." *Yale Review*, Spring 1981. Yale University Press.

Fuller, A. R. (1990). *Insight into value: An exploration of the premises of a phenomenological psychology*. State University of New York Press.

Hannush, M. J. (2002). *Becoming good parents: An existential journey*. State University of New York Press.

Levine, D. P. (2013). *The capacity for ethical conduct: On psychic existence and the way we relate to others*. Routledge.

Lynch, M. P. (2004). *True to life: Why truth matters*. The MIT Press.
Merkin, D. (2017). *This close to happy: A reckoning with depression*. Farrar, Straus and Giroux.
Merleau Ponty, M. (1962). *Phenomenology of perception* (C. Smith, Trans.). Routledge.
Nicholas, M. W. (1994). *The mystery of goodness and the positive moral consequences of psychotherapy*. W. W. Norton.
Symington, J., & Symington, N. (1996). *The clinical thinking of Wilfred Bion*. Routledge.
Waddell, M. (2002). *Inside lives: Psychoanalysis and the growth of the personality*. Karnac.

Part IV

The Capacities for Companionship and Aloneness

12

Companionship: The Capacity for *Companionship* and Friendship

I will begin by describing the essential features and functions of close friendship. After that, I will attempt to derive from these features and functions the defining core or essence of friendship. Lastly, I will delineate the therapeutic fruit of friendship while keeping a vigilant eye on its fragility.

The Essential Features and Functions of Close Friendship

Bolt and Dunn (2016) describe eleven essential dimensions or features of good friendship: attachment (a sense of connection made possible by closeness and liking), common activities (mutual enjoyment derived from time spent doing things together), exclusiveness (an elevation over other relationships made possible by the unique qualities of this special relationship), frankness ("honest self-disclosure of strengths and weaknesses as well as frank feedback about the other's actions"), giving (reciprocal provision of social support as well as material goods), imposition (a stance of reciprocal readiness to seek and provide help), knowing (understanding), loyalty (defending one another from attack from the outside), sensitivity (empathy), spontaneity (spontaneous self-expression), and trust (holding "each other's disclosures in confidence") (p. 211).

Moustakas (1995) describes the essential "themes" or "unique features" of "the experience of intimate bonding in friendships" (p. 38). Intimate friendships, according to Moustakas, are characterized by:

© The Author(s), under exclusive license to Springer Nature Switzerland AG 2021
M. J. Hannush, *Markers of Psychosocial Maturation*,
https://doi.org/10.1007/978-3-030-74315-4_12

1. A risk-involving choice to begin, maintain, and enhance an intimate relationship that will hopefully endure the test of time, knowing that there is always "an unpredictability factor that may lead to betrayal [or other deleterious consequences] and [thus] an end of the relationship" (p. 39).
2. "[S]udden, immediate openings [disclosures], freshness of dialogue and sharings, and connectedness and mutuality" (p. 38).
3. The exploration of ideas and *meanings*, the search into *reciprocal* thoughts and feelings, the discovery of *new shared meanings*, and the creation of new joint activities and projects.
4. A high degree of *comfort* with each other, an affirmation of each other, a feeling of at-homeness with each other, and the freedom to express oneself without monitoring one's thoughts and feelings, "knowing that one will be accepted and valued in one's own self-expression" (p. 38).
5. An "experience [of] joy in being together," a receptivity to the experience of adventure, surprise, and wonder (p. 39).
6. The discovery of one's own thoughts, feelings, and *meanings*—of "who they [as intimate friends] are together, what they are moving toward in being and becoming" (p. 39).
7. "[Being] there for one another in times of triumph and in times of tragedy and crisis" (p. 38).
8. An open-endedness in that it is "continually unfolding in new directions, new sharings, new ways of fulfilling its potentials" (p. 39).
9. An absence of "imposition of role, title, or authority" (p. 39); a *co-presence* of two equally empowered voices.
10. "[T]he promise for being and growing in solitary and mutually rewarding ways" (p. 39).

What functions do close friendships serve? Good friends contribute to our life satisfaction, psychological well-being, and happiness. As Bolt and Dunn (2016) put it, "good friends satisfy people's basic psychological needs" (p. 204). How do close friends contribute to each other's flourishing? What basic needs do friends satisfy? Friendship, elaborate Bolt and Dunn, satisfy our basic needs for belonging, *meaning*, mutual support, personal control (self-regulation), and self-esteem (worthiness).

Close friendship satisfies our basic communal need for belonging—for feeling a sense of oneness with one another. Life becomes *more meaningful* in the company of good friends. Friendship adds *depth to the meaning of life*. Friends meet each other's need for mutual social support. Bolt and Dunn (2016, pp. 203–204) describe three kinds of social support: *emotional, instrumental, and informational. Emotional support* is defined as the giving of "a listening ear for confiding painful feelings" (p. 203). *Instrumental support* refers to the extending of "tangible goods and services" (p. 204). *Informational support* means the offering of "expert counsel and advice" (p. 204). Good friends give and receive all three kinds of social support. Good friends strengthen each other's need for a sense of *agency.* I subsume "self-control," "self-regulation," and "willpower" under "agency." Paradoxically, then, friendship serves the seemingly opposite needs for agency *and* communion. Lastly, friends recognize and validate each other's inherent sense of worth.

Mutuality as the Defining Core of Friendship

After surveying the literature, Beverly Fehr defines friendship as a "voluntary, personal relationship, typically providing intimacy and assistance, in which the two parties like one another and seek each other's company" (cited in Bolt and Dunn, 2016, p. 211). "Sharing (intimacy) and caring (assistance)," conclude Bolt and Dunn (2016), "seem to be the central, perhaps even the defining, features of friendship" (p. 211). Viewed through the lens of lived experience, however, sharing-as-intimacy and caring-as-assistance are blurred, for caring, in its deeper meaning, can be understood to be a source and a byproduct of intimacy (love). Nevertheless, the concept of *mutuality* is implicit in Bolt and Dunn's (2016) description of the communal nature of true friendship—though they acknowledge that the strength of the *communal orientation* varies from person to person:

> Friendship is based on what it gives, not what it gets. It is motivated by love, not debt, and is willing to sacrifice without seeing or expecting a return… Friendship is a communal relationship in which partners are oriented toward each other's needs … Only when the benefits are voluntary, when partners freely give and receive, do we tend to view a relationship as true friendship or love. (p. 214)
>
> "Friends," they conclude, "share a communal relationship in which they are mutually responsive to each other's needs" (p. 216).

It is Cates (2005) who, in my view, captures the definitional core of friendship. She defines friendship as "a relationship of mutual and mutually known good will and beneficence. It is also a relationship of mutual and mutually known affection" (p. 36). However, I can go to Cicero (106 BC–43 BC) to find "mutuality" used as the defining essence of friendship:

> Friendship may be defined as a complete identity of feeling about all things in heaven and earth: an identity which is strengthened by mutual goodwill and affection. With the single exception of wisdom, I am inclined to regard it as the greatest of all the gifts the gods have bestowed upon mankind. … What we enjoy in a friend is not the profit we derive from him, but the affection. Any practical benefit that goes with this affection only gives satisfaction when it is the product of a warm heart. … friendship … is the noblest and most delightful of all the gifts the gods have given to mankind. (cited in Symington, 2016, p. 38)

It is *not* mutual utility, but mutual affection bodying forth from a "warm heart" that is the core of friendship. Friendship, for Cicero, is decimated when it serves a utilitarian need, when it ceases to be its own end, and becomes a means to some other end. Friends, Cicero adds, admire each other's "fine qualities" (Symington, 2016, p. 39).

Friendship, says Symington (2016), is a cardinal relational context in which a *healing conversation happens*: "I am stressing friendship because it is the supreme instance where communion between persons is valued for its own sake. … in friendship it is communication between one person and another that is being celebrated" (p. 40). Then, Symington suddenly shares an astounding reflection that is in synchrony with my own tacit thinking: "I have had the thought for some time that the burgeoning of psychotherapy and counselling in the present era is partly a function of the diminution of friendship in our present culture. If this is the case, then I think our culture is a very sick patient" (p. 40). For a long time I have thought that it becomes more difficult, but not impossible, to cultivate friendship, especially among males, in a culture that is *hyper*—busy, competitive, consumeristic, individualistic, materialistic, narcissistic, and, in short, utilitarian. Symington labels this as a "cultural disease" (p. 62). Or, to avoid the connotations of a medical model, I would hyphenate it into a "cultural dis-ease or dis-order."

Above and beyond culture, Symington focuses on the developmental origins of the capacity for affect-laden communication. For Symington (2016), "the capacity to communicate is present to the extent to which the individual him or herself has been communicated to by mother or, in the modern jargon, the primary caregiver" (p. 47). When an essential other, mother or primary caregiver, enters into communication with a distressed or joyful child, the child, elaborates Symington, builds up emotional capital, confidence, deposit, or resource. But, Symington continues, "'emotional capital' is built through a particular form of communication with another" (p. 63). There is no "critical period" for the building of such emotional confidence. Simply stated, "emotional growth occurs through communication with a person" (p. 63).

Communication between true friends, then, is "an end in itself" and does not serve the purpose of (optimal) individualistic survival. Here again is Symington (2016) writing on the "pleasure of friendship":

> Friendship has been defined as an association the purpose of which is the very communication between the two people themselves and not to further any other objective. Friendship becomes the high point in communication – communication for its own sake. The personal love that exists between two friends is the basis and reason for the association. (p. 36)

This heart-to-heart, center-to-center, core-to-core communication is generative in that it not only strengthens us emotionally (builds our "emotional capital"), but contributes to our mutual psychosocial development and growth. This is the potential fruit of creative communication. This is *how healing happens*. It happens through *a healing conversation* between friends. Of course, it happens in other relational contexts as well.

Tracing the Developmental Origins of *Mutuality*

Fascinatingly, as Erikson (1963) enlightens us, mutuality is the central relational process that resolves the early crises or tensions between trust versus mistrust and autonomy versus shame and doubt. In other words, through the mutual coordination of affection-laden giving-and-receiving that occurs between mother-and-child, the developing child learns to trust the essential m(other) and comes to perceive her or himself as trustworthy. Moreover, through the coordination of the love-laden resolution of the tension between holding-on (say, through protective hugging)-and-letting go (say, through allowing the child to stand on his or her own feet) between mother-and-child, the child learns to coordinate her or his (good) will with the (good) will of the (m)other. Moving beyond his or her dyadic relationship with the mother, the child must learn to include the father, his or her siblings, and peers in an expanding circle of mutual affection and good will. Simply stated, for Erikson, trust and autonomy, and, later, initiative, industriousness, identity achievement, intimacy, generativity, and integrity are all capacities or character strengths that are consolidated in the context of mutuality. True trust, for instance, emerges from the ground of mutuality of a caring relationship between a primary *caregiver* and a *care-receiver*. Here, in a pivotal passage, Erikson (1963) describes the foundation for the construction of the future capacity for friendship:

> The mutuality of relaxation thus developed [between mother-and-child] is of prime importance for the first experience of friendly otherness. One may say (somewhat mystically, to be sure) that in thus *getting what is given*, and in learning to *get somebody to do* for him what he wishes to have done, the baby also develops the necessary ego groundwork [or character strength] to *get to be a giver*. (p. 76)

"Healthy functioning," writes Welchman (2000), "involves a capacity for playful imagination and for mutuality in relationship" (p. 10). In fact, I would go so far as to say that playfulness in general is made possible by "mutuality in relationship." Additionally, mutuality is the configurational context which makes our capacity for "reconciliation or balance of opposites which are nevertheless necessary and complementary" possible (p. 11). The experience of mutual peaceful relaxation or mutual joyous excitement enables us to tolerate moments of troubling tensions.

Erikson (1964) elaborates on the concept of mutuality. Here he is reflecting on the origins of the gift of mutuality:

> Nothing in human life, however, is secured in its origin unless it is verified in the intimate meeting of partners in favorable social settings. The infant's smile inspires hope in the adult and, of course, only one physiognomic detail which indicates that the infant by his trustful search for experience and assurance, awakens in the giver a strength which he, in turn, is ready and needful to have awakened and to have consolidated by the experience of mutuality. (p. 116)

The optimal experience of mutuality generates preverbal, iconic, and linguistic memories that serve as the basis of trustfulness and hope. Hope, Erikson tells us, helps the child "approximate a measure of rootedness" (p. 117). "To the infant," Erikson continues, "his mother … must be the first verification [validator], which, later will come from wider segments of [social] reality [such as partners or best friends]" (p. 117). Throughout this text, Erikson makes references to "mutuality of mates and partners in a shared identity" (p. 128), "mutual verification" (p. 128), "mutual commitment" (p. 128), "mutual concern" (p. 128), "psychosexual mutuality" (p. 129), "mutual enhancement of experience" (p. 129), "mutuality of devotion" (p. 129), "mutual activation" (p. 165), "mutual influences" (p. 165), "mutual understanding" (p. 231), and "mutual arousal and response" (p. 231). Mutuality, for Erikson, is not only the "original source of hope," but also "the basic ingredient of all effective as well as ethical human action" (p. 231). This "mutual understanding," Erikson expands, "is the primal source of all moral motives" (p. 231). Erikson then goes on to state that we need to "endow the Golden Rule with a principle of mutuality, replacing reciprocity of both prudence and sympathy" (p. 231). Most psychologists equate mutuality with reciprocity. In Erikson's eyes, mutuality is much deeper than reciprocity. "Mutuality," in its refined form, note Newman and Newman (2018), "refers to empathic awareness of another, understanding self and other, and the ability and willingness to regulate one's needs in order to respond to the needs of one's partner" (p. 459). For Erikson (1964), mutuality, in its essential sense, means "mutual activation," where one person activates and is activated by another person. Two friends, for example, can activate care for one another. Here is Erikson describing how two equally unique different human beings depend on mutuality to potentiate each other:

> *truly worthwhile acts enhance a mutuality between the doer and the other – a mutuality which strengthens the doer even as it strengthens the other.* Thus, the 'doer' and the 'other' are partners in one deed ... Understood this way, the [Golden] Rule would say that it is best to do to another what will strengthen you even as it will strengthen him – that is, what will develop his best potentials even as it develops your own. (p. 233)

"Missed mutuality," for Erikson (1964), means arrested or stunted psychosocial and ethical development. "The failure of basic trust and of mutuality has been recognized in psychology as the most far-reaching failure, undermining all development" (p. 231). Here is my version of Erikson's amended Golden Rule of Mutuality applied to the context of friendship: "Do unto your friend that which will strengthen her or him as it strengthens you." The cultivated capacity for mutual activation is the foundational ground that makes the construction and deepening of friendship possible. Like infants and their mothers, friends are able to synchronize and harmonize their behaviors and mental states. Together, they are able to move fluidly from on mental state to another. They are able to enliven each other, say, through mutual smiling or mutual playfulness. And when they experience a mismatch in communication they are able to repair these relational ruptures quickly. They are able to restore their positive feelings of connection. As their sense of mutual pleasure and enjoyment increases, it leaves a memory of such precious moments to guide their future healing and communion-instilling conversations. Their capacity for trust in each other is strengthened.

Human life, in its deepest existential sense, states Erikson (1975), moves us "*outward* from self-centeredness to the mutuality of love and communion, *forward* from the enslaving past to the ... anticipation of new possibilities, and *upward* from the unconscious to the enigma of consciousness" (p. 39). In the affirming "configurational" (meaning) context of mutuality, "creative self-renewal in truly playful moments" is actualized (p. 39). Being attuned to the "configurational" or meaning context refers to being able to see the whole – say the importance of the friendship—in the parts—even the bad parts – say disagreeable argumentation.

"A friend, as opposed to an ally," says Symington (2012), "is someone I am with for his own sake or her own sake. There is no purpose beyond that I and the other enjoy each other's company" (p. 20). "When my friend dies," Symington continues, "I give it a ritual burial …; I place some flowers by it as a sign of beauty" (p. 20). "The value of the person for his or her own sake," Symington adds, "is expressed clearly by Homer when he describes Achilles's grief at the death of his friend, Patroclus" (p. 20). Long before Homer, we hear the depth of grief in Gilgamesh's devastated reaction to the death of his friend Enkidu. Symington concludes, the "supreme exemplar of communication for its own sake is realised in friendship" (p. 20). It is "communication for its own sake" that links the disparate parts of our personality—what Symington describes as the "'gathering in' [that] unifies the personality" (p. 20). But there is a double gathering that is made possible by communication for its own sake with which Symington would concur: a gathering within and a "gathering between." It is a form of communication that D. W. Black (1997), echoing the philosopher Giambattista Vico, describes as "communal making" (p. 53). To communicate this way is "to *make* common" (p. 53). It is to co-create "common consciousness" (p. 53). More than that, to communicate in this manner, is to refine our conscience, for "the fundamental tasks of communication is to create not merely a means for personal expression but a lasting sense of conscience" (p. 54). Put differently, authentic communication between friends cultivates not only a sense of communion, but also their moral (and I would add aesthetic) consciousness. "Although moral consciousness differs significantly from aesthetic consciousness, we cannot afford to isolate radically the energy of these interactive awarenesses" (p. 42). In his *Confessions*, Saint Augustine (1961) reflects on the act of stealing pears from his neighbor's tree as aesthetically ugly. He finds no "beauty" in the act (p. 41). In short, through genuine communication, friends contribute to the broadening and deepening of their consciousness, to the maturation of their conscience, and to the nourishment and refinement of their sense of beauty.

The developmental origin of the capacity for friendship can be traced back to the primordial relationship between primary caregiver and child. Two key concepts emerge here: the mother's capacity for *contemplation* and the child's *innate need for companionship*.

Contemplation, says Symington (2012), is a generative state of mind. It is a form of active mental indwelling. It is likened to an inner mirror. It is similar to, but more active and deeper than, Freud's "free-floating attention" of the analyst and Bion's maternal capacity for "reverie," whereby "the mother processes the anxiety coming from the baby and transforms it and gives it back in an acceptable form" (p. 146). The mother in this instance is "contemplating her baby and this contemplative act embraces the whole world of which the baby is a living part" (p. 146). "The contemplative act," Symington emphasizes, "reaches through from one person to the other" (p. 146). Symington provides us with a second instance of maternal contemplation. When the mother is able to create the mental space, which allows her to reflectively and calmly evaluate and then assimilate her own feelings about her past relationships or attachments, even if they were unsatisfactory, she can then "forgive and tolerate her own shortcomings" (p. 5). This in turn enables the mother to "relate to her own baby as an independent and separate person and to be sensitive to the baby's states of mind in such a way that the baby is likely to become securely attached" (p. 5).

This *contemplative* maternal mind, further elucidates Symington (2012), is characterized by its "liveliness and responsiveness, the quality of going out to meet the other/baby, not just to contain it" (p. 47). Having calmly reflected on what it means to be helpless herself as a child, she can now be understandingly attuned to the helplessness of her own child. She is able to enter into "a *harmony of the similar* – a similarity which respected the difference between us" (p. 38). This "harmony of the similar finds its similarity in the togetherness in truth of both participants" (p. 44). Although Symington does not say it, mother and child, fundamentally and primordially, are *two-in-relation-to-a-third*: truth. But I would add, the third can be not only truth, but also beauty, goodness, and above all, love. "Love," elaborates Symington, "embraces the elements of the personality creating them into a newborn unity" (p. 98). In such a hallowed relational space, where over time there is "a mutual indwelling" (p. 9), we move toward becoming our true selves. As Symington says, "if I am *relating* then the different parts [of my personality or emerging identity or selfhood] are inwardly connected and so there is a true *I*" (p. 45). Stated differently, I would say, a true "We" makes the movement toward the true "I" possible. "The person," asserts Symington, "is *in-relation* to the other and also inwardly connected within the self. The interpersonal and the intrapsychic [creative core] are two aspects of one thing" (p. 90).

Symington (2019) further explicates that the mental act of contemplation is fundamentally oriented to meeting or encountering the other, the baby. Contemplation, therefore, forms the basis for understanding the other/baby.

It is a basic intentional orientation of the mother's mind. It is a moment of meeting or encounter. It involves the mother's "*primary maternal preoccupation or riveted attention*" (p. 47), "This meeting," Symington says, "is more important than the nurture of the baby" (p. 47). He goes on to provide a lengthy quote from the work of the psychoanalyst Ian Suttie on the "innate need for companionship":

> '*I [Ian Suttie] saw the possibility that the biological need for nurture might be psychologically presented in the infant mind, not as a bundle of practical organic necessities and potential privations, but as a pleasure in responsive companionship and as a correlative discomfort in loneliness and isolation. … I imagined [self-]expression as an offering or stimulus directed to the other person, designed to elicit a response while* ***love*** *itself was essentially a state of* ***active harmonious interplay****. … [I am therefore] introducing the conception of* ***innate-need-for-companionship*** *which is the infant's only way of self-preservation. This need [results in] giving rise to parental and fellowship 'love.'*' (p. 47)

If we miss out on early *contemplative companionship* or on the "harmonious interplay" of "parental and fellowship love," Symington adds, there is no need to despair for it "can be repaired in later life" (p. 48). I humbly offer the view, and I believe that Symington would wholeheartedly concur, that *friendship is a natural relational context in which such repair can occur.*

The Fruit and Fragility of Friendship

Had we had good friends, we would *likely* not be in need of good therapists. It ought to not surprise us therefore to read, in a basic text on psychoanalysis, that "the psychoanalyst needs to be a consistent 'good friend to the patient'" (Barratt, 2013, p. 141). For Barratt, a "good friend" practices a sort of intimate "soul force," a "nonviolent truthfulness" and "loving-kindness" (p. 141). "The patient's love for the psychoanalyst," however, "is both genuine and iatrogenic" (p. 142) which needs to be deconstructed by way of "nonviolent truthfulness" and "loving-kindness." Although there are convergences, there are also significant divergences between the meanings of friendship inside and outside the consulting room. Suffice it to say that inside, there is an *asymmetrical mutuality*, whereas outside, there is a *symmetrical mutuality*.

Like therapists, friends are also challenged to enact a kind of "intimate soul force"—a "nonviolent truthfulness and loving-kindness" if their friendship is to flourish and if it is to contribute to their mutual growth. How does this happen? Guided by Symington's (2019) work, I will extrapolate a provisional answer.

Good friends communicate the truth to each other. They know it's the truth in their bones because they trust each other. By trusting each other they inhabit each other's inner worlds. They enter into each other's context of life-world meanings. The two friends join each other in creative harmony. Together they create a "shared endowment."

> Trust means what I give you give. There is a mutual giving to each other. We are in a shared world so a giving is not one way. I give to you and you give to me. When I trust you, ... you join arms with me. ... It was this mutual inter-giving that is described as trust.. ... It is a giving of myself into the care of the other. ... Trust indicates that this is done because of a faith in the good will of the other. (Symington, 2019, pp. 108–109)

Through trust I take in the loving care of my friend. In turn, I am empowered to provide my friend with my own loving care. I trust that my friend's primary purpose is a *regard* for me as a unique person. I know in my heart that she or he will not use me for her or his "self-enhancing advantage." Symington (2019) uses the terms "respect" and "almost reverence." My friend values me for who I am and not for the advantages I can offer her or him. I knowingly trust her or his master motivation. My friend "values me, my company" (p. 111). Further, it is this primordial trust that makes it possible for me to be generous toward and forgiving of my friend, and grateful for the gift of friendship, for our mutual love and enjoyment of each other. It is this foundational mutual trust that plants the potential for dyadic maturational growth.

"It is important to realize however," Symington (2019) cautions, "that no motive is ever entirely pure; there is always a mixture; what we want to know is which is dominant" (p. 111). Good friends keep their impure motives in check. Additionally, even though Symington does not make it explicit, the level of maturity of the two friends can limit their capacity for deepening their friendship. For instance, Symington says, "It would be trust misplaced if I expected someone to synthesize a variety of elements [in his or her personality] if I knew that the person in question was unable to unify [these, for example, contradictory elements]; if this was a function [or competence] that was poorly developed in him or her" (p. 112). Other undeveloped or underdeveloped functions or competencies that serve as barriers to deepening the capacity for friendship are *the incapacity to* imagine, feel, think abstractly, remember, relax, know on a tacit level, take in and create good experiences, bear the suffering of painful happenings, construct a coherent dyadic narrative, intuit, relate, like, and sympathize. Add to this list *the incapacity to* engage in contemplation, free-floating attention (or wide-unfocused attention), and to know "when the outer behaviour [of the potential friend] flows from … [a] united creative core [of her or his personality]" (p. 113).

The influence of friends, caution Bolt and Dunn (2016), is "not always beneficial" (p. 209). Friends, they add, "are like the buttons on an elevator – they can take you up or take you down" (p. 209). Friends, for example, are the best predictors of drug use. "Listening to another's [friend's] woes can make us feel superior" and "we can feel threatened by our friends' successes" (p. 220). Yet, a friend, says Fiumara (2013), is someone who can embrace the saintly and demonic sides of us. A friend is one who can see our shadows and then be a mirror for so much more than our shadows. Above all, friends need to be kind to each other. But a kindness that embraces the shadows requires a slow blossoming over years; this is the real measure of our adventures with one another.

"Imagine," asks J. Martin (2016):

> a friend asking you to accompany him or her through a difficult time – the loss of a job, the death of a parent, major surgery. You would see your friend at his or her most vulnerable, most naked, most honest. It would be a privilege to accompany your friend in that way – it's something that would change your relationship forever. (pp. 125–126)

My companionship helps my *trustingly vulnerable* friend feel less isolated and alone. I am at this moment worthy of her or his trust. "There are few things," Martin remarks, "as isolating as suffering, for everyone's suffering is largely incommunicable" (p. 119). Why? Because the "particular problems that you face in your family, for example, are so complex, so shot through with complicated family histories and relationships, as to be almost unexplainable to others" (p. 120). Moreover, "the struggles you face about almost any part of your life are so private, so personal, and so unique, that even when you do explain, you may feel that you've given someone the wrong impression" (p. 120).

There are times when I may feel that even my best friend may not understand the difficult issue I am struggling with because he or she has not gone through the same or similar difficulty. I may therefore feel ill at ease in wanting to open up. There will always be a dialectical tension between *revealing* and *concealing* ourselves even to our best friend. Ideally, the best of friends will hold *almost* nothing back from each other. I say "almost" because discernment in disclosure is necessary while remaining attuned to the sensitivities of the essential other—our friend. Still, there are parts of our lives, especially the darker sides of ourselves—our acquisitiveness, our vengefulness, our pettiness, our hyper-competitiveness, our enviousness, and so on, that we keep from even our best friend.

Ironically, we can only know ourselves by giving ourselves almost entirely to our best friend. It is in the giving-and-receiving of ourselves that we come to know our selves and each other. This is no easy matter. The mutuality of friendship is fraught with fragility. Yet, we need to take the risk of being fragile in order to become our truest selves. From my friend, who is outside me, I receive an image of what is inside me. In other words, through my friend the invisible becomes visible. Through my friend's mirroring presence and generative responsiveness, I acquire a clearer picture of my "I-world." His or her *word* expands my *world* and fuels my deepest desire to live in such a way that approximates this new "I-world" of mine with its promising possibilities.

"We long to be known," observe Bolt and Dunn (2016), "but also to remain hidden" (pp. 217–218). Although they emphasize the communal dimension of friendship, Bolt and Dunn add, as an aside, "Lasting friendships combine the need to belong [for communion] with the need for space [for privacy, solitude]" (p. 219). Furthermore:

> True friends are honest [truthful] with each other, but even when they reveal their foibles, they do so against the backdrop of unconditional acceptance. There is tremendous relief in being known and still being accepted. In telling the truth, friends spur us to growth. Most important, true friends bring out the best in us. They bring to light strengths that no one else looks hard enough to find. (p. 219)

This is easier said than done. Kierkegaard (1995) provides us with an illuminating account as to why the work of friendship is difficult. Kierkegaard views friendship (or romantic love) as an extension of (improper) self-love. "See, therefore," comments Kierkegaard, "erotic love and friendship *as such* are only enhanced and augmented self-love" (p. 267). Moreover, whether we admit it or not, there is always in friendship a limiting element of expectant positive *or* negative reciprocity: "If when another person says, 'I cannot love you any longer,' one proudly answers, 'Then I can also stop loving you – is this independence?'" (p. 39). Or, is this not malignant reciprocity? A mature person's response, should a friend say "I no longer lovingly care for you," would be, "Even so, my loving care for you will abide." This is easier imagined than said and done.

Some say that friendship love is the basis for all other kinds of love. For Kierkegaard (1995), it is love of one's neighbor, even if she or he is one's enemy, is the foundation of all other loves. Neighborly love makes proper friendship love possible. As I see it, both types of love—neighborly love and friendship love, can potentially fertilize each other. But it is Kierkegaard's genius to alert us to the transforming power of neighborly love on friendship love and romantic love. It is neighborly love that shields us from malignant reciprocity. Though neighborly love is the most difficult kind of love to practice, for Kierkegaard, it is the only kind of love that will teach us proper self-love, proper friendship love, and proper romantic or erotic love: "Just as this commandment [to love thy neighbor] will teach everyone how to love oneself, so it also will teach erotic and friendship love genuine love; in loving yourself, preserve love for the neighbor; in erotic love and friendship, preserve love for the neighbor" (pp. 61–62).

What, you might ask, makes neighborly love possible? The answer, for Kierkegaard (1995), is that love between neighbors is made possible by a mediating third or God (GOD = LOVE). "God is the middle term in … love [between neighbors and flowing from that between friends and between romantic lovers]" (p. 107). It is also this mediating third that enables us to love ourselves "because to love God is true self-love" (p. 107). The omitting of the middle term or the mediating third results in the "defraudation of love" (p. 107). *"To love God is to love oneself truly; to help another person to love God is to love another person; to be helped by another person to love God is to be loved"* (p. 107). And again: "it is God who by himself and by means of the middle term 'neighbor' checks on whether the love for wife and friend is conscientious. In other words, only then is your love a matter of conscience" (p. 142). Kierkegaard here is transposing the middle term or mediating third to embody the neighbor. And, "in turn love is a third thing by itself" (p. 260).

To expand on Kierkegaard, the building, sustaining, and enhancement of friendship love (or any other kind of love, including self-love) requires, in my eyes, *multiple thirds*: friends need to be together-in-love, together-in-beauty, together-in-goodness, together-in-truth. Love, beauty, goodness, and truth *are* the mediating thirds. By practicing non-preferential loving of our neighbor with all her or his imperfections, our capacity to love our friend is enhanced. It is this kind of love that forms the love that emanates from our mature, mindful heart. Here I depart from Kierkegaard. For me there seems to be a dialectical relationship between self-love and other-love, between love of neighbor and love of friend, and between friendship love and self-love. Deepening one enriches the other. It flows both ways. But what I retain from

Kierkegaard is that friendship love is sustained and strengthened through the multiplication of mediating thirds.

Allow me to conclude with what I deem to be a fiercely honest reflection on love and friendship. Perry (2017) concludes his musings on Michel de Montaigne with this:

> If reading and writing about Montaigne has taught me anything, it is not that I am on some path to perfection where I never again grab the [shock-delivering electrified] pig fencer. Montaigne *is* the pig fencer jolting me out of my absent-minded musing and into the recognition that through the examination of my *im*perfections I can better serve my obligations to others. … This above all, is what I take from Montaigne. … I am obligated. … I must do better. (p. 215)

Awakening to the accentuation of his obligation to others is one supreme illustration of what we have been calling a "middle term" or a "mediating third." Perry devotes a chapter on "Marriage," focusing especially on his own marriage to his wife, Anneliese. "It is Anneliese," he contemplatively reflects, "who *sees this family* [which includes their two daughters] *as a whole*" (p. 130). There is no doubt that Perry values and jointly shares this kind of *seeing*. This for me is another mediating third. Then there is this beautiful illustration of yet another mediating third, a heart-to-heart, center-to-center, core-to-core communication: "And perhaps the oddest comfort, but the deepest comfort? Anneliese knows my darkest secrets and innermost shames. There are no surprises for her. In my darkest hours this gives me peace of mind, lends me safety. With her I have nothing to hide" (pp. 130–131). "But," adds the perplexed Perry, "when couples say their spouse is their best friend, I wonder what that's like. Anneliese is my truest confidant, my one lover, my *utterly trusted* partner. But friendship? I struggle with that one. … And yet: *intimacy and esteem are not friendship*" (p. 136). Perry goes on to question his unconditional generosity in his relationship to Anneliese and to admit of "*halts and difficulties*" in the relationship which allow for no "*immediate remedy*," but then arrives at the realization that by not conflating the secondary with what is primary, these misunderstandings can be borne with *patience* and *forbearance*. Keeping one's eye on what is primary and not making the secondary primary, as Meister Eckhart advises us, is still another mediating third. And in my humble opinion, with all these mediating thirds, Michael Perry and his life partner, Anneliese, are on their way to becoming ever the best of friends. Intimacy and esteem (admiration), based on mutuality and trust, *are essential facets of friendship*.

References

Augustine, S. (1961). *Confessions*. Penguin.

Barratt, B. B. (2013). *What is psychoanalysis? 100 years after Freud's 'secret committee'*. Routledge.

Black, D. W. (1997). *Vico and moral perception*. Peter Lang.

Bolt, M., & Dunn, D. S. (2016). *Pursuing human strengths: A positive psychology guide* (2nd ed.). Worth Publishers.

Cates, D. F. (2005). Spending the day with a good friend: Autobiography, moral character, and the religious imagination. In P. Lamoureux & K. J. O'Neil (Eds.), *Seeking goodness and beauty: The use of the arts in theological ethics*. Rowman and Littlefield.

Erikson, E. H. (1975). *Life history and the historical moment: Diverse presentations*. W. W. Norton.

Erikson, E. H. (1963). *Childhood and society* (2nd ed.). W. W. Norton.

Erikson, E. H. (1964). *Insight and responsibility*. W. W. Norton.

Fiumara, G. C. (2013). *Psychoanalysis and creativity in everyday life: Ordinary genius*. Routledge.

Kierkegaard, S. (1995). *Works of love* (H. V. Hong & E. H. Hong, Trans.). Princeton University Press.

Martin, J. (2016). *Seven last words: An invitation to a deeper friendship with Jesus*. Harper Collins.

Moustakas, C. (1995). *Being-in, being-for, being-with*. Jason Aronson.

Newman, B. M., & Newman, P. R. (2018). *Development through life: A psychosocial approach* (13th ed.). Cengage Learning.

Perry, M. (2017). *Montaigne in barn boots: An amateur ambles through philosophy*. Harper Collins.

Symington, N. (2012). *The psychology of the person*. Karnac.

Symington, N. (2016). *A healing conversation: How healing happens*. Karnac.

Symington, N. (2019). *The growth of mind*. Routledge.

Welchman, K. (2000). *Erik Erikson: His life, work and significance*. Open University Press.

13

Aloneness: The Capacity to Be at Home with *Aloneness*, Silence, and Solitude

The "basis of the capacity to be alone," says Winnicott (1965), is "the experience of being alone in the presence of someone" and that it emerges as "the ego [self]-supportive environment is [progressively] introjected [internalized] and built into the individual's personality" (p. 36). "This capacity," emphasizes Winnicott, "is one of the most important signs of maturity in emotional development" (p. 29). Through the support of essential others, we internalize multiple maturational functions, one of which is the capacity to be alone. Growing up feeling well held by holding others (Winnicott's "holding environment") our weaknesses are, bit-by-bit, transformed into maturational strengths.

Winnicott (1965) traces the capacity to be alone to its developmental origins in childhood. He then grounds it in the experience of togetherness with the mother. Paradoxically, the capacity to be alone, therefore, has its origin in the "*experience of being alone, as an infant and small child, in the presence of mother*" (p. 30). Dialectically speaking, the experience of being at home with aloneness is made possible (goes hand-in-hand with) the optimal experience of harmonious *companionship* or togetherness.

The capacities for silence and solitude are an outgrowth of the capacity to be alone, while in the presence of essential others. The capacity for solitude, notes Nicholsen (2002), is born out of "the experience of being both separate and merged with the mother" (p. 23). We are first alone in the presence of our mother or another primary giver. Our capacity to be alone is a byproduct of our original bond with or attachment to our mother or our caregiver. This secure attachment or bond makes it safe for us to explore our play space on

© The Author(s), under exclusive license to Springer Nature Switzerland AG 2021
M. J. Hannush, *Markers of Psychosocial Maturation*,
https://doi.org/10.1007/978-3-030-74315-4_13

our own while being mindful of the security-producing presence of our m/other. And "it is this experience from which we develop the capacity for solitude" (p. 23).

In an analogous way, we learn, or better yet we feel or sense, our first "companionable silence" from the silent and relaxed togetherness experienced early in our lives with our essential others, especially our mother, our primal Other. It is originally a shared silence. It probably extends to our existence within our mother's womb. It is the silence of at-homeness. It contains the root of our movement toward healthy differentiation and individuation. It is also the first silence experienced as a response to the emerging *beauty* and *wonder* of the world. It is a quiet and quieting response of awe and wonder we experience in the presence of our mother's beautiful face and precious presence. Like staring at the sun, it may be too much to experience all at once. As a result, it has to be lovingly contained. The need to be protected from overexposure has to be understood and respected.

The capacity to be alone with oneself in silence and solitude needs to be nurtured and cultivated into maturation. It can serve as a counterforce to the other kind of silence that is tinged with tension—the silence that is characterized by agony, alienation, anger, anxiety, despair, embarrassment, fear, guilt, rage, secretiveness, shame, and terror. The latter type of silence can, of course, overwhelm the former kind of silence. Children who have been subjected to the "silent treatment" at the hands of their conditionally accepting parents are likely to experience this type of toxic silence.

Just as we need parents who themselves have cultivated the capacity to be alone with themselves in silence and solitude and the capacity to provide their children with the emotional holding and reflective containing needed for the children to develop their own nascent capacity for continuing to be at home with aloneness and silence, so does culture has to provide its members with rituals that will continue to sustain this precious capacity. We live in a culture that is talkativeness, and not silence, friendly. In fact we grow up in a cultural surround that is saturated with noisy distractions diverting us away from contemplative or companionable silence. This explains the relative popularity of meditation and mindfulness exercises that are to serve as rafts that will help us from drowning in a sea of noisy, idle chatter.

Speech emerges as a figure from the ground of speechless silence. Silence and speech have a figure-and-ground relationship to each other. When the ground of silence is underdeveloped, so is the figure of speech. How we are with silence will have an effect on how we speak. Respectful speaking will mirror our respect for silence.

"For to be alone," Twyman (2005) tells us, "offers the opportunity to follow the pathway of one's own thought" and this, she concludes, "may be the mature individual's use of time alone, a time of reflection, where thought can proceed associatively and connections previously unremarked can be found" (p. 259). The "capacity to be alone," adds Jacobs (1998), is "a vital developmental achievement" and the "avoidance of being alone," he continues, "can be understood as a difficulty" (p. 188). Similarly, seeking to be alone in excess "may indicate a defence against intimate relationships" (p. 188). "In any relationship," he continues, "there needs to be an ebb and flow between closeness and solitude" (p. 188). Dialectically speaking, therefore, there is a healthy and unhealthy way of being intimately together and there is a healthy and unhealthy way of being separately alone. There is a lonely way of being alone. Or, one can feel lonely and alone in the company of others. Additionally, one can be intimately, but unhealthily, enmeshed with an essential other, having lost one's sense of boundary, one's fluidly solid or solidly fluid sense of identity—one's identificatory integrity or relatively integrated identity. The "honest scrutiny of our conscience," remarks Rose (2005), "is essential in finding integrity" (p. 190) or what the early Erikson also calls "integration" and the later Erikson labels as "integrality." But "without a *truthful awareness*" of our contradictions and inconsistencies "we cannot realistically feel we have integrity" (p. 190). Jacobs (1998) poignantly quotes psychoanalyst Eric Rayner as having written, "'to find one's identity it seems centrally important to be able to be alone … alone with one's conscience'" (p. 188).

To achieve relative identity integration and wholeness, we need to cultivate the capacity to be relaxedly alone with our own maturing conscience. If it were an immature conscience, a so-called inner, condemning harsh critic, then we would defensively escape or engage in rationalizing maneuvers to silence this self-lacerating and self-flagellating inner voice. We cannot keep on maturing in the absence of listening and responding to the continuous call of our maturing conscience. We need to be able to be alone with our caring conscience in order to continue growing as co-participants-in-a-common-lifeworld.

Heidegger (1996) makes reference to the *call of conscience*. It is the existential call of our universal humanness. At times it is sensed as felt promptings and not necessarily as specific words, to live up to our ownmost potentiality for becoming our best human selves. "Conscience," specifies Heidegger, "gives us 'something' to understand, it *discloses* … A more penetrating analysis of conscience reveals it as a *call*" (p. 269). The call of conscience summons me to *care*, for that is of the nature of my human existence. Above all, it is *care-for-self* that potentiates my *care-for-others*, and my care for life itself. This caring includes the recognition of my effect on the well-*being* of others. The voice of my existential conscience calls me to be open and live up to my possibilities and potentialities. It beckons me to *listen* to the prodding of my *existential guilt* for owing something to existence. I can always be and do more until the day I die. It invites me to attend to my *existential anxiety*—being-ill-at-ease or experiencing discomfort in the face of (1) ultimately being responsible for making choices which in turn will contribute to the making of who I am as a person; (2) dimly sensing that I will never fully understand or be understood by others; and (3) realizing that I will always be tensely suspended between the polar meanings of human existence (e.g., connectedness versus separateness, dependence versus independence, revealing versus concealing, *communion* versus *aloneness*); (4) tacitly knowing that we are all fragile and vulnerable as we encounter or confront the vicissitudes (blessings and losses, pleasures and pains, joys and sorrows) of existence, including this ephemeral and transitory life itself. Above and beyond the comfort I derive from sharing my discomfort with essential others, I *alone* am ultimately responsible (response-able or able to respond) to the call of my existential conscience. I am forever challenged, while I am conscious and alive, to be tuned to this silent call's stirrings. Alone, in silence, I am summoned. In my aloneness, in silence, and away from idle chatter, I must pay attention. Paradoxically, then, we can *silence* the intimate voice of our existential conscience—the caring voice that beckons us to be and do more.

We are here making a distinction between life-suppressing silence and life-enhancing silence. Ultimately, states Schalow (2017), we need to learn to cultivate the art of "remaining silent, in order to preserve the mystery of human existence *as* a mystery for the individual to rediscover (for him/herself)" (p. 166). In this sacred space of silence, "the individual can first heed a call of [humbling] self-awakening … to an untapped potentiality, of 'who I can be'" (p. 172).

References

Heidegger, M. (1996). *Being and time* (J. Stambaugh, Trans.). State University of New York Press.

Jacobs, M. (1998). *The presenting past: The core of psychodynamic counselling and therapy* (2nd ed.). Open University Press.

Nicholsen, S. W. (2002). *The love of nature and the end of the world: The unspoken dimensions of environmental concern*. The MIT Press.

Rose, J. (2005). Work, identity, and love. In E. Rayner, A. Joyce, J. Rose, M. Twyman, & C. Clulow (Eds.), *Human development: An introduction to the psychodynamics of growth, maturity, and ageing* (4th ed.). Routledge.

Schalow, F. (2017). *Toward a phenomenology of addiction: Embodiment, technology, transcendence*. Springer.

Twyman, M. (2005). Being alone. In E. Rayner, A. Joyce, J. Rose, M. Twyman, & C. Clulow (Eds.), *Human development: An introduction to the psychodynamics of growth, maturity, and ageing* (4th ed.). Routledge.

Winnicott, D. W. (1965). *The maturational processes and the facilitating environment: Studies in the theory of emotional development*. Hogarth Press.

Part V

The Capacities for Self-Esteem, Flexibility, and Resilience

14

Self-Esteem: The Capacity for *Self-Esteem* Regulation

Self-esteem, say Cabaniss and her colleagues (2013), is "the respect or admiration we have for ourselves. Most of us begin life excited by our abilities – think of the joy on infants' faces when they say their first words or take their first steps" (p. 25). Yet, throughout life we are subjected to self-esteem threats. A self-esteem threat is anything that jeopardizes our good feelings about ourselves. Self-esteem regulation refers to the ability to handle self-esteem threats. Stated differently, it is the "ability to pick oneself up after disappointments or slights … and is an important part of how people function in the world" (p. 25). Our patterns of self-esteem regulation vary depending, at least in an important part, on what happens to us during life, especially during the early years.

Some of us are able to keep our "positive self-regard," when we are unexpectedly subjected to emotional wounding by others. We have relative *resilience* in the way we handle threats to our self-esteem. Some of us are much more fragile and are easily injured in the face of self-esteem threats. "Sometimes," continue Cabaniss and her colleagues (2013), "people have particular types of self-esteem threats to which they are especially vulnerable" (p. 26). For example, a person is able to handle criticism from a supervisor at work, but is very sensitive to criticism from a parent or partner. Another person may not be able to handle being unfavorably compared to others. In such situations this individual may become filled with envy-driven rage or may jealously want what the other possesses.

Our patterns of responsiveness to self-esteem threats can be adaptive or maladaptive, conscious or, mostly, unconscious. The aim of these patterns, which are established over time, beginning with childhood, is to regain our

© The Author(s), under exclusive license to Springer Nature Switzerland AG 2021

M. J. Hannush, *Markers of Psychosocial Maturation*,
https://doi.org/10.1007/978-3-030-74315-4_14

good feelings about ourselves when they are derailed. "More adaptive patterns," observe Cabaniss and her colleagues (2013), "restore positive feelings flexibly while maintaining other functions, such as relationships with others" (p. 27). The most adaptive pattern of responses to self-esteem injuries or threats are not only flexible, but they also "utilize the most adaptive defenses" such as altruism, humor, and sublimation (p. 28). "People with more adaptive self-esteem regulation strategies," they conclude, "are able to take advice, metabolize it, and make their own decisions. They take pleasure and pride in their accomplishments without relying exclusively on others for praise" (p. 29). Our need for praise can be subsumed under what Heinz Kohut calls "the need for mirroring," which includes the needs for admiration, affirmation, attention, praise, recognition, and validation. Part of our maturing process involves the internalization of the capacity for mirroring. We will always need others to positively mirror us to ourselves. However, this needs to be balanced with our own ability to admire, praise, and validate ourselves for our praise-worthy accomplishments and admirable conduct internally. It necessitates knowing when we have done a good job without needing to hear praise from others.

Acquiring a relatively resilient sense of self-esteem requires of us to have an accurate sense of our strengths and limitations. It requires that our assessment of our strengths and limitations is in general synchrony with the evaluation of essential others who know us well. This also applies to our overall sense of who we are. We need to be able to question ourselves directly about our talents, capacities, ambitions, and goals without becoming defensive and without engaging in self-deception and self-justification.

The capacity for self-esteem regulation is acquired early in life as we begin to construct a nascent sense of our talents and limitations. Accurate acknowledgment of our competencies and shortcomings enables us to regulate our sense of self-esteem. "Parents who appropriately **mirror** their children," say Cabaniss and her colleagues (2013), "are excited by what the children are able to do, without overinflating or downplaying it" (p. 95). Children thrive upon their parents' "empathic feedback or sensitive support" (p. 95). Provided with appropriate mirroring, they develop a core sense of self that is characterized by relative consistency and constancy. As adults, they do not rely excessively on the opinions of others "to keep their self-esteem afloat." They do not "swing back and forth between overly inflated views of their own abilities and deep-seated feelings of inferiority" (p. 95). They do not need to devalue others so that they can shore up their fragile sense of self. Having been provided with accurate "mirroring" of their true abilities and talents, they grow into early adulthood with a stable sense of their own worth—a solid sense of self-esteem.

They acquire the ability to persevere in solving tasks and in pursuing their life projects. Along with a healthy sense of self-esteem, they acquire a strong sense of self-efficacy.

Cultural factors, say Cabaniss and her colleagues (2013), can affect self-esteem development in young adulthood between the years of 18 and 23. "Imagine," they suggest as an example, "a first-generation young adult in a community of white Americans – will that person feel attractive? Shunned? Excluded? Will he or she be able to find a partner? Maybe 'yes' and maybe 'no,' … Religious [and cultural] differences can also affect the young adult's ability to form relationships during this period" (p. 118). Not being accepted for being culturally or religiously different can have a deleterious effect on the young adult's tenuous sense of self-esteem.

The capacities for trust, for secure attachment, for having built a solid or consolidated sense of self, and for forming good relationships in the earliest years can buoy our sense of self-esteem in times of turmoil and loss. A "generally positive sense of self-esteem," continue Cabaniss and her colleagues (2013), "characterized by an acceptance of our positive and negative qualities and the capacity to maintain good feelings about ourselves in a variety of contexts, including adversity or criticism from others" is essential for healthy psychological functioning (p. 182). They add:

> The development of healthy self-esteem is thought to depend both on inborn characteristics, such as resilience and optimism, and on relationships with early caregivers. How caregivers respond to their children's emotional states and developing physical and cognitive abilities plays a crucial role in helping children to feel good about themselves and to have a positive but realistic sense of their capacities and limitations. (pp. 182–183)

"Negotiating the discrepancies between ambitions and talents in a realistic way," continue Cabaniss et al. (2013), is a key ingredient in the acquisition of a relatively solid sense of self-esteem (p. 118). Accurate parental mirroring and realistic encouragement, praise of, and pride in children's abilities, achievements, and accomplishments strengthen the development of children's sense of self-esteem and self-efficacy. Bandura (1977) defines self-efficacy as "the conviction that one can successfully execute the behavior required to produce the outcomes" demanded in specific situations (p. 79). This "I-can" feeling, which is behind one's confidence in one's competence, opens up one's existential space of meaning-action possibilities. Moreover, parents who are psychologically able to mentalize and empathize with the emotional states and needs of their young children help them develop a secure sense of self-esteem. When parents help their children accept their limitations and acknowledge their strengths, children acquire a *realistic sense of self* that is not overly vulnerable to being easily wounded by the slings and arrows of life that are hurled at them as they grow older.

The capacity to regulate one's sense of self in general or one's sense of self-esteem in particular, contend Cabaniss and her colleagues (2013), is a byproduct of our earliest experiences with our caregivers. Adults whose earliest caregivers have recognized and acknowledged their abilities and have thus been adequately mirrored have learned to assess their capacities accurately and have felt good about themselves. They have had parents who have been realistically attuned to their capacities, limitations, and potentials. These caregivers have neither underestimated nor overestimated their abilities. As adults, they are not likely to experience achievement-related problems. They tend to function smoothly in their interactions with others, for they are not overly sensitive to criticism and do not feel easily blamed and attacked. They are not overly critical of themselves. They do not quickly become anxious, enraged, or devastated in the face of self-esteem threats. They are able to quickly regulate these self-esteem threats. They do not use and manipulate others to bolster their fragile self-esteem. They are not too harsh on themselves. They do not carry the heavy burden of a shame-based sense of self. They do not need to construct a *compensatory false self* that is caused by inadequate mirroring and a lack of acceptance of the *real spontaneous self*. They do not need to present a false front of arrogance and exaggerated confidence when they confront threats to their self-esteem. Instead, they have developed a "true" sense of self that is based on good-enough mirroring and more unconditional and lesser conditional acceptance. As adults, they can tolerate disappointments when some of their goals are not achieved. They do not become easily discouraged when they, on occasions, do not perform well or achieve their desired goals. They have acquired a realistic and healthy sense of themselves. They do not rely on "superficial markers of success" (p. 186).

Securely attached individuals, say Cabaniss and her colleagues (2013), are able to self-regulate. Our early dyadic relationship with our primary caregivers mediates "the development of fundamental capacities that allow the person to have a sense of self, form relationships with others, adapt to stress and anxiety, and self-regulate" (pp. 191–192).

We are born to become attached to essential others. It is the quality or pattern of our attachment that mirrors the degree of our security or insecurity. It is the protective nurturance that our parents provide us that makes us feel safe and secure. We come to experience our social environment as predictable and fathomable. We feel at ease and home-in-the-world. "The sense of safety [and security] that children get from their central caregiving relationship," add Cabaniss and her colleagues (2013), "helps them to develop the system of emotional regulation that they use to handle a wide variety of experiences … to develop relatively stable patterns of adapting to stress and regulating their responses to anxiety and affects" (p. 192).

Securely attached children are better able to tolerate separations and are more easily soothed and comforted. As adults, securely attached individuals are able to incorporate pleasurable *and* painful memories into their life narratives. They "can think about others in three-dimensional terms, and can look at emotions from other people's point of view. They find it relatively easy to become emotionally close to others and are comfortable both depending on others and having others depend on them" (Cabaniss, et al., 2013, p. 193).

Securely attached children's "caregivers," state Cabaniss and her colleagues (2013), "can understand and process their emotional experiences (this is also called mentalization …). … The caregivers' processing of emotion fosters the development of the child's ability to **regulate affect**, that is, the ability to handle basic emotions, such as fear, anxiety, insecurity, and excitement" (p. 194). The children of such sensitively attuned, responsive, and empathic parents become adept at self-regulation, especially in relation to "modulating their sense of self, their capacity for impulse control, and their reaction to anxiety" (p. 194).

Compared to insecurely attached adults, securely attached adults find more adaptive ways of managing separations, setbacks, and losses. They are secure enough to consider multiple ways of looking at a situation and alternative ways of managing their feelings about it. They are able to process and thus handle intense feelings more effectively. As a consequence of identifying with secure caregivers, they have internalized ways of observing and describing in a clear fashion what goes on in their minds and the minds of others. They are better able to modulate their affects and, thus, self-regulate.

In his "overall summary … [of] *the potentials realized in well or optimally functioning persons*, viewed from a person-centered perspective," Barrett-Lennard (1998) provides the following partial portrait:

> He/she is not weighted by conditions of worth and is not judgmental in stance toward self, although at ease in appraising self-capacities and goals. Basically, the person has an accepting and regardful or valuing attitude toward self. This is a primary, spontaneous self-esteem, not a reactive need to regard self as superior [or exceptionally special]. (pp. 180–181)

This distinction between *primary self-esteem* and *reactive self-esteem* is easily overlooked in the literature on self-esteem. It has a phenomenological resonance. This primary esteeming (accepting, regarding, and valuing) of the self is a primordial and pre-reflective self-world stance. Although he does not call it "primary," it is this that Hart (2009b) has in mind when he states that "esteem is not merely for the abstract 'myself' but the 'myself' as entelechy [or the *vital* principle guiding the development and functioning of an organism] working out one's 'personification' [embodiment in action]" (p. 201). "For Rogers," Hart continues,

> this is a balance between being and becoming. The ideally functioning person moves toward and through the process she inwardly and actually is and moves away from being any façade of herself. Such false versions of herself, as [phenomenological philosopher and psychologist Eugene] Gendlin would say, cause her to get 'stuck' and not be able to carry forward the process of her felt sense [or felt meaning]. She does not try to be more than she is in the sense of what is less true of herself; such acts lead to feelings of 'insecurity and bombastic defensiveness' which of necessity interfere with letting one's capacity carry one forward. Nor is it a move toward less than she is 'with the attendant feelings of guilt and self-depreciation.' Rogers believes that the work of sorting out and choosing the course of living to be the sort of person that she most values being is the truest expression of who she really is. (p. 201)

Hart (2009a), in concurrence with Saint Augustine, equates what we have been calling *primary self-esteem* with originary and pre-reflective *self-love*. For "Augustine this original self-presence prior to reflective acts may be thought of as a kind of original loving and knowing and understanding oneself" (p. 80).

For Hart (2009a), ipseity ("I-ness"), selfhood, and who one is (or who I am) are interchangeable. Further, "what the 'I' refers to is connected to my personal being and thus world, as the open field [of possibilities] and ultimate horizon of all *agency* and *perception [or interpretation or understanding of meaning possibilities]* within which my *personal self* unfolds, my deeds are launched, and everything comes to light" (p. 79). *Primary self-esteem* or *primordial self-love guides the bodily self's agentic balance-seeking among its lifeworld meaning possibilities and involvements.*

I will now go further by first making a distinction between what Bandura (1977) calls *self-efficacy* and what I label as *primary self-efficacy* and then link it to *primary self-regulation (or self-balance).*

Again, Bandura (1977) defines self-efficacy as a having confidence in one's competence. More specifically, it refers to the conviction that *I can* successfully respond to the demands of a given situation. Bandura theorizes, and provides experimental evidence for, four sources that contribute to judgments of self-efficacy: history of successful past experiences, vicarious participation in the successful enactments of others who serve as models, verbal encouragement, and felt bodily feedback. By *primary self-efficacy*, I mean that, under optimal conditions, the *I-can* felt sense is there to begin with; it is a pre-given. These four sources are simply echoes, resonances, or reverberations for our primordial "I-can" felt sense. The same applies to our primary self-esteem and primary self-regulation (self-balance). Here is Fuller (1990) describing an efficacious human hand competently stretching and reaching out for an apple: "One's sensible hand, one's body, is oneself being possible. One's hand *exists*, it has itself to be. One's hand is an 'I can,' and no 'it.' One's hand's space, that of oneself as a bodily self, is an existential space of possibility of significance [meaning]" (p. 68).

I, as human *being* [Dasein], am familiar with and competent in enacting everyday meanings that make up my lifeworld. A human *being*, writes Fuller (1990), is "an 'I am able to' with regard to the relational totality of world" (p. 53). *Being capable* is equivalent to *being possible*. Quoting Heidegger, Fuller adds, "'*I am, that is, I can*'" (p. 53). To exist is to be and become. I can not only be, but also I can do. The "I can do" is the other side of the "I can be." "The I can" signals an openness to what can realistically be done with lifeworld possibilities.

"All in all," concludes Fuller (1990), "the bodily self is a historically situated *center of meaning* … and meaning is a phenomenal event through and through" (pp. 164–165). The self is always directed toward positive, neutral, or negative meanings. Positive feeling-and-value-laden-meanings are "'to be reached,' 'to be supported,' 'to be maintained'" and negative feeling-and-value-laden-meanings are "'to be avoided,' 'to be changed in the positive direction,' 'to be eliminated'" (p. 140). Whereas positive meanings trigger peace, negative meanings elicit restless tension. We humans strive for balance by moving toward good meanings that provide us with peace and harmony and moving away from bad meanings that cause tension and strife. However, some seemingly good meanings can be upset by seemingly bad meanings. When the latter are absorbed and incorporated, the result can be the achievement of a better balancing and integrative meaning. Allow me to give an example. Being dependent means for me something uncomfortable that is to be avoided. Being independent means for me something comfortable that is to be attained. Finding myself safe, secure, and non-defensive in a loving relational context that affirms my original worthiness unconditionally (primary self-esteem) and my original competence (primary self-efficacy), I find myself open to the possibility of opening myself to stretching the meanings of "dependency" and "independency." Suddenly I "see" that "dependency" can have a "good" meaning and that "independence" can have a bad meaning. These are not simply "abstract" meanings. They are lived-action-meanings. They are embodied meanings to be enacted. They are *existential meanings lived out in existential space*. I have achieved a higher order form of primary self-regulation, a *self-world balance* – a balance between the seemingly polar meanings of dependence and independence. My lived meanings have undergone articulation and individuation. Simply put, my meanings (and the bodily self that is directed to these lifeworld meanings) have undergone psychosocial maturation.

References

Bandura, A. (1977). *Social learning theory*. Prentice-Hall.

Barrett-Lennard, G. T. (1998). *Carl Rogers' helping system: Journey and substance*. Sage.

Cabaniss, D. L., Cherry, S., Douglas, C. J., Graver, R. L., & Schwartz, A. R. (2013). *Psychodynamic formulation*. Wiley.

Fuller, A. R. (1990). *Insight into value: An exploration of the premises of a phenomenological psychology*. State University of New York Press.

Hart, J. G. (2009a). *Who one is, Book 1: Meontology of the "I": A transcendental phenomenology*. Springer.

Hart, J. G. (2009b). *Who one is, Book 2: Existenz and transcendental phenomenology*. Springer.

15

Flexibility: The Capacity for *Flexibility*

Horney (1970) describes three primary character structures or trends: moving toward, against, or away from others. "In a healthy human relationship," she asserts, "the moves toward, against, or away from others are not mutually exclusive" (p. 19). The mentally healthy individual can move flexibly between these relational modalities. Horney (1970) elaborates:

> The ability to want and give affection, to give in [move toward others]; the ability to fight [move against others], and the ability to keep to oneself [move away from others] – these are complementary capacities necessary for good human relations. But in the child who feels himself on precarious ground because of his basic anxiety [insecurity], these moves become extreme and rigid. Affection, for instance, becomes clinging; compliance becomes appeasement. Similarly, he is driven to rebel or to keep aloof, without reference to his real feelings and regardless of the inappropriateness of his attitude in a particular situation. The degree of blindness and rigidity in his attitudes is in proportion to the intensity of the basic anxiety [insecurity] luring within him … The three moves toward, against, and away from others therefore constitute a conflict, his basic conflict with others. In time, he tries to solve it by making one of these moves consistently predominant – tries to make his prevailing attitude one of compliance, or aggressiveness, or aloofness. (p. 19)

In the concluding chapter, Horney (1970) provides us with what she describes as a "streamlined summary":

> [The core of neurosis is] *a disturbance in one's relation to self and others* … [These relational disturbances] obstructed the child's unhampered psychic growth. Instead of developing a basic confidence in self and others, the child developed

© The Author(s), under exclusive license to Springer Nature Switzerland AG 2021
M. J. Hannush, *Markers of Psychosocial Maturation*,
https://doi.org/10.1007/978-3-030-74315-4_15

> basic anxiety, which I defined as a feeling of being isolated and helpless toward a world potentially hostile. In order to keep this basic anxiety at a minimum the spontaneous moves toward, against, and away from others became compulsive. While spontaneous moves were compatible, each with the others, the compulsive ones collided. The conflicts generated this way, which I called basic conflicts, were therefore the result of conflicting needs and conflicting attitudes with regard to other people. And the first attempts at [pseudo] solution were largely attempts at [pseudo] integration, through giving full reign to some of these needs and attitudes and suppressing others. (p. 368; pp. 366–367)

Kelman (1971) provides us with yet another way of describing these *relational moves*:

> In order to keep his basic anxiety [insecurity] at a minimum, the child's spontaneous moves toward closeness in affection, away from people to be by himself, and against others to affirm a stand become compulsive compliance, aggression and detachment ... While spontaneous moves are freely oscillating, the compulsive ones are rigid, absolute, and indiscriminate – attributes which make for ease and intensity of conflict. Horney called them 'basic conflicts' – the consequence of opposing needs and attitudes in regard to others. (p. 44)

Those individuals who express inflexible compliance, says Solomon (2006):

> attempt to reduce basic anxiety by evoking an affectionate reaction [from others]. They value unselfishness ... [Those] who show [inflexible] expansiveness strive for [hyper] mastery. They hate helplessness. Their prominent traits are arrogance, vindictiveness, and perfectionism ... [Those] who manifest [inflexible] detachment want [pseudo or false] freedom. They venerate self-sufficiency. They ... usually feel they are better than anyone else. Basic anxiety is dealt with by moving away from people. They live a rather narrow existence, asking very little out of life to avoid being disappointed. Above all else, they do not want to be bothered. (p. 111)

Solomon concludes by commenting: "In my clinical experience, seldom does a patient display exclusively one [pseudo] solution; rather most patients indicate a mixture of the major trends" (p. 110). Even though one inflexible pseudo-solution may be in the foreground, the other two potential pseudo-solutions are lurking in the background ready to replace the one in the foreground.

Teyber and Teyber (2017) refine and expand upon Horney's three major character structures or trends and their pseudo-solutions: (1) moving toward others with its pseudo-solution of complying, appeasing, and overly pleasing others while attempting to be perfect; (2) moving against others with its pseudo-solution of being aggressive, controlling, dominating, expansive, and always attempting to take charge in relation to others; and (3) moving away from others with its pseudo-solution of being detached, invisible, rigidly self-sufficient, conflict-avoiding, and seemingly free from others.

Instead of speaking in terms of "character structures" or character trends, Teyber and Teyber (2017) use, more aptly, the terms interpersonal coping strategies, patterns, or styles. They define *interpersonal coping styles* as "the habitual coping strategies employed in interpersonal relationships to ward off anxiety and maintain self-esteem" (p. 372). Inflexible coping strategies are "pervasively and rigidly overused – even in situations where it is not necessary or no longer adaptive" (p. 224). The "inflexible coping style," elaborate Teyber and Teyber, aims "to systematically elicit responses from others that may seem self-defeating yet have served to avoid anxiety or support self-esteem in the past. These eliciting maneuvers – or 'security operations' as [Harry Stack] Sullivan … has termed them – are interpersonal defenses" (p. 261). In contrast, the individual with a *flexible* coping style, while *tolerating ambiguity* and discomfort, remains non-defensive and resists the temptation to take refuge in "eliciting maneuvers" or "security operations."

The person with an immature interpersonal coping style habitually elicits less than optimal responses from others, responses that once served the purpose of eschewing anxiety or shoring up one's fragile self-esteem in the past. The mature person does not engage in such eliciting maneuvers, security-guarding operations, or interpersonal defenses. He or she uses flexible, in contrast to rigid, interpersonal strategies in attempting to resolve relational conflicts and to live harmoniously with others.

Healthy and flexible interpersonal coping strategies are the combined byproducts of secure attachments, effective child-rearing practices, and healthy structural family relations where boundaries between family members are respected and alliances are not skewed – where there is no triangulation (e.g., mother-son vs. father) and no parentification (child assuming premature caring responsibilities for parents in a role reversal). When experienced consistently, especially in the sensitive period of early life, these healthy and flexible coping strategies give rise to harmonious internal working models (representations or templates) of the relational world, adaptive and constructive beliefs about oneself, and discerningly benign, yet realistic expectations of others – a broad and flexible view of what will typically happen in intimate relationships. Having acquired a healthy and solid sense of self-esteem as a consequence, *maturing* individuals develop a flexible interpersonal coping style. They can differentiate between interpersonal situations that call for taking charge, accommodating and yielding, or avoiding and withdrawing. They are not fixedly stuck on the use of any one style of coping strategy. Their interpersonal coping style is pervasively adaptive and constructive.

Flexible individuals, state Teyber and Teyber (2017), are securely attached. Secure persons value close relationships. "**Secure** … adults [are] free from excessive anxiety in intimate or close relationships … [They] function independently but can seek help when distressed – they discuss relationships clearly and openly, exhibit reflective capacity, and show empathy for others and themselves" (p. 374). When they describe the role of attachments in their developmental histories, as they remember them, they do so in a non-defensive and non-distortive manner. "These coherent 'attachment narratives' … are based on having received a Safe Haven and Secure Base from their caregivers, which leads to a more integrated identity or coherent sense of self" (p. 186). "**Safe haven**," elaborate Teyber and Teyber, refers to "the empathy and emotional responsiveness that an attachment figure reliably offers when a young child is frightened, distressed or vulnerable" (p. 374). As adults, secure individuals are able to provide this experience of affirmation, attunement, empathy, perspective taking, recognition, and validation to essential others, especially when the others are distressed. "**Secure base**" refers to "the active support that caregivers offer to facilitate a child's exploration and increasing independence" (p. 374). As adults, secure individuals are able to explore independently while remaining related and at the same time encourage independence and exploration-seeking in essential others while they maintain close connections to them.

Secure adults, continue Teyber and Teyber (2017), think and relate flexibly. "Researchers find that secure adults are more efficacious, more flexible cognitively and interpersonally and more resilient – better capable of dealing with stress than [insecure adults]" (p. 187). They are able to "discuss relationships clearly and openly, exhibit reflectiveness (i.e., the adaptive capacity to think flexibly about their own – and other's – thoughts, feelings, and intentions)" (p. 187). Moreover, even when past experiences were not all positive, secure adults are able to "acknowledge the impact of childhood experiences realistically" (p. 187). Having had their attachment needs for the most part met, these individuals, all things considered, become autonomous and resilient in adulthood. They have acquired "the significant psychological strengths of emotional self-regulation, impulse control, empathy, and agency … they possess a positive IWM [Internal Working Model] of Self as being good or worthy of care, and that some carefully filtered Others are positive or trustworthy" (p. 187). Even those who had a shaky start in life and therefore were not securely attached in childhood can become secure adults after having "addressed their problematic experiences realistically and worked through them" thus "achieving or earning security (**earned security**)" (p. 187). This *earned security* unfolds in a relational context involving a secure attachment figure, a context that repeatedly provides a corrective or reparative relational experience. These "reparative relationships" can be with therapists or they can be "with aunts and uncles, friends, teachers, and mentors" (p. 230). In these reparative relationships, security-earning children, adolescents, or adults learn that needs and feelings can be expressed and directly dealt with – that attachment needs can be non-defensively addressed and met.

In short, the previously inflexible, defensive, and maladaptive interpersonal coping style of *security-earning* adolescents and adults is transformed into a flexible, non-defensive, and adaptive interpersonal coping style.

> Because life is stressful for everyone and all people need defenses, healthy individuals will also employ these three interpersonal styles [moving toward, against, and away] at times. When they do not become exaggerated or used pervasively, there are adaptive strengths features in them … However, they are not an identity or way of living for well-functioning people who use them flexibly to cope with a difficult person or problematic situation … [They] learn to discriminate or assess more realistically when and with whom they need to cope in one of these ways, and when and with whom they don't. (Teyber and Teyber 2017, p. 232)

Secure adults have learned that "*more flexible or varied interpersonal coping styles will serve them better*" (p. 233). They know when to move toward (please or yield), move against (take, gently and firmly, a confrontational stance), or move away (avoid or withdraw). They do not identify with or tie their identity to any of these relational stances. They *are not* their ability to please, to confront, or to avoid. They are more and other than these relational postures. Their sense of Self does not depend on their ability to please, achieve, or insulate oneself. They have developed "a wider experiential/interpersonal range" (p. 234). Having experienced a Secure Haven and "having had a Secure Base," they have learned to "venture flexibly into new relationships" (p. 235).

Flexibility is the core of the healthy and constructive coping style. But the capacity for relational flexibility itself requires the capacities for empathy and perspective taking. The mature person has the flexibility to decenter – to *bracket* or set aside his or her own perspective and enter and try to make sense of another person's subjective worldview or existential reality. Additionally, flexible individuals know when to relinquish control, yield, or serenely surrender. They can *tolerate the ambiguity* of not knowing what will transpire in a current relational transaction. They remain open to the unpredictable and the spontaneous. They are receptive to the possibility of the unfolding of a new direction in their encounter with the Other, a direction that may open up new horizons, possibilities, or domains of meaning. Kelman (1971) refers to this happening as "kairos" [the Greek God of opportunity]. Here he is quoting the existential theologian Paul Tillich to explicate the meaning of *kairos*:

> 'Kairos points to unique moments in the temporal process, moments in which something unique can happen or be accomplished. In the English word 'timing' something of the experience which underlies the term kairos is preserved. Timing means doing something at the right time ... Kairos emphasizes the qualitative experiential unique element in the [lived] temporal process.' (p. 426)

Kelman (1971) elaborates further:

> *Kairos* implies a right time in the course of events to do certain things that will favor a crucial happening; the necessity to be aware that there is such a right time so that it might be prepared for; and that is an opportunity which must be immediately recognized and ceased upon. The context of *kairos* must be experienced to be acted upon ...
>
> *Kairos* is a living palpitating process having direction leading to a peak of heightened tension following the relaxation of which new patternings obtain which have the characteristics of being more open, more flexible, more dynamic, and more spontaneous. (p. 427)

Flexibility, fluidity, or, more precisely, "proteanism," says Lifton (1993), is the key not only to our resilience, but also to our psychosocial *maturation* and to wise living in a fragmented and fragmenting age. Lifton provides us with a detailed portrait of *the protean self*. He defines "the self ... [as] one's inclusive sense (or symbolization) of one's own being" (p. 2). "If the self is a symbol of one's organism," he continues, "the protean self-process is the continuous psychic re-creation of that symbol" (p. 5). Even though this process is laden with confusion and treachery, "it allows for an *opening out* of individual life, for a self of many possibilities" (p. 5). Self-making, therefore, is a creative and re-creative process:

> Though variation is the essence of the protean self, that self has certain relatively consistent features. Central to its function is a capacity for bringing together disparate and seemingly incompatible elements of identity and involvement in what I call 'odd combinations,' and for continuous transformation of these ele-

> ments ... At the same time, the protean self must cope with, and sometimes even cultivate, feelings of fatherlessness [or parentless-ness] and homelessness associated with shifts in authority and mentorship ... One may take on the psychology of a survivor and undergo symbolic forms of death and rebirth that contribute further to shapeshifting. At the same time, one always seeks a degree of form, grounding, and cohesion. (p. 5)

Lifton (1993) lifts the capacity for "shapeshifting" – flexibility, fluidity, or proteanism, to a new heightened level of importance. It is now considered to be a prime marker of psychosocial maturity and mental health. But this protean self is not a chameleon-like identity at all. This capacity for proteanism is named after Homer's mythological figure Proteus who takes, among many others, the shape of a lion, a serpent, tree, or water. Lifton tells us that "shapeshifting can be equated with wisdom," and again, it suggests "the blending of radical fluidity, functional wisdom, and a quest for at least minimal form" (p. 5). A sense of absurdity, irony, humor, and mockery, especially self-mockery, "lubricate" the protean self's perception of and transaction with the lifeworld. His or her mind is laden with "'playful and self-ironizing' patterns" (p. 8). His or her emotions tend to be "free-floating, not clearly tied to cause or target" and are "embraced temporarily and selectively, with no promise of permanence" (p. 6). Similarly, the protean self holds his or her ideas tentatively, until further notice. Things could always be otherwise. He or she has the "capacity to sustain and live out moral principles in the midst of psychological flux" (p. 6). The protean self's "overall quest involves a struggle for larger human connectedness" (p. 6).

The protean self, Lifton (1993) tells us, is able to transform suffering (trauma) into "expressions of insight, compassion, and innovation" (p. 7). He or she derives energy from his or her pain. This remembered pain can be recollected, creatively and imaginatively. This involves a "'grounded imagination' – ideas and actions that transcend immediate arrangements while being rooted in personal and professional knowledge and experience" (p. 7).

The protean self, Lifton (1993) adds, is on a "quest for authenticity and meaning, a form-seeking assertion of the self" (p. 9). His or her *tolerance of ambiguity*, complexity, and uncertainty "may well represent a certain maturation in our concept of self" (p. 9). The protean self "presses toward human commonality" or a "connection to humankind" (pp. 11–12).

Flexibility tempers the proclivity toward destructiveness. "The protean self," notes Lifton (1993), "represents an alternative to violence" (p. 11). Flexibility decreases the likelihood of our aggressiveness. Our flexibility manifests itself in our "*open-ended behavioral repertoire*" (p. 13). We have "the capacity for flexible imagination and action" (p. 13). We can playfully transmute culturally or "historically transmitted *patterns of meaning*." Even our perception of time – which includes our conception of the future and our own finality, can be re-vision-ed. After all, "the knowledge that we die … is crucial to a sense of self" (p. 14). The protean self possesses "the capacity to symbolize, to make endlessly imaginative use of the self's cultural and psychological resources" (p. 14).

"Protean flexibility," states Lifton (1993), "enables one to move toward empathy or to return to it after a lapse … Proteanism enables men and women alike to call for that potential for weblike connectedness and empathic sensitivity" (p. 215). Through empathy – "thinking and feeling our way into the minds of others," we "assert our commonality … [we] include the other's humanity in one's own imagination … empathy is a key to species awareness … Crucial to the development of species awareness is empathy for [the] trauma and suffering [of others]" (pp. 214–215). What we need here is "an evolving species self" (p. 216). Our proteanism involves us in an "empathic circle," allowing us to "transform new traumas in a species direction" and thus expand our humanity (p. 216). Our proteanism or flexibility makes it possible for us to "create from suffering" (p. 217). It also connects us not only to other humans, but to nonhumans – animals or nature itself, of which we are a part.

The "protean mind," elaborates Lifton (1993), is characterized by "skepticism and openness" (p. 224). Other "protean characteristics … [are] shifts in ideas, work innovations, free-floating emotions and communities … [and] receptivity to broader human ties" (p. 225). "The protean self can transcend time and space – to contain simultaneously elements from highly divergent historical periods and equally divergent geographical and cultural places" (p. 225). "The protean self need not be here or there but can be here *and* there … [it can] leap from the individual mind to the shared aspirations and images of an entire historical era" (p. 225). While seeking independence from "prior ties," the flexible self does not cut him or herself off from such connections, but rather changes the nature of his or her dependence. The protean self is sustained by the image: "I am a human being," and, "However extensive or brief my own journey on the earth, I live on in humankind" (p. 226). For the flexible self, the "possibilities for improvisation are limitless" (p. 227). The fluid self is forever "struggling for a species mentality" (p. 227).

In line with our dialectical model, the flexible self, emphasizes Lifton (1993), seeks *balance*:

> The protean self seeks to be both fluid and grounded, however tenuous that combination … there is a continuous effort without clear termination.

> Proteanism, then, is a balancing act between responsive shapeshifting, on the one hand, and efforts to consolidate and cohere, on the other. (p. 9)
>
> [The protean self-process involves exploring] combinations of local identification (personal, familial, ethnic, religious, occupational, national) with principles of human commonality, to move back and forth between the two while at the same time blending them into an evolving species self. (p. 227)
>
> We modify the self to include connections virtually anywhere while clinging to a measure of coherence. The individual thus learns to develop a 'place for many places,' while prevailing historical forces propel the process toward ever greater inclusiveness ... Mutability and inclusiveness can replace, or at least undermine, the rigidity and exclusion inherent in the violent act. (p. 230)
>
> The [cultural] tradition provides a certain centering to balance the risky decentering inherent in contemporary forays, an element of cultural grounding necessary for the stretch toward the species. It is a tradition that provides a context for transcendence of context. The protean self, then, becomes a bridge between the modern and the postmodern, a source of continuity that takes in radical discontinuity. (p. 231)

It is our capacity for symbolization, representation, or meaning making, observes Lifton (1993), which makes our proteanism possible. It is "responsible for Mozart sonatas and the theory of relativity – and the basis for proteanism, for a sense of self that can be fluid and multiple" (p. 26). For Lifton, the *fluid self*, the *protean self*, and the *symbolizing self* are interchangeable. I would add the *dialectical self*, the *flexible self*, the *ironic self*, and the *playful self* to this interchangeable list of "selves."

> The principle of the symbolizing self helps resolve several false dichotomies: symbolizations are *both* "rational" and "irrational," relate to *both* "inner" and "outer" worlds, are *both* individual and communal. Similarly that principle enables us to engage the self's simultaneous involvement with proximate (or immediate nitty-gritty) experiences having to do with people and events on an everyday level, on the one hand; and with an ultimate level of larger human connectedness (or symbolization of immortality), on the other ... [It helps us resolve] our struggles with connection and separation, with movement and stasis, and with integrity [or relative integration] and disintegration [or deintegration]. (p. 29)

This "self," Lifton (1993) tells us, "operates 'in moral space,' from a 'frame or horizon within which I can try to determine from case to case what is good, or valuable, or what ought to be done, or what I endorse or oppose'" (p. 30).

Our self is, above all, oriented to the good. "That 'orientation to the good' can become hauntingly elusive, but remains integral to the protean enterprise" (p. 30). This moral orientation goes hand-in-hand with our capacity for self-world reflexive symbolization. "This ever-present capacity to divide oneself into observer and observed can all too easily lapse into forms of dissociation, but can also contribute to creative self-guidance" (p. 30).

"The essence of the protean self," Lifton (1993) informs us, "lies in its odd combinations" (p. 50). It lies in its capacity to *link* the different identity elements or sub-selves that sometimes seem irreconcilable. Still, amidst this discontinuous exploration, a sense of continuity is retained. The protean self "continually combines its fragments in order to avoid fragmentation" (p. 50). He or she is capable of constantly restructuring its self-world images. He or she possesses "the ever present capacity for emerging from 'stuckness'" (p. 51). His or her openness allows him or her to partake of "varied life experiences and to ways of responding to them" (p. 58). His or her mental health is contingent upon its continuous innovation. The protean self can "carve out new combinations of content and capacity" (p. 66). Proteanism is a "balancing act between grounding and fluidity" (p. 60). It is this grounded fluidity or fluid grounding that allows the flexible self to remain open to making "new and unexpected combinations of human beings, cultures, ideas, politics, movies, songs" (p. 73). From this confluence, new and creative combinations or fusions can be fashioned. The fluid self can even fashion a sense of location and at-home-ness in the midst of dislocation and homelessness.

The protean self, Lifton (1993) reflects, is "in touch with death and death-related experiences [such as losses and separations], a way that, in turn, contributes to his capacity for empathy and to his ethical and political energies" (p. 63). He derives hope even from adversity and is exquisitely attuned to the "relationship between suffering and creativity" (p. 63). Instead of falling apart, he or she takes a solid stance against the falling apart of the surrounding world. He or she constructively confronts collective threats to the survival of one's fragile and vulnerable world. He or she engages in acts of resistance to such threats from which he or she derives a feeling of freedom.

The protean self, Lifton (1993) elaborates, is committed to the enhancement of life even as he or she confronts pain, suffering, and the inevitability of death – one's own and those of his or her loved ones. The "*death guilt* that one feels from having survived where others have died … can become animating and transformed into various expressions of responsibility and moral concern" (p. 82). Instead of shutting down, as survivor, the fluid self opens out and makes oneself vulnerable to the experience of pain. He or she humbly accepts his or her limitedness in what is doable in the aftermath of survival.

The flexible self is helped by his or her affirmations that "include the basic satisfaction, even joy, in being *alive*, in not having died, along with the sense of having undergone an experience that is illuminating in its pain" (p. 82).

The protean self is in a continuous quest for integration. Lifton (1993) calls it "integrative proteanism." It "involves holding together, however loosely, disparate elements of the self" (p. 87). Total integration is never the aim of the fluid self; relative integration will do. "For the 'decentralized' protean self, the 'unity of consciousness ... is a necessary, but never fully attainable ideal" (p. 135). The fluid "self requires a modicum of inner continuity, and of coherence as well" (p. 88). One can be "intensely protean while at the same time holding fast to important experiences, principles, and connections" (pp. 88–89). For instance, a person may rely "on continuous self-examination to sustain her integrative process" (p. 89). Or, it could be sustained by an "energizing image." The steadfastness, which combines with fluidity, Lifton informs us, "requires the kind of energizing image" that carves out for "the self a course that is both fluid and ethically formed" (p. 91). "This image, this love, I compose myself/Of these" is a fragment of a poem by Wallace Stevens that is quoted in this context. For a Christian, for instance, the image could be that of the crucifixion and resurrection of Jesus Christ.

Although a relative sense of coherence can be sustained, says Lifton (1993), this feeling is "tenuous because the protean self does nothing in a completely linear, straightforward manner" (p. 93). His or her mind "darts and teases." His or her affects and links are not totally transparent. The fluid self "seeks always to maintain a certain poise or balance – an equilibrium or equipoise – to enable it to function in the world ... That poise is bound up with agility, with flexible adaptation" (p. 93). The flexible self has the ability to maneuver in diverse conditions.

> Such poise requires a series of additional psychological characteristics, ones that are crucial to protean existence. These include strong tendencies toward mockery and humor for 'lubricating' experience, emotions and communities that are 'free-floating' rather than clearly anchored, preference for fragmentary ideas rather than large belief systems, and continuous improvisation in social and occupational arrangements and expressions of conciliation and protest. No wonder that protean poise is demanding, always at issue, always required. (p. 93)

In light of the absurdity of our lives, to which he or she is sensitively attuned, the protean self makes repetitive use of irony and mockery – the mocking of the absurd in life, including self-mockery. This way, he or she gives assertive expression to his or her authentic feelings. His or her humor and irony serve as a source of vitality. They give her a wider perspective through which she *partially* integrates the diverse elements of her sense of self. I say "partially integrates" because the "protean self, even while adrift in its own emotions, can live with partial integration and partial trust in the possibility of constructive human actions" (p. 100).

Quoting the words of Czech statesman and writer Vaclav Havel, Lifton (1993) writes: "'you must have a healthy awareness of your own human ridiculousness and nothingness'" (p. 97). Our sense of absurdity allows a modicum of healthy detachment or distancing from our existential predicament. This "absurdity and mockery enable the protean self to do several things at once: articulate bitterness and anger while sometimes combining those with affection; provide 'interference' from every kind of inauthenticity; establish patterns of such lubrication [of experience] as a sustained [or sustaining] inner form" (p. 98).

"Doubt," asserts Lifton (1993), "is both mother and child of proteanism and can be a valued trait" (p. 107). The protean self is relatively at ease with uncertainty for "uncertainty can have the advantage of keeping the imagination open and thereby protecting one from emotions that are monolithic, suffocating, inauthentic" (p. 102). The fluid self is to some extent at home with homelessness for he or she is relatively adept in performing the "balancing act of multiple levels of belonging" (p. 105). The protean self struggles for *balance* of doubt and faith, of belonging and homelessness, of "order and disorder … [and of the] private and the universal [which are] inextricably entwined" (p. 112). He or she struggles to keep "an equilibrium between 'moral courage' and a reasoned tactical approach that avoids 'quick, emotional responses to events'" (p. 116).

The protean self, points Lifton (1993), is a Sisyphus-like figure who, "despite all his defeats, [remains] undefeated" (p. 118). He or she succeeds at failing and sees the potential for failure in success. "In the midst of flux," adds Lifton, "the protean self seeks connections … in ways that leave openings" (p. 120). The protean self is capable of "protean love," the kind of love that is at home with complexity and "uncertainty about expectations and assumed rules [and roles]," the sort of love that is open to "ad-hoc attitudes and behavior" (p. 123). The same can be said of "protean parenting," the kind of parenting that enacts flexible gender role socialization. "The protean self presses the limits of the life cycle, looks for ways of surmounting its constraints" (p. 124). Development, growth, and change can take place at any juncture during the life cycle. And "what happens in early life can be 'transformed' by later experience" (p. 125).

Lifton (1993) further depicts the protean self as someone who "seeks ethical commitment ... that allows for doubt and uncertainty and includes a stress on personal responsibility ... [Ethical commitment] brings one to larger human connectedness [or 'species consciousness']" (p. 127). Yet again, the "unity of consciousness ... is a necessary, but never fully attainable, ideal" (p. 135).

The flexible self, Lifton (1993) informs us, is capable of finding *balance* between centering and decentering, a balance that enables the self to be grounded and at the same time available to the other. This balance makes "the empathy act" possible:

> For that [empathy] act, one needs to be capable of *decentering*, of stepping back from one's involvements sufficiently to enter into the mind of another. And for decentering, one requires prior *centering*, a prior capacity for ordering of experience along various dimensions – temporal (past, present, and future), spatial (proximate and ultimate experience), and emotional (allocating or 'valencing' of the intensity of feelings and actions). (p. 206)

We are born to be empathically connected, says Lifton (1993). We are constructed to potentially embody the "principle of *commonality*: that of the characteristics we share as a species, and even more, the life experiences we share as well" (p. 213).

> All human cultures, at any historical moment, bring their bodies and minds to lovemaking and to childbirth, to pain and to sickness. We all must deal with the nurturing of the young, with family and sexual relationships, with adult responsibility and the reality of death ... 'A baby is a baby is a baby' ... We assert our commonality through our capacity for empathy, for thinking and feeling our way into the minds of others. (p. 214)

True individuation or maturation involves the cultivation of the capacities for empathy (including empathy for trauma and suffering) and connectedness (sense of commonality). "Proteanism enables men and women alike to call forth that potential for weblike connectedness and empathic sensitivity" (p. 215).

Lifton (1993) ends his concluding chapter with this summarized version of the portrait of the protean self: He or she is fluid, "tough-minded and morally committed" (p. 232). The fluid self is open to truth. The flexible self seeks authenticity. He or she has the capacity to "transform discontinuity and pain" and "allows the traumatized to speak and to be heard" (p. 232). The protean self reaches "toward global belonging" (p. 232). The protean path is a "path of hope." Why live? Well, here is at least a partial answer: "We live because there are a number of encounters ahead of us for the sake of which living is worthwhile" (p. 67). This reflects a fundamentally hopeful stance toward existence.

The Protean Self, named after the mythological Greek God of shapeshifting water, is, Lifton (1993) tells us, "the protector of the beautiful" (p. 5). Lifton would no doubt wholeheartedly concur that the *flexible self* is, in addition, the guardian of the *true* and the *good.*

"But in order to meet otherness," observes Melucci (1996), "one needs to change form" (p. 116). One needs to undergo a "metamorphosis." "We cannot communicate or relate to differences," continues Melucci, "by simply remaining ourselves" (p. 116). In order to meet the different Other and learn from the encounter and be changed by the meeting we need to cultivate "the capacity to keep and to lose, to cope with fears and resistances, but also with the ability of going beyond our given identities" (p. 116). Commonality is the other side of difference. From the point of view of our dialectical model, there is a positively and a negatively "valenced" difference and there is a positively and negatively "valenced" commonality (similarity). Our mental health, individually and collectively, lies in struggling to find a balance between positive difference and positive commonality (similarity). Melucci reflects, "extreme stress on differences … can bring in dramatic forms … of violence" (p. 116). This is an instance of a negatively charged difference or feeling of being different from the Other. Commonality (similarity) that erases differences results in enmeshment – the erasure of identity boundaries, and the eradication of uniqueness and singularity. "The problem," muses Melucci, "is never just difference, but rather the parallel necessity to overcome it, to make the constant effort of listening and understanding each other" (p. 116). Metamorphosis (changing form) or proteanism (shapeshifting) is an essential requisite for holding-and-resolving this dialectical tension, and thus finding a relative balance between our need to gain solidarity with the Other through our commonality (similarity) and our need to be different (unique) and to learn from the different Other.

Rogers (1989) describes the "*self-structure*" of "the fully functioning person" as "a fluid gestalt, changing flexibly in the process of assimilation of new *experience*" (p. 251). For Rogers, *flexibility*, *openness to experience*, *trust in one's own organism*, *living fully in the moment*, *freedom of choice*, and *creativity* go hand-in-hand. The opposite of flexibility is defensive rigidity. "Caring," says Rogers (1980) "is an attitude that is known to foster creativity – a nurturing climate in which delicate, tentative, new thoughts and productive processes emerge" (p. 160). *Caringly creative, and thus flexible, parents or institutions tend to beget caringly creative and flexible children.* Fully functioning, psychologically healthy, or psychosocially mature persons who are fully open to all experiences, who trust their own organisms, and who express themselves in creative products and creative living will inevitably display flexibility in their decisions and actions. Existentially, we can say, they are *open to lived meaning possibilities in their lifeworld.* Defensively rigid persons, in contrast, who lack feelings of freedom, are closed off from many experiences, live within determined guidelines, are neither spontaneous nor creative, will be fated to display inflexibility in their decisions and actions. Existentially, we can conclude, they are *closed to lived meaning possibilities in their lifeworld.*

References

Horney, K. (1970). *Neurosis and human growth: The struggle toward self-realization.* W. W. Norton.

Kelman, H. (1971). *Helping people: Karen Horney's psychoanalytic approach.* Science House.

Lifton, R. J. (1993). *The protean self: Human resilience in age of fragmentation.* The University of Chicago Press.

Melucci, A. (1996). *The playing self: Person and meaning in the planetary society.* Cambridge University Press.

Rogers, C. R. (1980). *A way of being.* Houghton Mifflin.

Rogers, C. R. (1989). *The Carl Rogers reader.* Houghton Mifflin.

Solomon, I. (2006). *Karen Horney and character disorder.* Springer.

Teyber, E., & Teyber, F. H. (2017). *Interpersonal process in therapy: An integrative model* (7th ed.). Cengage Learning.

16

Resilience: The Capacity for *Resilience*

Resilience refers to the capacity to recover from stress or the ability to withstand the effects of stressors that are typically associated with negative outcomes. Researchers "are now finding," say Cabaniss and her colleagues (2013), "that our capacity for resilience may also be hereditary… Genetic differences [which] regulate the metabolism of neurotransmitters … may affect an individual's response to early childhood maltreatment and trauma" (p. 86). "Individual differences in vulnerability and resilience in the face of trauma," they add, "may reflect neural and/or genetic predispositions and may influence the likelihood of developing symptoms of PTSD [Post Traumatic Stress Disorder]" (p. 144). Hagerty (2016) writes that research has uncovered support for "a genetic basis for resilience" indicated by the fact that some of us apparently are able to "bring stress hormones back to baseline more quickly (chemicals including cortisol, adrenaline, and noradrenaline) and particularly implicated is the neurotransmitter Neuropeptide Y [which] has been called the 'resilience hormone,' because it shuts down the alarm system quickly" (pp. 415–416).

In addition to reflecting neural and genetic predispositions, resilience is also a byproduct of our learning experiences, a result of cumulative experiences of psychosocial inoculation. Based upon research with people who have suffered all kinds of stresses and traumas, Hagerty (2016) concludes, resilience is now viewed as a "mixture of personality traits, biology and life experience, each part shaping the others" (p. 236). The available research yields a list of ten essential ingredients to resilience: realistic optimism; the ability to face fear; having a moral compass and altruistic instincts; possessing some religious or spiritual sensibilities; having social support; knowing resilient role models;

© The Author(s), under exclusive license to Springer Nature Switzerland AG 2021
M. J. Hannush, *Markers of Psychosocial Maturation*,
https://doi.org/10.1007/978-3-030-74315-4_16

being physically fit; staying mentally acute; remaining cognitively and emotionally flexible; and retaining a sense of meaning, purpose, and growth.

Although the majority of resilient people do not have all these traits, continues Hagerty (2016), researchers "have singled out optimism and social support as particularly critical" (p. 415). Re-viewing the ten traits, it occurs to me that a significant number of them – the capacity for realistic optimism (*hope*); the ability to face fear (*courage*); having a moral compass (*goodness*); the ability to establish relations with others (*positive relating*); the ability to remain cognitively and emotionally flexible (*flexibility*); and the ability to retain a sense of meaning, purpose, and growth (*seeking better life meanings*) – can be subsumed under the superordinate categorical concept of *psychosocial maturation*. This should not surprise us. The capacity for resilience is one of the *markers of maturity*. It is a part (resilience) of a whole (maturity). But it is a part that overlaps with other parts that belong to the whole. Just as a whole has an influence on the parts, likewise parts have an influence on the whole. And just as a whole is made up of parts, the parts themselves can act as wholes, having dynamic parts of their own. Moreover, a part can mirror the whole.

Hagerty (2016) gives yet another definition of resilience. It is "the ability to regulate one's response to fear" (p. 238). For some, she continues, it could be their "natural resilience." That is, their resilience is grounded in the capacity of essentially two brain centers to communicate with each other – the reasoning part of the brain (the prefrontal cortex) and the fear center of the brain (the amygdala). But I conjecture that "natural resilience" is inevitably intertwined with what I will call "nutrient resilience." I would further venture that securely attached children or adolescents, who have been properly "nurtured" will, over a developmental time-line, have brains whose parts, such as the amygdala and the prefrontal cortex, will be in better communication with each other than the same parts of the brain of insecurely attached children who have not been properly "nurtured." In other words, properly "nurtured" children will have a higher degree of "natural resilience."

Above and beyond their "natural resilience," which is inseparable from "nutrient resilience," resilient people, expands Hagerty (2016), "rely on other people to help them" (p. 239). Or, it could be that they rely on their calmness-providing religious or spiritual outlook. "For others, it could be natural optimism, trust in one's resourcefulness and ability to thrive, the support of friends, or even past experiences and training that reduce a towering mountain to a scalable hill" (p. 238). Hagerty notes, "The really highly resilient people tend to have very good social networks" and then adds, "They seem to instinctively know that their bodies demands friends" (p. 240). "Finding meaning in adversity," she concludes, "tracks closely with the quality most associated with resilience: optimism, that is, a realistic buoyancy that acknowledges the bad facts in front of you and is not consumed by them" (p. 241). Quoting a neuropsychological researcher, she adds, "'the resilient person maintains that kind of positive glow for a much longer period of time'... Not only does this reasoning part of the brain tamp down the fear center (amygdala), but it also keeps the ventral striatum, a region that is important for positive emotions, merrily engaged for longer periods of time" (p. 241).

"The key to psychological fitness," posits Seligman (2011), "is resilience" (p. 127). A resilient person is someone who espouses the opposite answer to the statement: "When things go wrong in my life, it generally takes me a long time to get back to normal" (p. 27). The core of Seligman's "Master Resilience Training" involves "building mental toughness, building strengths, and building strong relationships" (p. 167). To build "mental toughness" Seligman relies on Albert Ellis's rational-emotive-behavioral therapeutic strategies. This involves learning how to think rationally and realistically in an effort to counter irrational, unrealistic, and catastrophic thinking. It is not adversity, but our beliefs about adversity, that trigger our emotional and behavioral reactions. "After the mental-toughness skills, we turn to identifying character strengths [such as courage, integrity, and selfless service]... We then shift the focus to using strengths to overcome challenges" (pp. 171–172). Then we assign "Strengths in Challenges" scenarios and stories that provide us with the opportunity to apply our character strengths.

> Our final module focuses on how to strengthen relationships with others ...[at work] and at home. Our goal is to provide practical tools that build relationships and to challenge beliefs that interfere with positive communication... [When] an individual responds actively and constructively (as opposed to passively and destructively) to someone sharing a positive experience, love and friendship increases. So we teach the four styles of responding:
>
> Active constructive (authentic, enthusiastic support), passive constructive (understand and support), passive destructive (ignoring the event), and active destructive (pointing out the negative aspects of the event). We demonstrate each through a series of role plays... Finally, we teach assertive communication, describing the differences among passive, aggressive, and assertive styles. (pp. 173–174)

Not all children who are subjected to stressors such as family conflict and emotional or physical abuse, poverty, and "bad" neighborhoods and schools become troubled and troublesome as adults. "The ability to cope or recover quickly from hardships of this type," say McClure and Teyber (2003), "is called *resilience*" (p. 181). They go on to cite research that sheds light not only on the risk factors but also on the factors that contribute to these children's resiliency:

> Risk factors for negative outcomes under stressful situations include gender (boys exhibit more behavior problems than girls), difficult temperament, not having a good relationship with parents, poor planning ability, and poor social skills... Characteristics such as being intelligent, having an easy temperament, and having skills valued by society, such as being athletic or artistic are considered 'protective' ... In addition, having families who are warm and provide structure, having a supportive extended family, and having financial security are also considered protective and help children make good adjustments when exposed to traumatizing or challenging situations... This ability to adjust well under difficult circumstances is called resilience. (pp. 181–182)

Effective or proper parenting – the provision of adequate guidance and supervision, consistent discipline, and emotional responsiveness – is instrumental in producing children who are securely attached. "Secure attachment to a warm [affectionate and loving] and structured [limit-setting] caregiver," elaborate McClure and Teyber (2003), "affects children's beliefs about themselves and others (e.g., they feel worthy of being cared about and see people as trustworthy and dependable)" (p. 181). Such children internalize their parents' values and acquire the capacity for self-regulation (self-control), which includes emotional regulation. These children tend to make discerningly benign attributions to the *meaning* of other people's behavior. They are more likely to become good empathizers, perspective-takers, problem-solvers, and prosocial agents.

"In summary," conclude McClure and Teyber (2003), "positive attachment to a caring adult enhances resilience in several ways. These children will:

1. feel good about themselves;
2. trust others;
3. be more likely to see benevolent (positive) rather than malevolent (negative, hostile) intentions [meanings] in others' behavior;
4. be more likely to value affiliation or connection rather than dominance or revenge;
5. have empathy for others; and
6. be realistic about their own level of aggressiveness and its negative consequences." (p. 182)

The "resilience literature," holds Holmes (2010), "suggests that people vary in the extent to which they succumb to childhood adversity" (p. 78). "The presence of a supportive family (e.g., grandmother or aunt) or sympathetic adults such as a teacher; personal qualities such as good looks, sense of humour, sporting or artistic talents; and in adolescence and early adulthood forming a stable romantic relationship," elaborates Holmes, "all these protect people from the psychological ill-health that might be expected to be the consequence of childhood adversity" (p. 78). It is not adversity itself that causes psychopathology. Rather, it is "the way in which difficulties are, or are not, mediated, initially with the help of caregivers and later intrapsychically" (p. 78). "Resilience," Holmes concludes, is thus closely connected to "reflexive function; mentalizing [or accurate meaning making] is a crucial determinant of the outcome of adversity" (p. 78).

Holmes (2010) traces the origin of the acquisition of the capacity for reflexive functioning, mentalization, or mind-mindedness to mother's "ability to 'read' infant distress and to maintain a strong parental role" (p. 79). This accurate reading of the *meaning* of the child's distress and the consequent capacity to respond reparatively is a crucial determinant of infant security. Security strengthens the child's emerging *exuberant exploratory meaning-seeking drive.* Securely mentalizing or mind-minded mothers tend to beget securely mentalizing or mind-minded children. The mother's secure mind-mindedness "becomes internalised as an autonomous psychological [reflexive] function" (p. 79). This security-based high reflexive function plays a central role in strengthening the "psychological immune system ... whose function is to support psychological integrity [integration] by putting adverse experience to good effect ... it maintains continuity in the face of the inevitable disruptions and distortions of intimate relationships" (p. 79).

Phenomenologically, let us now focus on what Holmes has described as the *self's exuberant meaning-seeking drive* or, better yet, *directedness toward the life-world,* a lifeworld of *meaning possibilities.* For me, in this lies the root of so-called *resilience* or what I prefer to call creative *vitality.* "What is it," asks Jacobsen (2007), "that makes some people cave in when faced with moderate adversity while other persevere despite the most unbelievable difficulties?" (p. 9). The answer he provides is not what one expects, *resilience*; rather it is *life energy* or *vitality.* "*Life energy* or *vitality,*" Jacobsen states, "is the ability of the organism to survive even under difficult circumstances and to achieve longevity" (p. 11). Although, he admits, "the biological component is strong," he quickly adds that "our biology is woven into *patterns of meaning* and *intention* that *codetermine our life energy*" (p. 11). I would qualify this to say that, though grounded in our biology, our *vitality* lies in our primordial capacity for *exuberant meaning co-making*, which occurs in a relational *existential space* and not objective (bio-environmental) space. Vitality, says Jacobsen, is an *existential phenomenon*.

Anxiety and fear can be the enemies of the *exuberant meaning-seeking drive* that is fueled by our *creative vitality*. Anxiety and fear can weaken our resilience or vitality. Anxiety can close us to meaning possibilities in our lifeworld. Anxiety and insecurity can act as blinders that prevent us from gaining *insight into lifeworld meaning possibilities*. "Courage," states Tillich (1952), who was May's mentor, "is … the power of the mind to overcome fear" (p. 34). By "courage," Tillich means the *courage of being* or *the courage to be*, thus the title of his book. Anxiety and fear, Tillich elaborates, "are interdependent" (p. 35). The basic conflict in human existence, for Tillich, is between anxiety and courage. Anxiety in the face of nonbeing, however, is inherent in our being. May (1967) distinguishes between *normal anxiety*, *neurotic anxiety*, and *existential anxiety*. May defines *normal anxiety* as that "which is proportionate to the threat [to one's values], does not involve repression, and can be confronted constructively on the conscious level" (p. 80). "All growth," expands May, "consists of the [normal] anxiety-creating surrender of past values" (p. 80). We experience a normal degree of anxiety as we handle everyday hassles. We experience normal anxiety as we confront that which is novel, unfamiliar, and complexly ambiguous even in our creative moments. By *neurotic anxiety*, May means an unrealistic anxiety that is out of proportion to the source that is triggering it. More specifically, neurotic anxiety is defined as "a reaction which is disproportionate to the threat [to one's values], involves repression and other forms of intrapsychic conflict, and is managed by various kinds of blocking-off of activity and awareness" (p. 80) May defines *existential anxiety* as "the subjective state of the individual's becoming aware that his [or her] existence can be destroyed, that he can become 'nothing'" (p. 50). Existential anxiety is triggered not only by an awareness of one's nonbeing, but also by experiencing a threat to a value or meaning essential to one's existence or from confronting the challenge of fulfilling one's potentialities. In contradistinction to *neurotic anxiety* that requires therapeutic interventions so that it is reduced to normal anxiety, existential and normal anxieties, when courageously confronted and contained, can release the life energy of our *creative vitality*. It is this creative vitality that keeps us realistically hopeful and helps us cope constructively with the inevitable setbacks of everyday living.

References

Cabaniss, D. L., Cherry, S., Douglas, C. J., Graver, R. L., & Schwartz, A. R. (2013). *Psychodynamic formulation*. Wiley.

Hagerty, B. B. (2016). *Life reimagined: The science, art, and opportunity of midlife*. Riverhead Books.

Holmes, J. (2010). *Exploring in security: Towards an attachment-informed psychoanalytic psychotherapy*. Routledge.

Jacobsen, B. (2007). *Invitation to existential psychology: A psychology for the unique human being and its applications in therapy*. John Wiley and Sons.

May, R. (1967). *Psychology and the human dilemma*. D. Van Nostrand.

McClure, F., & Teyber, E. (2003). *Casebook in child and adolescent treatment: Cultural and familial contexts*. Thomson.

Seligman, M. E. P. (2011). *Flourish: A visionary new understanding of happiness and well-being*. Free Press.

Tillich, P. (1952). *The courage to be*. Yale University Press.

Part VI

The Capacities for Acceptance, Authenticity, and Responsibility

17

Acceptance: The Capacity for *Acceptance* of Self, Others, and Life Itself

Ogden (2012), while interpreting W. R. D. Fairbairn's work, states that we are born with a healthy nascent self. From the beginning this healthy nascent self is able to differentiate itself, be it on a rudimentary level, from others. From the start, this healthy nascent self is capable of a primitive perception of reality. It is in response to positive, good-enough experiences with the mother who loves and accepts him and, in turn, accepts his primitive love that this central self is enabled to develop, grow, and mature. The central, healthy nascent self is not only retained but also expanded upon.

The central healthy self, expands Ogden (2012), is the only part of our Self that is "able to engage in, and learn from experience with external objects [others]" (p. 71). The central self does not incorporate unsatisfactory, repressed, and internalized relations with essential others. The central healthy self includes only good internalized experiences with essential others such as our identifications with our good-enough parents who accepted, loved, and recognized us and whom we loved, even in our early limited ways, and the love we offered was in turn received and accepted. "Such identifications underlie feelings that include a sense of internal security, as well as background feelings of solidity and integrity [integration]" (p. 71).

When our parents accept, recognize, and love us, this contributes to our own self-acceptance, self-love, and self-recognition. We are freed from the need to always try to extract acceptance, love, and recognition from external, and later internal, others.

Ogden (2012) concludes with the following reflections on the role of acceptance for psychological growth and maturation:

© The Author(s), under exclusive license to Springer Nature Switzerland AG 2021

M. J. Hannush, *Markers of Psychosocial Maturation*,
https://doi.org/10.1007/978-3-030-74315-4_17

> Psychological growth, for Fairbairn (as I read him), involves a form of acceptance of oneself that can be achieved only in the context of a real relationship with a relatively psychologically mature person. A relationship of this sort … is the only possible exit from the [internal solipsistic] world … Self-acceptance is a state of mind that marks the (never fully achieved) relinquishment of the life-consuming effort to transform unsatisfactory internal object relationships [internalized representations of our relations with essential others] into satisfactory (that is, loving and accepting) ones. With psychological growth, one comes to know at depth that one's early experiences with one's unloving and unaccepting mother will never be other than what they were. It is a waste of effort to devote oneself to the effort to transform oneself (and others) into the people one wishes one were (or wishes they were). (p. 75)

All psychological growth and maturation involves the genuine acceptance of ourselves and, correlatively, of others. "That acceptance is achieved by means of the work of coming to terms with the full range of aspects of oneself, including one's disturbing, infantile, split-off identifications with one's unloving, unaccepting mother [or father]" (p. 72). Only this way can we then be open to experience and learn from others. Only this way will we be able to discover a relational world involving people outside ourselves, a world in which we can experience authentic feelings, including feelings of delight and disappointment. This openness is made possible by our self-acceptance. With this new relational orientation, we are not preoccupied with changing ourselves to fit the expectations of others or desperately trying to change others to match our own expectations.

The precondition for self-acceptance, concurs May (1958), is the compassionate acceptance of essential others. Similarly, for Rogers (1980), unconditional self-acceptance is contingent upon the unconditional acceptance of essential others, such as our parents. Human beings have a basic need to be accepted (loved and prized). They acquire the capacity for self-love when they are adequately (unconditionally) loved. Ultimately, as Kahn (1997) describes it, Rogers's therapeutic approach is "A Therapy of Love":

> By 'love' Rogers meant what the Greeks called 'agape … [which] is characterized by the desire to fulfill the beloved. It demands nothing in return and wants only the growth and fulfillment of the loved one. Agape is a strengthening love, a love that, by definition, does not burden or obligate the loved one … If the therapist successfully communicated the experience of agape, the client would change in the desired direction. (p. 39)

For Rogers (1980), "agapic" communication involves the ability to communicate *genuineness* (congruence, realness), *empathy* (attuned empathy, empathic understanding), and *unconditional positive regard* (unconditional acceptance). Rogers makes it abundantly clear that this type of communication is applicable to many other interpersonal domains outside the therapeutic context such as parent-child, teacher-mentor, or husband-wife relationships. Here is how Rogers summarizes the "CHARACTERISTICS OF THE PERSON-CENTERED APPROACH" (pp. 114–117):

> There are three conditions that must be present in order for a climate to be growth-promoting ... These conditions apply, in fact, in any situation in which the development of the person is a goal ... The first element could be called genuineness, realness, or congruence. The more the ... [person] is himself or herself in the relationship, putting up no ... personal façade, the greater likelihood that the ... [person] will change and grow in a constructive manner ... This means that the ... [person] is openly being the feelings and attitudes that are flowing within at the moment. The term 'transparent' catches the flavor of this condition ... As for the ... [person], what he or she is experiencing is available to awareness, can be lived in the relationship, and can be communicated if appropriate. Thus, there is a close matching, or congruence, between what is being experienced at the gut level, what is present in awareness, and what is expressed to the ... [other]. (pp. 115–116)

To be genuine, in other words, I need to have access to my own inner experiencing, my own feelings, moods, and attitudinal dispositions. I need to be aware of my feeling flow and the unfolding of my thought patterns. Sharing my access or awareness may invite my essential other to have access to or become aware of her own flow of feelings and thoughts. To become genuine, however, I need to assume responsibility (be *response-able*) for *enduring* the flow of my own inner experiencing.

Being aware of the flow of feelings and thoughts is not sufficient though. I need not hide my inner experiencing from my essential other. I need to be *non-defensively* transparent. I need to present myself to my interlocutor without any concealment. I can even do this without words. Or, I may choose to tell my partner-in-communication what I am feeling and thinking. But I need to express myself with care, concern, and respect for the Other. I must do it with empathy and warmth. If I make her defensive, then, at least for that moment, I have lost her. This moment can be described as an empathic failure, a failure in communication that can result in a relational rupture that, in turn, needs to be repaired. But if in a face-to-face encounter I am being genuine, the other will trust me and will be willing to expose herself to me. Rogers (1980) continues:

> The second attitude of importance in creating a climate for change is acceptance, or caring, or prizing – what I have called "unconditional positive regard." When the … [person] is experiencing a positive, acceptant attitude toward whatever the … [other] is at that moment, therapeutic [growth-promoting] movement or change is more likely to occur. The … [person] is willing for the … [other] to be whatever immediate feeling is going on – confusion, resentment, fear, anger, courage, love, or pride. Such caring on the part of the … [person] is non-possessive. The … [person] prizes the … [other] in a total rather than a conditional way. (p. 116)

Kahn (1997) comments that Rogers's:

> model for this attribute is the loving parent who 'prizes' the child. Such a parent has strong positive feelings for the child, feelings that are not possessive and do not demand that the child be a certain way. The parent gives the message that even though from time to time the child is likely to evoke annoyance, anger, disapproval, or disgust, the child is basically, essentially loved and lovable, no matter what. (p. 46)

Whether it is my child, partner, or friend, I need to give her or him "a great deal of room to be a separate and independent person" (p. 46). And if she or he discloses feelings or acts in ways that collide with my set of values or my aesthetic sense, then I have to keep in mind that our children, partners, or friends are "worthwhile human beings struggling gamely to find their way back to their birthright of growth and self development, and as such they should be prized" (p. 46). Of course, while remaining true to the spirit of Rogers's model, I am generalizing what Rogers and Kahn have to say about the client-therapist relationship to other relational contexts.

Only when we are bestowed upon with unconditional acceptance, love, or positive regard can we explore our deepest nature and become our true selves without having to disavow parts of our selves.

Rogers (1980) then describes the third necessary and sufficient condition for maturation and growth:

> The third facilitative aspect of the relationship is empathic understanding. This means that the … [person] senses accurately the feelings and personal meanings that the … [other] is experiencing and communicates this understanding to the … [other]. When functioning best, the … [person] is so much inside the

> private world of the other that he or she can clarify not only the meanings of which the ... [other] is aware but even those just below the level of awareness. This kind of sensitive, active listening is exceedingly rare in our lives. We think we listen, but very rarely do we listen with real understanding, true empathy. Yet listening, of this very special kind, is one of the most potent forces for change I know. (p. 116)

Suppose my wife is angry. To be empathic toward her anger, I need to imaginatively enter her private world, her subjective experience, or her context of lifeworld meaning. I need to try to understand her experience from her own point of view. My understanding of her anger cannot be simply cognitive in nature. My experience of her anger is more than that. It has an emotional component as well. To have empathy for my wife's anger, I need to experience her anger the way she is experiencing it, but with a caveat. I need to experience her anger without losing myself in it. I do not become angry myself. I can move in her angry world freely. So my empathy has what Rogers calls an "as if quality." I imagine myself "as if" I were in my wife's position. Then, to complete the empathic cycle, I need to communicate my understanding of her anger to her. I communicate it in a language sensitively attuned to her feeling, in a language that matches her mood and the content of what she has expressed, and in a language that expands on her awareness of all that is involved in her anger. In communicating my understanding of her anger clearly, my wife realizes (1) I take our relationship seriously; (2) I am aware of what she is feeling in the present; I am able to stay flexibly in tune with her shifting emotional state; I *non-defensively* correct my misunderstanding of her anger when she gives me more feedback that points to my empathic failure; I communicate the message that I am with her, that I am on her side, and that I have her back. Above all, as a result of my empathically attuned response, my wife *feels understood.* When my wife feels understood by me, she is likely to move in the direction of understanding herself better. My empathy toward her begets empathy toward herself and toward me. She can now move in the direction of grasping my experience in an *accepting* way, just like I acceptingly grasped her experience of anger. My wife now feels better about herself and about me. Her self-worth is affirmed and strengthened. I have communicated to her that she is worthy of my time and effort, of my loving understanding.

Rogers (1980) concludes his section on the characteristics of the person-centered approach with the question, "How does this climate which I have just described bring about change?" He then immediately proceeds to give a succinct answer:

> Briefly, as persons are accepted and prized, they tend to develop a more caring [accepting] attitude toward themselves. As persons are empathically heard, it becomes possible for them to listen more accurately to the flow of inner experiencings. But as a person understands and prizes self, the self becomes more congruent with the experiencings. The person thus becomes more real, more genuine. These tendencies … enable the person to be a more effective growth-enhancer for himself or herself. There is a greater freedom to be the true, whole person. (pp. 116–117)

Rogers, notes Kahn (1997), "did not think that any mortal would ever be perfect in any of these three [attributes]. Rather, he saw each of these attributes as a continuum" (p. 48). Becoming mature, along Rogerian lines, requires of us "developing one's capacity to move farther and farther along each of those three continua" (p. 48). And if I can be genuine, empathic, and (unconditionally) accepting of the other as she or he is, she will also be on her way to becoming mature.

A core existential belief that undergirds these three attributes, states Rogers (1961), is that the purpose of life is "to be that which one truly is" (pp. 163–182). In synchrony with this life principle, children have a most basic need to grow up in environments that make them feel that it is *acceptable* to be who and what they truly are. Such relatively optimal environments allow them to become themselves. Under such good-enough conditions, children experience respect for the persons they are and for the persons they are becoming. Children (and adults) need to sense in their bones that it is all right to be whoever they truly are. To reiterate, the purpose of life is to be one's true self. *Self-acceptance* is therefore the most precious gift that a parent can give a child.

We have been referring to the three attributes of maturation as if they are separate. This is far from the truth. These attributes interpenetrate and overlap with each other. There is no such thing as acceptance without congruence and empathic understanding. Acceptance always goes hand-in-hand with genuineness and attuned empathy. Moreover, to be genuinely known and accepted by an essential other not only leads to self-acceptance but also results in a feeling of self-integration. To be acceptingly known by a genuine other is to feel solidified and "together."

Mearns and Thorne (1999) define unconditional positive regard (acceptance) in the following "straightforward language":

> Unconditional positive regard is the label given to the fundamental attitude of the person-centered counsellor towards her client. The counselor who holds this

> attitude deeply values the humanity of her client and is not deflected in that valuing by any particular client behaviours. This attitude manifests itself in the counsellor's consistent acceptance of and enduring warmth towards the client. (p. 64)

"It is possible," they reflect, "to accept the client as a person of worth while still not liking some of the things he does" (p. 65). "Accepting," for example, that "violent behavior does not represent the whole of the human being helps the counselor to stay interested, concerned and even warm toward her" (p. 65). The behavior of the Other does not capture his or her whole being. Key terms such as affirmation, concern, interest, prizing, valuation, and warmth are subsumed under *unconditional acceptance*. "There are many words used to describe this interpersonal dimension. Already we have referred to *unconditional positive regard* and *acceptance*. Another which was once widely used was *non-possessive warmth*, and *respect*" (p. 66). To unconditionally value (accept) the deep humanity of another person entails valuing him or her as a person of worth even when he or she expresses a set of values that are different from our own. Unconditional acceptance "does not demand they [others] meet our needs" (p. 66).

Let us extrapolate. Mature parents who love their children display their mature love properly through their unconditional acceptance of them. Their unconditional acceptance manifests itself through their concern about the welfare of their children, through their deep interest in their children's evolving needs and potentials, through their immense valuation of their children, and through the oceanic affectionate warmth or warm affection they bestow upon their children. And just like clients who are unconditionally accepted by their therapists, children who are unconditionally accepted by their parents come to accept themselves and, by extension, others. But in a concluding commentary on the theme of unconditional acceptance, atypical in the literature on person-centered counseling and psychotherapy, Mearns and Thorne (1999) wisely caution:

> In this book we shall restrict ourselves to the use of the conventional label *unconditional positive regard*, with *acceptance* as a shorthand form, although it should be noted that in its literal sense it is impossible to achieve 'unconditional' positive regard. Every counsellor is human and fallible and therefore must have some 'personal limits' that might be exceeded by her client; the counsellor cannot therefore guarantee unconditionality. However, the person-centered counsellor is likely to be 'less conditional' than most other people with whom the client will relate. (p. 66)

To generalize, because we are fallible and are inevitably saddled with personal limits, we humans will not always be "consistent" and "enduring" in the giving of our unconditional acceptance to (essential) others. However, with maturity we can be/come "less conditional" in our acceptance. Moreover, what Mearns and Thorne (1999) miss is that in spite of our best intentions to be relatively unconditional or less conditional in our acceptance when we take a significant Other to task for a behavior, while trying our best to accept his or her whole being, she or he may still infer that our lack of acceptance of the behavior means a lack of acceptance of her or his being as a whole. Still, we can be less conditional in our acceptance of self and others as a general orientation in life.

As we learn the language or lexicon of our essential others, imply Mearns and Thorne (1999), their behavior becomes more understandable. The "person behind the behaviour becomes progressively easier to see and to accept" (p. 71). To this I say, "sometimes, yes; sometimes, no." Still, empathy paves the way to easier acceptance. Or, it may make acceptance less difficult. It can allow for the revision of earlier judgments regarding the unlikableness of a behavior.

With maturation comes the expansion of one's repertoire for communicating acceptance toward self and others. Our capacity for acceptance becomes more nuanced. We can show our acceptance in different ways with different individuals. For example, in initial encounters, our warmth, as a manifestation of our acceptance, is communicated in a *modulated* fashion in order to avoid being misinterpreted by the recipient of our acceptant disposition. We can also communicate our acceptance through touch, an essential expression of our acceptance and warmth. Touch, however, has to be *discerningly utilized* depending on the nature of the relationship to the target of our touching.

Accepting the seemingly unacceptable is a foremost facet of maturity. "Most forms of psychotherapy," says Cohn (1997), "see the non-acceptance of something which seems unacceptable, the turning-away from difficulties which cannot be mastered, the denial of aspects of life which cannot be integrated, as a source of conflict and disturbance" (p. 121). To put it differently yet again, "the facing and reintegration of an unaccepted or unacceptable aspect of life" is one of the major aims of existential psychotherapy (p. 119). What is true as a cardinal aim of therapy is also true as a major maturational life task.

According to the existential viewpoint, what is difficult to accept, the seemingly unacceptable, has to do with essential aspects of our everyday existence, such as *being thrown* into this lifeworld with this temperament and body, with these parents, in this community and culture, in this socio-economic and political context, and at this juncture in history. It has to do with confronting our sense of finitude, fragility, mortality, uncertainty, and vulnerability. It has to do with coming to terms with our decisional anxieties, post-decisional regrets, guilt over not living up to our potentials and falling short of becoming our better selves, negating ourselves or others, and the tensions arising from our contradictory and conflictual lifeworld meanings, meanings that make up who we are and that beckon balance and fulfillment. Additionally, it has to do with being saddled with the responsibility of deciding on how to respond to the call of our conscience, the call to maturation. We seem to be destined, not fated, to act upon our need to choose, the choosing to choose. Deciding not to choose is itself a choice. Being destined has the implication of an active sense of agency. Whereas, being fated has the connotation of a passive sense of "patiency" (passive suffering). Accepting the seemingly unacceptable requires countering our "fatedness" by assuming *responsibility* for our destiny. Our destined responsiveness – our responsible responsiveness to our fate – is a manifestation of the core of our being-in-the-world-with-others – the center of our "gravity," "initiative," and "openness." All this requires an abiding sense of vigilance against the pull of existential blindness, "closedness," denial, distraction, evasion, and unawareness. To accept or not to accept – these "givens" of our existence – that is the unceasing question that beckons a consistent answer.

"To live or to die?" – that is the question that she has agonizingly struggled with since her early childhood, says writer Daphne Merkin (2017), in her memoir. In her never-ceasing effort to accept her seemingly unacceptable life, Merkin has "written down a quote from Rilke's 'Ninth Elegy' … in which the poet acknowledges that while happiness barely exists except as a prelude to unhappiness, this world is all the same our one and only ticket" (p. 277). Merkin, as a middle-aged adult, comments:

> If could heed the poem's unsentimental message and last the dark season out – and the next one – there might be something durable, a more permanent holding:
>
> But because *truly* being here is so much; because
> everything here
> apparently needs us, this fleeting world, which in
> some strange way
> keeps calling to us. Us, the most fleeting of all.
> *Once* for each thing. Just once; no more. And we too,
> Just once. And never again. (p. 277)

Having resonated so deeply to the message contained in Rilke's poem, Merkin not only internalizes its meaning, but creates her own version of it, which she recites to herself like a secular prayer: "*O My Lord, what a tragic and terrible, weird and slightly wonderful life this is. My one and only, our one and only; hold it close, away from the worms, live it through, give it every chance you've got*" (p. 278).

Merkin (2017) longs to have had a life different from the one she got. She deeply desires to be properly re-parented. She wants her mother back, this time as a mature, loving mother. She wants her father back, this time as a caringly involved father. She dreams of conquering her depression once and for all. But she comes to understand that it is a permanent condition, a part of her just like her "literary bent." She comes to have a nuanced understanding of its meaning in her life. She no longer views it in either/or terms: "You are either depressed or happy." The "opposite of depression," she reflects, "is not a state of unimaginable happiness but a state of approximate contentment, of relative all-right-ness" (p. 283).

Merkin (2017) now intuits the link between accepting her depression and affirming her "literary bent." She holds "an underlying conviction that language can transmute personal pain into a shared grief about what living in the world entails" (p. 102). Additionally, Merkin sees, though dimly, the connection between the capacity for acceptance and the cultivation of the capacity for dis-identifying or not over-identifying with, what she calls, her "depressive self" or her "counter self."

> Meanwhile, I'm trying hard, really I am. What, you may ask, does 'trying' consist of? Primarily it involves separating myself from the me that is depressed – flying above it, so to speak, like a plane that has lifted off the tarmac. Trying is going on, is forced engagement with the trivial and less trivial forces of my everyday life. (p. 253)

I would have preferred the metaphorical use of a "helicopter" than that of a "plane," for the helicopter is capable of hovering atop of the over-identification with the "depressive self" and viewing it from a more detached, yet caring perspective and putting it in its proper place. This mature movement enables her to strengthen what has been her under-identification with her "self as someone stronger than I am, able to stand on her own two feet, do the things grown-ups with advantages like my own do" (p. 257). In progressive, forward-moving moments like this, "everything felt freshly come upon, as though my depressed self had stepped back in honor of my homecoming" (p. 267). In moments like this, Merkin understands the meaning of life as "a gift … a great gift." In moments such as this one there is an affirmation of life. In instances as this one, one is able to bear the contiguity of one's attraction to life with one's aversion to life.

> But perhaps I've all along understood the pull of life itself, slyly offering up its enticements. I tend to give short shrift to these enticements when I'm sinking, but they are very real. They would include but are not limited to the supreme diversion of reading and the gratifications of friendships, the enveloping bond of motherhood and the solace to be found in small pleasures ... Not to overlook my (mostly) inextinguishable sense of curiosity; a certain pleasure I take in beautiful things and aesthetic experience generally ... And yes, the tug of love, when I allow myself to feel it, for all those who help tether me to this world. (pp. 273–274)

"Freud," Safran (2012) tells us, "believed in the importance of shedding one's illusions and coming to accept the inevitabilities of life" (p. 50). Freud also encouraged patiently "allowing things to unfold in their own way" and not pursue the healing process with excessive zeal – with 'furor sanadi'" (p. 49). Freud, in other words, embraced a kind of Stoic stance: "a kind of acceptance," Bakewell (2010), tells us, "the Stoics called *amore fati*, or love of fate" (p. 113). "As the Stoic Epictetus wrote," she continues, "Do not seek to have everything that happens as you wish, but wish for everything to happen as it actually does happen, and your life will be serene" (p. 113).

There is something of a paradoxical nature about radical acceptance. The genuine acceptance of something about the self, the other, and one's situation is somewhat freeing. Acceptance makes us more amenable to change. On the one hand, we desire change. On the other hand, we resist change. Suppose I am an overly cautious individual. My over-cautiousness (excessive mistrust, hyper-vigilance, or suspiciousness) has contributed to my psychological survival in life. I over-identify with my over-cautiousness. My unconscious or not-so-conscious script that I live by and that shapes (or warps) who I am is: "Be ware; otherwise bad things will happen to me." I do not view it as a skewed stance for which I pay a heavy mental health price because of the partial payoff it has yielded in my developmental history. It is an extension of my way of being-with-my-self-and-others-in-the-world. It has become a natural part of my bodily dialect, jargon, lexicon, or context of meaning. Now, if I truly *accept* that my mistrustful stance is skewed and warped, I open myself up to the possibility of achieving a *balance* between being cautious, on the one hand, and being trustful on the other. My radical acceptance melts away my resistance to change.

In the last chapter of his *Essays*, Bakewell (2010) informs us, humanistic philosopher Michel de Montaigne writes: "I accept with all my heart and with gratitude what nature has done for me, and I am pleased with myself and proud of myself that I do. We wrong that great and all-powerful Giver by refusing his gift, nullifying it, and destroying it" (p. 147). Bakewell then comments:

> This [reveals a] comfortable acceptance of life as it is, and of one's own self as *it* is ... [As a skeptic] Montaigne places everything in doubt, but then he deliberately reaffirms everything that is familiar, uncertain, and ordinary – for that is all we have. Skepticism makes him celebrate imperfection ... To Montaigne ... escape [from humanity] is impossible. No one can rise above humanity: however high we ascend we take our humanity with us. (pp. 147–148)

Yet, paradoxically and ironically, for both go together here, Montaigne wrote the *Essays*, Bakewell tells us, to answer the existential question of "*How to Live?*" Montaigne, in other words, was perennially preoccupied with his quest for living well – for flourishing as a human being, for becoming better at being human, while never losing sight and being accepting of his limited and contradictory human nature. Montaigne muses that we can live a flourishing life when we can accept, among other matters, our inevitable, unavoidable, and humanizing situation – the dependent inconsistencies, not contradictions, in our character. Contradictions annihilate their opposites, whereas humanizing inconsistencies can live harmoniously side-by-side.

Affirmativeness, states Schachtel (1959), refers to the affirmation of the Other's total and unique being. It is a movement from gaining knowledge about the Other to acknowledging the existence of the Other in its own right. "In Hegel's thought it is the movement from knowledge to acknowledgement which constitutes love" (p. 226). "This is the reason why," Schachtel continues, "love sees more than hatred" (p. 226). Hatred narrows our perception and predisposes us to see only a partial, and thus distorted Other. When we are consumed with hatred we are unable to see the totality of the being of the Other. Love "wants to affirm others in their total and unique being. [Loving affirmation, however, is not blind to] the other person's limitations, weaknesses, and shortcomings, which are the lot of man" (p. 226). Moreover, this affirmative attitude extends to "every part of nature." Simply stated, to be affirming is to say an emphatic "Yes" to Life.

Our affirmativeness can only be sustained by feeling akin to others, by our "fellow-feeling." To feel akin to others is to experience them as a variation on our own humanness. The Other is my kin. The word "kin" is in the word "skin." The experiential origin of our basic feeling of kinship lies in the quality of inter-bodily (skin-to-skin) contact (touching-and-being touched) between infant and caregiver. It goes back to how we were handled and held. In being properly loved, we feel securely held. Being lovingly held is the *ultimate affirmation* we can receive from another human being. Having been lovingly held, we are able to lovingly hold, physically and metaphorically, not only our significant others, but also the generalized human Other. We can lovingly hold the Other, not only by giving him or her a hug, but also with a warm handshake, or even a loving, thus affirming, gaze. In the year 2016, a Syrian refugee stands, voluntarily blindfolded, arms extended seeking a hug in the middle of a central square of a major German city. German citizens, who are strangers to this young man, pass him by. Many stop to give him a hug. This is videotaped. It goes viral on YouTube. There is something about this "moving" picture that tears and touches the heart of the viewer. This blindfolded young man is welcomed and affirmed by the simple act of being hugged.

It makes sense then to surmise that one barrier to being able to affirm the Other is to not have been properly loved or to not have been loved at all. Other barriers include not being accepted by mainstream culture because of one's *skin* color, ethnicity, religion, sexual orientation, and so on. Negative affects and protective defensiveness are aroused. Affirmativeness "is made difficult or impossible," says Schachtel (1959), "by fear and arrogance – by fear because then the need to protect oneself by flight, appeasement, or attack gets in the way; by arrogance because then the other is no longer experienced as akin, but as inferior to oneself" (p. 227).

It needs to be stressed here, however, that the affirming "attitude is a relative rather than an absolute concept, matter of emphasis rather than of the exclusion of all and any autocentricity [or self-centeredness]" (Schachtel 1959, p. 227). We cannot, says Schachtel, make ourselves immune to fear or other negative emotions that interfere with our capacity for affirmativeness. But it is our immature attempts at escaping these negative emotions, rather than their existence, that prevent us from turning toward the whole being of the Other, with all his or her humanness, with our whole being. I would also add, the likeability or "lovability" of the Other or lack thereof makes it either easier or more difficult to approach him or her with an affirmative attitude. That in turn, depends on the relative maturity of both parties. There is also the element of risk that is involved in turning affirmatively toward the Other. We expose and make ourselves vulnerable to the rebuff of the Other. Given our human limitations and our need to make judicious judgments regarding the trustworthiness of the other, a discerning affirmativeness is the attitude to be cultivated.

"Two things seem to matter most in life," contends Kamler (1994): "finding love and becoming someone we like" (p. 1). Self-liking, for Kamler, is interchangeable with self-acceptance or self-satisfaction. What does it take to become someone we like? Kamler provides us with a succinct answer in the last page of his Conclusion:

> It takes maintaining a consistency about the character traits that our identificatory acts have brought into existence. Such consistency is no easy matter. … All of us, in fact, have within us the capacity to be satisfied with our selves. Of course it takes a certain vigilance, too (a strength of character?) to do all that's required for becoming someone we like, for being someone with whom we are satisfied. As autonomous identificatory creatures, the choice is certainly up to us. … We choose and rechoose [identificatory] images of the good life, but we simply don't always take our defense of those images as seriously as we might. We identify, but not fully. Nevertheless … it is only when we take identification as seriously as we can, and so choose to be as fully responsible as we can about our valuational images [the identificatory images that we value, that we care about], that we have a chance of being not just a character, but a character that is someone we like. (p. 304)

A "person who accepts both who he is and the value of who he is," Kamler comments, "is a person who most fully is who he is" (p. 212). This person's "self-empowerment is a phenomenological expression of self-responsibility" (p. 212).

Kamler elaborates:

> The nondefensive [mature] person … is someone who is *self-accepting*. The degree of a person's solidity and the degree of his self-responsibility is the degree of his self-acceptance. Such a person accepts the value or worth of the character self that he has sculpted through his identificatory valuations. He has self-respect and pride. He doesn't respond to challenges to the worth of his self by defending that worth. … He assumes his worth …. Persons who totally accept themselves in this fashion are a rare breed. We recognize them by their unflinching calm and sense of conviction when challenged. They *know* their worth. But most of us are this way only in degrees. (p. 211)

It is important to note that, for Kamler (1994), self-acceptance goes together with identificatory integrity or integration. When "a person drifts from consistently acting on one of his identifications, even just momentarily," Kamler cautions, "he suffers a certain amount of feelings of *lost integrity*" (p. 250). But what do humans *identify with*? We humans identify with almost anything. We can identify with that which we care about or attend to. We identify with our activities (playing sports, writing a book, or mountain-climbing), bodies, emotions (with strong emotions, selves are at stake), ideas (psychological theories or philosophical stances), ideologies (political or religious), inanimate objects (e.g., books, pens, and depicted figures in paintings), institutions, life projects, personal histories, traits ("traited ways of being," on an individual or group level), people (parents, friends, and other role models), values, vocabularies (repeated key words, phrases or other utterances of importance which designate who we are and with which we connect with or confront others), and "other kinds of beings – animals, fictional heroes, deities" (p. 119). Life provides us with unendingly varied identificatory opportunities. The traits or *character*istics we identify with deeply will come to constitute our character. More importantly, our identity is a byproduct of the strength of our internalized identifications. They become parts of our evolving self. "That is what identification is about. What an adult self is – i.e., its who-ness – is the activity of identifying" (p. 22). However, through mature identification (1) we are more conscious of the content of our identification, (2) we creatively adapt our identification to fit our uniquely emerging distinctive selves, and (3) we hold a balanced tension between being like (connected to) others and being unlike (separate from) others. As mature identifiers we sculpt who we are becoming as persons by selectively choosing and responsibly owning what Kamler calls our "identificatory valuations" – the value standards contained in the identifications we *choose* to live by. Because we are "multidimensional identifiers" (p. 163), our identifications may contain not only moral concerns, but also aesthetic and practical concerns. Above all, our identificatory acts have to match our identificatory images of our selves. The more the match between our images and acts the more the self-acceptance. Simply stated, "we *are* our identifications" (Kamler 1994, p. 204).

Our *true* identity, continues Kamler (1994), is defined by the degree to which we live up to our chosen and thus owned identifications. This is the kind of identity we are likely to like, be satisfied with, and accept. Our *true* or *mature* identity, to which we can say "yes" to, also requires the appropriation of identifications that cohere, that can be integrated:

> Just as the existential psychological payoff for becoming a personal identity is one's achieving a sense of integrity and self-esteem about a unified, coherent distinctive character self, the existential psychological payoff for becoming a social identity is her achieving a sense of belonging through varied feelings of solidarity, kinship, fellowship, fellow-feeling, camaraderie, and togetherness with group members. (p. 270)

We humans are destined to confront the existential tension between our individual versus our group identity, between our personal versus our social identity, and between our need for individuation (agency) and our need for communion (belonging). The "sharing of values (valued traits) … is required for genuine group identification" (p. 270). This has to be balanced with the "responsibility a person takes for sharing these values" (p. 270). This means that valued group traits that a person identifies with must be genuine and must allow the person to retain her or his sense of agency and the right to stand up for identificatory traits that have ultimate value, that speak to one's ultimate human concern. We can acquire a deep sense of our social self without sacrificing our individuated sense of self, while remaining inclusive, without becoming exclusive. Our "social identification as it mixes with personal identification … [contributes to] the making of the full character self" (p. 290). It is the kind of self that I can unconditionally accept. In such a mature identity, the "interpersonal truth is also the intrapersonal truth" (p. 291). Even if, in my identification with a universal value, I take a position contrary to that of my social group, I do so because of a commitment to my character self *and* my concern for the ultimate welfare of the social group to which I belong. Atticus Finch, the protagonist in Harper Lee's (1960) *To Kill a Mockingbird*, comes to mind here as an exemplar (see Hannush 2002).

We become our individuated selves through a lifetime of identifications and dis-identifications. We identify, originally, with our parents' qualities or traits in an effort to establish, maintain, and enhance our need to love and be loved by them, to be attached or connected to them. We identify with their strengths and shortcomings. The process of maturation involves keeping and refining the good identificatory qualities or traits and letting go of the bad identificatory qualities or traits. It also entails the continued addition of new identificatory traits or qualities. Individuation therefore necessitates the toleration of the tension between *holding on* to certain valued identificatory ways of being and the *letting go* of other disvalued ways of being.

Kamler (1994) reminds us that even in our beginnings in infancy, there is a need on the part of the infant to individuate and therefore separate from the loved-and-loving parent. There is loss and gain experienced in the process. When parents encourage the child's agentic or autonomous strivings toward separating from them while remaining connected, "the evolving self can accept separation without fear of dissolution" (p. 46). Separation, it needs to be noted, is a form of loss. With loss, even when it is accompanied by gain, there is inevitable pain. The trajectory of our unfolding lives is wound up with a series of painful separations and losses. But as Symington (2019) says, the "acceptance of pain enriches the personality" (p. 56). Pain that is not adequately suffered impoverishes our personality. "Painful happenings are part of life so to put energy into eroding pain is, at the same time, a subversion of life" (p. 56). Because pain is a part of life, to accept life we need to accept pain. We pay a mental health price for avoiding emotional pain. Psychological growth, Symington tells us, involves embracing the painful and the joyful, the good and the bad aspects of life. This is an integrative act or an act of integration.

Symington (2019) traces the capacity to suffer pain to its origins in infancy, although this ability to tolerate suffering can always be acquired later in life, however, with more difficulty. In a moving passage, Symington quotes from a letter sent to him by a friend and colleague two years prior to the friend's death:

> 'In my view what gave me life [what enabled me to say 'yes' to life including its painful and joyful aspects] or at least saved me from [psychological] death is the amazing fact that my mother had inborn tendencies to minister to my infant helplessness and that they were sufficiently supported socially and culturally for her to work the miracle. From my point of view this was a totally unmerited gift – Grace, in fact. Ave Maria! So the choices we have to make every day now in so far as they are very derived or developed forms of this very first relationship depend on how much we can acknowledge and honour this Gift (and become identified with it).' (p. 90)

At the core of this friend's identity as an affirmer of life, in its vicissitudes, is his *identification* with the Gift that his mother bestowed upon him when he was a *helpless* infant. This early Gift for which he is forever grateful has guided his later choices in life as a whole. His identification with the Gift of life "gathered" him and disallowed potentially aversive identifications from dispersing or fragmenting him.

Interestingly, both Symington (2019) and Kamler (1994) overemphasize the role of *conscious* "choice" in achieving integrative identification or identificatory integration which is necessary for the *acceptance* of self and of life. "For example," comments Gerhardt (2015), "Neville Symington talks about 'choosing the life-giver' and 'saying yes to life' as a choice a patient can make ... It is very dispiriting when clients fail to make progress and seem unable to make positive choices" (p. 110). Yet, in all fairness, Symington also says that psychological growth occurs only in the context of center-to-center, whole-heart-to-whole-heart, creative-core-to-creative-core healing conversations. Nevertheless, Gerhardt's critical comment is valid for it is abundantly substantiated in Symington's writings where he repeatedly emphasizes that the essential aspect of the creative core of personality is the capacity to choose.

Wachtel (2011) has this to say on this matter:

> Central to the effort at modifying the patient's representational [I would say, "intentional"] world is helping him to rework the identifications that form the core of his sense of self and his place in the world. These identifications mostly operate outside the range of critical reflection, shaping and constraining our sense of life's possibilities, imperatives, and desiderata. Beneath the level of awareness, and soaked in the psychic import of the early parent-child matrix, these identifications are highly value-laden. They import a sense of compelling necessity to our experience and lay our boundaries that we are forbidden to transgress. These boundaries are not merely with regard to behavior; they dictate what we may hope for and what we may believe. To see around them, much less to live on a different basis or with different assumptions and different internal imperatives, is extremely difficult. The distinction between description and value disappear at this level; it is the level of what *should* be, what *must* be. (p. 302)

Wachtel asserts that identifications form the core of our identity. We cannot live without our identifications. Some people's identifications are "tenuous or lacking in substance" (p. 302). As a consequence, they live empty, isolated, and meaningless lives. In effective therapy, the therapist becomes the object of the patient's identification. The psychotherapist needs to be comfortable in being identified with. Some patients begin to talk or even walk like their therapists! The therapist offers himself or herself as a "good-and-whole object" of identification. This will counter the patient's already existing contradictory, conflicting, inconsistent, or vacuous and pre-reflectively embodied and lived identifications. The therapist, Wachtel tells us, is faced with a balancing act of (1) fostering the *life-affirming identifications* with the therapist and (2) helping the patient cultivate her or his "capacity to rework those identifications and achieve a unique and independent selfhood" (pp. 302–303). In essence, therapy is about working through or reworking one's identifications – the building blocks of selfhood. This involves modifying identifications, letting go of others – a process involving dis-identification, and adding new, healthy identifications. Through it all, the therapist is helping the patient position him or herself to observe, examine, and gain *insight into* her or his *identifications*.

We are born to identify with others. More accurately, we are born with what I call the capacity for *identificatory resonance* that makes the capacity for the evolving mature forms of identification possible. Symington (2019) labels it as "sensitive affinity" (p. 41). In another context, Symington (2012) points to "*a harmony of the similar*, a similarity which respected the difference between us" (p. 38). This "harmony of the similar," he adds, "finds its similarity in the togetherness in truth of participants" (p. 44). By "truth" he means relational and emotional truth.

Existentially speaking, we are essentially co-beings or "with-beings." Or, we are beings-in-the world-with-others through and through. We inhabit or dwell with others. From the beginning, we are constructed to co-participate in a common lifeworld. As Paskow (2004) puts it:

> [Others] touch us … always, necessarily, and *essentially*. We are 'co-' as regards them … in that their basic endeavors are (as possibilities) *our* basic endeavors, that our question of who we are is ineluctably linked to our quest of who they are, that, in other words, our being is defined by their being (or what we take their being to be) – and vice versa. (pp. 94–95)

Our capacity for identificatory resonance, therefore, is an existential phenomenon or a trait fundamental to our existence. It makes our capacity for, what I call, "existential identification" possible. It is equivalent, but preferred to what Paskow (2004) calls "existential role-playing." Through existential identification I deal with the Other not as an object of utilitarian use but rather as a co-being who embodies my existential issues and concerns. I see the Other as my "alternative self." I see her or him as a meaning making co-participant in the flow of life. The Other incarnates for me what I might or should be. He or she exemplifies for me life's possibilities to which I aspire or with which I have not come fully to terms. She or he embodies for me "existential roles" or ways of being or doing which I might appropriate or find repugnant. She or he exemplifies for me the kind of person I could become or would rather not be or become. The refined or ripened Other incarnates for me the call of my *existential conscience* or what Paskow calls *Seinkonnen*, my potentiality to be.

Our existential conscience (Paskow's Heideggerian *Seinkonnen*) is:

> a dimension of our being suggested to us in first-person experiences … [it is] that which calls each one to become a psychically fully integrated and self-actualized … we should view our *Seinkonnen* [existential conscience] as the stimulus of one's creative expression (or action) … [It is] the source par excellence of creativity. (p. 120)

D. W. Black (1997) unearths the multiple meanings of *conscience*. Conscience, in its primeval meaning, is inseparable from linkage to "communication" and "consciousness." The "fundamental task of communication" is to generate "our first consciousness," "to *make* common" or "communal" and "to create not merely a means for personal expression but a lasting sense of conscience" (pp. 53–54). Then, in a circular fashion, he adds, "it is actually conscience that creates consciousness. One can see the non-theoretical genesis of ethics" (p. 54). Consciousness as a reflexive awakening generates our gradual awareness or "witnessing" – the observing and evaluating, of our emerging selves in action as co-participants with others in the lifeworld. It is the voice within us, mirrored through the (caring) voice from without, that beckons us to do and be more. We are forever challenged to *conscientiously* heed the *communicative* call of our *conscience* made possible by our *consciousness* (witnessing awareness) which in turn results in the deepening of our conscience, the broadening of our consciousness, and the authentication of our capacity for communication and communion.

The "Voice of Conscience," Symington (1996) says, "is the speech of the integrated part of the self addressing the actions of the unintegrated part" (p. 184). He continues, "ego-strength is built up each time someone follows conscience. In contradistinction to the harsh superego, conscience, for Symington, is the seat of the Lifegiver – the *life-affirming* voice. "The self," he adds, "is a construction, a self-construction, that is fashioned through acting towards transcendent values through conscience" (p. 200). There is a deep connection, Symington concludes, between "conscience and mental health" (p. 207).

Again, the more integrated we become, in response to the call of our maturing conscience, the more *accepting* we are of ourselves, of others, and of life itself. Lest we fall into a quest for perfection, we need to view the concept of integration through a realistic lens. Integration here is not viewed as the equivalent of perfect intrapersonal and interpersonal harmony, symmetry, or synthesis. The self is essentially a synthesizer. No self, however, is ever fully formed. We will always fall short of complete synthesis. There are degrees of falling, however. There are levels of intrapersonal and interpersonal alienation, compartmentalization, dispersal, fragmentation, or isolation. We humans are condemned to containing within and between us unconscious contradictions, inconsistencies, and unresolved conflicts. Correlatively, there are degrees of coherence, cohesion, communion, connectedness, or togetherness (within and between us).

The quest for full integration is a mirage. Symington (2019) refers to the blinding consequence of the "human *lust for [full] coherence*" for "reality is a mixture of clarity and hiddenness" (p. 102). Our inner and interpersonal lives are punctuated with complexity, untidiness, and asymmetry. Accepting ourselves requires of us humbly recognizing our limitations. It demands of us the acceptance of the identificatory dialectical tensions that are at the core of our selfhood: balance versus imbalance, coherence versus incoherence, cohesiveness versus non-cohesiveness (incongruity), harmony versus disharmony, and symmetry versus asymmetry. Still, for maturity to unfold, balance, coherence, cohesiveness, harmony, and symmetry will outweigh imbalance, incoherence, non-cohesiveness, disharmony, and asymmetry. The integrators, such as trust and, above all, love, will counter the disintegrators, such as mistrust and hate (or indifference). The unifying functions of personality, such as good judgment and emotional regulation, will outnumber the dividers, such as poor judgment and emotional deficit or excess. Fundamentally then, just as love is more primary than hate (or indifference), identificatory resonance is more primary than identificatory dissonance (repugnance), or identificatory resistance (opposition). Nevertheless, the dialectical tension between identificatory resonance and identificatory dissonance or resistance is all part of what it means to exist in an existential space of lifeworld meanings.

It is our capacity for identificatory resonance – our originary life-affirming capacity, that makes it possible for us to cultivate the capacities for communion, communication, empathy, sympathy mentalization, perspective taking, and sympathy possible. It is the mechanism through which we are able to see ourselves in others and others in ourselves. But above all, it is the instrument of psychosocial maturation. Through it we acquire our ever-expanding existential identificatory roles. Psychosocial maturation occurs in a relational context in which identificatory resonance unfolds between a maturing child and an accepting and caring mature adult. Commenting on the work of Fairbairn, Ogden (2012) concludes: "Psychological growth … involves a form of *acceptance of oneself* that can be achieved only in the context of a real relationship with a relatively psychologically mature person [who serves as an identificatory figure]. A relationship of this sort… is the only possible exit from the solipsistic World" (p. 75). Self-acceptance is from the beginning intertwined with the acceptance of the essential other. And there can be no acceptance of the Other without self-acceptance.

Although psychiatrist D. J. Siegel's (2012) evidence-based neuropsychological theory of *The Developing Mind* is ostensibly grounded in the "natural science" of the brain or in *How Relationships and the Brain Interact to Shape Who We Are,* allow me to conclude this chapter on acceptance with a quotation from Siegel's (2010) *Mindsight*:

> In short, when a person's [self] states are unintegrated he is internally distressed and inclined toward chaos and rigidity – or both; he is behaviorally compromised as well, unable to be flexible and adaptive in his interactions with others. … Healthy development is not about creating a single "self" that is a homogenized, uniform entity. Rather, healthy development is about coming to acknowledge, accept, and then to integrate one's various [self] states: to discover how disparate [self] states can link, and even collaborate as a unified whole of many parts. (p. 198)

Descriptively, as a clinician, Siegel can be incisively insightful about the process of "healthy development." His neuropsychological theory of the "developing mind," though seemingly based on biological facts about the brain in particular and the nervous system in general, is reductionistic. In a refrain that begins and repeats three times in a short song that is a play on the lyrics of a James Taylor song, "Carolina in My Mind," Siegel (2010) says or sings: "In my mind I'm driven by mirror neurons" (p. 223). I would rephrase the song to read: "In my mind, I am called by my identifications." My identifications, which are grounded in my fundamental capacity for *identificatory resonance* with people and things, are made possible by, but cannot be reduced to, my mirror neurons. Certain features of my affective life are experientially irreducible to my mirror neurons. My identifications are more and other than my mirror neurons. They can creatively gain *functional autonomy* from their original, biologically "driven" source. Analogously, *acceptance* leads to integration, but integration, in turn, results in *radical acceptance* of our evolving true self.

References

Bakewell, S. (2010). *How to live or a life of Montaigne in one question and twenty attempts at an answer*. Other Press.

Black, D. W. (1997). *Vico and moral perception*. Peter Lang.

Cohn, H. W. (1997). *Existential thought and therapeutic practice: An introduction to existential psychotherapy*. Sage.

Gerhardt, S. (2015). *Why love matters: How affection shapes a baby's brain* (2nd ed.). Routledge.

Hannush, M. J. (2002). *Becoming good parents: An existential journey*. State University of New York Press.

Kahn, M. (1997). *Between therapist and client: The new relationship* (Rev. ed.). W. H. Freeman.

Kamler, H. (1994). *Identification and character: A book on psychological development*. State University of New York Press.

Lee, H. (1960). *To kill a mockingbird*. Warner Books.

May, R. (1958). Contributions of existential psychotherapy. In R. May, E. Angel, & H. F. Ellenberger (Eds.), *Existence*. Basic Books.

Mearns, D., & Thorne, B. (1999). *Person-centered counselling in action* (2nd ed.). Sage.

Merkin, D. (2017). *This close to happy: A reckoning with depression*. Farrar, Straus and Giroux.

Ogden, T. H. (2012). *Creative readings: Essays on seminal analytic works*. Routledge.

Paskow, A. (2004). *The paradoxes of art: A phenomenological investigation*. Cambridge University Press.

Rogers, C. R. (1961). *On becoming a person*. Houghton Mifflin.
Rogers, C. R. (1980). *A way of being*. Houghton Mifflin.
Safran, J. D. (2012). *Psychoanalysis and psychoanalytic therapies*. American Psychological Association.
Schachtel, E. G. (1959). *Metamorphosis: On the development of affect, perception, attention, and memory*. Basic Books.
Siegel, D. J. (2010). *Mindsight: The new science of personal transformation*. Bantam Books/The Guilford Press.
Siegel, D. J. (2012). *The developing mind: How relationships and the brain interact to shape who we are* (2nd ed.). Guilford.
Symington, N. (1996). *The making of a psychotherapist*. Routledge.
Symington, N. (2012). *The psychology of the person*. Karnac.
Symington, N. (2019). *The growth of mind*. Routledge.
Wachtel, P. L. (2011). *Therapeutic communication: Knowing what to say when* (2nd ed.). The Guilford Press.

18

Authenticity: The Capacity for *Authenticity*, Congruence, Genuineness, and Realness

It seems to me that in attempting to unravel the meaning of authenticity for D. W. Winnicott, we find out that it is interrelated to or overlaps with other key capacities: aloneness, creativity (originality), I am-ness (going-on being), play-and-playfulness, realness, genuine relating, reparation, spontaneity, transitional being-ness (making use of transitional objects, spaces, or phenomena), and true selfhood.

For Winnicott, says Tuber (2008), "authenticity and originality are the hallmarks of mental health" (p. 82). This "capacity for realness," continues Tuber, "by definition, implies the creation and existence of a solitary, non-communicating place of solitude for the person to retreat to that is not just safe, but optimally relaxing" (p. 82). In other words, being authentic implies being able to be alone.

Winnicott traces the origin of authenticity to the early mother-infant relationship. "A baby with a 'good-enough' mother," explains Tuber (2008), "develops the capacity to be alone in the presence of another without distress and without falseness. This leads to the ability to hate the now separate mother and for her to optimally survive the 'hatred' in order for the baby to become fully fused or integrated" (pp. 226–227). The original source of authenticity, then, is early good-enough mothering. It involves growing up in a relatively distress-free and facilitating home environment in which the child cultivates the capacity to be alone, initially in the presence of the mother, which in turn enables the child to move toward building a true, spontaneous integrative self.

For Winnicott, Tuber (2008) tells us, the process of becoming an authentic, real, and true self involves two other elements: play and transitional space. Play spaces are also referred to as transitional spaces wherein the child plays

© The Author(s), under exclusive license to Springer Nature Switzerland AG 2021

M. J. Hannush, *Markers of Psychosocial Maturation*,
https://doi.org/10.1007/978-3-030-74315-4_18

with transitional objects. Play is pivotal for optimal development. The "capacity to play," says Tuber, "is the gold standard for eventual *[mental] health*. Play is made still more meaningful in the context of the creation of transitional phenomena, the arena for the growth of cultural life" (p. 227).

Winnicott grounds *spontaneity* in the lived body, in body-to-body communication, in the spontaneous gesture – the original attempt on the part of the infant to communicate with the primary caregiver. "By 8 months," note Newman and Newman (2018):

> infants use sounds like grunting and whining in combination with gestures to achieve a goal. Sounds combined with gestures and looks in a certain direction become part of purposeful communication. … A common first gesture is to raise the arms up toward the caregiver in a desire to be picked up … Gestures may also be used to express emotion or to get someone's attention …Three other communicative strategies emerge at about 9 to 11 months. Infants begin to seek adult interest and attention by *showing* … *giving* … [and] *pointing* …
>
> [All this testifies to] an infant's ability to set up a shared focus with another person … This is called **intersubjectivity** – a condition in which two conscious minds have the same thought or feeling. (p. 149)

In other words, the preverbal gestures of the infant play a pivotal role in the establishment of intersubjectivity. "**Representational skills**," such as the capacities for (playful) imitation, for playing with mental images and symbols, and for using language, which emerge in toddlerhood, "allow children to share their experiences with others … [and] free children from communicating only through **gestures**" (p. 197). Playful or practical spontaneous gestures may begin as solitary schemes, guided by reflexive templates such as the sucking scheme, the grasping scheme, or even the smiling scheme, and evolve into purposive and playful relational schemes.

In these spontaneous and playful gestures Winnicott discovers the original essence of authenticity. From these spontaneous gestures emerges our quest for authenticity. In them lie our future uniqueness, creativity, originality, or authenticity. Our optimal development, growth, or maturation is contingent upon the nurturance and cultivation of our "personal spontaneity." However, being incipiently dialectical, Winnicott (1965b) importantly adds that the trajectory of our *maturation involves balancing spontaneity with socialization*: "Maturity of the human being … implies not only personal growth but socialization. In health … the adult is able to identify with society without too great a sacrifice of personal spontaneity" (p. 83).

Just as spontaneity is an original dimension of authenticity, so is the related concept of emerging *true selfhood*. And just as spontaneity needs to be balanced with socialization, so too true selfhood needs to be balanced with false selfhood.

"Winnicott," state St. Clair and Wigren (2004), provides us with "a unique perspective on how the interplay between mother and child fosters or hinders the child's development of an authentic self" (p. 84). As is evident, the "true self" and the "authentic self" are interchangeable. Good-enough mothering facilitates the optimal maturation of the child. "Maturation" is therefore "defined in terms of relationships" (p. 69). Maturational processes are made possible by facilitating social environments. A facilitating mother is one who responsively and responsibly adapts to the changing needs of the developing child. A good-enough mother provides the child with an initial experience of omnipotence. "From illusions of omnipotence emerge a healthy or true self" (p. 70). By repeatedly affirming the child's spontaneous gestures and by empowering the child through meeting his need for initial, magical omnipotence, the mother "makes real the infant's hallucination" or primordial imagination; the "infant then can serenely enjoy the illusion of omnipotent creativity and control [or empowerment]" (p. 71).

True or false, the self emerges from the child's interaction with the social environment. The stage of "omnipotence" is made possible by the adaptation of the good-enough mother to the child's changing needs. This is a stage in which the mother is wholly "preoccupied" in adapting herself to the child's needs. In the stage that follows, the mother begins to gradually return to her ordinary self with its ordinary preoccupations. Correlatively, the child learns to gradually let go of his or her illusion of omnipotence. It is through this unfolding developmental process that the child discovers a "me" here and a "not-me" out there to whom he or she must "relate." "The true self," state St. Clair and Wigren (2004), "has a *me* and a *not-me* clearly established" (p. 71). Meanwhile, the good-enough mother must continue to protect her child from environmental impingements that are beyond the child's capacity to manage on his or her own. Should this not happen, the child develops a *compliant (false) self* that is severed from the child's emerging *spontaneous (true) self*. "This compliance," comment St. Clair and Wigren, "could lead to the isolation of the infant from his own spontaneous and lifegiving core" (p. 71). The false self can develop in the earlier stage when the child is not provided with adequate experiences of empowering omnipotence, when the child's spontaneous gestures are not repeatedly responded to in an attuned way, and when the mother imposes her own gestural being upon the being-ness of her child.

> When the mother's adaptation is not good enough … the infant remains isolated and lives falsely. A false self reacts compliantly to environmental demands and builds up a false set of relationships. The false self hides the true self and cannot act spontaneously. Only the true self can be spontaneous and feel real or genuine. The presence of the false self results in the person feeling unreal and futile and unable to be genuine in relationships. (St. Clair and Wigren 2004, p. 71)

Just as maturation entails, in part, *balancing* spontaneity with socialization, it also involves, in part, *balancing* the true (spontaneous) self with the false (compliant) self.

Although Winnicott does not put it as such, our dialectical model would differentiate between healthy and unhealthy spontaneity on one side of the dialectical continuum and healthy and unhealthy compliance on the other side of continuum. I can achieve a relatively stable *balance* between being spontaneous and being compliant depending upon the situation in which I find myself. As Fuller (1990) formulates it, "lifeworld tensions come to fittingly balance one another out in accordance with the demands of the situation's structure" (p. 160). The play of meaning's phenomenal tensions "come to balanced structural fulfillment" (p. 168). And "seeking a state of balance works to integrate new and disturbing meanings into existing wholes of meanings" (pp. 168–169). Our bodily selves will forever struggle to seek balance among "meaning's phenomenal tensions" (p. 167).

Erikson's concept of *optimal ratio* and Rogers's concept of *un/conditional acceptance* are relevant here. Maturation requires the cultivation of an optimal ratio between becoming and being a spontaneous (true) self and becoming and being a compliant (false) self. Unconditional acceptance allows for the flourishing of the authentic (true) self. However, socialization also requires *conditionality*, especially when it comes to how we *behave* in the social world. Pure and continuous unconditional acceptance is a mirage. It is when we come to *identify* with the false, inauthentic, compensatory self that we pay a mental health price. In this, we sacrifice our true, authentic, spontaneous self. The tragic thing is that when we *identify* with the false self, we come to take our false (distorted) emotions (e.g., ruminative worry), our thoughts (e.g., meaning misattributions), and even our actions (e.g., acting-out) as justified and real. Then again spontaneity can devolve into recklessness, and discerning compliance can be adaptive and civilizing.

Analogously, part of my maturation involves cultivating the capacity to be genuine in relationships. This necessitates that I relate to (see) the Other *as* Other, objectively as a variation on but separate from me. "With maturation," explain St. Clair and Wigren (2004), "the individual is gradually able to relate genuinely to objects [others], have vital contact with reality, feel real and alive, feel real in the world, and feel that the world is real and actual" (p. 72). Again, from the perspective of our dialectical model, maturation involves balancing authentic (genuine) relating and functional or instrumental relating.

Winnicott (1965b) points to a developmental transition in infancy and childhood from an amorphous one-body (infant-with-mother or infant-being-held-by-mother-in-a-state-of-absolute-unintegrated-dependence), to a two-body (infant distinct from mother or infant-living-together-with-mother--in-a-state-of-relative-dependence), and, finally, to a three-body (child-mother-father or child-living-together-with-mother-and-father-in-a-state-of-integrated-independence) awareness. This process entails significant qualitative shifts in the experiencing of the maturing child. The *capacity to be alone* emerges along with the shift from the one-body to a two-body awareness on the part of the developing infant and is further refined in the three-body awareness phase. The capacity to be alone is made possible by the internalization of the presence of the good-enough mother. We see early evidence of it in the mobile infant or child who becomes absorbed with an object or activity as he or she moves away from the mother only to check intermittently for the reassuring presence of the mother or going back to his or her secure base only to embark again upon his new exciting expedition alone. "Maturity and the capacity to be alone," emphasizes Winnicott, "implies that the individual has had the chance through good-enough mothering to build up a belief in a benign environment" (p. 32). Having internalized a good relationship with the mother and later the father, the child, even when alone, feels at home in the world.

The first thing that comes to mind when we hear of Winnicott's *transitional objects* are pacifiers and blankets that serve as substitutes for mother's safe, secure, and soothing presence. As his thinking evolves, however, these *transitional phenomena* take on a broader and much more encompassing meaning. In commenting on Winnicott's essay, "Transitional Objects and Transitional Phenomena" (Winnicott 1971), Ogden (2012) has this to say about the deeper and richer meaning of Winnicott's *transitional phenomena*:

> Of course, what is being introduced is the concept of 'transitional phenomena.' The 'moment of illusion' is a moment of psychological 'overlap' of the mother and infant – a moment in which the mother lives an experience with the infant in which she actively/unconsciously/naturally provides herself as an object that can be experienced by the infant at once as his creation (an unnoticed experience

> because there is nothing that is *not* what is expected) *and* as his discovery (an event with a quality of otherness in a world external to his sense of self). (p. 91)

Nothing short of a *new way of being-with* is revealed in this powerful paragraph. The infant/child is transitioning to a new way of being with mother. It is a new way of *being-with* that *paradoxically* combines creativity (illusion) with reality (otherness). It is a way of being alive that allows the child to become his or her unique or true self while connecting to the reality of the m/other. It makes it possible for the child to create coherence (integration) for him or herself. Winnicott is generating a kind of understanding "that is adequate to the paradoxical nature of human experience" (Ogden 2012, p. 77). Creation without reality meanders into madness.

Deepening the paradoxical meaning of transitional experiencing – this newly emerging way of being with the m/other is that this potentially creative-and-enlivening way of being-in-the-world-with-others remains with us as a potentiality throughout the trajectory of our unfolding lives. The "central organizing thread of psychological development from its inception," in Winnicott's work, says Ogden (2012), "is the experience of being alive and the consequences of disruptions to that continuity of being" (p. 90). Our capacity to transition, to shift to a new way of being-and-doing, "is an act of infusing experience with life" (p. 90). It is, in Winnicott's (1971) own quoted words, "'a capacity to conjure up what is actually available'" (p. 91). It is "a way of experiencing that is lighter, more full of energy, than other ways of experiencing" (p. 91). It is a byproduct of the convergence of the magical world of the infant and the "world of grounded consensual reality" of the mother.

We humans are gifted with the potential capacity to imbue our experience with our aliveness, creativity, originality, and uniqueness. It is always possible for us, under good-enough conditions or in facilitating social environments, to "transition" to this authentic way of being-and-doing, alone or, primordially, with others while remaining in contact with or grounded in reality. It is this ability to transition that makes poetry possible, both for poet and for reader. It is what makes any creative endeavor possible. Transitioning to this mode or mood allows me to "see" a raindrop as a teardrop, while "knowing" that in reality it is just a raindrop. I am able to ascribe my sense of aliveness not only to things, but also to others and the "space" we co-create between us. With the deepening of my love for my wife, the transitional space between us becomes imbued with our enlivening mutual intimacy. Or, I can think of the transitional space that is created while traveling in a family car by members of a family whose members, to use the words of Erich Fromm (1956), have creative love for each other – they *care* about each other; they are *concerned* about each other's welfare; they are *responsibly* responsive to each other's needs, and they respect and *know* each other's points of view, even when these views differ from one's own.

Again, this capacity to shift (transition) in experiencing is, according to Winnicott, made possible by a good-enough mother who, originally, makes up the child's facilitating environment. Being-good-enough-to-the-infant involves protecting the infant from "complications that cannot be understood" or impingements that cannot be defended against by the infant (Ogden 2012, p. 92). The facilitating mother brings "the world to the baby in understandable form" (p. 94). Moreover, from the beginning, mother and child "live [the mutually vitalizing transitional] experience together" (p. 92). In this initial joint experiencing, the mother represents reality at one pole and the child embodies the other, imaginative pole. "Creativity," comments Ogden, "is not only worthless, it is lethal (literally so in the case of an infant) when disconnected from objectivity – that is, from 'acceptance of external reality'" (p. 93). The "full blast of fantasy is made safe by a child's sturdy grasp on external reality" (p. 95). Here is how Ogden concludes his chapter on "Winnicott's 'Primitive emotional development'": "To be alive (in more than an operational sense) is to be forever in the process of making things of one's own, whether they be thoughts, feelings, bodily movements, perceptions, poems or analytic papers" (p. 96).

Longhofer (2015) describes the link between authenticity and true selfhood in Winnicott's work:

> Although Winnicott offered little clear definition of the sense of the true self, in general he describes a state of feeling connected, whole, real, alive, and spontaneous. This is a feeling of being real and alive in the mind and body: it is a state that produces the necessary conditions for intimacy and creativity. Winnicott did not imagine, however, that these were categorical distinctions, and because the true and false selves are potential states for everyone, he placed them along a continuum.
>
> The false self maintains relationships through the continual anticipation of the demands of others ... [In the absence of a facilitating environment] the false self emerges as a defence against unsafe and overwhelming environments ... With compliance and conforming behaviour, the infant is motivated to please the caregiver; the result is an inhibition of spontaneous expression of authentic feeling and thought. This may also occur when one conforms or complies with social codes, conventions or rules: over time mental life and relational patterns are organized around compliant adaptation to the environment. (pp. 178–179)

In his conclusion to a section on the "**true/false self**," Longhofer (2015) uses the work of Winnicott and other researchers in academic psychology to describe what has been called a state of authenticity: "Authentic states result when 'enduring propensities (e.g., attitudes, values, beliefs, personality) match cognition or action. Others have argued that [a] self-concordant (i.e. authentic) [state] results from a match between situational goal strivings and personal values'" (p. 179).

This last quoted definition of authenticity complements the implicit or explicit meanings that Kohut and Rogers attribute to authenticity.

Kohut (1977) describes the bipolar self as being pushed by ambitions, which is equivalent to "situational goal strivings," and pulled by ideals, which is equivalent to "personal values." The healthy authentic self is driven by realistic ambitions commensurate with one's potentials and is led by realistic ideals (goals and values or valued goals). Realistic ambitions unfold from the early healthy assertion of our initiatives. Our realistic ideals emerge from the early healthy admiration for and identification with the idealized figures in our lives. The energizing tension arc created between these two polar dimensions or aspects of our core or nuclear self, the bipolar self, propels us into action. The self, recognized as somewhat elusive in its operational definition, stands "for our sense of being an independent center of initiative and perception, integrated with our most central ambitions and ideals and with our experience that our body and mind form a unit in space and a continuum in time" (p. 177).

Kohut's authentic self is a byproduct of an *optimal ratio* of empathic attunements (successes) to empathic ruptures (failures) in responsiveness to our basic early needs for mirroring. Our *mirroring needs* are for the most part met when our early displays of aliveness, assertiveness, expansiveness, and magnificence, and our emerging grandiose ambitions, skills, talents, and other physical and mental attributes are admired, affirmed, confirmed, recognized, and validated with pleasure, joy, and delight. We are also mirrored when we receive a reparative response to our experience of a relational rupture or empathic disconnection. Our *idealizing needs* are met when we are blessedly allowed to merge with the goodness, reliability, soothing calmness, and strength – a merging from which we derive our own unique idealized goals, of our idealizable caregivers. When these two basic needs for mirroring and idealization are adequately met, we are enabled to form a consolidated and cohesive nuclear (core) self. Later, Kohut adds a third basic need, the *need for twinship* – of needing to be similar to essential others.

We should never forget, however, that the meeting of these three basic needs occurs in the context of vitalizing affirmations, empathic attunements, and enthusiastic participation in the child's activities. It is this *optimal ratio* of attunements-to-misattunements that makes it possible for us to achieve self-cohesion, self-continuity, and self-realization. This vibrant relational self is innately motivated to grow and move toward psychological health if its basic needs are significantly satisfied in a matrix of empathic attunement. Although Kohut uses the word "independent" in his definition of the self, this in no way means independence from others. The hallmark of maturity, he believes, lies in our mutually dependent relations throughout the life cycle.

After describing the "tripartite self" as "driven by ambition, pulled by ideals, and needing to recognize itself in similar others" (p. 174), Flanagan (1996) makes the link between empathy and *authenticity* in Kohut's self-psychology:

> there had to be an optimal balance of empathic gratification and empathic failure for the developing self to flourish and eventually experience itself as energetic and cohesive ... in life ... reactions to failures in empathy can be worked through if the disappointment and anger over unmet needs can be expressed and understood. This leads to a stronger and firmer sense of self. According to self psychology, empathic attunement is the necessary facilitator of development ... if you can name troublesome feelings you can begin to master and transform them, because you have a fuller, more accepting knowledge of yourself. Empathy does not necessarily make a person feel good, but it does help people feel genuine and authentic. (pp. 179–180)

Three sets of mature qualities emerge, expands Flanagan, as the needs of the tri-partite authentic self are properly met. (1) As children we make contact with our authentic self when our need for the assertiveness of our ambitiousness and specialness is sufficiently satisfied. The "mature qualities that derive from the pole of the grandiose [assertive] self ... are enthusiasm over appropriate goals and the ability to pursue these ambitions with joy and self confidence" (p. 185). (2) Contact with our emerging authentic self is further made when our need to merge with the admired qualities (calmness, competence) of our idealized essential others is optimally gratified.

> When there are sufficient selfobjects in a person's life to idealize, the mature qualities of the pole of the idealized parent imago can develop. These are the ability to delight in and grow from qualities in others and eventually experience pleasure and pride in one's own qualities, standards, and values. These qualities of the idealized self are taken into the self as a result of successful merger experiences. (p. 187)

(3) Contact with our evolving authentic self is further made when our need to feel similar to essential others is significantly satisfied. "The mature qualities that develop when the selfobject needs of the twinship pole are met are security and a sense of belonging and legitimacy. These enhance the nuclear [authentic] self and all its endeavors" (p. 189). Simply stated, we make contact with our authentic self when our mirroring, idealizing, and twinship needs are optimally met not only in early childhood, but throughout the life cycle.

The most concise description of the authentic self appears in an article written by Kohut and Wolf:

> The patterns of ambitions, skills and [valued] goals; the tensions between them; the program of action they create; the activities undertaken toward their realization; all are experienced in space and time; they are the [authentic] self, an independent center of initiative, an independent recipient of impressions. (quoted in Elson 1986, p. 12)

From a Kohutian perspective then, it is the optimal ratio of empathic-attunement-to-empathic-failures that stimulates the energy needed for becoming our authentic, healthy selves. When our basic needs for mirroring, idealizing, and twinship are optimally met, we become more fully our authentic selves. We are enabled to grow in an authentic way. The key mechanism that is instrumental in this process is what Kohut calls *transmuting* (transforming) *internalization*. Here is how Elson (1986) defines the concept of transmuting internalization:

> The process through which a function formerly performed by another (selfobject) is taken into the self through optimal mirroring, interaction, and frustration. Selfobjects [essential others] and their functions [are] replaced gradually by the self and its functions. Healthy functioning self is not a replica of selfobjects but a unique [authentic] self. (p. 252)

Transmuting internalizations, through which we "take in psychological nutrients from selfobjects," says Flanagan (1996), "potentiate our self-knowledge, growth, and cohesion in the nuclear [core] self, and very importantly, a sense of joy" (p. 190). But it is the "empathic attunement of selfobjects, including the willingness to admit and repair empathic failures, [that] is the necessary groundwork for transmuting internalizations to occur" (pp. 190–191). "Qualities and functions of selfobjects are taken in," concludes Flanagan, "by the process of transmuting internalizations; these help the self grow strong and whole, enjoying a sense of genuineness, authenticity, and individuality" (p. 196). For example, through the transforming internalization of the mature qualities of the parents with whom they identify, children acquire the capacities to soothe themselves, monitor their anxiety, reestablish cohesion, and display the beginnings of mature empathy toward themselves and others.

From a Kohutian point of view, our authenticity goes together with our mental health. When we are authentic, we experience ourselves as cohesive and whole. One's "mental health is defined by the subjective experience of well-being, cohesion, and vigor within the self" (Flanagan 1996, p. 194). We relate to the Other as whole being for we have been related to as a whole being by essential others. The authentic-and-healthy self has acquired the resilience to work through and come to terms with the inevitable empathic failures and disappointments of life. She or he has also cultivated the capacity to repair relational ruptures subsequent to empathic misattunements.

Our need for selfobjects continues to play an important role in strengthening our sense of self throughout our life cycle. "Indeed," says Elson (1986), "the capacity to find and enjoy selfobjects, who either perform a confirming role or permit idealization, is evidence of [mental] health" (p. 16).

> The capacity of the individual to seek and find appropriate selfobjects is the hallmark of [mental] health. As we mature, the selfobjects we seek for sustenance will include not only individuals, but also one's profession or vocation, particular skills or attributes, cultural and civic activities which reverberate to the standards, values, and beliefs of our core nuclear self. (p. 19)

It is evident that parents serve as selfobjects for their children. But it is easy to become forgetful of the fact that children can also serve as selfobjects to their parents (see Hannush 2002). Of course, as children become independent adults, mature parents turn to additional selfobjects, such as the pursuit of new civic activities and life projects other than their professions or vocations.

Our need for selfobjects that shore up the self continues throughout our life's journey. There are times, such as when the last of our young adult children leave home or when we unexpectedly lose loved ones, when we need to intensify our "search for sustenance by turning to new selfobjects … such as new pursuits and skills" (Elson 1986, p, 19). It is during times of transition involving loss of selfobjects that our sense of self is shaken. "It is the hallmark of a cohesive, vigorous, harmonious nuclear [authentic] self," says Elson, "to experience wide swings in emotion in response to these changes but to respond with maturing ability to regulate self-esteem, that is *healthy* narcissism" (p. 19). "As we learn the limits of our grandiosity, as we learn to temper our disappointments and redirect our efforts," Elson continues, "we find pleasure in strengthening enduring ideals or forging new ideals. However modest our role, serving as leaders to new generations, younger colleagues, is in itself invigorating and intensifies a sense of cohesion" (p. 19).

Let us take up Kohut's concept of healthy narcissism. For Kohut, the term *narcissism* in itself does not have a negative connotation. On the contrary, it is an important aspect of our evolving sense of self. It is a valuable energizer of our personality. It is the source of our aliveness. It manifests itself in the early years of life through the exuberant and expansive display of the emerging self. Kohut understands narcissism in terms of different levels of maturity. Narcissism, or self-love, is a vital resource to be nurtured so that it is transformed into its mature form. Self-love and love of others are complementary and not mutually exclusive categories. The maturation of narcissism is pivotal for the development of maturational capacities such as self-assertiveness, self-esteem regulation, and self-efficacy.

As children we revel in the age-appropriate gratification of our narcissistic needs through the mirroring, idealizing, and the twinship experiences our parents generously and lovingly provide us. As our narcissism matures, we are able to get these needs met ourselves. We learn to seek out people who can give us these gratifications. We cultivate the capacity to accept mature forms of gratifications when they avail themselves.

Authentic growth, says Kohut (1978), involves "the reshaping of the [immature] narcissistic structures and their integration into the personality – the strengthening of ideals and the achievement, even to a modest degree, of such wholesome [mature] transformations of narcissism as humor, creativity, empathy, and wisdom" (p. 270). To these qualities Kohut adds the ability to accept our transient existence or the inevitability of our own death. A. M. Siegel (1996) gives us a detailed description of these mature qualities:

1. **Creativity**: Creative persons, says Siegel, have a "child-like capacity to play imaginatively" with their surroundings (p. 62). Why? Because they are less psychosocially separated from their surroundings. (This Kohutian understanding of the selfobject, for there is no self without an object, is incipiently phenomenological in the sense that there is no bodily self without a world.) Our creative work becomes an extension of our self. Just as a mother was once a primary object to our self – for there is no self without a mother, so too the creative work becomes a selfobject – an object that

mirrors the self, an object that the self idealizes, an object that becomes a companion, just as our mothers mirrored us, idealized us, and once served as our primordial companion.

2. **Empathy**: "The best definition of empathy," states Kohut (1984), "is that it is the capacity to think and feel oneself into the inner life of another person. It is our lifelong ability to experience what another person experiences, though usually ... to an attenuated degree" (p. 82). "Kohut," says Siegel (1996), "considers empathy's origin to be the echoing of the mother's feelings and behavior in [or of] the experience of the developing self" (p. 62). Empathy, elaborates Siegel, emerges as an extension of the evolving self. What he means is that the self emerges in a relational matrix in which empathic attunement plays a pivotal part for (a) making the unfolding of selfhood possible, (b) strengthening the bond between mother and child, and (c) gradually appropriating the capacity (function) for empathy not only toward others but also toward oneself.
3. **Humor**: For Kohut, the capacity for nondestructive humor is a manifestation of mature narcissism. "When present," comments Siegel (1996), "humor contains a sense of quiet inner triumph, mixed with an undeniable melancholy that differs from the picture of fragmentary or defensive grandiosity and elation" (p. 62). As he does with *the selfhood that is made possible by empathic attunement*, Kohut does not emphasize enough the intersubjective nature of humor. Just like empathy, humor strengthens the bond between the child and the m/other. "Adults can easily be drawn, if they allow themselves to let go of the serious business of living, into the cheerful space of children. This special space is filled with playfulness, humor and laughter. In this space, games are played, rituals enacted, and loving bonds are strengthened" (Hannush 2002, p. 65).
4. **Wisdom**: For Kohut, the essence of wisdom lies in the letting go of our immature narcissism and in the acceptance of our mortality. Becoming wise, explains Siegel (1996), "is the result of a movement through life that includes the ideals cathected [invested into] in youth, the humor cathected in maturity, and the acceptance of transience established in old age" (p. 63).
5. **Transience**: The ultimate challenging maturational task, holds Kohut, is to accept the transitoriness of our lives. For this to happen, we need to let go of our quest for perpetual living. This acceptance of our vulnerableness requires of us the attainment of an advanced level of mature narcissism – a paradoxical mixture of pride and humility, a modest pride. In seeing the acceptance of transience as a hallmark of maturation, Kohut's self-

psychology is in synchrony with existential psychology, such as that of Rollo May. Becoming keenly aware of our *shared* human transitoriness and vulnerableness can contribute to the refinement of our self-compassion and our compassion for our vulnerable and transient fellow human beings.

For Rogers (1989), *authenticity* is equivalent to "realness," "genuineness," or "congruence." Although the meaning of congruence first emerges in Rogers's therapeutic work, it is later extended in its application to all kinds of human contact or encounter. Congruence is the "third condition" among three (the other two being *unconditional acceptance* or *positive regard* and *empathic attunement* or *understanding*) that are "*The Necessary and Sufficient Conditions of Therapeutic Personality Change*" (p. 219). Later, Rogers generalized the applicability of these necessary and sufficient conditions for psychological change, growth, and maturation to transactions in everyday life. Here is Rogers (1989) describing the meaning of *congruence*:

> The third condition is that the therapist should be, within the confines of this relationship, a congruent, genuine, integrated person. It means that within the relationship he is freely and deeply himself, with his actual experience accurately represented by his awareness of himself. It is the opposite of presenting a façade, either knowingly or unknowingly. (pp. 223–224)

Being congruent, as Rogers describes it, is easier said than done. It is therefore more realistic to think of congruence in terms of degrees – an *optimal ratio* relative to incongruence with which it is in constant tension. That would be more in line with the dialectical understanding of the meaning of congruence and its relation to the meaning of incongruence – seeing "the bodily self" as "a historically situated center of meaning" (Fuller 1990, p. 164) – a center that struggles to seek balance between "meaning's phenomenal tensions" (p. 167) and bring these tensions to "balanced structural fulfillment" (p. 168). In this instance, it involves seeking balance between congruent and incongruent ways of being with oneself and others, among many other meaning-laden modalities of existence.

Bugental (1978), like Rogers, equates being authentic with being "genuine" and "real." Bugental, however, places the accent on "genuine presence" or, put differently, on "being as wholly and as nakedly present as possible" (p. 104).

> *Presence* is the quality of being in a situation in which one intends to be as aware and as participative as one is able to be at that time and in those circumstances.

> Presence is carried into effect through the mobilization of one's inner (toward subjective experiencing) and outer (toward the situation and any other person/s in it) sensitivities … Presence is being there in body, in emotions, in relating, in thoughts, in every way. (pp. 36–37)

Again, in my view, the capacity to be present comes in degrees and is always in tension with being absent (not being fully there), as, for example, when one slips into absent-mindedness while in the presence of a fellow interlocutor. One could be physically, but not fully "there" due to fatigue, due to life concerns, or simply because of narcissistic immaturity.

"To the extent that we are able to live out our destiny," observes May (1981), "we experience a sense of gratification and achievement, a conviction that we are becoming what we were meant to become. It is an experience of authenticity, a feeling of being in accord with the universe, a conviction of genuine freedom" (pp. 93–94). May equates "destiny from within the person" with our "vital design" and places the emphasis on "destiny as destination, or the significant direction or conflict of directions each one of us senses within himself" (p. 93). Ultimately, we are our vital designs. May adds, "each of us to some extent falsifies, denies, or dodges his destiny" (pp. 92–93). We are called upon to creatively realize our destiny or vitalizing life design. "Destiny in this sense," continues May, "is that design of our lives that we spend our years trying to find, seeking and groping, trying this job and that one, loving this woman or man and that one … sometimes with success and sometimes with failure" (p. 93).

The American ethos, reflects May (1981), that we can be/come anything we want to be/come or that "we can change everything at any time we wish, that nothing in character is fixed or given … or that we can remake our lives and personalities over the weekend is not only a misperception of life, but is also a desecration of it" (p. 93). May elaborates:

> Often our pressure to deny our destiny [vital design] comes from such things as our insecurity, our dread of ostracism, our fear and anxiety, and lack of courage to risk ourselves. These in turn come from the pressure to conform [to gain acceptance, approval, and belongingness]: it is safer to be like everybody else. The vital design, the authentic pattern to which we are called can then be left behind. (p. 94)

I want to hasten to comment that a distinction needs to be made here between discerning risk-taking and reckless risk-taking, between constructive conformity and destructive conformity, and between the alright-ness of a degree of inauthenticity and the impossibility of living a perpetually authentic life.

The "authentic person," say Schneider and May (1995), "not only transcends himself in various ways; he also transcends his culture. He resists enculturation … He becomes a little more a member of his species and little less a member of his cultural group" (p. 94). They equate inauthenticity with "general phoniness" and "living by illusions and fear" (p. 97). In our dialectical view, the authentic person, just as he or she does with his or her familial strengths and limitations, holds on to the best that his or her culture (family) has to offer and lets go of the worst that his or her culture (family) embodies or identifies with, while adding, in small or not-so-small ways, his or her own creative contribution to the psychosocial evolution of his or her cultural (familial) identity.

The healthy individual, for May (1981), has the capacity to own up one's freedom by confronting one's destiny. In an earlier work, May (1967) states, "freedom is the individual's capacity to *know that he is the determined one*" (p. 175). Thus, implicit in May's view is the dialectical tension between freedom and limitation. In our freedom lies our potential for change, development, and growth. But freedom is made possible by facing and embracing our destiny – what we meaningfully make of our fatedness. May (1981) offers yet another definition of destiny: "*It is the design of the universe speaking through the design of each one of us*" (p. 90). May seems to confound the meanings of *fate* and *destiny.* My *fate* includes the fact that I am going to die. It also includes my genetic background, my temperament, my raw intelligence, my gender, my body shape, stamina, and strength, my familial background, and my cultural heritage. I carve out my *destiny* or destination through the meanings I make of my *fate.* My *destiny* creates the meaningful boundaries within which I can make choices. We cannot deny our fate, "but we can choose how we shall respond, how we shall live our talents which confront us" (p. 89). Paradoxically, freedom requires our destiny. Without destiny, there is no freedom, though limited it may be. In our freedom lies the possibility of change. Freedom "entails being able *to harbor different possibilities in one's mind even though it is not clear at the moment which way one must act*" (pp. 10–11). This places us in an anxiety-producing predicament that the authentic individual is able to manage. The authentic person, for instance, faces the inevitability of his or her death and realizes that it is an inseparable part of life.

With freedom comes responsibility, for we are ultimately responsible for the persons we become. To transform our fate into our destiny we need to be courageous. Such a transformation requires of us to be willing to make choices in the light of the kind of persons we want to become. To live authentically, the maturing person must carve out the path of his or her destiny by responsibly embracing his or her limited freedom in the here-and-now. The authentic individual is deeply connected not only to the social world, but also to the natural world – the world of objects and things and one's own biological drives (the natural phenomena of eating and evacuating, sleeping and awakening, and being born and dying).

Our psychosocial inheritance includes the internalization of familial and cultural values. "All growth," says May (1967) "consists of the anxiety-creating surrender of past values" (p. 80). We can freely choose to let go of the past values that we were fated to psychosocially inherit. Again, from the perspective of our dialectical model, we not only are challenged to surrender *some* past values but are also inspired to hold on to *some other* life-affirming past values and to add *some new values* to identify with and to live by. Living authentically means welcoming both our freedom and responsibility, while realizing that choice-making is anxiety-producing and thus difficult and painful.

Living authentically is the opposite of living pretentiously or in "bad faith" (a la Jean Paul Sartre). We are constantly in a state of potential maturation. Consciously or not so consciously, we are confronted with the awesome responsibility for our own process of maturation. We are response-able to *the call of maturity*. Our authenticity lies in whether we respond to the call of maturation or whether we avoid the anxiety that comes with living up to the responsibilities of continuing maturation and/or the guilt that comes with having failed to respond in a mature way in any given life situation. We cannot be authentic all the time. We inevitably oscillate between living authentically and living inauthentically. There are times when we need to put on pretentious airs in order to live harmoniously and function adaptively in our everyday life. When I am asked by an acquaintance or colleague that I do not know well how I am doing, I respond by saying that I am doing okay, thank him or her, and ask about their state of being for that day. This is how we grease the machinery of our everyday transactions so that they function efficiently in culturally sanctioned ways. But if my life is skewed excessively on the side of living pretentiously (inauthentically), I pay a mental health price. My maturation will become developmentally arrested. The weight of the balance ought to be on the side of authenticity.

Living authentically is one response to the awareness of our transitoriness, to our anticipation of the advent of our demise. Schalow (2006) provides us with Heidegger's definition of authenticity: "'*What we understand by authenticity … is that mode of human existence wherein man (authentically) appropriates himself,* i.e., *wherein he comes to himself and can be himself*'" (p. 14). Schalow (personal communication) elaborates on the meaning of authenticity:

> In regard to authenticity, … "owning," e.g., as in "owning up to," "taking ownership," and "coming into one's own," is an accurate rendition of appropriating or appropriation in this context. Moreover, the more literal rendering of the German word "Eigentlichheit," ordinarily translated as "authenticity," would be "ownedness." I like to use the example of the expression when we refer to someone, e.g., a student, "coming into his/her own." This is a basic sense of what Heidegger understands as "authentic selfhood." In my book [Schalow, 2017], I actually emphasize that aspect of "taking ownership," as a pragmatic rendering of what it means to be "authentic." It also fits well with contemporary English usage.

In my view, this definition of authenticity comes as close as possible to capturing the essence of the process of maturation. It implies the assumption of responsibility, or at least co-responsibility, in the co/creation of our sense of selfhood. This "bringing into one's own (… appropriation or 'owning') [which is instrumental in] gaining a sense of rootedness, predetermines [is prior to] all other senses of 'having,' possessing,' or 'owning' [in the materialistic meaning of the term]" (Schalow 2006, p. 14).The authentic person, continues Schalow, anticipates the kind of person he or she can optimally become and acts to realize this possibility. "The development of this authentic temporality [authentic-life-lived-in-time] occurs in tension with, but without denying, a parallel inauthentic temporality which exalts in the expediency and immediate gratification of the present as realized in technological life" (Schalow 2001, p. 10). I would qualify and say "as realized," not only in "technological life" but also in everyday life. In other words, the dialectical (back-and-forth) tension between authentic-versus-inauthentic living is an abiding tension of our everyday existence. We simply cannot always be authentic. It is a matter of degree. It is the *optimal ratio* of authenticity-to-inauthenticity that counts. In our everyday lives, we find ourselves *inevitably* treating others, in their functional roles, as means to end-goals. In those instances we are being inauthentic by not relating to them as ends in themselves.

Living in a hyper-materialistic and hyper-technological culture, a culture of diversion and distraction, while seeking certainty, freedom, and security, makes it difficult for an individual to cultivate a "profounder *ethos*." Paradoxically, in such a cultural climate, one is apt to lose one's freedom to become one's authentic self.

Our insecurity may unthinkingly propel us toward the inauthentic exercise of frivolous freedom, but it is the tolerance of insecurity that beckons the balance needed for heeding the call of authenticity and the voice of mature conscience.

Living authentically is seemingly the opposite of living pretentiously or in bad faith. We are constantly in a state of becoming mature. Consciously or not so consciously, we are confronted with the awesome responsibility for our own process of maturation. We are response-able to the call of maturity. Our authenticity lies in whether we respond to the call of maturation or whether we avoid the anxiety that comes with living up to the responsibilities of continuing maturation and/or the guilt that comes with having failed to respond in a mature way in any given life situation. We cannot be authentic all the time. We inevitably oscillate between living authentically and living inauthentically. But if my life is skewed excessively on the side of living pretentiously, I pay a mental health price. My maturation will become developmentally arrested. The weight of the balance ought to be on the side of authenticity.

To emphasize, in synchrony with our dialectical model, Heidegger's (1962) understanding of the existential tension between authenticity and inauthenticity is *not* to be viewed as a dialectical conflict between a positive pole (authenticity) and a negative pole (inauthenticity). We can find a relative balance between the two modalities of existence not by affirming authenticity and rejecting inauthenticity, but by modifying our identification with each pole. "Authentic Being-one's Self," holds Heidegger, "does not rest upon an exceptional condition of the subject, a condition that has been detached from the 'they'; it is rather an existential modification of the 'they' – of the 'they' as an essential existentiale" (p. 168). Behaving inauthentically is an inescapable part of our everyday social living. It is a matter of degree. Letting ourselves fall into conformity (with the "they") is an inevitable consequence of getting along with others. Then again, we can keep this tendency toward inauthentic fallenness in check by balancing it with the appropriation of an authentic (transparent and truthful) mode of being-with-others. The passion for transparency and truthfulness (authenticity) can be awakened by our awareness of our mortality. By opening ourselves to the reality of our own death, we discover our true Self. "Impassioned freedom toward death," Heidegger reminds us, is "a freedom which has been released from the illusion of the 'they' and which is factual certain of itself, and anxious" (p. 266). Why be anxious? It is because of my awareness of my mortality and my limitation. Paradoxically, tolerating this anxious awareness of my mortality enables me to become more authentic.

References

Bugental, J. F. T. (1978). *Psychotherapy and process: The fundamentals of an existential-humanistic approach*. McGraw-Hill.

Elson, M. (1986). *Self psychology in clinical social work*. W. W. Norton.

Flanagan, M. (1996). The theory of self psychology. In J. Berzoff, L. M. Flanagan, & P. Hertz (Eds.), *Inside out and outside in: Psychodynamic clinical theory and practice in contemporary multicultural contexts*. Jason Aronson.

Fromm, E. (1956). *The art of loving*. Harper and Row.

Fuller, A. R. (1990). *Insight into value: An exploration of the premises of a phenomenological psychology*. State University of New York Press.

Hannush, M. J. (2002). *Becoming good parents: An existential journey*. State University of New York Press.

Heidegger, M. (1962). *Being and time* (J. Macquarrie & E. Robinson, Trans.). Harper and Row.

Kohut, H. (1977). *The restoration of the self*. International Universities Press.

Kohut, H. (1978). P. Ornstein (Ed.), *The search for the self* (Vol. I). International Universities Press.

Kohut, H. (1984). *How does analysis cure?* International Universities Press.

Longhofer, J. (2015). *A-Z of psychodynamic practice*. Palgrave Macmillan.

May, R. (1967). *Psychology and the human dilemma*. D. Van Nostrand.

May, R. (1981). *Freedom and destiny*. W. W. Norton.

Newman, B. M., & Newman, P. R. (2018). *Development through life: A psychosocial approach* (13th ed.). Cengage Learning.

Ogden, T. H. (2012). *Creative readings: Essays on seminal analytic works*. Routledge.

Rogers, C. R. (1989). *The Carl Rogers reader*. Houghton Mifflin.

Schalow, F. (2001). *Heidegger and the quest for the sacred: From thought to the sanctuary of faith*. Kluwer.

Schalow, F. (2006). *The incarnality of being: The earth, animals, and the body in Heidegger's thought*. State University of New York Press.

Schalow, F. (2017). *Toward a phenomenology of addiction: Embodiment, technology, transcendence*. Springer.

Schneider, K. J., & May, R. (1995). *The psychology of existence: An integrative, clinical perspective*. McGraw-Hill.

Siegel, A. M. (1996). *Heinz Kohut and the psychology of the self*. Routledge.

St. Clair, M. with Wigren, J. (2004). *Object relations and self psychology: An introduction* (4th ed.). Brooks/Cole – Thomson Learning.
Tuber, S. (2008). *Attachment, play, and authenticity: A Winnicott primer*. Jason Aronson.
Winnicott, D. W. (1965b). *The maturational processes and the facilitating environment: Studies in the theory of emotional development*. Hogarth Press.
Winnicott, D. W. (1971). *Playing and reality*. Tavistock Publications.

19

Responsibility (Response-Ability): The Capacity for the Acceptance, Assumption, and Owning of *Responsibility*

The "accepting of responsibility," holds Fingarette (1963), "is a necessary condition of maturity, and those who do not, or 'cannot,' do so, for whatever reason, are in fact doomed never to have psychological and moral integrity" (p. 167). We must accept responsibility for integrating as much of our self-world as we can into a pattern that fits the best of our human purposes as the requisite for maturation. *Maturation ought to serve as our ultimate aim in life. Becoming mature is the purpose of life.* Here is more from Fingarette:

> This *ideal*, and not the past, is the ground for the harsh demand that we accept responsibility for what we are, even though we are in many ways morally evil and even though we could not help ourselves ... Guilt is retrospective, but responsibility is prospective. Responsibility is based on a willingness to face the world as it is *now* and to proceed to do what we can to make it the world as we would like it to be. To accept responsibility is to be responsible for what shall be done. (pp. 164–165)

Becoming mature goes hand-in-hand with becoming responsible. The path toward the achievement of autonomy-in-relatedness is through taking on the burdens of responsibility. We cannot participate in the making of a just world without being held responsible for the consequences of our actions. We need to accept responsibility for what we can control. The capacity to assume responsibility is also instrumental in the enhancement of our ability to develop our intimate relations with others.

© The Author(s), under exclusive license to Springer Nature Switzerland AG 2021

M. J. Hannush, *Markers of Psychosocial Maturation*,
https://doi.org/10.1007/978-3-030-74315-4_19

Ultimately, above and beyond assuming the burden and privilege of being responsible for the Other, we are pleasurably and painfully responsible, says Fiumara (2013), for having our own mind:

> The 'responsibility' of having one's own mind is more innovative and creative than we are prepared to appreciate; it takes [ordinary] genius [or maturity] to bear with oneself and to endure one's own pathology. And also, … [from what we know] about imitation, acting out, anaesthetising [sic] maneuvers, all this seems to suggest that there must be alternative modes of inner life in which action seems to proceed from the innermost part of the personality. Perhaps the repetitive, reactive patterns can only be observed when profiled against the unifying light of personal creativeness. (pp. 80–81)

Relative integration or wholeness makes the assumption of responsibility possible. The opposite of being relatively whole and integrated is being fragmented and split. "Splitting," notes Nicholas (1994), is "the mental polarization of 'objects' (affects, experiences, people, parts of people, ideas) into good and bad" (p. 133). Splitting, continues Nicholas, "happens naturally in the minds of babies and children and continues in adult functioning to some degree, as well" (p. 133). Infants and young children make sense of their world through the sorting-out process of splitting. This constitutes the start of their primitive moral differentiation. They begin to discriminate between "experiences that feel 'good' and those that feel 'bad'" (p. 134). Nicholas elaborates:

> Splitting is normal and necessary in infancy and early childhood, but with increased cognitive development and, given some patience and consistency on the part of the parent, considerable integration of good and bad objects [essential others] can be expected to take place during the course of the first three years. (p. 134)

All of us split sometimes as a way of relieving tension, especially during times of painful conflict and intolerable stress when we are unable to contain our contradictory feelings and impulses.

"Splitting," observes Nicholas (1994), "makes **justice** [or fairness], **responsibility**, and **egalitarianism** hard to achieve and sustain" (p. 134). She expands:

> As long as I see *only* the bad parts of myself or another and the good parts are split off, I will feel highly punitive toward myself or toward the other. As long as I only see the good parts of myself or of another, and the bad parts are split off,

> I will excuse immoral behavior in myself or the other. If, in dealing with two people, I see one as all bad and the other as all good, I am probably being unfair to the one I am seeing so negatively. (p. 134)

Splitting, therefore, is simultaneously an intrapersonal as well as an interpersonal phenomenon. From a phenomenological perspective, it is *intentionality* gone awry.

Intentionality means that I as a subject am always oriented toward an inner or outer object to which I struggle to attribute *meaning*, consciously or not so consciously. The origin of the unfolding of our *meaning-making* capacity is relational in nature. An early secure and loving relational context results in elastic intentionality, which is essential to maturation. An insecure relational context rigidifies my intentionality and thus constricts my meaning making possibilities. Whereas immature intentionality involves either/or meaning-making deficiency or interpretive incompetency, mature intentionality involves both/and meaning-making or interpretive competency. Intentionality applies to our relation to our selves as well as our relation to others—in addition to our relationship to our affects, ideals, and other objects of pre-reflective consciousness. From an existential point of view, we are ultimately responsible for refining or tuning up the quality of our intentionality so that it is in line with emotional, psychological, and relational truth, so that it is in synchrony with our relational reality.

In psychodynamic terms, maturation involves, as Nicholas (1994) puts it, "owning" the split-off parts of ourselves. "Resolving splitting," she comments, "takes enormous conscious emotional and mental effort, a difficult challenge for anyone at any time, but particularly when we are under stress" (p. 135). She elaborates:

> Only if we can own the parts of us that are split off can we feel whole and satisfied. This, of course, means facing things about ourselves that we would rather attribute to others. I might have to admit that not only was the other person greedy, mean-spirited and stubborn, but *I* was as well. While 'owning' my faults may temporarily cause me shame and guilt, it ultimately will help my self-esteem and feelings of connectedness with others, for I will realize that my faults are part of what makes me human, that no one else is perfect either, and that the proudest moments we have are when we can acknowledge our complete self, liabilities and all, without fear.
>
> ...
>
> Resolving splitting does not just mean admitting one's faults, but accepting one's good qualities as well … [such as facing] the parts of us that are loving, generous, and moral. (p. 135)

Proper parenting, says Nicholas (1994), makes it easier to reduce and resolve our early propensity for splitting:

> The conditions for learning to resolve splitting in childhood are similar to those necessary to learning how to feel appropriate guilt. In families where it is possible for children and parents to 'screw up,' apologize sincerely, be forgiven, and make amends, the child will begin to integrate the good and the bad, realizing that he and others have their bad parts and good parts, that one can love and hate the same person, and that the same person can be destructive and loving at different times. (p. 136)

It should not surprise us then to hear Nicholas state that, in adulthood, a "major purpose of therapy is to resolve splitting – to identify with what we have projected out and disclaim what we have erroneously introjected" (p. 138). Psychotherapy, continues Nicholas, "calls for relentless questioning of much that has previously been taken as morally incontrovertible, including knee-jerk attributions of responsibility and blame. In this way, the search for psychological truth through psychotherapy is … a moral venture" (pp. 138–139).

Frankl (1992, 2000) reminds us again and again that responsibility must follow freedom. It is not sufficient for me to feel free to choose. I must assume responsibility for the choices I make. Logotherapy aims at reminding me of my responsibility in this manner: I must live my life as if I am living for the second time and had acted as wrongly the first time as I am about to act now. Freedom entails not merely being free *from* something, but being free *for* the pursuit of those transcendent or ultimate values with which we identify. In short, freedom must be lived in light of responsibleness.

Responsibility is a central theme in the writings of Fritz Perls. In Perls's (1969) view, healthy or mature persons have the capacity for taking responsibility for their own lives. They are on their own. They do not shift the responsibility for who they are to other people such as their parents or partners. They do not blame their fate for their present predicament. They are *aware* that they and only they are responsible for what they make of their lives. In fact, Perls goes so far as to say that I am not responsible for others. As he notes in the infamous Gestalt prayer, "I do my thing and you do your thing" (p. 4). Taking responsibility for others *means*, for Perls, assuming an omnipotent and intrusive role in their lives and thus contributing to the diminishment of their sense of independence and depriving them from exercising their own sense of responsibility.

Post-Perlsian gestalt psychotherapists have a much more modulated understanding of responsibility toward oneself that is balanced with one's responsibility toward others. "Maturation," contend Korb, Gorrell, and De Reit (1989), calls for "a set of experiential steps that embraces … concepts, such as … *responsibility* for personal feelings, experiences, and behaviors and for the choice of appropriate responses to the environment" (p. 49). Maturation involves assuming responsibility for "experiencing and developing more of what is possible for each person" (p. 48).

"Being responsible for oneself," continue Korb, Gorrell, and De Reit (1989), "means being 'able to respond' to one's own expectations, desires, fantasies, and actions, and to those of others" (p. 49). Being responsible for oneself also entails discerningly knowing when one is *unable to respond responsibly* to the attitudes, behaviors, expectations, and feelings of others. This "restriction of responsibility in no way implies a lack of caring about the needs of other people nor does it imply an inability to respond to their needs" (p. 49). No one can respond or assume responsibility on my behalf unless I choose to allow it. It is in this sense that I am responsible (response-able) for myself. "This kind of responsibility derives from self-acceptance, acceptance of the environment as it is, and from the maturity to see both self and others in proper perspective" (p. 49). Responsibility, choicefulness, and freedom, on the one hand, and awareness, on the other, belong to the same maturational process. In order to be responsible, they conclude, I must be aware. The more aware I am, the freer I am to choose my own responses, which include my actions, attitudes, feelings, and thoughts. The more unaware I am, the less able I am to choose my own responses.

Authenticity, remind us Deurzen and Kenward (2005), "is based on an awareness of one's choices, one's potential and one's limitations" (p. 174). Moreover, they add, Martin Heidegger "speaks of existential **guilt** in relation to responsibility" (p. 174). Differently described, guilt is the felt experience of failed responsibility. Through re-constructive guilt, I feel and reflect on the *meaning* of my wrongdoing, struggle with the nature of the harm or destructiveness that I have perpetrated, the question of my responsibility, and the "fit response" of which I am capable in the given situation in which I find myself. The "fit response" ought to prevent the repetition of my failed response-ability in the past. Schrag (1997) provides us with an account of the transformation of "responsivity" into responsibility:

> [The] conversion of responsivity into responsibility [involves] the move from a state of affairs of being-with-others to the insinuation of ethico-moral requirements to respond in a fitting manner. The ability to respond, being able to

> respond, becomes aligned with a moral injunction to do so in the proper way. It is this that we understand by the phenomenon of responsibility – being responsible in our responding to prior action upon us – and it is this phenomenon that provides the space for what might appropriately called the 'ethic of the fitting response.' (pp. 91–92)

For Schrag (1997), to be responsible is to be ethical. A *fitting response-ability*—the capacity for "the fitting response," is contingent upon having a mature and wise conscience. Schrag makes a distinction between an "authoritarian conscience that is simply the voice of custom and convention" (p. 96) and a higher-order "conscience" which is "a mode of moral understanding; a manner of knowing one's way about in moral predicaments; a practical wisdom of what the situation requires, given the potentialities and constraints of our human nature" (p. 97). Such a higher-order conscience has an "integrative function" (p. 98). The "authenticity of resolute responsibility" (p. 95), the cumulative pattern of fitting responses, gathers our sense of selfhood together. "The self in action," Schrag continues, "is a unified self to the extent that it displays a constancy in discourse and action, in the keeping of its word and in the coherence of its actions, in the delivering of its past promises and in its pre-enactment of commitments for the future" (p. 64). For Schrag, the responsible self is an ethical self:

> The ethical has to do with *ethos* in the originative sense of a cultural dwelling, a mode or manner of historical existence, a way of being in the world that exhibits a responsibility both to oneself and to others. It is this that defines the bearing of the self as ethical subject, whose subjectivity is always that of an intersubjectivity. (p. 101)

A Heideggerian phenomenological approach, explains Schalow (2017), equates authenticity with "owning." The "self can either 'own up' to its existence or refrain from doing so, find guidance in the boundaries [limits] of its existence or transgress them in 'destructive' acts, and, ultimately, set the *priorities* of life or undermine them in the pursuit of a single indulgence [or multiple indulgences]" (p. 22). Becoming authentic involves struggling to achieve individuality without succumbing to the pressures of excessive conformity—to "fit in" to be a part of the crowd, and thus making "destructive choices." "'Owning up to' implies the self-disclosure that is necessary for the individual 'to be' responsible, e.g., to answer for (*antworten*) his choices" (p. 22). There can be no authenticity without responsibility—answerability to one's choices.

May (1953) speaks of *response-ability* as the capacity to be answerable. May writes:

> When one has consciously chosen to live, two other things happen. First, his responsibility for himself takes on a new meaning. He accepts responsibility for his own life ... as something he has chosen himself. ... The other thing which happens is that discipline from the outside is changed into *self-discipline*. He accepts discipline ... because he has chosen with greater freedom what he wants to do with his own life, and discipline is necessary for the sake of the values he wishes to achieve ... it is a lesson everyone progressively learns in his struggle toward maturity. (p. 173)

Without self-discipline, there can be no responsibility, and without responsibility there can be no maturity. To lack of self-discipline can be added lack of resoluteness, passivity, valuational vagueness, blind conformity, and immature conscience as obstacles to maturity.

"Insight," says Fuller (1990), "is responsible answering to meaning, a responding that disposes itself to the structural necessity of meaning events" (p. 196). "Responsibility," continues Fuller, "is an attitude of opening oneself to intrinsic values, preparing oneself for their advent, everrenewed [sic] process of becoming dimensionally responsive" (p. 196). To be insightful is to responsibly situate myself in my lifeworld. Becoming an authentic self has to do with the degree to which I, as a whole person, am able to insightfully discover, find, and responsibly situate myself in my lifeworld. How do I insightfully or responsibly situate myself in my lifeworld? (1) I do this through finding and investing myself in projects that *resonate with personal meaning.* Whether it is the project of writing a book or being-and-becoming a good husband, father, professor, or simply an art appreciator, I become my projects. These life projects *mean* a lot to me. I *interpret* them as being very important to who I am and the kind of person I want to become. I am my passion-and-value-laden meanings, which are insightfully taken up by me. I am the manner through which I responsibly pursue, take up, or own these *meaning-ful* projects of mine. (2) I do this by the way I position myself, as much as humanly possible, for what I actually come across in my everyday life, for what I encounter and "freely" move toward or move away from. "We are responsible," says Fuller, "for our own situatedness" (p. 185). It can be as simple as lingering while appreciating the beauty of a face or the kind gesture of a stranger. Or, it can be simply avoiding or turning away from ugly chatter or mind-numbing and reality-uglifying television programs. As Merleau-Ponty (1962) puts it, "What makes something be figure and something else be ground is the way we concretely relate to them in our act of looking" (p. 278).

References

Deurzen, E. V., & Kenward, R. (2005). *Dictionary of existential psychotherapy and counselling*. Sage.
Fingarette, H. (1963). *The self in transformation: Psychoanalysis, philosophy and the life of the spirit*. Harper and Row.
Fiumara, G. C. (2013). *Psychoanalysis and creativity in everyday life: Ordinary genius*. Routledge.
Frankl, V. E. (1992). *Mans' search for meaning* (4th ed.). Beacon Press.
Frankl, V. E. (2000). *Man's search for ultimate meaning*. Perseus.
Fuller, A. R. (1990). *Insight into value: An exploration of the premises of a phenomenological psychology*. State University of New York Press.
May, R. (1953). *Man's search for himself*. W. W. Norton.
Merleau-Ponty, M. (1962). *Phenomenology of perception* (C. Smith, Trans.). Routledge.
Nicholas, M. W. (1994). *The mystery of goodness and the positive moral consequences of psychotherapy*. W. W. Norton.
Perls, F. (1969). *Gestalt therapy verbatim*. Real People Press.
Schalow, F. (2017). *Toward a phenomenology of addiction: Embodiment, technology, transcendence*. Springer.
Schrag, C. O. (1997). *The self after postmodernity*. Yale University Press.

Part VII

The Capacities for Holding, Trust, and Hope

20

Holding: The Capacity for *Holding* and Containing the Self/Other

The capacity for *self-holding* generally refers to the ability to soothe and comfort oneself. This capacity has its roots in relational holding. It begins when our primary caregiver provides us with limitless holding experiences. Our essential caregiver "holds" us physically. But from the very beginning there is an "extra" in this holding. From the get-go, holding is imbued with symbolic meaning. Our bodies remember this "surplus" meaning. Being held, properly, may come to have for us multiple embodied (mostly unconscious) meanings. It may mean being loved, comforted, soothed, and protected from falling apart and fragmenting. These "surplus" meanings are originally grounded in our inter-bodily being-with our essential m/other.

Being-held can be implicated in multiple physical and, later in our development, nonphysical forms or contexts of meaning. Being-held physically can be demonstrated through the trans-actions of being burped, caressed, danced with, kissed, rocked, thrown-in-the-air-and-caught, and so on. Being-held symbolically can be experienced by being sung to (as in a lullaby), being read to, being spoken to soothingly and comfortingly, and in a myriad of other ways.

Although early in our lives we participate in this holding-and-being-held dance in allowing our nascently selved bodies to be welcomingly held, our active role in the dance does not equal that of our caregiver. Under relatively optimal conditions, we relaxedly participate in the dance of holding-and-being-held. Instead of resisting with an embodied "No," we willingly and welcomingly yield or later reciprocate with an embodied "Yes." As we get older, we become increasingly more active co-participants in the dance of holding-and-being-held.

© The Author(s), under exclusive license to Springer Nature Switzerland AG 2021
M. J. Hannush, *Markers of Psychosocial Maturation*,
https://doi.org/10.1007/978-3-030-74315-4_20

Winnicott (1965a) provides us with a succinct description of the function of *holding*:

> Still earlier, the infant is held by the mother, and only understands love that is expressed in physical terms, that is to say, by live human holding. Here is absolute dependence, and environmental failure at this very early stage cannot be defended against, except by the hold-up of the developmental process, and by infantile psychosis. (p. 147)

Phenomenologically, then, our original way of being-with-the-m/other is an embodied-being-with. Through being adequately physically held, we eschew the bodily sensation of falling apart, fragmentation, or annihilation. Through the reliable experience of being lovingly held, we feel anchored, centered, grounded, and rooted. Winnicott goes so far as to say that good-enough reliable holding leads to the creation of a core real, spontaneous, or True Self. Moreover, good-enough holding allows the baby to gradually feel distinct from the m/other who holds him. This kind of reliable holding permits the child to securely *attach* and healthily *detach*—to view the world as a benign and inviting place, to be relaxedly at home in the world, and to exuberantly explore the world. Becoming mature (*wise*), says Erikson (1982), is in the end a movement toward a kind of "informed and detached concern with life itself in the face of death itself" (p. 61). Dialectically rephrased, becoming mature involves acquiring a *balance* between healthy attachment and healthy detachment (separation), an optimal, yet precarious, balance learned from the crucible of experience in living beginning in infancy.

What I am contending here is that our emerging and evolving capacity of what phenomenological psychologists and philosophers call the *transcendental reduction*, the transcending and thus the decentering of our self-centered viewpoint and the concomitant *bracketing* of our biases, is grounded in our original experience of holding-and-being held, of loving-and-being-loved. Edmund Husserl, the founder of phenomenology, displays such an intimation of this sort in his later, unpublished manuscripts (see Hart 2009 and Hadreas, 2007 and Melle, 2002), by speaking of the *ethical epoche*. Here is Melle (2002) describing Husserl's *ethical epoche*: "The concern about my life as a whole becomes an ethical concern through an ethical epoche, a bracketing of my whole previous life and a universal critique of it oriented toward a radical renewal according to ethical ideals" (p 243). The ultimate ethical ideal, for Husserl, turns out to be "the absolute ought of our pure love" (p. 244).

Complementarily, I trace the origin of the developmental trajectory of the capacity for reflexive meta-meaning making or insightful interpreting of lifeworld meanings back to the early cumulative experiences of holding-and-being held, of loving-and-being loved. It is my conjecture that those of us who are deprived of good-enough holding-and-being held, thus becoming holding-and-love hungry, will be blocked on one end of the dialectical continuum and thus from eventually finding that delicate balance between caringly attaching and separating, a balance which allows for reflective distancing. Those of us who are possessively held-and-loved, on the other side of the dialectical continuum, will also be blocked from acquiring the capacity to seek and find a balance between loving (caring) in a measured and modulated way, while maintaining the right proportional distancing poise. In capsule form, what I am proposing here is that the maturing person's future capacity for *meta-meaning making*-gaining enough optimal distance in order to make empathically attuned yet reality-rooted interpretations that are as free from self-centered biases and prejudices as possible, is grounded in early embodied experiences of holding-having-been-held (Winnicott), containing-having-been-contained (Bion), and exploring-having-been-securely attached (Bowlby). The well-held bodily self is better positioned to interpretively release meanings in one's lifeworld. It is more open to actualize and organize more refined lifeworld meanings – meanings such as truth, goodness, love, and beauty.

Some say that the opposite of love is not hate, but indifference. From the perspective of our dialectical model, there is something missing about both assertions. Just as there are healthy and unhealthy variations on the themes of love and hate, the stance of indifference is an unhealthy variation on the theme of the open-minded and open-hearted stance of the *ethical epoche*. It is one thing to speak and believe *abstractly* and *intellectually* that one is capable of bracketing one's biases and decentering one's self-centeredness; it is another to *live* out this capacity when it is grounded in the early and later cumulative experiences of holding-and-being-held lovingly (caringly), physically and symbolically.

Fleeting failures in holding can be tolerated and can contribute to the infant's emerging sense of distinctness, separateness, and uniqueness. In order to effect genuine, heart-felt holding, says Slochower (2014), our original holders have had to *bracket their own subjectivity*. They provide us with "a holding experience by (unconsciously) excluding (bracketing) those disturbing aspects of … [their] 'separate' presence that leak through even when we try to hold" (p. 2). The holding experience needs to be attuned enough to the needs of the one being held to buffer the experience of separateness, as much as that is possible. The holding-and-being-held experience cannot be "emotionally disjunctive." It needs to be emotionally "conjunctive." Over time, the experience of holding-and-being-held requires of us "the capacity to tolerate our separate subjectivity" (p. 153). In light of our own dialectical model, I would modify and say, the experience of holding-and-being-held requires of us tolerating the existential tension between being connected (attached, at-one-with, being-like) and being separate (detached, differentiated, unique).

"Holding," continues Slochower (2014), "creates a protected space because it minimizes the danger of external intrusion" (p. 3). Holding not only shields us from experiences of impingement, but also reaffirms the continuity of our existence. It is a form of embodied affirmation, recognition, and validation of our singularly pulsating life, our promisingly unfolding life trajectory.

In childhood, we are held, not only physically, but also, to use Slochower's (2014) phrase, by our "parents' even responsiveness" to our varied agitated and agitating behaviors and the mental and emotional states that lie behind them. Along with dependency, these "states [such as 'self-involvement, ruthlessness, or rage'] – and people's need for moments of holding – pervade the life span" (p. 5). Our good-enough parents provide us with a "containing and relatively even emotional space within which to experience and express a range of difficult affect states" (p. 5). We are held when our parents tolerate our and, simultaneously, their own intense reactions.

Holding, therefore, serves a dual function. Becoming mature means being able to tolerate the tension between mutual holding-and-being held (which requires, within limits, *bracketing our own subjectivity*) and recognizing the separate existence of the other (which necessitates the letting-go and *acknowledging the limits of bracketing*). It means entering a relationship of "mutual recognition" and "collaboration." Slochower (2014) uses "the term collaboration to describe a relative tolerance for, and capacity to engage with the other's separate (if sometimes unwelcome) perspective" or presence (p. 154). It means tolerating the otherness of the other.

The experience of holding-and-being-held can be a source of reparation and, sometimes, even healing. Our primordial holder is at the same time our "reparative maternal object" (Slochower 2014, p. 10). Good-enough holding makes it possible for the developing person to find a balance between becoming healthily dependent and healthily independent. Holding-and-being-held can be instrumental in repairing our relational ruptures and healing our psychological wounds. "Disruptions (enactments) followed by repair [through holding-and-being-held] can be enormously strengthening" (p. 110). Attunement, recognition, collaboration, and synchronous interaction, which are all requisites for the experience of holding-and-being-held, invite the hopeful possibility of reparation.

To emphasize yet again, good-enough holding involves not only bodily holding, but also emotional and mental holding. It takes a "mind spacious enough," notes Nicholsen (2002), "to hold or contain [the developing child's] experience" (p. 17). Nicholsen elaborates:

> In Wilfred Bion's model of mental development, the mother, identifying with her infant's experience in reverie [or compassionate contemplation] 'holds' it for the infant and gives it meaning in her own mind before communicating it to the infant. Through this process the infant becomes able to symbolize experience and eventually put it into words. Emotional experience thus becomes usable for growth and development. (p. 17)

The holding and containing mother co-creates with her child a homeworld where life is continuous and where, in the beginning, body, time, and space (or place) are one. Both mother and child are in a holding and containing (existential or lived) space where, through passionate mutuality, they co-create a shared homeworld. The mother's capacity for reverie enables her to hold or contain her child's inchoate and unverbalized experience by *contemplating its meaning* and then making it palatable and less overwhelming for her child. This is what is meant by emotional-and-mental *containing*. As the child grows, she is able to feel feelings and think thoughts without becoming burdened beyond the point of forbearance. Growing up in a holding homeworld, the child is then creatively empowered to find refuge in multiple concrete and metaphorical holding environments, such as in kinship networks, books, cultural traditions, religious rituals, leaderships, nature, art, music, or other passionately pursued projects. A holding homeworld will be found where beauty, goodness, love, and truth abide. To complete the intentional arc, there is always a capacious and open mind, "one's own larger ego" or as Bion would put it "one's non-psychotic part," that is correlative to a holding homeworld—a beautiful mind seeking goodness, love, and truth. Just as we have our holding environments, we correlatively have our "internal mothers," our own holding and "containing capacities" which allow us not only to "face and feel the pain of adaptive challenges without being overwhelmed by the anxieties they generate" (p. 196), but also to be ready to experience wonderment in the face of that which is beautiful, good, loving, and true, modalities of being-with which from the beginning are embodied by the face of our lovingly holding m(other).

References

Erikson, E. H. (1982). *The life cycle: A review*. W. W. Norton.
Hadreas, P. (2007). *A phenomenology of love and hate*. Ashgate.

Hart, J. G. (2009a). *Who one is, Book 1: Meontology of the "I": A transcendental phenomenology*. Springer.

Melle, U. (2002). Edmund Husserl: From reason to love. In J. J. Drummond & L. Embree (Eds.), *Phenomenological approaches to moral philosophy: A handbook*. Kluwer.

Nicholsen, S. W. (2002). *The love of nature and the end of the world: The unspoken dimensions of environmental concern*. The MIT Press.

Slochower, J. (2014). *Holding and psychoanalysis: A relational perspective* (2nd ed.). Routledge.

Winnicott, D. W. (1965a). *The family and individual development*. Routledge.

21

Trust: The Capacity to *Trust* Self and Others

To trust is to believe in our heart of hearts that an essential other is reliably available when we need her or him. A trustworthy other is one who will be there to comfort, hug, and soothe us when we need comforting, hugging, and soothing. She or he is there for us when we need affirmation and validation. The trusted other is there to care and be concerned about our welfare. "Trust," say Cabaniss and her colleagues (2013), "is vital for forming relationships" (p. 92). With trust we can depend on others. As we grow older, this need to depend on others is balanced with our need for independence. I can be healthily dependent on my wife, while being healthily independent of her and the other way around. It is this critical capacity for healthy dependency that makes the essential capacity for mutual intimacy possible.

The origin of trust, continue Cabaniss and her colleagues (2013), in agreement with Bowlby, Erikson, and May, goes back to the primary dyadic relationship between caregiver and child. "When an infant's primary caretaker is reliably available and appropriately responsive to the baby's needs, the growing child develops **basic trust**—the core positive expectation that one's physical and emotional needs will be met and that other people can be depended on to provide comfort and safety" (p. 92). When the physical and emotional needs are consistently satisfied, the child develops a visceral conviction that the world is a safe and secure place. It is this early solidary dyadic relationship that forms the basis for the acquisition of the capacity to trust.

In the context of this evolving solidary relationship, the child is gradually learning to be increasingly dependable. Being dependable emerges as the complementary side of being dependent on others. Dependability and dependence require each other. In healthy or mature relationships they go

© The Author(s), under exclusive license to Springer Nature Switzerland AG 2021
M. J. Hannush, *Markers of Psychosocial Maturation*,
https://doi.org/10.1007/978-3-030-74315-4_21

hand-in-hand. I depend on you; I am also dependable. This is why, as we grow older, we are devastated by acts of betrayal and infidelity. They inflict, sometime an irreparable, tear in the fabric of our relational being. They violate our basic trust in one another, for trust and secure attachment (connectedness) are woven of the same fabric. In becoming securely attached, I learn to trust myself as I learn to trust my essential others.

Brothers (1995) defines trust as "the hope or wishful expectation of obtaining and providing the selfobject experiences necessary for cohesive selfhood" (p. 231). What are *selfobject experiences*? Under "the term *selfobject experiences* I include all those experiences essential for the establishment, preservation, and restoration of self-experience" (p. 33). *Selfobject experiences* enable us to "experience ourselves as cohesive initiators of activity, existing over time, and worthy of esteem" (p. 33). Again, "the term 'selfobject experience' refers to a vitalizing or cohesion-producing affective state" (p. 235). Moreover, "only those [essential others] experienced as *trustworthy* will be represented in selfobject fantasies" (p. 235). Additionally, we are very selective in our choice of providers of selfobject experiences. They need to be worthy of our trust. "Trustworthiness is determined by experiences that demonstrate affectively attuned responsiveness to selfobject need" (p. 232).

Trust, says Brothers (1995), has four dimensions:

1. Trust-in-others—the tendency to view others as trustworthy providers of selfobject experiences
2. Trust-in-self—the tendency to view oneself as capable of eliciting selfobject experiences from others
3. Self-as-trustworthy—the tendency to view oneself as a trustworthy provider of selfobject experiences for others
4. Others-as-self-trusting—the tendency to view others as trusting of their capacity to obtain and provide selfobject experiences (p. 232)

For Brothers, trust is the prime "glue" or the "organizer" of self-experience. "Everyone," however, "develops a unique … trust organization as a consequence of inevitable developmental traumas" (p. 232). Trust betrayals are disorganizers and disintegrators of the cohesiveness of self-experience. They create "black holes" in self-experience (p. 233). They result in "flaws in the self" (p. 233). Testing others, the flawed self either looks for confirmation of their lack of trustworthiness or distorts and unrealistically sees trustworthiness when it is not there in reality. As our capacity for trust matures, we become more realistic testers of the trustworthiness of others. Although we are born with it, *the capacity to trust* "matures over the course of development"

(p. 232). *Immature trust* manifests itself in "extreme diminutions and intensifications in the various dimensions of … trust" (p. 235).

Brothers (1995) describes four attributes, criteria, or dimensions by which we can evaluate *the degree of maturity of trust*: *realism, abstractness, complexity,* and *differentiation*.

1. *Realism*. A person with an immature capacity for trust has "phantasmagorical and perfectionistic notions about self and others" (p. 47). She or he perceives essential others as being "omnipotent, omniscient, and indestructible or possessing magical or supernatural powers" (p. 47). A person with a more mature capacity for trust will invest herself or himself in others who are "perceived as having more modest qualities" (p. 47).
2. *Abstractness*. An individual with an immature capacity for trust uses concrete (physical, external) and superficial attributes, criteria, or dimensions to test the trustworthiness of others, such as their "size, attractiveness, and material possessions" (p. 47). A person with a more mature capacity for trust will use abstract attributes, criteria, or dimensions to test the trustworthiness of others, such as their "truthfulness, sophistication, integrity, or the adherence to valued principles" (p. 47).
3. *Complexity*. The individual with an immature capacity for trust utilizes simplistic criteria for evaluating the trustworthiness of others that involve "black or white" or either/or thinking. People are either absolutely reliable or totally unreliable. They are either always truthful or always prevaricating. A person with a more mature capacity for trust utilizes complex criteria for the evaluation of the trustworthiness of others by taking into "account the multifaceted nature of human personality" (p. 47). People may be unreliable in one domain, but can be depended upon in other domains. Our friends, partners, parents, or children, for instance, can be depended upon to meet many, but not all, of our needs. The person with a mature capacity for trust can appropriately mistrust others when discernment calls for it. She or he is capable of combining a mix of healthy skepticism and doubt with realistic hope.
4. *Differentiation*. This refers to the "ability to discriminate between qualities of self and qualities of others. … Differentiation also refers to the ability to discriminate among other people" (p. 48). The individual with an immature and undifferentiated capacity for trust engages in sweeping "generalizations about the trustworthiness of others based, for example, on their inclusion in some ethnic or religious group or because they physically resemble someone who proved unworthy in the past" (p. 48).

In short, mature trust is realistic, abstract, complex, and differentiated. Immature trust, in contrast, is unrealistic, concrete, simplistic, and undifferentiated. In fact, Brothers reaches the conclusion that immature trust lies at the core of all psychopathology.

What, you may ask, is the "cause" of the immature capacity for trust? The answer, in the eyes of Brothers (1995), is simple and straightforward: *empathic failure*. "When failures in empathic responsiveness [on the part of essential others] … are severe enough," she concludes, "children come to experience themselves as potential betrayers of the trust placed in them to provide for the selfobject needs of others" (p. 211). What Brothers does not make explicit here is that underneath this blame and role reversal, children's own trust in others and in themselves has been shattered to begin with. This "shattering," which for Brothers is equivalent to "traumatizing," experience is doled in degrees. Such shattering alters self-world experience, with faults on the self-side and fissures on the world-side. None of us escapes this shattering of trust totally. Those of us who are "optimally frustrated" by the empathic failures of essential others can still move toward acquiring a trust that is for the most part realistic, abstract, complex, and differentiated. It is never too late, however, for those of us who are less fortunate to seek and partake in social situations that provide us with "transmuting" empathic experiences and, more generally, optimally nourishing selfobject experiences, which in turn promote the maturation of trust. Empathy, concludes Brothers, is "integral to selfobject experience" (p. 236). "Empathic responsiveness is an almost universal criterion for … trust. Those who fail to respond empathically are unlikely to be experienced as trustworthy … empathy is therapeutic to the extent that it promotes … trust" (p. 236).

Like Brothers, Nicholsen (2002) links the experience of trauma to the catastrophic loss of trust. The "trauma victim," Nicholsen writes, "suffers the loss of social trust and the loss of the background security," which ought to have been provided by essential others (p. 140). Such a trauma and the consequent overwhelming loss of social trust perpetrate a fault line in the self and a twin-tear in the fabric of one's world.

> The most basic feature of trauma is the destruction of some part of this fabric through betrayal of trust in something [or someone] beyond the self. In the betrayal there is a sense of the destruction of a broader authority, morality, or community. Trauma touches levels from the family to the community, to the society to humankind … Evil enters into every trauma, for what is betrayed is ultimately our trust in goodness or the capacity of goodness to withstand evil, the strength of life as such. (p. 132)

Trauma places blinders on the self and a constriction on one's world-horizons. The devastating constriction in one's circle of care may result in a desperate "search for just one trustworthy person to attach oneself to" (p. 138). Finding such a person may make all the difference in the trajectory of one's trust of others, of life itself.

The acquisition of the capacity for *basic trust*, says Erikson (1963), results from the learning that occurs in the beginning of life. It is the byproduct of a favorable ratio of *trust* to *mistrust* that is cumulatively experienced by the infant in his interactions with the primary caregiver, which is usually the mother. This favorable ratio is attained when the infant realizes that his mother will, for the most part, be consistently and reliably available to satisfy his basic needs. This realization is grounded in his oral-sensory or bodily interaction with the mother. A good example is when a child in distress regularly hears the pleasant, rhythmic, soothing, and "beautiful" voice of the mother, he comes to count on her as a source of soothing and comfort. In this and multiple other ways the child's basic trust in the mother is solidified. It is the favorable ratio of trust-to-mistrust that strengthens the child's ability to adapt to the demands of his environment. Regardless, growing up in an imperfect social world, there will be an inevitable crisis, collision, conflict, or tension between basic trust and basic mistrust – a vigilant mode of anticipating or readying oneself for danger, discomfort, disconnection, or distress. A favorable ratio of trust-to-mistrust ultimately results in the acquisition of the "virtue" or character strength of "primal hope" (p. 80). The antithesis of this primal hope is the acquisition of the strong tendency or orientation toward primal "doom" or despair (p. 80) and a deeply ingrained tendency toward *withdrawal* from active and spontaneous participation in relational life.

Trust is the name Erikson (1963) gives to the inner feelings of "certainty," "confidence," and "goodness," which co-inside with experiences of consistent, continuous, and predictable acts of provision by the *care*giver. These "remembered and anticipated sensations and images … provide a rudimentary sense of ego identity" (p. 247).

> The general state of trust, furthermore, implies not only that one has learned to rely on the sameness and continuity of the outer providers, but also that one may trust oneself and the capacity of one's own organs to cope with urges, and that one is able to consider oneself trustworthy enough so that the providers will not need to be on guard lest they be nipped. (p. 248)

The infant, Erikson continues, is constantly "tasting and testing the relationship between inside and outside," especially in times of distress and pain

(p. 248). When the *care* provider, on the whole, passes these tests, the child comes to acquire that sense of *basic trust* or, more precisely, that favorable ratio of trust-to-mistrust.

Hope, Erikson (1964) expounds, like the other "active qualities," or "inherent strengths" of *will, purpose, competence, fidelity, love, care, generativity, and wisdom* (pp. 115–134), is a virtue. True to its origin, in "Latin virtue meant virility" (p. 113). As a character strength, hope is enlivening and inspiriting. It is an "animated and spirited quality without which his [human's] moralities become mere moralism and his ethics feeble goodness" (p. 113). In our primal hope lies our *goodness*. Antithetically, in our hopelessness lies our badness (destructiveness or evilishness). Primal hope is the animating quality that mirrors the vibrancy of the state of our *mental health*.

Erikson (1964) grounds the origin of the *trust-hope-faith triad* not only in the bosom of the family, but also in the larger community (culture):

> It seems probable, then, that what we have called basic virtues emerging from the dealings of generations with each other have their counterparts in the spirit of those human institutions which attempt to formalize and safeguard such dealings. … From the stages and virtues such individual dispositions as faith, judiciousness, moral purpose, technical efficiency, ideological devotion, ethical responsibility, and detached integrity flow into the life of institutions. (p. 155).

Character strengths (virtues), such as hope, and character weaknesses, such as hopelessness, undergo an intergenerational transmission. Character weaknesses will continue being passed on from one generation to the next, unless certain mature adults generate an emergent mature community capable of successfully breaking the vicious cycle of intergenerational transmission of character weaknesses. Erikson prefers "weakness" over "vice." "Now, the negative of this kind of virtue cannot be vice; rather, it is a weakness, and its symptoms are disorder, dysfunction, disintegration, anomie" (p. 139). Moreover, he continues, "rage … accumulates whenever man is hindered in the activation and perfection of the virtues" (p. 139). For Erikson, primal hope is "that basic minimum without which the most highly valued and espoused hopes become irrelevant" (p. 140).

To summarize so far, for Erikson, the sacred triad of basic trust, primal hope, and deep faith forms the heartbeat of integrality—the ability to maintain a relative sense of wholeness in the face of bodily, mental, and psychological disintegration or deterioration. Having trust and faith in oneself is correlative to having trust and faith in others and in the community of which one is a part. Perceiving oneself as "good" is correlative to having a basic sense of the world as good. Viewed dialectically, healthy mistrust (caution) is compatible with healthy trust. Trust of others is requisite for being open to learning from them, while at the same time feeling comfortable in questioning them.

In the beginning of life, our *existential trust*, our *trusting openness to all that is*, is undifferentiated. Our *existential maturation*, our maturational movement toward the best that we as humans can become, is contingent upon the refinement or differentiation of this initial undifferentiated primordial *open* disposition toward the lifeworld. For instance, for the infant, there is, on a pre-reflective bodily level, no differentiation between the body as whole and its parts. It is not unusual to witness a ten-month infant circularly chasing his own leg. Analogously, on the lifeworld side, in the shape of the mother, there is no distinct differentiation between the face of the mother and the mother's embodied presence as a whole. The same lived and limited pre-logic applies to how the child lacks the capacity to differentiate between the nuanced foreground and the layered background of his existential space or between complex dimensions of his lived time—between present-and-past and between present-and-future. He is not even able to differentiate clearly between fantasy and reality. Interestingly, there are adults who are not capable of keeping in mind the lessons of the distant past as they apply to the present or the consequences of present actions on the distant future. *Mature existential living*, guided by *differentiated existential trust—ripened trusting openness to all that is,* illuminates and keeps lighted before us, especially when we are in the dark and have lost our way, that which is most important or primary in life. Differentiated openness to lifeworld meaning possibilities builds upon that original undifferentiated openness to all that is.

Primal presencing is yet another way of describing being trustingly open to all that is. In its differentiated form, it manifests itself in the capacity to be open to all that is Beautiful, Good, and True. To exemplify, I am attuned to the presencing of the beauty of the human face, the mountain, the blue color of the walls in my study, or the beauty in the character and conduct of Jesus Christ or in the broken beauty in the characters of psychologists Erik Erikson, Heinz Kohut, and Rollo May.

Primal presencing can also be viewed as a kind of sensual communion, an aesthetic reciprocity. This is what Paul Cezanne meant, having painted Mont Sainte-Victoire more than thirty times, by his statement: "The mountain and I are one." In these paintings, the line of demarcation between nature (mountain, sky, trees, and earth) and viewer is beautifully blurred, though temporarily, on a higher level of integration. The whole aesthetic phenomenon unfolding before our *trustingly open* eyes, where, as Paul Klee puts it, "one eye sees and the other one feels," is experienced as not only beautiful (*aesthetically trustworthy*), but also intrinsically good and true to life itself. As Merleau-Ponty (1962) would put it, for someone like me who resonates to J. S. Bach's musical compositions or Cezanne's paintings, they will acquire a special place in my life as long as I live, trustworthily shaping my whole aesthetic experience.

Rogers (1989) views trust as a natural byproduct of unconditional positive regard (acceptance, warmth, love). When I am unconditionally loved, I naturally become trustful of the unconditionally loving other. Why should I trust the Other when she or he offers me different forms of love and then repeatedly withdraws the offer? Let us bring to mind that for Rogers, in the fully functioning (mature) person, unconditional positive regard (acceptance, love), congruence (authenticity, genuineness, realness), and empathy (empathic attunement and understanding) are more integrated and inseparable. It is easier to trust someone who displays the three integrated "fundamental attitudes" of acceptance, congruence, and empathy. Moreover, deep trust is more likely to occur in relationships that are egalitarian and where co-presence, honesty, and mutuality abide.

The other side of learning to trust the Other is learning to trust oneself. Rogers (1989) traces the development of the capacity to trust oneself to infancy:

> As infants, we live in our experience; we trust it. When the baby is hungry, he neither doubts his hunger not questions whether he should make every effort to get food. Without being in any way conscious of it, he is a self-trusting organism. But at some point, parents or others say to him, in effect, 'If you feel *that* way, I won't love you.' And so he feels what he *should* feel, not what he *does* feel. To this degree, he builds up a self that feels what it should feel, only occasionally seeing frightening glimpses of what his organism, of which the self is a part, is actually experiencing. (p. 163).

In a section entitled "Speaking Personally," Rogers describes "some of his significant learnings" in his own life (pp. 17–29). The first of the learnings "which are less concerned with relationships" and has "more to do with my own actions and values … is very brief. *I can trust my experience*" (p. 23). "I have learned," writes Rogers, "that my total organismic sensing of a situation is more trustworthy than my intellect" (p. 23). Rogers admits that it has taken him a long time to acquire this basic learning and that he is "still learning" that "when an activity *feels* as though it is valuable or worth doing, it is worth doing" (p. 23).

References

Brothers, D. (1995). *Falling backwards: An exploration of trust and self-experience*. W. W. Norton.

Cabaniss, D. L., Cherry, S., Douglas, C. J., Graver, R. L., & Schwartz, A. R. (2013). *Psychodynamic formulation*. Wiley.

Erikson, E. H. (1963). *Childhood and society* (2nd ed.). W. W. Norton.

Erikson, E. H. (1964). *Insight and responsibility*. W. W. Norton.

Merleau-Ponty, M. (1962). *Phenomenology of perception* (C. Smith, Trans.). Routledge.

Nicholsen, S. W. (2002). *The love of nature and the end of the world: The unspoken dimensions of environmental concern*. The MIT Press.

Rogers, C. R. (1989). *The Carl Rogers reader*. Houghton Mifflin.

22

Hope: The Capacity for Realistic *Hope*

In Erikson's (1963) developmental model, all the stages have their corresponding virtues, which are consequences of the resolution of their respective crises. Resolving the core crisis, conflict or dialectical tension of *trust* versus *mistrust* in infancy results in the acquisition of the virtue of *hope.* "I will, therefore speak," says Erikson (1964), "of *Hope, Will, Purpose,* and *Competence* as the rudiments of virtue developed in childhood; of *Fidelity* as the adolescent virtue; and of *Love, Care,* and *Wisdom* as the central virtues of adulthood" (p. 115). These character strengths, Erikson hastens to add, are dependent on each other. "Will cannot be trained until hope is secure, nor can love become reciprocal until fidelity has proven reliable" (p. 115).

Although difficult to quantify and objectify, "he who has seen a hopeless child, knows what is *not* there" and "if life is to be sustained hope must remain, even where confidence is wounded, trust impaired" (Erikson, 1964, p. 115). "But," Erikson continues, "there is something in the anatomy even of mature hope which suggests that it is the most childlike of all ego-qualities, and the most dependent for its verification on the charity of fate" (p. 116). In a moving passage, Erikson (1964) describes the "physiognomic" or inter-bodily *meaning* of hopefulness that the smiling infant triggers in the smiling adult and vice versa:

> Nothing in human life, however, is secured in its origin unless it is verified in the intimate meeting of partners in favorable social settings. The infant's smile inspires hope in the adult and, in making him smile, makes him wish to give hope; but this is, of course, only one physiognomic detail which indicates that the infant by his trustful search for experience and assurance, awakens in the

© The Author(s), under exclusive license to Springer Nature Switzerland AG 2021
M. J. Hannush, *Markers of Psychosocial Maturation*,
https://doi.org/10.1007/978-3-030-74315-4_22

giver a strength which he, in turn, is ready and needful to have awakened and to have consolidated by the experience of mutuality. (p. 116)

The origin of hope, Erikson tells us, can be traced to the infant's "first encounter with *trustworthy maternal persons*, who respond to his need for *intake* [of food] and *contact* with warm and calming envelopment" (p. 116). Such a mature-enough maternal person is enabled and empowered by her own "experience of being mothered"; by the shared meaning she ascribes to motherhood; and by "an all-enveloping world image tying past, present, and future into a convincing pattern of providence" (p. 116).

Hope, Erikson (1964) informs us, begins "in that inner light of the mother-child world" (p. 117). In fact, "such light must continue to shine through the chaos of many crises, maturational or accidental" (p. 117). Thus, even though the child will inevitably experience "disappointed hopes," as she grows, "maturing hope not only maintains itself in the face of changed facts – it proves itself able to change facts, even as faith is said to move mountains" (p. 117). "*Hope is the enduring belief in the attainability of fervent wishes in spite of the dark urges and rages which mark the beginning of existence*" (p. 118).

As a virtue, hope is an "inherent strength" and an "active quality" (Erikson, 1964, p. 113). In its owning by the developing person it becomes a pervasive aspect of her or his identity—of *who one is*. It mirrors one's essence and "animates" one's sense of personhood. It vitalizes one's sense of agency—one's capacity to act in the world. Erikson (1964) points to the link between the absence of hope (and other basic virtues) and pathology: "We recognize … an inner affinity between the earliest and deepest mental disturbances and a radical loss of a basic kind of hope" (p. 112). Hope, like other basic virtues, contributes to our "ego-synthesis," self-consolidation, or personal integration. Hope, therefore, is an integrator that contributes to our *sense of balance* and subjective well-being. For Erikson, the cultivation of a sense of hopefulness is synchronized with and buttressed by the hope-laden images and narratives of our cultural heritage. A culture can be characterized as having an immature sense of hope (unrealistic optimism) or a mature sense of hope (realistic optimism).

Without hope, in Erikson's mature view, there can be no wholeness. "Throughout his lifetime of writing," Hoare (2002) informs us, "Erikson maintained that primal hope and faith are healthy outcomes of infancy, the first stage of life" (p. 72). "But," Hoare continues, "by his mid-life, he gave those strengths [hope and faith] preeminence as the best case resolution of the last stage of life as well" (p. 72). In his last "existential" and "experiential" period (1970–1985), Hoare tells us, it is no longer "wisdom" but rather "hope" that is the outcome of the successful resolution of the last core conflict of life: integrity versus despair. Erikson replaces "integrity" with "integrality"—a fusion of "integrity" and "integration" (the ability to keep things together) – emphasizing the "ethical" aspect of "integration," and exchanges the last virtue, "wisdom," with "hope." Integrality, born of generativity and discernment, is now seen growing in degrees and as having "enduring hope" as one of its essential and constant ingredients.

To Erikson, therefore, healthy development throughout life, though never reaching a point of completion, came to require the luminosity of hope as a life-affirming counterweight to life's negating darkness as it manifests itself through, among other things, mistrust, stagnation, and despair.

Throughout our developmental lives and into old age we carry within us, consciously or unconsciously, a maternal assurance that we were (hopefully) unconditionally loved—loved for the fragile, imperfect, helpless, and small beings that we were and not loved for living up to the promise of satisfying the false or unrealistic hopes of our narcissistic parents. This maternal memory provides us with the basis of realistic hope. "By old age," Erikson said, "hope is an 'attitude' that represents the revelation of creation in one's life now nearly complete, a simple sense that the created life 'is good,' as in 'and he saw that it was good'" (Hoare, 2002, p. 79). This primal hope is accompanied by a sense of faith or trust in the continuity of human life.

For Erikson, final integration or "integrality" entails bridging enlightened adulthood with "a child-like sense of wonder and joy in the immediate moment" (Hoare, 2002, p. 37). It is this arc or bridge that serves as the "existential nutrient" necessary for the maintenance of a hoped-for future. In Erikson's eyes, *wonder*—"the ability to see things delightfully anew" (Hoare, 2002, p. 113) – goes hand-in-hand with the capacity for hope (faith and trust), always grounded in the context of activating, playful, and self-and-other strengthening, and life-affirming *mutuality*. Erikson's *writing self* at its best embodies this blend of hope-inspiring wonder as it manifests itself in his ideational playfulness with the polar meanings of existence. It is mirrored in his abiding sense of awe at the ideational universe. He makes "purposeful use of the [writing] self as an agent of [life] affirmation" (Hoare, 2002, p. 181) .

Searles (1979) begins his classic paper, "The Development of Mature Hope in the Patient-Therapist Relationship," by informing us that one of the hardest developmental tasks of maturation is the realization and acceptance of hope as an "impure" phenomenon:

> One of the harshest maturational tasks the individual must accomplish, to be truly adult, is to realize and accept that his hope is "impure" in two ways: first,

> it is not unitary in nature but multifarious and permeated with ambivalence, with conflict (such that no one hope or set of hopes is completely fulfillable, for it is opposed by powerfully contrasting hopes); and second, many of these hopes are devoted not to loving, but rather to destructive ends. (p. 479)

When we are in a hopeful mode, Searles continues, we tend not to allow our ambivalence to enter our awareness for such allowance would contaminate the purity and power of what is hoped-for in our fantasied world. Part of the maturing process involves becoming cognizant that many of our "private hopes are mutually irreconcilable" and unloving "in nature than one's ideal self would have them be" (pp. 479–480). This is how we come to acquire what Searles calls *realistic* or *mature hope*.

The acquisition, maintenance, and growth of our *realistic hope*, Searles (1979) continues, can only come about if we are able to integrate our many and various types of conflictual hopes into a coherent core hope. This kind of "integration involves our working through our disappointments, and above all our infantile omnipotence-based frustration-rage and grief, as regards those of our hopes we have had to relinquish" (p. 480). Differently described, working through our impure hopes involves the recognition and acceptance of the inescapable presence of ambivalence in human relatedness. "This," Searles reminds us, "is a never finally completed maturational process" (p. 480).

In order to achieve relative fulfillment in life, we need to discover in ourselves, over and over again, what so far has been our repressed or *unconscious hopes* that may run counter to our *conscious hopes*. We may have to let go of single-mindedly hoped-for-goals. A parent, for example, will have to let go of the unrealistic, false, and unconscious hope of possessing her or his child. A parent may manically attempt to instill the hope of joy and determined optimism in her or his child, but infuse the child with her or his own unconscious depression or despair that are too threatening to acknowledge. All of us need to surrender the unrealistic hope that a fantasied psychosocial twin will understand us perfectly or that we will come to understand ourselves completely or that we will always be able to communicate our innermost feelings and motivations accurately.

Searles (1979) does not shy away from using his own life story to illustrate the power of unconscious self-destructive hopes. In his early years as a small child, Searles experiences his mother as both "loving," but at the same time as "hell to live with." "Thus any longing to recapture my early-mothering experience was impossible to differentiate from a hope to be living again in hell" (p. 483). When Searles enters his father's orbit in subsequent years, he "found him to be living largely in his private hell" (p. 483). This "private hell" includes depression, fear of insanity, psychosomatic symptoms, and other torments. "As regards my analysis," Searles discovers, "I do not doubt, in retrospect, that I *hoped* fully to join my father in hell, not only because I hated him and much unconscious guilt to atone for, as regards his suffering, but also because I loved him and wanted to rescue him from his hell" (p. 483).

In order to cultivate the capacity for mature, healthy, or realistic hope, it is necessary to integrate the disowned parts of the self—to face and successfully grieve our feelings of disappointment, discouragement, and despair. Realistic hope, in contradistinction to unrealistic hope which is unconsciously denial based, is founded in the capacity to experience and survive, through successful grieving, our cumulative losses. This is how hope triumphs over despair:

> One who has survived the griefs over losses, over disappointments in the past has known what it is for hope to triumph over – or to survive – despair. Also, he knows that hoped-for changes which the future may bring, no matter how "favorable" or "healthy" (in psychotherapeutic terms) these changes may prove to be, inevitably bring concomitant sense of loss in various regards – since, as he knows from his past experiences, the fulfillment of one hope is accompanied by loss feelings stemming from the necessary discarding of the hopes which have been opposing it. (Searles, 1979, p. 484)

Another way we become healthily hopeful, elaborates Searles (1979), is when we share our disappointment, discouragement, and despair with, especially, essential others. Not only do we become hopeful but our sense of relatedness is strengthened, and we no longer feel alienated, isolated, or stigmatized. Our hope can become unhealthily sadistic in nature when we repeatedly engender hope in another person and follow it up with disappointment. Hope can become skewed yet in another way when we communicate an implicit, subtle, and cruel demand upon another to fulfill our narcissistically driven hope.

The realm of realistic hope becomes manifest in the discovery of *new meanings* or in the discovery of *previously undiscerned meanings* in our relational patterns—in our ways of relating to one another. Hopelessness or false hopes are frequently byproducts of *rigidified meaning-making patterns* or insightless misinterpretations of lifeworld meanings—what social psychologists call "attribution errors."

Searles (1979) concludes his classic paper on "mature hope" with a summary:

> Maturation involves one's coming to realize and accept that one's hopes are multifarious, devoted variously to destructive as well as constructive ends, permeated with ambivalence, and in many regards mutually irreconcilable, and inherently, therefore, far from wholly fulfillable at best. Thus the accomplishment of this maturational task requires one's recognition and large-scale relinquishment of one's erstwhile unconscious fantasies [false hopes] of omnipotence.
>
> The integration in awareness of previously unintegrated, and largely unconscious feelings of hopefulness proceeds in pace with the working through of progressively intense feelings of disappointment, discouragement, despair, grief, and infantile omnipotence-based frustration-rage. This is a maturational process which is never finally completed. (p. 502)

"Mourning," notes Nicholsen (2002), "means relinquishing certain hopes, in particular the hope for a life without death and loss" (p. 181). Hope, she further elucidates, opens us to what is creatively possible in our future. Hope propels us toward what is novel and yet to be known. "Hope," elaborates Nicholsen, "as an orientation to possibility, is an emotional expression of the ongoing creative process of life. Despair, in contrast, feels like an internal process of destruction, something that attacks the very life in us and propels us toward death rather than toward a future" (p. 183).

Viewed dialectically, just as there can be healthy or unhealthy hope, there also can be constructive and destructive despair. Constructive despair is like a phosphorous light in the dark, a light that points in the direction of life-affirming hope. This is the kind of light that serves as the antidote to what Nicholsen (2002) and others label as *destructive narcissism.* "Dismantling this destructive narcissism," Nicholsen observes, "entails experiencing despair, both despair over what we have deprived ourselves of, and despair over what we have wrought in our delusion" (p. 179). I hasten to add that constructive despair contributes to making us more humble by acknowledging our limits and more compassionate and empathic toward similarly despairing others.

Nicholsen (2002) distinguishes between hope and optimism. Whereas hope is experienced intimately, optimism is based on the deluded belief that the future will inevitably and magically be good. The optimistic person willfully predicts a positive future that promises an unending abundance in whatever one is optimistic about. This kind of "progressive optimism" is founded upon denial of human limitation and finitude. Sooner or later, life will confront us with limits on our human freedom and thus puncture our sense of false and inflated optimism. In contradistinction to this false and unrealistic optimism, mature hope is realistic because it takes the contingencies of the past and present into account. Realistic hope is tempered with concern and disappointment—disappointment in the deluded ideas of infinite progress, deathlessness, and life without loss. Realistic hope does not ignore the present or the past for the sake of simply living exclusively in and for the future. It looks for what is realistically available in the present and for lessons learned from the past.

Despair is not simply the opposite of hope. In destructive despair, Nicholsen (2002) reminds us, there exists "an unwillingness or inability to desire" (p. 184). Unlike the falsely optimistic or the unrealistically hopeful individual, the realistically hopeful person looks for possibilities in the present. For the destructively despairing person, the future is foreclosed. A despair-ridden, traumatized individual "cannot think in terms of a future… cannot imagine a future or to want anything" (p. 184). Constructive despair, on the other hand, has its hopeful aspect. It can serve as a means for our psychosocial transformation. It can awaken us from our destructive narcissism. The full identification with our despair-producing suffering can become the humbling ground for our movement in a life-affirming direction. The hopeful side of constructive despair emerges with the acceptance of our dependency and suffering. Openness to realistic present and future possibilities becomes feasible. Along with this openness comes the capacity to wait with patience, while being mindful of the transformational potential of despair.

Marcel (1964) describes the meaning of *hope* by contrasting it to the meaning of *unhope*:

> The word *unhope* coined by Thomas Hardy … translated by a neologism *inespoir* [hopelessness], admirably renders that state of the soul apprehended in terms of what might be called its positive negativity. Unhope which is opposed to hope as fear is opposed to desire is truly a death in life, a death anticipated … It yawns before us as an abyss at certain moments and we are swallowed up by it as in a morass from which we do not possess the courage even of the most elementary kind to will our escape. (p. 54)

Hope, however, is much more than simply escaping our entanglement in a muddy morass. For Marcel, our integrity, salvation, and wholeness are at stake in confronting the dialectical tension between hope and unhope. Here our dialectical model differs from that of Marcel, for we make a distinction between healthy (realistic) hope and unhealthy (unrealistic) hope and between constructive hopelessness and destructive hopelessness. Regardless, what I value most about Marcel's (1950) understanding of hope is that he grounds it in a context of an optimal relational encounter. Hope is not only hope for oneself but a "spreading of one's hope, keeping its flame a radiance of hope burning around one" (p. 160). The relational ground from which hope originates and spreads is *presence* or, better yet, *co-presence*, which involves a loving attachment bond between two persons. Having been loved, I radiate hope.

References

Erikson, E. H. (1963). *Childhood and society* (2nd ed.). W. W. Norton.
Erikson, E. H. (1964). *Insight and responsibility*. W. W. Norton.
Hoare, C. H. (2002). *Erikson on development and adulthood: New insights from the unpublished papers*. Oxford University Press.
Marcel, G. (1950). *Mystery of being, Volume 2: Faith and reality*. Harvill Press.
Marcel, G. (1964). *Creative fidelity*. Noonday Press.
Nicholsen, S. W. (2002). *The love of nature and the end of the world: The unspoken dimensions of environmental concern*. The MIT Press.
Searles, H. F. (1979). *Countertransference and related subjects: Selected Papers*. International Universities Press.

Part VIII

The Capacities for Empathy, Relating, and Repairing

23

Empathy: The Capacity for *Empathy*

The word *empathy* is a translation of the German term *Einfuhlung*, which means "feeling into." "The philosopher Robert Vischer," says Hagman (2010), "who coined in 1872 the word 'empathy' (*Einfuhlung*), spoke of it as a feeling rather than a process of formal thought" (p. 115). The concept of empathy seems to have evolved to embody multiple overlapping definitions. One way of defining empathy is to view it as a form of attunement to the other's emotional experience. This is why the words "empathy" and "attunement" are frequently paired together: *empathic attunement*. Let us, however, cite more extensive definitions of empathy.

Akhtar (2009) defines empathy as "the ego's [self's] capacity to transiently identify with someone else in order to grasp his or her subjective experience" (p. 93). Moreover, an "altruistic elimination of one's personal agenda—to the extent this is possible—and attunement to the other's affect and fantasy are the hallmarks of 'empathy'" (p. 93). Additionally, "empathy originates in the amalgamation of constitutional talents for attunement and identification with devoted and empathic parents" (p. 94).

"**Empathy**," state Auchincloss and Samberg (2012), is "a complex affective and cognitive process of feeling, imagining, thinking, and somatically sensing one's way into the experience of another person" (p. 73). As a developmental process involving the interaction between the attuned responsiveness of parents and their children's inborn capacities, the capacity for empathy comes to assume a pivotal position not only in understanding and forming intimate relations with others, but also in building the developing person's basic sense of self. Empathy, elaborate Auchincloss and Samberg, overlaps with other concepts, such as mentalization, intersubjectivity, attunement, and reverie.

© The Author(s), under exclusive license to Springer Nature Switzerland AG 2021

M. J. Hannush, *Markers of Psychosocial Maturation*,
https://doi.org/10.1007/978-3-030-74315-4_23

Empathy, add Auchincloss and Samberg (2012), subsumes multiple, conscious or unconscious, components. They emphasize its developmental nature. "It may begin unprompted, as affective resonance and/or imitation, progressing to include hypotheses and reflection about another" (p. 74). Even as far back as 1921 Sigmund Freud had intuited a trajectory from imitation to identification ending in empathy, which then served as a means for understanding the mental life of another. Still, Freud, according to Auchincloss and Samberg, shied away from emphasizing the role of empathy lest it stood in the way of objective interpretation. Regardless, since empathy is a developmental process, then in its advanced (mature) form it becomes *generative empathy*, which is described as a "sublimated creative act" (p. 74). Interestingly, Erikson (1963) writes that one "synonym" for the concept of generativity is "*creativity*" (p. 267). But although the concept of *mutuality* is a central mechanism in the maturational process and in the achievement of integrative generativity or generative integrity—the pinnacle of maturity, to the best of my knowledge, Erikson never links mutuality with empathy. It is Edmund Husserl (see below) who makes this essential link. Nevertheless, Erikson links the mutual process of "confirming" and "being confirmed" between the generations (parents and their children) with "generativity" under which he subsumes the capacity for "regeneration" and "renewal":

> It is the young [adolescents] who, by their responses and actions, tell the old [middle-aged adults] whether life as represented to them has some vital promise, and it is the young who carry in them the power to confirm those who confirm them, to renew and regenerate, to disavow what is rotten, to reform and rebel. (Erikson, 1968, p. 258)

In other words, through the process of mutuality (confirming-and-being-confirmed), regeneration or renewal (the expansion of generativity) is made possible. Still, Erikson does not see that this is also a process that requires the *accumulation of mutual empathies* between the generations.

Cabaniss and her colleagues (2017) give us a more general definition of empathy:

> The ability to understand how another person experiences the world is a powerful ingredient in human emotional connections. Each of us has our own view of reality, but using our imagination and drawing on our experiences can give us an approximate sense of someone else's perspective. This ability is called **empathy**. (p. 129)

Teyber and Teyber (2017) offer us yet another definition of empathy:

> **Empathic understanding**: a genuine feeling of warmth, concern, and acceptance of others. This is accomplished by an accurate, specific and in-depth understanding ... [of others' expressions and viewpoints] within a developmental, familial and cultural contextualization... [This enables us] to make sense of ... [their] seemingly irrational responses. (p. 371)

Empathy plays a central role in Kohut's self-psychology. Strozier (2001) provides a description of Kohut's evolving definition and role of empathy in *healthy psychological functioning*:

> Here cure [healing of the self] begins (though does not end) with empathy, which at various times he [Kohut] named the 'recognition of the self in the other'; 'the expansion of the self to include the other'; 'the accepting, confirming and understanding human echo'; and the 'wordless psychological extension of the human environment' that separates us from death, the 'incomprehensible vastness of endless time,' and the 'barrier to meaninglessness, to pessimistic despair.' (pp. 345–346)

Kohut (1984) offers his most succinct definition of empathy as "the capacity to think and feel oneself into the inner life of another person. It is our lifelong ability to experience what another person experiences, though usually ... to an attenuated degree" (p. 82). Kohut went so far as to assert that empathy is the central ingredient in the provision of a corrective emotional experience for the suffering patient. More than that, empathy contributes to the stabilization, vitalization, and consolidation of the patient's tenuous, depleted, and fragmented sense of self.

Empathic attunement makes it possible for the therapist to see the world from the patient's point of view. Empathically attuned therapists let patients know that they are trying their best to understand how things look to them, that they are doing their best to see their situation from their own (patients') perspective. For Kohut, empathy achieves a kind of affective merger with the Other. I label this as an advanced form of affect-laden identificatory resonance.

Self-psychology teaches us that even our emerging and developing sense of self, in its origin, depends on the empathic responsiveness of our essential others. The acquisition of our capacity for empathy is made possible by having been consistently empathized with by our caregivers. Plainly put, empathic parents tend to beget empathic children. Having been empathically responded to in consistent and age-appropriate ways in our growing-up, early critical years, we become able to be empathic toward ourselves and toward others. Attuned and empathic responsiveness to our needs—to our physical, emotional, and mental states—contributes to the solidification of our evolving sense of self. We feel empowered, strengthened, individualized, vitalized, and exuberant about life and living.

Self-psychology informs us that our caregivers need not be perfect empathizers in order for us to become proficient at empathizing. In fact, it goes so far as to assert that sporadic empathic failures are not only human, but also necessary in expediting our internalization of our caregivers' functions that include, among other functions, the capacity for empathy toward self and toward others and the ability to realistically assess our capabilities and limitations. A balance of optimal indulgences and optimal frustrations, as manifested in cumulative successes and failures in empathic mirroring with the former far outweighing the latter, is necessary for the consolidation of a maturing sense of self.

Our parents' early, though not perfect, steady, empathic attunement; their capacity to mirror us accurately to ourselves; and their ability to allow us to idealize them and bask in this idealization, say self-psychologists, made it possible for us to internalize these empathic and mirroring functions. On the whole, they provided us with what we needed and desired in an age-appropriate and timely way. As we grew older we became capable of empathizing with our selves and others. We learned to nourish, shore up, and sustain ourselves in their absence while confronting trying times. We acquired measured expectations of ourselves and of others. On the whole, we began to offer ourselves and allowed caring others to offer us what we needed and desired in our adult years. Simply stated, we developed a steady, balanced, resilient, and healthy sense of self.

The capacity for empathy needs to be understood as part of a more encompassing caring or even loving stance toward the Other, a stance which communicates, to use Frommian terms, care, concern, respect, responsibility, and the wish to "know" the Other. Therefore, it is not just empathy that is powerful. The wish and effort to empathize sends a powerful message with multiple meanings. Through deep empathic attunement, I set aside my own preoccupations in order to come close to and connect with the Other. My devoted care or love for the Other makes it possible for me to suspend my everyday, ordinary self (what phenomenologists call the self with the "natural attitude" or I call the ordinarily preoccupied self).

Empathy overlaps with Wilfred Bion's concept of *reverie* and Donald Winnicott's concept of *mirroring.* Described differently, there can be no empathy without "reverie" or "mirroring." To be in a state of reverie is to be in a state of relaxed attentiveness. It is "a state of receptivity to one's own and the patient's [or the Other's] conscious/unconscious experience" (Ogden, 2012, p. 177). It requires the suspension, bracketing, or setting aside, as much as possible, of one's remembrances and anticipations or, as Bion (1984) puts it, "what is required is a positive act of refraining from memory or desire" (p. 31).

Winnicott (1971) describes, phenomenologically, the baby's experience: "Now, at some point the baby takes a look around. What does the baby see when he or she looks at the mother's face? … what the baby sees is himself or herself" (p. 112). What Winnicott is saying here is that when the good-enough mother is empathizing (identifying) with her baby, she is able to serve as a mirror for her baby's physical and mental states. She is able to transmit to the baby what she is seeing (grasping) while looking at her baby. This is a visceral transmission through her mirroring face. Her face relays her reading or deciphering the *meaning* of the baby's state of mind. Her facial expression is, more or less, matching what she sees, the baby's present experience. The baby then receives a relatively accurate mirroring of his experience. This results in "a significant exchange with the world, a two-way process in which self-enrichment alternates with the discovery of meaning in the world of seen things" (p. 113). For this to happen, as in exercising the capacity for reverie, the mother needs to keep her own moods or preoccupations from distorting her mirroring capacity. Being accurately mirrored enhances the baby's accurate or reality-based *meaning-making ability*. In this intersubjective or inter-intentional exchange lies the original source of the developing child's authenticity, realness, and originality. Simply stated, the mother's face serves as a mirror for the child's emerging sense of selfhood. "Wouldn't it be awful," comments Winnicott, "if the child looked into the mirror and saw nothing!" (p. 116). Accurate empathic mirroring unifies the emerging nascent self. Inaccurate, insufficient, or non-empathic mirroring distorts the child's sense of evolving selfhood. Accurate mirroring, notes Nicholsen (2002), is "a work of beauty" (p. 99). In its absence, we are left with a "nonself" or a "disintegrated self that was not in relationship, in an ugly environment" (p. 99). Contingent upon whether we were the recipients of good or bad empathic mirroring, the world itself will come to be seen as having a beautiful or ugly face.

For Winnicott, a "sign of health in the mind is the ability of one individual to enter imaginatively and accurately into the thoughts and feelings, hopes and fears of another person; also to allow the other person to do the same with us … When we are face to face … we are reduced to two human beings of equal status" (quoted in Fiumara, 2015, p. xxii).

There is therefore an element of beauty in optimal empathic mirroring. Hagman (2010) attributes the concept of "aesthetic empathy" to the early work of German philosopher Theodor Lipps. In his *Aesthetics of Space*, holds Hagman, Lipps characterizes empathy as the objective enjoyment of self. For Lipps, aesthetic or positive empathy is where the self is encountered in the object (e.g., the Other or a creative work of art), and negative or ugly empathy is where the self is repelled. "So," Hagman concludes, "empathy … is a special, transcendent form of union, a bond of beauty" (p. 115). Incidentally, Lipps had a profound influence on Husserl's theory on empathy.

Kohut (1971) traces the developmental origin of the self to the empathic mirroring that occurs between parent and child. He makes repeated reference to the "gleam in the parent's eye" (p. 116). The infant *finds (discovers)* him*self* empathically mirrored through the *beautiful* gleam he perceives in the parent's eyes. In this gleam lies the primal affirmation of the emerging loveable self. Though Kohut does not describe it as such, the arousal of the aesthetic sense cannot be severed from the experience of empathic mirroring, for there is indubitable relational beauty not only in the "gleam of the parent's eye" but also in the reciprocal gleam in the child's eye.

The distinction between what I call *symmetrical empathy* and *asymmetrical empathy* has, to the best of my knowledge of the literature on empathy, largely been ignored. This is at least in part due to the clinical bias where, in a therapeutic setting, it is asymmetrical empathy that is largely practiced. There is also the "developmental" bias. In the early years of development, it is the good-enough parent who mostly engages in asymmetrical empathy. The capacity for symmetrical empathy is a byproduct of maturation. It is in Husserl's unpublished transcripts where the importance of the phenomenon of symmetrical empathy is insightfully addressed. Hadreas (2007) describes Husserl's coined concept of *Nachverstehen* translated as empathic "understanding-following-after-another." More specifically, "Verstehen" is translated as "'to follow and understand', 'to understand in following', 'to follow in understanding' and 'to understand regeneratively'" and "Nachverstehen" is translated as "'following and understanding' and 'understanding-in-following another'" (p. 20). This is what I mean by *symmetrical empathic understanding*. It can also be termed as *inter-empathy*. In mature love, for instance, each lover, through inter-empathy, "arrives at the uniqueness and incomparable value of the beloved" (p. 102). Through symmetrical empathy, each lover "weaves one's own self in the life of the beloved" (p. 102). By way of "understanding-following-after-another," each lover partakes in "the strivings of the other" (p. 102).

For Husserl, Hadreas (2007) expounds, symmetrical empathy occurs only in the context of an "I-You" relationship:

> Husserl describes an 'I-You relation', as a relation in which two striving subjects come to be related to each other, one after another in mutual interactive affecting and being affected. In this [1921] manuscript we find three times in just three lines, that striving subjects interact, 'one after the other'... In fact, here we have a fundamental condition of the development of personal love ... Personal love requires what Husserl calls 'understanding-following-after-another' (*Nachverstehen*), which ... is a Husserlian neologism. It is this empathic understanding 'of one person following after the other' which makes the interrelationship with another person impossible to objectify. The beloved person remains more than can be collated into an object. (pp. 20–21)

Through *cumulative mutual empathy* lovers are disclosed to each other. "And here lies the transformative potential of *Nachverstehen*" (p. 25). The identities of the lovers can be transformed through "empathic acts of care and attentiveness, as determined by interactive *Nachverstehen*" (p. 37). The lovers conjoin their identities through "a series of empathies *vis-à-vis* the strivings and endeavors of the beloved, sharing in them ... The lover is *with* the beloved in her strivings, hopes and satisfactions" (p. 37). Although there arises a conjoining of identities, it is also "the uniqueness and the manner in which the other person [lover] becomes a source of [special and irreplaceable] value [that] arises through *Nachverstehen*" (p. 27). Through mutual empathy, or better yet, through the "building of inter-active empathies" (p. 28), the lovers come into contact with the essential *truth* of each other. "We [come to] know the *truth* by knowing ... the history of [the] other's conflicts and confrontations" (p. 28).

> Understanding a person's uniqueness as their *truth* involves understanding their trials. The other person's strivings and struggles are key. The concatenation of empathies of the other person is myriad. They might involve being stymied by a particular educational system, by the unique admiration of a father, by the hopes for romance with a particular love, by the death of a child, by the pride taken in a spouse's accomplishments, and so on. (p. 29)

For Husserl, then, there is a circular relationship between mutual love and mutual empathy. Just as a concatenation of empathies strengthens the love between the lovers, so does the strengthened love enhances the continuation of the building of mutual empathies.

As a manifestation of our capacity for identificatory resonance, empathy needs to be understood not as an all-or-none phenomenon but as a capacity that displays itself in degrees. Not only will we experience fluctuations in our ability to empathize with others in our everyday lives, but while taking these oscillations into account, our capacity for empathy mirrors our level of maturity. Just like maturity, the capacity for empathy requires vigilant cultivation throughout the life cycle. After all, the capacity for empathy is one of the markers of maturity.

The later work of Stern (2004) contains an integration of insights from evidence-based developmental psychoanalysis and phenomenology. In an earlier work, Stern (1985) first asks, "Is attunement close to what is generally meant by empathy? No" (p. 145). Why? "The evidence indicates attunements occur largely out of awareness and almost automatically," while empathy "involves the mediation of cognitive processes" (p. 145). This answer is premature and erroneous. First, there can be no empathy without attunement. Second, there are levels of empathy some of which occur consciously and some unconsciously. Moreover, as Ogden (2012)).makes clear, a view consonant with phenomenology, there is "a seamless continuity of conscious and unconscious experience" (p. 177).

"Empathy," according to Stern (1985), "consists of at least four distinct and probably sequential processes: (1) resonance of feeling state; (2) the abstraction of empathic knowledge from the experience of emotional resonance; (3) the integration of abstracted empathic knowledge into an empathic response; and (4) a transient role identification" (p. 145). "Affect attunement," acknowledges Stern, "shares with empathy the initial process of emotional resonance" (p. 145). "Attunement," however, "need not proceed towards empathic knowledge or response" (p. 145). Again, had Stern understood empathy as a developmentally layered process, the distinction he makes between "affective attunement" and "empathy" would evaporate. To repeat, one can speak of a visceral and affective layer or level of *empathic* attunement that then serves as a prelude for an understanding-based empathic response.

Stern (1985) brings to our attention the rich theoretical and clinical concept of *selective attunement.* Parents may selectively aim the beam of their empathic attunement toward one form of the child's experience and not another.

> In essence, attunement permits the parents to convey to the infant what is shareable, that is, which subjective experiences are within and which are beyond the pale of mutual consideration and acceptance. Through the selective use of attunement, the parents' intersubjective responsivity acts as a template to shape

> and create corresponding intrapsychic experiences in the child. It is in this way that the parents' desires, fears, prohibitions, and fantasies contour the psychic experiences of the child. (p. 208)

To extrapolate and exemplify, through selective empathic attunement, the face of the parents may light up when "mirroring" or "echoing" (terms that Stern himself uses as almost synonymous with attunement) their child's delight, enthusiasm, and joy, but *not* the child's lethargy and sadness.

In the process of exchanging identificatory resonances, parents and children engage in a mutual sharing of affects, cognitions, intentions, motives, and psychic states. It is a mutual exchange involving "intersubjectivity," "interaffectivity," and "interintentionality." It entails the mostly pre-reflective and inter-bodily communication of *affect-and-value-laden meanings*. It is akin to the co-creation of a shared lifeworld. What I find utterly fascinating in Stern's (2004) later work is that, in my eyes, he concretizes at the *micro*-level, Husserl's *macro*-notion of mutual inter-empathy. Here is what I get from Stern: the quality of mutual attunement or inter-empathy (a term Stern never uses in connection with attunement) at any given encounter between two human beings will reveal at the "moment of meeting" the history of their respective relational patterns, separately or together. At the same time, this *moment of meeting* can carry the seed of relational transformation. It contains within it the potential to begin a new inter-empathic pattern. The present moment, when pregnant with inter-empathic attunement (for Stern it is only attunement), is experienced on an inter-sensorial, inter-corporeal, or, as Merleau-Ponty would describe it, inter-fleshly level. The present moment promises the possibility of moving away from what Stern terms as "intersubjective anxiety" and "fuzzy [or frozen] intentionalizing," to "sloppy moving along," and thereafter toward a "moment of meeting" whereby one can experience an "intentional-feeling flow," a "shared feeling voyage," and an "altero [other]-centered participation" (pp. 241–246).

We conclude this chapter by pointing out the central role that empathy plays in the therapeutic approach of Carl Rogers. For Rogers (1989), the therapeutic attitude necessitates three interrelated requirements: acceptance (unconditional positive regard), congruence (genuineness, authenticity, or realness), and *empathy*. Just as Rogers focuses on the central importance of empathy from inside the humanistic movement, Kohut talks of empathy as a core therapeutic attitude from inside the psychoanalytic movement. For Rogers, empathy is simultaneously a bodily, emotional, and cognitive experience. To have empathy is to experience someone's world the way she or he experiences it, but to experience it without floundering in it, without losing sight of the "as if" quality:

> To sense [the client's] confusion or his timidity or his anger or his feeling of being treated unfairly *as if* it were your own, yet without your own uncertainty or fear or anger or suspicion getting bound up in it, this is the condition I am endeavoring to describe. When the client's world is clear to the counselor and she can move about in it freely, then she can both communicate her understanding of what is vaguely known to the client, and she can also *voice meanings* in the client's experience of which the client is scarcely aware. (Rogers, 1962, p. 93)

The empathic therapist communicates nonverbally to the client the message, "I am with you." More than that, the therapist communicates her or his understanding and experience to the client. Should the client indicate that she or he is being misunderstood, the therapist responds non-defensively by accepting and correcting her or his misattunements, misunderstanding, or empathic failure.

What is the therapeutic value of empathic understanding? When clients see that the therapist sees their world the way they see it, they feel encouraged to clarify and increase their understanding of themselves. The empathic therapist becomes a model for them with whom they can identify. They learn to be empathic toward themselves. They learn to understand their own experience in an accepting way, just like their therapist. They come to accept themselves. Rogers reminds us that lack of self-acceptance is at the core of psychopathology. With self-acceptance comes a strengthened sense of self-worth. After all, if therapists deem us worthy of their care-laden time and effort, then we come to perceive ourselves as worthy human beings.

References

Akhtar, S. (2009). *Comprehensive dictionary of psychoanalysis*. Karnac.

Auchincloss, E. L., & Samberg, E. (Eds.). (2012). *Psychoanalytic terms and concepts*. Yale University Press.

Bion, W. (1984). *Attention and interpretation*. Karnac.

Cabaniss, D. L., Cherry, S., Douglas, C. J., & Schwartz, A. (2017). *Psychodynamic psychotherapy: A clinical manual* (2nd ed.). John Wiley & Sons.

Erikson, E. H. (1963). *Childhood and society* (2nd ed.). W. W. Norton.

Erikson, E. H. (1968). *Identity: Youth and crisis*. W. W. Norton.

Fiumara, G. C. (2015). *Psychic suffering: From pain to growth*. Karnac.

Hadreas, P. (2007). *A phenomenology of love and hate*. Ashgate.

Hagman, G. (2010). *The artist's mind: A psychoanalytic perspective on creativity, modern art and modern artists*. Routledge.

Kohut, H. (1971). *Analysis of the self*. International Universities Press.

Kohut, H. (1984). *How does analysis cure?* International Universities Press.

Nicholsen, S. W. (2002). *The love of nature and the end of the world: The unspoken dimensions of environmental concern*. The MIT Press.

Ogden, T. H. (2012). *Creative readings: Essays on seminal analytic works*. Routledge.

Rogers, C. R. (1962). The interpersonal relationship: The core of guidance. In C. R. Rogers & B. Stevens (Eds.), *Person to person*. Real People Press.

Rogers, C. R. (1989). *The Carl Rogers reader*. Houghton Mifflin.

Stern, D. N. (1985). *The interpersonal world of the infant: A view from psychoanalysis and development*. Basic Books.

Stern, D. N. (2004). *The present moment in psychotherapy and everyday life*. W. W. Norton.

Strozier, C. B. (2001). *Heinz: Kohut: The making of a psychoanalyst*. Farrar, Straus and Giroux.

Teyber, E., & Teyber, F. H. (2017). *Interpersonal process in therapy: An integrative model* (7th ed.). Cengage Learning.

Winnicott, D. W. (1971). *Playing and reality*. Tavistock Publications.

24

Relating: The Capacity for Healthy *Relating*

"The capacity to have relationships," say Cabaniss and her colleagues (2013), "is central to the way people function and develop… By the time we are adults, we tend to form relationships according to certain patterns which can be more or less adaptive" (p. 32). They define relationships simply as "the interactions that we have with people in our lives" (p. 32). We have different types of relationships. We have relationships with our parents, siblings, extended family members, friends, classmates, teachers, mentors, partners, spouses, colleagues, and so on. Some of our relationships are fleeting and others may be more enduring. Some of us have many and others have few relationships. Our relationships may be deep or shallow. Relationships can be pleasurable, rewarding, and life–saving, or they can be confusing, frustrating, and demoralizingly disagreeable. They can also be both pleasurable and painful. Healthy relationships, assert Cabaniss and colleagues, are characterized by *trust, a three-dimensional way of understanding oneself and others, security, intimacy,* and *mutuality.*

"The ability to **trust** others," continue Cabaniss and her colleagues (2013), "is essential to having meaningful, mutually satisfying relationships… Trust allows people to count on one another, to believe that thy will be taken care of, and to have confidence in the consistency of their relationships" (p. 33). Our relational patterns develop early in our lives. "In normal development, children's interactions with caregivers who are consistent, loving, and empathic lay the groundwork for healthy relationships in later life" (p. 147). They are able to trust others and form secure attachments. The unfolding vicissitudes of life will also affect our relational patterns. "But having at least one or two people who you really trust is vital for adaptive functioning" (p. 33). Trusting

© The Author(s), under exclusive license to Springer Nature Switzerland AG 2021
M. J. Hannush, *Markers of Psychosocial Maturation*,
https://doi.org/10.1007/978-3-030-74315-4_24

that at least a few essential others care for and love us buffers us, at least to some extent, from the stresses and strains of everyday life.

"Being able to think about oneself and others in a three-dimensional way," elaborate Cabaniss and her colleagues (2013), "is critical to having healthy relationships." By three-dimensionality they "mean that the person can think about himself/herself and others as having… both bad and good qualities… separate and unique feelings, beliefs, needs, or motivations… [and] generally consistent feelings about self and others from past to present" (p. 34). When our "three-dimensionality" is in gear, we are open to hearing more than one side of a story, to seeing more than one aspect of another person. We cultivate an appreciation for the complex nature of the Other. We realize that there are multiple sides to other people's personalities, some of which we resonate to more than others. We do not see people as all good or all bad. We can imagine others as being separate from us. We can think about ourselves and about others in nuanced ways. Although we experience inevitable frustrations, we, for the most part, are able to sustain meaningful ongoing relations with others. We are also able to think about what might be going on in other people's minds. This ability can be subsumed under what has been called *mentalizing* or *mentalization*. "Mentalising," says Holmes (2010), "refers to the ability to reflect on thinking and thereby to grasp the perspectival nature of thought, and the experiential ground from which it arises" (p. 4). "Portmanteau definitions of mentalizing," he expands, "include: 'the ability to see oneself from the outside, and others from the inside', and 'thinking about feelings, and feeling about thinkings'" (p. 4). Coincidentally, adds Holmes, "psychological and physiological security are preconditions for mentalising" (p. 28). In other words, the capacity for mentalization is made possible by secure attachment.

Having a sense of security is the third characteristic of healthy relating. "The word **security**," state Cabaniss et al. (2013), "refers to the state of being safe in relationships; security in a relationship refers to feeling safe with another person… This means being able to feel that the relationship will persist even if there are … separations … disagreements … [and] other negative feelings" (p. 35). Securely attached people, they elaborate, are on the whole able to tolerate ambivalence toward others, have different kinds of relationships, and build relationships at a slow pace so that they gain gradual knowledge of others.

Intimacy is the fourth characteristic of healthy relationships. "**Intimacy**," state Cabaniss et al. (2013), "refers to closeness and familiarity. People are intimate with one another if they share things about themselves, such as feelings, experiences, wishes, and disappointments … [and] stories, hopes, and fears" (p. 35). By becoming intimate, we also become vulnerable. But if sharing is *mutual*, then we are equally vulnerable. Our mutual vulnerability attests to the precarious preciousness of our special intimate relationship.

Mutuality is the fifth characteristic of healthy relating. "Relationships are mutual," say Cabaniss and her colleagues (2013), "when both people involved are able to give and take" (p. 36). The concept of mutuality has a pivotal place in Erikson's psychosocial theory of development. "First experienced with the mother," says Hoare (2002), "mutuality was, to Erikson, the source of hope and of trust. This first source is essential to life, to mental health, and, when integrated on a higher developmental level in adulthood, to the ethical treatment of others" (p. 96). "*Mutuality*," continues Hoare, "means 'mutual activation' in which two persons ... are activated by one another... 'Mutual activation' was the 'crux' of mutuality to Erikson, an 'ego actuality' in which persons are 'inspired' to actively engage their selves, strengths, and abilities" (p. 96). "Mental health, ethical and spiritual health, and ego vitality are of the same cloth" (p. 96).

The foundations of our ability to navigate two- and three-person relationships, say Cabaniss and her colleagues (2013), go back to our earliest years. Under good-enough conditions, in a facilitating social environment, infants "establish a solid relationship with **one** person," what they label as a "**dyadic**, or **two-person relationship**" (p. 101). This allows the infant to "trust other people," to "form secure attachments," and to "maintain a stable sense of himself/herself and other people" (p. 102). During this phase, infants behave as though their primary caregivers are all theirs and probably a part of them.

As we leave infancy behind and enter toddlerhood, continue Cabaniss and her colleagues (2013), our world widens; it becomes more expansive. We become aware that there is another person with whom to share the primary caregiver. We thus enter the phase of **triadic relations**. This phase brings a complex constellation of feelings of exclusiveness, jealousy, and rivalry, intensified longing for love, and other conflicted and contradictory emotions. It is in this phase that we learn to navigate three-person relationships. Cabaniss and her colleagues expand:

> When this developmental phase goes well, the primary caregiver embraces the child's desires and affections in a safe and supportive way. The desired caregiver allows the child to demand the desired caregiver's attention, while also setting appropriate limits. Over time (usually months), children regain closeness to the rival caregiver, while perhaps keeping a special place for the desired caregiver. This is sometimes called **successfully traversing the Oedipal phase**... Three-person relationships are [later] seen in many constellations with many people, such as friends or teachers. (pp. 102–103)

> If things go well in the earliest years, they [children leave]... this period with a nascent sense of self and the capacity to have relationships with others based on secure attachments... In middle childhood, children develop the capacity to think about people as having relationships with each other as well as relationships with them. This allows them to feel like part of a family, and even a community... Learning to tolerate jealousy and competition is an important developmental goal of this phase. (p. 106)

When things have gone well in our childhood, as adults, we are better able to navigate the terrain of three-person relationships through our willingness to share, within the bounds of reason, "the special other" without becoming possessive or excessively jealous and rivalrous. Children who have developed trusting, secure, and thus stable relationships in the dyadic phase of their relationships with primary caregivers are better able to negotiate three-person relationships in middle childhood and beyond. As adults, they do not long for a much earlier dyadic relationship, a relationship in which they will be taken care of exclusively and one-sidedly by "one" other person. They are able to consolidate a secure dyadic relationship based on empathy and mutual care, a relationship in which they are able to *give and receive.* People with highly developed abilities for attachment, trust, and self-esteem regulation have no difficulties with commitment in adulthood. They do not long for perfection in a partner, a longing that is a residue from an early relationship. Moreover, when their rivalrous feelings from middle childhood are appropriately handled by their attuned and supportive parents, as secure adults, they will have an easier time balancing their competitiveness with their cooperativeness.

Object relations theory traces the roots of our capacity to have positive relations with others to our early relationships or interactions with important caregivers. From these early interactions, say Cabaniss and her colleagues (2013), we derive our "basic **templates** for relationships that affect all subsequent experiences" (p. 174). Basic templates refer to "internalized representations" of our earliest relational experiences. "These early relationship experiences," continue Cabaniss and her colleagues, "are **internalized** [taken into our experiencing and becoming part of ourselves] and exist in the individual's unconscious as he/she grows up" (p. 174). "Internalization of experience," they add, "occurs throughout the life cycle and, as people get older, is more often called **identification**" (p. 174). We develop "positive relationships templates" when our essential others satisfy our basic needs. "If children are more often satisfied than frustrated in their relationships with early caregivers," they elaborate, "they tend to learn to trust others and to develop healthy, balanced expectations of future relationships" (p. 174). As adults, having experienced a good match between what we needed as children and what our caregivers had to offer, we are equipped with a relational resilience that enables us to manage the inevitable disappointments of life. Thus, our early unconscious templates of our relationships with our caregivers, which contain our view of ourselves vis-à-vis our essential others, continue to influence the quality of our relationships in adulthood.

Our unconscious, emphasize Cabaniss and her colleagues (2013), contains multiple relationship templates. These relationship templates manifest themselves in the way we enact our roles. We can therefore experience ourselves in "either role of a relationship template – sometimes … [we] feel like the child and sometimes like the caregiver. This is because, as children, we identify with our caregivers" (p. 176). In my interactions with my daughter, for instance, having identified with my father, I may feel angry in the same way my father felt angry with me when I was a child. When our relationship templates are derived from mostly positive early experiences, our role enactments will seem seamlessly concordant—they will be smoothly coordinated instead of being experienced as confusing, contradictory, and perpetually conflict-ridden. I can easily shift, as an example, from being a good-enough husband, to a good-enough father, to a good-enough son, sibling, friend, colleague, and so on. Unconscious relationship templates, containing role-expectations, are activated when we enact adult roles. With early positive identifications contained in my relationship template, I expect, when I interact with my wife in my husbandly role, that, together, we can solve almost any problem.

Our "expectations of others," continue Cabaniss and her colleagues (2013), "are based on [our] early templates" (p. 177). Unrealistic expectations of others and the resulting feelings of inevitable disappointments in others can be viewed as acting according to the script laid out in our early relationship templates. They are formed in an effort to compensate for the reliable responsiveness to our needs that we did *not* receive in our early childhood experiences with essential others. Early reliable responsiveness to our needs results in the building of relationship templates that contain realistic expectations of others. Fortified with such positive relational templates, we are less likely to experience feelings of pervasive alienation in our current relationships. These early positive templates, which we continue to carry into our adult years, will also contain realistic expectations of ourselves. Should these self-expectations be unrealistic—as when expecting, as children, to behave like adults—our relation to ourselves will thereafter be one of restlessness and disaffection.

Dialectically described, *mature relating* involves connecting without merging or without the loss of personal boundaries. Mature relating entails the achievement of a relative balance between secure attachment (close relatedness) and relaxed detachment (healthy individuation and separation).

"Mature object-relations," writes Loewald (1991), a psychoanalyst and former student of Heidegger, "are not characterized by sameness of relatedness but by an optimal range of relatedness and by the ability to relate to different objects according to their particular levels of maturity" (p. 27). Moreover, just as a properly loving parent draws out the *more* mature vision of the child—a "vision, informed by the parent's own experience and knowledge of growth and future … a more articulate and more integrated version of the core of being that the child presents to the parent" (p. 26), properly loving partners *reach out and release the more mature vision or version in each other.*

Bugental (1978) puts forth a "prescription" for "An Existential-humanistic Ideal for the Client-therapist Relationship" (p. 66). We can strive to approximate this ideal even in our everyday relationships. The important characteristics or qualities of such an "ideal relationship" are *mutuality, honesty, respect, dynamism* ("the relationship is continually evolving and changing"), *vitality*, and *trust* (66–71). Bugental further emphasizes two separate qualities that are essential in therapeutic relationships and beyond: *presence* and *authenticity.*

"Presence is being there in body, in emotions, in relating, in thoughts, in every way" (p. 37). Further, Bugental (1978) identifies "two chief aspects" that belong to the quality of presence: *accessibility* and *expressiveness.*

> *Accessibility* comes about from one's having the intention to allow what happens in a situation to matter, to have an affect on one. It involves a reduction of the usual social defenses against being influenced or affected by others. It implies a measure of trust and vulnerability.
>
> *Expressiveness* arises from the intent to let oneself be known by the other in a situation, to make available some of the contents of one's subjective awareness without distortion or disguise. It implies a measure of commitment and a willingness to put forth some effort. (p. 37)

"Presence, accessibility, and expressiveness" adds Bugental, "are all continua – that is, they are all matters of degree" (p. 37). He equates *authenticity* with "genuineness" and "realness." Moreover, authenticity is inseparable from "being as wholly and as nakedly present as possible" (p. 104). Underlying authenticity and presence is the implicit mutual knowing that, extrapolated to everyday life, "I am on your side" and "You are on my side."

Being-with, a Heideggerian descriptor of human existence, Deurzen and Kenward (2005) remind us, is "more than the traditional synonym for presence" because it is "also concerned with absence" (p. 160). *Absence* "illuminates Being" (p. 161). Similarly, *authenticity*, another Heideggerian descriptor of human existence, is more and other than a synonym for congruence, genuineness, and realness. Moreover, authenticity (an owned way of living; owning one's possibilities) and inauthenticity (an unowned way of living; not owning one's possibilities) are complementary and equally important. In a state of inauthenticity, one may "fall into following the behaviour and thoughts of the **They**, or to absorb oneself in one's role and to neglect oneself, to have less **care** of oneself [and consequently of others] … [and alternatively to experience] **indifference**, being neither authentic nor inauthentic" (p. 11). Just like authenticity, inauthenticity belongs to our essential nature as human beings. What is critical is the movement toward achieving an optimal (balanced) ratio between being authentic and being inauthentic.

Iacovou and Weixel-Dixon (2015) encourage us to recognize "the freedom, choice and responsibility" we have within our relationships (p. 204).

> In order to achieve intimacy with others, we need to abandon the 'twin pitfalls of bad faith' … —an overemphasis on facticity (a conviction we can't control anything in our relationships) and an overemphasis on freedom (a conviction we can control everything in our relationships)—and be truly open to the 'otherness' of our partner. (p. 204)

Iacovou and Weixel-Dixon acknowledge "the inevitability of conflict in relationships" (p. 205). In the face of relational conflict, we are challenged to pursue mutual understanding "through the development of shared meaning and purpose in the relationship or, in some occasions, through an appreciation that shared meaning is not possible" (p. 205). As Fuller (1990) frames it, loving relations entail "reaching and releasing the being possible of the loved one" (p. 153).

References

Bugental, J. F. T. (1978). *Psychotherapy and process: The fundamentals of an existential-humanistic approach*. McGraw-Hill.

Cabaniss, D. L., Cherry, S., Douglas, C. J., Graver, R. L., & Schwartz, A. R. (2013). *Psychodynamic formulation*. Wiley.

Deurzen, E. V., & Kenward, R. (2005). *Dictionary of existential psychotherapy and counselling*. Sage.

Fuller, A. R. (1990). *Insight into value: An exploration of the premises of a phenomenological psychology*. State University of New York Press.

Hoare, C. H. (2002). *Erikson on development and adulthood: New insights from the unpublished papers*. Oxford University Press.
Holmes, J. (2010). *Exploring in security: Towards an attachment-informed psychoanalytic psychotherapy*. Routledge.
Iacovou, S., & Weixel-Dixon, K. (2015). *Existential therapy: 100 Key point and techniques*. Routledge.
Loewald, H. W. (1991). On the therapeutic action of psychoanalysis. In G. I. Fogel (Ed.), *The work of Hans Loewald: An introduction and a commentary*. Jason Aronson.

25

Repairing: The Capacity for *Repairing* Relational Ruptures

Based on his rigorous observations of parent-infant interactions, Stern (2004) came upon the conviction that the process of rupture – experiencing derailments, misattunements, missteps, and misunderstandings – and repair was of the essence of parent-infant *and* adult-adult dyadic interactions. Here is Stern in his own words:

> My observations of parents and infants have made me familiar with this process of constant derailing and repairing in dyadic interactions. There are many "missteps" every minute in the best of interactions, and the majority of them are quickly repaired by one or both partners. For certain stretches of interaction, rupture and repair constitute the main activity of mother and baby… missteps are most valuable because the manner of negotiating repairs, and correcting slippages, is one of the more important ways-of-being-with-the-other that become implicitly known. (p. 157)

Stern (2004) states, "life between people is directly lived at a relatively small scale: a sentence, a pause, a facial expression, a gesture, a feeling, a thought" (p. 149). Our relational dynamics has the potential to "move along" or move forward in real time – in the here-and-now of the present moment. Otherwise, it becomes repetitious and stagnant. The present simply repeats the past. Moving along, however, is not a clean, linear process. Plainly put, our relational dynamics is messy and sloppy. Moving along is a "loosely directed process of searching for and finding a path to take, of losing the way and then finding it (or a new one) again, and of choosing goals to orient to – goals that are often discovered only as you go along" (p. 150). "Moving along," Stern continues, "is driven forward, in large part, by the need to establish

© The Author(s), under exclusive license to Springer Nature Switzerland AG 2021

M. J. Hannush, *Markers of Psychosocial Maturation*,
https://doi.org/10.1007/978-3-030-74315-4_25

intersubjective contact" (p. 151). We sound each other in order to find if we are on the same relational wavelength. Mostly unaware, we test each other to find out where our relationship stands and where it is going. We share our experiences in order to be known and to know, in order to increase the overlapping parts of our relational circles, in order to enlarge our joint intersubjective field. Out of this emerges a "new way-of-being-with" our therapeutic other. This all becomes a part of our "implicit relational knowing." Of course, it can also become "consciously, verbally understandable" (p. 152). Lastly, we seek the Other in order to "define and redefine one's self using the reflection of the self from the other's eyes. One's own identity is reformed or consolidated in this process" (p. 152).

Whenever two minds meet in an effort to "cocreate and share similar worlds," says Stern (2004), sloppiness will inevitably result. Their interaction, as they engage in "relational moves," will be characterized by a "'hit-miss-repair-elaborate' fashion" (p. 156). Their lived present moment will be characterized by spontaneity and unpredictability as their interactive relational moves unfold. They will experience "many mismatches, derailments, misunderstandings, and indeterminacy. These 'mistakes' require a process of repair" (p. 157). To emphasize, "the manner of negotiating repairs, and correcting slippages, is one of the more important ways-of-being-with-the-other" (p. 157). The "essential catalyst" for mature negotiations, says Fiumara (2013), is kindness. Negotiations follow conflicts, from which further conflicts may arise. These additional conflicts may in turn be followed by further negotiations. Fiumara cautions, "failure [to repair-and-resolve conflicts] is often due to the absence of a metabolite – kindness" (p. 30).

Stern (2004) concludes, in the last page of his final chapter, "Therapeutic Change: A Summary," with the following:

> It is the doing-together that enriches experience and brings about change in ways-of-being-with-others through implicit processes … Here the implicit doing-together and altered implicit [relational] knowing frames the flow of explicit understanding and locks it home. (p. 227)

> Implicit relational knowing is [defined as] the domain of knowledge and representation that is nonverbal, nonsymbolized, unnarrated, and nonconscious. It consists of motor procedures, affect patterns, expectations, and even patterns of thinking … it is not unconscious in the sense of repressed. Rather, it has never, as yet, needed to be put into words and may never need to be. It is nonconscious in the sense of never becoming reflectively conscious. The vast majority of all we "know" about how to be with others (including transference) resides in implicit relational knowing. (p. 242)

"But to live a life, to come alive," says Bollas (2011), "a person must be able to use objects in a way that assumes that such objects survive hate and do not require undue reparative work" (p. 39). The attempted reparative and potentially transformative action follows the awareness that one's aggressiveness against loved ones has damaged them and that one needs and wants to redress the damage. Akhtar (2009) cautions, however, that there are three types of reparation: (1) manic reparation, (2) obsessional reparation, and (3) creative reparation (p. 245). The first two modes of reparation, which can easily be fused together as forms of pseudo-reparation, are unhealthy and non-transformative, for they may either be due to excessive and maladaptive guilt that is out of proportion to the reality of the injury or woundedness perpetrated upon the Other *or* they may be a consequence of a magical thinking aiming at undoing a not so easily forgivable cruelty toward the Other. Only the third mode, creative reparation, motivated by genuine concern and adaptive guilt, is likely to constructively restore the lost relational balance or equilibrium.

Akhtar (2009) provides a definition of *atonement* as "an act of reparation that is preceded by, and is accomplished through 'identification with the aggressed' or an unconscious joining with the victim in his suffering. It is through such empathic and pained 'at-one-ment' that the damaged object is repaired and forgiveness elicited from it" (p. 28).

Loewald (2000) emphasizes the importance of assuming responsibility for the harm we cause others, beginning with those who gave us life. This he calls an act of "atonement." Some destructiveness is inevitable as developing persons struggle for emancipation and individuation. Atonement is restitution for such oedipal and post-oedipal conflicts, conflicts between the generations. Through atonement induced by healthy guilt and proper mourning, a *mature conscience* is born, which in turn makes *mature relatedness* possible. To *atone*, Loewald reminds us, is literally to become *at one*, to bring about relational reconciliation, concordance, and harmony. All this can only unfold in a relational context characterized by love, understanding, and patience. From mature models, such as our properly loving parents, we take in (identify with and internalize) their best values as we continue the process of separating while enjoying our loving reunions.

May (1958), who has referred to his work as a *psycho-ontology*, describes three forms of ontological guilt. Ontological guilt is triggered when we (1) remain blind to our dependence on the natural world as we become more and more removed from nature; (2) deny or fail to live up to our potentialities, given that we will never completely fulfill them; and (3) fail to adequately perceive or interpret the needs of others, given that we will never be able to achieve total accuracy in our interpretation of their lifeworld meanings.

It is the third form of ontological or existential guilt that we will elaborate upon given our focus on *reparation of relational ruptures.* As finite humans, we can never be perfectly attuned to the needs of others. May (1958) writes, "this is not a question of moral failure … it is an inescapable result of the fact that each of us is a separate individuality and has no choice but to look at the world through [our] own eyes" (p. 54). The more we misperceive or misinterpret the needs of others, the more we violate their individual integrity, the more dismissive we are of their true identity. Because we are incapable of perfectly understanding and thus anticipating the needs of others, we frequently experience a sense of inadequacy in our relations with others. As a consequence, we experience an inescapable form of existential guilt. This condition is experienced by all of us to some degree. Still, the relative accuracy of our perception of the needs of others comes in degrees. Responding responsibly to our existential guilt, say through acts of atonement or reparation, modulates the degree to which we experience such guilt and paves the way for strengthening our capacity for attunement to the needs of others.

References

Akhtar, S. (2009). *Comprehensive dictionary of psychoanalysis.* Karnac.

Bollas, C. (2011). *The Christopher Bollas reader.* Routledge.

Fiumara, G. C. (2013). *Psychoanalysis and creativity in everyday life: Ordinary genius.* Routledge.

Loewald, H. W. (2000). The waning of the Oedipus complex. *The Journal of Psychotherapy Practice and Research, 9*(4), 239–249.

May, R. (1958). Contributions of existential psychotherapy. In R. May, E. Angel, & H. F. Ellenberger (Eds.), *Existence.* Basic Books.

Stern, D. N. (2004). *The present moment in psychotherapy and everyday life.* W. W. Norton.

Part IX

The Capacities for Irony, Joy, Love, and Work

26

Irony: The Capacity for Cultivating a Sense of *Irony*

"Mockery and self-mockery, irony [and self-irony], absurdity, and humor," says Lifton (1993), "enable the protean [fluid or flexible] self to 'lubricate' experiences and to express the absence of 'fit' between the way the world presents itself and the way one actually feels about it" (pp. 5–6). And again, "the protean self lives in a realm of absurdity, embraces a tone of mockery and self-mockery along with a spirit of irony and often bathes its projects with humor" (p. 94). Through the cultivation of a sense of absurdity, mockery and self-mockery, and irony and self-irony, elaborates Lifton, we make moves toward the assertion of our authentic feelings. "Irony," he elucidates, "implies an exposure of the discrepancy between intended and actual meaning, along with a separate stance of the self making the judgment" (p. 94). Irony tends to be accompanied by humor. Through irony, I am able to experience discordance "pleasurably with the self affirmed in its rejection of an assumed reality" (p. 94). Irony, along with playfulness and humor, are "a source of vitality." They provide us with a sense of perspective that in turn enables us to "integrate the varied components of … [our] sense of self" (p. 96).

"Irony then," states Melucci (1996), "can become a positive process and weds itself with benevolence, an ability to tolerate our own weaknesses and those of others" (p. 138). "Or," maintains Melucci, "we learn to use it to establish our boundaries, to defend them when they come under attack from others, to settle our scores straightforwardly without resorting to more indirect and covert means" (p. 138).

We "generally find something ironic," says D. W. Black (1997), "because it thwarts an anticipated experience, because we perceive within it a collision of opposites, and because the juxtaposition of these opposites conveys insight

© The Author(s), under exclusive license to Springer Nature Switzerland AG 2021

M. J. Hannush, *Markers of Psychosocial Maturation*,
https://doi.org/10.1007/978-3-030-74315-4_26

through its ambiguous imagery" (p. 103). Ironic truth, he tells us, is "topsy-turvy truth … that … yields … a new standpoint for coping with the unexpected developments of life" (pp. 104–105). Irony involves "felicitous reversals of fate." The life of Giambattista Vico, an Italian philosopher-rhetorician of the Age of Enlightenment, "reveals [ironic] truth" (p. 105). The most important events in Vico's life unfold not through planning or deliberate intending, but "by the flip-flop movement of fate … Vico's topsy-turvy world embodies the Dickensian trope: the worst of times can indeed become the best of times" (p. 105). For example, Vico credits his free-floating inventive thinking to the fact that it was "his *good fortune* in having [had] no teacher whose words he had sworn by … [consequently] he followed the main course of his studies untroubled by sectarian prejudice" (p. 105).

> However, perhaps the most well-known and important twist of fate upon which Vico built his good fortune was the traumatic childhood fall … He writes that 'as a result of this mischance he grew up with a melancholy and irritable temperament such as belongs to men of ingenuity and depth …' This represents the deepest and most extensive effect of providential irony. (pp. 105–106)

Thus, the ironist learns to see *new and positive meanings* in the felicitous twists of her or his fate. She or he learns to read the *ironic signs* of her or his unfolding life narrative. Ironists "possess the capacity for *double-mindedness* that allows them to review the bilateral meaning of [their developmental] history" (p. 107). They "recognize the double meaning of their own activity" (p. 108).

"Irony," elaborates Black (1997):

> is thus a gift from providence … irony helps [us] … comprehend the movement of providence … it provides insight into … [our] conscience … Irony can help each of us look for the 'occasions of fortune' that give us insight into the scheme of things. It can help the discursive mind re-energize itself … the ironic attitude actually gives our hardened consciousness 'a new lease of life.' The ironic attitude adjusts our basic and usual disposition … It offers a conscientious perspective. (p. 108)

Ironic laughter, explains Black (1997), constitutes "the highest reaches of laughter" (p. 109). "We laugh ironically when we find an opposition that we are at home with, an opposition that we can hold in an imagined contiguity … When we laugh, incongruity becomes not a problem but a meaningful relation" (pp. 108–109). Ironic contentment, for instance, involves "a sense of contented discord." "Even the etymology of the word *irony* – derived from the term *eiron*, which means *dissembler* – can be misleading … [A truer meaning] is in the semblance of dissemblance" (p. 104).

Through irony, continues Black (1997), humorous or otherwise, we gain a *relative distance and a detached perspective*. Irony readies us for *living a conscientious life*. It contributes to the cultivation of a *mature conscience*. We can find "narrative analogies for conscience in irony, contiguity, rhythm, and place" (p. 143). Even moral concepts need to be placed in their "rhythmic place." Conscience is not only "a place-bound memory of moral purpose," but also a rhetoric-bound dialogue with self or other in the present which is "central not only to the genesis but to the subsequent care of conscience" (pp. 171–172). Though born of playful consciousness or unconsciousness, ironizing requires imaginative discipline.

Ultimately, Black (1997) sees irony and dialectics as belonging to mutually exclusive domains of existence. "The difference is best expressed by distinguishing a consciousness of *contiguity* from a consciousness of *reconciliation*" (p. 183). Whereas irony employs *moderation*, dialectics makes use of *mediation*. For instance, in the realm of affect, "moderation … directs its activity toward a regulating emotion … moderation manufactures a commonplace … moderation fine tunes the emotions. In a moderate disposition, the emotions blend to form a suitably human place" (p. 183). *Mediation* "aims at a concept … mediation effects a categorical synthesis … Mediation … fashions a consistent account of moral [or affective] experience, a description that will hold true in any number of places" (p. 183). A moderate disposition helps us see things comprehensively – as a continuous, and not unified pattern, a perception that places us in a harmonious order. "Unity [which is the aim of a dialectical (mediation-seeking) disposition] means to *make one*. Continuity [which is the aim of an ironic (moderation-seeking) disposition] means to *hold together*" (p. 183). Individuals with an ironical-and-rhetorical disposition "possess a sensitivity to contiguity, rhythm, and moderation; they are able to think outside the bounds of dialectic" (p. 184). Mediators impress us with the "technical" expertise; moderators inspire us.

To illustrate Black (1997) offers the reader the example of the Aristotelian "courageous soldier":

> Aristotle's courageous soldier does not discover the virtuous mean by generating logically mediate unification of cowardice and rashness. A courageous consciousness does not employ dialectic … Courage is not a reconciliation of rashness and cowardice. Aristotelian courage arises when one holds together in a

> moderate disposition the feelings of too much and too little fear, when one holds two polar emotions in a meaningful contiguity. The emotions are held together without denying the conscientious force of either emotion. The Aristotelian mean approximates a balancing act. The virtuous [wise or mature] mind attends to two things at once. (p. 184)

In our view, in contrast to Black's sharp distinction between the ironic orientation and the dialectical orientation, ironic consciousness is made possible by our dialectical consciousness. Our dialectical orientation, in its broadest sense, is a back-and-forth movement of the mind that aims at *both* mediation *and* moderation. In our dialectical model, a "courageous consciousness" *does* employ dialectic, but not the kind of narrow dialectic that Black has in mind. The tension that the courageous soldier must resolve, relatively speaking, is not between "rashness" and "cowardice," but rather between boldness and fear. Rashness is simply reckless boldness (the taking of excessive or irrational risk). Cowardice is simply excessive or unrealistic fear. Consequently, in our model, through "mediated moderation," the courageous soldier is able to find a precarious balance between rational boldness and realistic fear. He or she is able to maneuver both ends of the continuum. He or she is able to mediate-and-moderate, unify-and-hold-together his or her bold self (identity) and fearful self (identity). He or she is able to identify with the mediated-and-moderated versions of both polar identities. Yet, he or she is able to simultaneously dis-identify with the exaggerated versions of both polar ends – the recklessly bold self and the excessively fearful self. Yes, *I am both* realistically fearful *and* discerningly bold. No, *I am* not frozen by my irrational fear, *and* No, *I am* not on the verge of acting rashly on reckless impulse. My dialectically inspired ironic orientation allows me to transform my potential character weaknesses into strengths, my liabilities into assets. Of course, endowed with a diffused, compartmentalized, fragmented, and splintered identity, I can find myself transforming my potential character assets or strengths into character weaknesses or liabilities. Think of the individual gifted with exceptional intelligence that is put in the uncreative service of self-destructiveness or the destructive exploitation of others.

Mota-Strasser (2005) describes how Socrates embodied the ironic orientation in his everyday philosophizing: "The ability to use humor about a very serious subject was one of the ways in which Socrates used irony … He frequently said one thing and meant its opposite" (p. 101). Here is an example of an ironic humor: "Don't take life too seriously; it's only a temporary situation!" Socrates, I surmise, would have reacted with an ironic smile. In "Socratic irony," say Deurzen and Kenward (2005), "the philosopher affects ignorance in order to draw out knowledge" (p. 106). Socrates has purportedly said, "All I know is that I know nothing," to which, Sextus Empiricus, the Roman philosopher in the second century, CE, added, "And I am not sure about that!" Becoming mature involves, in part, adopting the ironic attitude of perpetually acknowledging our not-knowing while pursuing self-and-relational knowledge.

References

Black, D. W. (1997). *Vico and moral perception*. Peter Lang.

Deurzen, E. V., & Kenward, R. (2005). *Dictionary of existential psychotherapy and counselling*. Sage.

Lifton, R. J. (1993). *The protean self: Human resilience in an age of fragmentation*. The University of Chicago Press.

Melucci, A. (1996). *The playing self: Person and meaning in the planetary society*. Cambridge University Press.

Mota-Strasser, L. (2005). Dialogue and communication. In E. V. Deurzen & C. Arnold-Baker (Eds.), *Existential perspectives on human issues: A handbook for therapeutic practice*. Palgrave Macmillan.

27

Joy: The Capacity for *Joy* and En*joy*ment as Manifested in Humor, Laughter, and Playfulness

Where there is humor, laughter, and playfulness, there is enjoyment and joy. A psychologically healthy "life," states Gay (2001), "should move from joy to mourning, and back to joy" (p. 211). The presence of joy in our lives is a manifestation of psychological maturation and well-being. The absence of joy reflects the state of our arrested development and neurosis. Gay's basic thesis is this:

> The absence of joy, I suggest, evokes in children a lifelong quest for repair and restitution. Because they are children, they believe that only a concrete, actual thing, like money or sexual victories or self-inflicted pain, can replace this lost object [an unavailable essential Other] … neurosis is primarily the *absence* of joy. (p. x)

And what is the primal source of joy? The answer Gay (2001) provides is startlingly simple, conceptually, but exceedingly challenging in practice: "mutual regulation." Joy "occurs when a child enjoys the grace of 'mutual regulation'" (p. 184). He extracts this concept from Erikson's "master theory of ego development." Gay (2001) elaborates, while quoting Erikson himself:

> Erikson notes that the nursing pair of happy mother and happy nursing infant, for example, is paradigmatic of benign human relationships because neither party dominates. Both regulate the other's body, self-state, and form a social 'pair.' … [They are both involved, as Erikson puts it, in a] 'world of participation, shared with a minimum of defensive maneuvers and a maximum of mutual activation. Mutual activation is the crux of the matter… the person actuates

© The Author(s), under exclusive license to Springer Nature Switzerland AG 2021
M. J. Hannush, *Markers of Psychosocial Maturation*,
https://doi.org/10.1007/978-3-030-74315-4_27

> others even as he is actuated… the person is 'inspired with active properties,' as he so inspires others. This is ego actuality; largely preconscious and unconscious.' (p. 185)

The meaning of *joy* needs to be broadened. We need to stretch our understanding of what it means to be joyful in this difficult-and-delightful life. We can think of gradations of joy or experiences that share a family resemblance to joy. The "opposite of depression," says Merkin (2017), "is not a state of unimaginable happiness but a state of approximate contentment, of relative all-right-ness. Perhaps depressives expect too much of life when they're *not* feeling depressed, have too exalted an idea of what the standard is" (p. 283). There is something deeply satisfying and subtly pleasurable in feeling "a state of approximate contentment" or "relative all-right-ness." To reiterate Gay's (2001) words, a healthy life is a movement "from joy to mourning, and back to joy" (p. 211). This means that the capacity for joy goes hand-in-hand with the capacity for mourning, for coming to terms with the inevitable losses of life.

Moving to tragicomic attunement and humor, Marcus (2013a) comments that:

> tragicomic attunement and skillfulness—the ability to discern the comic in the tragic and the tragic in the comic—can be very helpful, if not life-saving, defence against those 'extreme situations'… in which one is hurled into an experience where one is inundated with death anxiety and other crippling affects. (pp. 88–89)

"Thus, in psychoanalytic terms," continues Marcus, "tragicomic humour at its best can be conceptualized as a triumphant re-affirmation of one's 'healthy' narcissism through an adaptive ego-regression" (p. 90). I would quickly add that it is "an adaptive ego-regression" that is in the service of adaptive, creative, and healing *ego-progression*. Through tragicomic humor we are enabled to endure our life's pain, while at the same time partaking of the "pleasure in the amusing moment" (p. 95). Such humor can be "deeply moral" in that it can embody our "dearly held values and beliefs, those inner convictions that" help us maintain our sense of agency, our feeling of solidity, and our human integrity (p. 100).

Tragicomic creativity, says Marcus (2013a), makes it possible for us to "rediscover and restore" our true strengths and talents. It empowers us to actualize our potentials, "to facilitate what is not yet in consciousness" (p. 107). Like great art, tragicomic creativity "reconfigures relations, … opens up new horizons, contexts, and worlds by creating and evoking different sensations. In other words, … [it] has the capacity to change our very relationship to the world, 'to transform and re-create the very potentiality of life'" (p. 108). It changes our "narrative of self identity," which is constituted by a "cluster of affects, percepts, and experienced embodiment" (p. 108). To think creatively is to "think otherwise." It is to create novel and original food for thought that opens up "new possibilities for inventively living" (p. 108). The "application of tragicomic creativity is a way of living life as a 'work of art'" (p. 108). Our tragicomic attunement and skillfulness or creativity shift "the ground of our way of thinking, feelings, and acting" (p. 108). It strengthens our integrative power and thus our sense of agency. It allows us to produce "a new world of meanings that express and affirm the humanising valuative attachments of Beauty, Truth, and Goodness" (p. 108). Our emotional truth can be manifested in the kind of enhanced self-understanding that enables us to maintain our core self, our "authentic self-identity" without being corrupted or destroyed by our everyday ordeals. Goodness is aroused by the deep consolation that we derive from creative tragicomic humor and by the deep compassion for and sense of solidarity with our fellow sufferers.

Tragicomic creativity, concludes Marcus (2013a), is "a vital aspect of the art of living the 'good life'" (p. 109). It keeps us powerfully and productively in touch with the "values that we most dearly hold and cherish" (p. 109). It re-centers us, in that it allows us to return to our embodied center in the here-and-now. It lessens our inordinate centration on our past or future. Instead, especially in times of tragic suffering, it steers us away from our natural and habitual orientation toward the past (memories) and toward the future (projected plans). Instead, we live "solely within the here and now" of our "laughter, a merciful reprieve from [our] tears" (p. 109).

Just as our relational difficulties represent the dark side of life, playfulness, humor, and laughter are our sources of "de-light," the light side of life. They lighten our relational loads. They help us cope more effectively with our everyday relational hassles. More importantly, they intensify the closeness between us. Playfulness, humor, and laughter are corollaries of the capacity to love. Cultivating our capacities to be playful, to use humor, and to laugh together strengthen our attachment bonds. They stretch the depth and range of our ability to love. They enable us to love more deeply, widely, and wisely.

Through playfulness, humor, and laughter we can better manage our daily difficulties. If in the midst of heated argumentation or conflict with our partner we can still be playful with each other—we can still find a way to use humor and laugh together, then the chances increase that we will find creative solutions to our relational problems. Our capacity for playfulness becomes a marker for our relational maturity. When we are playful, we feel more relaxed, safe, and secure. When we use heart-felt humor and laugh *with* each other, we feel affirmed, validated, and revitalized. Our vital centers, and thus our true selves, are energized and enlivened.

At its best, humor humanizes us. At its purest, it makes us more moral. As Marcus (2013a) puts it, humor and ethics go hand-in-hand. We are more likely to treat each other well, when we laugh together. As we habitually share laughter, we become more "beautiful," "good," and "true" in each other's eyes. Humor has the potential to help us cultivate an aesthetic life. Humor assists us to live a life in which emotion and reason become integrated. Through humor we are enabled to affirm and say, "Yes" to life, even when we are surrounded by sadness. "Man," says Ricoeur (1986), "is the Joy of Yes in the sadness of the finite" (p. 140).

Heart-felt humor can heal us. It can deepen our love for each other. Humor gathers us together. When we make each other laugh, says Marcus (2013a), we make each other, at least temporarily, more fully ourselves—our relaxed, spontaneous selves. During these precious moments of joint or shared laughter, we feel present to each other in a special and immediate way. It is as if we have been touched by grace—a gift from a source larger than ourselves has been bestowed upon us.

The impulse toward playfulness, states Lemma (2000), precedes and pervades the capacities for humor and laughter. Relational playfulness comes before solitary playfulness. Humor is "a form of playing which originates in the earliest exchanges between mother and baby and which confers significant advantages to our adaptation" (p. 6).

From the beginning, the capacity for playfulness, of which humor is a subset and the products of which are laughter and the social smile, serves an adaptive value for the human infant. It is the baby's way of communicating with the primary caregiver. Just think of the powerful impact of a baby's smile or laughter on the parents. It invites an irresistible joyful response from them: a reciprocal smiling or laughing response. These wonderfully escalating reciprocal smiling and laughing responses build, on an inter-bodily level, positively affirming traces and anticipations of more joyful future moments of mutual validation and recognition.

Beginning with the first months of life, shared laughter between parent and child leads to play, and circular playfulness permeates the spiritedness of shared laughter. Playful laughter is not only a means of communication and adaptive survival, but also a vehicle for strengthening the attachment bond of love between parent and child. Similarly, playful laughter strengthens the loving attachment bond between adult partners.

Playfulness, laughter, and humor ease and enliven social interaction. Circularly, easy, and enlivened social interaction creates a climate that is conducive to playfulness, laughter, and humor. If we are lucky enough, we internalize this circular predisposition early on in our lives in our interactions with our parents, siblings, and other close familial and non-familial persons in our extended radius of relationships. Plainly put, we internalize the ability to enliven and be enlivened, to make others and to allow others to make us feel at ease and relaxed, and to make others smile and laugh while being receptive to smiling and laughing at the invitation of others.

We humans construct various barriers to defend ourselves against painful self-knowledge. Getting to know our selves requires an assumption of responsibility in relation to that which needs to be understood and the consequences of such knowledge. To cultivate refinement in our humanness entails a constant struggle with an acceptance of who we are, who we are not, and who we may or may never be. Many of our symptoms embody and symbolize that which has been disavowed and thus perpetuate our state of ignorance. Our symptoms encrypt a narrative about what we do not want to face up to, our *disowned lifeworld meanings.*

Through humor we can face the truth of our pain. We need to achieve a delicate balance between identifying and dis-identifying with our pain at some level so as to find it amusing. Over-identifying with our pain would plunge us in depression and in the constriction of our horizon of possibilities. Quickly detaching or dis-identifying ourselves from our pain or suffering and then projecting it onto (seeing it in) the Other and thereafter demonize her or him for that which we have disowned only perpetuate our ignorance, numbness, and potential for cruelty.

Because our unhealthy narcissism overrules our tolerance for criticism, the semblance of self-awareness quickly translates a narcissistic wound into defensive over-seriousness. Hence, we seldom laugh freely at our own shortcomings or absurdities as we do at other people's faulty slippages. This is one way of differentiating mature from immature humor, refined from crude and cruel laughter, and the "well-tempered" from the supercilious smile. We need to cultivate the capacity to stand back and be amused by our own shortcomings, rather than feel overpowered or persecuted by them. This can start in infancy, when the baby, with the help of the mother, learns to take pleasure in inadequacy. The baby's first laughs may be at his own expense, but they are to his benefit as the mother imparts the rudiments of the capacity to accept and even be amused by his limitations and faulty slippages as well as her own.

The ability to recognize our own shortcomings and the capacity for forgiveness are intimately related to our ability to adopt a humorous attitude toward our predicament. A mature sense of humor involves humility, a healthy narcissism, and a broadened view of the self. It requires an acceptance of one's own limitations and the 'givens' of existence without being unduly defensive or arrogant as a means of coping with our life predicaments. In mature humor we laugh at ourselves and *with* others. Mature humor conveys a willingness to share and be open about our vulnerabilities. It invites others to support us through laughing *with* us at what ostensibly concerns us. Mature humor manages skillfully to convey both self-effacement and self-worth. It fuses a feeling of significance with an awareness of insignificance. Mature humor can be viewed as a manifestation of an *existential posture* that embodies the acceptance of uncertainty. It views laughter as freedom's possibility to escape, even if temporarily, from its struggles with fatedness. It involves a freeing movement from monocular to *binocular vision* that allows us to "see" *multiple meanings* of our life's situations. The hallmarks of this existential stance entail the willingness to put oneself into question, to stand back, to look at things from an alternate perspective, and to be ready to be surprised with amusement and de*light*, as in the smile or laughter of recognition. *Playing with one's possibilities responsibly* constitutes the essence of the *existential posture. Playing with lived meanings in general and lived polar meanings in particular in existential space captures the heart of an existential-dialogical-dialectical disposition toward life. Playing with meanings' tensions not only requires endurance, but is also an exciting, exuberant, and ecstatic lifelong venture.* After all, the root of the verb "to exist" is derived from the Latin *existere*, which means to stand out or to come into being. There is a sense of playful excitement in the movement of lifeworld meanings coming into being.

Bollas (2011) traces the origin of our playfulness, humor, and laughter to our earliest interactions with our mothers. We are born with a readiness to smile and then to laugh. Our mothers, to varying degrees, stimulate us to smile and then to laugh. Thus, the circular dance of playfulness is put into motion very early in our lives. When we are infants, our mothers exaggerate their facial features and tone of voice to elicit our smiles and later our laughter. They make use of multiple age-appropriate "playful pushings" to make us smile and laugh.

Something needs to be said about Friedrich Nietzsche's (1961) ruminations on joy and laughter. We can find joy, Nietzsche instructs us, by accepting (loving) our fate, by embracing all of life as it is wholeheartedly. It involves Yes-saying to life, when we know that we will experience agony, pain, and suffering again and again. For Nietzsche, joy is also brought about by the acquisition of wisdom (truth). We cannot say that we have gained a truth if we cannot laugh about it. We cannot be open to discovering and appropriating emotional and relational truths if we are overly serious. "And when I beheld my devil," reflects Nietzsche, "I found him serious, thorough, profound, solemn; it was the Spirit of Gravity – through him all things are ruined" (p. 68). Moreover, "he who wants to become light and a bird must love himself" (p. 211). Like Zarathustra, Nietzsche's alter ego, we need to learn to laugh in the face of suffering. We need to learn to relax, and thus overcome, our *resistance* to the difficulties we encounter in our everyday lives. When something bad happens to us, we ask pleadingly, "Why me?" When something good happens to us we do not raise the very same question. "Joy," for Nietzsche, explains Kellenberger (1997), "is deeper than agony ... but ... joy includes the experience of agony" (p. 104). To summarize, "Zarathustra creates his joyfulness through the resolution of his will, and it is for this reason that Nietzsche can urge others to follow him with their own joyful acceptance through a like exercise of their own wills" (p. 104). Kellenberger points to a "dialectical tension between ... two modes of acceptance" (p. 95). It is between "weary acceptance" and "joyful acceptance," with Nietzsche (Zarathustra) *willing* the latter (pp. 95–96) rather than surrendering to the former. As alluring as this *resolute willing of joyful acceptance* may seem, it does not fare well from the perspective of our relational dialectical model. The embracing of joy needs to be balanced with a surrender to sorrow, a delicately balanced deep expressiveness that is to be *shared* with essential others, again and again. Just as there is a joyful *or* weary acceptance on one side of the dialectical pole, there also is reparative *or* weary (melancholic or depressive) surrender on the other side of the dialectical pole. A *singular will to joy* is unlikely to lead to an agony-absorbing joyful existence. We can only hope for being surprised by joy upon leading a relatively balanced *relational* life of joyful acceptance *and* reparative surrender.

Allow me to conclude this subsection with Critchley's (2002) musings on the ironic and sublime smile:

> For me, it is this smile – deriding the having and not having, the pleasure and the pain, the sublimity and suffering of the human situation – that is the essence of humor. This is the *risus purus*, the highest laugh, the laugh that laughs at the laugh, that laughs at that which is unhappy, the mirthless [ironic] laugh .... Yet, this smile does not bring unhappiness, but rather elevation and liberation, the lucidity of consolation. This is why, melancholy animals that we are, human beings are also the most cheerful. We smile and find ourselves ridiculous. Our wretchedness is our greatness. (p. 111)

Through ironic and "finely tempered" smiling—the phosphorous light of the worlding bodily self, which procures for us some dignified distance from our immediate predicament—we are able to achieve a precarious balance between our lived polar meanings of existence, such as potency and impotence, authenticity and inauthenticity, being and having, the physical and the metaphysical, the sacred and the profane, pleasure and pain. Such an ironic smile transforms our self-world understanding. Our capacity to smile amusedly at our ridiculousness is made possible by our *caring conscience*. It is the expression of "the child that has become the parent: wiser and wittier, if slightly wizened" (p. 103), a conscience which has become one's "amigo."

References

Bollas, C. (2011). *The Christopher Bollas reader*. Routledge.

Critchley, S. (2002). *On humor*. Routledge.

Gay, V. P. (2001). *Joy and the objects of psychoanalysis: Literature, belief, and neurosis*. State University of New York Press.

Kellenberger, J. (1997). *Kierkegaard and Nietzsche: Faith and eternal acceptance*. St. Martin's Press.

Lemma, A. (2000). *Humour on the couch: Exploring humour in psychotherapy and everyday life*. Whurr.

Marcus, P. (2013a). *How to laugh your way through life: A psychoanalyst's advice*. Karnac.

Merkin, D. (2017). *This close to happy: A reckoning with depression*. Farrar, Straus and Giroux.

Nietzsche, F. (1961). *Thus spoke Zarathustra* (R. J. Hollingdale, Trans.). Penguin.

Ricoeur, P. (1986). *Fallible man*. Fordham University Press.

28

Love: The Capacity to *Love* and Be *Love*able

"Love," says Fromm (1956), is "the crowning achievement of maturity" (p. 82). "Beyond the element of giving," asserts Fromm, "the active character of love becomes evident in the fact that it always implies certain basic elements, common to all forms of love. These are *care, responsibility, respect* and *knowledge*" (p. 24). To *care* is to be concerned about the welfare of the other. It includes the willingness to take care of the other. To *respect* the other is to treat the other as an equal, as another "I," to accept the other as she or he is, and to refrain from attempting to change him or her. *Responsibility* entails a willingness and ability to respond to the needs of the other. *Knowledge* has to do with knowing the other from the inside out. It means being able to see the other from his or her own point of view. Although Fromm incorporates "concern" into the care element in love, I prefer the autonomous meaning that Nicholsen (2002) gives it: "Concern is the effort to make oneself worthy of what one loves. It is expressed in working to know and appreciate the beloved and to preserve its value" (p. 46). For Fromm (1956) "mature love is *union under the condition of preserving one's integrity*, one's individuality. … In [mature] love the paradox occurs that two beings become one and yet remain two" (p. 19).

In a later work, Fromm (1981) repeats the definition of love as a "union with somebody, or something outside oneself *under the condition of retaining the separateness and integrity of one's own self*" (p. 3). Love, therefore, resolves the dialectical tension between the need for connectedness (closeness or intimacy) and the need for separateness (autonomy or independence). Mature love maintains and enhances one's *integrity* through *integrating* two seemingly oppositional needs. What Fromm does not make explicit is that the cultivation of the capacity to *integrate* the seemingly bipolar needs for connectedness

© The Author(s), under exclusive license to Springer Nature Switzerland AG 2021

M. J. Hannush, *Markers of Psychosocial Maturation*,
https://doi.org/10.1007/978-3-030-74315-4_28

(closeness; secure attachment) and separateness (autonomy; differentiation; individuation) is made possible by the nurturance and nourishment of these needs on both sides of the polar continuum very early in life. As children, and as adults, we all need to have both basic needs for secure attachment *and* autonomy accepted and adequately met.

Fromm's definition of love is very close to that of Erikson (1963) who views love as a basic strength of young adulthood that emerges as a result of the resolution of the crisis of intimacy versus isolation. However, for Erikson, the capacity to resolve this crisis is contingent upon the resolution of the previous crises of trust versus mistrust of infancy, autonomy versus doubt and shame of early childhood, initiative versus guilt of play age, industriousness versus inferiority of school age, and identity achievement versus identity confusion of adolescence with the respectively resultant basic strengths of hope, will, purpose, competence, and fidelity. Interestingly, the basic strength of care, according to Erikson, follows developmentally, in adulthood, the basic strength of love and is the outcome of resolving the crisis of generativity (the ability to creatively "generate" ideas, products, relationships, and future generations) versus stagnation. As we have described earlier, for Fromm the capacity to care is an essential ingredient of the ability to love. For Rollo May, there is a circular relationship between love and care.

M. W. Martin (1996), like Fromm, includes *caring* and *respect* (self/mutual) as two of the elements of love and adds *fidelity* (faithfulness/commitment), fairness (equality/shared autonomy), honesty, intimacy, wisdom, courage, gratitude, obligation, joy, appreciation, and wonder. Recall that Erikson posits the virtue of *fidelity* as a requisite for the virtue of love, but the virtue of wisdom, that is the outcome of the resolution of the crisis of integrity versus despair, belongs developmentally to old age, the last stage of the life cycle.

Keen (1997), like Fromm, includes care, under which he subsumes *responsible* action, and knowledge as two (three in two, really) of the elements of love and adds attention (noticing and focusing), desire (erotic attraction), sensuality (physical touching), empathy (loving imagination), compassion (sympathetic suffering), enjoyment (sympathetic pleasure), storytelling (loving narrative), repenting (forgiving and renewal), self-love (solitary communion), commitment (willing to love), co-creation (fertility and fruition), adoration (wondering love), sexuality (carnal love), and enchantment (renewal in the face of disillusionment).

Kernberg (2012) delineates several essential dimensions that he subsumes under "the capacity to love." These are: interest in the life project of the other, basic trust, capacity for authentic forgiveness, humility and gratitude, a common ego ideal as a joint life project – that is, a dedication to the love relationship itself as a joint life project – mature dependency, permanence of sexual passion, acceptance of loss, jealousy, and boundary protection, and, lastly mentioned is, a capacity to mourn, which is potentially an enhancer of the capacity to love.

In *Becoming Good Parents* (Hannush, 2002), I delineate ten elements as ingredients of love: *attention* (attuned presence which requires care, disciplined effort, embodied mindfulness, openness to experience, the relative overcoming of our unhealthy narcissistic tendencies, the affirmation of the differentness and uniqueness of the other, and the willingness to share enjoyable mutual objects of attention), *imagination* (imagination-based relational creativity, empathy, sympathy, and perspective-taking; the ability to "see" and hold onto what is beautiful, good, and true in oneself-and-in-the-loved--other), *compassionate detachment* (sympathetic distancing or unsentimental contemplation which requires courteousness, endurance, patience, perseverance, self-control, and tolerance – all in balance with "passionate attachment"), *humility* (which requires having a realistic perspective on one's own strengths and limitations while recognizing and respecting the independent reality of the Other), *unselfishness* (which involves placing the self in its modest or proper perspective and the absence of defensive self-inflation), *fairness* (which refers to being egalitarian, just, and fair-minded and which involves treating the Other as one would like to be treated, protecting the rights of the Other, while assuming an assertive stance when one's own rights have been infringed upon), *truthfulness* (which refers to being honest, tolerating emotional and relational truths, and the pursuit of accurate knowledge about oneself, the Other, and one's relationship to the Other, while acknowledging the ultimate personal truth has to do with becoming a good person and that the ultimate relational truth has to do with loving-and-being-loved; seeking the resolution and synthesis of the seeming opposites with which we identify), *cheerfulness* (which includes having a sense of playfulness and humor and having a sunny disposition or good-spiritedness; it also involves the proclivity to be amused, especially by that which is contradictory, ironic, and paradoxical), *courage* (resoluteness, resilience, and steadfastness), and *wisdom* (discerning judgment and reverence for, learning about, and abiding by relational knowledge or truth; understanding and living by love's qualities or virtues).

Love as Acceptance (Loving Is Accepting of Self-and-Other)

The optimal relational climate for maturation and growth, asserts Rogers (1989), is constituted by *acceptance*, *congruence*, and *empathy*. Although, for Rogers, these necessary and sufficient conditions for change and growth are intertwined, in this subsection I will focus, as much as possible, on acceptance as a manifestation of love. Children's maturational growth is facilitated when they are unconditionally accepted or positively regarded by their parents. In such an accepting home atmosphere, children feel safe to explore their inner and outer worlds. Above all, children who are unconditionally accepted develop a deep sense of unconditional self-acceptance. Self-acceptance and *self-love* are interchangeable. Self-acceptance (self-love) and acceptance of others (love of others) go together. Here is Rogers (1951) linking self-acceptance to acceptance of others: "*When the individual perceives and accepts into one consistent and integrated system all his sensory and visceral experiences, then he is necessarily more understanding of others and is more accepting of others as separate individuals*" (p. 520). A person needs "to accept the locus of evaluation as residing within himself" (p. 151). Moreover, "acceptance," adds Rogers, "is an emotional phenomenon, not an intellectual one" (p. 165). This kind of self-acceptance not only makes the acceptance of others possible but enables us to love the Other:

> It seems to me that we can love a person only to the extent that we are not threatened by him; we can love him only if his reactions to us, or to those things which affect us, are understandable [and thus acceptable] to us and are clearly related to those basic motivations within us all which tend to bring us closer to compatible and meaningful relationships with other people and with the world. (p. 161)

Acceptance of the self means that the person tends

> to perceive himself as a person of worth, worthy of respect …; to perceive his standards as being based upon his own experiences …; to perceive his own feelings, motives, social and personal experiences without distortions of the sensory data; to be comfortable in acting in terms of these perceptions. (pp. 138–139)

Acceptance, says Rogers (Rogers and Freiberg, 1994), is a requisite attitude for becoming "successful at facilitating learning" and for change, growth, and maturation. He continues,

> I think of it as *prizing* the learner – prizing her feelings, her opinions, her person. It is caring for the learner, but nonpossessive caring. It is an acceptance of this other individual as a separate person who has worth in her own right. It is a basic trust – a belief that this other person is somehow fundamentally trustworthy. Whether we call it prizing, acceptance, trust, or some other term, it shows up in a variety of observable ways. … What we are describing is a prizing of the learner as an imperfect human being with many feelings, many potentialities. The facilitator's prizing or acceptance of the learner is an operational expression of her essential confidence and trust in the capacity of the human organism. (p. 156)

So far Rogers uses the term *acceptance* to mean "nonpossessive caring," "prizing," and "trusting." Earlier, "love" is directly linked to "understanding" and indirectly to "acceptance." In another context, cited by Barrett-Lennard (1998), Rogers fuses warmth and acceptance into "warmth of acceptance" (p. 11). But it is in *A Way of Being* that Rogers (1980) links *acceptance* not only to admiration, appreciation, caring, liking, prizing, tenderness, and warmth, but also to *love*. In a seemingly autobiographical style, Rogers writes: "I shall share with you some of the things I have learned for myself in regard to [growth-enhancing] communication [a communicative encounter or a meeting moment]. These are personal learnings growing out of my own experience" (p. 6). He adds: "perhaps you can check what I say against your experience and decide as to its truth or falsity for you" (pp. 6–7). The first learning has to do with *hearing* (understanding) and *being heard* (understood) *empathically*. The second learning is about being *real* (congruent or genuine). "I can be real," he explains, "when I can be close to whatever it is that is going on within me" (p. 14). It means to "get close to what I really am and feel and think" (p. 16). It also means "to permit another person to be his own realness and to be separate from me" (p. 18). It is allowing the Other to be/come "a separate person with ideas, purposes, and values which may not be identical with my own" (p. 18). It is to be understood that for Rogers all these personal learnings are interrelated. The third and last learning involves *acceptance*. Rogers then provides us with a most moving personalized description of *acceptance as a form of love*:

> I want to move on to another area of my learning in interpersonal relationships – one that has been slow and painful for me.
>
> I feel warmed and fulfilled when I can let in the fact, or permit myself to feel, that someone cares for, accepts, admires, or prizes me. Because of elements in my past history, I suppose, it has been very difficult for me to do this. For a long time I tended almost automatically to brush aside any positive feelings aimed in

> my direction. My reaction was, 'Who, me? You couldn't possibly care for me. You might like what I have done, or my achievements, but not me.' This is one respect in which my own therapy helped me very much. I am not always able even now to let in such warm and loving feelings from others, but I find it very releasing when I can do so. I know that some people flatter me in order to gain something for themselves; some people praise me because they are afraid to be hostile. But I have come to recognize the fact that some people genuinely appreciate me, like me, love me, and I want to sense that fact and let it in. I think I have become less aloof as I have been able to take in and soak up those loving feelings. (pp. 19–20)

"Thus," Rogers summarizes,

> prizing or loving and being prized or loved is experienced as very growth-enhancing. A person who is loved appreciatively, not possessively, blooms and develops his own unique self. The person who loves nonpossessively is himself enriched. This, at least, has been my experience. (p. 23)

Rogers then concludes by pointing to the interrelatedness between the three elements culminating in the ability to "give and receive love":

> I trust that you will see in these experiences some of the elements of growth-promoting interpersonal communication that have had meaning for me. A sensitive ability to hear, a deep satisfaction in being heard; an ability to be more real, which in turn brings forth more realness from others; and consequently a greater freedom to give and receive love – these, in my experience, are the elements that make interpersonal communication enriching and enhancing. (p. 26)

Mearns and Thorne (1999) inform us that in the final analysis, Rogerian or person-centered therapy is "All About Loving" (p. 20):

> 'Really, when you get down to basics, person-centered counselling is very simple: It's all about loving. It's about being free to treat other people in a loving way. It's trying to put the loving into helping.' … What is more, person-centered counsellors in training can see that the process they are going through is one which is gradually freeing their loving selves with the first stage often being that of helping them to be able to 'love' themselves, to achieve the self-acceptance which they hope to facilitate in their clients. (p. 66)

And again,

> For the person-centered counsellor the ability to love herself is the cornerstone for her therapeutic practice. … It is impossible to offer a client acceptance, empathy and genuineness at the deepest level if such responses are withheld from the self.
>
> Self-love is not easily attained and it needs frequent tending once established. Essentially it requires a willingness to give oneself time, attention, and care … out of responsibility to clients [and to oneself]. (p. 24)

The achievement of self-love is also contingent upon the awareness and the questioning of one's values and the differentiation between those that one has introjected and those that one has responsibly chosen and owned. The latter set of values will form "a firm foundation in her own psychology" (p. 79). One has to face one's own irrational fears and unreasonable needs for they not only can be traced to the early excess of parental conditional demands but also can "channel her into conditionality" (p. 80). "Uncovering and facing our own needs and fears is of course part of the therapeutic process which is associated with developing self-acceptance [or self-love]" (p. 80).

Yet, we can only be *relatively unconditional.* Mearns and Thorne (1999) quickly caution that practicing *total* "*unconditional positive regard* with *acceptance* as a short hand form" (p. 66) is humanly unachievable. Substituting love for acceptance, prizing, or warmth, it is literally impossible to achieve total unconditional love. To extrapolate from therapist to parent and from client to child, a good enough parent is "human and fallible and therefore must have 'personal limits' that might be exceeded" by her or his child (p. 66). The parent "cannot therefore guarantee unconditionality. However … [the mature enough parent] is likely to be less conditional" compared to immature parents (p. 66).

We can say then that the unconditional positive regard of good enough parents will be manifested in their relatively consistent acceptance and enduring warmth toward their children. As holders of this fundamental attitude of warm acceptance, these mature enough parents deeply value the humanness or personhood of their children. This relatively consistent acceptance that is always coupled with enduring warmth will be tryingly tested by their children's external behaviors, which at times can be very unpleasant and even cruel. Children's objectionable behaviors do not represent their whole humanness, personhood, or selfhood. But can good enough parents, who are "authoritative," but are neither "authoritarian" nor "permissive," assert their differential power, set boundaries and limits, and apply their farsighted wisdom to the long-range welfare of their children without the exercise of conditionality?

The answer provided by Thomas Gordon, a colleague of Carl Rogers and the originator of "person-centered parenting," reports Barrett-Lennard (1998), is "No." "Gordon does not believe it is possible to be unconditionally accepting, especially at the level of behaviours, but means to refer to the generally prevailing attitude and response" (p. 193). Similarly, Barrett-Lennard cites the work of parenting experts B. G. Guerney and L. F. Guerney whose parenting repertoire of strategies oscillate between empathic "acceptance of the child's viewpoint" and "a full assertion of adult authority when it is unrealistic for the child's wishes, feelings, and so on to control the outcome" (p. 196). Parents are to "exercise wisely a special power-of-responsibility" (p. 196). They believe, for instance, that "'reinforcement cannot be avoided, that it is at work in the real world all the time, in every situation'" (p. 196). Consequently, it behooves parents to "'harness the power of this phenomenon' to achieve desirable competencies and maturity in children" (p. 196). "Parents need to learn 'how to balance the exercise of acceptance with the enculturation of prosocial and adaptive behaviors'" (p. 196). From all this we can conclude, as with parents, mature partners are never absolutely unconditional in their love for each other; they are simply *less conditional* in their love than immature partners.

Love as Aesthetic Experience

Leffert (2017) traces the developmental origins of our *aesthetic being*:

> To the extent that early aesthetic being exists, it must involve the very young child's experience of the mother's body, her appearance, her smell, her skin texture, and the texture and colors of her garments. However aesthetic being begins, it must begin altercentrically, remaining inseparable from the Social. Aesthetic experiences from these periods include the pleasant surprise and wonder of repetitive or spontaneous discoveries … and the toddler's wondrous reflections on how she can repetitively cause things to happen. (p. 73)

Repetitiveness breeds familiarity. "Such aesthetic familiarity can be soothing, calming, and satisfying as it takes us into a different world" (p. 67). Although Leffert acknowledges that developmental failures and psychological disturbances serve as barriers to the acquisition and cultivation of our "aesthetic being" (our capacity for aesthetic experience and aesthetic competence) and even though he traces the developmental origins of aesthetic being to the child's experience of the mother's body, he does not focus on the mother's *love* that manifests itself through her inter-bodily communicative connectedness or communion with her child – through touching-and-being-touched, tasting-and-being-tasted, smelling-and-being-smelled, hearing-and-being-heard, and seeing-and-being-seen, as when the elated child sees the gleam in the mother's eyes and lovably beautiful face, partakes in the experience of aesthetic reciprocity, and responds with a gleam in his own eyes.

"Aesthetics," for Leffert (2017), "refers first to a specific kind of being, a kind of Dasein" (p. 69). It points to a way of "being-open." Aesthetic competence is therefore a mode of human existence. To be human is to be open to aesthetic experience. One way of being-in-the-world is by way of an aesthetic presence or participation. "Aesthetics," continues Leffert, "is a state of the holistic Self" (p. 69). From a Heideggerian viewpoint, "aesthetic being is fundamental to Dasein, to human existence … aesthetic competence is a necessary part of Human Being" (p. 71). We, therefore, existentially pay a high mental health price for dulling our aesthetic being. Phenomenologically, we are aesthetically oriented to take "something out of the world (be it a painting, sculpture, or sunset) for aesthetic purposes" (p. 69). We are constructed to image or imaginatively fashion the world in an aesthetic and hyper-real sense. In other words, "what the aesthetic image represents is imminent and emergent to the [actual] image" that we experience in the world (p. 69). Using the complementary work of Maurice Merleau-Ponty, Leffert adds that our aesthetic being is "an embodied engagement with World, an involvement that is active rather fixed and passive" (p. 70). Aesthetic being helps us in "the actualization of truth" (p. 70). It can aid us in living more truth-fully. For example, the impulse to express oneself through singing or dancing can be curative and healing. This is a kind of embodied-and-lived truth. Our bodily "being is inseparable from the aesthetic, perhaps its most fully revealed truth" (p. 70).

The bodily based reciprocal communication and communion between infant and mother and between adult partners, elaborates Leffert (2017), is itself an aesthetic experience that contributes to the "development and integration of the self":

> In the vein of good-enough parenting, there is also good-enough 'infanting' that involves reaching out to a mother aesthetically in a way that, in the case of lesser maternal psychopathology, is also therapeutic.
>
> Mothers appear to be hardwired (dating to their infancy?) to sing or make musical sounds to their infants while the infants display intense interest in the 'musical prosody of motherese' … as both members of the mother-infant couple strive to synchronize their facial expressions to each other and the musical rhythms. Body movements of the [adult] partners are an integral part of this [same] process, which also contributes to the development and integration of the self. (pp. 74–75)

Meltzer and Williams (1988) describe the potentially conflictual impact of the "beauty and mystery" of the mother on her very young infant. They point to the importance of "aesthetic reciprocity" for the healthy development of the child. By "aesthetic conflict," they are referring to the too-much-ness of the mysterious beauty of the mother if, I hazard to interpret, the encounter between mother-and-infant is excessive or prolonged. It is like not being able to turn one's gaze away from the blindingly beautiful sun. I prefer to make sense of this aesthetic encounter in terms of a dialectical tension between too-much-ness and not-enough-ness. A mature mother senses how to optimize the aesthetic encounter without veering into not-enough or excessive aesthetic stimulation. A good enough mother knows intuitively how to calibrate and thus achieve a just-right-ness in the aesthetic intensity experienced with and by her child. Aesthetic impingement or impoverishment can result in repressed or not-so-repressed rage (violence) or apathetic passivity and withdrawal. Phenomenologically, the free-flowing, spontaneous, and creative intentionality of the child becomes constricted. His or her *meaning-making capacity* is compromised. His or her aesthetic being is depleted, becoming arid, fixed, fixated, and rigidified.

Yet again, aesthetic co-being in the co-world that is opening up between mother and child does not occur in a vacuum. Aesthetic encounter occurs in the context of tender, *loving* care and concern. "The child," says Schindler (2004), "in his awakening both to himself and the world with the unsurpassable goodness of his mother's love … is a beginning that is … a *historical* embodiment of the comprehensive whole" (p. 111). In others words, the child's embodied embeddedness in the mother's goodness-and-love is a movement toward relative integration and wholeness. Schindler then quotes Hans Urs von Balthasar: "'The little child awakens to self-consciousness in his being-called … by the love of his mother'" (p. 111). This "means," continues Schindler, "that the self comes *to* itself only by coming *out* of itself or, more concretely, only by going *to another*, indeed, by being raised up *by* the other, *to* the other" (p. 112). Therefore, "transcendence means being outside of oneself" (p. 113).

In the Balthasarian scheme, states Schindler (2004), there is a reciprocal relationship between love and beauty. The relationship between love and beauty is that of circular causality: "love is an *effect* of beauty, but, on the other hand, love is the *cause* of the experience of beauty. … [And again,] love is the cause of beauty … beauty is the cause of love" (p. 409). Beauty "inspires love" and love inspires the perception of beauty. "One loves best in revealing the other as supremely loveable" (p. 410). Goodness, adds Schindler, contains "beauty and truth." But then again, relational truth contains elements of beauty and goodness. However, above all and from the very beginning of our early lives, the goodness and truthfulness of the loving mother are embodied in her beauty. In the loving encounter or the "life-giving exchange" between mother and child, there is beauty, goodness, and truth (existential pre-knowledge or pre-reflective, embodied knowing). Beauty, goodness, and truth are the fruit of love. Picture this simple scenario: a distressed child is being lovingly comforted and successfully soothed by his mother. There is something beautiful, good, and true to how life ought to be conducted. As witnesses, we behold an aesthetic competence in the loving containment of the distress of a vulnerable child.

Lastly, the Heideggerian link between care-and-concern, beauty, goodness, and truth, on the one hand, and our "potentiality-to-be," on the other hand, needs to be explicated. Here is how Paskow (2004) describes the link:

> For our 'potentiality-to-be,' is, in a manner of speaking, 'the good,' 'the beautiful,' and 'the true' for every human being ... a never wholly realizable felt horizon of possibility that claims each of us individually and, in conjunction with a grasp of our mortality, provokes a global stance, a coming to terms with, in one form or another, the meaning or Significance of our lives. (p. 238)

A "basic feature of our humanity," elaborates Paskow, "makes possible a certain kind of care for ourselves that we are born with and that becomes structured with ever greater complexity as we mature" (p. 18). Our "potentiality-to-be" this or that kind of person is for Heidegger an essential human trait. "Heidegger's theory of *Seinkonnen* [potentiality-to-be]," explains Paskow, is "that feature of our being that ... makes the deepest emotional demand on oneself" (p. 79). Even paintings can speak to this feature of our being. Vermeer's *Woman Holding a Balance*, for example, depicts a woman with "a kind of religious patience, concentration, and tenderness" (p. 160). Even though this woman is a figure in a painting painted around 1866, she still calls upon us to become more patient, attentive (mindful), and tender in the way we live our everyday lives. This woman then assumes a "real" *meaning* or significance in our world. Paskow expands upon his reflections on the *Woman Holding a Balance*: "As such she has qualities that may stimulate the recrudescence of an important concern for our lives, as well as aid us to define and emotionally and intellectually clarify it. Such concern is real to us not only in being 'out there,' but in being central to who we are, to what our world is" (pp. 174–175).

Our experience of this *balance*-holding woman helps us face the dialectical tension between the light and dark sides of our lives, for the painting, in a beautifully balanced fashion, contrasts this woman's embeddedness at the midpoint between lightness and darkness. "What is light in our lives? What is darkness? *We feel* light, for example, as truth, being, wholeness, the Way, salvation, we feel darkness as confusion, nonbeing, lostness, evil, death" (pp. 176–177). This beautifully balanced woman has found a way of integrating the forces of lightness and darkness without contradicting herself. "In fact, her facial expression and demeanor [reinforced by the interpenetration of the light and dark colors of her attire and the floor underneath her] imply that she has accomplished her task with modesty and grace" (p. 177). We are inspired to achieve a similar balance in our lives.

Vermeer's *Woman Holding a Balance cares* and is *concerned*, not only about the kind being (person) she is and wants to become – her "potentiality-to-be" – but also, pregnant that she is, she *cares* and is *concerned* about the kind of mother she is going to be, the kind of child she is going to raise, and her hopes for facilitating the kind person her child is going to become – his "potentiality-to-be." We human beings are constructed in such a way as to *care-and-be-concerned about* the kind of persons we can become and about our role in co-contributing to making our co-world a better place. There is (moral) beauty, goodness, and (existential) truth in such a way of being-in-the-world-with-others. We are fated to never fully realize our "potentiality-to-be"; we are destined, however, while taking into account our transitoriness and the contingencies of our lives, to try to actualize our "felt horizon of possibility that claims each of us" and thus attain "meaning or Significance" in our lives. To conclude, if we take *care-and-concern* as essential elements or manifestations of our loving orientation to our world, then we can now see the link between love, on the one hand, and relational beauty, goodness, and truth, on the other.

Love as Attachment

John Bowlby's (1982) attachment theory provides a developmental model that supports the existential-phenomenological perspective which holds that care is the source of human flourishing in general and the capacity to love in particular. Here is Bowlby (1982) connecting sensitive maternal care to optimal development:

> An easy newborn may assist an uncertain mother to develop a favorable pattern of care. Conversely, a difficult unpredictable newborn may tip the balance the other way. Yet all the evidence shows that a potentially easy baby is still likely to develop unfavorably if given unfavorable care and also, more fortunately, that

> with only few exceptions a potentially difficult baby can develop favorably if given sensitive care. The capacity of a sensitive [or sensitively caring] mother to adapt to even a difficult unpredictable baby and thereby enable him to develop favorably is perhaps the most heartening of all recent findings in this field. (p. 368)

A pattern of sensitive care results in favorable development. What does favorable development entail? Simply stated, it involves becoming securely attached. "*Attachment* refers to an enduring affectional or emotional tie between infants and their caregivers" (Hannush, 2002, p. 137). *Secure attachment* refers to a (mostly) positive emotional bond between caregiver and child. Now, it seems that for Bowlby secure attachment and love are interchangeable. "Indeed," as Karen (1998) puts it, "to Bowlby, attachment was much closer to the idea of love, if not identical with it" (p. 90). "For Bowlby," concurs Holmes (2010), "attachment and love were synonymous" (p. 6). Sensitive parental *care* results in secure attachment or secure love. The quality of our early caregiving shapes our emerging capacity to love. All things considered, being-and-becoming securely attached means being-and-becoming loved, loveable, and loving.

For Bowlby, *attachment* is a dynamic relational orientation. The key descriptive phrase *attachment pattern* or *attachment style* in attachment theory does not refer to a trait that is bestowed upon the child by a caregiver. It refers to the *quality of the relationship* between caregiver and child. It denotes a relationship of reciprocal influence. The need to attach, connect, link, or love is universal. "Virtually all children, even abused children," says Karen (1998),

> love their parents. It's built into the nature of being a child. They may be hurt, disappointed, caught in destructive modes of being that ward off any possibility of getting the love they yearn for, but to be attached, even anxiously attached, is to be in love. Each year the love may become a little more difficult to access; each year the child may disavow his wish for connection more firmly; he may even sear off his parents and deny that he has any love for them at all; but the love is there, as is the longing to actively express it and to have it returned, hidden like a burning sun. (p. 230)

Attachment, then, is a dynamic relation of loving connectedness. But, according to attachment theory and research, the "loving" in "loving connectedness" can become unhealthily twisted. Recall, even abused children have a relation of loving connectedness to their caregivers. It is a kind of loving that has gone awry.

With affection, attunement, availability, consistency, patience, sensitivity, and warmth, the developing child builds up a set of positive expectations and an internal representation or template "of the way love works" informs us Karen (1998, p. 231). The child develops "faith in the possibility for an open and loving connection and persists in his newfound responsiveness" even in the face of occasional letdowns (p. 231). Thereafter, the healthy child continues loving and expects to continue being loved in spite of occasional slippages on the part of the parents. When the distressed child needs a hug, the attuned parents are, for the most part, there to provide the child with an affectionate, comforting, reassuring, and soothing embrace. The child comes to rely on this anticipated response. Properly loving parents treat the child with respect and "steadfastly demand respect" (p. 231). When it comes to discipline, good enough parents "discipline a child in a moderate way; neither indulge, seduce, manipulate, nor explode" (p. 231). Mature enough parents do not trespass upon the child's vulnerability – his or her utter dependence, helplessness, and relative powerlessness. That is how they handle one side of the dialectical continuum. Secure enough parents celebrate the child's preciousness and radiant magnificence. That is how they handle the other side of the dialectical continuum.

As maturely loving parents, says Karen (1998), we are able to "shield our children from the damaged parts of ourselves – the fears, the unmourned injuries, the unbearable longings" (p. 377). Through self-reflection or mentalization these "parents do the one thing they most need to do – gain a deeper understanding of their own motivations, conflicts, and inner needs" (p. 378). They are able to let the past into their consciousness. "The problem we have as parents," Karen comments, "is not usually a lack of love or good intentions, but more often an unwillingness to face who we are" (p. 378).

"People who grow up hating their parents," reflects Karen (1998), "invariably hate themselves" (p. 56). Conversely, then, people who grow up loving their parents invariably love themselves as well. A "strong sense of having been loved and having the confidence in one's essential ability to love and be loved, enables one to both enjoy solitude and to confidently seek nourishment when one needs it" (p. 382). In other words, having been properly loved and therefore having acquired the ability to love and be loved make it less difficult to resolve the dialectical tension and find a balance between the need for close intimacy and the need for solitude. More than that, such a solid secure base (foundation in love) makes it easier to resolve the dialectical tension between meeting one's need for independence and self-reliance, on the one hand, and satisfying one's need for dependence and interdependence, on the other hand. In a lecture given on "Self-Reliance and Some Conditions That Promote It,"

John Bowlby is quoted by Karen as having said that secure attachment (or secure love) in adulthood, which is based on an internalized secure base (foundational love) from childhood and beyond, shapes our entire emotional and social life: "'Evidence is accumulating,'" Bowlby says, "'that human beings of all ages are happiest and able to deploy their talents to best advantage when they are confident that, standing behind them there are one or more trusted [loved and loving] persons who will come to their aid should difficulties arise'" (quoted in Karen, 1998, p. 381). Bowlby calls the "trusted person" an *attachment figure* and I call her or him the *loved-and-loving figure*. This loved-and-loving figure offers us a secure base to stand on. Bowlby believes that as we get older, this secure attachment figure gradually shifts to other loved-and-loving figures, such as our partners and friends.

The essential qualities of secure attachment (Karen, 1998) include having a feeling of all-rightness, a healthy sense of independence and a correlative healthy sense of dependence and interdependence, a basic sense of trust, rational faith, realistic hope, a solid sense of self-efficacy, self-reliance, and confidence in one's ability to love and be loved. Another "key quality" of secure-autonomous adults is having a flexible and open way of reflecting on their past and present attachments. To "be self-reflective" and "to be more appreciative of the mental states of others … have been found to be key ingredients of the secure adult" (p. 403). Such securely attached adults are in touch with their true feelings about their relationships. Most reassuringly, insecurely attached adults can *earn* the status of security in spite of wounded childhoods. It is never too late, though it may be more difficult, to change from being insecure to being secure in our confidence in loving and being loved. We can always learn to "let the past rest and move on" with our lives (p. 401).

Attachment theory makes a distinction between secure and insecure attachment. From our perspective secure attachment is equivalent to secure (mature) love, whereas insecure attachment is the same as insecure love. Insecure attachment or love manifests itself in different styles of relating: avoidant-dismissive, ambivalent-preoccupied, and disorganized-unresolved.

Avoidant-dismissive adults pretend that loving relations are not that important as a way of protecting their independence and personal control over their lives. They focus instead on their achievements and personal preferences. They deemphasize the role of emotions and overemphasize the role of reasoning in their lives. The "**Dismissive Adult**," according to Karen (1998), dismisses the "importance of love and connection"; he or she often "idealizes parents, but actual memories don't corroborate"; he or she displays "shallow, if any self-reflection" (p. 445).

Ambivalent-preoccupied adults overemphasize the role of relationships, emotions, and dependency needs and deemphasize the role of reasoning in their lives. The "**Preoccupied Adult**," says Karen (1998), remains "embroiled with anger and hurt at parents." He or she is unable "to see [his or her] own responsibility in relationships." He or she dreads "abandonment" (p. 445).

Disorganized-unresolved adults tend to unconsciously relive their own past disorganized, dysregulated, and dysfunctional relationships in present ones. Their extreme fear of abandonment or rejection and their shame-based sense of self make them incapable of repairing relational ruptures. They are easily prone to sudden disruptive and disorganizing behaviors the origin of which can be traced to unresolved relational conflicts from the past. They are thus rendered incapable of reflecting objectively and coolly on their hot emotional outbursts when experiencing relational conflicts. These unconscious and unresolved relational conflicts are simply acted out rather than reflected on. The **Unresolved** attachment pattern is sometimes viewed as a subset of either the **Dismissive** or the **Preoccupied** attachment pattern.

The "**Secure Adult**," states Karen (1998), has easy "access to [a] wide range of feelings and memories, positive and negative." He or she has a "[b]alanced view of parents. If insecure in childhood, [he or she] has worked through hurt and anger" (p. 445). But none of us is totally secure in our capacity to love and be loved. As a consequence, comments Karen, we need to vigilantly

> remain conscious of ourselves and of the pull of early models, even if hang-ups of various kinds remain, as inevitably they must, we have a better chance of creating satisfying relationships with our mates and secure relationships with our children. To that extent it seems that in emotional life, much as in history, we are only doomed to repeat what has not been remembered, reflected upon, and worked through. (p. 208)

In my view, we all have insecure holes in our relational templates, for none of us has come from a perfect family or has grown up in a perfect relational world. Existentially, we are never wholly secure. We are all, consciously or unconsciously, aware of our fragility and finiteness. We are all vulnerable to the vicissitudes of existence, including the possible loss of people we love and rely on. We are all inevitably subjected to unfair criticisms, harsh treatments, and frustrating failures. We all fall short of our potentiality-to-be. All this is a source of what I call *existential insecurity*. Being secure or insecure in our love comes in degrees. It depends on genetics, luck, resilience, communal context, and the degree to which we were subjected to proper or improper parenting. More than *earned security*, becoming mature additionally involves learning to accept and tolerate our *existential insecurity*.

Attachment theory postulates that early parent-child relations lay the foundational template for our emerging attachment or loving style. "The first emotions that the parent deals with," asserts Karen (1998), "are the attachment emotions themselves – the baby's desire for connection, his need to be taken care of, his need to be responded to when hungry, when in pain, when wanting love or attention" (p. 243). The good enough parent tolerates, contains, and responds sensitively and in an attuned fashion to the child's rage and distress. The mature parent is able to respond effectively to the child's need for comfort, security, and care. The child does not have to develop devious and manipulative ways of getting his needs satisfied. He does not feel desperately hungry for love. He does not have to disavow or repress painful feelings or memories associated with his longing for proper love. He does not have to habitually avoid and withdraw in order to shield himself from neglect, rejection, or harsh discipline. He does not have to develop a shame-based sense of self, with its accompanying fury in response to anticipated rejection and pervasive pattern of unacceptability, to not mattering. In short, he does not have to be forced to choose a *compensatory false self* for the purpose of psychosocial survival and the attainment of skewed conditional love. He does not have to forsake his *congruent, genuine, natural, organismic, real, spontaneous, or true self*. His fundamental experience is that of acceptance, lovability, and mattering.

Basically, Bowlby, concludes Karen (1998), begins with a simple and self-evident concept: "a child needs to be lovingly attached to a reliable parental figure and that this need is a primary motivating force in human life" (p. 441). Our lives revolve around the pleasures and pains of being linked to others. "But the need for proximity [physical and emotional closeness], for felt security, for love; the need to be held [physically and emotionally], to be understood [known], to work through [mourn] our losses; these basic themes of attachment [love] are to some degree built into us biologically" (p. 441). Bowlby "saw himself as an evolutionist and believed that the formation of affectional ties – the development of love – was one of the greatest achievements of human evolution" (p. 427).

Love as Care

Many psychologists and philosophers view care as a component of love. According to Erikson's (1963) linear developmental model, the character (ego) strength of love precedes the character strength of care. We need to develop the ability to love before we can *generatively* care for others.

Caring, says Mayeroff (1971), has the "major ingredients" of *knowing* (learning about one's own and the Other's needs, strengths, and limitations in order to allow for one's own growth and that of the Other; understanding one's own unfolding life narrative with which one identifies), *alternating rhythms* (moving back and forth between doing and experiencing or between assuming a narrow and broad perspective), *patience* (giving self/other time to ripen; tolerating times of chaos and confusion), *honesty* (being authentic and true to self and acting in good faith), *trust* (having faith that essential others will be there when needed; being responsibly trustworthy; having confidence in one's capacity to change by listening to one's organismic valuations; openness to the unfamiliar and the unknown), *humility* (acknowledging one's limitations while not being self-effacing regarding one's strengths; admitting one's not-knowingness), *hope* (expecting that the future is laden with realistic possibilities to be actualized), and *courage* (willing to discerningly approach the unfamiliar and the unknown).

"Care," for May (1969), "is a state in which something [or someone] does *matter*; care is the opposite of apathy. Care is the necessary source of eros [love], the source of human tenderness" (p. 286). May traces the origin of care to infancy: "care is born in the same act as the infant" (p. 286). Maternal care is essential, not only for biological survival, but also for living a "good life." May then connects care to (maternal) identification with the pain of the child.

> Care is given power by nature's sense of pain; if we do not care for ourselves, we are hurt, burned, injured. This is the source of identification: we can feel in our own bodies the pain of the child or the hurt of the adult. … but care must become a conscious psychological fact. *Life* comes from physical survival; but the *good life* comes from what we care about. (p. 286)

Having described how care is the source of love and empathic identification with the pain of the Other, May (1969) goes on to connect care with will. He acknowledges his indebtedness to Martin Heidegger who asserts that, in May's words, "care (*Sorge*) is the source of will" (p. 286). Will is not a mental faculty. "It is a function of the whole person" (p. 286). "When we do not care, we lose our being; and care is the way back to being" (p. 286). When I care, I become integrated in my being, my selfhood. My capacities to wish and will are "founded on care" (pp. 286–287). I cannot wish or will if I do not really care to start with. "Willing is caring made free, says Heidegger" (p. 287). "The constancy of the self," continues May, "is guaranteed by care" (p. 287). Guided by Heidegger, May connects care to human transitoriness: "The fact that we are finite makes care possible. Care also, in Heidegger's conception, is the source of conscience. 'Conscience is the call of Care,' and 'manifests itself as Care'" (p. 287).

Our will, which is a mature form of our wish, is rooted in our care, explicates May (1969). Care is intentional in its structure; "care is always caring *about* something" (p. 288). When I care, I am involved. I have decided to do something regarding that which I care about. This is why care and will are paired together and are parts of the same experience.

Again, May (1969) emphasizes, care "is ontological and refers to a state of being" (p. 288). To not care is to be uninvolved. Using Heideggerian language May states, "man is ontologically constituted by care" (p. 289). To play on the Cartesian dictum, *I care, therefore I am*. Our *quest for enlivening meaning* entails finding something or someone we care about – something or someone that matters. I care when I genuinely wish you well. I care when what happens to you matters to me. The origin of the word "care," states May, "lies in the little term 'tend'" (p. 289), which also happens to constitute the root of the term "intentionality," of which care is a particular type. May defines "intentionality" as "the structure by which experience becomes meaningful" (p. 299). We are constituted by intentionality in that we are always *tending toward* something or someone outside of ourselves. "Tend means a tendency, an inclination, a throwing of one's weight on a given side, a movement; and also to mind, to attend, to await, to show solicitude for. In this sense, it is the source of both love and will" (p. 289). Touchingly, the term "tend" is in the word "*tend*erness."

For the mature person, then, both love and will entail reaching out or tending toward another person or thing. Care is the common denominator for both love and will. Both involve choice or resolute decision-making, action, and the assumption of responsibility. In the absence of care, there is no love. What we are left without care, May comments, is vacuous sentimentality and fleeting sexual arousal (tumescence) followed by a state of quiescence (detumescence). May (1953) defines love as a "delight in the presence of the other person and an affirming of [that person's] value and development as much as one's own" (p. 206).

For Heidegger (1962), ontologically (from the vantage point of what it means to be a human being), care is an essential structure of human existence. Differently described, we humans are constructed to care – to care about something or someone. How we care – the quality of our care – will be manifested, says Schalow (2017), in how we live time (how we make sense of our past, how we conduct ourselves in the present, and how we approach our future), how we live in our existential space (how we inhabit or dwell in our surroundings), and how we live bodily (how we express ourselves through our bodily comportment). For instance, if I truly care about someone, I will treasure my memories of our times together; I will come alive and enjoy being with this person in the present; I will look forward to being with this person in the future. Together, we co-create a safe and secure dwelling place in which we are playful, relaxed, warm, and at home. Our natural, organismic and spontaneous self-expression – our bodily being-with each other – will communicate our valuation of one another.

Care colors our wishes, wants, and desires. When our care is true, what is perceived as realizable and within reach in our lived space and lived time becomes wide and fluid. Our intentional arc is expanded. There is more freedom in our choice-making. Our meaning-making ability becomes more flexible and creative. In contrast, when our care is diverted, distracted, or disordered, what we perceive as within reach in our lived space-and-time is narrowed and fixed. Our intentional arc is contracted. The spectrum of our desires and choosing is restricted. Succinctly stated, the way we care structures the way we live time, space, and our body – all three of which are interwoven in the way we live our lives. When our caring is diverted or dissevered, our desires get twisted. Portions of our existence are disowned. We take less ownership and responsibility for our actions. We obsessively over-identify with narrowed desires and impulses. Our *meaning horizons* shrink. Our capacity for "choosing to choose" (our freedom) diminishes. We become less open to *alternative meanings and possibilities.* Our unfolding life narrative becomes stuck (repetitive) and loses its dynamism. We become less answerable or responsive to the call of our true self, which is to say, we become less responsible (response-able) to the call of our *caring conscience.* The responsibly resolute response to the call of our caring conscience is always available to us in the present – the present moment, which is potentially pregnant with possibilities – with *alternative meanings to be actualized* by us. For example, a man who has not been a caring father could cease the present moment and in resoluteness decide to become a truly caring father. As a consequence his lifeworld takes on a new meaning.

In most of his works, Heidegger rarely speaks of love, except in a series of lectures on Schelling in 1936, says Schalow (2001, p. 39). Love is a derivative of our human capacity to care. It is a refined rendition of care. How I care will shape how I love. In other words, twisted care results in warping our capacity to love. Authentic care becomes a part of wise (mature) loving.

Love as Concern

"Concern," notes Nicholsen (2002), "is the effort to make oneself worthy of what one loves. It is expressed in working to know and appreciate the beloved and to perceive its value" (p. 46). The object of one's love can not only be another human being, but also a project or a natural object, an object of nature. "The Bushmen," for example, "dance as long as the moon is up to show the moon that they care about it" (p. 29).

From the beginning of my life, I am not totally separate from the essential others for whom I am the object of care and concern. Soon after, I begin to feel my similarity to and continuity with them. As I get older I start to emphasize my separateness and difference in order to sense my I-ness, who *I am*. The "*I am*" emerges from the once amorphous "*we are*." "As we become more mature," states Nicholsen (2002), "we grow the capacity to acknowledge and experience our kinship with what is most different from us, 'holding the sameness and difference delicately in mind'" (p. 35). Under relatively optimal conditions, we learn to tolerate the dialectical tension between our connectedness and similarity to and our separateness and difference from others. Nicholsen then makes the link between the experience of attachment, identification, kinship, and love, the consequent suffering, loss, pain, and destructiveness, on the one hand, and *concern*, which includes awareness of separateness and responsibility, on the other:

> The feelings of attachment and identification we develop early in our lives – the feelings that give rise to our sense of home – become the basis of our later recognition of kinship. We know attachment and identification because we have experienced it; it is the matrix from which the self develops. But it is only by suffering the loss of those early bonds – and enduring the pain and destructiveness that were in any case bound up with the love in them – that we become able to feel concerned for what we love, a concern that includes the knowledge that we are also separate and responsible. (p. 35)

As we mature we tolerate the tension between the self-like and the unself-like in the Other, and manage to make the Other an object of concern. But what makes this evolving concern possible is the bedrock of our original lovely home, a home whose meaning deepens and widens as we mature.

> 'Abiding loveliness' speaks both to the sense of continuity over time that the home place provides and also to the ability to see and experience that place as saturated with the love that has circulated within it, a love that flows not only from person to person but between other beings as well. (p. 36)

Nicholsen (2002) points to a circular relationship between our maturing capacity for concern – making ourselves worthy of that which we love – and our capacity for relatedness to others and to the world. Thus, she writes, "if we pay more attention, make ourselves worthy, we may become purified. Purification may in this case mean a transformation in our sense of relatedness" (p. 42). Purification, however, does not occur in a vacuum. It has to be balanced with mourning our losses. The first loss we have to mourn is the loss of childhood. As I become more and more a separate self, I am subliminally aware of my loss of childhood, the loss of my relatively undifferentiated sense of oneness and my secure dependency. When I grieve what I have lost, I am reminded that I was once part of a kind of fused relatedness. It is in my struggle to mourn my loss of childhood, among other losses, while holding on to my emerging and evolving autonomous and separate selfhood, that I come upon a creative solution: I become a *concerned self*, a self that attempts to be worthy of that which I love. It is a concern born of reparative guilt for my acts of destructiveness that accompanies my attempts to carve out an independent and separate self. Think of that collateral damage consequent upon the toddler's tyrannical "no-saying." Looking back, I feel guilty because I have failed those whom I have loved. I now respond to my guilt constructively by purifying myself through striving to be worthy of those I love most. "Concern," reflects Nicholsen, "encompasses the emotional complexity of relatedness in separateness" (p. 47). Described differently, in my concern I resolve the dialectical tension between my need for relatedness and my need for separateness. By proving myself worthy of that which I love again and again, I become capable of a more *mature* form of relatedness. Just as my self becomes more differentiated, so does my homeworld. I am reminded here of Goethe's definition of happiness: "'We are happy when for everything inside us there is an equivalent something out there' – a world 'alive and sentient, responding to the imagination in shapes of terror and joy'" (quoted in Nicholsen, 2002, p. 44).

Concern, Nicholsen (2002) tells us, can be viewed as a "labor of gratitude" for the gift of love we have received. In gratitude, I open my mind and heart, my mindful heart, to the Other. My labor of gratitude extends to learning how to use the gifts I have received creatively and constructively. I first receive the gift – a talent for example – and consequently I have to earn the gift through its creative and constructive use. "Making the return gift is … [my] labor of gratitude" (p. 89). I then perpetuate and pass on this ritual of receiving-and-giving and giving-and-receiving. Nicholsen exemplifies the concept of concern as a labor of gratitude through the use of the words of a Sioux elder: "'If men would pay more attention to … [their] preference and seek what is best to do to make themselves worthy of that toward which they are attracted [love], they might have dreams which would purify [transform] their lives'" (p. 90). Just as giving is a gift, so is receiving, including being receptive with an open mind and heart. By making use of the gift of receptivity, I open myself to the new and different. This means that I am willing to sacrifice my old habitual patterns, my old self. This process of change involves sacrifice and suffering. By deepening and widening my circle of concern, I am widening my "identification with the whole of life" and I am also experiencing "an increase in love and caring" and "concern" (p. 91).

Love as an Integrator of Opposites

Marcus (2010) provides us with "a dialectical formulation, where love is viewed as a wedding of opposites, perhaps best illustrated in the [Freudian] love-death theme" (p. 158). "Love relations," maintains Marcus, "like all human relationships are messy and complicated, laced with contradictory feelings and attitudes, as Freud noted, as most honest and self-aware people, at least in Western society, will tell you" (p. 160).

In a brief essay written in 1915, entitled "On Transience," Freud (2005) succinctly equates *love* with *libido* (sexual or life energy):

> We possess, as it seems, a certain amount of capacity for love – what we call libido – which in the earliest stages of development is directed towards our own ego. Later, though still at a very early time, this libido is diverted from the ego to objects, which are thus in a sense taken into the ego. If the objects are destroyed or if they are lost to us, our capacity for love (our libido) is once more liberated; and it can either take other objects instead or can temporarily return to the ego. (p. 217)

Freud provides us with an "instinctivist" model of love (eros). As a manifestation of a life force, the aim of the sexual instinct is survival (including reproductive success) and sexual satisfaction. For Freud, even the purpose of the power motive is ultimately love (sex) – the survival and perpetuation of our selfish genes. In this Freudian model, we humans are basically and fundamentally egotistic pleasure seekers and pain avoiders. We are driven to maximize our pleasures and minimize our pains. As Marcus puts it, according to the Freudian view, "all love is essentially love of a need-satisfying object. … In this view, all forms of love, including in their sublimated expressions, as, for example, in love of God, music, an idea, or one's dog, are construed as derivative of instinct and their main purpose is to give instinctual gratification" (Marcus, 2010, p. 160).

Mature lovers will feel affectionate admiration and adoration for their special loved ones and will acknowledge and affirm their separateness and uniqueness, including their special characteristics, competencies, interests, and potentials. Mature lovers can relax with and into one another without needing constant affirmation and validation. Moreover, for the post-Freudians, mature love requires "object constancy." "**Object constancy**" is defined as "the capacity to maintain a stable, balanced, and accurate mental image of another" (Frankland, 2010, p. 178). Additionally, the capacity for mature loving "requires a well-developed sense of autonomy and integration (e.g., a good sense of self-cohesion, self-continuity, and self-esteem, among other elements)" (Marcus, 2010, pp. 160–161). "'Loving and being loved,' the 'union of mental and bodily satisfaction,'" Freud is quoted as saying, "is perhaps the best way for achieving 'a positive fulfillment of happiness'" (quoted in Marcus, 2010, p. 161). Our love's maturity in adulthood depends on our good enough loving relations with our caregivers in early childhood. Such an early advantage helps us cultivate the capacity to manage our inevitable ambivalences in our adult love relations. Whereas in his theoretical assertions Freud is reductionistic in his understanding of love, his experience-near, informal declarations about love are startlingly insightful and truer to life.

Most critically, the capacity for mature love, says Marcus (2010), depends, among other factors, on

> the ability to "manage" one's ambivalence, ambivalence broadly described. Love requires the mingling or balancing of opposites, for example, the reasonable needs and desires of the self vs. those of the Other, closeness vs. distance, dependence vs. independence, and, of course, affection vs. hostility. The latter opposites are the sharpest expression of ambivalence, a derivative of the love-death that underlies all … love relations. … Put simply, unless one can live within the dialectical tension between Eros and Thanatos, ideally with a tilting towards the positive side of the ambivalence, towards Eros, one is not going to be able to adequately sustain a [mature] love relation with a significant Other. (pp. 161–162)

Of course, there are many more opposites or *polar meanings* beckoning balance that are not touched upon by Marcus. Moreover, in our own dialectical model, there is no need for always tilting to the so-called positive side of the ambivalence – at least not for all the seeming opposites. For instance, in mature love, I can be healthily dependent on and healthily independent from my significant other. I do not need to tilt toward dependence or independence. Moreover, sometimes tilting may go in either direction without the need for the positive or negative labeling of sides. For instance, for a person growing in an individualistic culture that overemphasizes independence especially for males, a healthy movement is needed to be made in the direction of the dependence side of the dialectical continuum in order to achieve balance or integration; whereas for a person growing in a communal culture that overemphasizes dependence, a healthy movement is needed to be made in the direction of the independent side of the dialectical continuum so as to acquire balance or integration. But these tilts do not stabilize at an absolute balancing midpoint; rather they hover around a range that is optimal for the given contingencies of the cultural context.

Not all ambivalences are amenable to balancing or integrating. Deep and intense ambivalences need to be modulated before they can be balanced or integrated. Take (immature) love that can quickly turn into (immature) hate, for example. A Kleinian perspective would describe this as an instance of splitting. A Gestalt-phenomenological viewpoint would describe this as an instance of a figure-ground reversal involving an either/or or dualistic meaning making. Only when one is able to widen his or her horizons of meaning making can mature love become relatively integrated with constructive hate.

Marcus (2010) raises a most critical question: "how does one keep the redemptive vision of love alive and present in the face of its death-tinged opposite" (p. 162)?

> The answer, or at least an important aspect of the answer, is to learn how to reside in what William Wordsworth called the 'border states,' the space between love and death. This imaginary place, the boundary between two people, I call 'moment love/moment death' is best known by its experienced paradoxes. … For example, 'fidelity to oneself' leads to being faithful to the Other; recognizing and admitting personal limitations and faults creates a deeper understanding and acceptance of the Other's limits and inadequacies; honesty with oneself fosters greater realism with the Other; to be reasonably loving of oneself liberates new caring capacities that can be utilized for the best interests of the Other; to nurture oneself creates new resources of support for the Other. And, of course, to do all of these things encourages the significant other to be 'forgiving, realistic, honest, loving, and nurturing' in return. (p. 162)

Lastly, Marcus (2010) concludes, there are three important elements in mature love relations that enable us to *modulate the dialectical tension between the life* versus *death forces* within and between us, between moment love and moment death. They are the "redemptive triad" of hope, faith, and forgiveness.

Hope Marcus (2010) quotes Kierkegaard in his description of hope as "'a passion for what is possible'" (p. 163). Hope is "a necessary sense of destination to somewhere better, the space between dreams and reality" (p. 164).

"Moreover, paradoxically, hope is also the reward for one's faith in the Other, in the Other's infinite goodness" (p. 164).

The structure of hope, expands Marcus (2013), is made up of thoughts and feelings that something desirable is likely to happen, even under difficult and trying circumstances. The hopeful person, while holding "deference to uncertainty and doubt," loosens the "interpretive grip" of the past "through imagining a better future" (p. 63). "[Gabriel] Marcel says," continues Marcus, "that patience and humility are crucial aspects 'of authentic hope which is at the same time trust and love (for these are not separable)' … patience and humility are two of the crucial elements of hoping. … Humility … [is] that quality of mind and heart of being modest and respectful to others and things" (p. 62). Humility, in turn, is part of "availability," a central Marcelian concept. Availability is a kind of other-directed open-minded and -hearted disposition that makes room for mercy and love.

"'Availability' … [is] manifested in absolute 'fidelity,' a total commitment to the best interests of others" (p. 16). "Most important, perhaps, hope is always rooted in 'availability' …, a dynamic, sensitive receptivity and 'communion,' the self's participation in [the lightness of] being, or being-with, that is, with a deeper and wider capacity for loving" (p. 43).

Even *grace*, elaborates Marcus (2010), requires of us a certain kind of availability or readiness, "a certain kind of openness and receptivity to the other, as exemplified, for example, in love, fidelity, faith, and hope" (p. 74). Grace requires "patient awaiting." It "necessitates a readiness to respond in the moment to that which is other than oneself, whether animate or inanimate" (p. 74). Being open to grace means being "permeable" or "porous." Porosity involves giving or offering up of self for the sake of participating in the "reciprocity of presence" (p. 75). To be available is to "'place oneself at the disposal of [the Other]'" (p. 123). By far, "love is that ultimate experience of being, of emotional 'availability' … and connection, of disclosure and presence, the realm where two people acknowledge and affirm the eternity and absolute value of each other" (p. 180). Love breaks "'the tension between the self and the other'" (p. 180).

As has been described earlier, Harold Searles makes a distinction between *realistic* and *unrealistic* hope. It is *realistic hope* that mediates and modulates the dialectical tension between opposing meanings in our everyday experience. Here again is a summary of Searles's reflection on *realistic hope*:

> Any realistic hope – as contrasted to unconscious denial-based, unrealistic hopefulness – must be grounded in the ability to experience loss. One who has sur-

vived the griefs over losses, over disappointments in the past has known what it is for hope to triumph over – to survive – despair. In the same regard, hope comes into being when one discovers that such feelings as disappointment and despair can be shared with a fellow human being – when one discovers, that is, that the sharing of such feelings can foster one's feelings of relatedness with one's fellow human beings. (quoted in Mitrani & Mitrani, 1997, p. 76)

The root of "realistic hope" or "unrealistic hopefulness" goes back to our early childhood relationships with our essential caregivers. The realism or unrealism of our hopefulness depends on whether or not we were properly loved. Viewed dialectically, unrealistic hope could easily slip into its opposite: destructive despair; whereas realistic hope has the resilience to withstand and absorb moments of despair the meaning of which is transformed into a constructive force. Constructive despair then becomes the complementary counterforce to realistic hope.

Faith. Faith, states Marcus (2013), is "an attitude of openness, especially to the truth, fused with an absolute trust" (p. 163). The fusion of *faith* and *trust* matches Erikson's linking of the two phenomena together. For Erikson, *faith* and *hope* are the healthy results of *basic trust.* Hoare (2002) writes of this linkage:

Principled behavior defines advanced adult identity in Erikson's view. To him, ethical adults are those who, in most instances, affirm judiciously instead of negating arbitrarily. Ethical adults hold positive, life-affirming values. They involve themselves actively in the work of their world, honor their commitments, and eschew moralizing and blaming. They also have faith without which "wholeness" [integration or integrality] is impossible.

Throughout his lifetime of writing, Erikson maintained that primal hope and faith are healthy outcomes of infancy, the first stage of life. But by his mid-life, he gave those strengths [aspects of maturity] preeminence as the best case resolution of the last stage of life as well. … By age 80, Erikson was a decidedly existential thinker; he had to give faith its due. Faith then became an alternate term for integrity [or] … 'integrality,' the tendency to keep things together … integration is shown by the ability to find meaning in life. (p. 72, 90, & 192)

In one of his last publications, Erikson (Erikson et al., 1986) once again writes on the linkage between hope and "mature faith": "Evolving from lifelong experiences of hopeful confidence and cautious skepticism, [mature] faith that is sturdy and firm need not itself be questioned" (p. 238). One can have faith and trust in oneself, in others, in family, in generational cycles, in industriousness (work), in nature, in religion, in the future of the human species, and in the continuation of the cosmic world of which one is a part.

"The practice of the art of loving," asserts Fromm (1956), "requires the practice of [rational] faith" (p. 109). Rational faith, he elaborates, "is a conviction which is rooted in one's own experience of thought or feeling" (p. 110). It is "a character trait pervading the whole personality" (p. 110). It "is rooted in productive intellectual and emotional activity" (p. 110). It is anchored "in reason and visions of truth" (p. 110). It is grounded "in the confidence in one's power of thought, observation, and judgment" (p. 111). It is steeped in "productive" or reason-based thinking. It is a way of knowing that is based on accurate assessment of reality. A productive thinker aims at seeing happenings and people as they are out of interested concern. A productive thinker knows oneself for *who one is*. He or she has no need for distortion of psychosocial reality.

"Having 'faith' in another person," says Fromm (1956), "means to be certain of the reliability and unchangeability of his fundamental attitudes, of the core of his personality, of his love" (p. 111). "In the same sense" continues Fromm, "we have faith in ourselves" (p. 111). Having faith in myself enables me to make and keep my promises to myself and others. "What matters in relation to love," adds Fromm, "is the faith in one's own love; in its ability to produce love in others, and in its reliability" (p. 112). When I have faith in others, I also have faith in their potentialities – "potentialities to love, to be happy, to use … reason, and more specific potentialities like artistic gifts" (p. 112). A productive (healthy, mature) loving orientation on the part of my parents, which includes having faith in my potentialities, enables me to grow up having faith in my own potentialities. Moreover, growing up having "faith in others has its culmination in faith in *mankind*" (p. 113). Being treated lovingly, affectionately, caringly, concernfully, responsibly, and respectfully as a human equal enables me to have faith in a future built on the principle of justice, equality, and love.

"*The basis of rational faith*," emphasizes Fromm (1956) again and again, "*is productiveness*; to live by our faith means to live productively" (p. 113). "It follows," he continues, "that the belief in power (in the sense of domination) and the use of power are the reverse of faith" (p. 113). "To have faith," he adds, "requires *courage*, the ability to take a risk, the readiness even to accept pain and disappointment" (p. 114). "To be loved, and to love, need courage, the courage to judge certain values as of ultimate concern – and to take the jump and stake everything on these values" (p. 114). "To take the difficulties, setbacks and sorrows of life as a challenge which to overcome makes us stronger, rather than as unjust punishment which should not happen to *us*, requires faith and courage" (p. 115). My practice of faith and courage starts with me attending to the details of my everyday life. I need to learn to notice when, where, and with whom I lose my faith and thus become weakened which sets me up in turn to further betray my own faith in myself and/or others. Fromm concludes by linking faith, hope, and love: "To love means to commit oneself without guarantee, to give oneself completely in the hope that our love will produce love in the loved person. Love is an act of faith and whoever is of little faith is also of little love" (p. 115).

We are now ready to link ambivalence to faith. From a Kleinian point of view, the trajectory of maturation and mental health involves a developmental movement away from extreme ambivalence, culminating in splitting "an immature defense mechanism that reduces anxiety by keeping notions of good and bad separate in the person's mind" (Frankland, 2010, p. 179), to a position or a mode of being characterized by the tolerance of ambivalence and the relative integration of love and hate. While this mature position involves acknowledgment of the reality of loss, pain, and coming to terms with destructiveness through acts of atonement or reparation, it is at the same time a source of resilience and faith or confidence in oneself and in one's relationship to others. There seems to be a negative co-relationship between ambivalence and faith: the less the ambivalence, the more the faith; the more the ambivalence, the less the faith in oneself or others.

Forgiveness Marcus (2010) defines forgiveness as "the capacity for pardoning the significant other for a mistake or wrongdoing directed toward oneself" (p. 164). Hoffman (2011) makes reference to the work of the psychoanalyst Sandor Ferenczi, whose psychoanalytic thinking was partly shaped by "Kierkegaardian understandings of love, truth, and intersubjectivity" (p. 198). Ferenczi, she holds, has an "abiding capacity for, and belief in, love" (p. 198). She quotes him as having said, "Psychoanalytic 'cure' is in direct proportion to the cherishing love given by the psychoanalyst to the patient; the love which the psychoneurotic patient *needs*, not necessarily the love which he thinks he needs and therefore demands" (pp. 198–199).

Ferenczi, according to Hoffman (2011), has also written about "the need for forgiveness between patient and analyst. The analyst must recognize complicity in treatment impasses. When the analyst falls into some of the same attitudes as the traumatizing parents, he must confess to the offense at hand, and also vicariously for the patient's parents' offenses, and be forgiven by the patient" (pp. 199–200).

Let us extrapolate and apply what Ferenczi is saying here to everyday life outside the analytic setting. When I catch myself doing to my wife, child, sibling, friend, or a vulnerable stranger what was unfairly done to me by my parents as a child, when I engage in the same traumatizing actions that my parents perpetrated upon me, just like their parents perpetrated upon them, then I need to apologize and ask for forgiveness. I ask for forgiveness not only on my own behalf but also on behalf of my parents and my parents' parents. Following Ferenczi, as described by Hoffman, it is not enough for me to make a confession to, say, my wife. She wants me to truly "see" how much pain and suffering I have caused her. She wants me to correct my cruelty by no longer acting out or repeating the same harsh and remorseless actions that copied my parents' sadistic responsiveness. It is only then that my wife is in a position to truly forgive me. Now that I am forgiven, I enjoy, in my relationship with my wife, what was denied me in my relationship to my parents, what had hardened my heart and predisposed, better yet condemned me to repeat my parents' harsh pattern. To quote the words of Kierkegaard, "'when love forgives, the miracle of faith occurs'" (quoted in Hoffman, 2011, p. 200). Authentically asking for and receiving forgiveness for one's destructive behavior, which includes the element of lasting correction, restores faith in the forgiven and the forgiver. This restoration of faith is an essential prerequisite for the maturation of my capacity to love. "'But why,'" asks Kierkegaard, "'is forgiveness so rare?'" He answers his own question: "'It is … because faith in the power of forgiveness is so small'" (quoted in Hoffman, 2011, p. 200). When faith in forgiveness or faith in the Other has been shaken, it either withers or is transformed into erratic faith that can easily be overturned. But when faith is anchored in mature loving, then it ripens and is transformed into solid or, what Fromm calls, *rational faith*. Similarly, when the capacity to ask for forgiveness and to forgive is rooted in mature loving, then it is transformed into a mature form of forgiveness – forgiving and being forgiven. Otherwise, even if present at all, this capacity remains shallow, inauthentic, and without transforming power, for it is not rooted in maturing love. Plainly put, there is a dialectical relationship between mature loving and mature forgiving.

Something needs to be told about the developmental origins of our capacity or incapacity to *handle* our dialectical tensions between the seemingly opposing forces or polar meanings in our lives. Culbert-Koehn (1997) provides us with a pivotal passage from the work of Frances Tustin illustrating the importance of integrating the opposites of hardness versus softness through the mediation of the infant's experience of the mother's body:

> In the sense-dominated state of early infancy the infant's primary distinctions are between 'comfort' and 'discomfort,' 'pleasure' and 'unpleasure.' 'Soft' sensations are pleasurable and comfortable. 'Hard' sensations are unpleasurable and

> uncomfortable. ... When on the basis of a cooperative suckling experience, 'hard' entering nipple and tongue are experienced as working together with 'soft' receptive mouth and breast, there is a 'marriage' between 'male' and 'female' elements that takes place. Out of this union of hard and soft sensations a new way of functioning is born. (p. 112)

In my eyes, there is no need to label the hard and soft sensations as, respectively, "male" and "female" elements. Shall we label the "hard" nipple of the mother's breast "male" or "female"? Shall we label the male infant's receptive "soft" mouth "female" or "male"? Or, shall we label the female infant's tongue "male" or "female"? What is important here is that in the context of "a cooperative suckling experience," an optimal fusion of hard (uncomfortable and unpleasurable) sensations and soft (comfortable and pleasurable) sensations is made possible. A "new way of functioning" is born. The infant can now tolerate and absorb the hard-into-the-soft, the uncomfortable-into-the comfortable, and the unpleasurable-into-the-pleasurable experience. The young child has acquired the capacity to modulate the tension between the hard and the soft, the pleasurable and the unpleasurable, and the comfortable and the uncomfortable. It is the loving relational context of mutual cooperation and recognition, grounded in unconscious inter-bodily communication and communion, which makes this "new way of functioning" possible.

The origination of this "new way of functioning," I believe, is the primordial source of our emerging capacity or incapacity for love. It forms the (metaphorical) prototype for how we *handle* the "hardness" in our unfolding lives. Both mother and child can be hard (harsh) and soft (tender). This dialectical tension can be modulated and mediated through their inter-bodily loving cooperation, with the weight of responsibility lying more on the shoulders of the mother. With attuned responsiveness (response-ability), the mother draws on her capacity for, as Wilfred Bion (1962) puts it, "reverie" (p. 36) – the mother's capacity to contain the infant's anxiety as well as her own while continuing to *think* as she confronts her child's seemingly unfathomable distress and protest and at the same time making optimal use of her own resources. Put differently, the mental stance of *reverie* refers to "the capacity of the 'good object' (the good mother) to manage her own emotions and adopt a stance of accepting everything that comes from her baby, thinking about it and giving it back in a digestible form," that is more livable with (Frosh, 2012, p. 158). The mental stance of reverie parallels a "kind of free floating attention" (Frosh, 2012, p. 168) or a "state of relaxation" (Symington & Symington, 1996, p. 168). While in this mental state of relaxation or free and evenly hovering attention, the mother is able to register the infant's mental states and then to "think about what they mean and respond accordingly, in a loving and calm way" (Frosh, 2012, p. 202). The mother here is in pursuit of emotional and relational truth lovingly. Both mother-and-infant minds mature in the pursuit of emotional and relational truth in a loving way. It is not surprising then to hear the Symingtons (1996) say: "Bion … values truth and the achievement of love above all else … some insights are only possible to the one in whom the values of truth and love are central … the mind is healed by truth [and love]" (p. 22).

For Ricoeur (1986), our primal capacity for "Joy" is infinitely more central to the core of our being than our finite or temporary experiences of "sadness" (p. 140). The dialectical tension between "joy" and "sadness" is here resolved in favor of the life-affirming "Yes" to Joy. Our joyous affirmation of life is a primal position that enables us to absorb the sadness-inducing disappointments of everyday life. The seeming opposite of "Yes" is "No." Developmentally, the "No" gains ascendance in toddlerhood, approximately in the second and third years of life. The toddler's favorite word then is "No." The dialectical tension here is between Yes-saying and No-saying. When the No-saying of the toddler is *handled* properly by the parents, this loving handling mediates the resolution of the tension between the "Yes" and the "No," between the desire to assert the autonomy of the emerging separate self and the desire to cooperatively coordinate one's will with the will of essential others. In a discerningly caring context, the young child, over time, is enabled to learn to know when to rightfully assert the self (say "No") and when to cooperate, surrender, or yield, without feeling broken, humiliated, or shamed. There is no reason for him or her to become stubbornly willful or passively will-less.

Fascinatingly, Ricoeur equates the phenomenological concept of *intentionality* with *will.* In phenomenology, intentionality refers to the orientation of human consciousness, which includes unconsciousness, to something or someone outside of itself. Or, it is the directedness of the bodily self toward the lifeworld meanings we experience and enact (actualize) in existential space. Our thoughts and feelings are ultimately relational in nature. The bridge that connects the arc of intentionality (consciousness is one side of the arc and the object of consciousness is on the other side of the arc) is our capacity for (pre-reflective or reflective) meaning making while being cognizant of how meanings make us. I am, therefore, always oriented to meaningful (purposive) people or projects. In the beginning, I am above all oriented to essential others. The primordial meaning toward which I am, at first, pre-reflectively-and-bodily directed is a loving and loveable Other. My capacity for free-flowing meaning making goes awry and gets twisted when the object of my consciousness (or unconsciousness), the essential m/other, repeatedly frustrates my quest to love and be loved. My intentionality is damaged. My capacity to orient myself toward loving and loveable objects, which Ricoeur calls *will*, goes askew.

For Ricoeur (1995), there will always be a fissure between my *capacity* and *incapacity* to actualize my purposeful projects. Thus, there will always be a limit to achieving my meaningful destiny. In this gap lies my proclivity for evil (destructiveness). Ricoeur defines evil as "the incapacity belonging to the capable man, the incapacity that does not abolish capability but presupposes it as the very thing that has ceased to be available to man as we know him historically" (p. 569). For me, what is critical in this passage is the dialectical tension between *capacity* and *incapacity* and the fact that our *incapacity*, under relatively optimal or good-enough conditions, presupposes our *capacity*. In this primordial capacity lies our *loving orientation* and our *orientation toward goodness*. It is only in the twisted version, where our incapacity outweighs our capacity, which only ensues under less than optimal or not-good-enough conditions, that we become oriented to evil (destructiveness). Our secondary incapacity triumphs over our primary capacity for love-and-goodness. As a consequence, our incapacity translates into an orientation to hate-and-harm (evil). Part of our maturational journey requires us to acknowledge and affirm our capacities while at the same time humbly and realistically accept our incapacities. From this precarious balance emerges a healthy integration of healthy pride and humility while eschewing false pride or degrading self-effacement.

Love as an Integrator of Hate

In our ambivalence, we both love and hate our fellow human beings. The developmental origin of this deep ambivalence begins in infancy and childhood. Both Melanie Klein and D. W. Winnicott point to the growing awareness, acknowledgment, and tolerance of hate as a pivotal maturational step that allows the developing person to experience, more deeply and widely, the counterpart of hate which is love as well as other constructive emotions and impulses. Of course, all this can only evolve in a "facilitating" social environment as embodied in the caregivers who are understanding and tolerant of the child's original ambivalence.

Describing the Kleinian view of love-as-a-counterforce-to-hate, Altman (2010) writes:

> The Kleinian depressive [mature] position occurs when people take responsibility for their destructiveness and recognize that they can have destructive feelings, impulses, fantasies, and actions toward people whom they also love. Thus arises guilt, which in constructive [healthy] form can give rise to reparative actions. A relationship that accommodates hatred and provides for reparative action is stronger than one that denies hatred and thus becomes brittle. Denial of hatred very often implies denial of love. We can acknowledge our hatred when we recognize our love as a counterforce, when the motivation for repair is also strong. (p. 150)

The "maturity and strength of a person or a people," continues Altman, "is measured by the degree to which they can acknowledge [tolerate, and discerningly atone for] painful truths" such as having hateful feelings, thoughts, and actions (p. 121).

Schalow (2001) offers us a phenomenological understanding of the dialectical tension between love and hate. His approach is guided by the philosophies of Martin Heidegger and Friedrich W. J. Schelling. Schelling, we learn, has had a profound influence on the later thinking of Heidegger on love, a topic of rarity for Heidegger, although *care*, which is close to *love*, has a central presence in his philosophy. The core of our "being," holds Heidegger (1996), "reveals itself as care" (p. 182).

Love and hate, explicates Schalow (2001), ground our way of knowing our world. In other words, the way we love-and-hate shapes how we get to know others; how open we are to learning about them; and how capable we are in identifying with them and taking their point of view. Moreover, how I love will be reflected in how I hate and the other way around. Schalow quotes Schelling in this respect: "'For every nature can be revealed in its opposite – love in hatred, unity in strife'" (p. 42). In fact, the mediated and modulated opposition between love-and-hate, among other oppositions, marks the site of my creativity and freedom. The deeper my ambivalence, the less creative and free I am. My mature love, which absorbs and contains my hate, opens up and expands my possibilities. Conversely, my immature love, which cannot contain my hate, shrinks and contracts my possibilities. For instance, the way I love will be manifested in how I communicate with others. My mature loving orientation, which is capable of modulating my hateful orientation, allows me to be flexible and open in my communication with others. This is why for "Schelling love is a communicative field" (p. 44). Mature loving permits me to partake of a "narrative of reconciliation." I am much more inclined to repair my relational ruptures when my love is resolute and thus my hate is contained. My "faith" in a "narrative of reconciliation" is much stronger for it is anchored in the solid ground of resolute or mature love.

The resoluteness or maturity of love is tested and vindicated, states Schalow (2001), "in face of the tendency toward divisiveness and egoism" (p. 43). Resolute or mature love is able to surmount its antagonist, hate, and its derivate or other guises such as destructiveness and evil. "According to Heidegger, Schelling arrives at the paradoxical conclusion that love welcomes evil" (p. 45). By finding its antagonist, love realizes itself. Love's test lies in its achievement of reconciliation in its conflict or dialectical tension with hate (destructiveness, divisiveness, egoism, or evil). Such resolute love is also able to reconcile the conflict or dialectical tension between similarities and differences. With such a mature loving orientation, we are able to join "self and other by welcoming the differences as well as the similarities" (p. 45).

Resolute love achieves harmony within conflict. The "expression of love is always bound with the depths of human conflict" (46). Mature love has the power to "gather together opposites, and allows them to flourish in their delicate balance, i.e., harmony" (p. 46). "Harmonia is the attuned element and vibrating dimension of intimacy [love] as it traverses the chasm of alterity [otherness]" (p. 46). With this traversing we arrive at a way of loving that incorporates otherness – the differentness of the other. To do so we need to be able to "endure the tension of this transformation" (p. 48).

Once again, humility is the key to this openness and receptivity to the otherness of the Other. To be attuned to the Other, we need to learn to listen and be silent. Schalow (2001) adds, "silence is a form of attunement" (p. 87). Such attunement honors the differentness of the Other. We allow the Other to be – we let him or her be, even if he or she is seemingly opposite to us. Resolute love "seeks conciliation in the face of defiance" (p. 110).

We human beings, elaborates Schalow (2001), need to "walk the tightrope between good and evil" (p. 112) or to coordinate the opposites of love and hate, polarities that mark the site of our freedom. Walking this tightrope involves inevitable pain and suffering. Such intense "suffering invites the profoundest compassion and hatred summons the need for forgiveness" (p. 113). So we see that resolute "love always grows out of the tension of opposites" (p. 113). The movement between opposites is itself a creative process.

Resolute love, following Schalow (2001), solidifies our sense of self and makes us feel at home in the world. It allows us to follow "the natural rhythm of breathing" and readies us "for an experience of 'releasement'" and harmonious dwelling (p. 139). Harmonious dwelling, however, is not a perpetual state of contentment. It is rather the ability to endure the counterbalance of its opposite: the absence of harmony. For a concrete instance, we need to learn to "bear the inordinate weight of the [dialectical] tension of identity [similarity] and difference" (p. 150). Parents and partners must learn to walk the tightrope, balancing their similarities and differences. The letting-be of the opposite (hate, etc.) "allows love to shine" (p. 151). Resolute love "is sensitive to the magnitude of human suffering, to the plights of the 'flesh' as well as the soul" (p. 154). At the same time, mature love has an element of compassionate detachment (distancing), when balanced with passionate attachment (closeness), allows one to remain centered. Mature love, concludes Schalow, "makes us more resilient in our suffering and enables us to stand resolutely within the expanse of possibility" (p. 162).

Through resolute or mature love, we are granted a special form of freedom, the freedom to "let be." As Heidegger (1962) puts it, authentic caring is a way of "leaping ahead" by which he means allowing the Other to discover her or his possibilities or choices, rather than "leaping in for" in an attempt to control or impositionally enable the Other. The "leaping in for" way of being with others is a manifestation of inauthentic caring or parasitic paternalism. The "leaping ahead" way, in contrast, is a manifestation of authentic solicitude, which for us is a part of mature loving.

McGrath (2012) provides us with a succinct condensation of Schelling's understanding of love:

> The failure of personality, both in madness and in lifeless understanding, is the failure of freedom to achieve love. Personality is only fully realized, and understanding only fully alive, when it loves. Precisely because love effects the integration of the negative and affirmative ipseity [identity] and alterity [otherness], love is madness regulated, ground [the unconscious] moderated by [conscious] existence. We are only truly ourselves when we love, that is, when we love ourselves, others, and God. … Schellingian love is both erotic and agapic because it is as self-centered as it is other-centered. Love unites two that are really distinct. (p. 188)

Schelling makes a distinction between a healthy and unhealthy lightness (consciousness) and a healthy and unhealthy ground (unconsciousness). Whereas our destructive unconscious is "demanding" and "willful" (p. 33), our productive unconscious enlivens, empowers, and potentiates our consciousness. And whereas the destructive ground disallows the present to eject its beam upon the past, the creative ground allows the present to shed light upon the past. The past "subsists in the self as a grounding potency" (pp. 32–33). Love is facilitated by our creative and productive ground and obstructed by our destructive and unproductive ground.

In the healthy mode of self-relating, I am able to throw light on an aspect of my personality that until now has been part of my dark unconscious. I am now able to gain "distance" from it, acknowledge it, tolerate it, and "sublate" or assimilate it. What has been severed from my wider consciousness (which includes my dark unconscious) is now integrated and can be put to creative use. My capacities for optimal distancing and assimilating empower my ability to love maturely. The dialectical tension between the darkness of the background of my unconscious and the lightness of the foreground of my consciousness is relatively resolved because whereas before it has been a part of my unconscious which is severed from my consciousness, but now has become a part of the whole of my wider consciousness.

"According to Schelling," elucidates McGrath (2012), "the dark ground [unconscious], when it acts in accordance with love, *holds itself back*; it defers to the light [of consciousness] not because its desires are out of proportion to the modicum of pleasure reality can afford [Freud], but because only by subordinating itself to consciousness can it participate in love" (p. 183). "In the healthy individual," McGrath continues, "ground [the unconscious] freely subordinates itself to existence [consciousness] in a spontaneous act that Schelling likens to the unreflective decision whereby a person in danger 'knows' just what to do to save his or her own life" (p. 183). If this does not happen, then the dark unconscious dims the lightness (aliveness) of our personality. It is, McGrath concludes, like a psychological virus that devours its host.

Wirth (2003) calls the secretive and silent coordination of opposed affect-laden intentionalities, such as life versus death, health versus sickness, and love versus hate, the "conspiracy of life." "In the same way that all living is always already a dying, health and sickness form a complication, a conspiracy" (p. 174). "The conspiracy," Wirth states, "is a simultaneous expiration and inspiration, and each thing of nature is both inspired yet expiring. That is what I call the conspiracy of life, that is the life beyond and within life and death" (p. 2). Interestingly, the word "spire" is in the word "conspire." *Conspiro* means to breathe together. *Spiro* means spirit or breath. Analogously, through extrapolation, love and hate form a complicated conspiracy. How I breath-in and breath-out love conspires with how I breath-in and breath-out hate. Love is revealed in its opposite, hate. Concealed within me is my capacity for love. Wirth quotes Schelling as saying, "'the soul of all hate is love'" (p. 174). Wirth elaborates, "just as love is topsy-turvy hate … hate is perverse love" (p. 174).

At the center of our selfhood, expounds Wirth (2003) on Schelling's theory of love, is our orientation toward goodness, health, and love along with their counterforces of evil, sickness, and hate or wrath. When we speak from the perspective of goodness, health, and love our "speaking is fundamentally affirmative, the 'holy yes-saying' [to Life]" (p. 180). We are inspiringly guided by "the will to love." When we speak from the perspective of evil, sickness, and wrath (hate), we subordinate our human center to the perverse power of the periphery of our consciousness. "Wrath [or hate] is the paradox of narcissism" (p. 180). It is love's intentionality gone awry. We now love ourselves too much or too little for that matter. Our mature conscience can redeem us by calling us back to our healthy center, to love's healthy intentionality, by loving ourselves and others. Our loving center orients us toward embracing "the conspiracy of life." We are responsible for attending to and attenuating our movement away from our center and toward the periphery. Our egoism or false pride severs us from our center and renders us ungrounded. Proper love grounds and solidifies us; it holds us together. Mature love allows us to affirm the present moment. We love things as they are. To love is to live in synchrony with our own organismic temporality. We live in accord with the ground of our existence. There is relative harmony between our conscious and unconscious self, as between our dreaming and non-dreaming self-states and between sleeping and awakened modes of being-in-the-world. Our unconscious and un-coercive will, "the will that wills nothing" releases us to love freely and maturely.

Let us take a last look at the conspiracy between love (goodness) and hate (evil) and how love (goodness) can be deepened by the acknowledgment of hate (evil). Extreme hate (cruelty, destructiveness, or evil) can reveal to me, if I am open to confronting the painful existential truth, I too can be, though on a smaller scale, hateful, cruel, and destructive. This awareness can then make me less harshly judgmental of hatefulness, cruelty, and destructiveness in others. I can no longer view myself as an innocent victim, the target of other villainous people's insensitive cruelties. I am now more patient than I used to be. I try to reduce my own pettiness. In the context of this new awareness, I find myself placing myself in question. I now experience an adaptive form of guilt realizing how I have already betrayed my potential for goodness, a guilt that prepares me for acts of reparation. This new awareness has led me to a new existential truth. As Merleau-Ponty (1962) puts it, it is like "bringing truth into being" (p. xx). I am, like a true and wise philosopher, he continues, "relearning to look at the world" (p. xx). I am a "perpetual beginner" for I have to relearn again and again until the truth sinks in.

Love as a Creative Fusion of Multiple Meaning Systems

Lichtenberg et al. (2011) devote a chapter on "Love: A Motivational Systems Perspective" (pp. 75–93). They hold that "love as an experience … involves multiple shifting motivations operating for the individual in dyadic, triadic, and multiple interactions across a very wide spectrum of life's opportunities and challenges" (p. xviii). Love as motivational system intersects or overlaps with other key motivational systems: affiliation, aversive, caregiving, exploration/assertion, physiological regulation, and sensual/sexual systems. They assert that

> as a particular feeling, in its origin in infancy, love (noun) involves mainly the attachment and caregiving systems for which safety and affection are foundational. Additionally, the development of love as an experience involves the sensual, physiological and exploratory systems. Once established, a feeling of affection and attraction, and the activity of cherishing and desiring can be experienced in any motivational system where the role of treating another, oneself, a group, and any setting or object lovingly (adverb) has great exploratory and survival significance. Despite all the positive qualities of love for human vitality and survival, affection, attraction, and desire easily activate possessiveness, envy, insensitive domination, and exploitation, and expose the lover to possible humiliation, shame, and embarrassment. (p. 75)

"Systems," add Lichtenberg and his colleagues, "exist in *dialectic tension* with other [motivational] systems, and as perturbations approach chaos, tipping points lead to reorganization" (p. 14). From a phenomenological perspective, we could rephrase this to say that meanings exist in dialectical tension with one another. Meanings initially emerge from the coming together of parent-and-child and communicating, first, on an inter-bodily, pre-reflective, and preverbal level. Shared meanings emerge from this primordial inter-bodily dialogue between parent and child. These meanings leak into one another. My mother feeds me and thus enables me to regulate my bodily (physiological) system. But she feeds me protectively and lovingly. Consequently, I feel safe-and-secure in her presence. I become affectionately "attached" to her as she becomes affectionately "attached" to me. I flourish and thrive when she mirrors and partakes with me the emergent shared meanings between us, be they feelings, thoughts, bodily actions or objects in my newly forming world, even though initially I do not fully understand them. She encourages my assertive and exploratory initiatives. And she comforts and soothes me as she contains my distress and outbursts of rage in response to need frustrations, misattunements, and empathic failures. Along with these positive experiences, I undergo negative experiences like uncontainable distress, failures in communication, relational ruptures, and the mystifying inscrutability of my mother. She is not always there when I am hungry, in distress, or in need of stimulation. What she *means to me* as a companion, container, holder, soother, stimulator, and lover, and later, as a discipliner and limit-setter, keeps shifting. Over time, my mother's capacity to serve multiple loving functions or meanings stabilizes my self-world perceptions. My stabilization absorbs those occasional destabilizing moments involving shocking shifts in meanings. Her love-and-care anchors me in my emergent and meaningful self-world.

"For all the forms of love," state Lichtenberg and his colleagues (2011), "whether between child and parents, devoted friends, or lovers, the essential prerequisite experiences are the same":

1. A sense of safety based on the assurance that distress will be recognized and, to the degree possible, relieved
2. An ability to send, recognize, and respond appropriately to clear signals of need, desire, and intention
3. A shared current of sensual pleasure
4. An appreciation and admiration of the physical and mental attributes, capacities, and achievements of the loved one, the self as lover and loved, and what the dyad cocreates. (pp. 77–78)

For Lichtenberg and his colleagues (2011), in contradistinction to Bowlby, secure attachment facilitates, but is not love. A "secure base experience makes mutual love more likely to develop" (p. 79). Yet, they slip and make inadvertent reference to the child's "loving attachment to each parent" (p. 83). And, they "regard the sparkling positive emotional experience of mother and baby to be love" (p. 79). Regardless, in degrees, insecure attachment, anger, anxiety, fear, hate, sadness, and shame are added to the exchange of love. There is now a significant overlap between the motivational systems of attachment/love, affiliation, exploration/assertion, physiological regulation, and sensual (sexual) stimulation, on the one hand, and the aversive motivational system, which includes the negative affects as well as the fight-freeze-flight response system, on the other.

"The securely attached four-to six-year olds' love," expound Lichtenberg and his colleagues (2011), "is apt to contain the vibrancy of a full repertoire of positive and negative feelings" (p. 81). They, however, do not employ "coyness and clingy dependence." They are not preoccupied with the mind states of their caregivers, the consequence of which is the propitiation of both "the rival and parent of desire." They do not "restrain and dismiss their desire for pleasurable contact" with their caregivers (p. 81). They do not coercively, compulsively, demandingly, and tyrannically desire inclusion in the erotic life of their parents. Their eroticism does not play out "in domination-submission and sadomasochistic polarized forms" (p. 82). "For the securely attached oedipal-age child, romantic affection predominates toward the parent of desire and a playful aversive/affection toward the rival" (p. 82). Her or his romantic affection does not vie with or lose out "to fear and anger and the defensive manifestations of the aversive system" (p. 82). As secure adults their loving relationships are not entangled with collusive compliance or "collusive possessiveness, envy and jealousy, exploitation for the purpose of power and dominance" (p. 82).

Securely attached children, continue Lichtenberg and his colleagues (2011), have ample "opportunity for joyous intersubjective play" in their triadic relationships with both parents regardless of their heterosexual wins or losses. "Rivalry can stimulate a child's creative pursuit of successful strategies. Competitive skills become honed in the exploratory/assertive [motivational] system through rivalries in games played out in peer groups and between siblings" (p. 83). Envy and jealousy do not introduce a lasting aversive element into the rivalry. "Envy and jealousy can be contained within an essentially loving romantic triangle, adding spice to it" (p. 83). The overall dispositional style of the child is not colored by the aversive system and consequently does not become dominant. The secure child, or adult for that matter, does not doubt his or her "effectiveness in being able to elicit and retain a loving sensual or sexual response" (p. 84).

Beginning in infancy, elaborate Lichtenberg and his colleagues (2011), securely attached children, for the most part, experience a complementarity between their temperamental sensitivities and the sensitivities of their parents. Regardless of the ease or difficulty of their temperament, these children feel loved and accepted by their parents in their bones. Their parents essentially love what they have and who they are as they are, "even those with hypersensitivity to arousal and colic" (p. 85). Even though "all children, teens, and adults take many hits to their self-esteem," some take much more than others beginning with infancy and continuing far beyond. Children are resilient, but with a limit – a threshold beyond which they suffer narcissistic "injuries about appearance and performance" (p. 85). When these limits are not repeatedly violated, when the threshold is not crossed again and again, they do not result in an "impediment to forming or sustaining attachment, affiliative, romantic, and lustful love" (p. 85). "Learning to bear the slings and arrows of outrageous fortune is a lifelong experience that begins in infancy as the sensitivity of caregivers meshes or does not mesh with the temperament of the child" (p. 85).

It is not until the oedipal period (four to six years), say Lichtenberg and his colleagues (2011), that, in the context of sensitively attuned parenting, children develop the "confidence in their ability to love emotionally and physically and to be accepted and lovable" (p. 86). This acquired confidence is foundational to the future adult's capacity to love and be loved and to be loveable. Oedipal children are especially vulnerable to loss of confidence. This "vulnerability to loss of confidence as lover and rival … derives from oedipal-age children's mix of pretentions and limitations" (p. 86). Children gain confidence "in the ability to love *emotionally*" from "the romantic-tinged responses of the parent of desire and the status of little rival from the other parent" (p. 86). Children, however, also become painfully aware of the limitation imposed by their littleness. "Size matters." They come to recognize that there is a discrepancy between their desires and ambitions and their capacities. "Ambition is a powerful spur to creativity and enterprise, but also a potential source of disappointment and the destroyer of confidence when the bubble of grandiosity bursts" (p. 86). Parents who *handle* their oedipal children sensitively by navigating a *balance* between prideful affirmation of their children's oedipal (love-and-lust tinged) strivings and appropriate limit-setting enable their children to emerge from this period with a "dispositional reservoir of … positive oedipal relations" with their parents that they can tap into as they grow into adulthood (p. 89).

"The many mental [and emotional] states that are referred to as love (noun or verb)," comment Lichtenberg and his colleagues (2011), "alter in complexity throughout life" (p. 90). There is interplay between attachment, caregiving, sensuality, and love that is grounded in "security and mutual mirroring." These motivational systems (or positive meaning modalities) intersect with aversive motivational systems (or negative meaning modalities).

> The divide in the sensual/sexual system between approved of body pleasure intentions and disapproved of personal and interpersonal intentions involves regulation imposed through the aversive system conveyed by shaming and prohibiting authorities. Many children, adolescents, and adults form a successful strategy of sexual intentions enhanced by transgressive (aversive system) excitement that is incorporated along with attachment into romantic and lustful love. (p. 90)

"Love," expand Lichtenberg and his colleagues (2011), "in its success or failure in any of its forms, involves many motivational systems – as to be expected of any complex amalgam of mental [and emotional] states" (p. 90). This complexity that is love-in-relation-to-other motivational systems unfolds in unpredictable spurts. In infancy dyadic love is nascent. Beyond infancy, dyadic and triadic love becomes central as it plays out the complexity of multiple motivational systems. Love's success does not typically focus on *aversiveness* in the affiliative, attachment, caregiving, and sensual motivational systems.

Love's success, however, "depends on prior and current regulation of the aversive system" (p. 90). It is also contingent upon increased self-reliance and "self-selection" (p. 91). The aim of agentic self-selection – the assertion, exploration, and the selective pursuit of "preferences in learning and recreation" – is to deepen and broaden one's creative fusion of multiple intentions serving multiple motivational systems (or meaning functions) even though "the basic pattern [has been] established in the oedipal phase" (p. 92).

> The dyadic form of adult love characteristic of the attachment motivational system drives much of its lasting power from continuity with the foundation of intimacy and affection that begins infancy: security, approval, commonality, admiration, and sharing of information [meanings] that allow each to know the other deeply. The dyadic form of attachment love consolidates its lasting power from shared activity in each of the other [motivational] systems. (p. 92)

Two partners share their bodies through sensual, sexual, and mutually comforting and physiologically regulating contact. They may also share political, recreational, religious, and other social affiliations. Additionally, they may share caregiving in their relations to their own children, their pets, elderly parents, relatives, or friends. Individually and together they may explore and then share their separate or joint interests in art, literature, movies, music, sports, television, travel, and world events. They may even or inevitably gossip (positive or negative, preferably the former) as a way of intensifying their attachment bond.

"Aversiveness," assert Lichtenberg and his colleagues (2011), "is an integral aspect of any successful lasting commitment – how to 'play at' shifting roles of domination, argue fairly and know when to withdraw, and most of all, how to repair disruptions" (p. 92). Moreover, "while expressions of inevitable differences of opinion add spice to the attachment, an abiding sensual current is a necessary ingredient for maintaining a satisfying level of affection, even if romantic and lustful love have diminished" (p. 92).

The answer to the question *Can Love Last?* – a question that has been raised by Mitchell (2002), say Lichtenberg and his colleagues (2011),

> can best be derived from an appreciation of the intentions and goals of the attachment system (the strength of the dyadic relationship), the sexual system (the strength and pitfalls of the triadic relationship), and the persistence of the sensual system (the link that connects attachment, romance, and sexuality). Stated differently, an appreciation of love as a complex experience of different mental [and affective] states requires an understanding of the dyadic and triadic relationships playing out in different motivational systems. (pp. 92–93)

To be true to their theory of love, the answer ought to have included motivational systems other than simply the attachment and the sexual/sensual motivational systems. "Systems," they say early in their work, "exist in dialectical tension with other systems" (p. 14).

Allow me to extrapolate the practical implications of Lichtenberg et al.'s (2011) theory of love. To understand my need for love (attachment), I have to comprehend how it interacts or is in dialectical tension with other needs (motives, intentions, or meaning systems). How this interplay plays out in different relational contexts and over time affects how I love, how I am loved, and my lovability in my eyes and in the eyes of my essential other. If I smother my significant other with parent-like care, the quality of my love for her and her love for me will be compromised. If I don't engage in enough caring acts, then our love will suffer. If I am too controlling of my partner or the other way around (touching on the aversive system), our love will be negatively influenced. If we do not jointly and separately explore and pursue interests, our love will be undermined. If we do not touch each other enough sensually and sexually, our love will be emptied. The tensions between our different motivational or need systems (meanings) are beckoning for balance. We need to listen to the call for balance across our motivational systems (or meaning modalities) if our love is to grow.

Let us now take up Mitchell's (2002) question: *Can Love Last?* The attempt to understand love, says Mitchell, propels us inevitably into "the dialectics concerning fantasy and actuality, love and hate, the controlled and the uncontrollable, pathos and guilt, safety and risk" (p. 29). As we read further in Mitchell's text, we discover that the struggle to comprehend love involves a range of other polarities: rest versus motion (p. 49), security versus insecurity (p. 49), safety versus adventure or risk (p. 49; p. 51), aloneness versus connection (p. 50), predictability versus unpredictability (p. 51), vulnerability versus invulnerability (p. 51), controllability versus uncontrollability (p. 51), permanence versus impermanence (p. 51), and love versus desire (53). The dialectical tension between love and desire receives special attention by Mitchell.

"Love and desire," says Mitchell (2002), "generate the arc of tension within which romance emerges, and, like all our experiences, love and desire are partly [social or cultural] constructions." "They are not completely constructions," he adds, "and they are certainly not subject to our conscious will" (p. 53). Modern life, expounds Mitchell, makes it difficult to integrate love and desire. "Vitality and meaning are not easy to come by" either (p. 25). This con-fusion or lack of fusion (integration) is passed on from parents to children for we "become, inevitably and irreversibly, extraordinarily like the caregivers we require to nurture us through a lengthy dependency" (p. 26).

Additionally, we live in a hyper-competitive, hyper-individualistic, hyper-materialistic, and hypersexual culture that makes the integration of love and desire very difficult.

Mitchell's focus is on *romantic love* as a fusion of love and desire. This is very similar to a portion of Sternberg's (1998) *triangular theory of love.* According to this theory,

> love can be understood as comprising three components: intimacy, passion, and commitment. Different kinds of love comprise different combinations of these components. For example, romantic love was characterized by intimacy plus passion, fatuous or foolish love by commitment fueled only by passion, and consummate or complete love by the combination of all three. (pp. ix–x)

Passion is "driven by physiological arousal" (p. 161). But over time, like an addiction, an "opposing force starts to come into being, moderating the experience of passion" (p. 162). "What started out as a positive feeling is now an attempt to stave off a negative one – withdrawal symptoms" (p. 162). Being *intimate* means emotionally investing oneself in a relationship for the purpose of deepening the connection or closeness between two people. Being *committed* means cognitively deciding to stay in the relationship. There is a correlative narrative (story) that goes with each of these elements of love: intimacy, passion, and commitment. "Love is synthetic rather than analytic – literally synthetic in the sense that we synthesize" (p. 24) the stories that we partly construct and partly breathe in from our familial and cultural air in disjointed fragments.

To repeat, for both Sternberg (1998) and Mitchell (2002), romantic love is synthesis of intimacy (love) and passion (desire). Mitchell asks: *Can Love* Last? This question should really be rephrased to read, *Can Romantic Love Last?* The subtitle of Mitchell's book, *The Fate of Romance over Time*, reveals the true subject of the work at hand. But here is my objection: Romance or romantic love in my eyes is a variation on the theme of love and not the other way around. His concluding paragraph to the book, though with *few qualifiers*, makes sense to me:

> The cultivation of [loving] romance in relationships requires two people who are fascinated by the ways in which, individually and together, they generate forms [vitalizing meanings] of life they hope they can count on. It entails a tolerance of the fragility of those hopes, woven together from the realities and fantasies [as forms of polar lifeworld meanings], and an appreciation of the ways in which, in the rich density of contemporary life, realities often become fantasy and fantasies often become reality [polar meanings are transformed into one another]. (p. 201)

There are times when Mitchell (2002) describes love's tensions as unresolvable, as when he discusses the theme of attachment. Our so-called secure attachment, with its promise of permanence and buffered protection is illusory. Still, we believe in it because it defends us "against the vulnerability inherent in romantic love" (p. 45). "Thus," surmises Mitchell, "'secure attachment' is not a terribly useful model of mutual, adult romantic love, except in fantasy, illusory, security-bolstering dimensions. Love, by its very nature, is *not* secure; we keep wanting to make it so" (p. 49). Here Mitchell does not entertain the possibility of the existence of *degrees* of secure attachment and *degrees* of insecure attachment. Yet, there are times when Mitchell understands that love's tensions are reducible, as when he describes the relationship between authentic passion and the longing for the predictability of security and between spontaneity and steady commitment:

> Genuine passion, in contrast to its degraded forms, is not split off from a longing for security and predictability, but in a continual dialectical relationship with that longing. In order for romantic involvement [for romantic love] to remain vital and robust over time, it is crucial that the commitment not be so rigid as to override spontaneity and that spontaneity not be so rigid as to preclude commitment. (p. 199)

Analogous to the previously touched-upon concept of *self-selection*, Mitchell (2002) lyrically links love to the dynamic concept of *agency*:

> When two people say 'I love you' to each other (or something equivalent), they are not just reporting on what has happened but contributing to determining what sort of agents they can become for themselves and each other, determining whether and how their relationship may deepen and whether certain paths of development will be foreclosed. (p. 196)

Love as a Dialectical Dialogue Between Meaning Attributions

I am, at least in part, the agent (co-author or co-subject) of my unfolding love story (meaning-saturated narrative). I am the inheritor of my familial and multicultural love stories that I have been *subjected to* in my developmental history. I am the "co-author" in the developing script of how I have *appropriated* the love stories I have acquired through my psychosocial inheritance. I am the dialectical tension that seeks the semblance of balance between being the subject of my developing love story and of being or having been and continue to be subjected to the love stories that surround me. I am inhabited with polar or polyphonic voices embodying love's dialectical tensions, voices that are seemingly opposite to one another, voices that are contiguous or stand in contrast to one another, and voices that are harmonic with one another. Outside voices dwell within me. I give expression to these voices in my interaction with others, especially my essential others.

In concurrence with Sternberg (1998), *love is a story*. As a story, love is a most essential constituent of a larger story, the story of who we are and who we want to become. It is a most important part of our self-realization through, though *limited*, self-selection. Our familial and cultural stories make us; we selectively contribute to the making of our own stories. As Habermas (1987) describes it, agency and responsibility go hand-in-hand in the creative construction of our life story in general and, I would add, our love story in particular:

> To the extent that the adult can take over and be responsible for his own biography, he can come back to himself in the narratively preserved traces of his own interactions. Only one who takes over his own life history can see in it the realization of his self. Responsibility to take over one's own biography means to get clear about *who one wants to be*, and from this horizon to view the traces of one's own interactions *as if* they were deposited by the actions of a responsible author, of a subject that acted on the basis of a reflective relation to self. (pp. 98–99)

By *answer*ing the *question*, which is a form of a dialogue with oneself, about who or what kind of person I want to be, I make it possible for myself to reflect on my past interactions as being problematic. What Habermas (1987) is describing is really a blueprint for *becoming mature* or *maturational becoming*, which above all involves assuming responsibility for my own biography. The hallmark of maturity for Habermas is what he calls communicative or interactive competence, which involves becoming competent in how I communicate with my self and others. But my capacity to interact with my self and others competently involves "the choice of a life project" of integrating my disparate and disintegrated identities:

> Ego-identity proves itself in the ability to integrate a series of concrete – partly disintegrated, partly superseded – identities into a life history taken upon oneself [integrated in a new way]. … An autonomous conduct of life depends in turn on the decision – or on successively repeated and revised decisions – as to "who one wants to be." … [This is] a complex obscure process [that moves from

> obscurity or unconsciousness] into a conscious, spontaneously exercised choice. In any case, the answer to the question, who does one want to be, cannot be rational in the way a moral decision can. … There is an indissoluble element of arbitrariness … in the choice of a life project. (p. 109)

Analogously, our dialectical movement toward an *integrative love story* results in the reduction of our contradictory identifications, strengthens the integration of our identity, and leads to the acquisition of communicative competence. There is always a dialectical dialogue going on within and between us and others, forming an arc of intentionality, involving *meanings*, beliefs, decision scripts, feelings, goals, thoughts, and so on, that are either fixed and static or dynamic and generative. Generative meanings are open to re-vision. When revised, love-imbued meanings open up new possibilities for relating lovingly and more maturely with our selves and others.

In "any intimate relationship," holds Holmes (2010), " – spousal, parent-child, sibling, close friendship – highly specific meanings derived from the minutiae of a person's life are co-created" (p. 48). Once articulated, "meanings can be considered … from all possible angles: tested, refined, held onto, modified or discarded as appropriate" (p. 48). Emergent meanings, especially those that are developmental, relational, and initially implicit (unconscious), transcend mere cognition and ultimately derive from bodily experiences, such as one's dimly apprehended overwhelming dependency upon a maternal figure for survival and comfort or one's own archaic need for the nurturing body of the mother. Such generative meanings can only emerge in a jointly co-created secure space in a communicative context of a secure and coherent narrative where meanings communicated are not oversaturated (enmeshed-hyperactivating); are not undersaturated (dismissive-deactivating); and are not incoherent, disorganized, illogical, and wildly disjointed. Moreover, *how* the loving partners talk about themselves and their lives is just as, if not more, important than *what* they talk about. A secure narrative style facilitates an open-ended discourse where meaning is inherent in the interactive mutuality of the dialogue in the moment. This kind of dialogue encourages the exploration of *mutual meanings*. The loving partners are "able to balance affect and cognition in ways appropriate to the topic discussed" (p. 49). It is the movement from private to *shared meanings*, where *meta-meanings* – meanings about meanings (about sensitive subjects) – are explored and played with, that enables the loving participants to feel solidly secure and strengthened in their love for each other. Loving partners are able to companionably share and explore mutual meanings. They are able to enhance each other's secure narrative style – way of expressing their meanings. It is the fruition of a creative synthesis between conscious and unconscious meanings. Such a narrating style is fluid, open-ended, and polysemic. Securely shared meanings beget a secure base from which to venture into new meaning-ful domains. To summarize, the "*capacity to find/make shared meanings*" enables loving partners to "come together in a meaningful shared 'present moment' … it is the *mutuality of meaning-making* that matters" (p. 53).

The dialectical mind, at its maturational best, in our view, is akin to what Bollas (2018) calls the "democratic mind" (Chapter 11, pp. 79–92). Quoting John Stuart Mill, an individual with a democratic mind is one who "'has kept his mind open to criticism of his opinion and conduct. Because it has been his practice to listen to all that could be said against him … [for it is] the only way in which a human being can make some approach to knowing the whole [truth] of a subject'" (p. 81). "This statement," continues Bollas, "could easily be the credo of the psychoanalyst" (p. 81). A good enough psychoanalyst, who wants to understand the patient's "unconscious truths," subjects herself to all aspects of the patient's emotional life as well as, I would add, her own emotional reactions to the patient's telling of emotion-laden life narrative. With an open mind, the psychoanalyst listens to the patient with an evenly hovering attention, while the patient associates freely, expressing anything that comes to mind. Imagine approximating this dialectically dialogical model in everyday life. Two close partners (parents or close friends), who have love for each other, alternate between listening with an evenly hovering attention while the other expresses freely what is on his or her mind. I believe that this would only intensify the bond between the two while getting to know (the truths) about each other. This kind of dialectical dialogue is likely to elevate their mutual love to a higher level of integration.

"Above all else," elaborates Bollas (2018), "free associations reveal how full of contradictions we are" (p. 84). Interestingly, I myself may not be conscious of many if not most of my unconscious contradictions. However, as I freely associate without fear of being subjected to harsh judgment thereby rendering me defensively unfree, my essential other becomes conscious of my unconscious contradictions. My unconscious is in the consciousness of the Other. When this is gently and caringly brought to my attention at the right time when I am ready, I become enlightened and my knowledge of the truths about myself expands. I am on my way to reducing my contradictions and moving toward further maturation. Similarly, my partner may read my bodily tension before I myself become aware of it. She then moves to hold me and lovingly ameliorates my tension. I am thankful. I am blessed. I hope to become a better listener to my own body – what my body is trying to tell me. I hope to listen to her body – to the embodied meanings that emanate from her in the shared relational context of our life together, and respond kindly, understandingly, and lovingly.

Any "mind," states Bollas (2018), "could simultaneously house many speakers [voices or selves], talking to various [imagined or real] others about all kinds of things" (p. 87). Just as the self is part of a community, the self is also a community unto itself. The "concept of democracy," continues Bollas, "was applicable to our internal world as it was to conflicts amongst groups and nations" (p. 87). Bollas elaborates:

> we all have a "representative drive": an urge to express our views. This drive arrives out of the *jouissance* of the infant and toddler over expression and then speech. We might see this drive, so necessary to the self's expression of idiom [unique subjectivity], as the psychic foundation of the force behind democracy; something that arrives, not because it has been handed down over the centuries, but because it exists within all of us as an intricate feature of the need to speak freely. (87)

The "reasoned self evolves gradually out of an *internal* democracy of many competing ideas that, in the beginning, might more accurately be described as mental chaos" (p. 88). For Bollas, the mind is seen as being inherently dialogically dialectical – always *questioning* and *answering*. There is a dialectical dialogue between mind (person) and world. There is a blurring between the internal and the external. This is why the inherent democracy of our mind can be easily compromised by powerful authoritarian contexts. "Whereas the democratic frame of mind will happily house many diverse ideas – 'democratic vistas,' to quote Walt Whitman – the totalitarian frame of mind will shut down the divergent voices of our inner democracy to follow a narrow, rigid set of views" (p. 89). Growing up and living in familial and communal contexts that encourage "inclusiveness, discussion and compromise" will incline us "to exercise a democratic frame of mind" (p. 91). Although this existential democratic frame of mind may be suppressed or repressed because of rigidly polarizing familial or communal conditions, "the democratic process remains a *potential* in all beings, even within the most totalitarian self" (p. 91). *The capacity for love* is more likely to grow (ripen) in the soil of democracy where dialectical dialogue is allowed to freely flourish.

Altman (2010) asserts that it is time to depathologize the psychoanalytic concepts of projection (externalization) and introjection (internalization) and begin to view them as part of the dialectical relationship between self-and-world. Making them part of ordinary life goes some way toward the view that multiplicity, instability, and discontinuity (coexisting dialectically with stability, coherence, and continuity) are inherent to human mental life. Seeking a sense of *existential mastery*, for instance, entails the avowal of our own sense of helplessness. Only then does the experience of helplessness become "integrated with the experience of mastery" (p. 103). The "*maturity* and strength of a person or a people," continues Altman, "is measured by the degree to which they can acknowledge painful truths" (p. 121). And "whoever cannot tell himself the truth about his past is trapped in it, is immobilized in the prison of his undiscovered self" (p. 121). Maturity requires of us the ability to tolerate our shame and guilt regarding our past destructive acts, even toward essential others whom we love. Maturity necessitates that we assume responsibility for the harsh and harmful actions we perpetrate upon the people we love. Maturity demands of us that we acknowledge and assume responsibility for our hateful feelings and actions; that we respond to the voice of our guilty conscience by taking reparative action. As a consequence our loving relations are strengthened. We must "acknowledge our hatred" in order to "recognize our love as a counterforce" (p. 150).

"Dialectics refers to the art of dialogical discussion and the interplay of ideas" (Hannush, 2007, p. 9). The "dialectical approach," writes Wrightsman (1994), includes three major points:

> 1. the idea of opposing forces, or polarities
> 2. the unity of opposites, in the sense that opposites define each other, or lend meaning to each other (Without hate there can be no love.)
> 3. the dynamic relationship between opposites, or their struggle for control, hence necessitating constant change. (p. 150)

Dialectics, adds Marra (2005), is a dialogue about

> *meaning* and purpose in life. The dialogue centers on the fundamental nature of reality which involves thesis and antithesis, balance and imbalance. Each imbalance offers an opportunity for rebalance. … Psychological dialectics involve conflict and opposition … as the needs of the person are frequently in conflict with the demand characteristics and contingencies of the [social] environment at the moment. (p. 84)

Meanings and purposes, our own and in relation to those of others, collide. As the reader will have noticed, I consider the Hegelian dialectical tension or conflict between thesis and antithesis seeking balance and rebalance applies only to a segment of human experience. Some dialectical tensions are balanceable; others are not. A thesis (meaning) might have multiple antitheses (contrasting or oppositional meanings) and the other way around.

What a close wife, daughter, sibling, cousin, and best friend mean to me may not synchronize or may only partially converge with the *meanings they ascribe to these social roles* with which most of us *identify*. As a result we may experience conflicts and collisions as we enact these variant meanings. To reduce or sometimes even enhance these meaning tensions, we seek, in order to find a good-enough *match in meaning*, new shared meanings that enrich our relational lives.

When attempting to understand love relations, we need to focus our attention on the tensions that inhere in relating. "As people come together," say Baxter and Montgomery (1996), "in any social union, they create a host of dialectical forces" (p. 15). "Dialectical interplay," they continue, "may work 'backstage' beyond partners' mindful awareness, nonetheless contributing to relational dialogue" (p. 15). Although Baxter and Montgomery do not, to the best of my reading, mention love relations (except in passing reference to the context-dependent meaning shifts of the utterance of "I love you"), they devote a chapter on "Rethinking Closeness" (Chapter 4, pp. 79–105) and another chapter on "Understanding Interactional Competence in Relationships" (Chapter 8, pp. 185–206).

Two people who love each other will inevitably, if they are honest with each other, experience interpersonal conflict. Conflict is of the essence of human life. They will experience a nonsynchronous moment, what Baxter and Montgomery (1996) call a "momentary experience of a contradiction" (p. 15). This involves an "antagonistic struggle" "such that one person aligns his or her interests with one pole and the other person aligns his or her interests with another pole" (p. 15). They provide the example of a close couple, where one partner desires more autonomy and independence, which constitutes one pole, and the other partner desires more connection and interdependence, which constitutes the other pole. Thus, there is antagonistic asynchrony between the two partners. They label the conflictual collision (the intentional arc of dialectical or back-and-forth tension) between the two poles as a *contradiction*. They then illustrate the possible patterns that may ensue from the dialectical exchange between these prototypical relational partners:

> Many possible patterns of dialectical change result from a pair's communicative choices. For example, a pair that perceives too little interdependence and too much partner autonomy in their relationship could respond in any of several ways, ranging, for example, from naively optimistic efforts to gloss over or ignore the tension, to efforts that emphasize increased interdependence and decreased autonomy, to fatalistic efforts to accept the inevitability of their situation, to efforts to redefine what they mean by togetherness and separation.

> Whatever their choices at the moment, their future interactions will be constrained by those choices. (p. 14)

Messiness is the essence of our relational lives. Our "social life," say Baxter and Montgomery (1996), "is a dynamic knot of contradictions, a *ceaseless interplay* between contrary or opposing tendencies" (p. 3). I need to be independent and separate from my partner *and* simultaneously I need to be interdependent with and connected to him or her. I desire predictability and certainty at the same time that I desire for some unpredictability, uncertainty, and mystery in my intimate close relationship. I want disclosure and openness, yet I need to use discretion and protect my privacy. A "both/and," not an "either/or," way of responding to these seemingly contradictory needs is necessary for the well-being of our relationship, for our love to flourish. A "healthy relationship is one in which the parties manage to satisfy both oppositional demands, that is, relational well-being is marked by the capacity to achieve 'both/and' status" (p. 6).

Not only are they intrinsic to our relational lives, "contradictions," elaborate Baxter and Montgomery (1996), "are the basic 'drivers' of change" (p. 7). "The term 'contradiction' … refers to the dynamic interplay between unified oppositions" (p. 8). Change and stability, in turn, form a unified opposition. "Put simply, dialectical change is the interplay of stability and flux" (p. 10). Oppositions, however, are likely to function, not in a binary, but in a multivoiced way. There are likely to be multiple oppositions on each side of a polar continuum operating simultaneously. Moreover, contradictions or incompatibilities not only oppose but also require each other. This is why they "must be simultaneously unified or interdependent on each other" (p. 9). "Connection with others," for instance, "is necessary in the construction of a person's [separate] identity as an autonomous individual … just as a relational connection is predicated on the continuing existence of the parties' unique identities" (p. 9).

Our sense of "self," itself, state Baxter and Montgomery (1996), "is constituted out of two contradictory necessities – the need to connect with another (the centripetal force) and the simultaneous need to separate from the other (centrifugal force)" (p. 25). The "self," they continue, "is in a perpetual state of becoming as a consequence of the ongoing interplay between fusion and separation with others" (p. 11). They expand:

> personal close relationships … are always composed of both fusion with and differentiation from, both centripetal and centrifugal forces, both interdependence and independence. Within each is the seed of the other. From a relational

dialectics perspective bonding occurs in both interdependence with the other and independence from the other. (p. 43)

How love relations grow, stagnate, or deteriorate requires our "understanding of the processes by which couples create, realize, and deal with dialectical tensions" (p. 44). Those who truly desire to move toward the maturation of their capacity to love must learn to tolerate the tensions triggered by the simultaneous opposition and unity of their contradictions. We must learn "to live on 'friendly terms' with paradox, contradiction, and multivocality" (p. 60). We need to learn to be at home with the ironic nature of our incongruous lives. We must cultivate "an attitude and action of ironic appreciation" (p. 60).

We need to learn to recalibrate, balance, and integrate our lived contradictions if we want our love to ripen. By recalibrating we come to see that "the opposing forces are no longer regarded as oppositional to one another" (Baxter and Montgomery, 1996, p. 65). We come to realize that balancing and integrating our seemingly oppositional modes of being-in-the-world-with-others are never absolute. Our relational lives are characterized by a dynamic flux involving multiple vocal tensions, including the tension between stability and change. "Contradictions do not go away in a relationship" (p. 65). We, as lovers and loved ones, need to repeatedly reaffirm our acceptance that "contradictory polarities cannot be reconciled" once and for all (p. 66).

We need to learn to flexibly confront, cooperate, coordinate, compromise, and creatively improvise as we negotiate our dialectical dilemmas and our multiple tension-producing voices if we are to deepen our love for each other. "Relationships," assert Baxter and Montgomery (1996), "*are* slippery processes, constantly on the dynamic edge between order and disorder, sameness and difference, repetition and newness, linearity and cyclicity" (p. 69). There are, however, "turning points in a relationship's history when the pressures of dialogic interplay are of sufficient intensity that a major quantitative and qualitative change occurs for the pair" (p. 72). "A relationship's dialogic complexity," they add, "is captured by the simultaneous moreness *and* lessness on a variety of contradiction-based characteristics – for example, more and less interdependence, more and less openness, and so forth" (p. 73). The moreness or lessness is context related. For instance, a couple may become more and more connected in their body-to-body tender expressivity, but less and less connected when it comes to their finances or work activities. "Thus, dialogic change is multidirectional in nature" (p. 73). We need to keep our dialectical dialogue or dialogical dialectic alive, lively, and enlivening.

As participants in close relationships, explain Baxter and Montgomery (1996), we are poised, quoting Mikhail Bakhtin, "'*on the boundary between [our own] and someone else's consciousness, on the threshold ... and in this tension-filled encounter lies ... the highest degree of sociability*'" (p. 79). In this encounter with our loved one, at the boundary or threshold of our consciousnesses, "the both-and-ness" of *closeness* (connectedness, interdependence, unity) and *distance* (differentiation, individuation, separation) needs to be negotiated on an ongoing basis. The quality of my closeness to my loved other can only be understood or mirrored in the quality of my distance from her or him. My loved one and I share similarities and have differences. There is tension in that awareness. This awareness of our similarity and difference animates our ongoing dialogue. My awareness of my similarity to my loved one indicates to me that s/he and I have a shared lifeworld of meanings. Knowing that my loved one and I are similar in a very deep way and that we both are fairly identical in the meanings we give to things is very, very important to me. I am also continually aware of our differences, of unshared lived realities. With an orientation of acceptance, openness, and tension-tolerance this differentness or the otherness of the other can be a potential source of enrichment and growth. Yet, it can also be alienating and distancing, especially when the differentness of my essential other makes me feel misunderstood, alienated, alone, lonely, and isolated.

Like a pendulum, observe Baxter and Montgomery (1996), there will be "qualitative shifts in what 'connectedness' and 'separateness' mean to the pair" – to the close partners in their joint dialogical trajectory in lived space-and-time (p. 99). For instance, there will be a "qualitative shift" in *what love means* to the dialogical partners as their relational history unfolds over time. Of course, it depends, at least in part, on how they *handle* the tensions in their ongoing dialectical dilemmas; for a concrete instance, how they have *handled* the tension between "We Time" and "Me Time" at different phases of their partnership.

Maturely loving partners do not ignore a particular contradiction by "privileging only one polarity," say connectedness. For "before long," reflect Baxter and Montgomery (1996), "the exigence of the neglected demand for autonomy [separateness] will become salient to the pair" (p. 100). We cannot gloss over "the presence of autonomy-connection tension" without paying a relational, maturational, and mental health price. Close and loving pairs who have successfully calibrated-and-recalibrated, balanced-and-rebalanced, and integrated-and-reintegrated their seeming contradictions will talk about communal and individual themes – things that they enjoy doing together and things that they enjoy doing separately. They are committed to both connectedness and autonomy. They have been able to balance their communal and individual goals. They are comfortable talking about themes of union and themes of separateness. "Dialogic closeness is built upon *both* partner connectedness *and* partner autonomy or separation" (p. 104). Their polyphonous or multi-voiced "communicative practices … collectively give voice to the interplay of connectedness and separateness" (p. 105). This is love-in-action, a calibrated, balanced, and integrated transaction.

Relationships are co-created, assert Baxter and Montgomery (1996), "at the gap between utterance and response" (p. 189). Interactional competence has to do with how well close pairs or partners manage their patterns of spiraling dialogue at the gap of utterance and response as they "*deal with themes like openness, certainty, and closeness*" (p. 193). Extrapolating, in order for our love to deepen and widen, we need to acquire the capacity for "interactional competence." We need to efficaciously deal with dialectical tensions produced by polar themes or modes of being-with-each-other such as being-open versus being-private, seeking certainty versus being comfortable with uncertainty, and being-close versus maintaining a healthy distance. We need to deal effectively with other polar themes, "like politeness versus assertiveness, communality versus instrumentality, attention to long-term versus short-term goals, even appropriateness versus effectiveness" (p. 196). We need to cultivate interactional competence in the context of our ongoing and open-ended dialogue around these and other tension-producing polar themes that are central to our everyday lives.

Even angry, deceptive, degrading, derogatory, embarrassed, and shame-based interactions, note Baxter and Montgomery (1996), can "be important to relational well-being" (p. 197). Such interactions "can help couples to change and renew their relationship in healthy ways" (p. 197). This can be done so long as the couple is able to meet the "first principle of realizing, reflecting, and re-creating the dialectical nature of social reality" (p. 198). "In summary, communicating well in personal relationships means communicating in ways that acknowledge, respond to, and re-create contradiction" (p. 199). By "recreating contradiction" they mean transforming the either/or contradiction to a both/and dialectic. They assert, yet again, "interactional competence is signaled by actions that contribute to the fluidity of dialogue, that is, that keep the conversation going" (p. 200). "Blocking, precluding, or discouraging dialogue are, however, signals of [interactive] incompetence" (p. 201).

We need to cultivate "the abilities not only to advance a position," elaborate Baxter and Montgomery (1996), "but also to take the other's view, to adapt, to work *with* an opponent as much as against, sometimes to even change the rules to come up with the new, and, always, to continue the process [of dialogue]" (p. 202). When we are able to remain open when our own meaning attribution (interpretive expression) is countered with an opposing meaning attribution, then "'we are fulfilling a truly human, if incomplete, side of our natures'" (p. 202). If we want our love to deepen and widen, then we need to welcome our loved ones to oppose our meanings with their own counter-meanings, when they do not share our meaning attributions. "'*A meaning only reveals its depths,*'" Bakhtin is quoted as saying, "'*once it has encountered and come into contact with another, foreign meaning; they engage in a kind of dialogue, which surmounts the closedness and one-sidedness of these particular meanings*'" (p. 207).

How are we to enter the meaning world of another who is different from us, an Other who contradicts our meaning with a counter-meaning? Baxter and Montgomery (1996) respond by referring us to Richard Rorty's description of "liberal irony." "Irony," they tell us, "entertains both belief and doubt, both hope and despair, both seriousness and play" (p. 224). As an ironist, using Rortyian language and extrapolating on the discourse on love, my loved one and I can raise doubt about our own "vocabulary of meanings." We can place our meanings in brackets and question them. This way we do not over-identify with and imbue them with uncontested emotional or relational truth. We can at the same time view each other's vocabularies of meanings with an attitude of fascination and intrigue. My loved one and I can reaffirm our dyadic solidarity by trying out different vocabularies of meanings. We can, using a direct quotation from Rorty, "'redescribe ourselves, our situation, our past … with alternative [vocabularies of meanings] … to make the best selves for ourselves that we can'" (pp. 203–204). This process enables us to imaginatively identify with each other's lifeworld, which is not only different from, but also similar to our lifeworld. Our lifeworlds now become "'in the range of 'us''" (p. 204).

Perceiving the "strong poet" as one who is exquisitely attuned to the ironic in life, Rorty (1989) writes:

> We shall see the conscious need of the strong poet to *demonstrate* that he is not a copy or replica as merely a special form of an unconscious need everyone has: the need to come to terms with the blind impress which chance has given him, to make a self for himself by redescribing that impress in terms which are, if only marginally, his own. (p. 43)

Every person has the potential to cultivate the capacity to become a "strong poet." An individual does not have "to accept somebody else's description of oneself"; one can always "tell a story about one's causes in a new language" (p. 28). From this I can derive the understanding that I can always tell my own love story in a novel language. Suppose I grew up in a family and a culture that linked love with money. Unconsciously, I "inherited" this familial and cultural narrative of love and loving.

Or, imagine that I grew up in a family and a culture where love was contingent upon "success" in small and not-so-small ways. Yet again, picture growing up with narcissistic parents who lacked the capacity to bestow upon me the generous gift of a surplus of unconditional love counterbalanced by a lesser conditional love. Their love was severely skewed in its conditionality upon my "success." I now find myself blindly enacting these familial and cultural scripts through my unconscious attempts to satisfy my twisted longing for "love" through my "success" strivings.

Frazier (2006) agrees with Rorty's thesis that

> the critically reflexive person is much farther down the path of novel self-creation. She has more autonomy, for as she recognizes the web of contingencies that she is, in a profound respect she gains a perspective on herself and others that is liberating just by virtue of the fact that she gains some critical distance from the inherited identity and is able to see it in a different light. … Indeed, such a person comes to recognize clearly a [life] project that is implicated in all her more specific pursuits of self-creation: the project of coming to terms with her inherited identity. (p. 97)

Recognizing, facing, acknowledging, and, then painfully, *owning* the emotional truth about the contingencies of our lives that constitute our "inherited identity" is liberating. This is a daunting life project that has ripple effects on how we live our everyday lives.

From a Rortyian perspective, asserts Frazier (2006), our "identity is revisable" (p. 195). For Rorty, however, to be a true practitioner of the ironic way of life – to be amusedly attuned to the inconsistencies or incongruities in our beliefs, desires, and ideals from which we repeatedly fall short when compared to how we actually live our lives – we must be committed to freedom of expression, truthfulness, and peacefulness or the avoidance of harming others. We cannot practice the ironic way of living if we cannot refrain from harming others. Simply stated, we cannot practice irony cruelly. This is what constitutes our commitment to liberalism – a liberal democracy.

Frazier (2006) views Kierkegaard as more of the pure ironist than Rorty. Why? Although for both irony holds a central place in (ethical) life, Kierkegaard maintains that our capacity to be cognizant of the incongruities of our personal lives and acting ethically upon this awareness is an existential given – a universal human potential. There is no further need to link this capacity for living the ironic way of life to a socially constructed phenomenon like liberal democracy. I respectfully differ from Frazier. I see here a concordance between Rorty's "liberalism" and Christopher Bollas's (2018) understanding of the "democratic mind." In my eyes, both would hold the assumption that a "liberal" or "democratic" mind is an existential and universal given. Our human mind has evolved to a place where it is inclined, at least potentially, to think, feel, and behave liberally or democratically. The liberal or democratic mind is a dialogical-dialectical-ironic mind. Our capacity for playfulness – for amusement and humor (smiling and laughing) – is born of this frame of mind. Love and laughter thrive when there is mutual attunement to the ironies of our lives. True ironists make good lovers. Love flourishes in an atmosphere of liberalism, democracy, or, simply, egalitarianism. Lovers are more likely to grow together when they are both of a democratic mind.

For Husserl too, our consciousness operates dialectically. Everything we experience, we experience as beautiful or ugly, good or bad, true or false, meaningful or meaningless. For Husserl, Hart (1994) exemplifies, "the rational depends upon the irrational and … the rational requires a kind of irrationality for its sustenance" (p. 286). It is analogous to saying that our sanity depends and requires a flicker of insanity or a spark of madness for its nourishment. "Our susceptibility to the irrationalities of everyday life and the accidents of fate challenge our rational life" (Hannush, 2007, p. 9). Hart (1994) comments that it was "increasingly evident to Husserl that these forms of 'irrationality' were essential, perhaps dialectical features of the meaning of rationality" (p. 288). Many of our basic beliefs, ideals, and worldviews are, in some sense, irrational because they are not based on veridical evidence. Rather, they are, at least partly, grounded in desire and faith. Moreover, we humans can be rational to the point of irrationality. "In these respects, rationality and irrationality are contrast concepts" (p. 288). "That is to say, reason itself can seem to be madness, caprice, or absurdity" (p. 289). Though contrasting, they are functionally related phenomena that require each other. Let us go back to the theme of love itself, which the later Husserl perceives as the fundamental problem of phenomenology that beckons elucidation. Our loves are never grounded on pure rationality or factual reasoning; they are additionally anchored in our desire and faith. Love, in other words, requires a kind of *rational faith* or *sane madness*. No wonder that we sometimes use the word "crazy" or "mad" to describe the intensity of our love for one another.

Writing on his later ethics, Melle (2002) reminds us that, for Husserl, the aim of all life is a life of blissful love. That is the true life. "Such a life begins with a decision for radical renewal" (p. 242). "'Renewal of the human being,'"

Melle quotes Husserl, involves "'both the single person and the community'" of which one is a part (p. 242). This, Husserl asserts, "'is the chief aim of ethics'" (p. 242). The "will to renewal" must be continuously renewed. Consequently, the ethical life entails "methodical self-cultivation, self-discipline, and self-control" (p. 242). A rational ethical life is based on true knowledge, not only of the facts at hand, but also of one's aims and values.

Following Husserl, Melle (2002) then delineates three essential characteristics of personhood. "First, persons make themselves into what they are by their freely chosen acts. They are responsible for their own being" (p. 243). Second, persons are historical through and through. They have a hi*story*. Persons are *concerned* about their hi*story*. Each person is concerned "about her life as a whole. Therefore, the ethical question is always twofold: 'What to do in this particular situation?' and 'How to transform my life as a whole into an ethical life?'" (p. 243).

Genuine concern about my life as a whole, continues Melle (2002), requires an *ethical epoche* – "a bracketing of my whole previous life and a universal critique of it oriented toward a radical renewal according to ethical ideals" (p. 243). Looking forward, I decide that from hereon I will live "a life with no regrets" (p. 244). I myself am responsible for the kind of life I am going to live, a life that is guided by my *caring conscience*. I will be resolutely true to the radical renewal of the self I want to become, a self that shines through all my acts. What characterizes me in everyday life will be a reflection of my true character.

"A person – and this is the third essential characteristic [of personhood or what it means to be a person] – is who she is most inwardly by her love and calling" (Melle, 2002, p. 244). Love is the ultimate value we live by. "Such a value is an absolute 'ought'" (p. 244). And, quoting Husserl, "'to go against this value is to be untrue, to lose oneself, to betray one's true "I," [which is equivalent to living] an absolute contradiction'" (p. 244). To realize our true selfhood, we need to heed the *call of our caring conscience*, the voice of our deepest self. We must be guided by "the absolute ought of our pure love" (p. 244). *The call to love maturely is at the heart of the call of conscience.*

In these unpublished manuscripts, Melle (2002) tells us, Husserl provides two prototypical examples of *the call to love*: the mother's calling to love her child and professional calling. Both are forms of vocational calling. Husserl comments that whereas a mother's calling has a biological basis, a professional calling does not. Still, motherly love has to be "refined into a pure love" even if it has an instinctual basis (p. 244). The call to love maturely has to be cultivated and refined throughout life.

Love, to quote Husserl, is "'a personal decision of the active heart'" (Melle, 2002, p. 244). Love, for Husserl, is more than a feeling because it involves choice. Love's value precedes all other valuations. Here again is Husserl in Melle: "'Over and against a value that is absolutely rooted in the "I" itself and that has arisen from love (as absolute love), over and against such a value an objective value counts for nothing'" (p. 244). "And," elaborates Melle, "since I am who I am by loving such a value absolutely, I sacrifice myself in sacrificing this value" (p. 245).

A true community, for Husserl, operates like a person, though it has a higher-order character of its own. "The community of love," explicates Melle (2002), "is a community where all the members mutually help each other to realize their true selves" (p. 246). Although for Husserl true love is rational or reasoned, Melle tells us that Husserl does not reflect systematically on the relationship between reason and love in his discourse on love in these unpublished manuscripts. But if love is "a personal decision of the active heart" and love-and-reason are fused together, love then is a personal decision of the active *mindful heart.*

In pursuing the ethical ideal of love, I will always fall short of perfection and I will have "to cope with regular setbacks" (Melle, 2002, p. 247). I strive toward an approximation of the ethical ideal of love. Being fallible and finite, I will never achieve its full realization. Whenever I slip, I pick up the pieces and begin again. That is what "radical renewal" is all about. There are married couples who renew their vows on love and fidelity every ten, twenty, or fifty years. From a Husserlian point of view, we need to renew our vow to love maturely everyday. Moreover, because "I am who I am by loving," my "world," when I am properly in my loving-and-being-loved mode, "must be beautiful and good; it must be a universally teleological world" (p. 247).

For Husserl, love, as an ultimate value, absorbs and fuses other values such as beauty, goodness, and truth (accurate knowing). Hart (2009a) reinforces the link between love and reasoned decision-making. "Husserl," Hart exclaims, "once stated that it [love] can be understood as 'absolutely deciding for the Other.' The lover decides for the beloved and ultimately 'in her beauty'" (p. 215). Hart then builds on Husserl's conception of love as incorporating beauty, goodness, and truth:

> The 'truth' of the beloved's beauty and lovableness, i.e., the beloved's remarkable and endearing properties, can be made more readily manifest in love whereas this 'truth' is hidden from one incapable of such love. It is true both that love uncovers the beloved's loveable properties, and that typically it is the properties which are the way the radiant lovableness of the person is manifest. (p. 241)

Although Hart does not use the word "dialectics," my selective emphasis points directly to the dialectical relationship between "love" and "loveable properties," between "properties" and the "radiant lovableness of the person." In other words, the qualities of my beloved lead me to love her or him. More than that, these qualities lead me to my beloved's essence, or what Hart calls *ipseity* (Who She Is). In different contexts in his text, Hart defines *ipseity* as "the innermost center of the I" (p. 206), as "an awareness of oneself which is not dependent on being aware of anything else besides oneself" (p. 234). Hart (2009b) elaborates on the meaning of *ipseity* as "the 'myself' of the Other" (p. 276). This unique "I-ness" holds our "essential goodness" or "unique goodness" (p. 277). In the core of the "I" lies our capacity for "centering and gathering" (p. 276). And again, *ipseity* refers to "the propertyless 'myself' … that establishes each of us in an irreplaceable, incommunicable uniqueness" (p. 367). Simply stated, ipseity refers to the core or unique essence of our personhood. Even though it is manifested in qualities or properties, unique or shared, that I display in my everyday comportment, it can never be reduced to them. The core of my I-ness is more and other than my behavioral characteristics or traits even when as a constellation they comprise the unique-and-not-so-unique me. This reminds us of Carl Rogers's distinction between "person" and her or his "behavior." Rogers exhorts us to love the person unconditionally, but not necessarily her or his behavior, which can be abhorrent and unacceptable. Rogers distinguishes the essential personhood of the doer from her or his deeds.

Hart (2009a) admits, "distinguishing the ipseity from the deeds and character of the person is a dance few are capable of. And this difficulty is intelligible precisely because we cannot presence the ipseity apart from the person who is manifest in the character produced by her deeds" (p. 241). It is much easier to confuse the sort of person one truly is (who one is in her essence), which is ultimately non-sortable with the sortable or "sortal self," the self that can be sorted out according to its properties. Described differently, it is easy and even natural, for example, to hate the essence of the Other because of her or his hated properties. Hart, like Rogers, asserts that it is still possible to love in a way that allows "the Other's negative qualities [not] ever to obliterate the transcendent incomparable splendor of the essential fullness of the Other's 'I-ness.'" The shortcomings and weaknesses can, though with difficulty at times, be balanced by the incommensurate goodness of the Other's "I-ness." Hart's "thesis is that love indeed aims beyond the personal presentation in so far as it targets the ipseity as more than the properties and signature style of the [other] person" (p. 237). That is, true "love's intentionality … does not stop at their [others'] personal qualities. Rather, it heads toward who it is who is there having these properties" (p. 233). The *telos* or purposive intentionality "does not aim at the distinguishing properties the beloved has but at her*self*" (p. 233).

Doubtless, Hart (2009a) reflects, "we find it easier to love someone with 'loveable' qualities" (p. 231). This is to be distinguished emphatically from "Who one is … *profoundly* (i.e., in our center or core, what we will call Existenz)" (p. 238). We are called in a primal way to identify with our Existenz. We pay the price of inauthentic existence, false-selfhood, and living in bad faith (a la Sartre) if we live our lives identifying exclusively with our attributes, properties, qualities, or traits. There is beauty, goodness, and truth in living a life in which we are invested in who we *are* and not what we *have*. "In sum, love reveals how love is beyond the qualities or properties of the Other and aims at the other ipseity's life" (p. 225). To be lovingly attuned to the essence of the Other's personhood – her "myself," the other *person herself* (her center or her core), or, as she is properly herself, her ownmost self – involves being "attuned to her I-can, her horizon of possibilities. This would mean that we would be sensitive to what obstacles would lie in the way of her actualizing her potentialities. Love would therefore be a form of making-room for the beloved to be her truest self" (p. 215).

Hart (2009a) agrees with Husserl that love "is the single individual's unique calling" (p. 205). "Love … reveals the innermost center of the I of the one loving [and being loved]" (p. 206). It is more than an emotion for it is "founded on the position-taking of empathic perception … i.e., the presencing of the Other as an other self-experiencing" (p. 206; p. 207). "Love," Hart reiterates, "is an intentional act, based on an act of 'empathic perception'" (p. 209). Love is always at the center of what matters to us most. Hart then embarks on delineating the positive features of love: rejoicing in the existence of the Other; affirming the reality of the Other; renouncing the impulse to control and have power over the Other; the "letting-be" of the Other; valuing (esteeming) of the Other; experiencing admiration, aesthetic resonance, celebration, delight, enhancement, enthrallment, entrancement, and joy in the presence of the Other; experiencing communion in the bodily proximity of the Other; experiencing mutual knowledge of oneself and the other; experiencing solidarity and union with the Other; experiencing "a kind of common consciousness through a common life which, nevertheless keeps distinct the individual consciousness" (p. 217); experiencing humility and grace in the presence of the Other; experiencing the radiance and splendor of the Other; experiencing tender intimacy with the Other; experiencing "compassion toward the frailty and vulnerability of the ipseity present in the fleshly comingling" (p. 221); experiencing "pleasure that borders pain and a pain that verges on pleasure" (p. 221); experiencing the transformation of "the bodily presence of the Other into "a 'cipher' of an essential transcendence which infinitely eludes one's efforts to comprehend and have charge over her" (p. 222); experiencing a resoluteness to solicitously be there for the Other; and delighting in the signature bodily presence and the essential mystery of the Other.

Hart (2009a), however, cautions that because "we are essentially inadequate to ourselves [and others]" (p. 21 6), "love is always in the proximity of danger" (p. 219). But from where does this essential inadequacy in loving my or the Other's ownmost I-ness originate? We can infer the origin from the following description by Hart (2009b):

> Existenz, as one's ownmost self facing what is unconditionally important, is most basically manifest in love. Love, as the most centering, unifying, and comprehensive act, the position-taking that in and of itself is unconditioned and does not know of its possible termination or invalidation, is inseparable from one's most proper essence and reveals the bottomless ground and innermost center of I-ness of both the beloved and lover. There is thus revealed in love an infinity not only in terms of the unfathomable depth of the other ipseity but also in terms of the lover's capacity for dedication. (p. 324)

From what I infer from the above, for Hart, like Rogers, the primary barrier to loving the essential I-ness of the Other is early exposure to conditionality. For Rogers, the barrier to our capacity to love unconditionally is a consequence of our early subjection to conditional acceptance, regard, or love. Insecurity and defensiveness, which result from improper loving, both Hart and Rogers agree, make it extremely difficult to love the essential I-ness of self and Other. Other consequences of being raised with conditional love are (1) the proclivity to identify with distracting, scattering, and negativistic emotions, motives, characteristics, qualities, and personal properties and not being able to dis-identify from these narrow emotion-laden predispositions and (2) the tendency to make decisions (reflecting a defective will that is severed from love and a damaged intentionality) that betray and move one away from one's essential I-ness. Under such conditions, the self is no longer a planned life project responding to the call of love or the will to love. *Intentionality*, the ability to invest one's actions and projects with meaning, loses its elasticity.

Just as Rogers prioritizes the unconditional self, Hart (2009a, 2009b) prioritizes the propertyless I. Loving is, for both, of the essence of the unconditional self or the propertyless I. For me, there is an intrinsic, tension-tinged dialectical relationship, a relation of reciprocal influence, between the loving I and my own characteristic ways of showing love. Hart would label these characteristic ways of mine as properties, qualities, or traits. Regardless, as I stretch my repertoire of loving acts, I become more deeply in touch with my loving I-ness. Its oceanic depth is tapped into. Correlatively, as I tap deeper into my loving I-ness, the range of my repertoire of loving acts and characteristic ways of showing love expands.

Just as there is a dialectical relationship between individuals and society, in that individuals shape society and in turn society shapes individuals, there is a dialectical relationship between individuals in loving relationships. Persons who love each other open themselves, though not consciously, to being influenced by each other. At the same time, they allow each other to be. Partners who have loved each other for years, in part, *become* each other. One partner may say to the other with a tone of amused wonder, "I am becoming like you," as one catches oneself saying or doing something the other would say or do.

For Merleau-Ponty, states Hamrick (2002), even our "will is an intimate complex dialectic of the voluntary and the involuntary" (p. 292). Similarly, we can say that love is a complexly intimate dialectic of the voluntary and the involuntary, individuality and communality, morality of the heart (compassion and care) and morality of responsibility (fairness and justice), knowledge (knowing) and practice (doing), expressive spontaneity and deliberate discernment, happiness and the absence of happiness, egoism and generosity, similarity and difference, attachment and detachment, pleasure (joy) and pain (suffering), and ambiguity and clarity.

For Merleau-Ponty, says Bahler (2016), my experience of "disagreements and disunity" with others can only take place in the context of "my desire for community" (p. 128) and, I would add, communion. The Other who disturbingly criticizes me can also decenter my perspective, thus "expanding my possibilities and my sense of objectivity rather than by destroying me" (p. 128). Of course, the criticism has to be *lovingly handled.* Such a delicate, caring correction can orient me to move in the direction of "a more full life" (p. 128). This is what happens between a maturely loving parent and a loved child. "Both parent and child are altered by their newfound experience in encountering one another and their view of the world is expanded. … This is love" (p. 128). During the encounter, at the moment of the parent's constructive criticism of the child, the child experiences tension in the form of discomfort and disturbance. But the child's felt sense of criticism-in-the-context-of-care ("My mother is telling this because she loves me and wants the best for me") resolves the tension in the direction of psychological maturation and growth.

For Merleau-Ponty, the dialectical relationship between mother and child involves a two-way directionality. Just as the child is dependent on the mother for survival and for love, the mother is dependent on the child, not only for (limited) affection and love, but also for a new identity (motherhood) and a new *meaning* (purpose) in life. Both mother and-child come to view each other over time as not only extensions of each other, but also independent and separate from each other. The mother "draws her cues on how to care for the child, what the child wants, or what the child is trying to say *from* the child" (Bahler, 2016, p. 154). The child derives his cues of how to elicit attending, caring, and loving responses and later how to respond caringly, concernedly, and lovingly, *from* the mother. This is the *dance of dialogical dialectics*. Take the seemingly simple breast-feeding situation. It requires a continuous mutual and reciprocal inter-bodily adjustment or position-taking on the part of both mother-and-child in order to achieve the harmonious giving-and-receiving of milk. This is the fertile soil from which love grows. From this and countless other repeated patterns of interactions, the child builds corporeal and, later, mental schemas of his *I-can* possibilities in the time-space of his relational world. "I can, in my fleshly co-being, love-and-be-loved." This "I-can" constitutes for Merleau-Ponty the essence of our wider consciousness, which includes our unconsciousness. It captures the heart of our fleshly way of being-in-the-world-with-others.

"'The child's attachments to adults,'" writes Merleau-Ponty, "'are evoked by the adults; it is a reciprocal situation. If the child is loved, he loves. Children experience in their own life the repercussions of the other's affectivity'" (quoted in Bahler, 2016, p. 165). Good dialectical spirals happen when a positive or negative action is responded to in a manner that results in integrative and harmonious resolution, as when a child's anger is responded to in an attentive, attuned, and understanding fashion by the caregiver or as when a child's plea for a playful response is fully and wholeheartedly reciprocated by the parent. Good dialectical spirals also take place when call-and-response result in surprising outcomes that are filled with creative and meaningful possibilities and constructive outcomes, as when interactions between parent and child simply lead to creative discord that is a spur to maturation and growth. Sometimes, good things can come out of seemingly negative or disagreeable interactions. Then again, sometimes not. Bad things can come out of seemingly well-intentioned relational initiatives. Dialectical spirals do not always yield positive outcomes. Disingenuous, inauthentic, and incongruent interactions can spiral negatively out of hand.

Unlike Ogden's (1986; pp. 88–91) distinction between immature ambivalence and mature ("achieved") ambivalence, Merleau-Ponty (1964) makes the movement of maturation as that from "ambivalence" to "ambiguity." "Ambivalence," he writes, "consists in having two alternative images of the same object, the same person, without making any effort to connect them or to notice that in reality they relate to the same object and the same person" (p. 102). Ambiguity involves the acknowledgment that the same person who is loving can also be hateful. It also involves the courage to confront the contradictions, including our ambivalences, that we find in ourselves and others.

Mature persons, Merleau-Ponty (1964) asserts, undergo a psychosocial movement from the immature stance of intolerant "ambivalence" to the relatively mature stance of tolerant "ambiguity." This movement, however, will always be dialectical in nature. There will always be a residue of immature ambivalence in our most mature loving relations. It is the learning of the tolerance of the ambiguity of life that allows us, as Ogden (1986) says, to *own* our "feelings of sadness involved in mourning, guilt, and the renunciation of omnipotence" (p. 89). It is our relative at-homeness with the ambiguity of life that permits us to acknowledge our vulnerability to the loss of loved ones. It is our synchronicity with the ambiguity of our lives, with its accompanying sense of humility, that makes it possible for us to atone or make up for the harm we have done and we cannot change. Tolerance of ambiguity enables us to accept our finitude in the light of which our life projects will always remain unfinished. It is through being in tune with life's ambiguity that we can more or less reconcile the dialectical tension between our sense of agency – our experience of ourselves as subjects; our sense of authorship, personal power, and responsibility in shaping our destiny – and our "patiency" – our experience of our selves as objects who are subjected to uncertainty, unpredictability, and susceptibility to the vicissitudes of the twists and turns of fate. The capacity for the tolerance of ambiguous complexity involves learning to become humbly accepting of the always existing gap between experience and full (total) experience, between meaning and full (total) meaning, while courageously working toward reducing the size of the gap. The capacity to love maturely requires the cultivation of the capacity for the tolerance of ambiguity.

Love as Giving (Loving as Being Generous)

"A mature form of friendliness or love," says Dilman (1983), "is above all giving. Even the appreciation and gratitude with which it responds to what it receives is outgoing and giving" (p. 182). There may be, Dilman conjectures, a biological basis for generosity in children. But these early unlearned generous "reactions have to be co-ordinated and built on. They will only add up to generosity with a growth of the self from which they come, a growth involving the consolidation of a 'giving' orientation which has thought for other people at its centre" (p. 196). "It is," continues Dilman, "a moving away from impulsive action and involves the development of responsibility and self-control. It is this that makes generosity an expression of maturity" (p. 196).

"There is such a thing," continues Dilman (1983), "as compulsive giving, but then the giving is a way of seeking something for oneself, whereas true generosity is an expression of love and concern" (p. 195). Genuine generosity requires "emotional learning." It requires outgrowing "the self-centered orientation that belongs to … greed" (p. 195). All "emotional learning," adds Dilman, "involves some curbing and frustration" (pp. 173–174). This is how we learn self-control, self-discipline, self-mastery, and self-regulation. These interrelated and overlapping capacities are requisite for cultivating the healthy giving or generous orientation.

For Melanie Klein, Hoffman (2011) tells us, love is embodied in our giving mother. The child, whose giving mother withstood his attacks, comes to hold her with deeply appreciative eyes. By gratefully receiving the gift of love from our giving mothers, we become potential givers of the same gift of love to others. Our mothers not only survive our destructiveness, but forgive us our acts of destructiveness as well. Analogously, our mothers are themselves not perfect. Looking back, we too forgive our mothers' failures. But in the beginning, we are not in a position to forgive or even be aware of our parents' limitations. Additionally, we are unable to respond reciprocally to our mothers' forgiving generosity. From Klein's perspective, we can only perform reparative work to make up for the suffering our mothers endured vis-à-vis our earlier destructiveness. But our mothers bestow upon us the gift of forgiveness freely without retaliation or expectations of compensatory redress. Their superabundant love favors forgiveness over equivalent justice. We are not only grateful for the gift of love that we received, but also for the empowering trust, hope, and faith that are engendered by a freely given forgiving love. These empowering virtues, made possible by the free gift of love, enable us to tolerate the tension of their complementary opposites: mistrust, despair, and doubt. We are summoned instead to cycle the gift of love to others, thus completing the circle of generous loving.

According to our own dialectical model, under a less than optimal familial-and-cultural context, I may end up skewed or tilted on either the side of giving or the side of receiving. My life-long task of balancing these polar meanings becomes a very difficult developmental project.

Nicholsen's (2002) understanding of the phenomena of giving-and-receiving is incipiently dialectical. Take the case of excessive giving or unbridled generosity. Erich Lindemann, whose work on unresolved grief Nicholsen references, calls it "self-dispossession." People with unresolved grief and "uncalled for generosity" end up not only harming themselves, but also family members and friends. Here is Nicholsen describing the work of Lindemann:

> [Patients engaging in self-dispossession] with uncalled-for generosity, give away their belonging, are easily lured into foolish economic dealings, lose their friends and professional standing by a series of 'stupid acts,' and find themselves finally without family, friends, social status, or money. This protracted self-punitive behavior seems to occur without awareness of excessive feelings of guilt. It is a particularly distressing grief picture because it is likely to hurt members of the family and drag down friends and business associates. (p. 43)

We can now look at the other extreme of giving (generosity): one-sided receiving. Here Nicholsen (2002) makes use of Neville Symington's theory of narcissism. For Symington, the narcissist is someone who has unconsciously rejected the Lifegiver, the source that gives us life. In the beginning the Lifegiver is on the outside – for example, our mother or our parents. We internalize the generosity of our Lifegiver. Upon the internalization of the Lifegiver, the gift of life becomes creatively our own. We actively appropriate it. It becomes part of our own creatively generous disposition. Parents themselves perceive the fruit of their union as a miraculous gift that has been bestowed upon them. But, suppose that, upon my birth, my parents did not perceive me as a blessing, but rather as a burden. Instead of being wholeheartedly welcomed to the world, my whole being is rejected. This is fertile ground in which the seeds of inauthenticity and narcissism are planted. With this primal rejection comes the birth of a future narcissistic self. "In fact," notes Nicholsen (2002), "there is no deep self there for the narcissist to love, since narcissism is precisely a rejection of that which allows a deep authentic self to develop – the Lifegiver" (p. 175). In the absence of a deeply loved self, the narcissist's openness to emotional learning is curtailed. The openness to receiving "emotional knowledge" as a consequence of the "transformative gift" of love-and-life is constricted. "Symington's Lifegiver is an internal source of generosity. It makes initiatory action possible. … initiatory activity [is described by Symington] as a 'creative fashioning of the social environment'" (p. 175). Emotional knowing enables me not only to receive, but also to give the gift of life and love to others. I am able to make use of my parents' generosity by developing my own capacity for receiving and, in turn, giving. All this is part of my labor of gratitude which acknowledges my indebtedness to my healthy dependency upon my essential others while affirming my own separateness from them. "The Lifegiver has become an internal source of generosity that makes the person's own creative leadership possible" (p. 176). "Again," Dilman (1983) reminds us, "while generosity is an expression of love, selfishness is not. By generosity I understand the ability to give and share willingly without any condition" (pp. 85–86).

Love as Goodness (Loving Is Embracing the Good of Self-and-Other)

"Goodness," notes Nicholas (1994), "is defined here as *the capacity to behave with love and concern toward others*" (p. 4). Morality and virtue, she continues, are two aspects of goodness. Whereas morality involves the ability to distinguish between right and wrong, virtue comprises the ability to be positive and act positively in the world. These virtues provide us with a frame of reference in what we perceive as good, important, and true. Altruism (generosity), egalitarianism (respectful mutuality), honesty, justice (fair-mindedness), and responsibility are expressions of interpersonal virtues. They are the primary "principles of goodness" (p. 87). Nicholas's primary premise is this: Goodness is a major manifestation of maturity and mental health. Her aim is to demonstrate that "increased virtue often means improved mental health. … increased virtue denotes and promotes enhanced interpersonal functioning" (p. 15). She further equates goodness with "healthy conscience."

> [A] healthy conscience … is continually growing, is responsive to crises that challenge, is alert to its own blind spots and to new areas of human need; it is integrated – aware of the wholeness of the human; it is caring and nurturing of others; it is socially responsible, with a global inclusiveness to its caring; it is androgynous (i.e., egalitarian and mutually respectful with regard to gender); and it is concerned with the survival of mankind. (p. 15)

"Each virtue [altruism, responsibility, egalitarianism, or justice]," Nicholas tells us, "operates along a spectrum from the private to the public domain. For instance, one might be altruistic [generous] with one's spouse, but stingy with one's time and money in one's community, or vice versa" (p. 4). When deeply appropriated, Nicholas elaborates, these virtues become integrated into our self-concept. Take responsibility for an example. By habitually assuming responsibility for making my needs known to my wife or taking responsibility for the impact of my words and behavior on her, I am making these new responsible ways of behaving a part of my self-concept. I begin to think of myself as a responsible person. Becoming a responsible person is part of becoming a good-and-loving person.

What is the source of our goodness? Nicholas (1994) makes use primarily of object-relations and attachment theories in response to this question. The "rationale for goodness," she says, "stems from object relations theory and holds that being good to others is a natural outgrowth of a … biologically based need – the need to attach and to give and receive love" (p. 120). From an object-relations point of view, "morality is relational … and … it is motivated by the desire to give and receive love, rather than by a fear of punishment" (p. 128). "The object relations model," continues Nicholas, "holds that morality is largely voluntary rather than defensive, although the threat of loss of love, care, and approval, can be a powerful motivation for acts of goodness" (p. 128). It is the early and consistent love one receives from essential others and the subsequent responsible acts of desiring to be worthy of that love which makes it possible to develop care, concern, respect, and responsibility for others. If the capacity for goodness – "*the capacity to behave with love and concern toward others*" (p. 4) – is sufficiently nurtured at home in the early years of life, the probability increases significantly that it will continue growing as one's radius of relationships expands in the larger world.

"Goodness," notes Nicholas (1994), "begins at home in infancy. For the child to develop morally, in the object relations framework, he must have satisfactory early attachment experiences from the very beginning of life" (p. 129). From the start, children need to feel taken care of and accepted by their reliable and trustworthy caregivers. By being properly loved, children form a preconscious knowledge of goodness – the goodness from within and from without, although initially the source of goodness is indistinguishable. The consistent trustworthiness of the caregivers builds basic trust in oneself and others. Children develop what Gendlin (1978) calls a "felt sense" or "felt meaning" of loving goodness.

Concern for others, which can be defined as making oneself worthy of the loving goodness of others, manifests itself through an atonement-inducing healthy sense of guilt and the accompanying desire to make amends or reparations. In fact, Nicholas (1994) reminds us that for object-relations theorist Melanie Klein, the capacity for such concern is evidence of a developmental movement from an immature "paranoid position" to a mature "depressive" or reparative position. When operating from a paranoid position, the child fabricates fantasies of revenge against the parent who has seemingly caused her frustration. When operating from a depressive or reparative position the child is able to hold on to the image of the parent as a loving person even in the aftermath of being enraged and wishing the annihilation of the same parent. Additionally, the more mature child is now capable of feeling sorry for having hurt the parent in a moment of reactive rage. In attempting to repair the relational rupture and restore the state of being worthy of her parent's love, the child, at her own level, may not only ask for forgiveness, but may also extend to the parent what she believes is a gift of restitution. The child is attempting to restore relational harmony through an act of compassion. The maturing child is learning "to read the cues of another's pain and suffering" (p. 131). She is beginning to assume responsibility for having acted cruelly or harshly toward the parent. "This effort," comments Nicholas, is aimed at making "'the object whole again through love'" (p. 130). Nicholas also points out that the parent in turn needs to reciprocate in kind when he or she slips and mistreats the child. Then the child's learning to repair relational ruptures is reinforced through modeling and, more deeply, through identification.

> In families where it is possible for children and parents to 'screw up,' apologize sincerely, be forgiven, and make amends, the child will begin to integrate the good and the bad, realizing that he and others have their bad parts and good parts, that one can love and hate the same person, and that the same person can be destructive and loving. (p. 136)

Only if we face and own the parts of us that we would rather project onto others, such as our faults, can we feel lovingly connected with others. Just as others make mistakes, so do I. Just as others can be unfair, so can I. You and I are humanly imperfect. It is in such moments of honest and humbling acknowledgment of our limitations that we feel compassionately connected with one another. At the same time, we need to remain affirmingly in touch with our good qualities. We readily own the good-and-loving part of our selves.

Love as Identification with a Loved and Loving Other While Retaining One's Distinct, Separate, and Unique Identity

"Once we begin to enter the lifeworld," says McIntosh (1995), "a new set of processes arises, in which person, self, and other intermingle in new ways. … Various terms have been used for these processes. Freud's overall term was 'identification,' and I will follow him in this" (p. 119). "It is via such identification," continues McIntosh, "that the child learns to look at the world and herself through the eyes of [George Herbert] Mead's 'generalized other,' as represented most importantly by the parents and so enters the lifeworld" (p. 69) – the world of everyday experience in which she *partakes*. McIntosh makes a distinction between *vertical identification*, which is one-directional, as that between child-and-parent, and *lateral identification*, which is bidirectional, as that between siblings and peers. Although this distinction may have some experiential validity from a developmental perspective, I question its absoluteness. In its most primal sense, identification is an "intermingling," a co-resonance, or co-vibration between self and (essential) others. A more nuanced, object-relations-based understanding, offered by Kamler (1994), describes identification in terms of its development as a *maturational* phenomenon.

> Identification is, in part, a way of a person's being psychologically connected to qualities or traits of an external object, but not in the way we have understood defensive object relating. The identifier isn't trying to hold onto the object as a helpful external agency. He is trying to make traits just like the object's into his own. He is trying to internalize them and make them into his own agency. He acknowledges that the object's version of those traits is fully the object's. In this regard, he is on his way to the eventual attitude of what theorists call 'mature object love,' an appreciation of the object for what it is in its own right. (p. 54)

There is therefore developmentally a movement from defensively identifying in order "to maintain one's primordial feeling of being loved by a central entity to which one is attached" (p. 35) to autonomously identifying with essential others which allows for both separateness and connectedness, agency and relatedness, individual differentiation and mature love. "In fact, a lot of what goes on in an adult character change is wrapped up in their taking on new identifications and weakening the tie of [or disidentifying with] old ones" (p. 307).

Nicholsen (2002) notes, "love is a form of identification" (p. 48). She adds that "identification … [is also] a basis for concern" (p. 48). I would further add, along with being the basis for care and concern, identification is also the basis for such capacities as empathy, perspective-taking, mentalization, and sympathy. All these abilities are in turn required for cultivating the ultimate competence: the capacity to love. Here is Nicholsen linking the capacity for identification, which she equates to kinship, and concern, love, responsibility, separation, suffering, and maturity:

> As we become more mature, we grow the capacity to acknowledge and experience kinship [identification] with what is most different from us, 'holding the sameness and difference delicately in mind.'
>
> The feelings of attachment and identification we develop early in our lives – the feelings that give rise to our sense of 'home' – become the basis of our later recognition of kinship. We know attachment and identification because we have

experienced it; it is the matrix from which the self develops. But it is only by suffering the loss of those early bonds – and enduring the pain and destructiveness that were in any case bound up with the love in them – that we become able to feel concerned for what we love, a concern that includes the knowledge that we are also separate and responsible. … in maturing, we discover, and rediscover, both as self-like – kin – and as an object of our concern. (pp. 35–36)

"Identification," Nicholsen (2002) continues, is "the extension of the self in continuity with the other … [and] in that extension we also become able to perceive the selfhood in those others" (p. 50). "Identification, and the concern based on it," she emphasizes once more, "are evoked most strikingly, perhaps, by suffering" (p. 51). She offers the example of how the cry of an infant in distress automatically elicits suffering in us. I would add that it also arouses distress in other babies who are subjected to the cries of the first crying baby. This latter example of mine provides an experiential evidence for a biological basis for identification. While our capacity for identification differentiates as we mature, in that we become responsible for our identifications, our original and undifferentiated capacity for diffuse identification remains in the background as an abundant re-source we tap into in the form of co-resonance or co-vibration as we move and are moved by the Other.

To broaden one's identification is, for Nicholsen (2002), to widen one's sense of kinship:

[In] widening our identifications – that is, in expanding our participation in the larger whole, the Self – we are in effect displaying an allegiance to our true nature. *In suo esse perseverare* – to persevere in one's own being, acting out of one's own nature or essence, in a phrase from Spinoza that resonates with [poet Girard Manly] Hopkins's 'selving' – is to broaden our identifications with other beings. As Harold Searles said, relatedness to what is most unlike oneself requires the highest order of maturity. (p. 53)

"Shifting our sense of self," Nicholsen concludes, "to include a broader identification with the whole of life in its cyclical form means not only an increase in love and caring, but also an increase in concern – and the loss, disequilibrium, and suffering entailed in such a deep psychic change" (p. 91).

I would temper the degree to which the larger Self partakes of the larger whole, made possible by the broadening of our identifications. Yes, the larger the Self, the larger its World. But human perception (experience), as Merleau-Ponty reminds us, is perspectival. The Self, no matter how broadened its identifications, will always fall short of attunement to the total Whole of which it is a part. This is the Achilles's heel of Buddhism and its western counterparts. Additionally, there are times when Nicholsen (2002) fails to make a distinction between differentiated and undifferentiated identification as when she conceives of "identification … as a pure merging of self and other" (p. 54). That is why she views "concern" as "more complex than identification" (p. 54). For her it is concern that is "the work of maturity" (p. 54). Yet, she concedes that concern "develops out of the original love and attachment that are early forms of identification" (p. 54). We view concern as one of the elements of a maturing loving orientation. In its mature form, concern reduces one's ambivalence, suffers from the pain of others, acknowledges one's own destructiveness, and pursues acts of creative atonement and reparation. This early demonstration of the capacity for concern needs to be accepted by the essential Other who forgivingly survives the child's destructiveness and allows the child to make a creative contribution in order to assuage his or her reparation-inducing guilt. Through loving concern, the child finds new ways of reestablishing her or his attachment bond with the loved Other.

Complementarily, Fisher (2002) writes that

> psychological maturity celebrates a central analogy of self and world in ever-widening spheres of meaning and participation. … The principle is that we are innately moved to differentiate and enter into progressively more encompassing realms of otherness, to dialectically widen out the ground of our being, the spheres of our understanding, thus developing an ever-growing horizon of awareness. It refers to the opening out of a life process, the moving into deeper and wider contact with the world, the building up of a sense of common ground or belonging with others ('the widening and deepening of love'), in the process of which we ourselves emerge, step by step, as the unique persons we are called to be. That human psychological development or individuation progresses as a relational project, as a process of bonding with and then separating from others, is well-recognized. (p. 122)

Differentiation means opening up a space for myself while I remain connected to others. "'This connection to others, based on early incorporations [or gradually differentiating identifications], in turn enable us to feel that empathy and confidence that are basic to recognition of the other as a self'" (p. 123).

The developmental unfolding of the maturational process of identification involves an ever-present dialectical tension between identification and dis-identification. When an acquired unconscious identification is not in the service of Life-giver – in the service of deepening and widening love, then it needs the counter-movement of disidentification. It is Freud who first pointed out the growth-inducing power of identification as a resolver of the developing child's oedipal conflict and as a creator of conscience. But suppose a child's identification is with an aggressive and cruel parent. Then, in order for this child to grow into a loving young person, he or she needs to transform "identification with the aggressor into identification with the victim, and, into compassion toward and an interest in helping the victim" (Nicholas, 1994, p. 131). This developing individual is faced with the challenge of letting go of his old identification with the aggressor – a process called disidentification – and cultivating a new identification with a more loving orientation – one that is characterized by concern, compassion, empathy, and identification with and responsibility for the victim. This movement from old identification-to-disidentification-to-new-identification is crucial for the process of maturation. "This" process, says Nicholas, "requires identification with the compassionate nurturer" (p. 132). Through identification with the loving nurturer the developing person is "able to form [other] positive identifications and avoid, or at least manage to resolve, splitting" (p. 132).

"Splitting," Nicholas (1994) says, is "the mental polarization of 'objects' (affects, parts of people, ideas) into good and bad" (p. 133). "Everyone," she continues, "splits sometimes" (p. 134).

> Splitting is normal and necessary in infancy and early childhood, but with increased cognitive [and emotional] development and, given some patience and consistency on the part of the parents, considerable integration of good and bad objects can be expected to take place during the course of the first three years [and beyond]. (p. 134)

Proper loving on the part of the parent enables the child to move beyond being a defensive splitter of "good" versus "bad" self or other. Splitting, while dispersing us, relieves tension from inner and outer conflicts "such as wanting to be close but fearing to trust because of the threat of abandonment" (p. 134). But "a child who identifies with and idealizes one who treated him with love, consideration, and respect, will probably not be inclined to [split and] abuse [oneself and/or] others" (p. 133). Children who are assured of love's constancy are able to remain anchored in their inner feelings of lovingness and lovableness even when they experience occasional hateful feelings toward themselves or their parents. Having been reared on mostly consistent love, these children develop the awareness that we are all a mix of goodness and badness. We first learn about love at home and upon acquiring this learning, we become at home with ourselves and in the world. Growing up in such a loving home, we experience, for the most part, affection, constancy, consistency, fairness, firmness, flexibility, safety, security, and space-and-time to think things out on our own (see Hannush, 2002).

As I see it, the two best tests for finding out the degree to which we are splitters is to reflect on how we *handle* situations when we are undergoing psychosocial stress or when we are in the midst of a heated conflict with another person, especially a loved one. If under these circumstances we *perceive* the Other as all bad and become forgetful of his or her good qualities we are high splitters. Heidegger says, "'perceiving is responding (resonating)'" (quoted in Fisher, 2002, p. 243). We can respond or resonate positively or negatively to that which we perceive (interpret). I am of the view that our original undifferentiated identification is a form of resonance or reverberation. In the realm of interpersonal relations, we either resonate positively – thus identifying with the Other – or negatively – disidentifying with the Other. Non-splitters, while disidentifying, can maintain their positive identification with Other. Even though she is unlike me (unself-like) in one respect, she is still a variation on my humanity (self-like). The kind of identification that allows breathing space for disidentification when it is called for makes the prospect of being cruel toward the Other less likely. It makes it possible to sustain one's love for the Other while disagreeing with or even experiencing hateful feelings toward her or him.

"Splitting," in contrast, elaborates Nicholas (1994), "makes **justice, responsibility**, and **egalitarianism** hard to achieve and sustain" (p. 134). Simply stated, splitting makes the sustaining of goodness ("*the capacity to behave with love and concern toward others*") impossible. On the contrary, splitting makes being bad and acting badly toward the self or Other much more likely. Only if we *own* our split-off parts – the faults we see in others but not in ourselves – can we love maturely, for then our love is able to contain our hate. "Resolving splitting," expands Nicholas, also means "accepting one's good qualities" and acknowledging "the parts of us that are loving, generous, and moral" (p. 135).

Properly loving parents can help their children learn to resolve splitting by allowing themselves and their children to make mistakes, apologize with sincerity, forgive and be forgiven, and make reparations. As a consequence, the child is enabled to integrate the *modulated* (both/and) *meanings* of goodness (lovingness) and badness (hatefulness or destructiveness) within oneself and in others. Such loving parents encourage their securely attached children to contemplate multiple points of view at the same time.

To resolve our splitting tendencies as adults, notes Nicholas (1994), we need to "identify with what we have projected out and disclaim what we have erroneously introjected" (p. 138). To integrate our splitting as grown-ups, we need to learn to "dis-identify with the aggressor, to identify with the victim and then gradually, to identify with the compassionate nurturing position" (p. 139). We then learn to "'suffer with' an increasing number of others … with a love that is 'distanced' enough to allow 'the expression of pity, compassion, and solace without having to [actually] become the victim'" (p. 139). "Morality [based on love]," adds Nicholas, "begins at home, but if it stops there, society suffers, for when one only applies love and compassion to one's own, insularity and subgrouping result" (p. 139). As representatives of our original home, we become a loving presence in the world. We are able to "think and act more lovingly" (p. 214). We are able to

> expand or generalize the objects of one's love beyond one's intimates or children to include one's community and even to persons with whom one has no personal relationship. One has greater compassion toward one's fellow man, which automatically generates generosity (**altruism**) and fairness (**egalitarianism**, **justice**) toward persons less fortunate or more vulnerable than oneself, and as well as more responsibility in all kinds of relationships. (p. 214)

Loewald (1988) says that the tension between self-love and other-love is "counterbalanced, modulated, tempered, by sublimation" (p. 20). "Sublimation is a kind of reconciliation of the subject-object dichotomy – an atonement for that polarization (the word *atone* derives from *at one*) and a narrowing of the gulf between object libido [other-love] and narcissistic libido [self-love], between object world and self" (p. 20).

Through "advanced" sublimation, Loewald (1988) elaborates, we achieve a "kind of union[,] a reconciliation of polarities, of separateness [and union]" (p. 23). To sublimate is to engage in a dialectical act of resolving the seemingly opposite basic orientations, positions, or stances of existence: loving union versus differentiating individuation. For Loewald, there is a "point" at which the developing child undergoes an alienating differentiation from his or her psychosocial matrix – the unitary field involving mother-and-child. This jarring juncture of alienating differentiation is reversed through sublimation:

> In genuine sublimation this alienating differentiating is being reversed in such a way that a fresh unity is created by an act of uniting. In this reversal – a restoration of unity – there comes into being a *differentiated unity* (a manifold) that captures separateness in the act of uniting, and unity in the act of separating. (p. 24)

Through sublimation, Loewald (1988) reiterates and expands, we achieve

> a reconciliation – with the return, on a higher level of organization, to the early magic of thought, gesture, word, image, emotion, fantasy, as they become united again with what in ordinary nonmagical experience they only reflect, recollect, represent, or symbolize ... sublimation [may] be both a mourning of lost original oneness and a celebration of oneness regained. (p. 80)

Loewald describes the movement from *original oneness* to the *regaining of oneness* as a process of *atonement* (*at-one-ment*). In other words, the sublimatory activity of atonement results in a higher-level integration, "to celebration and self liberation, as well as to [reconciliation of] love and hate – in sum to the higher emotions" (p. 82).

Traditionally, observes Loewald (1988), sublimation has been viewed as a "successful" defense, a compromise. Inspired by Freud's later work, Loewald sees sublimation as a psychological movement that contributes to the building of a healthy, vibrant ego – a creative "I" which is capable of reconciling the polar meanings of our lifeworld, including love-and-hate, which we must all confront in our journey toward maturation. Loewald likens the sublimatory self to Winnicott's transitional self – the self-in-transitional-space. "Understanding ourselves, our fellow beings, our world," notes Loewald, "is sublimation in action" (p. 82). Our world is reorganized or restructured through the actions or life projects of our sublimatory self, life projects with which we identify. We are our sublimatory life projects. We are most authentically at home in the world – in our homeworld, when we are being our sublimatory selves. But for Loewald, life is a "dialectic of irrationality and rationality, as well as ... [a] dialectic of shame [inauthenticity] and authenticity" (p. 82). These are the last words in Loewald's little book on *Sublimation.*

Loewald (1991) likens the psychoanalyst's love for her or his patient to the parent's love for her or his child.

> The parent-child relationship can serve as a model here. The parent ideally is in an empathic relationship of understanding the child's particular stage in development, yet ahead in his vision of the child's future and mediating this vision to the child in his dealing with him. This vision informed by the parent's own experience and knowledge of growth and future, is, ideally, a more articulate and more integrated version of the core of being that the child presents to the parent. This "more" that the parent sees and knows, he mediates to the child so that child in identification with it can grow. The child, by internalizing aspects of the parent, also internalizes the parent's image of the child – an image that is mediated to the child in thousand different ways of being handled, bodily and emotionally. (pp. 25–26)

This primal identification is part of self-development. In its earliest version it is built up through introjecting, among other qualities, the mother's image of the child as she sees, feels, smells, hears, touches him. Introjection, for Loewald, is not simply an intrapsychic activity.

> The bodily handling of and concern with the child, the manner in which the child is fed, touched, cleaned, the way it is looked at, talked to, called by name, recognized, and rerecognized – all these and many other ways of communicating with the child, and communicating to him his identity, sameness, unity, and individuality, shape and mold him so that he can begin to identify himself, to feel and recognize himself as one and as separate from others yet with others. The child begins to experience himself as a centered unit by being centered upon. (p. 26)

This phenomenological description by Loewald, in my eyes, points to a form of mature parental love in action, a kind of love that not only communicates to the child his or her emerging identity but also enables him or her to feel centered at the core of his or her being. Maturely loving parents provide the child with "an optimal range of relatedness" (p. 27). Such parents are able to relate to their children "according to their levels of maturity" and "always from the viewpoint of their potential growth, that is from the viewpoint of the future" (p. 27). Children, like patients, need a "relatedness with a consistently mature object" (p. 27).

"Identification," believes Breger (1974), "is central to the process of moral growth as, indeed, it is to the wider growth of self" (p. 256). For Breger, "identification describes the process whereby the social gets inside the individual as the self develops by adding roles modeled on others" (p. 330). Between the ages of two and five, "*Imitation has begun to be identification – an incorporation of parental roles into the self*" (p. 142). Whereas imitation aims at specific acts, gestures, or sounds, identification aims at reproducing a *total role*. By "identifying with her mother," for instance, the child is "incorporating a more complex role – with the motivation to be like a loved person" (p. 143). Through such positive, security-enhancing identifications the developing child becomes "more loving and lovable" (p. 143). Additionally, the child acquires a sense of *self-efficacy* – a feeling of confidence in his generalized competence. "He is open to the idea that the way to competence lies in becoming like the more skillful older siblings and adults" (p. 143). "Common to all the forms of identification … is an expansion of self by the imitation, assumption, and eventual internalization of new roles" (p. 144). Like Erikson,

Breger believes that a significant portion of our *identity*, which he equates with our sense of self, is a byproduct of our cumulative and, hopefully, fairly integrated *identifications*. Identifications can be conscious or unconscious and relatively integrated or dissociated. Breger makes a critical distinction between *identification based on anxiety* and *identification based on love*:

> Since identification involves an internalization of an external relationship (a change in self by the incorporation of a new role), it follows that the child will feel the same way toward the new part of himself as he did toward the parent he is identifying with. When he adds the role of a parent out of love or the wish to be powerful, he comes to love or be proud of the new part of himself. But when he adds new roles out of anxiety or anger he will experience these emotions in regard to parts of himself. Identification of this sort leads to an *inner ambivalence*. (p. 145)

Moreover, "identification based on love," Breger later elaborates, "lead[s] to a 'loving conscience'" (p. 257). Identification based on love is free from deep ambivalence. In contrast, "ambivalent – both angry and loving – parent-child interactions becomes internalized [identified with], producing an intense ambivalence about one's own impulses" (p. 256).

Although it is not made explicit, Breger (1974) would concur that a distinction needs to be made between healthy and unhealthy anxiety-based identifications. Upon separating from his mother, the child, having identified with his mother, "assumes an imaginary mother role as a way of alleviating the anxiety aroused by separation. This is [a healthy use of] identification based on anxiety" (p. 144). Identification with the aggressor is an example of unhealthy identification. "This arises when one is controlled, frustrated, or mistreated in situations where there is no escape" (p. 144). Though enraged, the child is "trapped by his dependence on these same parents, [consequently] the child attempts to gain their power by making himself like them" (p. 144). Similarly, following our dialectical model, a distinction has to be made between healthy and unhealthy love-based identifications. Breger focuses on love-based identification. Again, Breger would agree that a growing child can identify with an immature way of loving and being loved.

The self develops, grows, and matures through healthy identifications. External love becomes internal love by way of identification. The child acquires the capacity for love by *identifying with and internalizing* parental love. Love and the anxiety over its loss, states Breger (1974), motivate the developing child to *identify* with her or his parents:

> Love and [separation] anxiety [or anxiety over loss of love] are two of the powerful motives for such identification. In simple form, we may say that the child comes to love himself modeled after the way his parents have loved him. … One's sense of self is shaped by the way others treat one. … Identification describes the growth of the self by the internalization of external relationships. (p. 198)

The consistently loved child internalizes his parental love "in the form of a secure self-image, a sense of trust, or high self-esteem" (p. 198). In the tolerable absence of the good-enough parent, the well-loved infant becomes a "seeking and assertive" child who is able to enact the loving parental role, with which he has identified, by providing himself with the love that he has internalized. Deviations from this consistency arouse anxiety over loss of love. Repeated deviations may lead to a deep inner ambivalence. This deep inner ambivalence may become a more or less permanent part of the self. Breger elaborates:

> The mother's love for her child becomes internalized as his love – what Erikson terms "basic trust" – for himself. Loss of this love arouses anxiety and this component of the external relationship also becomes internalized through identification.
>
> … identification … [is] an ongoing process not a single event. Growth of the self by imitation and modeling, motivated by competence and admiration, occurs more or less continually throughout childhood and later life as well.
>
> Finally, it is important to note that much of identification is unconscious. (p. 245)

Without ignoring the importance of later identifications, early identifications, which are typically unconscious, shape the direction of personality development. The form or quality of identification used is contingent upon the manner in which successive core conflicts (e.g., security vs. anxiety, aggression and its control, dependence vs. independence, or desire and its renunciation) encountered at different stages of life are resolved.

The core conflicts or "central dimensions of human life," Breger (1974) tells us, are to be *dialectically* understood:

> The central dimensions of human life – what I have earlier called the core conflicts – are bipolar. Individuals, families and whole societies tend to emphasize one pole and deemphasize the other. To be independent one must give up the gratifications of dependence; to satisfy curiosity and the need for excitement, one sacrifices security. People desire love and admiration, yet their very ambi-

tions, sensual longings and aggressiveness bring about disapproval and the loss of love. (p. 236)

Movement toward maturation and growth involves vacillation between poles representing the major dimensions of existence. An "exaggeration of one pole," says Berger, results in "a concomitant submersion of the other" (p. 237). To use our own dialectical phrasing, each skewing or tilting is accompanied by an over-identification with one pole and a correlative under-identification with the other pole. "All [these dialectical vacillations] represent the search of the developing person for an identity within which the different aspects [or internalized identifications] of his nature can be integrated with social demands and values" (p. 237).

Because of its relevance for our present theme – love as identification – we will focus on Breger's (1974) core conflict of security (secure attachment, love) versus anxiety (insecurity, insecure attachment), which, he repeatedly emphasizes, are, among other social emotions, the prime motivators of identification. With relatively optimal external interpersonal relationships, which become internalized, there results "some balance of security and anxiety … in which the person feels secure (good about himself, a sense of 'basic trust,' high self-esteem) or [otherwise becomes] anxious about what exists 'inside,' about what [or who] he is" (p. 196).

The core conflict of security versus anxiety, elaborates Breger, "underlies the whole process of psychological development" (p. 195). To develop is to change. To change means to give up the security of the familiar for an unfamiliar future. To be born, to survive, and to thrive is to become attached (loved). To become detached or separated, in the early years of our lives, is to become anxious. Our separation anxiety aims at restoring our attachment and the regaining of our secure love. At the same time, our drive to detach or separate is part of the natural momentum of differentiation and growth.

From beginning of our lives, across cultures, states Breger (1974), love is bound up with attachment to essential others within the family and, later, with others outside the family. Love also becomes fused with sensuality, sexuality, and sexual reproduction. "The central force of the motive system of human love," states Breger, "is its *emotional* or *affective* quality. Attachment, love, and sexuality all involve qualities of pleasurable experiences that arise from the stimulation of various parts of the body" (p. 87). Early in life, attachment and love are fused with Sigmund Freud's "oral pleasure," Jean Piaget's sensorimotor (exploratory) pleasure, Harry Harlow's "contact comfort," and George S. Klein's "sensual pleasure." Original attachment (love) is rooted in inter-bodily activities such as suckling, holding-and-being-held, cuddling, tickling, caressing, kissing, smelling-and-being smelled, and touching-and-being-touched. Multiple bodily zones yield sensual pleasure throughout the life cycle. There are parallels between the interactive sensual stimulations of infants and children and the interactive sensual and sexual stimulations of adolescents and adults. We can describe forms of love which evolve developmentally and sequentially from a Piagetian perspective: sensorimotor (bodily and inter-bodily) love, preoperational (magical, iconic, or symbolic) love, concrete love (a love that is tied to concrete transactions of exchange, of tangible acts of giving and receiving), formal (abstract, ideological, or ideals-based) love – a love anchored in the deep awareness of the distant past and the anticipated future, including the potential loss of the loved one; a love, therefore, that is attuned to the preciousness and possibilities of the present moment.

The conflict between anxiety and its vicissitudes (original fear of separation, abandonment, and loss of love and the accompanying core social affects of first despair and rage, and, later, grief, guilt, and sorrow) versus love and its vicissitudes (original security-producing attachment and its later manifestations through acceptance, approval, recognition, and validation and the accompanying affects of relief, triumph, and elation), asserts Breger (1974), is a developmentally unfolding life-long dialectical tension beckoning resolution on higher levels of integration. The infant's anxiety over separation from the mother grows into anxiety over loss of her love and then develops into anxiety over her disapproval. "Later, the child comes to feel anxious about the disapproval of the social group. … anxiety about group disapproval replaces the earlier anxiety over loss of parental love, which, in turn, rests on the still earlier separation anxiety of infancy" (pp. 89–90). "As the child progresses from separation anxiety to fear of parental disapproval to conformity to the group," Breger expands, "rules, taboos, and standards are progressively [identified with and] internalized" (p. 90).

Under relatively optimal familial conditions, it is the consistent love of the constant parent for the child that is ultimately identified with and internalized. This is what psychoanalysts label as *object constancy*. The constancy of the love of the Other results in the constancy of the love of the Self. Similarly, ambivalent parental love is also identified with and internalized by the child. The inconstancy of the love of the Other results in the inconstancy of the love of the Self. Just as a holistic love of Self has its correlate in one's unambivalent love of Life, so too does the ambivalent love of Self has its correlate in a mixed, love-and-hate, feeling toward Life itself.

We can now conclude that whereas *insecure identificatory love* – deeply ambivalent and dissociative love – is dysfunctionally encapsulating and enslaving, *secure identificatory love* is not only containing of ambivalence and thus tolerant of ambiguity, but, above all, is *functionally freeing*.

Identifying with and internalizing the mature love of essential others makes the harmonious integration of roles and identifications or identificatory roles possible. There is a lesser contradiction or inconsistency among the identifications that make up my identity. I am enabled, as Kernberg (1984) puts it, to autonomously or selectively replace my archaic identifications with "sublimatory identifications":

> Individuation includes replacement of primitive introjections and identifications with partial *sublimatory identifications* fitting into the overall concept of self. Emotional maturity is reflected in the capacity for discriminating subtle aspects of one's own self and other people in increasing selectivity in accepting and internalizing the qualities of other people. (p. 74)

"Mature friendships," for instance, continues Kernberg, "are based on such selectivity and the capacity to combine love with independence and emotional objectivity" (p. 74).

Just as secure attachment enables the developing child to explore one's physical, mental, and social world, so does secure identificatory love free the growing person to be "selective" in one's identifications. This makes it possible for us to, more or less, balance, harmonize, or *integrate* our important identifications and minimize or reduce our contradictory or conflicting identifications, without drifting too far away from acting consistently on our essential identifications, without losing our psychosocial *integrity* or *integrality*. To illustrate, my secure identificatory love enables me to find a balance between my independent self – the self that identifies with being independent – *and* my dependent self – the self that identifies with being dependent. To conclude this subsection, just as secure identificatory love allows one to function more freely, so does Heidegger's "care" structure make it possible to actualize one's potentiality to be and become one's ownmost identity – who one is.

Love as Joy

Gay (2001) states, "[N]eurosis occurs when one cannot recollect joy … neurosis is primarily the *absence* of joy" (p. x). Gay emphasizes this theme throughout his text: "neurotic persons have little joy. … For to be neurotic is, perhaps, to be the opposite of joyful. It is to be miserable and suffer in a special kind of way. To be neurotic is to say 'I'm my own worst enemy,' 'I'm always working against myself,' or as the song puts it, 'I can't get no satisfaction'" (p. 21).

To reverse Gay's (2001) logic, if mental disorder involves "the *absence* of joy," then we can say that mental health presupposes the *presence* of joy. Gay subsumes under "instances of 'joy,'" descriptive terms such as "balance," "wholeness," "integrity," peace," and "playfulness" (p. 27). "Joy," he elaborates, "contrasts to neurotic suffering because it rests upon a different sense of temporality and connectedness" (p. 28). A different way of living time is inevitably intertwined with a different way of living space and living with others. In contrast to the self-world of neurotics, joyful persons' mode of being-in-time, being-in-space, and being-with-others is qualitatively different. To be more concrete, approaching the future with realistic hope typifies the way the joyful person lives time. She or he views her or his lived space as a *true home*. The joyful person is at home in the world. Her or his way of relating with others is grounded in basic trust. In general, the joyful person moves toward others in a relaxed and welcoming way.

Joy arises out of one's loving relationships, whether it is one's primal relations to essential others, to oneself, or to nature. For instance, "romantic poets say joy arises out of one's *relationship* to nature which they portray as a source of solace even though it is the source of our destruction" (Gay, 2001, pp. 32–33). The poet John Keats reminds us that the "poet's task is to respect the presence of loss" and that this "capacity to welcome melancholy makes joy possible" (p. 33). The poet Percy Bysshe Shelley links love to beauty and, indirectly, to joy: "'The great secret of morals is love; or going out of our own nature, and an identification of ourselves with the beautiful which exists in thought, action, or person, *not* our own'" (p. 32).

Additionally, Gay (2001) elaborates, "joy arises out of transience and affirmation of the ego's [self's] integrity in the face of certain destruction, namely one's own death and the ineluctable pull of time" (p. 34). Joy can also be "the product of aesthetic contrasts" (p. 49). "Sitting by the window in Michigan the contrast between noisy family life and sudden quiet was part of *my* pleasure at that time" (p. 49). Joy can arise out of our "reflection upon the flow of complex moods and multiple registrations of time" and out of "a unified contemplation of diverse experience and diverse aspects of the self" (pp. 49–50). "By creating ritual space and suspending the rules that govern ordinary time and ordinary social intercourse," Gay continues, "we make possible a new kind of joy" (pp. 51–52). Another kind of

> joy is available to persons able to tolerate and sustain dual registrations of past and present, of warm bed and frosty air. To know that one must leave the warm

> bed, that dreams will fade, that the frost patterns are occult signs, is to know a certain kind of fullness that depends upon loss. The bed is delightful because it lets us savor the cold air against which it protects us. The frost patterns are exciting because they let us inscribe upon them scenes from our internal world. Like the good hour or the happy moment of artistic pleasure we find in them objective referents to otherwise invisible realities. (p. 53)

Developmentally, Gay (2001) explicates, joy arises out of "the grace of 'mutual activation'" (p. 184). Just as parents "activate" joy in children; so too children "activate" joy in parents. Just as parents contribute to the growth of their children, children contribute to the growth of their parents (Hannush, 2002). "Erikson notes," expands Gay, "that the nursing pair of happy mother and happy nursing infant is paradigmatic of benign human relationships because neither party dominates. Both regulate the other's body, self-state, and form a social 'pair'" (p. 185).

Mutuality or *mutual activation*, Erikson (1964) states, is first experienced in our relationship to our early caregiver. The "mutuality of adult and baby is the original source of hope, the basic ingredient of all effective as well as ethical human action" (p. 231). Our ethical self and our loving and loveable self come into being in the context of mutuality – a mutuality based on (relative) equality. Here is Erikson describing a beautiful moment of love's joy made possible by the dance of mutual activation:

> A baby's first responses can be seen as part of an actuality consisting of many details of mutual arousal and response. While the baby initially smiles at a mere configuration resembling the human face, the adult cannot help smiling back, filled with expectations of a 'recognition' which he needs to secure from the new being as surely as it needs him. (p. 231).

In summary, mutuality is essential for our psychosocial maturation. It is the origin of our future ethical conduct, for it forms the basis for relationships based on care, concern, and love. In its origin, it involves the giving-and-receiving, on an inter-bodily and pre-reflective level, of mutually strengthening love between primary caregiver and child. It is our original source of joy. In the words of Shakespeare, in the "mercy speech" of the *Merchant of Venice*, "It blesses him that gives and him that takes." I bring out the loveable-ness and the lovingness in others, as I love and am loved by them. Therein lies the source of our primal joy.

Love, says Schindler (2004), lies in the interplay between giving and receiving. Under good-enough conditions, "'The little child awakens to self-consciousness in his being-called … by the love of his mother'" (Schindler, 2004, p. 111). The child comes, lovingly, to him or herself by going to or being called out by the love of the mother. "The mother's smile," continues Schindler, "is the outward expression of her *love* for the child and thus her 'self-gift' to the child" (p. 114). In smiling at her child, the mother is giving of her self in the smile.

The "love of the mother," avers Schindler (2004), "is a *creative call*; it is a spontaneous receptivity that gives rise to a receptive spontaneity" (p. 115). The mother's welcoming love activates in the child his "primal impulse toward his mother" (p. 115). The mother's smile communicates love in the form of an affective-and-value-laden *felt meaning* to her child. The child grasps, on an inter-bodily and pre-reflective level, "'that this love is the highest good and is absolutely sufficient and that a priori, nothing higher can be awaited beyond this'" (p. 115). The child responds joyfully to the love of his mother with his whole being. In this joy lies the child's "heart of freedom, namely, ek-static being with another and so being infinitely more than oneself" (p. 118). When I am wholeheartedly loved, "I have joy in Being" (p. 126).

So far we have shown that through being loved, the child comes to him or herself. Differently described, the child comes to gradually – first bodily-and-pre-reflectively – grasp the *truth* about himself and, later, the m/other. Additionally, along similar lines, the child comes to equate love with *goodness*. Lastly, for the child, there is beauty in the gleam in the mother's loving eyes. Just as the child sees his mother's face as beautiful, so does the mother see her child as the embodiment of beauty. In the context of love, beauty, goodness, and truth are linked together. The mother's love, as it is expressed in her smile, touches the child at the core of his or her being. The child is called to respond with his or her whole being. The mother experiences being loved in the act of loving. The mother loves the whole child. The child experiences worthiness (goodness) in being loved as a whole.

Bion emphasizes the importance of the mother's reverie for *containing* the child's distress. "According to Bion," says Frosh (1991), "what enables the infant's desperate aggression to be managed and integrated into her or his psyche, is the mother's ability to maintain a state of 'reverie' – an intense empathic connection with the child which nevertheless leaves the mother separate enough for her to retain her own emotional centre and hence to survive what might otherwise feel like murderous attacks" (pp. 71–72). Waddell (2002) explains it this way: "This mother's capacity to hold her baby's anxiety and her own, to go on thinking in the face of puzzling and increasingly intense protest and distress, drawing on and offering her inner resources, beautifully exemplifies what Bion … called 'reverie'" (p. 33). This is what Bion means by *containment*.

Allow me to suggest another kind of *reverie*, a positive and reciprocal reverie between mother and child. Mother and child, casually observed, will often enter an open space in which both are participants in a prolonged exchange of meditative glances. For the observer it is a co-presence that is beautiful to behold. Here is how Schindler (2004) describes it: It is "both contemplative and active"; it is a manifestation of "superabundant positivity"; it is a call and a response; and it is a "giving" and a "receiving" of the whole beings of both mother and child. Although Schindler focuses more on the mother's call and child's response, I am centering on the reciprocal dance between mother and child. It is not just the mother that is calling for a response, but also the child calling for the mother's response. The child comes to the dance of mutuality equipped with a pre-reflective, a pre-meditative, bodily based capacity for positive and reciprocal reverie. This capacity for *reciprocal reverie* is a manifestation of a primordial predisposition to *identificatory resonance.*

A parent's oceanic love for her or his child emanates from the self as a center of abundance (and simultaneously a center of insufficiency). The underside of "too-much-ness" is "not-enough-ness." The principle of abundance beckons balance with the "principle of insufficiency" which I take from the work of Georges Bataille, as interpreted by Parvulescu (2010):

> [For Bataille,] 'there exists at the basis of human life a principle of insufficiency.' … This principle is unsurpassable. We do not complete our selves through community, as if filling a lack. There is nothing tragic about insufficiency, thus there is no need for a project of becoming sufficient. We have nonetheless created mechanisms that give us the illusion that we are separated, isolated, self-sufficient individuals. Bataille insists that we need to be reminded of our insufficiency. Some states (laughter) expose us to it, and thus expose the very 'essence' of community. (p. 88)

In contrast to Balthasar and Bataille, our dialectical model holds that there are healthy *and* unhealthy ways of being abundant-and-insufficient. Our perspective differs in two ways: (1) It perceives the self as positioned between existential abundance *and* existential insufficiency; (2) it asserts that, under good-enough conditions, the polar meanings of abundance and insufficiency are lived (taken up) in a balanced and complementary way. Under less than good-enough conditions, the proclivity to abundance and insufficiency deteriorate into maladaptive and exaggerated ways of being-in-the-world-with--oneself-and-others. I become either falsely self-satisfied with my sufficient abundance or I end up becoming obsessively preoccupied with my insufficient lot in life. Both positions are inimical to the experience of authentic joy.

Let us return back to love-and-joy. When a child is properly loved, she or he can derive joy from her or his abundance *and* insufficiency. Mother and child share in the abundant joy that being-together brings. The love of the mother, states Schindler (2011), is what awakens the (positive) consciousness of the child. Thus, "consciousness *is* essentially joy – *in its very structure*" (p. 127). "In short, far from representing a 'neutral' *objective capacity*, consciousness, as attunement to Being, is essentially a participation in the joy of Being. Consciousness … is thus by its nature a *positive* inclination toward reality" (p. 127). There is abundant joy in the reciprocal heart-to-heart call-and-response between mother and child. "Joy, in other words, is itself another word for reciprocal causality" (p. 407). "Greater than Angst [basic anxiety or dread]," continues Schindler, "is joy and joy is especially tied to beauty, because joy is ek-stasis and surprise [– that ecstatic sense of wonder that lifts us beyond ourselves] of genuine mutuality" (p. 407). "Being," concludes Schindler, "is most revealed in the joy of mutual, and thus dramatic, relation between beings" (p. 427).

A good-enough mother can model the derivation of joy (and laughter) from her own failures and slippages and invite her child to derive joy (and laughter) from her or his own failures and slippages. The child learns not to take her or himself too seriously and to derive amusement from her/his sense of insufficiency. In the process of laughing at their respective failures, the loving communion between mother and child is enhanced. The loving attachment between them is strengthened. "We laugh at ourselves," writes Parvulescu (2010), "when we laugh at the falling man; laughter is a common experience of 'failure.' It is this failure, exposing us to our common insufficiency, that founds community" (p. 91). "We laugh our 'happiest' laugh," adds Parvulescu, "at a child falling in front of us, because a child is insufficient, joyfully so. In this, of course, we laugh at adult insufficiency which masquerades as sufficiency" (p. 187).

Something needs to be said about "*loveable-ness*" or the capacity for *being loveable*. Being loved properly (in a mature way) brings out the loveable-ness in us. Thereafter, it makes it easier for us to love others *and* for others to love us. It makes it smoother for us to alternate cyclically between being loving, being loveable, and being loved. "When some kindness prevails," says Fiumara (2013), "we can attempt a sequence of full cycles, from being loved, through becoming lovely and all the way to being a source of love. This is required for psychic [and interpersonal] life to go on and flourish" (p. 92).

Love as Playfulness

Bollas (2011) provides a graphic description of the developmental origin, meaning, and function of playfulness (amusement, humor, laughter) between mother and child in the early years of life:

> Watch the mother engage with the baby. If you look at her face, you will see someone who exaggerates human expression – wide-open eyes, a great smile, lengthened – and goofy – vocalizations, upper body swaying back and forth, head thrown back at a tilt, song and dance.
>
> The literature on mothers emphasizes her holding and containing functions, which soothe the infant, that is for sure. But mothers also transform themselves into figures with exaggerated human characteristics in order to stimulate their babies into smiling and even laughing. While it is frowned on to tickle a baby with a 'gitchy gitchy goo,' a mother will still stimulate a baby with incremental increases in hilarity, from the moment the baby wakes – 'Ah! Look who is awake now!' – gradually to playful pushings of the baby's feet and 'Well! Who does he think he is? Who does he think he is? Who does he think he is?' – bringing gurgles, chortles, and laughs.
>
> But whether or not the infant finds Mother amusing will largely depend on her timing and spacing. If the timing is poor and if she comes too close to or too far from the infant, she will not develop his sense of humor. (pp. 143–144)

Bollas (2011) goes on to state that an optimal comic approach on the part of the mother elicits, over time, the child's spontaneous, true self. By identifying with her comic approach, the child comes to "inherit the mother's sense of timing and spacing" (p. 144). The mother succeeds in transferring to her child the unconscious aesthetic practice of playfulness and humor. Both mother and child find amusement in each other.

Making a baby laugh serves yet another important function. The mother attempts to make the baby laugh not only during tranquil but also conflictual times. "Cracking up baby, then," continues Bollas (2011), "is a useful way to neutralize a power conflict" over feeding, toilet training, and discipline (p. 145). In this farcical space, mother and child treat each other as equals, in spite of the mother's superior power. The mother derives pleasure from her vulnerable child's endearing frailty. In this space, the sensitively caring mother transforms inequality into equally experienced pleasure. Moreover, the good enough mother "shows how amusement at one's plight can generate a special sense: the sense of humor. … In its origins a sense of humor takes pleasure in inadequacy" (pp. 145–146). The sensitively attuned mother finds her child amusing and invites him to laugh at himself without even realizing consciously what is comical. She is assisting him in developing "a sense of amusement in the human predicament well before the self comprehends his condition. The sense of humor precedes the sense of self" (p. 146). "Amusement in the self and in the other may be a vital constituent part of a comprehensive perspective on life" (p. 147).

The sense of humor, elaborates Bollas (2011), serves multiple functions. Above and beyond its probable survival function, humor contributes to the origin of the self. It serves a mirroring function that affirms, recognizes, solidifies, and validates the emerging sense of self out of the bits and pieces of experience. Additionally, it enables both mother and child to transform their intermittently experienced intense hate and rage into mutually acceptable, benign, and palatable aggression. It simultaneously deflates the child's sense of grandiosity and the mother's sense of superiority. It acknowledges identity and difference for it intensifies the identificatory resonance between mother and child and at the same time recognizes the essential differentness of each participant in this play space. It helps both develop "a strange balance … between the languid pleasure of being and the stiffening frights of life" (p. 148). It enables both to take "pleasure in the contradictory movements of two objects (two people, or a person and the environment, or a word and its other meanings)" (pp. 147–148). The contradictions within ourselves become the object of self-amusement. Lastly, humor teaches mother and child to *play with social reality* and the absurdities, ironies, and paradoxes of life.

In teaching her child to find humor in adversity, to derive pleasure from one's plight even before the self is fully born, the mother is bestowing upon her child the highest form of *refined love*. It is easy for a mother to love her child when the going is easy; it is much more challenging to love a child when the going is tough. This is where humor comes in. This is a most valuable life lesson that a mother can lovingly impart to her child. This is a com-passionate playfulness born of a refined (mature) act of loving.

Love as Responsibility (Response-Ability)

Levinas (1969) provides a radical *maternal ethics of love* as an asymmetrical, nonreciprocal, and unconditional responsibility for the Other. The irreducible face of the Other – the Other who will always exceed my capacity to understand him or her – demands of me to care for him or her. The face of the Other summons me: "You shall not commit murder" (p. 199). The face of the Other commands me not to let him die alone. The meaning of *totality* in the title of Levinas's text, *Totality and Infinity*, refers to the summons not to totalize the Other – to refrain from categorizing and objectifying the Other. *Infinity* has a double meaning. The first meaning has to do with the infinite demand that the face of the Other places upon me. The Other confronts me with an infinite demand for protection and care. I am called upon to be my brother's and sister's keeper. I am held responsible and cannot get away from this calling to care for the Other. The second meaning has to do with the infinite mystery of the Other that far exceeds my capacity to know and understand him or her exhaustively. "The way in which the other presents himself," explains Levinas, "exceeding *the idea of the other in me*, we here name face" (p. 50).

The Levinasian maternal ethics of love entails not only responding to the call of responsibility for the Other, but also the related call not to harm the Other. "The Other," Levinas (1969) says, "whose exceptional presence is inscribed in the ethical impossibility of killing him in which I stand, marks the end of [my egoistic] powers. If I can no longer have power over him it is because he overflows absolutely every idea I can have of him" (p. 87). In my lived social space, I place the Other on a higher plane. This Levinas labels as the "primary curvature" of being-in-the-world-with-the-Other. It results in privileging the Other.

Levinas (1969) uses the metaphor of "home" to elaborate on his maternal ethics of love. When we are truly at home in the world, we experience delight, enjoyment, gentleness, hospitality, intimacy, non-possessiveness, and welcoming hospitality. We not only feel that our kinship (identity to others) is recognized, but also that our differentness and separateness (alterity or otherness) is respectfully valued. "The interiority of the home," expands Levinas, "is made of [non-possessive] extraterritoriality in the midst of the elements of enjoyment with which life is nourished. This extraterritoriality has a positive side [of welcoming hospitality]" (p. 150). In contrast to possessiveness and territoriality, welcoming hospitality is

> produced in the gentleness or the warmth of intimacy [love], which is not a subjective state of mind, but an event in the oecumenia [oceanic sense] of being – a delightful "lapse" of the ontological order [whereby] … gentleness comes to the separated being from the Other. The Other precisely reveals himself in his alterity negating the [egoistic] I, but as the primordial phenomenon of gentleness. … in founding the intimacy [love] of home the idea of infinity provokes separation not by some force of opposition and dialectical evocation, but by the feminine grace of its radiance. (pp. 150–151)

In our dialectical model, we do not view the "dialectical evocation" as an intractable "force of opposition." On the contrary, we see it as an invitation to reconciliative resolution the aim of which is a maturational movement to a higher level of integration or reorganization. The allusion to "the feminine grace of radiance" is worth noting here. This Levinasian maternal ethics of love seems to point to a type of love that a self-sacrificing mother bestows upon her children. In the Levinasian view, this kind of love ought to be modeled by all of us. We are, from the very beginning of our lives, affected by others, engaged with others, and called by others not to do harm or violence to them, to be concerned about their welfare, to care for them by attending to and responding to their needs. This is what is demanded of us.

I become my true self only through living up to my obligation toward the Other, be it a significant other or a stranger, especially the suffering stranger. This is how I acquire my sense of agency. This is how I come to dwell or inhabit my world truthfully. My life is most meaningful when I act responsibly upon encountering the face of the Other. The demanded self is a moral self. It is a for-the-other self. Morality (ethics) is of the essence of my selfhood. The Other is always capable of "de-nucleating" my sense of coherent (nuclear) self – putting my self into question, destabilizing my sense of self. My sense of self can easily become discontinuous and thus interrupted. But this state of disequilibrium or imbalance in my selfhood in the face of the Other can be viewed as an occasion for assuming greater responsibility toward the Other. We are born with a sensibility that predisposes us to being vulnerable in the presence of the Other. Although this vulnerability can make us susceptible to being wounded, it is also an openness for an I-You encounter with the equally vulnerable Other.

Our adult relations ought to follow the model of the optimal relation between children and their good-enough mothers. We are more than our mothers can handle. We are more than they have bargained for. Yet our mature enough mothers respond to our too-much-ness with equanimity. They are always there to take our pains away. They are ever ready to die for us. They are always prepared to give, give, and give. In giving our mothers receive. But they do not give so that they receive. In giving, our mothers become themselves, their true whole-hearted selves. They are (almost) always available and responsive (response-able). They are there for us unto death. Their sense of self is elevated through giving, through timely responsiveness to their children's needs. Because of their responsible responsiveness, they feel free. Their freedom is born out of this heightened responsibility (response-ability). As Goodman (2012) puts it, "freedom is borne from its [the self's] responsibilities to the other. Freedom is being encumbered by goodness. Freedom is found in love, and love can be nothing less than responsibility and holiness" (p. 143). This is what the Levinasian maternal ethics of care and concern is all about. It is above all the *call to serve with love.*

At the same time our good mothers know deep in their hearts that they are always falling short of living up to their responsibilities for their children. They can always do more for their children. So they double and triple their efforts by doing more for them. Our good mothers are pulled out of themselves and thus out of their concern for themselves. They are forever grateful for the gift of their uniquely precious children.

For Levinas, the impulse to love (the obligation or summons to respond to the call of responsibility) is more primary than the impulse to exist as a monadic self. "The beginning of wisdom," observes Goodman (2012), "is to be found in … [an] evocation of love wherein the other is loved through a recognition of and attention to his or her needs" (p. 103).

> Love allows the other to interrupt the narcissistic processes inherent in ego function, and mourn the loss of sovereignty. 'It brings into question the "self-care" that is natural to beings, essential to the *esse* [essence] of beings' [Here Levinas is being directly quoted.] It involves carrying the weight of the other's existence, not a preoccupation with one's own. Levinas … writes, 'Suffering the weight of the other man, the "me" [*moi*] is called to *uniqueness* by responsibility.' (p. 103)

Marcus (2010) distills Levinas's thoughts on love as revealed in a series of interviews: Responsibility for the other grounds our capacity to love. Love is not a sentiment, but rather an obligation. Authentic love aims at the otherness (differentness, uniqueness) of the other. The way to approach this unique Other is with welcoming warmth. Our acts of goodness and self-sacrifice emanate from our care and concern for the welfare of the Other. Love is not simply knowledge of someone; it is being kind to the other. More than that, it is when the being and the nonbeing (death) of the other are more important than my own. This, Levinas believes, is our calling. The boundlessly compassionate, devoted, forgiving, and self-sacrificing mother is an exemplar of the Levinasian conception of love. The good mother epitomizes the supreme motherly figure who, responsibly, protectively, and caringly, devotes herself to her child's interests before her own. That is why his is called a maternal ethics of love.

The Levinasian conception of love as responsibility, though alluringly inspiring, is simply too idealistic, unrealistic, and, for most if not all of us, unattainable. Its inspiringly alluring aspect has to do, at least in part, with the resonance with which we respond to its elements, especially for those of us who have experienced good enough mothering or for those of us who long for it. Above all, it speaks to the best in us – our best selves. Viewed dialectically, Levinasian Other-love is enhanced rather than diminished by self-love. Responsibility to the Other and responsibility toward the self are two sides of the same psychosocial coin.

References

Altman, N. (2010). *The analyst in the inner city: Race, class, culture through a psychoanalytic lens* (2nd ed.). Routledge.
Bahler, B. (2016). *Childlike peace in Merleau-Ponty and Levinas: Intersubjectivity as dialectical spiral.* Lexington Books.
Barrett-Lennard, G. T. (1998). *Carl Rogers' helping system: Journey and substance.* Sage.
Baxter, L. A., & Montgomery, B. M. (1996). *Relating: Dialogues and dialectics.* Guilford.
Bion, W. (1962). *Learning from experience.* Heinemann.
Bollas, C. (2011). *The Christopher Bollas reader.* Routledge.
Bollas, C. (2018). *Meaning and melancholia: Life in the age of bewilderment.* Routledge.
Bowlby, J. (1982). *Attachment and loss, Volume I: Attachment* (Rev. ed.). Basic Books.
Breger, L. (1974). *From instinct to identity: The development of personality.* Prentice-Hall.
Culbert-Koehn, J. (1997). Analysis of hard and soft: Tustin's contribution to a Jungian study of opposites. In T. Mitrani & J. L. Mitrani (Eds.), *Encounters with autistic states: A memorial tribute to Frances Tustin.* Jason Aronson.
Dilman, I. (1983). *Freud and human nature.* Basil Blackwell.
Erikson, E. H. (1963). *Childhood and society* (2nd ed.). W. W. Norton.
Erikson, E. H. (1964). *Insight and responsibility.* W. W. Norton.
Erikson, E. H., Erikson, J. M., & Kivnick, H. Q. (1986). *Vital involvements in old age: The experience of old age in our time.* W. W. Norton.
Fisher, A. (2002). *Radical ecopsychology: Psychology in the service of life.* State University of New York Press.
Fiumara, G. C. (2013). *Psychoanalysis and creativity in everyday life: Ordinary genius.* Routledge.
Frankland, A. G. (2010). *The little psychotherapy book: Object relations in practice.* Oxford University Press.
Frazier, B. (2006). *Rorty and Kierkegaard on irony and moral commitment: Philosophical and theological connections.* Palgrave Macmillan.
Freud, S. (2005). On transience. In M. V. Unwerth (Ed.), *Freud's requiem: Mourning, memory, and the invisible history of a summer walk.* Riverhead Books.
Fromm, E. (1956). *The art of loving.* Harper and Row.
Fromm, E. (1981). *On disobedience and other essays.* Seabury Press.
Frosh, S. (1991). *Identity crisis: Modernity, psychoanalysis, and the self.* Routledge.

Frosh, S. (2012). *A brief introduction to psychoanalytic theory*. Palgrave Macmillan.
Gay, V. P. (2001). *Joy and the objects of psychoanalysis: Literature, belief, and neurosis*. State University of New York Press.
Gendlin, E. T. (1978). *Focusing* (2nd ed.). Bantam Books.
Goodman, D. M. (2012). *The demanded self: Levinasian ethics and identity in psychology*. Duquesne University Press.
Habermas, J. (1987). *The theory of communicative action, Volume two: Lifeworld and system: A critique of functionalist reason* (T. McCarthy, Trans.). Beacon Press.
Hamrick, W. S. (2002). *Kindness and the good society: Connections of the heart*. State University of New York Press.
Hannush, M. J. (2002). *Becoming good parents: An existential journey*. State University of New York Press.
Hannush, M. J. (2007). An existential-dialectical-phenomenological approach to understanding *cultural tilts*: Implications for multicultural research and practice. *Journal of Phenomenological Psychology, 38*, 7–23.
Hart, J. G. (1994). The study of religion in Husserl's writings. In M. Daniel & L. Embree (Eds.), *Phenomenology of cultural disciplines*. Kluwer.
Hart, J. G. (2009a). *Who one is, Book 1: Meontology of the "I": A transcendental phenomenology*. Springer.
Hart, J. G. (2009b). *Who one is, Book 2: Existenz and transcendental phenomenology*. Springer.
Heidegger, M. (1962). *Being and time* (J. Macquarrie & E. Robinson, Trans.). Harper and Row.
Heidegger, M. (1996). *Being and time* (J. Stambaugh, Trans.). State University of New York Press.
Hoare, C. H. (2002). *Erikson on development and adulthood: New insights from the unpublished papers*. Oxford University Press.
Hoffman, M. T. (2011). *Toward mutual recognition: Relational psychoanalysis and the Christian narrative*. Routledge.
Holmes, J. (2010). *Exploring in security: Towards an attachment-informed psychoanalytic psychotherapy*. Routledge.
Kamler, H. (1994). *Identification and character: A book on psychological development*. State University of New York Press.
Karen, R. (1998). *Becoming attached: First relationships and how they shape our capacity to love*. Oxford University Press.
Keen, S. (1997). *To love and be loved*. Bantam Books.
Kernberg, O. F. (1984). *Object relations theory and clinical psychoanalysis*. Jason Aronson.
Kernberg, O. F. (2012). *The inseparable nature of love and aggression: Clinical and theoretical perspectives*. American Psychiatric Publishing.
Leffert, M. (2017). *Positive psychoanalysis: Meaning, aesthetics and subjective well-being*. Routledge.

Levinas, E. (1969). *Totality and infinity: An essay on exteriority*. Duquesne University Press.
Lichtenberg, J. D., Lachmann, F. M., & Fosshage, J. L. (2011). *Psychoanalysis and motivational systems: A new look*. Routledge.
Loewald, H. W. (1988). *Sublimation: Inquiries into theoretical psychoanalysis*. Yale University Press.
Loewald, H. W. (1991). On the therapeutic action of psychoanalysis. In G. I. Fogel (Ed.), *The work of Hans Loewald: An introduction and a commentary*. Jason Aronson.
Marcus, P. (2010). *In search of the good life. Emanuel Levinas, psychoanalysis, and the art of living*. Karnac.
Marcus, P. (2013). *In search of the spiritual: Gabriel Marcel, psychoanalysis, and the sacred*. Karnac.
Marra, T. (2005). *Dialectical behavior therapy in practice*. New Harbinger.
Martin, M. W. (1996). *Love's virtues*. University Press of Kansas.
May, R. (1953). *Man's search for himself*. W. W. Norton.
May, R. (1969). *Love and will*. Dell.
Mayeroff, M. (1971). *On caring*. Harper Collins.
McGrath, S. J. (2012). *The dark ground of spirit: Schelling and the unconscious*. Routledge.
McIntosh, D. (1995). *Self, person, world: The interplay of conscious and unconscious in human life*. Northwestern University Press.
Mearns, D., & Thorne, B. (1999). *Person-centered counselling in action* (2nd ed.). Sage.
Melle, U. (2002). Edmund Husserl: From reason to love. In J. J. Drummond & L. Embree (Eds.), *Phenomenological approaches to moral philosophy: A handbook*. Kluwer.
Meltzer, D., & Williams, M. H. (1988). *The apprehension of beauty: The role of aesthetic conflict in development, violence and art*. Clunie Press.
Merleau-Ponty, M. (1962). *Phenomenology of perception* (C. Smith, Trans.). Routledge.
Merleau-Ponty, M. (1964). *The primacy of perception*. Northwestern University Press.
Mitchell, S. A. (2002). *Can love last? The fate of romance over time*. W. W. Norton.
Mitrani, T., & Mitrani, J. L. (Eds.). (1997). *Encounters with autistic states: A memorial tribute to Frances Tustin*. Jason Aronson.
Nicholas, M. W. (1994). *The mystery of goodness and the positive moral consequences of psychotherapy*. W. W. Norton.
Nicholsen, S. W. (2002). *The love of nature and the end of the world: The unspoken dimensions of environmental concern*. The MIT Press.
Ogden, T. H. (1986). *The matrix of the mind: Object relations and the psychoanalytic dialogue*. Jason Aronson.
Parvulescu, A. (2010). *Laughter: Notes on a passion*. The MIT Press.
Paskow, A. (2004). *The paradoxes of art: A phenomenological investigation*. Cambridge University Press.
Ricoeur, P. (1986). *Fallible man*. Fordham University Press.
Ricoeur, P. (1995). *Figuring the sacred*. Fortress.

Rogers, C. R. (1951). *Client-centered therapy: Its current practice, implications, and theory*. Houghton Mifflin.

Rogers, C. R. (1980). *A way of being*. Houghton Mifflin.

Rogers, C. R. (1989). *The Carl Rogers reader*. Houghton Mifflin.

Rogers, C. R., & Freiberg, H. J. (1994). *Freedom to learn* (3rd ed.). Macmillan College Publishing Company.

Rorty, R. (1989). *Contingency, irony, and solidarity*. Cambridge University Press.

Schalow, F. (2001). *Heidegger and the quest for the sacred: From thought to the sanctuary of faith*. Kluwer.

Schalow, F. (2017). *Toward a phenomenology of addiction: Embodiment, technology, transcendence*. Springer.

Schindler, D. C. (2004). *Hans Urs von Balthasar and the dramatic structure of truth: A philosophical interpretation*. Fordham University Press.

Sternberg, R. J. (1998). *Love is a story: A new theory of relationships*. Oxford University Press.

Symington, J., & Symington, N. (1996). *The clinical thinking of Wilfred Bion*. Routledge.

Symington, N. (1996). *The making of a psychotherapist*. Routledge.

Waddell, M. (2002). *Inside lives: Psychoanalysis and the growth of the personality*. Karnac.

Wirth, J. M. (2003). *The conspiracy of life: Meditations on Schelling and his time*. State University of New York Press.

Wrightsman, L. (1994). *Adult personality development: Theories and concepts* (Vol. 1). Sage.

29

Work: The Capacity for Generative *Work*

In this chapter, I will focus primarily, but not exclusively, on the capacity for work, developed under optimal conditions, as a marker of maturity and mental health. I will center, for the most part, on the ability to work as it evolves from a confluence of an actualized potential (competencies, proficiencies, talents, and learned skills), a freely chosen vocation that is in synchrony with one's actualized potential—a work that engages the creative-and-productive self, and a nurturing and supportive work environment. I know that this is an ideal, but the concrete realization of this ideal in the real world can come in degrees.

Ultimately, observes Levine (2010), we humans have a basic need for cultivating "the capacity … to do work that engages the self and its creative potential" (p. 1). We tend to work as a means of achieving other ends. Levine elaborates:

> We work when we form ideas … this forming of ideas is an essential part of all work, including work that eventuates in a physical product. Because work is the forming and shaping of something, it is an inherently creative act. At the end of work something exists that did not exist before. (p. 1)

Obviously, Levine acknowledges, the term work has multiple and sometimes conflictual *meanings*. His focus, however, is on work as:

> the effort to form or shape a product that realizes an idea. I will consider the imaginative element in work crucial; and since I consider the production of something as vital, I treat work as an expression of the human creative potential,

© The Author(s), under exclusive license to Springer Nature Switzerland AG 2021
M. J. Hannush, *Markers of Psychosocial Maturation*,
https://doi.org/10.1007/978-3-030-74315-4_29

> which I consider inextricably bound up with the self. Work understood this way creates something objective in the sense that it exists not only for the worker but for others; it has both a psychic and an inter-psychic reality. I take it that having inter-psychic reality is an important part of what we have in mind by being of use to society. (pp. 2–3)

Either we can experience the world as a theater for the projection of our internal dramas and the enactments of our fantasies or we can experience "that world as a setting for the realization of an idea. Only the latter involves real work in large part because ideas are not subjective fantasies" (p. 4). The urge to work goes hand-in-hand with the urge to create. "Where work expresses human creativity, the ability to tolerate not knowing must, indeed, be a crucial element of work" (p. 8). "Through work," notes Levine (2010), "we seek primarily satisfaction of the self, which for some reason we cannot achieve simply by the exercise of imagination" (p. 11). Our capacity for imagination is then placed in the service of our sense of agency. "Thus, being a self begins when we imagine that we are" or that we could be (p. 11).

For Levine, imagination or the "imaginative construction of an object is the first step in the direction of work" (p. 15). The second step involves the impulse to find satisfaction in the real world: the "capacity to imagine a world, and the impulse to find satisfaction there. This combination of impulse and capacity forms the basis of work" (pp. 14–15). A distinction is to be made between raw fantasy and refined imagination. Refined imagination involves a movement toward the appropriation of the capacity for conceptualization or abstract thinking. This movement from imagination to abstract conceptualization Levine calls the capacity for forming an idea. Ideas are invested with potentials. "Ideas," elaborates Levine (2010), "are potentials and this quality connects them to the investment of meaning in experience" (p. 15). It is *meanings* (or ideas) that have potentials or possibilities. Such meanings suggest possibilities of implementation in the world of work.

At times, Levine (2010) falls into the Cartesian dichotomization of body and mind, for he speaks of authentic work as serving the desiring mind but not the desiring body as if the mind is not embodied or the body is not mindful. Still, on the whole, his exposition of the phenomenon of work is for the most part true to lived experience. It captures *essential meanings* of work and their unconscious underpinnings. It is also existential in that it aims at elucidating the purpose of work for our optimal human functioning.

Levine (2010) remains, ironically, phenomenological by his attempt at overcoming the false dichotomy between "being" and "doing," an error commonly committed by so-called humanistic and popular psychologists, and new-age propagandists. I say "ironically" because of his occasional slippage into dichotomizing mind (being) and body (doing). Inspired by the work of D. W. Winnicott, Levine says that "being alive is the being that requires doing if it is to fulfill its promise" (p. 18). And we feel most "real" when we are most "alive."

Correlative to the world of the self-as-subject (self-as-agent), in here, is the world of possibilities, out there. A person with a denuded sense of agency (initiative) or with a crippled sense of self-as-subject will see limited or no possibilities or opportunities in his or her outer world. An impoverished inner world co-relates with a sterile outer world. The way our world is co-constituted will be manifested in the way we approach our work. "It does so," states Levine (2010), "essentially by defining the reason we work."

> We may work to realize the potential embedded in a [meaningful] idea and thus to make our subjectivity [the subjective pole of our intentional world] real [the objective pole of our intentional world]. Or, we may work to repair fantasized damage done to the good object [Other] and thus deal with our sense that we are responsible for the failure of our environment to provide us with adequate nurturance [thus skewing our intentional initiative]. Finally, we may work to service our greed, and thus in an effort to compensate for [or mirror] an impoverished inner world. The three reasons we work need not operate independently, and while they define different kinds of work they can also be present to different degrees within any given work setting, so what we do might be driven by all three, the balance among them determining the overall meaning work has for us. (p. 30)

When our social environment provides adequate nurturance—when it is good enough, states Levine (2010), "work becomes the doing that creates the good" (p. 18). The good we do out there is in synchrony with the good we experience in here. "In creating the good in the world outside, we realize and affirm the good we hold internally. That is work's [optimal] purpose" (p. 18). The good is originally represented (embodied) by the loving-kindness of our mothers, fathers, relatives, and peers; our peers' parents, teachers, mentors, and other subcultural, cultural, or transcultural models, fictional or real. Plainly put, growing up in a relatively good social environment nurtures the impulse in us to create good in the world. When we are treated as being worthy of love, we are inclined to attempt to be worthy of that love through our good work. To use Levine's object-relations language, we become our selectively and creatively synthesized internalized identifications. The way we work parallels the externalization of these internalized identifications. Good internalized identifications beget good externalizations (work). Our ability to create good work stems from having a secure self, "from our ability to experience ourselves as a locus of the good" (p. 54). Impaired internalized identifications beget either self-negation or self-aggrandizement that results in either inertia or a compensatory (greedy or compulsive) approach to work.

> Our identification with the bad internal object [the inner representation of the non-nurturing Other] obstructs our effort to make contact with the self. It is this contact with the self that makes what we do real; and it is our failure to make contact that lends a sense of unreality to our activities, relationships and attachments. Real then means rooted in an internalized agency. (p. 55)

"One of the basic premises of life," declares Deurzen-Smith (1997), "is that we have to earn our keep and work for our living and our survival" (p. 108). "Freud and Marx," she comments, "recognised that the very effort of work and direct replenishment originally gave instant joy, but that this gratification had to be postponed in order to assure greater future gratification" (p. 108). This, for Deurzen-Smith, results in more than just alienation from our drives. "That is more than alienation, it is a reversal of the natural process which makes living a joy" (p. 109). I may find it difficult to motivate myself upon awakening in the morning and do my work because it is so far away from the paycheck at the end of the month. "It is often difficult to remember that, in effect, every minute of work one does represents a bit of nurturance and is therefore potentially pleasurable" (p. 109). Instead of experiencing the joy of work in the moment, my consciousness becomes oriented to the future, where anticipated pleasure is artificially associated with *consumption* and *leisure*. This state of affairs puts me "out of touch with the essential cyclical nature of our existence" (p. 110). This essential cycle of hunger-effort-pleasure of satiation is now symbolically experienced as missing. It is not surprising then that on weekdays, I look forward to my weekends and on weekends and vacations, I find myself itching to get back to work.

"Unfortunately," reflects Deurzen-Smith (1997), "few of us are blessed with jobs that remind us of the pleasure of literally making a living ourselves. Broadly speaking, the lust for labor is lost" (p. 110). No wonder then that many of us compensate for the loss of the "lust for labor" by artificially associating effort with pleasure through trivial trips to shopping malls. Still others derive vicarious leisurely pleasure from watching sports, where their teams exert their greatest effort the aim of which is to achieve direct and concrete winning results. Although Deurzen-Smith does not say it directly, the implication from her analysis of our prevalent work orientation is for us to cultivate the capacity for deriving joy from our productive and creative efforts in the moment, while intermittently contemplating the transitoriness of our lives. We need to hold on to the belief in "a natural balancing mechanism, which allows pain [drudgery] to be eventually turned to pleasure [joy] but which accepts that life ultimately leads to death" (p. 111).

Some of us are blessed enough to derive joy from our work. Self-actualizing persons, says Maslow (1971), approach their work with a sense of dedication and a sense of mission. They become absorbed in their work. Plainly put, they love their work. As it is for a couple who are deeply in love, the work and the person seem to be "meant for each other … the person and [the] job fit together and belong together perfectly like a key and a lock" (pp. 301–302). Of course, for some us, work is a mixed blessing!

"Work," notes Luijpen (1969), "not only makes a man but also makes him a fellowman" (p. 247). Luijpen stresses the importance of *mutuality* in work. "Thus work really is mutual," for it always involves a division of labor (p. 247). "Man would simply disappear if he did not work" (p. 247). Luijpen reminds us, "*existence is co-existence*" (p. 267). "*Co-existence* in work also constitutes the interconnection in mankind's history" (p. 247). We humans are "permeated with, and dependent upon the past" (p. 247). The present generation serves "as a starting point for the work of future generations" (p. 247). Man is "the creator and the creature of history, and in this [common] history work occupies the central position" (p. 248). It is through the continuity of work that the "bond between men … is secured" (p. 248). Guided by Marx's description of work, Luijpen concludes by placing "emphasis on work as man's self-realization" (p. 248). Rather than being "purely a means to a goal … work is a goal in itself" (p. 248). Just as we cannot reduce eating and drinking to simply a means to survival—for eating and drinking are a *way of living*, a goal in itself—so too we cannot reduce working to simply a means to making a living. And even though Luijpen recognizes that "the character of work as a means can never be totally eliminated from work," work to a certain extent must remain a goal in itself—"as man's self-realization" (p. 248). "To work *is* to become man" (p. 248). Working, as a manifestation of our self-realization, *is* essential to our refinement as human beings; it is part of the process of our becoming more mature persons.

Fromm (1947) believes that above and beyond being able to give-and-receive, preserve and exchange things with others, healthy people are able to reason, love, and work *productively*. For Fromm, the mature person is one who has cultivated a *productive orientation* toward reasoning, loving, and working. The productive person works toward realizing her or his potential.

Only by practicing my *productive orientation* can I resolve my basic existential, dialectical dilemma of, on the one hand, wanting to unite and be connected with others and, on the other hand, desiring to maintain my individuality, separateness, and uniqueness. It is through productive reasoning, love, and work that I am able to more or less achieve a balance between these polar meanings in my lifeworld.

As a healthy person, I value my work not only as a means of making a living, but, above all, as a manifestation of my creative self-expression. I do not work for the purpose of exploiting others, marketing myself, accumulating unneeded material possessions, or withdrawing from other people.

For Husserl, informs us Melle (2002), we are defined by our "love and calling" (p. 244). In his unpublished manuscripts, Husserl gives two examples of "love and calling":

> The love of the mother for her child and the professional calling to be a scientist, an artist, or a politician. It may be that Husserl thought of motherhood as being analogous to a professional calling. He does point out that the love of the mother for her child has an instinctual ground that is absent in the professional calling. A purely instinctual love can, however, be refined into a pure love. (p. 244)

From a Husserlian point of view, then, our challenge in life is to do our best, given the contingencies of our lives and the meanings we attribute to them, to determine and respond responsibly to our vocational or "professional calling."

References

Deurzen-Smith, E. V. (1997). *Everyday mysteries: Existential dimensions of psychotherapy*. Routledge.

Fromm, E. (1947). *Man for himself: An inquiry in the psychology of ethics*. Holt, Rinehart, and Winston.

Levine, D. P. (2010). *Object relations, work, and the self*. Routledge.

Luijpen, W. A. (1969). *Existential phenomenology*. Duquesne University Press.

Maslow, A. H. (1971). *The farther reaches of human nature*. Viking.

Melle, U. (2002). Edmund Husserl: From reason to love. In J. J. Drummond & L. Embree (Eds.), *Phenomenological approaches to moral philosophy: A handbook*. Kluwer.

Part X

The Capacities for Suffering and Mourning

30

Suffering: The Capacity to Endure *Suffering*

The "underlying theme" in Fiumara's (2015) text on *psychic suffering* is "the creative use of human suffering" (p. xiv). This requires creative "coping with our limits and finitude … [and necessitates paradoxical] coexistence with pain and adversity" (p. xv). We need to "uncover the beneficial aspects of our unavoidable suffering" (p. xvi). We have to learn "to coexist with our very imperfect condition" so that "we could live far more intensively … we must become accomplished virtuosi survivors" (p. xxi). Our individual (and communal) growth can be facilitated "if we understand and manage suffering more holistically" (p. xxi). We must learn to relate to suffering creatively. Adversity could be viewed positively. Something of value can be extracted from pain and suffering. We can learn to manage "our affective problems … as potentially creative experiences" (p. xxiv). Like any other human experience, the nature of our suffering is influenced by how we respond to it. Instead of viewing it as something that needs to be anesthetized and eliminated, we can view pain as a resource. We can respond to it in a way that releases its *positive meaning* or purpose. We can learn to relate to suffering with courage rather than fear and cowardice. "Loss and disappointment are, after all, inevitable human experiences" (p. xxv). Suffering can be perceived "as a necessary signal to transform our quality of life – a 'message' that should be heard rather than ignored … [We can] respond to suffering as the natural accompaniment of a vital impulse to maturation" (p. xxv). Using the words of D. W. Winnicott, suffering can be viewed as a "'tribute to the fact that life is difficult'" [and not necessarily an illness] … "A tribute is a payment or a contribution we make to the challenge of life" (p. xxv). Our mental health lies in responding creatively to our pain and suffering in a way that "may contribute to self-formation, *or*

© The Author(s), under exclusive license to Springer Nature Switzerland AG 2021

M. J. Hannush, *Markers of Psychosocial Maturation*,
https://doi.org/10.1007/978-3-030-74315-4_30

even self deconstruction, when necessary" (p. xxvi). There are creative forces that can be derived from human suffering.

"Friedrich Nietzsche," state Iacovou and Weixel-Dixon (2015), "called upon each of us to be 'artists of life' … this is a call to the passionate life" (p. 200). "Greatness," they continue, "'involves putting pain to work'… We are called upon to do just that: not just to accommodate the pain, but to make it useful, if not 'beautiful'" (p. 201).

In his "memoir," Alexie (2017) describes how he attempts to come to terms with relentless pain and suffering: from pain, to story, to home. Through creative storytelling, Alexie is able to feel more at home with his pain and suffering, more at home in the world.

Frankl (2000) tells the following story "in order to illustrate how suffering may be bestowed with meaning" and to view "meaningful suffering in terms of sacrifice."

> It is the story of a physician who suffered from severe depression after his wife died. I embarked on a short Socratic dialogue by asking him what would have happened if he had died first. 'How much she would have suffered,' he answered. What was now left to me was simply to respond, 'Your wife has been spared this suffering, and after all, it is you who are sparing her this suffering – to be sure, at the price that now you have to survive and mourn her.' At the same moment, he could see a meaning in his suffering, the meaning of a sacrifice. There was still suffering, but no longer despair. Because *despair is suffering without meaning.* (pp. 132–133)

This is a beautifully uplifting story. However, I have two caveats to make. First, as Merleau-Ponty (1962) points out, we humans are always meaning-bound. We may experience ambivalent, ambiguous, contradictory, fuzzy, or inaccurate meanings. They are meanings nevertheless. Even so-called meaninglessness *makes sense* against the backdrop of meaningfulness. *Despair is not "suffering without meaning."* Despair is meaningful to the person experiencing it. Frankl is making the mistake of an "either-or" understanding of a shift in movement from meaninglessness to meaningfulness. What is actually transpiring is a shift from one form of meaning making to another form of meaning making. I would conjecture that the physician-patient in the above story told by Frankl experiences a widening and deepening of what his love for his departed wife *means* to him. He now experiences a higher form of love, a love that involves the capacity to sacrifice and suffer for the sake of his beloved wife who died before him. The second caveat has to do with Frankl's propensity, at times, to "having 'imposed' meanings and values on the patient" (p. 133), a charge that he contests, but seems in my eyes as apt.

Frankl (2000), however, has known deep suffering that taught him the importance of *waiting with hope*, a lesson he "learned in three years spent in Auschwitz and Dachau" (p. 135). He has also learned another important lesson: although suffering is unavoidable, a distinction needs to be made between *necessary suffering* and *unnecessary suffering*. "Masochism," Frankl states, "means accepting unnecessary suffering" (p. 123). The distinction is critical, though the line of demarcation between necessary and unnecessary suffering needs to be understood as elastic. There may be an emotional continuum between necessary suffering and unnecessary suffering.

Much has been written about *necessary suffering*, but not enough about *unnecessary suffering*, a theme that appears in disguise abundantly as, for example, in the *repetition compulsion*. We tend, for instance, to repeat familial and generational maladaptive relational patterns that bring suffering to ourselves and to others.

Because it is universally experienced as part of our embodied humanity, suffering is necessary, inevitable, and unavoidable. It is one of the existential givens of life. We suffer because we know we, and our loved ones, are going to die. We love; therefore, we suffer. "'*We are never so defenseless against suffering*,'" Freud reminds us "'*as when we love, never so helplessly unhappy as when we have lost our loved object or its love*'" (quoted as an epigraph to the text in Goldberg, 1999).

We suffer because we all experience *existential anxiety* (over decision-making), *existential guilt* (about not living up fully to our potential-to-be), and *existential isolation (loneliness)*. This is because no one can "be" us. No one can die or become sick on our behalf. No one can decide for us. Even when we relegate decision-making for someone else, we are still making decisions. No one can undergo atonement, expiation, or reparation on our behalf. No one can understand us fully. We cannot even understand ourselves completely. Even our closest partners cannot become our identical psychosocial twins. The price of all this is necessary suffering. "For that reason," reflecting on the universality of suffering, Fromm (1986) concludes, "a suffering person who recognizes how widespread suffering is can feel the consolation of human solidarity" (p. 148). "Sympathy," he adds, "is inseparable from love for humanity" (p. 148).

Sympathy, like joy, is a mode of encounter. "The hardship," that we suffer requiring sympathy, explains Melucci (1996), "and the joy of the encounter thus stand in a delicate equilibrium" (p. 102). Three abilities need to be brought to this encounter: (1) "the ability to remain anchored in a self that is our own and to bridge the void between that self and the other's [sic]" (p. 102),

(2) the "ability to see things from the other's point of view" (p. 102), and (3) the ability to empathize-and-sympathize with the other.

> The encounter brings two regions of meaning together, two fields of energy at different frequencies which we adjust until they resonate with each other. The encounter is sym-pathy; it is com-passion, feeling-with-another; it is the discovery that meaning does not belong to us but rather given in the encounter itself; although at the same time only we can create it. (p. 102)

In short, where there is shared empathy, shared sympathy, and *shared meaning*, there is less suffering. Com-passionate and sym-pathetic sharing reduces, but does not eliminate, the burden of suffering. Reciprocal receptivity to each other's (more or less) optimal unconditional love is an authentic response to personal suffering.

Where there is no love there can be no sympathy. "Indifference," says Fromm (1986), "is the opposite of sympathy" (p. 148). Our "capacity for sympathy," Fromm laments, "has shrunk in our century" (p. 147). Why? It is because people "are so alienated from themselves that they are no longer fully conscious of their suffering" (p. 147). Though repressed, alienation from our embodied self is in itself a source of suffering. Suffering is also the pain we pay for our separation, individuation, and uniqueness. Additionally, we experience the suffering of our own reflexive nature, which typically takes the form of a lonely discourse. We alone are ultimately responsible for the lonely *call of conscience*. We suffer the anxiety of being alone. Loneliness is emotionally painful. (I am here focusing on existential or ontological loneliness—loneliness due to awareness of nonbeing and due to the existential requirements of being). Loneliness can also be due to everyday cares, frustration, and stresses that are of a personal, familial, political, or sociocultural nature.

Existential loneliness is attenuated but not dissolved through loving relatedness, reflexivity, and levity. Again, with awareness and love come inevitable suffering. Through the mediation of reflexivity and relatedness, we wobble back and forth seeking a shaky balance between suffering and joy, with the core belief in the center of our embodied being that joy can absorb the suffering. Similarly, our capacity for levity lessens the burden of undergoing life's suffering, but does not eliminate it. "Laughter and weeping," says Melucci (1996):

> are located on the same emotional continuum. The one may merge with the other because they are the two aspects of the same experience, a contact with reality in which pleasure and pain are present at once. They are human dimen-

> sions of experience which are inseparate. Occasional laughter may then be transformed into good humour, a cheerful attitude to life which coexists with pain. The relationship between laughter and weeping grants access to a space of gratuitousness and play, to the element of childishness [or childlikeness] inherent in all of us. (p. 138)

Although we may yield to suffering, levity in the form of good humor and laughter, especially as in *laughing with others* and *at ourselves*—the kind of laughter that grants us the space to fluidly look at ourselves from a different perspective—the "distance between laughing [joy] and weeping [suffering] narrows and we may begin to pass from one to the other more frequently" (p. 138).

Necessary suffering also includes the inevitable and unavoidable experience of bodily pain in our daily lives. Here I have in mind what Melucci (1996) calls the *minor ailments* of everyday life: "The distinctive feature of our minor ailments is the fact that they belong to the body: we suffer from stomachache, headache, and the like" (p. 75). Melucci goes on to describe how these minor ailments have relational, temporal (durational), and spatial (place-bound) dimensions. "Each of us could plot a map of our minor ailments along these dimensions; a spatio-temporal [sic] map and a relational map of the body's minor afflictions" (p. 75). Although they could be alarming, annoying, frightening, menacing, and unwelcome, these minor "ailments are our boring, faithful companions, our constant partners as we move through daily life" (p. 75). Even though we may attempt to ignore them, try to forget them, or pretend they are not there, they are experienced as "the harbingers, the signals of potentially more suffering, the first steps toward Disease [and, I would add, Decay and Death] with a capital D" (p. 76).

Melucci (1996) encourages us to take cognizance of our lived body—the body as we live it in everyday life. It is the body that serves as the locus for our identity as distinct individuals. Bodily awareness "brings to light neglected or unknown levels of experience" (p. 74). By familiarizing ourselves with our lived body—"with its weight and lightness, its suffering and pleasure … we seek to summon up force to resist external pressure, to steer our energies in the direction that we feel corresponds to our needs, to affirm that we are distinct individuals" (p. 73). Melucci further advises us to be attuned to the ongoing bodily changes we experience in our everyday life. Such awareness brings us in touch with neglected or unknown levels of experience. Hidden issues bubble up to the surface. "The body," Melucci mentions, "is a message to be listened to, to be deciphered, to be answered. The body speaks, and not only through its public display, but personally to each one of us through its signals" (p. 74). "Paying attention to the body," is essential because "it also constitutes a provisional stage along the road to awareness, one point of view that may reveal another and bring hidden questions to the surface" (p. 74). This kind of listening may "point out ways to respond, as ways to responsibility" (p. 74).

"Freud believed," states Safran (2012), "that life by its very nature involves various forms of suffering: illness, loss of loved ones and friends, disappointments, and ultimately death" (p. 48). "It is essential," Safran goes on to caution, "to distinguish what might be termed *existential suffering* from self-imposed neurotic suffering. From Freud's perspective, one of the goals of psychoanalysis is to help people learn to grapple with life's inevitabilities with a certain degree of equanimity and dignity" (pp. 48–49).

Even movement toward positive change and growth, notes Nicholsen (2002), elicits suffering, for it entails the sacrifice or death of an old form of the self:

> Shifting our sense of self to include a broader identification with the whole of life in its cyclical form means not only an increase in love and caring, but also an increase in concern—and the loss, disequilibrium, and suffering entailed in such a deep psychic change. … we must acknowledge this suffering and the anxiety it causes if we are to appreciate our profound resistance to the very possibility of a deeper intertwinement with the natural [and social] world. (p. 91)

This suffering becomes bearable when it is acknowledged, shared, and reflected upon. But even suffering that is precipitated by traumatic experiences can become more bearable when shared and understood. These traumatic experiences are allowed to be felt, transformed into words, contained, and mourned. They are no longer shameful secrets to be suffered in silence. The *unknown-known* becomes known (as food of emotional truth for the hungry mind), and the not-yet-experienced becomes *experienced* (as feelings felt and thoughts thought). Suffering shared is suffering attenuated. Suffering that cannot be acknowledged festers and suffocates. When our suffering is not heard, we are rendered unable to hear the suffering of others. When our cries are not heard we become numbed to the cries of others. We become self-destructive and/or destructive of others.

Our original suffering, observes Nicholsen (2002), can be traced to "the pain of the mother's absence … [which] is also necessary" (p. 23). She alludes to the notion that our capacity for suffering accompanies, what I call, our *identificatory resonance* with the suffering of the Other. Here Nicholsen focuses on "identification with other life," such as the cry of the caught catfish. When this suffering is too much to bear, harking back to the *unnecessary* absence of the mother, we are disposed to put "an end to suffering through destruction on the other" and through identification with the destructive forces of life (pp. 136–137).

> When trauma or catastrophe destroys our sense of a safe, good, and strong world that can hear and bear our pain, we ourselves become unable to suffer that pain. We cannot experience it, digest it, and contain it within our larger selves. And if we have no way to suffer our pain, we cannot mourn the dead [our losses]. Without mourning, we have no way to move on within a world that remains meaningful. (p. 137)

In short, *unnecessary suffering* erodes and unravels our sense of identity or selfhood. It elicits our defensive destructiveness. It counters our original proclivity to constructive identification with essential others with destructive identification. But just as we needed to make use of the strengths of our essential others who provided us with original care, we now need to make use of the strengths of new others who extend their care and concern to us.

Lastly, Nicholsen (2002) offers us another slant on suffering. We suffer when we encounter the numinous in our lives. We find ourselves "at the very edge of awareness" when, in awe, we encounter something "so much greater than our present selves" before which we humbly kneel (p. 18). "The self needs a measure of strength to bear awe and its attendant suffering" (p. 18). What happens when this experience of awe is too much for us to bear? "Suffering will then either be avoided altogether, or it will miscarry and turn into bitterness, criticism, and despair" (p. 18).

Orange (2011) states that "receptivity and suffering [are] inherent in the process of understanding" (p. 23). Although Orange's focus is on the therapeutic relationship between patient ("the suffering stranger") and analyst, I will extrapolate and apply her insights to our existential human situation in everyday life.

I am called to emotionally participate not only in the suffering of my essential others, but also in the suffering of strangers, my fellow humans, and other living organisms. In the process of trying to understand my essential Other, I place myself at risk. I permit the Other to have an impact on me, influence me, and question my assumptions and my habitual ways of being. Without consciously knowing it, I may even change for the Other's sake. At the same time, I make myself susceptible to being disappointed and misunderstood by the Other. The Other can make me miserable. More than that, the Other awakens my finitude—my awareness of my human limitations. Yet, through it all, I may learn and grow through my suffering.

I, as finite human, will never be able to fully grasp and gain mastery over my suffering. However, even partial understanding may alleviate some of my suffering. Otherwise, I will never learn through suffering. Regardless, I sense that there is a difference between "useless and useful suffering" (Orange, 2011, p. 69). What I make of this distinction is that there are times when we are so overwhelmed with suffering that the Other's protective and caring presence is useless. At other times, the suffering Other is receptive and thus suffers less because I am there to, reliably and consistently, offer protection, understanding, and care. My compassion radiates in my suffering with the Other. By being involved, I will inevitably be affected to the core of my being by the suffering of the Other. This is what happens in a naturally holding-and-healing environment—an environment in which I "hold" the Other emotionally and even bodily, as in a com-passionate embrace, where two mindful hearts touch and are touched by each other.

What should we do if we find ourselves contributing to the suffering of the Other? "We have to," again extrapolating from the therapeutic context, "change our way of being with the … [essential Other] from the inside out. We have to find a way to love" (Orange, 2011, p. 101). We "must allow ourselves to be known, criticized, and changed by them" because "understanding … [is] a two-way street" (p. 101). Only "together can we enter the path toward healing and reintegration" (p. 102). There is always the risk of re-wounding each other as a consequence of mutual misattunements or misunderstandings. I look at the contorted face of the Other. I keep my defensiveness in check. I respond to the Other's implicit call, "Don't harm me, I am another You" or better yet, "Accept me; love me, I am another You." What we both desire is to live a good life in suffering with and suffering for the Other, in loving-and-being-loved by the Other.

In our reenactments of earlier familial dramas or scenarios, says Gay (2001), we carry with us lessons we learned in what Freud calls "this school of suffering" (p. 50). The family forms our early place of not only joy, but also emotional pain and suffering. Thereafter, in less than optimal familial circumstances, I can escape my suffering only "through some attack upon myself or upon another person" (p. 50). The line of demarcation between necessary (inevitable or existential) and unnecessary suffering—a suffering that could have been prevented in a more equitable lifeworld—can at times be ambiguously blurred. Still, a good-enough home environment is a place where unnecessary suffering is kept to a minimum.

Mann (1994) writes on "Psychiatric Pain and Deliberate Suffering" (pp. 94–112). "In psychiatric illness," Mann tells us, "the distinction between *patient* and *agent* is maximally vague" (p. 95). It is from this that "psychiatric suffering derives in part" (p. 95). It is widely believed, he informs us, that psychiatric suffering is "self-induced" or "self-inflicted." With a strong sense of "agency," "patiency" could have been circumvented. Our painful fate could have unfolded differently had we identified and internalized a more benign external authority. We could have been spared *neurotic suffering* as our fate, a fate that predisposed us to compulsively repeat painful past patterns, patterns which brought *unnecessary* pain to ourselves and others.

In *neurotic suffering*, bad (maladaptive) habits come to replace authentic relating. "It is human relatedness," Mann (1994) explains, that is "the aspect lacking from [maladaptive] habitual deeds" (p. 100). "And it is precisely relationships of [healthy] dependence that a great many habits replace. They [habits] become dependent relationships in themselves, with the sustenant person replaced by a ritual, an addictive substance, and so on" (p. 100). "Habit," in short, "conceals the facts and thereby obviates the need to relate" (p. 101). The neurotic sufferer has not come to terms with the painful facts of life. The unconscious and perverse "will to suffer" exacts a one-person solution—a symptomatic habit is a sort of answer to a problematic situation, to a two-person problem. "Alcohol dependency," for example, "replaces human dependency" (p. 104). It is "a ready replacement for relatedness" (p. 104).

Although Mann (1994) does not explicitly frame the neurotic sufferer's dilemma this way, I believe he would wholeheartedly concur: in addiction we find a failure in resolving a dialectical dilemma. The addict is unable to come to terms with the conflict between dependence and independence and between agency (ownership) and patiency (passive disownment):

> One assumes ownership of feelings by controlling them, and by experiencing them oneself. By making himself the agent as well as the ground of his suffering, the addict takes possession of it. By taking opiates, for a brief time he can both vanquish his pain and make it recur—he is in control. While this control lasts, it perfects his ownership. Unfortunately it does not last long. (pp. 104–105)

What we have here is dependency and patiency gone awry on one side of the dialectical continuum. Agency, independence, and ownership have gone askew on the other side of the dialectical continuum. The neurotic sufferer—be it an addict, a depressive, or an anorexic—has failed to achieve a balance between these dialectically related polar meanings of existence. The neurotic sufferer "*cannot tell the difference* between choice and fate. Here is the ambiguity against which we struggle to assume ownership" (p. 108). This ambiguity is mirrored in the sufferer's frozen capacity for reflexivity. "The states of dysreflexia," explicates Mann, "manifest as errors of ownership – the results of disowning and misowning diverse regions of the self [-world]" (p. 109).

By owning one's fate, always while humbly acknowledging one's limits, the sufferer clears the way for new *possibilities* and new ways of relating and relatedness. "This new self," concludes Mann (1994), "is simultaneously subject (ego) and object (in relation to itself as well as to others)" (p. 111). Balancing agency with patiency, always precarious, is a lifelong maturational task. Patiency itself, to my mind, is related to patience. Similarly the word "patient" denotes someone who suffers. "Patience," which is derived from the Latin *patiens* meaning "suffering," refers to the capacity to endure distress uncomplainingly. Patiency gone awry denotes extreme passivity and will-less-ness in the face of a seemingly intractable fate. Agency gone awry connotes being totally in control of one's embodied-being-in-the-world-with-others and thinking of oneself as the willful force behind one's unfolding destiny. Authentic agency requires facing the world realistically and truthfully. Lifton (1993) defines "genuine agency" as "the self's capacity to mobilize inner power, act effectively, and initiate constructive behavior" (p. 207). Contrastingly, "combinations of early trauma and a violent death [or destructiveness] – saturated environment contribute to strong patterns of numbing and to disturbances in meaning that lead to bizarre, destructive behavior" (p. 207). Lifton's *psychic numbing* is equivalent to passivity or patiency gone awry. He defines "psychic numbing" as a "diminished capacity or inclination to feel – and a general sense of stasis" (p. 10). True patience, in contrast, requires an increased capacity or inclination to feel—especially compassion for self and others, and a general sense of vitality. It is a supreme state of *active passivity*, of waiting hopefully with com-passion, realism, and understanding.

Dokecki (1996) has this to say about existential or necessary suffering:

> *The most general feature of our human condition is its tragic character* … The term *tragic* refers to a situation in which the conditions of well-being require and are interdependent with situations of limitation, frustration, challenge, and suffering … necessary conditions of creativity, affection, the experience of beauty. (p. 54)

Suffering and well-being are intertwined. The essence of existential suffering lies in our vulnerability. "Vulnerability," observes Dokecki, "'is the capacity of a living creature to undergo harm,' defined as 'the frustration of the needs and desires of that creature and the pain and suffering that accompany that frustration'" (p. 55). When "our elemental passions lead us to attempt to achieve the unachievable," explains Dokecki, "we suffer and experience frustration and anxiety" (p. 61).

Because we are tragically imperfect, we will always be frustratingly disappointed, and in turn we will inevitably frustrate others by disappointing them. We will always experience domains of incompatibility even with those whom we love and love us most. Perfect harmony will always elude us. We will forever, to some degree, fail to live up to our obligations or responsibilities toward others and vice versa. We can never fully transcend our narcissism. This, however, does not prevent us from trying our utmost to respond to the summons of the Other, to answer the *call of conscience*, to compassionately assume our responsibilities to the Other, and to ourselves, to the best of our abilities. Our limitations do not stand in the way of pursuing mutually meaningful projects and thus together partaking in relational beauty, goodness, and truth. We can live reflexively and respond discerningly in the face of our existential suffering. Dokecki (1996) defines human development, "as the growth and broadening of a person's experience over the life span" (pp. 60–61). This building and broadening of experience is contingent upon, what Wilfred Bion calls, being open to *learning* from experience. This kind of growth "entails both an increase in the quantity [and quality] of our experience (progressive differentiation) and changes in the ordering of experience toward coherent meaning (hierarchic integration). We come to experience more and more of our world more and more meaningfully" (p. 61). Our understanding of our lifeworld is deepened.

Thompson (1994) describes "psychopathology" as "a *flight* from suffering" (p. 272). Reality is a "necessity" that we need to reckon with and accept. A part of this reality is painful and thus a source of suffering. We will never understand our social reality fully. "We come to know it through our *encounter* with it" (p. 273). "Reality," however, "isn't 'external'; it invites me to *belong* to what's separate and to make it a dimension of my life" (p. 273). Fate, as a dimension of our reality, plays a role in shaping us, but we have the potential to transform this fate, within limits, into our owned destiny. We have a hand in directing our destination. Similarly, the unconscious dimensions of our selves that we have "inherited" as part of our historical reality can be modulated through our insight-driven actions. "Our conscious choices help determine what becomes unconscious as well … The line between the two isn't so easy to define" (p. 274).

Thompson (1994) too sees the difference between unnecessary (bad) and good suffering. There are patients, he observes, that appear to "prolong their suffering inexorably" (p. 261). Then there are people who demonstrate "the higher forms of love that involve the pleasure of sacrifice and the capacity to bear suffering in deference to the object of one's love" (p. 262). In neurotic suffering which is precipitated by "neurotic conflict," one "substitutes one form of suffering for another" (p. 263). Neurotic suffering "stifles our capacity to enjoy life because we're so obsessed with evading it" (p. 263). By "trying to escape suffering, we become even more alienated from ourselves" (p. 263).

Thompson (1994) makes an important distinction between, what I label as, *existential ambivalence* and *neurotic ambivalence*. *Existential ambivalence* "is axiomatic" to life and living. It is one source of existential suffering. *Neurotic ambivalence*, in contrast, is a manifestation of a "splitting" of self-world (into good versus bad) in an effort to defensively adapt to an overwhelmingly harsh social reality. We can only build our character, explains Thompson, by coming to terms with our existential suffering and by learning to tolerate the anxiety that comes with it. Above all, a healthy way of facing and coming to terms with our existential suffering is "to feel good by *being* good; by endeavoring to be truthful and accepting realities" (p. 267). This is the "fundamental aim in life" (p. 267).

Equating reality with "life," Thompson (1994) asks, "What, then, epitomizes the realities [life exigencies] we're unable to accept?" (p. 268). "Basically," he answers, "it comes down to feeling unloved" (p. 268). We consequently compensate for being unloved or for losing love by twisting reality—*distorting life's meanings*. This involves being-and-becoming deceitful (untruthful) in order to avoid the pain of our social reality. This leads us to "conceal the truth about lost loves" or about not having been properly loved (p. 130). "The truth about one's [compensatory or deceitful] behavior can only be determined [countered] by *being* who one is … [by] becoming a more honest human being [which] is not an easy thing to do" (p. 132). "Truth," however, "is what being human is all about … Knowing the truth is what it means to be a person, a being who's always showing [revealing] and hiding [concealing] who that person is" (p. 63).

We cope constructively with our existential suffering by cultivating the capacity for "*fidelity to revelation*" of our unfolding emotional and relational truths. We get at "the truth of experience," observes Thompson (1994), by "learning to accept the realities of a sometimes tragic existence" (p. 131). Truth's accomplices are "the secrets we endeavor to conceal" (p. xxiv). The "only way of overcoming the suffering we conspire to evade is to know the reality we deny, and face it" (p. xxiv). Thompson provides us with a practical Socratic dictum to live by: "Know your own mind and be your own person, and the truth will make you free" (p. xxiv).

"Beauty," states Sartwell (2004), "always bears within it the poignancy of loss" (p. 4). "The loss that lingers in every beautiful thing," he continues, "intensifies desire. Indeed if we did not age, if things did not disintegrate, the experience of beauty would be impossible" (p. 4). Loss, aging, and disintegration are all intimations of vulnerability, fragility, and finitude that we all have to suffer and endure. We experience beauty in our transactions with objects we encounter in the natural or cultural world, including human artifacts and human faces and bodies. "We also appreciate ... [the] beauty of character, of saints and sages, or people with more simplicity, serenity that we ourselves possess ... [We have an appreciation for] the beautiful soul or personality" (p. 10). Moreover, "beauty is something we make in cooperation with the [social] world" (p. 5). What is implied here is that in the absence of such "cooperation," relational *ugliness* ensues. And because perfect cooperation is a mirage, we are doomed to suffer ugliness in human relatedness. Our maturational and lifelong task is to seek to increase the beauty (goodness or purity) and decrease the ugliness (badness or destructiveness) of our character, personality, or soul. With the ripening of the beauty of our personhood comes the "relaxation into oneself" and the attainment of the capacity to "find peace where all along ... [it] already was" (pp. 130–131). "Though death itself is often ugly," Sartwell concludes, "we must be grateful to it as the source of the possibility of beauty" (p. 150). Again, "beauty is made possible by temporality, as loss is made inevitable by it" (p. 150). The "possibility of beauty is everywhere all the time, and beauty can encompass even ugliness, even terror, even evil" (p. 151). Beauty is born of the consciousness of temporality and finitude. Our challenge is to "expand" into beauty, an expansion that involves "an exercise in awareness, a way to keep finding what we've lost" and at the same time allowing for "the loss of awareness at the moment of its [beauty's] real expansion" (p. 152).

References

Alexie, S. (2017). *You don't have to say you love me*. Little, Brown and Company.

Dokecki, P. (1996). *The tragi-comic professional. Basic considerations for ethical reflective-generative practice*. Duquesne University Press.

Fiumara, G. C. (2015). *Psychic suffering: From pain to growth*. Karnac.

Frankl, V. E. (2000). *Man's search for ultimate meaning*. Perseus.

Fromm, E. (1986). *For the love of life*. The Free Press.

Gay, V. P. (2001). *Joy and the objects of psychoanalysis: Literature, belief, and neurosis*. State University of New York Press.

Goldberg, J. G. (1999). *The dark side of love: The positive role of negative feelings.* Transaction.

Iacovou, S., & Weixel-Dixon, K. (2015). *Existential therapy: 100 Key point and techniques.* Routledge.

Lifton, R. J. (1993). *The protean self: Human resilience in an age of fragmentation.* The University of Chicago Press.

Mann, D. W. (1994). *A simple theory of the self.* W. W. Norton.

Melucci, A. (1996). *The playing self: Person and meaning in the planetary society.* Cambridge University Press.

Merleau-Ponty, M. (1962). *Phenomenology of perception* (C. Smith, Trans.). Routledge.

Nicholsen, S. W. (2002). *The love of nature and the end of the world: The unspoken dimensions of environmental concern.* The MIT Press.

Orange, D. M. (2011). *The suffering stranger: Hermeneutics for everyday clinical practice.* Routledge.

Safran, J. D. (2012). *Psychoanalysis and psychoanalytic therapies.* American Psychological Association.

Sartwell, C. (2004). *Six names of beauty.* Routledge.

Thompson, M. G. (1994). *The truth about Freud's technique: The encounter with the real.* New York University Press.

31

Mourning: The Capacity for *Mourning* and Working Through Loss

Loss and its consequent pain is an inescapable universal human experience. To mourn means to be able to bear the pain and to come to terms with loss. The impulse to evade the pain is ubiquitous. The price for such evasion is pathology. Wilfred Bion goes so far as to say that eluding pain is the hallmark of psychosis. Incidentally, for Bion, all of us have psychotic pockets—delusions (false beliefs) and illusions (false perceptions). Here is Ogden (2012) describing Bion's idea of our proclivity to pain evasion: "Bion … uses the idea of evasion to refer to what he believes to be a hallmark of psychosis: eluding pain rather than attempting to symbolize it for oneself … and doing psychological work with it – lies at the heart of mourning" (p. 28).

Reading "Freud's 'Mourning and Melancholia' [Depression]" creatively, Ogden (2012) elaborates the meaning of successful mourning:

> The individual capable of mourning succeeds in freeing himself from the struggle between life and death that freezes the melancholic [depressive]: 'mourning impels the ego [the 'I' or Self] to give up the object [Other] by declaring the object to be dead and offering the ego the inducement of continuing to live' … So the mourner's painful acceptance of the reality of the death of the object is achieved in part because the mourner knows (unconsciously and, at times consciously) that his own life, his own capacity for 'continuing to live' is at stake. (pp. 29–30)

According to Ogden's (2012) interpretive reading of Freud, what arrests the process of mourning involves a deep ambivalence "between the wish to go on living and the wish to deaden oneself in an effort to be with the dead" (p. 31).

© The Author(s), under exclusive license to Springer Nature Switzerland AG 2021

M. J. Hannush, *Markers of Psychosocial Maturation*,
https://doi.org/10.1007/978-3-030-74315-4_31

The mourner faces the (unconscious or not-so-conscious) choice of living a relational life that has either an "enlivening quality" or a "deadening quality." The "self-imprisoned melancholic [depressive] ... survives in a timeless, deathless (and yet deadened and deadening) internal object world" (p. 32). In the successful mourner it is the sense of aliveness or continuing to be alive that ultimately triumphs.

Whereas the self-esteem of the depressive person who is unable to mourn is diminished, the self-regard of the mature mourner remains intact. Low self-esteem prevents the depressive individual from mourning adequately and adaptively. Similarly, insecure attachment stands in the way of successfully mourning the necessary and not so necessary losses of life. Mature mourning requires a basic feeling of secure attachment and a solid sense of self-esteem.

Losses can come in different forms. Bollas (2011) describes how a child can lose his or her "peace of mind." The parent of this child steals his or her "peace of mind" by "putting unwanted parts of oneself into" the child (p. 20). The parent temporarily experiences a "peace of mind" at the expense of the child "who is left in confusion." As he or she grows older, the child may engage in "unconscious mourning" through perpetrating upon others the unjust injury or injurious injustice that was inflicted upon him or her. This kind of acting-out is a manifestation of arrested or immature mourning. "Much of psychoanalytic theory," concludes Bollas, "is concerned with loss – and loss of the object [Other] in particular" (p. 120). "The therapists all try to evoke," reflect Summers and Barber (2015), "a healing process that translates anger and hurt to sadness and loss, and ultimately to love and gratitude" (p. 50).

From an object-relations perspective, write Berzoff and Hayes (1996), the person who can mourn successfully is able to "sustain an emotionally useful, enduring object representation in the absence of the lost loved one" (pp. 375–376). Of course, they add, one has to take into account "the developmental level of representations at the time loss occurs" (p. 376) for "the effect of losses" differ "at different stages of development" (p. 376). These "representations of others (literally, the mental representations of the absent person) undergo developmental progressions from the infant's fleeting, poorly differentiated (between self and other) images to the adult's enduring, well-differentiated, multifaceted representations" (p. 376). Actual losses may be incurred as a consequence of emotional unavailability, physical absence, or death.

Our mental health or maturation involves being aware of the possibility of loss and, upon experiencing loss, accepting and coming to terms with it. Here is Frosh (1991) delineating the object relations-Kleinian view:

> This is, in miniature, the full trajectory of development and indeed of mental health: from intense anxiety to projective and splitting defences that lead to the world being experienced as an abusive, threatening arena (the paranoid-schizoid position); to gradual integration of love and hate, with a tolerance of ambivalence, but with an acute awareness of the possibilities for loss and guilt (the depressive position). Finally, with the recognition of the internal sources of destructiveness and the damage which we can bring to those we love through the intensity of our passion, comes the creative force of reparation, defined by Klein as 'the variety of processes by which the ego [self or "I"] feels it undoes harm done in phantasy, restores, preserves and revives objects' [internalized mental representations or memories of significant others]. (pp. 50–51)

In the Kleinian vision, says Frosh (1991), the social environment (outer world) "possesses the ability to 'contain' the child's [or the adult's] destructiveness sufficiently to make it tolerable and to reduce anxiety enough to allow for greater integration – a model both of mothering [parenting] and psychotherapy" (p. 51). Moreover, in:

> Kleinian thought there is an emphasis on the reparative potential within individuals—and for the Kleinians it is reparation rather than sublimation that is at the root of the creative process. As long as destruction is balanced by love, envy by gratitude, it is possible to feel depression and loss, to do more than flit superficially through an isolated existence. Rebuilding after destruction, making good, asserting the viability of the self: these are Kleinian virtues; depth remains. (p. 53)

In other words, reparation maintains self-world integration and makes genuine mourning over loss possible. Under this condition, the meaningfulness of the lifeworld is deepened as it is experienced by a bodily self. The capacity for mourning or "the ability to feel depressive feelings – to experience loss, guilt and reparation – is a central designator of mental health, because it presupposes abilities to form committed relationships and to experience others as integrated, ambivalent objects [others with good and bad qualities, with strengths and limitations]" (p. 76). "It is also dependent upon," continues Frosh, "a reasonably successful negotiation of the paranoid-schizoid position, that is, upon an encounter with a maternal reverie that enables the infant's destructive impulses to be contained and that facilitates the projective-introjective processes" (p. 76).

From the beginning, says Frosh (1991), our maturation or "mental health is marked by the advent of depression [the depressive position], of a sense of the fullness of loving that is necessary for loss to be truly felt [and mourned]"

(p. 12). This kind of depression or *concern,* continues Frosh, is "built on the recognition of the reality of pain and loss and yet on the belief that it is worth creating and maintaining links with the world and relationships with others" (p. 12). A "depressive" or *concernful* way of being-in-the-world-with-others is what allows us "to construct a self which possesses some content, some energy, some particular individuality"—a uniquely social self (p. 12).

As an aside, I have always been jarred by the term "depressive" used to delineate a radical, though gradual, shift toward maturation. Now, I see its use as pointing toward the giving-up or loss of something, as in "paradise lost"—a diffused state of oneness and omnipotence. But what the term includes, but does not fully signify, is the tremendous maturational gain acquired through the loss or envisioned relational damage that can lead to loss. One gains the birth of selfhood, the recognition of the Other as separate and vulnerable, and the *capacity for concern* for the welfare of the Other as evidenced through acts of reparation.

Rustin (1991) tells us, "guilt in Klein's 'depressive position' arises from the recognition of the pain suffered by or inflicted on others, and as an essential part of relatedness" (p. 20). "Capacity for moral feeling, therefore," he continues, "in more or less benign forms, is seen as a defining attribute shared by human beings, rather than an unavoidable external constraint upon them" (p. 20). Internal conflict can be resolved and harmony restored through "the recovery and restoration of 'damaged and lost internal objects'" or, in other words, through "symbolically commemorating and preserving the relation to a loved other" (p. 22).

Constructing a self, holds Frosh (1991), is an "act of faith" requiring the affirmation of the possibility of a meaningful life against the backdrop of a chaotic and destructive lifeworld. "Creating a self is like creating a work of art; it may not be worked on as consciously, although sometimes it is …, but just as art to some degree involves taking bits and pieces of the world and fitting them to say something, so does the self. The self, then, is an affirmation of what is humanly worthy and creative" (p. 13). Our sense of selfhood, our identity, is made up of "identifications with deeply loved internalized others" and deeply cherished values (p. 85). *Maturation* involves holding on to many of these cherished identifications, the letting-go (loss) of some of these identifications and the adding (gain) of new identifications. Letting-go of identifications is a painful process. It is a kind of loss that needs to be worked through and mourned. We identify not only with roles, but also with values, familial rules, beliefs, and even emotions. A young woman identifies with her mother's dysthymia, a chronic, low-level depression. In a perverse unconscious way this identification provides her with the semblance of a sense of closeness to her mother. The two are made one through depression. It is one thing to acquire an intellectual insight into this *emotional truth*. It is another to act upon the insight by letting go of this form of toxic identification. For another example, a young man becomes an alcoholic just like his father. Again, unconsciously, he feels perversely connected to a father who was emotionally unavailable while the young man was growing up. Something needs to fill the emptiness when this identification is given up. Working through the loss (mature mourning) will be a painful process that will require a compassionate containment of vertiginous void experienced upon the severance of a compensatory connection, as the young man moves toward establishing a more constructive way of relating to his father.

We humans, says Fiumara (2015), have the natural propensity to flee from anticipated or remembered loss, pain, and suffering. She defines "loss aversion" as "the relative strength of two motives: we are driven more strongly to avoid losses than to achieve gains" (p. xxvi). For an everyday example, "positive thoughts are far weaker than negative ones. Thus, worrying can become a constant attitude, even if it wastes quality time and energy. Even if worrying is useless, we fear that if we stop, negative things are sure to happen" (p. xxvi). But, paradoxically, when loss, pain, and suffering are endured and tolerated, they can be productively utilized. Such endurance and toleration can put us on the path toward growth, maturation, and creative living.

Loss aversion favors the maintenance of the status quo. It keeps us stuck where we are. It anesthetizes us. It acts as a barrier to change. It makes us self-destructive and/or destructive of others. It distracts from living an enlivened life. Even so-called success can be used as a distraction from loss awareness and from creative suffering. However, those of us who are lucky enough to have had our earliest loss, pain, and suffering – beginning with our primal separation-induced loss, *contained* – are positioned to better absorb the inevitable pain of later losses. The Armenian phrase "tsavet danem," is a term of endearment literally meaning, "let me take your pain away." This phrase is mostly reserved for those we are close to and care about. "I care for you so much that I am ready to do anything I can to take your pain away." This phrase captures beautifully the essence of *containment*. The mother identifies and contains, through her tender loving care, not only the child's pain, but more challengingly the child's utter helplessness and frustration in handling his pain.

Fiumara (2015) states, "working through loss is a process that has no clear ending and is, in fact, sustained by a cultivated familiarity with inner pain" (p. 105). "A capacity for tolerating frustration," Fiumara cites Bion as remarking, "enables the psyche to develop thought as a means by which frustration is tolerated and is itself made more tolerable" (p. 105). "The 'alchemic' transformation of pain into creative suffering," or working through loss, adds Fiumara, "can be more realistically attempted in an atmosphere of empathy rooted in authentic listening" (p. 85). She defines "creative suffering" as that which "unfurls" us and "facilitates some kind of healthy change" (p. 10). But "this maturational creativity depends on our capacity to endure psychic distress" (p. 10). This in turn depends up on our movement from the "paranoid-schizoid" to the "depressive position"—"that is, the endurance of the inner coexistence of good and evil within our own mind" (p. 55). Under relatively optimal conditions, the child learns, in moving to the depressive position, to "tolerate the guilt and anxiety (that is, inner pain) that arise from concern about having injured a person he loves" (p. 23). By coming "through with the struggles of the depressive position, we would certainly gain in terms of creativity and relatedness" (p. 111). We would learn to endure the psychic paradoxes of the depressive position. "Why paradox? Because it is a question of recognizing and holding together the contradiction of being both good and bad" (p. 112). Learning to tolerate "our inner paradoxes allows for creative psychic actions, propelled by a search for [emotional] truth … [which in turn is] conducive to *mental health*" (p. 113). *We gain when we contain pain.*

Working through loss can strengthen our capacity to love. For, "there is no greater love than accepting our psychic pain and sparing our partners [others] the burden of carrying it in our stead" (Fiumara, 2015, p. 89). Moreover, as Homans (1989) puts it, individuation is the creative result of mourning, and "the outcome of individuation is in turn the creation of meaning, a building up of new structures of appreciation born of loss" (p. 263).

Lastly, a culture that is anesthetic to loss, pain, and suffering—a fetishistic culture, a culture that constantly diverts us from becoming familiar with our loss, pain, and suffering through a one-sided focus on *smiling and succeeding*, and a culture that urges us to cultivate the *having*, not the *being* mode of life – makes it very difficult for us to work through our losses.

The way we love will have a crucial bearing on how we react to loss. Loss is love's other side. When one has lost a loved one, says Yalom (1980), "the survivor has not only suffered an 'object loss' but has encountered the loss of himself or herself" (p. 56).

When we suffer a loss, observes Jacobsen (2007), we simultaneously experience a crisis in the face of our adversity *and* a potential for the "opening-of-existence" (p. 72). Jacobsen describes four kinds of losses (pp. 73–75): (1) *physical loss* (e.g., the loss of a bodily presence of a loved one); (2) *psychological loss* (e.g., when a loved one adopts "wholly new characteristics, values or manners" or when one emigrates to a new country leaving an old country behind);

(3) *loss of meaning and world view*, such as the way one views the world subsequent to the experience of severe trauma; (4) and *existential loss*. Existential loss involves the severance of existential space of meaning that had been co-constituted between the survivor and his or her lost loved one. One misses one's manner of dwelling with the other.

A crisis-triggering loss, writes Jacobsen (2007), "provides the option of opening up to the depths of existence ... it is as if a crevice opens in the ground that was previously covered with sand ... The crevice allows the individual to look deep into something very significant" (p. 77). "In this way," continues Jacobsen, "the crisis becomes existential and can become a personal turning point, a new life philosophy" (p. 77). Yalom (1980) reminds us that a life-disrupting adversity can serve as a trigger for repositioning ourselves vis-à-vis the four basic existential dimensions (or tensions) of our lives: (1) our orientation toward life versus death, (2) our posture toward freedom versus determinism, (3) our disposition toward isolation versus communal connectedness, and (4) our stance toward finding life either meaningful or meaningless (fixed versus open meanings, according to our own dialectical model).

Permit me to conclude this chapter by making two points. (1) It is meanings that we recall, recollect, and dwell upon when we remember a lost loved one. Here is Fuller (1990) describing this point: "When we recall the loss of something of significance to us, it is the loss itself that has come to life once again in its impact. The loss itself is what is paying us a visit and weighing us down, the loss itself that we are coming back to and not some objective or subjective in-itself" (p. 269). It is the *meaning* of the loss that returns to us. (2) This *meaning* is laden with action *possibilities* regarding our *re-membered* loved one. The meaning of the lost loved one can be re-membered (re-configured). For example, the meaning of my deceased mother can now be "imbued for the first time with its essence: something which is never captured or fully realized in the normal course of lived existence" (Lou Andreas-Salome, cited in Holmes, 2010, pp. 162–163).

References

Berzoff, J., & Hayes, M. (1996). Biopsychosocial aspects of depression. In J. Berzoff, L. M. Flanagan, & P. Hertz (Eds.), *Inside out and outside in: Psychodynamic clinical theory and practice in contemporary multicultural contexts*. Jason Aronson.

Bollas, C. (2011). *The Christopher Bollas reader*. Routledge.

Fiumara, G. C. (2015). *Psychic suffering: From pain to growth*. Karnac.

Frosh, S. (1991). *Identity crisis: Modernity, psychoanalysis, and the self*. Routledge.

Fuller, A. R. (1990). *Insight into value: An exploration of the premises of a phenomenological psychology*. State University of New York Press.

Holmes, J. (2010). *Exploring in security: Towards an attachment-informed psychoanalytic psychotherapy*. Routledge.

Homans, P. (1989). *The ability to mourn: Disillusionment and the social origins of psychoanalysis*. The University of Chicago Press.

Jacobsen, B. (2007). *Invitation to existential psychology: A psychology for the unique human being and its applications in therapy*. John Wiley and Sons.

Ogden, T. H. (2012). *Creative readings: Essays on seminal analytic works*. Routledge.

Rustin, M. (1991). *The good society and the inner world: Psychoanalysis, politics and culture*. Verso.

Summers, R. F., & Barber, J. P. (Eds.). (2015). *Practicing psychoanalytic therapy: A casebook*. The Guilford Press.

Yalom, I. (1980). *Existential psychotherapy*. Basic Books.

32

Conclusion

Allow me to conclude with a dialectical deconstruction of the concept of maturity. In synchrony with the spirit of the dialectical approach, psychosocial maturation is never fully completed. It is a never-ending process. It will never be an accomplished feat. "A mature person," Boelen (1978) reminds us, "can have integrity even though he stumbles … [Maturity] can only be attained at the cost of a lifetime of self-discipline, constant struggle, arduous effort, and even occasional failure" (p. 168).

Psychosocial maturation will always be in conflict or tension with its seeming opposite, with immaturity. In fact, from a dialectical perspective, as we shall see, "positive" immaturity (not-being-there-yet) can be viewed as complementary to and, when appropriated, an essential constituent of maturity, the kind of maturity that is always in the process of freeing itself, fluctuatingly, from immaturity.

Becoming mature is always a dynamic process involving an ongoing dialogue with our immature ways of being, which in itself is indicative of openness to further maturation. We will never attain a perfect state of maturity. We will always have psychosocial blind spots. Our developmental task is to become aware of them and, hopefully, as much as humanly possible, reduce them. There can be no maturity without immaturity and there can be no immaturity without the potential for maturity. Maturity and immaturity can be understood only in relation to one another. And just as there are degrees of maturity, there are, correspondingly, degrees of immaturity. Maturity and immaturity are not either/or, but rather both/and conceptions. Although they seem as oppositional phenomena, they are two sides of the same psychosocial coin. They are complementary phenomena. Their integration lies in the

© The Author(s), under exclusive license to Springer Nature Switzerland AG 2021

M. J. Hannush, *Markers of Psychosocial Maturation*,
https://doi.org/10.1007/978-3-030-74315-4_32

attainment of balance in their complementarity. Just as there is a healthy open orientation to maturity, there is also an unhealthy foreclosed orientation to maturity. And just as there is an unhealthy, disintegrative, disordered, and fixated or stuck way of being immature, there is also a healthy, "not there yet" disposition to immaturity. The healthy orientations to maturity and immaturity are complementary concepts. The more open I am to the "not yet" aspect of my immaturity, the more I am predisposed to movement toward maturity. Healthy (not-yet-aspect of) immaturity (my potentiality-to-be, the realistically "more" that I could become) is an essential integrant of healthy (openness to) maturity.

Our entire life, at least potentially, is a process of development, growth, and maturation. We have the potential, after we are born, to be psychosocially reborn again and again. We are never totally fixed once and for all. Our development, as Erikson (1963) describes it, extends across the whole lifespan. Consequently, even in the later stages of life, we continue to be on the road toward further maturation. As Boelen (1978) puts it, we never outgrow our earlier stages; "we simply integrate them as constituent elements into our personal maturity which is not the end of growing, but rather the full-grown way of growing" (p. ix). As maturing persons, we never outgrow our earlier developmental stages; we simply incorporate them into higher and higher levels of personal integration. For example, the conscience of our childhood, though still part of us in adulthood, becomes, under relatively optimal maturational conditions in adulthood, less rigid and more flexible and friendly – our superego which "speaks such kindly words of comfort to the intimidated ego" (Freud as cited in Critchley, 2002, p. 103), our "amigo" (Critchley, 2002, p. 103), or our "loving and beloved superego" as described by Roy Schaffer (cited in Carveth, 2018, p. 19).

The pursuit of maturational perfection is an illusory life project. We can be less or more mature, but we can never be completely mature. We will always have pockets of immaturity within and between us. Part of our maturing task involves becoming increasingly aware of our pockets of immaturity. To put it differently, bit-by-bit, we need to become as conscious of our unconscious predispositions toward immature thinking, feeling, and acting as possible. Maturity is always in a tension-tinged dialectical (back-and-forth) relation to immaturity. Again, as Boelen (1978) delineates it, the mature person is "essentially involved in a living dialogue with his own immaturity, with the child in himself, with the fixity of his character, and the fixation of some measure of disorder [dis-order]. Immaturity is an essential constituent of maturity" (p. ix). For instance, developmental and clinical psychologists have shown, again and again, that the first six or seven years of life are pivotal in shaping our evolving personality. But this influence can be modulated through our ongoing dialogue with our childhood memories or the child within us, especially when shared with a caring listener, a listener who listens to our re-collected childhood narrative *care*-fully. This continuing dialogue with our immature self is itself an essential part of our maturational development and growth.

This tension-tinged dialogue between our mature and immature dispositions or ways of being with our selves and others is part of a more pervasive proclivity of our conscious or unconscious way of being-in-the-world. Allowed to free-associate, our mind, consciously and unconsciously, oscillates between existential polarities: between being ("I am glad to be alive") and not being ("I am sad knowing that I and my loved ones will die"); between being this kind person ("Say it straight") and that kind of person ("I have to come up with a white lie in order not to hurt my essential other"); between being and doing; between being independent of others ("I want to be self-sufficient") and being dependent on others ("I want to be able to lean on your shoulder in times of need"); between being attached or connected ("I need to be close to you") and being detached or separate ("I want to be my own person"); and so on. Being human means being condemned to oscillate between these voices within us that give expression to universal polar meanings of existence. Maturity requires of us to find that optimal point of integration between these polar meanings of our lifeworld. The process of maturation involves being able to tolerate the tension that arises from moving back-and-forth between (seemingly) opposite ways of being-in-the-world with our selves and with others; it involves resolving our *existential dialectical dilemmas*. Immaturity involves becoming unhealthily stuck on one side of the polar continuum. For example, consciously or, more likely, unconsciously, I needily decide to become unhealthily (excessively) dependent on my partner. I foreclose my quest toward maturation by giving up on the side of me that wants to be healthily independent. I am skewed. I am tilted toward one side of the polar dimension of my existential identity. I lack *balance* in this domain of my life. I can say the same thing about finding *balance* or optimal point of integration between being healthily attached or connected to my partner and, at the same time, being healthily detached and separate from her.

Being dependent *and* independent or being connected *and* separate are *lived meanings*. "Meaning," reminds us Fuller (1990), "is an action, 'loaded with tension'" (p. 269). We humans are characteristically directed to these phenomenal meanings. We are naturally disposed to reduce and or enhance these tensions with which meanings are loaded in an effort to find in them a "balanced fulfillment of meanings" (p. 150). A relatively balanced bodily self is one that is directed to relatively fulfilling lifeworld meanings. We need to cultivate an insightful way of being that is creatively and relaxedly disposed and open to emergent lifeworld meanings, connections between meanings, and transcendent meanings that will enable us to surpass seemingly contradictory or inconsistent meanings, such as being *either* connected and dependent *or* separate and independent. We need to keep on seeking more beautiful, better, and truer meanings—excellent meanings, which will bring us more peace and harmony, such as being *both* healthily connected and dependent *and* healthily separate and independent. We need to learn to become expert tightrope walkers in our life's journey.

Personal maturity emerges out of how we respond to the dialectical tensions of everyday life. Here is a brief example of a dialectical tension we inevitably face in our daily lives. It is the tension that arises between how we live out the seemingly polar meanings of *self-assertion*-in-relation-to-*self-surrender*. There is an aggressive and insistent self-assertion that is unproductive and unhealthy, and there is a non-aggressive and less insistent and less rigid form of self-assertion that is constructive and healthy. Similarly, there is not only a healthy form of self-surrender—reasonable yielding but also an unhealthy form of surrender—a futile form of giving up prematurely out of passivity or fear. Becoming mature involves finding that precarious balance or integrative fulcrum while walking the high-wire tightrope navigating the pole now on the side of healthy self-assertion and, in another instance, navigating on the side of healthy self-surrender.

Psychosocial maturity has to do with seeking, attaining, maintaining, and enhancing relative integrative balance in our lives. Above and beyond *integrative balance*, other words or phrases have been used to give us the connotation of maturity: cohesion (a cohesive sense of self), continuity (a continuous sense of self across lived space and over lived time), ego strength (flexible adaptability and resilience), mental health (vitalized and vitalizing sense of well-being), organization (organized or ordered sense of self), solidity (consolidated sense of self), stability (a firmly grounded sense of self), and unity (a relatively unified sense of self). Achieving such *existential mastery* is not an easy life task in our developmental life journey.

Maturity is an inexhaustible *creative* process. We are always, potentially, capable of becoming more mature until the day we expire or begin to lose our mental faculties. We are saddled with the *responsibility* of creatively sculpting our evolving selves and fulfilling our potential by making optimal use of our talents and competencies. We are forever challenged to *refine* our ways of being-in-the-world with ourselves and with others.

The mature person is one who orchestrates her or his life, give or take, according to lived action-meanings, meanings that involve us in the lifeworld.

The mature individual's character embodies, relatively speaking, these *lived meanings*—for example, embodying and living what *love, work,* or *playfulness* means to one. Each of the thirty meanings of maturity described in this text is a byproduct of an oscillating dialectical process that plays an essential part in making up a relatively integrative whole that we call the *maturity syndrome.* Becoming mature is a never-ending developmental life project. It will always be an unfinished business. It is a primal *existential calling* that beckons us to be more. It calls us to keep on *selving* or, better yet, *co-selving,* for maturation is above all an interpersonal process. Becoming mature involves, among other dimensions of selfhood or meanings of maturity, *aesthetic selving* (becoming a beautiful person), *ethical selving* (becoming a good person), and *veridical selving* (becoming a truthful person).

The impetus or impulse toward maturation is born of wonder. The response to the call of maturation unfolds naturally under relatively optimal conditions whereby the developing person experiences a favorable balance between experiencing her or his *wondrousness* on one side of the polar continuum and her or his *vulnerability* and *limitedness* on the other.

Though maturity provides its own solid ground, it is a precariously shifting ground. We are forever suspended between oscillating modes of maturity and immaturity while progressively, but not linearly, freeing ourselves from immature modes of existence. Mature existence is essentially an incomplete life project. Yet, the impulse toward progressive maturation belongs to our essential nature. We are forever challenged to responsibly respond to the *call of maturation.* We will never answer the call with total finality. We will always experience the dialectical tension between the polar meanings of existence. Ironically in the conflict of seeming opposites lies the source of our creative dynamism. The primal conflict is that between celebratory wondrousness of those small everyday "peak" moments whereby we experience the harmonious goodness of positive emotion-and-value-laden meanings well lived, on the one hand, and the work of laboriously, sometimes agonizingly, and unendingly reducing (and sometimes enhancing) the conflict perpetuated by negative emotion-and-value-laden meanings that are difficult to live by. And yet, tension enhancement, as in a fair fight with a loved-and-loving partner, can lead to the further articulation of new, higher-order meanings that are conducive to reconciliatory understanding and to the advancement of our maturational progress and harmonious living.

Meanings of maturity and immaturity commune with each other as we commune with them. How we interpret, appropriate, and enact them, as emotion-laden values and disvalues, into our lives will co-determine *who we are being-and-becoming* as unique and communal individuals.

Permit me to end with a musical metaphor. In her commentary on a piano composition entitled *Musica ricercata* no. 7 in B flat major by the Hungarian composer Gyorgy Ligeti (1923–2006), the classical music critic Clemency Burton-Hill (2018) has this to say: "I give you the right hand with its smooth, serene, high notes; underneath, meanwhile, witness relentless chaos bubbling away ...That roiling left hand certainly injects the piece with a restless, antsy momentum" (p. 360). Ligeti's creative gift lies in his beautiful synthesis of the symbolic right hand with the symbolic left hand. We are all endowed with the potentially transformative gift of this capacity for creative synthesis of the polar meanings of our lives. We can display our gratitude for the gift by using it in our lifework of integrating the orderly (right) forces and the chaotic (left) forces in our lives. This capacity for integration will offer us moments of harmony, healing, holiness, and wholeness, validating the experience that life is beautiful in spite of its ugliness. And sometimes, we are able to transform the ugly into the beautiful, making the beautiful more beautiful, the fair fairer, and the true truer.

References

Boelen, B. J. (1978). *Personal maturity: The existential dimension.* The Seabury Press.

Burton-Hill, C. (2018). *Year of wonder: Classical music to enjoy day by day.* HarperCollins.

Carveth, D. L. (2018). *Psychoanalytic thinking: A dialectical critique of contemporary theory and practice.* Routledge.

Critchley, S. (2002). *On humor.* Routledge.

Erikson, E. H. (1963). *Childhood and society* (2nd ed.). W. W. Norton.

Fuller, A. R. (1990). *Insight into value: An exploration of the premises of a phenomenological psychology.* State University of New York Press.

Correction to: Creativity: The Capacity for *Creativity* and Creative Living

Correction to:

Chapter 7 in: M. J. Hannush, *Markers of Psychosocial Maturation*, https://doi.org/10.1007/978-3-030-74315-4_7

The original version of the chapter was inadvertently published without the reference list. The chapter has been now corrected and approved by the author.

The updated version of the chapter can be found at
https://doi.org/10.1007/978-3-030-74315-4_7

© The Author(s), under exclusive license to Springer Nature Switzerland AG 2021

M. J. Hannush, *Markers of Psychosocial Maturation*,
https://doi.org/10.1007/978-3-030-74315-4_33

References

Adams, M. (2009). *Change your questions, change your life: 10 powerful tools for life and work*. Berrett-Koehler.

Akhtar, S. (2009). *Comprehensive dictionary of psychoanalysis*. Karnac.

Alexie, S. (2017). *You don't have to say you love me*. Little, Brown and Company.

Alford, C. F. (1997). *What evil means to us*. Cornell University Press.

Altman, N. (2010). *The analyst in the inner city: Race, class, culture through a psychoanalytic lens* (2nd ed.). Routledge.

Armstrong, J. (2004). *The secret power of beauty*. Penguin Books.

Auchincloss, E. L., & Samberg, E. (Eds.). (2012). *Psychoanalytic terms and concepts*. Yale University Press.

Augustine, S. (1961). *Confessions*. Penguin.

Bahler, B. (2016). *Childlike peace in Merleau-Ponty and Levinas: Intersubjectivity as dialectical spiral*. Lexington Books.

Bakewell, S. (2010). *How to live or a life of Montaigne in one question and twenty attempts at an answer*. Other Press.

Balthasar, H. U. v. (1998). *The glory of the Lord: A theological aesthetics, Volume I: Seeing the form*. Ignatius.

Bandura, A. (1977). *Social learning theory*. Prentice-Hall.

Barratt, B. B. (2013). *What is psychoanalysis? 100 years after Freud's 'secret committee'*. Routledge.

Barrett-Lennard, G. T. (1998). *Carl Rogers' helping system: Journey and substance*. Sage.

Baxter, L. A., & Montgomery, B. M. (1996). *Relating: Dialogues and dialectics*. Guilford.

Berzoff, J., & Hayes, M. (1996). Biopsychosocial aspects of depression. In J. Berzoff, L. M. Flanagan, & P. Hertz (Eds.), *Inside out and outside in: Psychodynamic clinical theory and practice in contemporary multicultural contexts*. Jason Aronson.

© The Author(s), under exclusive license to Springer Nature Switzerland AG 2021

M. J. Hannush, *Markers of Psychosocial Maturation*,
https://doi.org/10.1007/978-3-030-74315-4

Bion, W. (1962). *Learning from experience.* Heinemann.

Bion, W. (1984a). *Attention and interpretation.* Karnac.

Bion, W. (1984b). *Transformations.* Karnac.

Black, D. W. (1997). *Vico and moral perception.* Peter Lang.

Bloland, S. E. (2005). *In the shadow of fame: A memoir by the daughter of Erik H. Erikson.* Viking.

Boelen, B. J. (1978). *Personal maturity: The existential dimension.* The Seabury Press.

Bollas, C. (2011). *The Christopher Bollas reader.* Routledge.

Bollas, C. (2018). *Meaning and melancholia: Life in the age of bewilderment.* Routledge.

Bolt, M., & Dunn, D. S. (2016). *Pursuing human strengths: A positive psychology guide* (2nd ed.). Worth Publishers.

Bowlby, J. (1982). *Attachment and loss, Volume I: Attachment* (Rev. ed.). Basic Books.

Breger, L. (1974). *From instinct to identity: The development of personality.* Prentice-Hall.

Brothers, D. (1995). *Falling backwards: An exploration of trust and self-experience.* W. W. Norton.

Browning, D. S. (1975). *Generative man: Psychoanalytic perspectives.* A Delta Book/ Dell Publishing.

Buber, M. (1970). *I and thou.* Charles Scribner's Sons.

Bugental, J. F. T. (1978). *Psychotherapy and process: The fundamentals of an existential-humanistic approach.* McGraw-Hill.

Burton-Hill, C. (2018). *Year of wonder: Classical music to enjoy day by day.* HarperCollins.

Cabaniss, D. L., Cherry, S., Douglas, C. J., Graver, R. L., & Schwartz, A. R. (2013). *Psychodynamic formulation.* Wiley.

Cabaniss, D. L., Cherry, S., Douglas, C. J., & Schwartz, A. (2017). *Psychodynamic psychotherapy: A clinical manual* (2nd ed.). John Wiley & Sons.

Carveth, D. L. (2018). *Psychoanalytic thinking: A dialectical critique of contemporary theory and practice.* Routledge.

Cates, D. F. (2005). Spending the day with a good friend: Autobiography, moral character, and the religious imagination. In P. Lamoureux & K. J. O'Neil (Eds.), *Seeking goodness and beauty: The use of the arts in theological ethics.* Rowman and Littlefield.

Charles, M. (2004). *Learning from experience: A guidebook for clinicians.* The Analytic Press.

Civitarese, G. (2016). *Truth and the unconscious in psychoanalysis.* Routledge.

Cohn, H. W. (1997). *Existential thought and therapeutic practice: An introduction to existential psychotherapy.* Sage.

Critchley, S. (2002). *On humor.* Routledge.

Culbert-Koehn, J. (1997). Analysis of hard and soft: Tustin's contribution to a Jungian study of opposites. In T. Mitrani & J. L. Mitrani (Eds.), *Encounters with autistic states: A memorial tribute to Frances Tustin.* Jason Aronson.

Deurzen, E. V., & Kenward, R. (2005). *Dictionary of existential psychotherapy and counselling.* Sage.

Deurzen-Smith, E. V. (1997). *Everyday mysteries: Existential dimensions of psychotherapy*. Routledge.
Dickens, C. (2001). *Great expectations*. Modern Library.
Dilman, I. (1983). *Freud and human nature*. Basil Blackwell.
Dokecki, P. (1996). *The tragi-comic professional. Basic considerations for ethical reflective-generative practice*. Duquesne University Press.
Elson, M. (1986). *Self psychology in clinical social work*. W. W. Norton.
Embree, L., et al. (Eds.). (1997). *Encyclopedia of phenomenology*. Kluwer.
Erikson, E. H. (1975). *Life history and the historical moment: Diverse presentations*. W. W. Norton.
Erikson, E. H. (1963). *Childhood and society* (2nd ed.). W. W. Norton.
Erikson, E. H. (1964). *Insight and responsibility*. W. W. Norton.
Erikson, E. H. (1968). *Identity: Youth and crisis*. W. W. Norton.
Erikson, E. H. (1980). *Identity and the life cycle*. W. W. Norton.
Erikson, E. H. (1981). The Galilean sayings and the sense of "I." *Yale Review*, Spring 1981. Yale University Press.
Erikson, E. H. (1982). *The life cycle: A review*. W. W. Norton.
Erikson, E. H. (1985). *The life cycle completed*. W. W. Norton.
Erikson, E. H., Erikson, J. M., & Kivnick, H. Q. (1986). *Vital involvements in old age: The experience of old age in our time*. W. W. Norton.
Fairbairn, R. W. D. (1952). *Psychoanalytic studies of the personality*. Routledge.
Fingarette, H. (1963). *The self in transformation: Psychoanalysis, philosophy and the life of the spirit*. Harper and Row.
Fisher, A. (2002). *Radical ecopsychology: Psychology in the service of life*. State University of New York Press.
Fiumara, G. C. (2013). *Psychoanalysis and creativity in everyday life: Ordinary genius*. Routledge.
Fiumara, G. C. (2015). *Psychic suffering: From pain to growth*. Karnac.
Flanagan, M. (1996). The theory of self psychology. In J. Berzoff, L. M. Flanagan, & P. Hertz (Eds.), *Inside out and outside in: Psychodynamic clinical theory and practice in contemporary multicultural contexts*. Jason Aronson.
Fonagy, P. (2001). *Attachment theory and psychoanalysis*. Other Press.
Frankl, V. E. (1969). *The will to meaning*. World Publishing Company.
Frankl, V. E. (1992). *Mans' search for meaning* (4th ed.). Beacon Press.
Frankl, V. E. (2000). *Man's search for ultimate meaning*. Perseus.
Frankl, V. E. (2006). *Man's search for meaning*. Beacon Press.
Frankland, A. G. (2010). *The little psychotherapy book: Object relations in practice*. Oxford University Press.
Frazier, B. (2006). *Rorty and Kierkegaard on irony and moral commitment: Philosophical and theological connections*. Palgrave Macmillan.
Freud, S. (2005). On transience. In M. V. Unwerth (Ed.), *Freud's requiem: Mourning, memory, and the invisible history of a summer walk*. Riverhead Books.

Fromm, E. (1947). *Man for himself: An inquiry in the psychology of ethics*. Holt, Rinehart, and Winston.
Fromm, E. (1956). *The art of loving*. Harper and Row.
Fromm, E. (1981). *On disobedience and other essays*. Seabury Press.
Fromm, E. (1986). *For the love of life*. The Free Press.
Frosh, S. (1991). *Identity crisis: Modernity, psychoanalysis, and the self*. Routledge.
Frosh, S. (2011). *Feelings*. Routledge.
Frosh, S. (2012). *A brief introduction to psychoanalytic theory*. Palgrave Macmillan.
Frost, R. (1965). *Selected poems of Robert Frost*. Holt, Rinehart and Winston.
Fuller, A. R. (1990). *Insight into value: An exploration of the premises of a phenomenological psychology*. State University of New York Press.
Gay, V. P. (2001). *Joy and the objects of psychoanalysis: Literature, belief, and neurosis*. State University of New York Press.
Gaylin, W. (2003). *Hatred: The psychological descent into violence*. Public Affairs Books.
Gendlin, E. T. (1978). *Focusing* (2nd ed.). Bantam Books.
Gendlin, E. T. (1997). *Experiencing and the creation of meaning: A philosophical and psychological approach to the subjective*. Northwestern University Press.
Gerhardt, S. (2015). *Why love matters: How affection shapes a baby's brain* (2nd ed.). Routledge.
Giorgi, A. (2018). *Reflections on certain qualitative and phenomenological psychological methods*. University Professors Press.
Goldberg, J. G. (1999). *The dark side of love: The positive role of negative feelings*. Transaction.
Goodman, D. M. (2012). *The demanded self: Levinasian ethics and identity in psychology*. Duquesne University Press.
Greenberg, J. R., & Mitchell, S. A. (1983). *Object relations in psychoanalytic theory*. Harvard University Press.
Habermas, J. (1971). *Knowledge and human interests*. (J. J. Shapiro, Trans.). Beacon Press.
Habermas, J. (1987). *The theory of communicative action, Volume two: Lifeworld and system: A critique of functionalist reason* (T. McCarthy, Trans.). Beacon Press.
Hadreas, P. (2007). *A phenomenology of love and hate*. Ashgate.
Hagerty, B. B. (2016). *Life reimagined: The science, art, and opportunity of midlife*. Riverhead Books.
Hagman, G. (2010). *The artist's mind: A psychoanalytic perspective on creativity, modern art and modern artists*. Routledge.
Hamrick, W. S. (2002). *Kindness and the good society: Connections of the heart*. State University of New York Press.
Hannush, M. J. (1999). An interview with Rollo May. *Review of Existential Psychology and Psychiatry*, Numbers 1, 2, & 3 (pp. 129–141).
Hannush, M. J. (2002). *Becoming good parents: An existential journey*. State University of New York Press.

Hannush, M. J. (2007). An existential-dialectical-phenomenological approach to understanding *cultural tilts*: Implications for multicultural research and practice. *Journal of Phenomenological Psychology, 38*, 7–23.

Hannush, M. J. (2010). Playing with polarities of existence: Toward understanding a pivotal passage in the life and work of Rollo May. In T. F. Cloonan & C. Thiboutot (Eds.), *The redirection of psychology: Essays in honor of Amedeo Giorgi* (pp. 137–162). CIRP.

Hart, J. G. (1994). The study of religion in Husserl's writings. In M. Daniel & L. Embree (Eds.), *Phenomenology of cultural disciplines*. Kluwer.

Hart, J. G. (2009a). *Who one is, Book 1: Meontology of the "I": A transcendental phenomenology*. Springer.

Hart, J. G. (2009b). *Who one is, Book 2: Existenz and transcendental phenomenology*. Springer.

Heidegger, M. (1962). *Being and time* (J. Macquarrie & E. Robinson, Trans.). Harper and Row.

Heidegger, M. (1996). *Being and time* (J. Stambaugh, Trans.). State University of New York Press.

Hermans, H. J. M., & Kempen, H. J. G. (1993). *The dialogical self: Meaning as movement*. Academic Press.

Hoare, C. H. (2002). *Erikson on development and adulthood: New insights from the unpublished papers*. Oxford University Press.

Hoffman, M. T. (2011). *Toward mutual recognition: Relational psychoanalysis and the Christian narrative*. Routledge.

Holmes, J. (2010). *Exploring in security: Towards an attachment-informed psychoanalytic psychotherapy*. Routledge.

Homans, P. (1989). *The ability to mourn: Disillusionment and the social origins of psychoanalysis*. The University of Chicago Press.

Horney, K. (1970). *Neurosis and human growth: The struggle toward self-realization*. W. W. Norton.

Howard, S. (2011). *Psychodynamic counselling in a nutshell* (2nd ed.). Sage.

Iacovou, S., & Weixel-Dixon, K. (2015). *Existential therapy: 100 key points and techniques*. Routledge.

Jacobs, M. (1998). *The presenting past: The core of psychodynamic counselling and therapy* (2nd ed.). Open University Press.

Jacobs, M. (2010). *Psychodynamic counselling in action* (4th ed.). Sage.

Jacobsen, B. (2007). *Invitation to existential psychology: A psychology for the unique human being and its applications in therapy*. John Wiley and Sons.

Johnson, S. M. (1994). *Character styles*. W. W. Norton.

Joyce, A. (2005). One to two years old: Junior toddlers/Two to three years old: Senior toddlers. In E. Rayner, A. Joyce, J. Rose, M. Twyman, & C. Clulow (Eds.), *Human development: An introduction to the psychodynamics of growth, maturity, and ageing* (4th ed.). Routledge.

Kahn, M. (1997). *Between therapist and client: The new relationship* (Rev. ed.). W. H. Freeman.
Kamler, H. (1994). *Identification and character: A book on psychological development*. State University of New York Press.
Karen, R. (1998). *Becoming attached: First relationships and how they shape our capacity to love*. Oxford University Press.
Keen, S. (1997). *To love and be loved*. Bantam Books.
Kellenberger, J. (1997). *Kierkegaard and Nietzsche: Faith and eternal acceptance*. St. Martin's Press.
Kellerman, H. (2014). *Psychoanalysis of evil: Perspectives on destructive behavior*. Springer.
Kelman, H. (1971). *Helping people: Karen Horney's psychoanalytic approach*. Science House.
Kernberg, O. F. (1984). *Object relations theory and clinical psychoanalysis*. Jason Aronson.
Kernberg, O. F. (2012). *The inseparable nature of love and aggression: Clinical and theoretical perspectives*. American Psychiatric Publishing.
Kierkegaard, S. (1995). *Works of love* (H. V. Hong & E. H. Hong, Trans.). Princeton University Press.
Knowles, R. T. (1986). *Human development and human possibility: Erikson in the light of Heidegger*. University Press of America.
Kohut, H. (1971). *Analysis of the self*. International Universities Press.
Kohut, H. (1977). *The restoration of the self*. International Universities Press.
Kohut, H. (1978). P. Ornstein (Ed.), *The search for the self* (Vol. 1). International Universities Press.
Kohut, H. (1984). *How does analysis cure?* International Universities Press.
Korb, M. P., Gorrell, J., & De Riet, V. V. (1989). *Gestalt therapy: Practice and theory* (2nd ed.). Allyn and Bacon.
Lee, H. (1960). *To kill a mockingbird*. Warner Books.
Leffert, M. (2017). *Positive psychoanalysis: Meaning, aesthetics and subjective well-being*. Routledge.
Lemma, A. (2000). *Humour on the couch: Exploring humour in psychotherapy and everyday life*. Whurr.
Lessem, P. A. (2005). *Self psychology: An introduction*. Jason Aronson.
Levinas, E. (1969). *Totality and infinity: An essay on exteriority*. Duquesne University Press.
Levine, D. P. (2010). *Object relations, work, and the self*. Routledge.
Levine, D. P. (2013). *The capacity for ethical conduct: On psychic existence and the way we relate to others*. Routledge.
Lichtenberg, J. D., Lachmann, F. M., & Fosshage, J. L. (2011). *Psychoanalysis and motivational systems: A new look*. Routledge.
Lifton, R. J. (1993). *The protean self: Human resilience in age of fragmentation*. The University of Chicago Press.

Loewald, H. W. (1988). *Sublimation: Inquiries into theoretical psychoanalysis*. Yale University Press.
Loewald, H. W. (1991). On the therapeutic action of psychoanalysis. In G. I. Fogel (Ed.), *The work of Hans Loewald: An introduction and a commentary*. Jason Aronson.
Loewald, H. W. (2000). The waning of the Oedipus complex. *The Journal of Psychotherapy Practice and Research, 9*(4), 239–249.
Longhofer, J. (2015). *A-Z of psychodynamic practice*. Palgrave Macmillan.
Luijpen, W. A. (1969). *Existential phenomenology*. Duquesne University Press.
Lynch, M. P. (2004). *True to life: Why truth matters*. The MIT Press.
Mann, D. W. (1994). *A simple theory of the self*. W. W. Norton.
Marcel, G. (1950). *Mystery of being, Volume 2: Faith and reality*. Harvill Press.
Marcel, G. (1964). *Creative fidelity*. Noonday Press.
Marcus, P. (2010). *In search of the good life: Emanuel Levinas, psychoanalysis, and the art of living*. Karnac.
Marcus, P. (2013a). *How to laugh your way through life: A psychoanalyst's advice*. Karnac.
Marcus, P. (2013b). *In search of the spiritual: Gabriel Marcel, psychoanalysis, and the sacred*. Karnac.
Maroda, K. J. (2010). *Psychodynamic techniques: Working with emotion in the therapeutic relationship*. The Guilford Press.
Marra, T. (2005). *Dialectical behavior therapy in practice*. New Harbinger.
Martin, J. (2016). *Seven last words: An invitation to a deeper friendship with Jesus*. Harper Collins.
Martin, M. W. (1996). *Love's virtues*. University Press of Kansas.
Maslow, A. H. (1968). *Toward a psychology of being* (2nd ed.). D. Van Nostrand.
Maslow, A. H. (1970). *Motivation and personality* (2nd ed.). Harper and Row.
Maslow, A. H. (1971). *The farther reaches of human nature*. Viking.
May, R. (1953). *Man's search for himself*. W. W. Norton.
May, R. (1958). Contributions of existential psychotherapy. In R. May, E. Angel, & H. F. Ellenberger (Eds.), *Existence*. Basic Books.
May, R. (1967). *Psychology and the human dilemma*. D. Van Nostrand.
May, R. (1969). *Love and will*. Dell.
May, R. (1972). *Power and innocence*. W. W. Norton.
May, R. (1981). *Freedom and destiny*. W. W. Norton.
May, R. (1985). *My quest for beauty*. Saybrook.
Mayeroff, M. (1971). *On caring*. Harper Collins.
McClure, F., & Teyber, E. (2003). *Casebook in child and adolescent treatment: Cultural and familial contexts*. Thomson.
McGrath, S. J. (2012). *The dark ground of spirit: Schelling and the unconscious*. Routledge.
McIntosh, D. (1995). *Self, person, world: The interplay of conscious and unconscious in human life*. Northwestern University Press.
McWilliams, N. (2004). *Psychoanalytic psychotherapy: A practitioner's guide*. Guildford.
Mearns, D., & Thorne, B. (1999). *Person-centered counselling in action* (2nd ed.). Sage.

Melle, U. (2002). Edmund Husserl: From reason to love. In J. J. Drummond & L. Embree (Eds.), *Phenomenological approaches to moral philosophy: A handbook*. Kluwer.
Meltzer, D., & Williams, M. H. (1988). *The apprehension of beauty: The role of aesthetic conflict in development, violence and art*. Clunie Press.
Melucci, A. (1996). *The playing self: Person and meaning in the planetary society*. Cambridge University Press.
Merkin, D. (2017). *This close to happy: A reckoning with depression*. Farrar, Straus and Giroux.
Merleau-Ponty, M. (1962). *Phenomenology of perception* (C. Smith, Trans.). Routledge.
Merleau-Ponty, M. (1964a). *The primacy of perception*. Northwestern University Press.
Merleau-Ponty, M. (1964b). *Sense and non-sense* (H. L. Dreyfus & P. A. Dreyfus, Trans.). Northwestern University Press.
Merleau-Ponty, M. (1973). *Adventures of the dialectic* (J. Bien, Trans.). Northwestern University Press.
Mitchell, S. A. (2002). *Can love last? The fate of romance over time*. W. W. Norton.
Mitchell, S. A., & Black, M. J. (1995). *Freud and beyond: A history of modern psychoanalytic thought*. Basic Books.
Mitrani, T., & Mitrani, J. L. (Eds.). (1997). *Encounters with autistic states: A memorial tribute to Frances Tustin*. Jason Aronson.
Mota-Strasser, L. (2005). Dialogue and communication. In E. V. Deurzen & C. Arnold-Baker (Eds.), *Existential perspectives on human issues: A handbook for therapeutic practice*. Palgrave Macmillan.
Moustakas, C. (1995). *Being-in, being-for, being-with*. Jason Aronson.
Newman, B. M., & Newman, P. R. (2018). *Development through life: A psychosocial approach* (13th ed.). Cengage Learning.
Nicholas, M. W. (1994). *The mystery of goodness and the positive moral consequences of psychotherapy*. W. W. Norton.
Nicholsen, S. W. (2002). *The love of nature and the end of the world: The unspoken dimensions of environmental concern*. The MIT Press.
Nietzsche, F. (1961). *Thus spoke Zarathustra* (R. J. Hollingdale, Trans.). Penguin.
Ogden, T. H. (1986). *The matrix of the mind: Object relations and the psychoanalytic dialogue*. Jason Aronson.
Ogden, T. H. (2012). *Creative readings: Essays on seminal analytic works*. Routledge.
Orange, D. M. (2011). *The suffering stranger: Hermeneutics for everyday clinical practice*. Routledge.
Parvulescu, A. (2010). *Laughter: Notes on a passion*. The MIT Press.
Paskow, A. (2004). *The paradoxes of art: A phenomenological investigation*. Cambridge University Press.
Perls, F. (1969). *Gestalt therapy verbatim*. Real People Press.
Perry, M. (2017). *Montaigne in barn boots: An amateur ambles through philosophy*. Harper Collins.
Phillips, A., & Taylor, B. (2009). *On kindness*. Farrar, Straus and Giroux.

Rayner, E. (1995). *Unconscious logic: An introduction to Matte Blanco's bi-logic and its uses*. Routledge.

Rayner, E. (2005). Three to five years old. In E. Rayner, A. Joyce, J. Rose, M. Twyman, & C. Clulow (Eds.), *Human development: An introduction to the psychodynamics of growth, maturity, and ageing* (4th ed.). Routledge.

Reeves, C. (1977). *The psychology of Rollo May*. Jossey-Bass.

Ricoeur, P. (1966). *Freedom and nature: The voluntary and the involuntary*. Northwestern University Press.

Ricoeur, P. (1967). *The symbolism of evil*. Beacon Press.

Ricoeur, P. (1986). *Fallible man*. Fordham University Press.

Ricoeur, P. (1995). *Figuring the sacred*. Fortress.

Rodman, F. R. (2003). *Winnicott: Life and work*. Perseus.

Rogers, C. R. (1951). *Client-centered therapy: Its current practice, implications, and theory*. Houghton Mifflin.

Rogers, C. R. (1961). *On becoming a person*. Houghton Mifflin.

Rogers, C. R. (1962). The interpersonal relationship: The core of guidance. In C. R. Rogers & B. Stevens (Eds.), *Person to person*. Real People Press.

Rogers, C. R. (1980). *A way of being*. Houghton Mifflin.

Rogers, C. R. (1989). *The Carl Rogers reader*. Houghton Mifflin.

Rogers, C. R., & Freiberg, H. J. (1994). *Freedom to learn* (3rd ed.). Macmillan College Publishing Company.

Rorty, R. (1989). *Contingency, irony, and solidarity*. Cambridge University Press.

Rose, J. (2005). Work, identity, and love. In E. Rayner, A. Joyce, J. Rose, M. Twyman, & C. Clulow (Eds.), *Human development: An introduction to the psychodynamics of growth, maturity, and ageing* (4th ed.). Routledge.

Rustin, M. (1991). *The good society and the inner world: Psychoanalysis, politics and culture*. Verso.

Safran, J. D. (2012). *Psychoanalysis and psychoanalytic therapies*. American Psychological Association.

Sartwell, C. (2004). *Six names of beauty*. Routledge.

Scarry, E. (1999). *On beauty and being just*. Princeton University Press.

Schachtel, E. G. (1959). *Metamorphosis: On the development of affect, perception, attention, and memory*. Basic Books.

Schalow, F. (2001). *Heidegger and the quest for the sacred: From thought to the sanctuary of faith*. Kluwer.

Schalow, F. (2006). *The incarnality of being: The earth, animals, and the body in Heidegger's thought*. State University of New York Press.

Schalow, F. (2017). *Toward a phenomenology of addiction: Embodiment, technology, transcendence*. Springer.

Schindler, D. C. (2004). *Hans Urs von Balthasar and the dramatic structure of truth: A philosophical interpretation*. Fordham University Press.

Schneider, K. J., & May, R. (1995). *The psychology of existence: An integrative, clinical perspective*. McGraw-Hill.

Schrag, C. O. (1997). *The self after postmodernity*. Yale University Press.

Searles, H. F. (1979). *Countertransference and related subjects: Selected Papers*. International Universities Press.

Segal, H. (1979). *Melanie Klein*. Penguin Books.

Seinfeld, J. (1991). *The empty core: An object relations approach to psychotherapy of the schizoid personality*. Jason Aronson.

Seligman, M. E. P. (2011). *Flourish: A visionary new understanding of happiness and well-being*. Free Press.

Siassi, S. (2015). Kindness, altruism and forgiveness: Three facets of healthy human relatedness. In S. Akhtar (Ed.), *Human goodness: Origins, manifestations, and clinical implications*. Rowman & Littlefield.

Siegel, A. M. (1996). *Heinz Kohut and the psychology of the self*. Routledge.

Siegel, D. J. (2010). *Mindsight: The new science of personal transformation*. Bantam Books/The Guilford Press.

Siegel, D. J. (2012). *The developing mind: How relationships and the brain interact to shape who we are* (2nd ed.). Guilford.

Slochower, J. (2014). *Holding and psychoanalysis: A relational perspective* (2nd ed.). Routledge.

Solomon, I. (2006). *Karen Horney and character disorder*. Springer.

Spinelli, E. (1989). *The interpreted world: An introduction to phenomenological psychology*. Sage.

St. Clair, M. with Wigren, J. (2004). *Object relations and self psychology: An introduction* (4th ed.). Brooks/Cole – Thomson Learning.

Staub, E. (2003). *The psychology of good and evil: Why children, adults, and groups help and harm others*. Cambridge University Press.

Stern, D. N. (1985). *The interpersonal world of the infant: A view from psychoanalysis and developmental psychology*. Basic Books.

Stern, D. N. (2004). *The present moment in psychotherapy and everyday life*. W. W. Norton.

Sternberg, R. J. (1998). *Love is a story: A new theory of relationships*. Oxford University Press.

Strozier, C. B. (2001). *Heinz Kohut: The making of a psychoanalyst*. Farrar, Straus and Giroux.

Summers, R. F., & Barber, J. P. (Eds.). (2015). *Practicing psychoanalytic therapy: A casebook*. The Guilford Press.

Symington, J., & Symington, N. (1996). *The clinical thinking of Wilfred Bion*. Routledge.

Symington, N. (1996). *The making of a psychotherapist*. Routledge.

Symington, N. (2004). *The blind man sees: Freud's awakening and other essays*. Karnac.

Symington, N. (2012). *The psychology of the person*. Karnac.

Symington, N. (2016). *A healing conversation: How healing happens*. Karnac.

Symington, N. (2019). *The growth of mind*. Routledge.

Tageson, C. W. (1982). *Humanistic psychology: A synthesis*. The Dorsey Press.

Teyber, E., & Teyber, F. H. (2017). *Interpersonal process in therapy: An integrative model* (7th ed.). Cengage Learning.

Thompson, M. G. (1994). *The truth about Freud's technique: The encounter with the real.* New York University Press.

Tillich, P. (1952). *The courage to be.* Yale University Press.

Tuber, S. (2008). *Attachment, play, and authenticity: A Winnicott primer.* Jason Aronson.

Twyman, M. (2005). Being alone. In E. Rayner, A. Joyce, J. Rose, M. Twyman, & C. Clulow (Eds.), *Human development: An introduction to the psychodynamics of growth, maturity, and ageing* (4th ed.). Routledge.

Wachtel, P. L. (2011). *Therapeutic communication: Knowing what to say when* (2nd ed.). The Guilford Press.

Waddell, M. (2002). *Inside lives: Psychoanalysis and the growth of the personality.* Karnac.

Wallulis, J. (1990). *The hermeneutics of life history: Personal achievement and history in Gadamer, Habermas, and Erikson.* Northwestern University Press.

Welchman, K. (2000). *Erik Erikson: His life, work and significance.* Open University Press.

Winnicott, D. W. (1965a). *The family and individual development.* Routledge.

Winnicott, D. W. (1965b). *The maturational processes and the facilitating environment: Studies in the theory of emotional development.* Hogarth Press.

Winnicott, D. W. (1971). *Playing and reality.* Tavistock Publications.

Wirth, J. M. (2003). *The conspiracy of life: Meditations on Schelling and his time.* State University of New York Press.

Wrightsman, L. (1994). *Adult personality development: Theories and concepts* (Vol. 1). Sage.

Yalom, I. (1980). *Existential psychotherapy.* Basic Books.

Name Index

© The Author(s), under exclusive license to Springer Nature Switzerland AG 2021
M. J. Hannush, *Markers of Psychosocial Maturation*,
https://doi.org/10.1007/978-3-030-74315-4

V

W

Y

Subject Index

© The Author(s), under exclusive license to Springer Nature Switzerland AG 2021
M. J. Hannush, *Markers of Psychosocial Maturation*,
https://doi.org/10.1007/978-3-030-74315-4